Library Programs and Services

LIBRARY PROGRAMS AND SERVICES
The Fundamentals

Eighth Edition

G. Edward Evans,
Margaret Zarnosky Saponaro,
Holland Christie, and Carol Sinwell

Library and Information Science Text Series

LIBRARIES
UNLIMITED™
An Imprint of ABC-CLIO, LLC
Santa Barbara, California • Denver, Colorado

Library of Congress Cataloging-in-Publication Data

Evans, G. Edward, 1937-
  [Introduction to library public services]
  Library programs and services : the fundamentals. — Eighth edition /
G. Edward Evans, Margaret Zarnosky Saponaro, Holland Christie, and
Carol Sinwell.
       pages cm. — (Library and information science text series)
  The first-fourth editions of this book authored by Marty Bloomberg
were published under the title Introduction to public services for library
technicians. The fifth-seventh editions authored by G. Edward Evans
and others were published under the title Introduction to library public
services.
  Includes bibliographical references and index.
  ISBN 978-1-61069-637-1 (pbk : alk. paper) — ISBN 978-1-61069-638-8
(ebook)
  1. Public services (Libraries) 2. Library resources. 3. Libraries—
Activity programs. 4. Libraries—Information technology. 5. Library
administration. I. Saponaro, Margaret Zarnosky. II. Christie,
Holland. III. Sinwell, Carol. IV. Title.
   Z711.B63 2015   025.5—dc23   2015003548

ISBN: 978-1-61069-637-1
EISBN: 978-1-61069-638-8

19 18 17 16 15   1 2 3 4 5

This book is also available on the World Wide Web as an eBook.

Visit www.abc-clio.com for details.

Libraries Unlimited
An Imprint of ABC-CLIO, LLC

ABC-CLIO, LLC
130 Cremona Drive, P.O. Box 1911
Santa Barbara, California 93116-1911

This book is printed on acid-free paper ∞

Manufactured in the United States of America

Contents

Preface to the Eighth Edition

The first incarnation of this book appeared in 1972 with the title *Introduction to Library Public Services for Library Technicians*. It was 251 pages in length, including eight pages of indexing. As you might expect, the focus was on manual systems and print materials necessary for carrying out public service activities. Of note is the fact there was only one index entry of something "technological" in character—"computers, p. 218–219."

The last edition of this book (*Introduction to Library Public Services*, seventh edition, 2009) had 382 pages of text and an 18-page index. That edition also reflected the impact that technology has had on library programs and services. There were 39 technology-related entries in just the A-D sections of the index. Perhaps the index entry "technostress" most clearly reflected the changing nature of libraries' efforts to meet service community needs in the digital world.

This edition continues to reflect the changing world of library public services. We have made a number of changes in this edition; so many in fact that we thought a new title was appropriate (*Library Programs and Services: The Fundamentals*). One obvious change is there are three new coauthors. Another new feature is that we employed a five-member advisory board. These kind, or perhaps foolish, individuals agreed to read and comment on the manuscript as it was prepared. Their thoughtful input is a key element in whatever quality there is in the book's content.

Between the four authors and the five advisory board members there are a great many years of public service experience represented in the text. The experience covers academic, public, and school library environments. That experience is reflected throughout the book in sidebars that provide examples of "real-world" situations that have, can, and will arise during a person's library career when working with the public. Additional sidebars appearing throughout the text suggest material to read to learn more about the topic under discussion or provide links to online sites that also reflect a real-world context.

Perhaps the features that drove the decision to have a new title for the book involved the restructuring of how we present the content and several new chapters. We organized the work into four broad categories: Part I—Background, Part II—Core Programs and Services (covers the programs and services almost every library offers in some form), Part III—Specialized Programs and Services (this part addresses programs and services that many, but not all, libraries offer), and Part IV—Operational Issues in Library Programs and Services (this part discusses the many topics that influence how libraries go about providing programs and services). The new chapters are:

Print Collections
Media Collections
E-Resources
Computer Access
Social Media and Library Programs and Services
Legal Aspects
Ethical Issues
Fiscal Concerns
Library as Place

We owe a very special thank you to our advisory board members. Their comments and suggestions were invaluable in preparing this edition. Members were:

Ruth Kifer, Dean of the University Library, San José State University
George Oberle, History Liaison Librarian at George Mason University
Jackie Gropman, retired regional children's branch manager of Fairfax County (Virginia) Public Libraries
Jenny Shanker, Library Media Specialist, Arlington (Virginia) Public Schools
Jean Wallace, retired school librarian, Clinton (Illinois) Public Schools

In addition, special thanks must go to Jamie Edwards and Celina McDonald, University of Maryland Libraries; Cinthya Ippoliti, Oklahoma State University Library; Sari Warren, Fairfax County Public Schools; and the reference staff at Northern Virginia Community College.

We hope this edition will prove useful to students and instructors alike.

G. Edward Evans
Flagstaff, Arizona

Margaret Zarnosky Saponaro
Rockville, Maryland

Holland Christie
Flagstaff, Arizona

Carol Sinwell
Oak Hill, Virginia

Part

I

Background

1

Introduction

> I think we all agree . . . that the key ethical principle of our profession is service to the client, getting them what they want and what they need first, last, and always.
>
> —*Barbara Quint, 2013*

> Before describing our vision for our future library, it is worth asking "who are our future clients?" We can point here to research into emerging technologies or evidence of changing social, information seeking and learning habits; however, we take these, the basis of the Web 3.0 world, as a given. . . . If we are to build a new library to accommodate the needs of our future clients, we must understand the effect of these trends in technologies, information, and education on our specific community and tailor what we deliver to meet their needs.
>
> —*Mal Booth, Sally Schofield, and Belinda Tiffen, 2012*

> Libraries do not have to invent their own future. But we do have to create an environment in which the rest of the world can make everything out of libraries that can be imagined.
>
> —*David Weinberger, 2014*

What type of library you do or will work in is determined by its organizational environment. With few exceptions, libraries are part of a larger parent organization; therefore, the library reflects the mission and goals of its "parent" in what it does and how it structures its activities. Both the parent organization and its library must change as their external environment changes; if they do not, they lose their relevance and place in society.

We seldom think of our work in a library as being part of an information ecology/environment; however, what we do is in fact tightly linked with what takes place in our society at large and our local community in particular.

Without question, the greatest change in today's libraries' environment is information technology and the rapid changes occurring in the e-world. To quote from Francisco-Javier Garcia-Marco, "In the midst of the digital revolution, we need a dock to anchor our reflections. This anchor could be the function that libraries—digital or not—perform: helping in the transfer of culture among and inside generations" (2011, p. 107).

There are some people who doubt that libraries will survive much longer in the electronic world of today. Such individuals believe all relevant information will be available wherever and whenever a person needs access through hand-held or even worn devices (e.g., Google Glass was test marketed to a select group of "explorers" in mid-2013, and became available to the general public in mid-2014). However, the library as we know it or as it has been perceived during the twentieth and early twenty-first centuries may disappear, but we only have to look to past predictions, for example, the "paperless library," to know this is not the case. Some college libraries were "designed" to be paperless, but paper eventually worked its way into these facilities.

It is quite possible there is some correlation between administrators thinking you can "Google" everything you want now and what these planners think the future of information and libraries will look like. To ensure that the future holds brighter days for libraries, librarians must proactively repurpose library physical spaces and enrich library digital spaces so that long-held customer service standards continue to keep the library a vibrant institution in our society.

Why are we optimistic about the library's future? The major reason is, it appears to us, that those who predict the demise of libraries have a lack of understanding of libraries' adaptability and ability to respond to change, and important role libraries play in society. For example, public libraries are active agencies providing user-driven information resources and public space. Academic libraries are intellectual crossroads that bring people together with ideas and information to create new knowledge and preserve it. Thomas Jefferson, a librarian at heart, knew this and placed the first library for the University of Virginia in the Rotunda located at the heart of the university (University of VA magazine). School librarians have to defend their library programs and their professional skills. They need to proclaim "we are *indispensable*" and that their libraries are an integral part of the changing educational picture.

Check This Out

The Center for the Future of Libraries, from the American Library Association, has created a trend library to "help libraries and librarians understand how trends are developing and why they matter." The library is regularly updated and is well worth a look: http://www.ala.org/transforminglibraries/future/trends.

The identity of what a library is shifts over time. Libraries have changed over time in order to respond to changing environments and needs. Hal Grossman (2011), when writing about how people think about the future, commented,

"When writers have tried to divine the future and how it will affect the library's role in society, a number of factors have come together. Their notions of the future have been shaped by how they understand the past, what gains they believe they had won, and what dreams remain unfulfilled" (p. 102). Many years ago, a prominent spokesperson for libraries (Jesse Shera, 1933) made the point that "the all important fact to be remembered is that the library is distinctly a social phenomenon and as such is susceptible to all the influences that react upon our social structure" (pp. 352–353).

The following is a more recent statement about libraries and their value to society: Libraries are one of our most important community institutions because they express our enduring commitment to education, culture, family, basic human freedoms, and historic preservation. . . . Even during trying fiscal times, let's never forget that our taxpayer investment in libraries is an invaluable investment in education and lifelong learning." (Barotz, 2013, p. A5) Celia Barotz, a Flagstaff, Arizona city council member, wrote the preceding during a debate about the city's upcoming budget.

Libraries are social constructs with a very long history—nearly 5,000 years. Looking at library history, we see that libraries have served and continue to serve the public, parent institutions, and society in four basic ways. First, libraries meet society's information needs by *acquiring* (licensing) the materials deemed valuable or useful to some or all of the people. Second, they provide a physical location/virtual location and an environment for *storing and preserving* those items. Third, libraries add value to the items acquired by *organizing* them in some manner to make access more efficient. Fourth, the library's staff improves access by *providing assistance* to individuals in locating desired information. All these functions involve public service personnel to a greater or lesser degree.

Increasingly libraries are providing access to information whether in physical or digital format and are less concerned about acquisition and ownership. The role of the library is moving toward curation of digital content found online, often in open access format. This requires the knowledge and expertise of staff. As noted by Lewis (2007), "For most libraries, the migration from purchased resources to curated content will require an input of staff" (p. 429).

Throughout history, libraries have added or adapted many technologies in order to carry out their societal role of collecting, organizing, and preserving information. Early Middle Eastern societies stored their information on clay tablets and created "libraries" to house the collection. At some point in history, there was probably concern when a new technology—the scroll—came on the scene, in that it did not seem very permanent. That concern was obviously overcome, as Egyptian libraries' collections were papyrus scrolls, while Roman libraries' collections were vellum scrolls. When the codex or book appeared, another transition was necessary.

During the Middle Ages, the vellum manuscript books were so costly to produce and preserve that books were literally chained down—the ultimate in a non-circulating collection. The development of paper-based books and the printing press presented another new technological challenge for libraries. It is likely that just like the times of the scroll versus clay tablets, there was more than a little skepticism about the impact of books on the need for libraries. Some people may have gone so far as to suggest there would be no need for libraries as anyone could afford to own many books and create a personal library. Although personal libraries did arise, libraries became even more important as the volume of information increased. Just as for those of us who enjoy reading and owning paper-based books, in time we run out of space to store them and money to purchase everything we would like to read. It is then that we turn to libraries to fill in the gaps. Even e-readers have a finite amount of storage space, and libraries are offering the chance to gain access to digital titles we'd like to read but not keep.

Libraries also provide diversity of information choices. Even a person who is widely read will typically have a limited scope and understanding of the information universe, and benefit from the serendipitous discovery of something that is beyond his or her information universe. As a result, the library becomes the place where surprises can and do happen. The "unanticipated finding" that is beyond awareness of a person is something that goes beyond a personal library. As a result, people will always try to group together to share their own personal collections within the public sphere. As Secretary General of the United Nations Ban Ki-moon said at a 2013 ceremony establishing a school library in Addis Ababa, Ethiopia, "A library is not just a building full of books. It is a garden to cultivate individuals" (UN News Centre, 2013).

These examples show how libraries have changed and adapted over time, but their basic functions have remained constant. Perhaps James Mullins (2012) best summed up today's changing library environment when he wrote, "it is no surprise to us who work in libraries, whether school, public, special, college or university, that the role we play in supporting the learning, discovery, and information needs of our clientele have changed" (p. 18). Paul S. Piper (2013) further reflects our thoughts about the future of libraries by noting, "By the beginning of the 21st century, several trends in the evolution of libraries had emerged—collaboration was a key to survival; technology would play an integral role; library as 'place' would supersede a warehouse function; and digitization would prevail" (p. 22).

This is as good a place as any to discuss the words used to refer to the individuals who access libraries and their services. Words such as *patron, client, user,* and *customer* appear in library literature in reference to such people. The labels have even generated a modicum of heat among the people who use one of the variations. "Patron" is one of the longest-standing terms; however, for some people that label is thought of as demeaning to libraries as well as to their staffs. (One can view patronage as suggesting something is unable to exist on its own and requires a special person[s] to underwrite its existence.) "Customer," although it is in many ways the most appropriate term—as in "customer service"—is viewed by some in the field as too profit/commercially oriented to use for a public service/good like a library. "Client" also carries a stigma of commercialism for some—lawyers or brokers have clients, not a library. "User," for a few people, suggests a person with some bad habits. So, where does this leave us? Based on our years of library experience, we believe either "customer" or "user" best reflect what public services are all about. After some debate, we have elected to employ "user" in this work to refer to the people who come to the library or remotely access online library services/collections.

LIBRARY ORGANIZATIONAL STRUCTURE

Earlier in the chapter we made the point that libraries and their parent organizations interact with their environment. In fact, what differentiates types of libraries is the nature of their parent organization. Libraries come in a variety of "flavors"—academic, corporate, public, school, and special at the very broadest level—they all share, regardless of category, the same basic functions. What makes the difference between these types is their environment/parent organization. How the library modifies those basic services and functions to fit its user community's needs is what places it into one of broad categories. Throughout this book we attempt to provide a general focus rather than attempting to treat libraries as category-specific variations. However, when the activity is unique to one or more institutional categories, we do cover the specifics. Some examples of the narrower focus are children's services, reserve collections, and special/archival collections. One reason for the more general approach is there are a number of texts that address category-specific environments.

From the Advisory Board

Advisory board member Ruth Kifer, San José State University Library, reminds us that while there are four basic categories of libraries, "Not all libraries fit nicely into one 'flavor' or 'type.' For example, the Dr. Martin Luther King Jr. Library in San José, California is a joint university and public library. Opening as the largest joint-use library in the world in 2003, the library serves as the downtown branch of the San Jose Public Library and the San José State University Library. The library provides access to library resources and services to library users from the general public and also from the university community. The library supports lifelong learning for library users including toddlers and young children in its children's room, tweens and high school students in the teen center, university students throughout the library and through its digital presence, and adult and senior members of the broader community. Physical library materials circulate equally to all and staff from both library organizations serve library users at jointly staffed public service desks. The joint library has one integrated library system and integrated online public catalog. Although this kind of collaborative library venture has not been replicated broadly within the United States, there are several such libraries across the country and numerous examples of joint-use libraries in Europe and Australia."

In the not-all-too-distant past, libraries were a classic example of the hierarchical organization, that is, many levels with units/departments carrying out a relatively narrow range of activities. An organization chart would look rather like a pyramid, with a wide base and narrow peak. Hierarchical structures based on preserving status don't adjust well to change. There's little incentive to take on new roles when you have a fossilized job grade and pay scale.

On the other hand, there are also jobs that once were critical to a library's functioning that are less necessary or time-consuming now, but still exist, while new tasks—such as creating and populating digital collections or data curation—are becoming more and more common. These newer positions are embraced by library leadership as a badge of innovation, but then are starved of resources. People asked to take on these tasks may well wonder why there isn't more resource reallocation, but that requires that decision makers to do some scary things, like explaining to people who do not want to hear it that the work they do is no longer as demanding or important as it once was, and they will need to do other things now. HR processes often make this difficult—like insisting that if the duties change, that job has to be advertised. (That's a great way to make people fear change: telling them that they have to learn new things, and the prospect of competing for their job, since their old position just became a new position.) Today's library structures are flatter; that is, there are fewer organizational levels. The flatter structures are intended to make the libraries more responsive to their environment by allowing frontline and mid-level staff and librarians the ability to make decisions and implement changes, rather than sending them "up the chain of command" to be discussed and reviewed by higher authorities.

How libraries change their organizational structure has been and is driven by several factors. Perhaps the two most difficult factors for libraries to handle are poor economic conditions followed by ever-changing technological developments. A third factor is increased demands for more services from their users. Another reason for changes in the number of or the kind of service points is the changing information-seeking behaviors of library users, due in part to technological change but also as a result of broader societal changes and expectations of students and other library users. Changing demographics of communities and an expectation that a wider cross-section of society receives a higher education have also impacted the kinds of services required by sometimes underprepared students.

A rather widely employed statement that sums up the situation for libraries is, "We must do more, better, and faster, with less." It is important to note libraries were and are not the only organizations faced with these challenges. Technology is both a benefit and a challenge. It has allowed libraries, more or less, to do more with existing resources, assuming they have funds to acquire that technology. Even when they have the funds for technology, each new technology/upgrade means staff must spend time, apart from their other duties, learning to use the new technology effectively. Technology also adds a level of competitive anxiety. Staff may be technologically adept, but feel undervalued by elders, or those who consider themselves technologically inept may sense younger staff are deriding them. In libraries, learning new technology is inescapable, but that doesn't stop some librarians and library staff from trying.

The need to do more with less has caused libraries to rethink how they do things and structure their activities. A study entitled *Reconfiguring Service Delivery* (Vyhnanek and Zlatos, 2011) conducted by the Association of Research Libraries (ARL) reported on the results of a survey of ARL libraries regarding changes in "service points" between 2008 and 2010. (Note: a service point is defined as "a fixed location within a library or information service staffed to provide a specific service to users, for example the circulation desk, reference desk, interlibrary loan office, etc." [Rietz, 2004, p. 653].) The researchers asked if there had been any additions, closures, consolidations, or "otherwise reconfigured" service points, including branches, during the study years.

Because the data only reflects changes in the research library environment based upon the responses of 59 ARL libraries, the data may underrepresent what took place in other types of the libraries during this time period. However, it still provides some interesting insights. Some of the study results were as follows:

- 88% had reconfigured one or more service points or branches.
- 47 libraries reported 149 changes were made to service points.
- 56 libraries reported consolidations.
- 53 libraries reconfigured services.
- 27 libraries closed a service point or branch.
- 16 added a service point (2011, p. 12).

The data suggests there were vastly more reductions in service points than expansions. The data is not too surprising given the economic conditions of the time frame. Although the data is representative of a small subset of libraries, it rather clearly illustrates what happens when libraries have to find ways to do more with less. It also suggests the reporting libraries flattened their organizational structure.

WHAT CONSTITUTES LIBRARY PUBLIC SERVICES?

Barbara Quint's opening quotation spells out what today's libraries are about, as well as the purpose of this book: the need to and how to provide service to the library's community. There is really little point to a society creating a library that does not provide service of some kind that the society values. Just as libraries have evolved, so have the services they provide.

One evolution in the thinking about service has been in who might have access to a library and how often. The earliest libraries were for a select few—government and religious officials. Later it was expanded to the noble class and then slowly grew to today's open access model.

An example of one such change would be the academic library. In the eighteenth and early nineteenth centuries, academic libraries were open only a few hours each week. Generally, students had to have permission to examine a specific book in the library. Even that usage required the direct supervision of a professor and was limited to a short time period. As colleges grew and attitudes about students as well as teaching methods changed, hours and access increased. A student could read a library book without being supervised. Today, through offsite access to databases and e-books, parts of a library collection can be accessible to users 24/7.

User assistance is an even more recent phenomenon. U.S. public libraries began staffing reference desks in the late nineteenth century. However, it was not until 1914 that Harvard business students recommended creating a library reference department, and it was the late 1930s before Widener Library (Harvard College library) provided even minimal reference assistance (Carpenter, 1986, p. 2). As late as World War II, some financial officers and library boards questioned the need for reference assistance, much as some people today question the need for libraries in an e-world.

Another reason for changes in the number of or the kind of service points is the changing information-seeking behaviors of library users, due in part to technological change but also as a result of broader societal changes and expectations of students and other library users.

A spin-off of reference assistance and the need to do more with less was "user instruction." The more the user learned about how to conduct library research, the less one-on-one assistance he or she would need. Public and academic institutions are eliminating or minimizing their physical reference desks by combining the circulation and reference desks. In some cases, a new service point focused on using media and/or technology services is emerging. Traditional reference service may be handled by online chat reference, instructional sessions, or appointments. Combined service desks in public and academic libraries mean traditional circulation staff now perform at least basic reference service. (This is a hard transition for many librarians, as doing reference was a big reason they became librarians.) These changes and the increased use of technology mean libraries continue to provide assistance, but can serve more people with the same or less reference staff members. The instructional aspect has evolved in terms of what is covered as well as what it is called—changing from bibliographic instruction to library instruction to information literacy.

Even the notion of free access is relatively recent; early "public" libraries in the United States were subscription based. A person paid an annual fee to be a member because there had to be some source of funding to acquire and house materials. The notion of tax support for libraries took some time to develop. For example, the Free Library of Philadelphia's name arose to distinguish it from the local subscription and/or restricted access libraries.

Free public library service, supported by local, regional, or national funding, has been the tradition in many countries. However, the notion of totally free has changed to something more akin to mostly free. As you might expect, technology has helped drive the change. Today no one thinks twice about charging or paying for photocopying service. Years ago, the idea of paying for an interlibrary loan (ILL) or document delivery was a topic of heated debate. (See chapter 5 for a discussion of these topics.) Today such charges to libraries and users are fairly common. That is not to say the notion that it should be free is dead. In 2012, Mark Norman wrote about a controversy he stirred up when suggesting an ILL fee for the public library system: "quite a few people were upset when I recommended to Swift NSW libraries that fees for interlibrary loans (ILL) should be around $18.00—close to the fee indicated by its own professional association, Australian Library and Information Association, and adopted by many academic libraries" (p. 95). Similar debates about ILL fees and other services that might be free or fee based were and are common in U.S. libraries.

From the Authors' Experience

Sinwell notes that as library users' behavior and use of technology has evolved, many libraries are now seeing a drop in revenue from photocopying and printing services in their facilities. Many library users e-mail e-content found online to themselves via e-mail, copy e-content to USB drives, and expect the library to provide a scanner for them to convert printed material to digital to copy to an USB drive.

Each new information technology seems to generate added and often unexpected costs for the library. More and more of these costs are being passed on to the person requesting the information or using the service. A newer typical charge is for printing material from online databases and the Internet. Initially libraries did not charge for such printing, but as the volume of printing has increased, more and more libraries have started charging for each page printed just as they did with photocopying.

The reality for libraries, their governing boards, funding agencies, and other stakeholders is there is no thing as a "free lunch." Everything a library does have some type of cost associated with it, be it time, space, or money. The challenge lies in trying to decide what should be free to the users, what should carry some cost, and deciding what the user's share can/should be. Even when there is a fee, libraries rarely recover the full costs associated with the service provided. For example, going back to the Mark Norman ILL fee, the amount set was just $6 rather than his recommended $18—a figure that the professional association also recommended (p. 95). The balancing of costs and service is always a challenging process. (We explore cost, budgets, and other financial issues in chapter 18.)

Not all technological developments result in passing on costs to users, at least not yet. One such example, which we explore in more depth in chapter 5, is the statewide resource-sharing network (e.g., OhioLINK) that allows end users to generate their own document delivery requests. Although free to end users, such programs do add significant costs to library operations.

One type of fee that has not yet become part of the U.S. library scene is payments to authors whose works are circulated by libraries. Public lending right (PLR) fees exist in a number of countries, including Canada and the United Kingdom. U.S. authors have at times attempted to have a PLR program implemented in the United States, with no success to date. Presently PLR national pools (funds from the government) pay the fees to the authors, not monies collected from libraries or readers. However, it is not inconceivable that in the future the fees might be a direct tax on libraries and borrowers. Although completely free library services are becoming a thing of the past, libraries still offer many free services, and charges seldom recover the full cost of any of the services provided.

From the Authors' Experience

Evans spent the better part of a year teaching and doing research in Iceland. There was one aspect of Icelandic library service that did and still does impress him that relates to free and fee service.

In the United States, almost all libraries offer users the option of checking out items from their collections, not every item such as reference items, but the vast majority of the materials. They provide this service free of charge. Not so in Iceland; there a person purchases a borrower's card that allows the individual to check out a fixed number of items before buying a new card. The card was similar to what you might get at a coffee shop that offers a free coffee after you buy x number of cups and they stamp or punch your card after each purchase. Icelandic library users referred to the card as the "clippacard." Based on his interviews with library users, Evans found the people both approved of the borrowing fee and felt strongly that it had to be maintained. The library generating the fee was able to use those monies to purchase new materials for their collections.

The system was/is very much like the early "subscription" libraries in the United States. The libraries had and do make a clear case for the fee, and the service community supports the concept, an example of sound library/user communication.

Today's libraries realize they face new and serious competition in what had been an almost monopolistic service area. Obviously the biggest competitor is the Internet (it is also in many ways a great asset for libraries) and sites such as Google and Yahoo!, not to mention Web 2.0 technologies and resources. What libraries must do is find an effective means to differentiate their information services from those of the Googles and Yahoos of the Internet world that offer only unevaluated information (or even the wikis that offer user-generated/moderated content). The key is to show that the differences that exist *do* matter in the long run. Steven Watkins of the Library 2.0 network proclaims, "Libraries need to be able to take reasoned risks to push the envelope when a clear trend emerges and a different way of envisioning and delivering services makes sense" (Casey and Savastinuk, 2007, p. xxi).

BASIC FUNCTIONS OF PUBLIC SERVICES

Library public service staff have several broad ongoing goals. The first is to provide access to informational materials. A second goal is to provide assistance to users in identifying appropriate materials. This goal requires trained and knowledgeable staff who possess excellent customer service skills. Other goals are to promote the value of learning, how to use information, to foster an enjoyment of reading, and to benefit from the knowledge and experiences of humankind as recorded and preserved through time. The American Library Association's (ALA) *Code of Ethics* (http://www.ala.org/advocacy/proethics /codeofethics/codeethics) summarizes the overall philosophy of library public service. It identifies the key service elements—collections, suitable loan conditions and service policies, and staff who are knowledgeable and who provide unbiased service to all. During periods of restricted or shrinking budgets, such as the one that has taken place recently, implementing or maintaining appropriate services creates several challenges. Maintaining high levels of service is an obvious challenge when there is a hiring freeze and staff vacancies cannot be filled. A less obvious, but very important challenge, is maintaining staff morale, especially when staff members know services could be better. Yet another challenge is maintaining the traditional concept of free services.

Another ALA document, the *Library Bill of Rights* (http://www.ala.org /advocacy/intfreedom/librarybill/), provides additional insight into what public service activities ought to address. Again, assuming you looked at the Web pages, you noted that the *Code* and *Bill* address many of the same topics. In terms of collections, it makes the point that collections should include all points of view on a topic and that complaints about collection content should have a review procedure that is fair and objective. Essentially, the document lays out the parameters for providing free, balanced, accurate information to all library visitors.

Many libraries have built upon the ALA's documents or ones generated by other professional information groups and posted their positions where anyone can view the policy. The following are some library Web sites that address user service policies and issues:

Falmouth Public Library (Massachusetts)
http://www.falmouthpubliclibrary.org/?/services/policies/customer-
    service-policy/
This is an example of a customer service pledge.

Chelmsford Public Library (Massachusetts)
http://www.chelmsfordlibrary.org/library_info/policies/2–1_publicser
    vice.html
This is an example of a governing board's policy that spells out its expecta-
    tions for the staff when providing service to users.

Jefferson County Public Library System (Colorado)
http://jeffcolibrary.org/policies
This is an example of a page outlining service policies and expectations.

Madison Public Library (Wisconsin)
http://www.madisonpubliclibrary.org/policies/behavior-policy
This is a sample of a specific user behavior policy.

Santa Monica City College (California)
http://www.smc.edu/AcademicAffairs/Library/Pages/Email-Reference-
    Service-Policy.aspx
This is a sample of an e-mail reference service policy for a community
    college.

Cocalico School District (Pennsylvania)
http://www.cocalico.k12.pa.us/lib/hs_services_policies.html
This is a sample of a site that lists a variety of high school library services
    and policies.

Nevada Middle School Library (Iowa)
http://nevadamslibrary.weebly.com/policies-services.html
A sample of listing of services available to middle school students.

University Laboratory High School (Illinois)
http://www.uni.illinois.edu/library/policies/
Outlines circulation policies for students at University Laboratory High
   School.

University of Maryland Libraries
http://www.lib.umd.edu/about/privacy
A sample privacy policy for library users.

As you can see, the issues regarding access to library services cover almost
every library type and vary in content.

Try This

Review three or more of the aforementioned Web sites and compare what
they identify as service with what is suggested in ALA's *Code of Ethics* and
Library Bill of Rights documents. Where do they match and differ? Can you
think of valid reason for the differences that you see?

A recent report (2013) authored by Kathryn Zickhr, Lee Rainie, and Kristen
Purcell and the Pew Internet and American Life project provides interesting
reading about what citizens think and how they make use of libraries. The
data was collected in October and November 2012 from a representative sample of U.S. citizens. The focus was on people's interactions with libraries in the
past 12 months. Fifty-nine percent (p. 5) of those surveyed reported they had
used a library in some manner in the past 12 months. Eighty percent said that
being able to borrow books was a very important library service. A similar percentage rated reference services as being very important. Seventy-seven percent believed that having free access to computers and the Internet is very
important.

The following are the top 14 reasons citizens gave for interacting with a
library:

1. Browse collections
2. Borrow printed books
3. Research a topic
4. Secure assistance from the library staff
5. Read, study, rest
6. Watch or listen to media
7. Access databases
8. Bring a child to attend an event/program
9. Borrow a DVD or videotape
10. Read a print magazine or newspaper
11. Attend a non-library event/program in the library's public meeting room
12. Attend a library class, event/program for adults
13. Borrow/download an audio book
14. Borrow a music CD. (p. 6)

The reasons identified as to why people used libraries were much wider than the items listed here (p. 5). Just about every service topic we cover in this book appeared somewhere in that report, and it is well worth reviewing.

Public services revolve around collections, circulation, document delivery, instruction, programming, and reference activities. Users judge a library on the basis of their experience with public services. Every public transaction adds to or detracts from the library's image. Keeping this in mind, especially when it is busy and pressure builds, is difficult; yet this is when library personnel must try hardest to provide top-notch service. We look at service quality in chapter 2, and discuss ethics and values in public services in chapter 14.

The primary purpose of circulation is to allow users to borrow collection items while assuring a degree of fair and equal access to all users. One part of assuring fair access is to limit the number of items checked out at one time and lending times. There are usually penalties (fines) for not complying with library usage policies. Collecting such fines can create strong emotions on both sides of the service counter. In today's library world the circulation service point has more duties than the basic checking out and in of items. In the case of academic and school libraries, the desk may also handle course/class reserve materials and borrowing services. (Chapter 6 covers circulation and reserve operations, while chapter 13 deals with such legal issues as copyright, contracts, and licenses.)

ALA's *Code of Ethics* states that "appropriate . . . collections" are one of the important elements of an ideal library public service program. Generally, the collection decisions are the responsibility of librarians with substantial input from the user community. Today's collections are a mix of formats, both physical and virtual. Although the content of the collection is beyond the scope of this book, how the collection is managed and maintained is a topic we cover in chapters 7, 8, and 9.

Document delivery service—DDS (a.k.a. interlibrary loan or ILL)—is a cooperative activity that, at least in theory, is capable of expanding the walls of the library to encompass the world's library collections. UNESCO's Universal Availability of Publications (UAP) Program expands on the concept. The goal of UAP is to have any publication available to any person anywhere in the world. The practical limits of DDS make its scope much smaller, but the potential for expanding customers' access to other libraries' collections is still great and is an important public service. (DDS activity is covered in chapter 5.)

Instructional activities of libraries vary widely. School libraries tend to focus on basic library usage practices, at least at the lower grades. Today's academic libraries tend to focus on accessing and evaluating e-materials and basic "information literacy." (The Association for College and Research Libraries [ACRL] provides standards for academic instruction.) Public libraries have the broadest range of instructional services, from basic English language literacy skills to classes in how to use common computer programs. Chapter 4 focuses on "formal" classes, while less formal instructional efforts appear in chapter 10.

Programming activities are limited only by the library staff's imagination, support from administration, and funding. Educational institution libraries tend to limit their programming to activities that link to some aspect of the institution's educational mission and goals. Public libraries are the most varied, ranging from such traditional activities as story hours and summer reading programs to costumed role-playing events. We address a variety of programming activities in chapter 10.

Answering questions and assisting people in identifying useful material is the focal point of reference service. Inquiries can be simple directional questions such as, "Where are the restrooms?" or "Which computers provide Internet access?" Or they can be information questions such as "Where are the craft books?" that sometimes morph into reference questions upon further probing (as you learn the true nature of the query was to find an article on the history of calligraphy). They can also be research questions that require several hours or even days to answer properly, if at all. Chapter 3 explores the issues and challenges of reference service. Other responsibilities of reference service may include instruction in using library resources, compiling bibliographies, or research guides.

From the Authors' Experience

Not long ago, Evans had to try to answer the following reference question, "What is the design of the tattoo behind the left ear of a White Mountain Apache male, which he gets when he becomes an elder?" That might not seem like an actual question, but it was; after several days of searching he did not find an illustration or description of the design, just that it was done. In our experience such questions are the most fun to work on even when, at times, there is no conclusive answer.

There are necessary support activities for the aforementioned basic services. One such activity is library security. Security issues can include both people and items (e.g., collection materials, equipment, and furniture). Natural and man-made disasters can injure people and damage or destroy thousands of items in a short period. Part of security is having a plan in place for handling such situations should they arise. There are also "quiet" disasters, such as insect infestations and the kind of deterioration of materials that time, uncontrolled environmental factors, and the bad habits of humans can cause. Constant vigilance, staff and customer education, and good planning are the best antidote to these threats to the library. (Chapter 16 covers these aspects of library security in depth.)

Without funding, there would be no library or services. Securing the requisite funds is a challenge. Chapter 18 looks at how to gather evidence of benefits for instances when funding agencies require proof that money is being spent wisely. Staffing is another crucial activity in the provision of service, and is covered in chapter 15. Budgetary and fiscal issues are the focus of chapter 18. You may be surprised to learn just how much of your work in public services involves securing funding. In chapter 12, we explore how libraries employ social media to enhance their various activities, from marketing to building and maintaining a community of users and supporters.

At least for the lifetime of this edition, we believe the library "as place" will continue to exist—a physical facility where staff and users congregate and interact. However, existing facilities must be managed and rethought from time to time to provide better service (remodeling, expanding, or creating a new facility). Chapter 19 covers these and other space-related concerns, while chapter 11 covers computer access.

CLOSING THOUGHTS

Throughout their long history, libraries have demonstrated the ability to adapt to a changing society and technologies. Society has also seen a value in maintaining libraries that provide a valued benefit to its members. We are confident that libraries will continue far into the future because people still believe in the usefulness of libraries. Early in this chapter we discussed a Pew Research Center study about libraries and the digital world of today and the fact that almost 60 percent of the survey respondents had gone to a library at least once in the past 12 months. Another Pew study, *Parents, Children, Libraries and Reading* (Miller et al., 2013), provided still more evidence that U.S. society values its libraries. Well over 90 percent (94%) of the parents surveyed said libraries are "important for their children;" of that group, 79 percent rated libraries as "very important." Over 80 percent of the respondents' primary reason for the importance of libraries was that "libraries provide their children with information and resources not available at home" (p. 2). Although the data is not that surprising (parents with young children have always been one of the largest groups of library users), the results certainly indicate that even in this digital world the library is viewed as an important resource.

The library service philosophy evolved over time from very limited access to open access for all. While technology has brought about a host of changes in the services provided, it has not changed the idea that any authorized person should have access to courteous, professional, and unbiased service.

Libraries are a fundamental part of society that need support from all constituencies so they have the resources to provide excellent service. As libraries evolve, they need to be respected and valued, as Chicago mayor Richard M. Daley is quoted as saying (Schmich, 2013): "Some people say libraries are old-fashioned, they're lost in a new society. No. It's all learning in a new environment."

We conclude this chapter with a quote from Keith Fiels (2013), executive director of the American Library Association, who noted:

Libraries of all types are currently undergoing changes that most agree are transformative.

But what do we mean when we talk about "transforming" libraries? We mean we are not dealing with quantitative change—doing more, for instance—but with qualitative change. This means fundamental change in the very nature of what we do and how we do it. . . .

As communities have changed, so has the relationship of the library to the community. (p. 6)

Chapter Review Material

1. Thinking about the changes that have occurred in libraries over time, what do you think are the requirements for libraries to prosper in the digital world?
2. What are the four ways libraries serve their societies?
3. What are the major factors in libraries' longevity?
4. Describe how libraries have adopted new technologies throughout their history.
5. What are the pros and cons to the various labels people apply to individuals who are served by libraries?
6. Describe the components of the two traditional library organizational structures.
7. Describe the public services a person can expect to find in almost any type of library.
8. Discuss how ALA's *Code of Ethics* and *Library Bills of Rights* influence library public services.

REFERENCES

Barotz, Celia. 2013. "Libraries Are Vital to the Community." *Arizona Daily Sun*, April 24, A5.

Booth, Mal, Sally Schofield, and Belinda Tiffen. 2012. "Change and Our Future at UTS Library: It's Not Just about Technology." *Australian Academic & Research Libraries* 43, no. 1: 32–45.

Carpenter, Kenneth E. 1986. *The First 350 Years of the Harvard University Library*. Cambridge, MA: Harvard University Press.

Casey, Michael E., and Laura C. Savastinuk. 2007. *Library 2.0. A Guide to Participatory Library Service*. New Jersey: Information Today.

Fiels, Michael Keith Michael. 2013. "Defining 'Transformation.'" *American Libraries* 44, no. 5: 6–7.

Garcia-Marco, Francisco-Javier. 2011. "Libraries in the Digital Ecology: Reflections and Trends." *Electronic Library* 29, no. 1: 105–120.

Grossman, Hal B. 2011. "A Comparison of the Progressive Era and the Depression Years: Societal Influences on Predications of the Future of the Library." *Library & Cultural Record* 46, no. 1: 102–128.

Lewis, David. 2007. "A Strategy for Academic Libraries in the First Quarter of the 21st Century." *College & Research Libraries* 68, no. 5: 418–434.

Miller, Carolyn, Kathryn Zickuhr, Lee Rainie, and Kristen Purcell. 2013. *Parents, Children, Libraries and Reading*. Washington, D.C.: Pew Research Center's Internet & American Life Project. http://libraries.pewinternet.org/2013/05/01/parents-children-libraries-and-reading/.

Mullins, James L. 2012. "The Changing Definition and Role of Collections and Services in the University Research Library." *Indiana Libraries* 31, no. 1: 18–24.

Norman, Mark. 2012. "Frail, Fatal, Fundamental: The Future of Public Libraries." *Aplis* 25, no. 2: 94–100.

Piper, Paul S. 2013. "The Library's Future Is Digital: HathiTrust and the Digital Public Library of America." *Online Searcher* 37, no. 2: 22–26.

Quint, Barbara. 2013. "The Searcher's Voice." *Online Searcher* 37, no 1: 33–34.

Rietz, Joan. 2004. *Dictionary for Library and Information Science*. Westport, CT: Libraries Unlimited.

Schmich, Mary. 2013. "Daley Settles (Not Entirely) into Life as a Regular Chicagoan." *Chicago Tribune*, April 28. http://articles.chicagotribune.com/2013–04–28 /news/ct-met-schmich-0428–20130428_1_downtown-high-rise-maggie-new-office.

Shera, Jesse. 1933. "Recent Social Trends and Future Library Policy." *Library Quarterly* 3, no. 4: 339–353.

UN News Centre. 2013. "Power of Books Celebrated by UN Chief as New Library Opens in Ethiopian Capital. January 31. http://www.un.org/apps/news /story.asp?NewsID=41096&Cr=ethiopia&Cr1=#.Uel6Q1nD8dU.

Vyhnanek, Kay, and Christy Zlatos. 2011. *Reconfiguring Service Delivery*. Spec Kit 327. Washington, D.C.: Association of Research Libraries.

Weinberger, David. 2014. "Let the Future Go." *Library Journal* 139, no. 15: 28.

Zickuhr, Kathryn, Lee Raine, and Kristen Purcell. 2013. *Library Services in the Digital Age*. Washington, D.C.: Pew Research Center's Internet & American Life Project. http://libraries.pewinternet.org/2013/01/22/Library-services/.

SUGGESTED READINGS

Albrecht, Karl, and Ron Zemke. 2002. *Service America in the New Economy*. New York: McGraw-Hill.

Alvite, Luisa and Barrionenuevo, Leticia. 2011. *Libraries for Users: Services in Academic Libraries*. Oxford: Chandos.

Black, Alistair, and Simon Pepper. 2012. "From Civic Place to Digital Space: The Design of Public Libraries in Britain from Past to Present." *Library Trends*, 61, no. 2: 440–470.

Coffman, Steve1. 2012. "The Decline and Fall of the Library Empire." *Searcher* 20, no. 3: 14–47.

Cooper, Tom. 2007. "Are We Helping the Information Have-Nots?" *Public Libraries* 46, no. 1: 18–19.

Craig, Barbara L. 2011. "The Past May Be the Prologue: History's Place in the Future of the Information Professions." *Libraries & the Cultural Record* 46, no. 2: 206–219.

Greifeneder, Elke, and Michael Seadle. 2012. "Interactions between Libraries and Technology over the Past 30 Years: An Interview with Clifford Lynch." *Library Hi Tech* 30, no. 4: 565–578.

Grief, Terri. 2014. "The Constancy of Change." *Knowledge Quest* 43, no. 1: 4–5.

Herrera-Viedma, Enrique, and Javier López-Gijón. 2013. "Libraries' Social Role in the Information Age." *Science* 339, no. 6126: 1382.

Malachowski, Margot. 2011. "Public Libraries and Health Literacy." *Computers in Libraries* 31, no. 10: 5.

Matheson, Nina W., and William H. Welch. 2013. "The Idea of the Library in the Twenty-First Century." *Journal of the Medical Library Association* 100, Supplement: 1–7.

McDowell, Kate. 2011. "Children's Voices in Librarians' Words, 1890–1930." *Libraries & the Cultural Record* 46, no. 1: 73–101.

Robinson, Michael. 2008. "Digital Nature and Digital Nurture: Libraries, Learning, and the Digital Native." *Library Management* 29, no. 1/2: 67–76.

Williment, Kenneth. 2011. "It Takes a Community to Create a Library." *Public Libraries* 50, no. 2: 30–35.

Woodward, Jeannette. 2009. *Creating the Customer-Driven Academic Library.* Chicago: American Library Association.

Yap, Sylvia, and Gabriel Yeo. 2007. "Reaching Out, Building Bonds." *Library Management* 28, no. 8/9: 569–576.

Zabel, Diane, and Lorraine J. Pellack. 2012. "Now Serving Customer 7,528,413." *Reference & User Services Quarterly* 51, no. 4: 316–318.

Chapter 2

Customer Service

If you walked out on the street today and randomly asked someone to talk about a recent service experience, good or bad, chances are the person would recount a story of deep disappointment. . . . And yet we should be living through the Century of Service—so what's going on?

—*Frances Frei and Anne Morriss, 2012*

Have you ever thought about how the school library is like a supermarket?

—*Barbara Bowling, 2012*

The word *customer* in customer services is one that causes a shudder in some more traditional members of the library profession. . . . The fact that libraries shy away from referring to their users as *customers* is an indication of the difficulty with which libraries have adapted to the new consumer approach to higher education.

—*Erika L. Gavillet, 2011*

No matter what business you're in, the customer is king. And customer service is the key to success or failure. That means customer service training is one of the smartest investments a company can make.

—*Margery Weinstein, 2013*

We concluded chapter 1 with a quotation from Michael Fiels (2013). We begin this chapter with another quotation from Fiels's essay, where he noted: "Another area of transformation is that of user expectations and user services. . . . Increasingly users expect services 24/7" (p. 6). He listed seven areas in which libraries are undergoing changes. We address the following six of the seven areas from his list in various chapters of this book:

- The composition of service communities
- The way libraries interact with their communities

21

- The variety of services communities want
- The nature and content of library collections
- The physical space and its usage by libraries
- The composition and skills of the library workforce

Each of the areas has an impact on what services libraries provide and how they go about providing those services.

Service is not a very long word, but like so many short words it has a surprising number of meanings and people use it in many different ways. Look up *service* in a reasonably comprehensive dictionary, such as *Webster's Third New International Dictionary* (Springfield, MA: G. & C. Merriam Company), and you find 20 or more definitions. Different types of organizations as well as individual people assign different meanings when they use the word *service*.

What libraries and other nonprofit organizations mean by service differs significantly from that of for-profit organizations. For example, a utility company's "service" is a product that is available to you, if you have the money to pay its fees and abide by its rules. Further it can stop the service at will and with little notice as well as raise its prices. Retail stores such as supermarkets and bookstores have a vested interest in good customer relations and service, but they too are free to set a price on their products and often top-notch customer service comes with a higher price for the product. Just think about the difference in prices and quality of service between Wal-Mart and a high-end department store.

Libraries certainly have products and services—story hours and course reserves, for example—but they typically offer those products to anyone in their service community regardless of the person's ability to pay. The vast majority of products are free of cost and for those where there is a charge, the price rarely comes close to recovering all the library's expenses for providing the product or service. About the only time a library stops providing a service is when the demand for that service ceases. (However, in some library organizations, there is a reluctance to let go of traditional library services or practices, even when they are no longer in high demand, for example, the bookmobile.) Overall, libraries adapt to the changing needs of users and continually explore offering new services.

In the business world, the professional/formal concept of customer service dates from at least the late nineteenth century. The desire was for retail stores, hotels, and restaurants to develop a loyal customer base that would provide repeat business. Beginning in the 1980s, many retail businesses paid renewed attention to customer service because market research indicated it was an effective way to attract and retain customers. Much research and hundreds of articles and books have been devoted to meeting customer needs. By the 1980s, libraries began to address the findings of this research, and adapt and apply these practices to improving their customer service practices.

WHY DOES CUSTOMER SERVICE MATTER?

As we noted earlier, attracting and retaining customers through programs specifically designed to produce loyalty to an organization's product or service (e.g., the "club card") became a popular marketing trend in the 1980s. Every organization needs repeat customers to survive and prosper. However, customers tend to remain loyal only as long as they are satisfied with the quality of the service or product provided. If these do not measure up or keep pace with changing customer preferences, expectations, and needs, then repeat use cannot be ensured. As Lynn Jurewicz and Todd Cutler (2003) observed, "We have seen in our own lives that as customer habits have changed, savvy businesses have changed their service strategies in an attempt to anticipate customer needs. . . . Too busy to go the mall? Buy from a catalog online and we'll send it to your door. Need to know when to update your online auction bid? Sign up for our service and we'll notify you. Want to know where your package is? Check our website and we'll track it for you" (p. 2).

Something to keep in mind about customer service is that it is not the same as customer satisfaction. *Customer satisfaction* is what a person remembers about his or her service experience. For example, in a library context, a person may know that the end result of the service process was exactly what was needed; however, what he or she remembers about the process may be very negative. Essentially, the person's perception of the service focuses on the interpersonal and relational process rather than the outcome. Thus, service is a perception and is often strongly influenced by human personality, sensitivity, or temperament, both on the part of individual customer and the library staff member.

A clear example of the impact of this is to think about a recent experience you had when standing in a service line—such as the grocery store, post office, or library—for a long time. The longer the wait for the service, the less patience most of us have. The result is, even if the person providing the service is courteous and efficient, many of us leave feeling dissatisfied. We may feel less dissatisfied if the person apologized for the long wait, but we may still retain negative thoughts about the "service."

Organizations that know there will be lines and customer frustration with long waits have tried several approaches. Having a single line with multiple service points is effective as long as each service point has someone providing service. If anything, people become even more frustrated when there is a substantial line and several service points are unstaffed. With shrinking budgets, keeping all service points fully staffed is a challenge. A relatively recent effort to address such challenges is "self-service" points. Many libraries now have some self-service checkout stations available to help users handle the checkout process on their own. As long as the stations are easy to use, in good working order, and if there are staff nearby for troubleshooting, such equipment can mitigate poor customer service experiences caused by long lines or by library staff with customer service deficiencies.

Check This Out

Advisory board member Ruth Kifer identified the Self-Service Nation page from East Lansing Public Library, which discusses the use of self-checkout systems:
http://www.elpl.org/blog/self-service-nation.

Keep in mind that perceptions of service quality are influenced throughout the process, not just at the start and ending points of the transaction. For example, the reference process has a number of points that can create a positive or negative impression—fielding the question, assessing what is wanted, and finding the answer are a few such points. Then there is the fact that a user may engage in several service processes during a single visit. Unfortunately, one negative experience is likely to offset several positive experiences. It is true that you can't do very much about the user who arrives in a negative mood, but if the public service staff understand the importance of their own disposition and efforts in providing good service—both perceived and actual—you are on the way to successful service.

You can view customer service interactions as either transaction based or relationship based. "Transaction-based" service occurs at point of need; for example, when a person checks out a book or media item. This is the kind of service that most organizations, including libraries, typically focus on. However, the realization that building loyalty is the best way to retain customers has caused many organizations to focus on "relationship-based" service. Transaction-based service is seen most clearly in the relationships that the public services staff sometimes develop with their user communities. Establishing a relationship with our customers through learning their reading or viewing interests allows us to recommend new titles as they arrive or new Web sites or databases.

From the Advisory Board

Advisory board member Jean Wallace is a school librarian who ran a single-person junior high school library. Jean indicated that it was especially important to make conscious, deliberate efforts to be friendly to all teachers whether or not she personally connected with them in the library space. Her opinion was that it was too easy for staff to avoid the library, but if they found her to be congenial, they'd be more apt to bring their classes to the library.

The American Association of School Librarians (AASL) found the following points of service excellence in common among recent award-winning libraries: collaborating with teachers in curriculum planning which enabled teaching librarians to tailor their programs to meet needs and interests of students; innovative use of technology; and assessments that validated connections to student success (see Elizabeth Marcoux's 2013 essay "Winning Characteristics for the National School Library Program of the Year" in *Teacher Librarian* 40, no. 4: 34–36).

Many communities of users populate the library arena. In public libraries, although relatively little is written about service to children, they are customers. Collection development and programming for them are major service components. In academic institutions, librarians often develop collegial relationships with faculty and are able to offer specialized assistance with their research and teaching. Many Web 2.0 initiatives, described later in this chapter, are aimed at personalizing library services in an effort to make them more useful and attractive to library customers. Doing so increases the library's usefulness to its customers and the value they place on library services.

The idea that libraries are businesses is anathema to many librarians. It implies a paradigm shift. Businesses exist for the bottom line—to make a profit—and libraries clearly are not in the money-making business (usually far from it). Libraries provide intellectual, recreational, and cultural value to their users, only some of whom pay for it through taxes, tuition, or user fees. This intellectual value, many argue, is a public good that enriches their communities beyond dollars and cents. Further the argument follows, this may equate or reduce libraries to the level of a capitalist enterprise transforming libraries from cultural icons to something more like retail storefronts.

We don't dispute that libraries are not a societal good whose value goes far beyond any measure that society can derive such as cost analysis or return on investment. However, it is also true that libraries, like all organizations, are under enormous pressures today to demonstrate evidence of accountability. Part of that accountability is being effective public stewards of the resources provided to the library. As Darlene Weingand (1997) stated,

> Librarians who flinch at the word *customer* are operating out of an outmoded paradigm. This older paradigm portrays the library as a "public good," with as high a ranking on the "goodness" scale as the national flag, parenthood, and apple pie. As a public good, the library "should" receive public support. However, today's library is in increasingly tight competition for declining resources, and unless it adopts and masters the language and techniques of its competitors, it faces a future of declining support and significance. (p. 3)

Valerie Gross, CEO and president of Howard County Library System (HCLS), and a 2013 Gale/LJ Library of the Year, posited that the library blends the best of the academic and business worlds. Like successful business, the library stands for excellence, accountability, and extraordinary customer service (the "wow" factor as it is called in some circles). The exceptional service that is the hallmark of HCLS is spelled out in its customer service philosophy: "When we put on our name badges and step behind a customer service or research desk, we personify our customer service philosophy. We prize its values, operate from its assumptions, and model its behaviors" (Berry, 2013, p. 30).

Something to Ponder

Businesses have made it a priority to focus on positive user experiences by cultivating a "wow" factor for their customers. As noted by Denise Baril (2011), "Impact is everything. With the speed of technology and our lives, we are constantly being bombarded . . . so that nothing stands out" (p. 6). Libraries need to work toward developing their own "wow factor" by considering the external environment, information and education trends, and the needs of library customers themselves (Kunneke, 2007, p. 3). Baril and Kunneke's articles are worth reviewing:

Baril, Denise. 2011. "How to Wow." *Sales & Service Excellence* 11, no. 5: 6.
Kunneke, Kathy. 2007. "Creating and Marketing a WOW-Library." *IFLA Conference Proceedings 1–14.*

Consider what it would take for your local public, academic, or school library to build and cultivate a "wow" factor. Who should be involved in this process? How would you know it had been achieved? How would you maintain this experience for users?

In their "Top Ten Assumptions for the Future of Academic Libraries and Librarians," (ACRL, 2008) the ACRL Research Committee listed as number seven, "As part of the 'business of higher education,' students will increasingly view themselves as 'customers' of the academic library and will demand high-quality facilities, resources, and services attuned to their needs and concerns" (p. 2). Another rationale, from a public library perspective, was provided by Sueanne Walters (1994) when she stated that "good service will result in customers voting for bond elections, contributing private dollars, and volunteering to support libraries. Poor service will result in lost elections and lost funding. It is as simple as that. Good customer service pays" (p. 1).

You may or may not agree with Weingand's and Walter's perspectives, which have taken on greater urgency with the appearance of information providers and book purveyors such as Google and Amazon; however, borrowing and adapting the principles of customer satisfaction from the corporate world is a pragmatic way to improve library services and better serve our communities. It is also a way to demonstrate to those demanding accountability the value of the library to their home organization or community. Stewart Saunders (2007) observed, "Imposing a business model on libraries has been beneficial for library management" (p. 24). It is important for library staff to know what their customers want and need from their libraries, and how customers value the resources and services they receive. The reason for this, summarized by Schlachter (2006), is that "excellence in customer service leads to greater use of library services, better coordination with other departments, and a greater chance of ensuring the security of library funding" (p. 8).

WHAT USERS WANT

Knowing the service community's interests is a critical component in creating and maintaining valued library services. There are a number of methods for gathering such information as well as nomenclature for the process. We will look at some of the methods in more detail in later chapters. Some of the methods used for the data-gathering activities are community analysis, community study, information audit, needs analysis, and needs assessment.

There are three important concepts related to service that we should define—needs, wants, and demands. We employ these concepts not only in this chapter but several other chapters as well. *Needs* are issues for the community, institution, or person that require one or more solutions; it does not always follow that a need is something the community, organization, or person wants. *Wants* are things that the group or person is willing to expend time, effort, or money to acquire; it does not necessarily follow that the want is good for those wanting it. *Demands* are wants that a group or person is willing to take action to achieve (e.g., paying for it, writing letters requesting it, making telephone calls, testifying, or demonstrating). From a library perspective, the ideal outcome of a service community study is identification of needs that are wanted and demanded.

These terms are generic in character. Because the literature of librarianship, including this book, makes frequent use of the term "need," the following breaks down that term into more discrete meanings. Jonathan Bradshaw (1972) discussed four types of social needs: normative, felt, expressed, and comparative that have had wide acceptance within the social sciences.

Normative needs often are based on expert opinion. One commonly cited normative need is the need to increase the level of literacy of the community. Teachers, librarians, and others, in their professional roles, express a desire to address this normative need. To some degree, the general public understands this need; however, finding adequate funding to address the need is often a challenge. This is due to the fact the community/society does not perceive the importance or scope of the normative need.

Felt needs (wants) come from the community based on its belief about a problem or issue. How appropriate or realistic felt needs may be is often debatable; nevertheless, such needs are a reflection of a community's perception of a situation. Just as normative needs are not always what the community thinks is important, felt needs do not always reflect what is good for the community.

Expressed needs (demands) reflect behavior. Individuals often say they want or need something, but their behavior shows they really want or need something else. Libraries tend to respond well to expressed needs. That is, libraries are more likely to meet a greater percentage of the active customers' expressed needs than they are to the needs of infrequent users. A needs assessment project can reveal whether the library is overresponding to active users' needs.

Comparative needs are the result of comparing the service population to other like populations. From the library perspective one such comparison might be the number of items circulated per capita. When making such comparisons, the service level or collection relevance for the two groups must be the same. One advantage of focusing on comparative needs is that they usually result in some quantitative measures that can be useful in setting goals for new services or programs according to the results of the assessment project.

The foregoing is a general discussion of theoretical need types. They do have applications to the library environment, assuming you take into account library missions, goals, and values. When a library can identify an expressed, normative, and felt need that also reflects other practices, that is an ideal situation. Usually you have to address only a few of the needs in order for customers to realize their requests are being taken seriously.

It is useful to remember, both during data collection and analysis of the data is that as the importance of the information wants increase, so do the amounts of money, time, and other resources community organizations or individual people are willing to expend to secure accurate information. From the individual to the largest organization, all information seekers place a value on each type of information used, often without being fully aware that they are doing so.

Several factors influence the information's value; one factor is its importance for pending decisions. The type and format of information wanted may also play a role in the valuation process. Another factor is accessibility and the effort required to gain access to information—sometimes labeled the "law of least effort."

According to the law of least effort, people and organizations expend as few resources as possible (time, money, or effort) to secure information. Frequently when a person is preparing a document, there is a need for more or updated information. A typical reaction is to turn first to materials at hand. Most people try this even when they know where they can secure more appropriate and relevant information, because taking the steps to find the more relevant information may be less convenient. Today, the process follows some variations:

- Check existing files/materials at hand (both physical and digital storage).
- Check the Internet—search Google or Amazon.
- Ask a friend or colleague (the "invisible college").
- Check with the local library and its databases.
- When all else fails and the need is great enough, request the library to secure the material from some other source (document delivery).

Experienced reference staff members are well aware of a sequence such as the above.

In chapter 17, we describe a number of data-gathering instruments used by libraries for various kinds of assessment purposes. The following are the methods, quantitative and qualitative, used most often by libraries to ascertain service community needs and wants.

Check These Out

Here are several Web sites worth reviewing that provide selected resources and examples of assessment activities:

Library Research Services: Resources for Community Analysis
http://www.lrs.org/data-tools/public-libraries/resources-for-commu
nity-analysis/
Library Research Service is located in Colorado and provides data for
studies.

South Carolina State Library: Community Needs Assessment
http://statelibrary.sc.libguides.com/community-needs-assessment
This site provides access to an assessment manual, as well as resources
   for South Carolina demographic information.

Richmond Public Library: Library Needs Assessment (2009)
http://www.rplf.org/download/Richmond_Needs_Doc_090216_sm.pdf
From the Richmond, California Library Foundation. This is an example
   of a study that employed almost all of the data collection techniques
   we describe in this chapter.

Surveys

Surveys or questionnaires are the data-gathering methodologies most often
used to ascertain customer needs and satisfaction (or dissatisfaction).
Although most library staff are not trained in survey methodology, it is easy
to find examples in the library literature of customer surveys conducted by
all types of libraries. Survey instruments may be administered via the Web,
mailed, e-mailed, or distributed in person to people in the library, on a street
corner, or shopping mall. A survey can reach more people than interviews and
focus groups, for example.

Interviews

Interview data-gathering involves an interviewer asking questions of one or
more individuals, usually one at a time. Carefully structured questions limit
the range of responses for interviewees to the areas of interest and make data
analysis easier. Interviewing has gained increased popularity as library staff
members have become more knowledgeable and skilled with focus group
methodology.

Focus Groups

Used since the 1920s by businesses, focus groups are essentially group
interviews. They involve open-ended questions/topics that are designed to
generate in-depth discussions with small groups, usually between 6 and 10
individuals. The participants are purposely selected and led (ideally) by a
trained facilitator, although resources do not always make this possible. The
groups explore a predefined topic in a nonthreatening and semistructured
setting. The goal is to obtain data about a single topic or limited range of
topics from a library user's perspective. The entire group answers questions
together.

Libraries frequently employ focus groups to determine customer satisfaction and to explore the reasons behind their satisfaction or dissatisfaction with
library services. While focus groups can provide a rich source of qualitative
data about library services, the methodology is labor intensive to perform and

that limits its wider use. Focus groups are frequently used in conjunction with surveys to gather both qualitative and quantitative data about service.

Observation

Observation of customer and library staff behavior has been a popular data-gathering method since at least the 1960s. One popular method, called unobtrusive observation, involves someone (referred to in the business world as a "secret shopper") posing as a library customer and asking typical questions in a reference or other service setting, then judging the quality of the staff member's response. Some libraries have used extensive observation programs, including videotaping, to assess service behavior and quality. However, observation is most commonly used informally by managers seeking quick information about customer service interactions.

From the Authors' Experience

Saponaro worked in a library that employed many techniques for customer feedback, including a suggestion box and Web site comment forms. One additional technique of gathering feedback as to user needs and experiences was Web site usability studies, which were conducted periodically in order to determine if changes to the library Web site were needed. In such studies, users were asked to perform a set of specific tasks and their attempts to do so were observed both in person, and with the use of eye-tracking software installed on test machines. Results were analyzed and reviewed by the committee responsible for Web site maintenance.

In addition to these methodologies, customer requests and complaints are also an important source of information about their wants and needs. These requests or complaints may be made informally to library staff while they are assisting users or more formally through suggestion boxes, Web sites, or other Web 2.0 communication vehicles such as Facebook. Repeated requests or suggestions for particular services or resources should be taken seriously by the library administration.

CUSTOMER SERVICE PLAN

The most effective way to establish and maintain a customer service orientation is to plan for it. A good plan can improve customer relations and internal operations by refocusing staff on customer needs. Peter Hernon and John Whitman (2001) offered the following steps toward mobilizing a service plan:

1. Determine and take control of the factors that influence service quality and satisfaction.
2. Set expectations for customer service based on what can reasonably be delivered.

3. Define the relationship between the customer and the library.
4. Empower the employees to satisfy customers.
5. Ask for customer feedback.
6. Respond to customers individually and collectively. (p. 77)

Some years ago, Susan Wehmeyer, Dorothy Auchter, and Arnold Hirshon (1996) distilled from the literature the following consensus items about customer service plans:

- *Frontline staff are vital to the plan's success.* Frontline staff are usually the only library employees customers see, so their responsibility for the success of customer service is key.
- *Service is a product.* Great service not only enhances the reputation of an organization, but adds value to the organization's services by enabling customers to use the resources effectively.
- *Understand your customer.* Formal research such as surveys and focus groups is important in helping the organization determine which services are important to its customers.
- *There is no quick fix.* Long-term, reliable, and effective customer service depends on regularly reviewing procedures, careful planning, and employee training. (p.174)

Check This Out

The *ALA Policy Manual* section that addresses library service responsibilities is a good starting point for thinking about your service plan:
http://www.ala.org/aboutala/governance/policymanual/updated
policymanual/section2/52libsvcsandrespon.

Glen Holt (2006), although addressing service to low-income families, outlined several key components for an overall service plan:

- Solicit information from members of poor households about the services they want and need.
- Organize quality services based on the information gathered.
- Decide the limits of the services you will provide.
- Deliver services at times convenient to users.
- Deliver services at the right locations.
- Make partnerships with agencies who know their neighborhoods and constituencies.
- Publicize services in neighborhood venues like billboards, buses and rapid transit vehicles and stops, and ethnic and satellite radio stations.
- Recognize that kids lead.
- Organize family experiences.
- Organize performance venues for kids. When kids perform, lots of adults attend. (pp. 184–185)

Two interesting examples of customer service plans are those of the Stettler Public Library, Alberta (http://www.municipalaffairs.alberta.ca /documents/lcvss/stettlerplanofservic87828.pdf) and the Brooklyn Public Library(http://www.bklynpubliclibrary.org/sites/default/files/files/pdf/about /PlanService2012–2016.pdf). The Stettler document contains material about the library's community survey activities as well as its service plans, while the Brooklyn document outlines assessment activities for measuring the success of each plan element.

SERVICE QUALITY

Jan Ferri-Reed (2011) identified several key reasons why libraries should think about service quality:

- Unhappy customers will tell 8 to 16 people about their bad experience.
- Unhappy customers rarely come back.
- Unhappy customers will stay customers, if you make an attempt to immediately address the issue.
- Unhappy customers are five times less costly to keep than to attract new customers. (p. 30)

Although the writer's focus was on for-profit organizations, her points do apply to the nonprofit sector as well. In the case of libraries, keep in mind that between 20 and 40 percent of the service community population does not use libraries (Becker et al., 2010, p. 26). Turning a non-library user into a library user probably is more than five times as costly to achieve, if you can do that at all.

Another factor to consider is that our "customers" are in a constant state of change. What was viewed as good quality yesterday may not be tomorrow. That means you must constantly monitor user behaviors and consider the implications of what you observe. And, libraries should monitor other industries and customer expectations in those arenas, so that best practices from other venues can be applied to libraries as possible and appropriate.

An important aspect of customer service is service quality. Service quality has been defined from at least four perspectives:

- Excellence
- Value
- Conformance to specifications
- Meeting and/or exceeding expectations. (Hernon and Nitecki, 2001, p. 690)

Many library researchers looking at service quality focus on the last perspective. Quality is usually assessed by employing "gap analysis," that is, determining the gap between customers' expectations for a particular service or for the library in general, and the customer's perceptions about the library and its services. Service quality is a means of reducing the gap between customer expectations and needs. If the gap between expectations and perceptions is too great, this is defined as poor service. This model offers greater utility for decision making and planning than simple satisfaction surveys.

Both service quality and customer satisfaction may be ends in themselves, but quality is often the antecedent of customer satisfaction. Better quality service usually results in higher levels of customer satisfaction. Determining and trying to improve the quality of the services offered is therefore an important part of a commitment to customer service. A paradigm of excellent service quality encourages library staff to identify user expectations and desires and commit the resources necessary to satisfy high priority expectations.

Each library needs to determine for itself how to define quality customer service. Valerie Zeithaml, A. Parasuraman, and Leonard Berry (1990) identified 10 dimensions of service quality:

- *Tangibles*—Appearance of physical facilities, equipment, staff, and information materials;
- *Reliability*—Ability to perform the promised service dependably and accurately;
- *Responsiveness*—Willingness to help customers and provide prompt service;
- *Courtesy*—Politeness, respect, and friendliness of staff;
- *Empathy*—Caring and individualized attention that the firm provides its customers;
- *Competence*—Required skills and knowledge to perform the service, believability, and honesty of the library;
- *Security*—Freedom from danger, risk, or doubt;
- *Access*—Approachability and ease of contact;
- *Communication*—Keeping the users informed in language they can understand and listening to them; and
- *Understanding the customer*—Making the effort to know users and their needs. (pp. 22–23)

Customers will have different expectations regarding each dimension and component of quality service, and library staff cannot meet every one of these. Priorities will have to be established based on a particular library's customer needs and resources.

A distinction should be made between service quality and customer satisfaction. Customer satisfaction is only one component, albeit an important one, of service quality. Certainly our customers are the best judge of whether, and how much, they are satisfied with library services. However, if a user is satisfied with a reference transaction, but the answer he or she received is wrong, is this quality service?

In chapter 17, we describe many ways libraries work to evaluate the quality of their operations. The idea of determining quality has been extended from numbers measuring inputs and outputs to the relationship between customers and the library. Outcome measurement is one way of describing this relationship, and customer satisfaction is another way. Customer assessment should be employed along with outcome measures in order to determine a balanced picture of a library's service quality.

TECHNOLOGY AND CUSTOMER SERVICE

One of the ways businesses are improving customer satisfaction is by using technology to enable customers to shop for products and services. Libraries also use technology to empower their customers to gain access to services. Libraries employ the Internet and Web sites as a major part of their information delivery systems. Library Web sites have evolved from simply linking to their OPAC to offering online reference services, homework help, technology access per Americans with Disabilities Act, blogs, RSS feeds, wikis, meeting room reservations, online research guides, digital newsletters, and various commercial and in-house databases, among other things.

The prevalence of Web 2.0 tools allows new opportunities for libraries to provide services and to satisfy changing customer needs and expectations. Web 2.0 refers to the evolution of the Web to being user centered in that it allows users to create, change, interact, and publish dynamic online content. It is essentially not a Web of textual publication but rather a Web of multimedia communication. In a library context, sometimes termed Library 2.0, these tools allow customers to participate in creating the resources and services they want.

Jack Maness (2006) described the following elements of Library 2.0:

- It is user centered.
- It provides a multi-media experience.
- It is socially rich.
- It is communally innovative. (p. 140)

As library users change, from the technologies they use to their demographics and expectations, libraries must change along with them. Web 2.0 tools allow libraries the flexibility to adapt to changing environments. As noted by Steven Bell (2014), "Rather than create a specific type of experience, the current thinking in UX [user experience design] is to design for an environment that will instead make it possible for any user to derive satisfaction from his or her personal experience" (p. 373). Michael Stephens (2006) listed some of the uses libraries are making of Web 2.0 "social software" tools "in creating conversations, connections, and community:"

- Openness
- Ease of uses
- Innovation
- Social interaction
- Creation of content
- Sharing
- Decentralization
- Participation
- Trust (p. 32)

No doubt more tools like those described in the preceding list will be forthcoming.

As you might guess, allowing our service community to access library resources that were formerly the exclusive domain of library staff is not without controversy. Some argue that we are in danger of deprofessionalizing libraries by allowing too much creative participation by our users. Web 2.0 technology is most effective if it is viewed as supplementing, not replacing, traditional library expertise. For example, allowing users to "tag" entries in our OPACs with their own descriptors, comments, reviews, and ratings does not replace the cataloging expertise required to assign controlled vocabulary subject headings. Tagging does, however, offer an additional means for customers to discover the contents of our OPACs and improves their utility. Using Web 2.0 tools is a customer-centered paradigm that seeks to reduce barriers to information, increase library knowledge of customer wants and needs, and improve customer satisfaction and interaction with library services and resources.

Providing access to productivity tools (e.g., Google Docs and Google Spreadsheets) has a dual advantage for libraries, especially small libraries. As noted by Gordon and Stephens (2007), online productivity software "allows library users to write resumes, compose letters, create newsletters, share documents and carry out other tasks" (p. 30) usually performed via the Microsoft Office or Apple suites. Further, online software allows users to create, store, access, and share their documents online for free, anywhere they can access a network connection. Empowering people to customize their own Web-based services in this way can be an important step to lessening the technology gap between haves and have-nots, and will certainly create a loyal base of library supporters who utilize these services. Offering online productivity software is also an advantage for the library. It can be expensive to keep up with new versions of commercial office productivity software (e.g., Microsoft and Apple), both the software and hardware requirements, and providing access to, and training in, the alternative free software can allow the library to provide user services they could not otherwise afford (Gordon and Stephens, 2007, p. 31).

In adapting new technology, libraries need to be careful to avoid "technology lust" for new tools just because they are new. Technology is a tool; it is never a good reason to employ it just because you can. Tools should be adopted selectively, to meet identified user needs, and regularly evaluated as part of the library's assessment program.

Check These Out

More and more, library services are digitally based. A problem for organizations, profit oriented or not, that offer some form of frontline or online service(s) is the danger of thinking that online service requires less thought about customer relations than does face-to-face service.

Two resources to review that concentrate on online customer service are Marsha Collier's *The Ultimate Online Customer Service Guide* (Hoboken, NJ: John Wiley & Sons, 2011) and Donald Barclay's *Serving Online Customers: Lessons for Libraries from the Business World* (Lanham, MD: Rowman and Littlefield, 2014).

CUSTOMER SERVICE TRAINING

In order to be sure that all employees have the same "baseline" knowledge regarding customer service, libraries need to provide an orientation or training session on customer service for all new hires, even those with prior library experience. Each library has a particular set of values and philosophy of service on how it expects staff to carry out public service activities, and should provide this orientation for all new hires, regardless of prior experience. However, it is not a given that all libraries provide such training. Kate Laughlin (2012) noted, "During the many years when I worked within different levels of library service, I marveled at how few of us were required to have any basic training in providing effective customer service. In the work I do with libraries statewide, I see that this is a common disconnect. For example, not every library intentionally targets service excellence in its recruitment process. It is as if there is an assumed mastery of skills" (p. 29).

Most customer service training is typically done by circulation and reference supervisors, often including classroom instruction, role-playing, computer-based instruction, and unsupervised instruction involving audio, written, or video materials.

From the Authors' Experience

The University of Maryland Libraries launched a unique customer service training program in fall of 2014. The program includes a module-based training in the campus course management system, which provides participants a digital "badge" when the course is successfully completed. All public services staff are required to complete the training over the course of the academic year. The online program is supplemented with in-person workshops on topics such as conflict management.

The program required extensive prework and preparation on behalf of a group of library staff—including volunteer "pretesters" of the online modules. (Saponaro served as one of the pretesters.) Cinthya Ippoliti reviews the process used to create and implement the system in her article "Are You Being Served? Designing the Customer Service Curriculum" (*Public Services Quarterly*, 2014, 10, no. 3: 177–192).

One of the most common, and important, components of customer service training is how to handle so-called difficult customers. People often come to the library with a specific need and try to find information unassisted. Some find what they want but many try unsuccessfully until their frustration and confusion builds up into the very real condition known as "library anxiety." Since the 1980s, a number of studies (see, for example, Mellon, 1986; Jiao and Onwuegbuzie, 1999; Nikolaison, 2011) have identified some of the causes of library anxiety, including the size of the library, lack of knowledge about how to find information, where things are located, how to begin looking for information, and what to do to get help. Unfortunately, some people are reluctant to ask for help because they fear that would reveal a perceived inadequacy.

Library anxiety can affect the young or the elderly, the affluent as well as the poor, the college-educated and the marginally literate, and especially the recent immigrant or the person with limited proficiency in English. The ability to assist such clients with patient and sympathetic listening, giving helpful but not patronizing responses, and reformulating and modulating their questions as necessary is an important skill; it will almost always enable the staff person to help the anxious requestor find what is needed.

There are, of course, customers who are impatient, confused, or angry for reasons other than simple anxiety. The physical and emotional makeup of individuals differs widely. Some people are on medication; others may have severe health problems. There are, sadly, people with substance abuse or emotional or mental health problems. Public libraries in some areas have been heavily impacted by a growing homeless population, or latchkey children who gather in libraries after school lets out. We explore these and other such issues in the chapter on security (chapter 16).

From time to time all these people visit libraries, especially public libraries. Community colleges and universities open to the public also encounter "challenging" individuals. More and more students at all levels have emotional problems or exhibit high anxiety due to academic stress. If they act appropriately, everything can proceed as normal. Sometimes customers may express apprehension, perhaps for no reason other than a person's appearance, mumbling, or other relatively harmless reasons. Especially in public libraries, there must be reluctance to take any punitive measures on two counts: first, because the person in question has a right to use the library as long as he or she does not infringe on another's rights; and second, because trying to evict the person may create more of a problem than just letting him or her be. Often, an unconventional customer will have a real interest in a particular library resource, such as browsing periodicals or trying to identify information about survival skills or coping. If help is asked for, it should be given with the same respect any person receives. We explore the challenges of handling "difficult" people in more detail in the chapter on security (chapter 16).

Another aspect of the training is focusing on how to handle user complaints. As noted earlier, market research shows that the vast majority of unhappy customers do not complain, but take their business elsewhere. They also generally share their negative views with friends. Public services staff need to be aware of this, and the likelihood that every reported complaint probably represents the experiences of several other customers. Staff should be aware of the most frequent complaints made by users of their library and should pass these complaints on to their supervisors.

What types of problems are brought to the attention of a public services staff member? A review of the literature through the years reveals some common themes. In academic libraries, the principal problems reported relate to an inability to find materials listed in the catalog electronically or on the shelves and lack of notification about overdue materials. Circulation limits on reserve items and restrictions on renewals, as well as dissatisfaction with strict application of circulation rules, were other problems. The most frequent complaints of public library users tended to be insufficient numbers of desired titles and not being notified about their overdue materials. Borrowers were also unhappy about short loan periods, limited renewals, fines, and the use of collection agencies. The most frequent complaint of students using school libraries was that materials they wanted could not be found. Students also wanted to be notified about their overdue materials, and they disliked receiving overdue notices for materials they believed they had returned. Like other library users, students were annoyed at limited loan periods and restrictions on their library privileges. We will cover complaints about collection content in chapter 9.

From the Advisory Board

Ruth Kifer noted that complaints at a joint university and public library arise from two sides: "University students often complain about the appearance, odor and behavior of homeless public library patrons or pornography-watching public library patrons who loiter in the library."

She also noted "public library patrons complain about noisy university students in what they believe should be a quiet library and also complain about not having remote access to databases licensed by the university for student remote use only (all patrons, both public and university have access on-site)."

We offer the following as tips for handling unhappy users:

- Plan some of your first responses to common problems in advance.
- Choose your words with care.
- Avoid using words that may be heard/interpreted as talking down, jargon, slang, and so on.
- Keep your tone neutral.
- Try to remain calm, even when the person directs the unhappiness at you personally rather than the library.

Libraries should have complaint management policies in place to guide staff and managers in effectively handling complaints. Rebecca Jackson (2002) recommended that such a policy include the following:

- *Offer opportunities to complain.* Many people do not know where to complain, or to whom. Opportunities like physical and online suggestion boxes, frequent customer surveys, and encouraging customers to let staff know of problems they encounter are important.
- *Prepare library staff.* Frontline staff should be thoroughly oriented to the building and its services. They need to understand how important they are to the perceptions our customers have of the library. They also need to know how flexible they can be in resolving a customer's complaint.
- *Plan for complaint management.* Written policies and procedures for speedy and fair complaint resolution are necessary.
- *Respond to complaints.* Complaints should be tracked so decisions can be made to improve customer satisfaction. A mechanism for public response to repeated complaints, like the library Web site or a bulletin board with written responses, will let your customers know that you have heard them.

- *Follow up on complaints.* Acknowledge the effort a customer has made to complain rather than just leave the building. An e-mail stating thank you and explaining how you are working on the problem is appropriate. You may not be able to solve every complaint, but the customer may be happier to know that you care and are interested in their satisfaction. (pp. 212–215)

We will conclude this section with Darlene Weingand's (1997) 10 "magic phrases" that should be a part of the customer service culture of any library:

1. Of course we can try to get it for you.
2. How may I help you?
3. Of course we'll waive the fines. . . .
4. I'll be happy to make that call to _____ for you . . .
5. Did you find what you wanted? How well does the information meet your needs? Is there something else that I can find for you?
6. Is this what you are looking for, or shall I investigate further?
7. There are several possible ways to address your question. . . . Can you give me a little more background?
8. I'm with another customer at the moment. . . . May I call (or IM or text or chat) you back in a few minutes?
9. Yes, that item is in and I'll be happy to hold it for you for forty-eight hours.
10. Thanks for using the "XYZ" library. (pp. 93–95)

These phrases cannot guarantee good customer service, but if used consistently by all public services staff, they will demonstrate the service culture of the library.

Check These Out

An interesting article about customer service, libraries, and staff personalities is Robin Milford and Tania Wisotzke's "Introverts and Customer Service in the Library: An Unexpected Fit" (*OLA Quarterly*, 2011, 17, no. 3: 22–26).

One article that provides insights into customer service from the evening/night shift perspective is Chad J. Pearson's "Customer Types and the Empathetic Response" (*Reference Librarian*, 2014, 55, no. 3: 256–261).

Two good books on customer service are Peter Heron and Joseph R. Mathews's 2011 *Listening to the Customer* (Santa Barbara, CA: Libraries Unlimited) and Charles Harmon and Michael Messina's 2013 *Customer Service in Libraries: Best Practices* (Lanham, MD: Scarecrow Press).

VOLUNTEER TRAINING

Volunteers are a vital part of the workforce of many libraries and perform a variety of important roles. Whether they carry out simple or the most advanced and complicated work, volunteers are a part of the library staff and must be trained, developed, and evaluated in customer service.

Customer service training for volunteers involves certain challenges not present for paid employees. Volunteers may enter the organization wishing to perform particular, narrowly defined work responsibilities and not be interested in, or expecting, extensive training beyond their primary job responsibilities. Another challenge is time. Volunteers typically work less than 20 hours per week, sometimes much less, and finding time for training may be difficult. Nevertheless, customer service should be addressed very early in the volunteer's orientation and training. Todaro and Smith (2006) recommended providing the following information to volunteers:

- The library's vision and mission statements
- The library's values statement
- The library's commitment to extraordinary customer service for external and internal customers
- The definition of the library's service community
- The definitions of internal customers (other employees of the umbrella organization [city, county, school, company, college, and so forth], all library employees, all volunteers in the umbrella organization, all volunteers in the library)
- How volunteer jobs interact with customers
- Any volunteer job descriptions
- Any management expectations for volunteers (the reason for this customer service training requirement, since it might not be as clear to volunteers)
- Any scripts appropriate to volunteer work responsibilities
- The volunteer evaluation form and how it addresses customer service expectations for volunteers (pp. 41–42)

Todaro and Smith's volume is well worth the read.

CLOSING THOUGHTS

With increasing demands on libraries for accountability, and competition from other information sources like Amazon and Google, libraries need to prove their worth to funding authorities. The customer service movement in libraries involves adopting certain concepts from the business marketing research in order to find out more about library users and improve customer satisfaction. Finding out more about our users' wants and needs allows library administrators to do better planning, and satisfied customers tend to vote for library bond issues and become library supporters.

Having a customer service plan is an important part of providing consistent quality service. In order to foster continuous improvement, the plan should consist of a customer-focused mission statement, an assessment of customer wants and needs, an action plan for meeting the highest priority customer needs, and a regular assessment and analysis of how the plan is working.

Service quality is an important antecedent of customer service. While customer satisfaction is one measure of quality service, other types of assessments are necessary to get a true, comprehensive picture of a library's service quality. Each library will need to define quality service in terms of its own mission, goals, and objectives.

Technology offers new and challenging ways to improve quality and customer satisfaction. Making access to information and resources easier, faster, and more convenient should be a major goal. Examples include fully employing social media tools such as chat reference service and making access to library resources available on mobile devices. Customers now expect to interact more personally with the library and the information resources provided to them.

Libraries, media centers, learning resource centers, and information centers exist to provide service. The kind and degree of service will vary from library to library. At one end of the spectrum is the "archive-museum" library, which provides only research and preservation services. At the other end is the information brokerage, which locates and delivers specific pieces of information to its customers. School libraries strive to meet the educational needs of students and teachers while also serving parents and other staff. These user groups influence county funding for staff and resources. Public libraries serve the widest myriad of users and are dependent on customer satisfaction to champion adequate funding for facilities, staffing, and resources. Academic libraries have struggled to meet the high demand for scholarly resources that will meet students' and faculty's educational goals. Knowledgeable and cordial teaching librarians and staff make this happen.

Chapter Review Material

1. Name at least two reasons for libraries to pay attention to customer service.
2. Why are some library staff uncomfortable with calling library users "customers"?
3. What are some ways libraries use to ascertain customer needs and satisfaction?
4. What are the differences between customer wants, needs, and demands?
5. What are some elements of a customer service plan?
6. Explain the relationship between customer service and service quality.
7. What are some ways of defining service quality?
8. What is Web 2.0, and how has it affected customer service?
9. What are some sources of customer dissatisfaction?
10. What are some ways staff can diffuse irate customers?

REFERENCES

Association of College and Research Libraries Research Committee. 2008. *Environmental Scan 2007*. Chicago: American Library Association.

Becker, Samantha, Michael D. Crandall, Karen E. Fisher, Rebecca Blakewood, Bo Kinney, and Cadi Russell-Suave. 2010. *Opportunity for All: How the American Public Benefits from Internet Access at U.S. Libraries*. Washington, D.C.: Institute of Museum and Library Services. http://permanent.access.gpo.gov/gpo33008/OppForAll2.pdf.

Bell, Steven J. 2014. "Staying True to the Core: Designing the Future Academic Library Experience." *Portal: Libraries & the Academy* 14, no. 3: 369–382.

Berry, John. 2013. "Pillar of Community Education: 2013 Gale/LJ Library of the Year: Howard County Library System, MD." *Library Journal* 138, no. 11: 30.

Bowling, Barbara. 2012. "Focusing the School Library on Students." *School Library Monthly* 29, no. 3: 30–32.

Fiels, Michael Keith Michael. 2013. "Defining 'Transformation.'" *American Libraries* 44, no. 5: 6–7.

Ferri-Reed, Jan. 2011. "Driving Customer Service Excellence." *Journal for Quality & Participation* 33, no. 4: 30–32.

Frei, Frances, and Anne Morriss. 2012. *Uncommon Service*. Cambridge, MA: Harvard Business Review Press.

Gavillet, Erika L. 2011. "The 'Just Do It' Approach to Customer Service Development: A Case Study." *College & Research Libraries News* 72, no. 4: 229–231, 236.

Gordon, Rachel Singer, and Michael Stephens. 2007. "Tech Tips for Every Librarian: Promoting Productivity." *Computers in Libraries* 27, no. 5: 30–31.

Hernon, Peter, and Danuta A. Nitecki. 2001. "Service Quality: A Concept Not Fully Explored." *Library Trends* 49, no. 4: 687–708.

Hernon, Peter, and John R. Whitman. 2001. *Delivering Satisfaction and Service Quality: A Customer-Based Approach for Libraries*. Chicago: American Library Association.

Holt, Glen E. 2006. "Fitting Library Services into the Lives of the Poor." *The Bottom Line: Managing Library Finances* 19, no. 4: 179–186.

Jackson, Rebecca. 2002. "The Customer Is Always Right: What the Business World Can Teach Us about Problem Patrons." *The Reference Librarian* 75/76: 205–216.

Jiao, Qun G., and Anthony J. Onwuegbuzie. 1999. "Self-Perception and Library Anxiety: An Empirical Study." *Library Review* 48, no. 3: 140–147.

Jurewicz, Lynn, and Todd Cutler. 2003. *High Tech High Touch: Library Customer Service through Technology*. Chicago: American Library Association.

Laughlin, Kate. 2012. "Excellent Customer Service: Nature *and* Nurture." *ALKI* 28, no. 1: 29–30.

Maness, Jack M. 2006. "Library 2.0 Theory: The Next Generation of Web-Based Library Services." *LOGOS: The Journal of the World Book Community* 17, no. 3: 139–145.

Marcoux, Elizabeth. 2013. "Winning Characteristics for the National School Library Program of the Year." *Teacher Librarian* 40, no. 4: 34–35, 79.

Mellon, Constance A. 1986. "Library Anxiety: A Grounded Theory and Its Development." *College and Research Libraries* 47, no. 2: 160–165.

Nikolaison, Jeanne. 2011. "The Effect of Library Instruction on Library Anxiety in the Public Library Setting." *Current Studies in Librarianship* 31, no. 1: 7–19.

Saunders, E. Stewart. 2007. "The LibQUAL+ Phenomenon: Who Judges Quality." *Reference & User Services Quarterly* 47, no. 1: 21–24.

Schachter, Debbie. 2006. "The True Value of Customer Service." *Information Outlook* 10, no. 8: 8–9.

Stephens, Michael. 2006. "The Promise of Web 2.0." *American Libraries* 37, no. 9: 32.

Todaro, Julie, and Mark L. Smith. 2006. *Training Library Staff and Volunteers to Provide Extraordinary Customer Service.* New York: Neal-Schuman.

Walters, Suzanne. 1994. *Customer Service: A How-to-Do-It Manual for Librarians.* New York: Neal-Schuman.

Weingand, Darlene E. 1997. *Customer Service Excellence: A Concise Guide for Librarians.* Chicago: American Library Association.

Weinstein, Margery. 2013. "Service with a Smile." *Training* 50, no. 2: 24–28.

Wehmeyer, Susan, Dorothy Auchter, and Arnold Hirshon. 1996. "Saying What We Will Do, and Doing What We Say: Implementing a Customer Service Plan." *The Journal of Academic Librarianship* 22, no. 3: 173–80.

Zeithaml, Valarie A., A. Parasuraman, and Leonard L. Berry. 1990. *Delivering Quality Service: Balancing Customer Perceptions and Expectations.* New York: Free Press.

SUGGESTED READINGS

Bradshaw, Jonathan E. 1972. "The Concept of Social Need." *New Society* 19, no. 496: 640–643.

Bueno, Bolivar J. 2012. *Customers First.* New York: McGraw-Hill.

Chen, Yen-Ting, and Tsung-Yu Chou. 2011. "Applying GRA and QFD to Improve Library Service Quality." *Journal of Academic Librarianship* 37, no. 3: 237–245.

Coleman, Chris, and Kit Hartley. 2012. "Working Together to Close the Civic Engagement Gap: The St. Paul Story." *National Civic Review* 101, no. 4: 15–17.

Edgar, William B. 2006. "Questioning LibQUAL+™: Expanding Its Assessment of Academic Library Effectiveness." *portal: Libraries and the Academy* 6, no. 4: 445–465.

Hatcher, Greg. 2011. *55 Steps to Outrageous Service.* Little Rock, AK: Parkhurst Brothers.

Huff-Eibl, Robyn. 2014. "Understanding the Voice of the Customer: Practical, Data-Driven Planning and Decision Making for Access Services." *Journal of Access Services* 11, no. 3: 119–134.

Kwanya, Tom, Christine Stilwell, and Peter G. Underwood. 2012. "Library 2.0 versus Other Library Service Models: A Critical Analysis." *Journal of Librarianship and Information Science* 44, no. 3: 145–162.

Lightman, Harriet, and Qiana Johnson. 2014. "Reimagining or Revisioning? How One Library Studied Information Services." *College & Research Libraries News* 75, no. 8: 445–448, 462.

Long, Dallas. 2012. "'Check This Out:' Assessing Customer Service at the Circulation Desk." *Journal of Access Services* 9, no. 3: 154–168.

Murphy, Sarah Anne, ed. 2014. *The Quality Infrastructure: Measuring, Analyzing, and Improving Library Services.* Chicago: American Library Association.

Nguyen, Linh Cuong, Helen Partridge, and Sylvia L. Edwards. 2012. "Towards an Understanding of the Participatory Library." *Library Hi Tech* 30, no. 2: 335–346.

Ottolenghi, Carol. 2013. "A Customer Is a Patron Is a Client . . . But Not Really." *AALL Spectrum* 18, no. 1: 17–19.

Pellack, Lorraine. 2012. "Now Serving Customer 7,528,413." *Reference & User Services Quarterly* 51, no. 4: 316–318.

Tierney, Susan. 2013. "Become the Apple of Your Customers' Eye." *Incite* 34, no. 1/2: 36–37.

Todaro, Julie Beth. 1995. "Make 'Em Smile: 10 Essentials for Successful Customer Service." *School Library Journal* 41, no. 1: 24–27.

Woodward, Jeannette. 2009. *Creating the Customer-Driven Academic Library*. Chicago: American Library Association.

Part II

Core Programs and Services

Chapter 3

Reference Services

Although times and tools have changed significantly in the past 130+ years . . . reference librarians today still instruct users, answer information questions, recommend resources, and promote the library and its services.

—David Tyckoson, 2011

Although most public libraries . . . continue to share the Deweyan democratic purpose of informing and enlightening their publics, today's public libraries are also constantly adapting themselves to compete in the information-rich spaces of the social web.

—Mary F. Cavanagh, 2013

A night librarian position is a good place to explore experimental reference approaches involving interdisciplinary thinking and relationship building. Most librarians concur that reference service has undergone a constant redefinition over the years.

—Chad Pearson, 2014

Most traditional library reference work and services are conducted within library walls. Community librarianship, also called embedded librarianship, has another goal: to get librarians into the surrounding neighborhood where they can help the local population wherever they need information.

—Michelle Lee, 2013

It goes without saying that reference assistance has long been considered one of the most valuable services offered by the library. In fact, even non-library users know—perhaps without knowing the official name—that librarians answer questions and that there is a centralized location for information, that is, the reference librarian. It therefore sets a standard that users consider when assessing their library service experiences.

Despite what has historically been an emphasis on the importance of reference work within libraries supported by the librarian's collection authoritative information sources, the Association of Research Libraries (ARL) reported that reference transactions have dropped 51 percent since 1991 (Martin and Park, 2010). This decline has forced many libraries to reexamine what was considered traditional reference work—answering reference questions and showcasing a librarian's expertise in locating and evaluating resources—and to reevaluate programs and services in order to meet the changing needs of their communities and patrons.

While libraries continue to address how to serve their patrons, a variety of new approaches have emerged. Embedded librarianship, mixed service desks, online and chat reference, and roaming reference are just a few of the ways libraries are adapting to the change in user needs and expectations. Additionally, the ever-increasing role of technology presents other new opportunities and challenges seemingly daily, and is a significant driver of change within the field of librarianship.

Whatever guise reference work takes, it is obvious that most people coming to or contacting the library still expect good service and become disappointed when that does not materialize. As alluded to in chapter 2, few people are willing to give a library a second chance if their last experience was unsatisfactory. They seldom assess or consider whether or not the problem was something the staff could control—that the information just does not exist in the desired form or that the ISP was having trouble maintaining Internet connectivity are but two such examples. Thus, there is a strong pressure on reference staff to do whatever they can to satisfy each information inquiry.

Check This Out

The Reference and User Services Association (RUSA), a division of the American Library Association, originally prepared a series of *Guidelines for Behavioral Performance of Reference and Information Service Providers* in 1996. Since that time, the guidelines have been regularly reviewed and revised, and were last approved by the RUSA Board in mid-2013. The guidelines cover five main categories: visibility/approachability, interest, listening/inquiring, searching, and follow-up, and cover both in-person and remote reference transactions. The *Guidelines* are well worth reviewing: http://www.ala.org/rusa/resources/guidelines/guidelinesbehavioral.

As mentioned in the opening quotation by David Tyckoson (2011), many of the fundamental tasks performed at the reference desk have remained unchanged—helping users with their queries, finding appropriate resources, instructing patrons, and promoting the library. What has changed is how these tasks are accomplished. Librarians and support staff provide reference assistance most directly by delivering personal service in response to requests for information. This personal service takes three primary forms:

1. Finding information to answer specific questions
2. Helping users find information for themselves
3. Teaching people how to use library resources and how to do library research

This chapter will introduce you to the traditional and innovative components of reference service common in libraries today.

Personalized reference service as we know it is a comparatively new addition to libraries (Rothstein, 1989). Only in the twentieth century did libraries become something other than storehouses for books, and librarians more than book collectors, catalogers, and custodians. In the latter part of the nineteenth century, public librarians began to realize that many users needed assistance to use the library effectively. Samuel Green, librarian of the Worcester Free Public Library in Massachusetts, published an article in *Library Journal* advocating personal assistance and service by librarians to library readers (Green, 1876). Green realized that assistance of this sort would increase the popularity of the library and its support by library users. After 1890, the reference function had gained sufficient popularity to become formalized as a distinct department in the larger public libraries.

In university libraries, acceptance of this new concept was slower. In general, reference service in academic libraries followed the path blazed by the public libraries. Personal assistance was first provided on a part-time and occasional basis. Increased demand for the service resulted in reference work becoming a specialized function, with that function eventually gaining the status of a separate department in libraries. However, the rate of advance was slower than in public libraries.

By 1900, reference service had become a common feature in both public and university libraries. In the early years of the twentieth century, reference service was generally limited to teaching and guidance, implying a policy of minimal assistance and emphasis on the librarian as instructor. However, librarians soon found themselves increasingly drawn into "fact finding" and providing direct information service.

The 1960s and 1970s saw two developments that expanded the reference staff's ability to provide service, while placing greater demands on the librarian's professional expertise. As libraries became larger and more complex with the need to house increasing amounts of information, the need for assistance in using the library grew among all users. Many reference librarians recognized the need to reassert the traditional emphasis on instruction in library use. *Bibliographic instruction* (later, library instruction or information literacy instruction), defined as teaching students how to do library research for themselves in order to facilitate lifelong learning, became an important part of reference responsibility beginning in the 1970s.

The second development was technology, starting in the 1960s, that began to change reference service. Computerized reference services began with bibliographic databases (containing references to periodicals, books, and other documents). Services then expanded to include online catalogs, mediated searching of online databases, CD-ROM (compact disk-read only memory) sources, networking of libraries and library systems, end user searching of online databases, full text retrieval, and the Internet. These and other innovations expanded the library's ability to provide diverse and complex information services. This trend continues into the twenty-first century as online information places ever-increasing demands on libraries to provide more varied and sophisticated reference services.

Today, reference departments in public, academic, and school libraries attempt to offer at least moderate levels of service in all three areas of reference service (finding information, helping others to find information, and teaching the use of the library), while departmental, professional school, and research institute libraries offer reference service of a quality and depth approaching that of a special library.

In today's world, technology forms the foundation for the majority of the services provided at a reference desk. This can be both a blessing and a challenge for reference staff. It provides faster and more convenient access to more information. It also adds to the complexity of providing the information. Today's reference librarians must not only be fluent in the resources offered by the library, such as online databases and e-books, but must also be comfortable and willing to address computer and technology issues that do not necessarily impact a user's ability to access library resources.

The ability to use electronic resources increases the professional competence of reference staff. To provide quality service, reference staff must know both the existing printed sources and also know about the available online resources, the different (and ever-changing) database interfaces, how to navigate the Internet, the intricacies of the online catalog, and even how to use many of today's e-readers. Librarians must know how to troubleshoot problems with word-processing software, such as Microsoft® Word, know how to create an account within a social media site, such as Facebook, and know how to help a user create an e-mail account. A by-product of this increased expertise and ability to answer questions may be greater esteem for library services and staff on the part of library users.

Staff members who provide remote service via IM, chat, texting, or e-mail must work to establish and maintain effective behavioral aspects of reference service when the usual visual and verbal cues are not available as well as be able to troubleshoot technology issues when they arise. Reference staff must learn numerous databases and searching protocols in addition to the knowledge required for reference work with existing printed sources, while maintaining performance in other duties such as collection development, instruction, readers' advisory, and other tasks. Conscientious staff members have to work harder, smarter, and longer to raise and maintain their level of expertise to take full advantage of the new and evolving resources available. It may be that the quality of performance and the ability to remain current with developments in the profession decline as the amount and sophistication of responsibilities increase.

Access to online sources in some cases changes the definition of quality reference service. Professional ethics require that reference staff give accurate information. (See chapter 14 for a discussion of ethical issues and public services.) Today, accurate (i.e., the most up-to-date) information is often only available online. Using print sources to answer a question when online alternatives are available may mean giving the user less current data. In the last decade of the twentieth century, for example, an inquiry for current financial data on a corporation required reference staff to know about financial publications from publishers such as Moody's or Standard & Poor's, or perhaps have access to annual reports for the most recent available data. Now the staff member must know how to search one or more of the financial databases to retrieve the most up-to-the-minute—that is, most accurate—information. In addition, the staff member must know what information is available on the Web and must be able to gauge its reliability. The reference staff member who does not know how to use online resources effectively is in the frustrating position of not being able to provide the best information available.

Along with the advantages inherent in electronic reference sources, however, there are two dangers that are, paradoxically, in opposition to each other. The first is that the uncritical or unskilled user may inadvertently miss much available material. The speed, power, and ease of using OPACs, online databases, and the Web create the assumption in some users that assistance by the reference staff is no longer necessary. These users assume that they know how to search a database or Web site effectively enough to reveal its contents, and that the retrieved information accurately reflects the contents of the library or database.

In fact, to use digital reference sources effectively, one must know more than how to "Google." One must at least understand the limits of the database or Web site searched. Users are often uncritical about which databases they search for information on a particular subject. Left alone, they will often choose an inappropriate resource (e.g., search a community forum for information on health issues) and retrieve far less relevant information than they would using an appropriate source, including a printed one. And yet, research indicates that users seem to be satisfied no matter how much they retrieve from the Web.

Many users are also not aware of the specialized searching procedures that enhance the effectiveness of electronic databases. The untutored user, for example, does not comprehend the technique of combining terms using Boolean logic (combining terms with the words "and," "or," and "not" to refine a search). The ability to limit searches (by date, language, refereed journal, etc.) for more precise retrieval is another characteristic often not understood. Even the most user-friendly systems do not provide enough instruction for some individuals to use the systems effectively, so they miss many of the advantages of digital reference sources.

The other danger resulting from the revolution in digital reference sources is the opposite of the first: that the speed and power of electronic references will generate too much material and drown the user in information. Many library users do not need or want the scope and quantity of information that the Web gives them. These users may be better served by the traditional printed references available in all reference collections. Many people, too, lack the training to critically examine the mass of data presented and select the best quality information. Staff should use the reference interview to judge the user's need for information with these two considerations in mind, and give the user neither too much nor too little information.

Digital reference is a permanent and essential part of reference service and will become more important as libraries adapt to the changing needs of their users. Reference managers should recognize the demands of the technology on staff and reduce the demands in other areas so that people have the time to acquire and maintain the expertise necessary to perform digital reference. Identifying training opportunities and making the time and resources available so that staff can take advantage of them are incumbent on the manager. Individuals planning a career in reference services should take every opportunity to improve their computer literacy.

It is important to keep in mind as you read this chapter that we can only touch on the highlights of reference work in this book. There are entire courses devoted to the subject and therefore it is beyond the scope of this book to address the full range of library programs and services.

TYPES OF REFERENCE QUESTIONS

Reference questions come from every variety of human inquiry and curiosity, but most can be classified under the following categories:

1. *Directional questions* are information or explanations of library policies and procedures. Examples are "Where can I get a drink of water?" "Where do you keep your magazines?" "How do I log onto the computer?" "How do I get a library card?"
2. *Ready reference questions* are usually simple factual questions that ask for information, such as: "What is the population of China?" "Who is our state representative?" "How many pounds make a ton?"
3. *Reference questions* are more involved inquiries and usually require several steps to answer, for example, "I need all the information I can find on General Motors." "I need to write a term paper on whales."
4. *Research questions* are reference questions involving several categories of tools for a comprehensive look at what is available on a particular topic. Research questions are differentiated from reference questions by degree, rather than methodology. Preparing an extensive bibliography of sources both in the library and beyond; working with the user to develop one or a series of strategies to accomplish a research task; helping the requester search several databases; and locating hard-to-find specific references by extensive manual or online means are examples of research librarianship. Research questions often require extended time, referral, or follow-up contact with users.
5. *Technical and mechanical questions* primarily involve using the computing, printing, and copying technology now ubiquitous in libraries. These questions may involve how to use various applications like word-processing programs, how to download a document to a flash drive, how to send a print job to the local printing system, or how to purchase a copy card.

A person's information need might fall into several of these categories, sometimes in a steady progression as the individual's questions become more specific as the research progresses. For example, directional questions often evolve into reference questions as the librarian determines through the reference interview that a user needs information beyond the original request. Both reference and research questions might involve instruction, as the staff member shows the user the step-by-step procedure to acquire the desired information.

THE REFERENCE INTERVIEW

Anyone who has ever worked at an information desk—whether within a library or another organization—knows that the question asked by an individual is often not the question he or she *really* needs answered. Requesters are often uncertain or unclear about what information they want. Sometimes it is because they have trouble expressing themselves. Often it is because they are not sure in their own minds what they want or need. For example, the individual who wants to search Google to find information on a corporation may really prefer a database like *Business Source Premier* or a corporate annual report to answer his or her question; the high school student asking for college catalogs might be better served with a directory of college majors. How does the reference staff member determine a person's true information need?

The *reference interview* is the process whereby the staff member communicates and interacts with the user to determine how best to answer an informational need. The interview is used to determine the true nature of a question before the staff member goes into action. It is an interactive process in which both staff and user ask questions and provide answers. The need may be a simple one, and the interview therefore short and sweet; for example, a group of children come up and one shyly asks, "Where's the bathroom?" "Boy's or girl's?" asks the staff member. "Both!" answers another child.

On the other hand, some questions are incomplete in terms of actual needs, and the reference staff member must guide the user in a series of steps just to get the process going: choosing a topic, thinking about the topic, and making decisions about limiting the search to find what is really needed. For example, a young adult (YA) comes in and announces to a reference staff member:

YA: "I have to write a term paper."

S: "Oh, that sounds interesting. On what topic?"

YA: "Oh, I don't know. Anything, I guess."

S: "Did your teacher give you something that describes the assignment, like a handout?"

YA: "Yes, but I left it at home."

S: "Do you remember what it said?"

YA: "No, just to write a paper is all."

S: "What subject are you taking with this teacher?"

YA: "Well, history."

S: "History of what? The U.S.? European history? Asian history?"

YA: "European history."

S: "What are you interested in writing about?"

YA: "Oh, I don't know. Anything, I guess."

S: "What are you studying in that class now?"

YA: "About the civil war."

S: "Which civil war?"

YA: "You know, the civil war."

S: "Do you mean the English civil war? Cromwell and all that?"

YA: "Yeah, I guess so."

S: "So would you like to write about the Roundheads or about the cavaliers?"

YA: "Who?"

S: "You know, the soldiers of Oliver Cromwell or the army of the king of England."

YA: "Well, how about Robert E. Lee?"

S: "Robert E. Lee? He fought in the *American* Civil War. Here, in the U.S.A."

YA: "That's what we're studying."

S: "You mean about Abe Lincoln and Jefferson Davis and Stonewall Jackson and Ulysses S. Grant?"

YA: "Yeah, that stuff."

S: "Oh, okay. Let's go over and look at a couple of good sources on Robert E. Lee to get you started. . . ."

The reference interview is a critical step in providing quality service. Being given insufficient, incomplete, incorrect, or even too much information presents serious problems to library users. Identifying several sources with a variety of points of view, when appropriate, is usually good practice. For less complex needs, a good, balanced, and clear overview of a topic, such as what may be found in general encyclopedias, may be all that is needed. In the example posed earlier, the "term paper" might be just that, with several sources beyond the encyclopedias required. It might also turn out to be a three-page handwritten essay on qualities the student admires in a historical personage, an "opinion" paper requiring little research.

From the Authors' Experience

Sinwell recalls two memorable reference transactions:

First, after working with a student for several weeks, I learned one early morning that this quiet, reserved 38 year old was a refugee from a war torn country. She and her two sons lived in a shelter, after being abandoned by her husband. She needed help with research techniques for her group presentation. After the project concluded, she returned to thank "all of us" in the library for our assistance. She especially wanted us to know that having such a supportive resource center on campus helped

her succeed and strengthened her resolve to persevere. She amazed me
with her grace and drive in the light of so many obstacles—but this is
the profile of many community college students across the country.

The second instance involved a reference phone call from a community patron who was writing a book on tugboats of Baltimore, MD. We
came to find out tugboats were used every time a dignitary had a pro-
cession into the city docks. The reference staff worked with him on "how
to do research" and developed a long term relationship with him. As
with other authors we've helped, the author recognized the assistance
of the staff in the "preface" to his book.

These show that each reference experience is unique in its own way.

Reading a user's nonverbal cues is also part of the reference interview. This
is especially true when assisting someone with a limited command of English.
As Ajit Pyati (2003) observed, "Communicating with LEP [limited English pro-
ficiency] users is not only a question of language, but a question of culture as
well" (p. 266). It is not always possible to have staff available who are fluent in
the various language groups represented in a library's community. Sensitivity,
patience, and a user-friendly approach are very important in these circumstances. Reading a user's body language, gestures, facial expressions, and so
on, may give clues to alert reference staff about whether he or she is effectively
communicating with the individual or whether the person is satisfied with
the information being given. Cultural values are a significant factor when it
comes to "reading" nonverbal signals. It requires a sound understanding of
the characteristics of the various constituencies of the service community. For
example, eye contact alone may or may not be a sign of satisfaction, because
in some cultures direct eye contact is considered rude.

Check These Out

A number of resources exist to assist librarians in conducting the reference interview. Four worth consulting are:

Conducting the Reference Interview: A How-to-Do-It Manual for Librarians
by Catherine Sheldrick Ross, Kirsti Nilsen, and Marie L. Radford. 2nd
ed. (New York: Neal-Schuman Publishers Inc., 2009),

The Ohio Reference Excellence Reference Interview module—http://www
.olc.org/ore/2interview.htm,

The Reference Interview Today by Susan Knoerr (Santa Barbara, CA:
Libraries Unlimited, 2011), and

*The Reference Interview Today: Negotiating and Answering Questions Face
to Face, On the Phone, and Virtually* by Dave Harmeyer (Lanham, MD:
Rowman & Littlefield, 2014).

In addition, the Colorado State University Libraries have developed a guide for patrons to use to help them in their interactions with reference staff entitled "Asking Good Research/Reference Questions." It is well worth a look: http://lib.colostate.edu/howto/askgood.html.

Asking that one additional question may be the difference between reference "success" and confused failure. Confusion may be expected in the requester, but the reference staffer should not be the person confused. Quiet and patient persistence will usually enable a staff member to get to the heart of the matter by helping the requester define the true informational need.

REFERENCE SERVICE CATEGORIES

There are a variety of common services offered at most library reference desks beyond answering questions of the type discussed earlier in the chapter. The following is a small sampling of common reference services.

Readers' Advisory

Readers' advisory service, broadly defined, means helping readers find what they want by recommending specific titles or types of titles. In this context, it is something that all reference staff, and perhaps even all library staff, occasionally do. Readers often ask for suggestions on what books to read on a particular topic, in a specific genre (e.g., mysteries), or by a certain author. If we happen to know about the subject or writer requested, it is satisfying to be able to refer the user to a particular title we know is a "good" one.

However, readers' advisory also refers to a specialized service usually found in public libraries. The users of this service tend to be adult fiction readers, but range from children to housebound seniors. Underlying readers' advisory is the belief that reading has intrinsic value and that readers are well served by a good collection and knowledgeable staff who are able to guide them in pursuing their interests. (Reader's advisory is related to another activity that is sometimes practiced in school settings—bibliotherapy. This topic is beyond the scope of this book as those who practice this have specialized training.) The reading of fiction is very popular in public libraries, and their collection development budgets reflect this interest. Given the high demand and resource commitment, libraries attempt to address the demands of readers in a structured way.

Currently, readers' advisory is practiced most in public libraries. Librarians advise borrowers primarily on recreational reading, and predominantly on fiction. Readers' advisors try to be familiar with popular literature and best-sellers lists and respond with perception and insight to the reading interests of their users. Staff are now assisted in this endeavor by print and online resources specifically designed to enhance readers' advisory service. Sources like EBSCO's *NoveList®* (a searchable database of fiction and nonfiction titles, including print and audiobooks—http://www.ebscohost.com/novelist) and *NoveList®* K-8 Plus (http://www.ebscohost.com/novelist/our-products /novelist-k8) are helpful in identifying resources.

There are also a number of published guides that are useful in providing such assistance. There are a series of titles that grew out of a Libraries Unlimited, Inc., title (*Genreflecting*), which provides guides to popular titles in genres like adventure, crime, horror and by age group—picture book/easy readers, middle school, and teens, for example.

There are a number of online resources that can aid in readers' advisory activities, such as GoodReads (http://www.goodreads.com/) and LibraryThing (https://www.librarything.com/). A Web 2.0 innovation, adopted from business sites like Amazon and employed by an increasing number of libraries, allows readers to enter their own tags, reviews, ratings, and reading suggestions in the library OPAC and library blogs. Readers and staff may use these sources to begin with books they have read and discover similar titles and authors. Some databases allow readers to enter words and phrases to describe a book they would like to read and search for books that contain the words or phrases in their subject headings. Readers may also explore titles in specific genres and examine lists of award-winning literature.

Referral Services

A *community information and referral service* refers to a particular service offered in public libraries. Its goal is to provide a link between people and services, activities, information, or advice outside the library that can meet the user's needs. According to Joan Durrance and Karen Pettigrew (2000), the service "covers information about human services (health care, financial assistance, housing, etc.), as well as information on recreation programs, clubs, community events, and all levels of government, including participation in the political process" (p. 44). The service ordinarily involves using a paper or online directory of community resources and information about them, which supplements information in other sources like government or social services directories or the Web. Technology enhanced the ability of libraries to provide information and referral services. Libraries create collections or, increasingly, searchable databases of community information, which citizens may search from remote locations any time of the day or night to find the information they seek.

Community information and referral services generally fall into two main categories: online community directories and community calendars (Rogers, Fombon, and Reynolds, 2005). Many libraries use their integrated library systems (ILS) to manage their information and referral systems, and the major vendors support software for this purpose. These databases are searchable by keyword and other search options. Other libraries have begun building their own customized information and referral databases to better meet the needs of their users.

Check These Out

Memphis Public Library (http://www.memphislibrary.org/linc/comminfo.htm) and Detroit Public Library's The Information Place (TIP; http://www.detroit.lib.mi.us/specialservice/tip) provide two examples of community information and referral services programs.

This type of service is especially important for people or groups with special needs, such as the poor, recent immigrants, or individuals who speak limited English. In the underserved areas of communities, this service may be the only means people have for obtaining needed information. Community information and referral programs can help forge a stronger relationship between the library and local ethnic communities.

Networks, consortia, and cooperative agreements to share resources among libraries, made more effective by technology, are increasing. Networks may be local or limited to libraries of the same type, for example, the public libraries in a city or rural area. They may also be expansive, multitype networks encompassing libraries of different kinds across counties or states or regions. Many networks are formed to allow libraries to take advantage of economies of scale in subscribing to or purchasing online services like periodical databases and even e-books. Interlibrary loan is the most common evidence of resource sharing within a network, often enhanced by interlibrary courier service. Cooperative reference services are also established in many areas. These permit the referral of difficult queries or those submitted when the library is closed by Web form or e-mail, typically to a central location or directly to other consortium members, where answers are found and delivered later.

Some networks have formalized the referral process. Specific steps and protocols are agreed on and followed by each participating library. This avoids duplicating work since the second library is told what works were consulted, strategies tried, and so on, by the referring library. Libraries share holdings information through a network, considerably improving access, guaranteeing better service, and minimizing delays and trouble for both users and staff.

E-mail, chat, Twitter, and e-mail reflector lists allow staff in local or national networks to communicate almost instantaneously with colleagues in any location. Staff may consult with scores, even hundreds of reference staff at a time through these networks, holding the promise of greatly facilitating the referral process.

Embedded Librarianship

As mentioned earlier in the chapter, a variety of new approaches to reference services have emerged in recent years. These include combined service desks, roaming reference, and embedded librarianship. While the combined service desk model seeks to both lower administrative costs and create better workflow by consolidating services and staff, and roaming reference strives to put librarians in the stacks in order to facilitate reference questions, embedded librarianship takes the idea of providing service at the point of need even further. This model, as mentioned in chapter 6, takes the librarian out of the library building and either into the classroom, as is the case in academic libraries, or into the community. Many libraries see this as a way to not only provide better service, but also as being a way to promote the library among community or academic organizations.

When librarians leave the library, they look for areas where their expertise would be needed and to "be where the user is and to be user-centric" (Kesselman and Watstein, 2009, p. 385). Using librarians within the classroom to collaborate with the instructor and develop curriculum is one method that is used frequently within school libraries, while public libraries must be slightly more creative. One option for public libraries is to send librarians to city council and other city-centric meetings, and allowing the librarian to discern the need once he or she is "embedded" in that environment.

A successful embedded librarian can advocate for the library while providing professional expertise. In a true embedded atmosphere, librarians "demonstrate the many ways it is possible to transcend traditional roles and underscore the unique value we add as institutions and individuals" (Kesselman and Watstein, 2009, p. 398). Research has shown that this model can drastically improve reference statistics. One example is Bennett and Simning's (2010) analysis of reference traffic at Capella University. After Capella adopted an embedded librarianship model, reference transactions went up 400 percent (p. 443).

From the Authors' Experience

Saponaro has served as an embedded librarian in two institutions. In one case, the role was formalized as part of her job responsibilities, and she had a private office in one of the academic units she served, where she spent most of her workweek. Students and faculty could drop by at any time to meet or ask a question regarding library services. She only went to the campus library for meetings or reference desk hours.

At another institution, her role as an embedded librarian evolved gradually from teaching an occasional class in the unit to requesting permission from the associate dean of the program to maintain weekly office hours in the departmental reading room during the academic year. She sent regular updates on library services and programs to the students, faculty, and staff via e-mail. She also made an effort to teach a majority of her instructional sessions in the department—where students and faculty were more comfortable and familiar with the equipment, and attended departmental faculty meetings. Outside of office hours and instructional sessions, she remained available to faculty, staff, and students via e-mail and phone. She also held in-person consultations by appointment.

Although the two instances operated very differently, in both cases faculty and students appreciated her proximity and availability.

Remote Services

Part of the reference staff's duties may include service to off-site users. Libraries are available by telephone, letter, fax, e-mail, chat, text messages, and IM for both ready reference and research information, often on a 24/7 basis. The request might be for library hours, for the date of the sinking of the *Titanic*, or for a citation to an obscure article for which the requester has very little information. Some colleges and universities have sizable distance education programs and student populations who depend on the library's off-site services. Sometimes, a staff member from a distant library may contact the library with a question that cannot be answered with local resources. A library known for particular subject strength, or the largest (or only) library in town, will receive a large number of these inquiries.

In general, staff should give an off-site requester, especially one who may be physically unable to visit the library (e.g., homebound individuals or those who lack transportation), as full an answer as possible within the constraints of time and the reference policy. In most libraries, the users who are physically present have first priority. Staff should decline unreasonable requests (those that take an inordinate amount of staff time or effort to answer) in a professional manner, with patient explanation and an invitation to visit the library and obtain guidance in performing the necessary research.

The reference policy should address the issue of conflicting priorities regarding off-site versus in-person requests. For example, staff will look up no more than "X" number of books in the OPAC, or spend no more than "Y" number of minutes looking for an elusive statistic. During very hectic periods, such as term-paper season in an academic library, it may be necessary for staff to log the question or save it to be answered later. The staff person contacts the requester (or asks the requester to call back) at a specified time, by which the reference staff will have attempted to find the answer. Some libraries have a separate telephone line or e-mail reference address or an IM account, with a staff member dedicated to answering queries for directional and reference questions.

Staff who provide remote service via IM, chat, texting, or e-mail must work to established procedures as well as keep in mind that the visual clues that exist in face-to-face transactions are lacking and may well impact the outcome. Conscientious staff members have to work harder, smarter, and longer to raise and maintain their level of expertise in terms of the remote access technology that constantly change in number and characteristics.

Check These Out

Two sources worth consulting for more information on virtual reference programming and services are:

Virtual Reference Adventure—Choose Your Own Experience—http://cs.ala.org/ra/vr_adventure/about.htm

From the Statewide Virtual Reference Project—Washington State Library. A self-paced learning experience for individuals engaged in virtual reference activities.

Virtual Reference Companion—A Guide for VR Coordinators and Librarians—http://www.ala.org/rusa/vrc/resources

From the Reference and User Services Association (RUSA), a division of the American Library Association. Sections include those addressing planning, assessment, marketing and staffing virtual reference programs.

In the academic setting, the combination of intercampus delivery systems and online collections offered through subscription databases can help students and faculty who are physically remote from the main campus attain a good measure of library access. With the increase in distance education offerings by universities around the country, many libraries find themselves called on to supply services to local students enrolled in programs offered at distant campuses. Some of these institutions contract with libraries to supply services to their students in particular areas, but this is not always the case. The library's reference service policy should address the level of service that is appropriate to deliver in support of distance education programs.

Like telephone, chat, text messaging, and IM reference, written, faxed, or e-mail correspondence needs the fastest feasible attention, and should be handled as thoroughly as other duties allow. Responding with a partial answer, with apologies and a notice that a fuller answer will take longer than one has time for at present, is an appropriate procedure when staff time is short. If it is known that the chances of answering soon are slim, a short reply politely stating this condition and an estimated date of reply would be welcomed by most researchers. Well-worded automated responses or form letters may be used if the backlog becomes a problem.

ORGANIZATION OF REFERENCE SERVICES

The organization of reference services can take several forms. The three most popular are *central* or general reference, *divisional* reference, and *departmental* reference. (See Figures 3.1, 3.2, and 3.3.) The organization of reference depends on many factors, the more important ones being philosophy of the library, physical layout of the building, size of the library's collection, abilities of the staff, type of library and type(s) of user, and financial resources.

A central or general reference department organization brings together all reference material in one physical location. Some arguments for this organization follow:

1. Reference materials are easier to locate because they are shelved together.
2. Because knowledge is interrelated and interdisciplinary, it is easier to do reference work if all the material is kept together.
3. It is not necessary to purchase duplicate materials or to duplicate services.
4. It is possible to make more economical use of staff at one service point rather than staffing several service points.

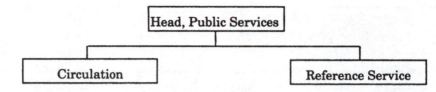

Figure 3.1 Central or General Reference Organization

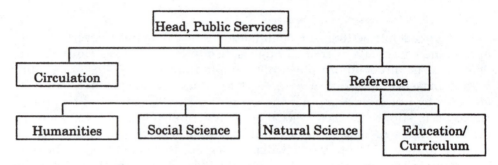

Figure 3.2 Divisional Reference Organization

Nearly all small libraries and most medium-sized libraries use a central or general type of organization.

Divisional reference organization may be found in larger libraries and brings together the reference materials for a group of related subjects. A divisional reference organization may divide the collection into social sciences, humanities, and natural sciences, or any other arrangement best suited to the library. Some of the arguments in favor of divisional reference organization follow:

1. A smaller reference collection is easier to use.
2. The reference materials and the general collection on a particular subject are often closer together in a divisional arrangement, allowing easier access to both types of materials.
3. Reference staff who are subject specialists can utilize their talents and provide better service for specialized reference inquiries when they work in their area of expertise.

Departmental libraries may be found in larger libraries in addition to a central reference collection or divisional reference collections. The collection in a departmental library is usually restricted to one subject area, such as physics or philosophy, and different departments may have a reference collection and reference services of their own, often in different buildings. The advantages of this organization are the same as those stated for divisional reference organization.

In-House Reference Training

It is essential that any staff person called upon to work the reference desk be well trained in library programs, services, collections, and technology, as

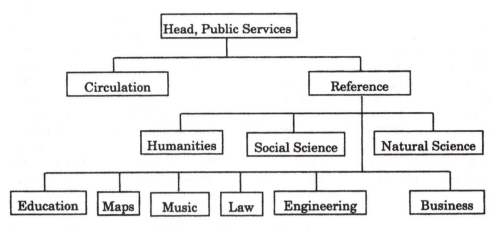

Figure 3.3 Departmental Reference Organization

well as be prepared to deal with problem behavior calmly and efficiently. The amount and kind of training given to the new reference employee will depend, of course, on his or her qualifications and on the specific duties of the position. The reference supervisor provides at least a general orientation to the department, the collection, departmental and library personnel, and policies and procedures of which the employee needs to be aware. The administrator often delegates specific training in such things as online searching, collection development, and library instruction to the staff who share responsibilities for these services. A significant portion of the new employee's time is spent getting acquainted with the reference collection and observing and assisting at the reference desk (or observing online reference sessions), preferably with different members of the staff. Not until the administrator is satisfied that the staff member can comfortably handle desk duty "solo" should the employee be scheduled alone, and then only with the assurance that, if needed for consultation, assistance is close at hand. Occasional meetings thereafter will reinforce new skills and help the supervisor gauge any need for further training. It is also the opinion of the authors that reference training never truly ends; there will always be a new technology or a new issue that will test even the most seasoned reference librarian.

Check This Out

Developing training programs is a complex topic. One resource to consult is Barbara Allan's *The No-Nonsense Guide to Training in Libraries* (London: Facet, 2013). It includes a review of approaches to learning and teaching, as well as chapters on various methods of making training interesting to participants and ways to incorporate technology into a training program.

Ongoing staff development is also important to maintain the reference staff's effectiveness. Acquisitions of new reference titles and databases, and regular changes to the interfaces of familiar databases, require that reference staff constantly keep up to date in order to be most effective. Regular staff meetings to review new and revised databases and other reference sources are an effective means of keeping current. Meetings of local, regional, and national professional associations often include programs on new reference sources and techniques. Regional organizations sometimes sponsor free Webinars highlighting new reference services and resources. Vendors' representatives are sometimes invited to come to the library and describe a new database and the administrator routes or e-mail relevant articles to the staff. It is the administrator's responsibility to make sure that reference staff members have the opportunity to continually develop their reference skills.

Scheduling

Because most public and academic reference staff (special libraries may differ) are typically available during all hours the library is open, library managers must allow great flexibility in scheduling reference staff. Staff schedules often must vary from day to day and week to week in order to maintain reference service. Subject to the dictates of an institution's personnel policy or union contract, late arrivals, early departures, and long breaks are generally accepted to compensate for the occasional 10-hour day and working weekend. The administrator who is not flexible with staff scheduling will have difficulty obtaining the loyalty and cooperation necessary to maintain services in times of great activity or staff shortages.

The library administration establishes the amount of time that reference service is provided. At a minimum, management considers three variables: the number of hours the library is open, the number of staff available, and the information needs of the library's users. School libraries are open for the shortest periods and have assistance available the greatest proportion of hours. Public libraries usually have reference help available from opening to closing. Academic libraries are open the longest amount of time, often more than 100 hours per week; however, in-person reference service is seldom available all the time. Late-night and some weekend hours, especially, may not have scheduled reference service. Institutions that have a large population of resident students, or have active programs of evening and weekend classes, need to provide more hours of reference service than colleges or universities that are largely commuter campuses.

Smaller libraries schedule one person at a time at the reference desk, while larger libraries have multiple staffing. Some libraries, responding to decreased demand for face-to-face reference service, schedule "on-call" service some or all hours. When busy, it is a good idea to rotate desk coverage frequently to prevent fatigue. Hours "on the desk" vary, based on number of service hours offered, individuals skills and knowledge, and the number of available staff. A survey of reference desk staffing patterns in academic and public libraries showed considerable variations, both between the two kinds of libraries and within each type of library (Bunge, 1986). Although this survey was performed some time ago, the patterns of reference desk staffing remain largely the same. Common practices include weekday desk shifts of two hours, with longer evening hours and on weekends (usually three to four hours).

Typically a person in reference works between 7 and 21 hours per week on the desk. Public library reference personnel work a greater percentage of hours on the reference desk than their academic colleagues. Nearly three-quarters of public library staff surveyed worked over 18 hours per week on the desk, while almost two-thirds of academic library staff worked less than 16 hours on the desk. This difference can be explained by the aggregate quantity of off-desk duty performed by academic reference librarians, especially information literacy instruction and issues related to library and campus governance, or "academic citizenship," and service in professional organizations. In both public and academic libraries, evening and weekend hours often have to be covered. These "off hours" are rotated among the staff, assigned regularly to a few individuals, covered by part-time staff hired for the purpose, or some combination of the above.

Check This Out

The use of part-time librarians at the Valley Library at Oregon State University is reviewed in Valery King and Sara Christensen-Lee's "Full-Time Reference with Part-Time Librarians" (*Reference & User Services Quarterly* 2014, 54, no. 1: 34–43.

Who Should Staff the Reference Desk?

With statistics indicating a decrease in reference questions, many managers must often defend the use of professionals at the reference desk. The profession has been debating about employing support staff on the reference desk since the 1970s. This was largely the result of the demand for more specialized reference service. Because there were often not enough librarians to meet the increasing demand, it was necessary in many libraries to delegate some reference functions to paraprofessional staff. Arguments both for and against the practice can be found in the library literature, and there are valid arguments on both sides (Courtois, 1984). Proponents of staffing the reference desk with non-librarians point to the well-established fact that the majority of questions asked at the typical reference desk are directional. Answering questions about library hours or policies and giving directions to various locations in the library does not, of course, require a graduate degree. Further, as noted by Nims, Storm, and Stevens (2014), "Librarians are pulled in many directions today. Therefore, with a decreasing number of reference questions being asked at the reference desk, it seems appropriate to reduce the number of hours that librarians work and schedule trained students and staff instead" (pp. 6–7). The paraprofessional and, some say, even student workers should be used to screen these nonreference questions, freeing the librarian to use his or her expertise answering reference questions and doing other professional-level work (where library schools exist, employing the students in reference may be mutually beneficial). Some libraries that use multiple staffing on the reference desk include paraprofessionals with librarians. Other libraries assign paraprofessionals to the desk during less busy periods.

The traditional model of providing reference service involves direct staff–user interaction at some physical service point. Decreasing numbers of reference questions and increasing demands of providing digital reference services are prompting some libraries to consider alternative models. Some advocate a tiered service model, usually involving an information desk staffed by paraprofessional staff and students. The information desk personnel filter out simple directional questions and refer reference questions to librarians.

Rather than having librarians sit at the reference desk, some academic libraries use support staff at the desk with the librarians available in their offices to take referrals or have consultation appointments users. This is the "research consultation model" pioneered by Brandeis University Libraries in 1990. Some libraries, responding to decreased demand for "face-to-face" reference service in many libraries and the increasing demands on reference staff, schedule "on-call" service some or all hours. Decreasing numbers of reference questions have even prompted some to call for the elimination of the reference desk entirely (e.g., see Bell, 2007). Some libraries have merged the reference and circulation desks into one service point (in some cases only to "unmerge" them later; see Fritch, Bonella, and Coleman, 2014). Librarians spend their reference shifts working on other projects, for example, answering questions asked via IM, chat, or text messaging; designing Web sites; preparing instruction; and so forth until circulation staff call them to answer in-person reference questions.

Opponents of the practice of nonprofessional reference staffing, while conceding that many questions are directional and can be answered by non-librarians, nevertheless argue for the professional nature of reference work. Many reference questions, they assert, begin as apparent directional questions. "Where can I find a comparison of dog breeds?" for example, often evolves into a research question. It takes a librarian's professional training and expertise, they say, to analyze a readers' request for information, ask the right questions, and answer a requester's true information need rather than contribute to the requester's ignorance of the library by giving him or her only what is asked for. The primary concern about using paraprofessionals to provide reference service has been their performance effectiveness. Several studies on the effectiveness of paraprofessionals at the reference desk, including both user satisfaction and accuracy of answers, indicate mixed results (Rieh, 1999, p. 180).

In practice, surveys show that it is common in many libraries for support staff to serve on the reference desk. Many libraries have both paraprofessional and professional assistance available. Given the increasing demands of implementing new technology to meet users' needs, pressures to document accountability and assess reference service effectiveness, and changing patterns of reference demand, it is likely that support staff will continue to find their talents for providing reference services on demand. This allows reference departments to enjoy the benefits of employing non-librarians to answer non-research questions, while making better use of the knowledge and experience of the librarians.

Check This Out

The Nims, Storm, and Stevens title referenced earlier (*Implementing an Inclusive Staffing Model for Today's Reference Services: A Practical Guide for Librarians.* Lanham, MD: Rowman & Littlefield, 2014) includes a section on selecting and training staff for the reference desk. They suggest 10 desired characteristics for individuals at the reference desk, including approachability, knowledge of the library, and what they call "the teaching impulse"—an ability of a person to provide basic instruction (pp. 73–74). The full title is worth consulting.

CLOSING THOUGHTS

Reference librarianship, with its traditional emphasis on personal service and new emphasis on technology, potential for positive feedback from satisfied users, flexible hours, and wide variety of subjects, duties, and responsibilities, is perhaps the most rewarding and most demanding area of library service. With changes in the delivery of reference services, it is also the most interesting and challenging. Chapters 7 through 9 of this text explore the different types of resources reference staff members use to answer questions.

Chapter Review Material

1. What are the three primary roles of reference services?
2. What duties do reference staff members commonly perform?
3. What are the types of questions asked at the reference desk, and how do they illustrate the different levels of reference service?
4. Describe the "reference interview" and tell why it is important.
5. What are some of the potential problems reference staff must be prepared to deal with when working with the public?
6. Discuss the place of referrals in reference work.
7. What are some of the advantages of digital reference services? What are some of the challenges?
8. What is a "readers' advisory service"?
9. What is embedded librarianship?
10. What factors influence reference desk scheduling?
11. What are the pros and cons of staffing the reference desk with non-librarians?

REFERENCES

Bell, Steven J. 2007. "Who Needs a Reference Desk?" *Library Issues* 27, no. 6: 1–4.

Bennett, Erika, and Jennie Simning. 2010. "Embedded Librarians and Reference Traffic: A Quantitative Analysis." *Journal of Library Administration* 50, nos. 5/6: 443–457.

Bunge, Charles A. 1986. "Reference Desk Staffing Patterns: Report of a Survey." *RQ* 27, no. 2: 171–179.

Cavanagh, Mary F. 2013. "Interpreting Reference Work with Contemporary Practice Theory." *Journal of Documentation* 69, no. 2: 214–242.

Courtois, Martin. 1984. "The Use of Nonprofessionals at Reference Desks." *College & Research Libraries* 45, no. 5: 385–391.

Durrance, Joan C., and Karen E. Pettigrew. 2000. "Community Information: The Technological Touch." *Library Journal* 125, no. 2: 44–46.

Fritch, Melia Erin, Laura Bonella, and Jason Coleman. 2014. "Nothing Is Permanent but Change: The Journey to Consolidation and Back." *College & Undergraduate Libraries* 21, no. 1: 2–18.

Green, Samuel. 1876. "Personal Relations between Librarians and Readers." *Library Journal* 1: 74–81.

Kesselman, Martin A., and Sarah Barbara Watstein. 2009. "Creating Opportunities: Embedded Librarians." *Journal of Library Administration* 49, no. 3: 383–400.

Lee, Michelle. 2013. "Reference on the Road." *Library Journal* 138, Reference 2014 Supplement: 18–20.

Martin, Pamela N., and Lezlie Park. 2010. "Reference Desk Consultation Assignment: An Exploratory Study of Students' Perceptions of Reference Service." *Reference & User Services Quarterly* 49, no. 4: 333–340.

Nims, Julia K., Paula Storm, and Robert Stevens. 2014. *Implementing an Inclusive Staffing Model for Today's Reference Services: A Practical Guide for Librarians*. Lanham, MD: Rowman & Littlefield.

Pearson, Chad. 2014. "Understanding the Work Dynamic of the Reference Night Shift." *The Reference Librarian* 55, no. 1: 89–93.

Pyati, Ajit. 2003. "Limited English Proficient Users and the Need for Improved Reference Services." *Reference Services Review* 31, no. 3: 264–271.

Rieh, Soo Young. 1999. "Changing Reference Service Environment: A Review of Perspectives from Managers, Librarians, and Users." *The Journal of Academic Librarianship* 25, no. 3: 178–186.

Rogers, Tim, Atabong Fombon, and Erica Reynolds. 2005. "Community Information, Electrified." *Library Journal Netconnect*, Winter: 4–9.

Rothstein, Samuel. 1989. "The Development of Reference Services through Academic Traditions, Public Library Practice, and Special Librarianship." *The Reference Librarian* 25/26, no. 11: 33–156.

Tyckoson, David A. 2011. "Issues and Trends in the Management of Reference Services: A Historical Perspective." *Journal of Library Administration* 51, no. 3: 259–278.

SUGGESTED READINGS

Ademodi, Olugbenga. 2011. "Reference Service in Academic Libraries: Accommodation of International Students." *Library Philosophy & Practice* April: 1–10. http://unllib.unl.edu/LPP/ademodi.pdf.

Anwyll, Rebecca, Brenda Chawner, and Laurel Tarulli. 2013. "Social Media and Readers' Advisory." *Reference & User Services Quarterly* 53, no. 1: 18–22.

Case, Donald Owen. 2012. *Looking for Information: A Survey of Research on Information Seeking, Needs and Behavior*. 3rd ed. Bingley, UK: Emerald Group Pub.

Clark, Larra, and Mary Hirsh. 2014. "How to Get the Edge on Technology Access." *American Libraries* 45, nos. 1/2: 36–39.

Coonin, Bryna, and Cynthia Levine. 2013. "Reference Interviews: Getting Things Right." *Reference Librarian* 54, no. 1: 73–77.

Dali, Keren. 2014. "From Book Appeal to Reading Appeal: Redefining the Concept of Appeal in Readers' Advisory." *Library Quarterly* 84, no. 1: 22–48.

Dewdney, Patricia, and Gillian Mitchell. 1996. "Oranges and Peaches: Understanding Communication Accidents in the Reference Interview." *RQ* 35, no. 4: 520–535. (Note: This is a classic article on the importance of communication in the reference interview.)

Dodge, Heather. 2013. "'Hi, R U There?' Adventures in Chat Reference Librarianship." *Public Services Quarterly* 9, no.1: 81–88.

Doerksen, Brad. 2013. "A Different Kind of Embedded Librarian: More than Just a New Office." *Christian Librarian* 56, no. 2: 80–82.

Frost, William J. 2013. *The Reference Collection: From the Shelf to the Web*. Hoboken, NJ: Taylor and Francis.

Hock, Randolph. 2013. *The Extreme Searcher's Internet Handbook: A Guide for the Serious Searcher*. 4th ed. Medford, NJ: CyberAge Books.

Kallio, Jamie. 2012. *Read On—Speculative Fiction for Teens: Reading Lists for Every Taste*. Santa Barbara, CA: Libraries Unlimited.

Katopol, Patricia F. 2014. "Avoiding the Reference Desk: Stereotype Threat." *Library Leadership & Management* 28, no. 3: 1–4.

Lanning, Scott. 2014. *Reference and Instructional Services for Information Literacy Skills in School Libraries*. Santa Barbara, CA: Libraries Unlimited.

Leonard, Elizabeth, and Erin McCaffrey. 2014. *Virtually Embedded: The Librarian in an Online Environment*. Chicago: Association of College and Research Libraries, American Library Association.

Lin, Chi-Shiou. 2010. "Neutral Questioning: A Sense-Making Technique for Reference Interview." *Journal of Librarianship and Information Studies* 2, no. 1: 1–15.

Lohmeier, Kerry, and Anne Mostad-Jensen. 2014. "Creative Reference." *AALL Spectrum* 18, no. 6: 22–23.

Mackenzie, Alison, and Lindsey Martin. 2014. *Mastering Digital Librarianship: Strategy, Networking and Discovery in Academic Libraries*. London: Facet Publishing.

Miles, Dennis B. 2013. "Shall We Get Rid of the Reference Desk?" *Reference & User Services Quarterly* 52, no. 4: 320–333.

Moyer, Jessica E., and Kaite Mediatore Stover. 2010. *The Readers' Advisory Handbook*. Chicago: American Library Association.

O'Gorman, Jack, and Barry Trott. 2009. "What Will Become of Reference in Academic and Public Libraries?" *Journal of Library Administration* 49, no. 3: 327–339.

Pearson, Chad. 2014. "Maximizing the Evening/Night Reference Transaction." *The Reference Librarian* 55, no. 2: 175–179.

Riedling, Ann Marlow, Loretta Shake, and Cynthia Houston. 2013. *Reference Skills for the School Librarian: Tools and Tips*. Santa Barbara, CA: Linworth.

Schonfeld, Roger C. 2014. *Does Discovery Still Happen in the Library? Roles and Strategies for a Shifting Reality.* [New York]: Ithaka S&R. http://www.sr.ithaka .org/sites/default/files/files/SR_Briefing_Discovery_20140924_0.pdf.

Schwartz, Howard R., and Barry Trott. 2014. "The Application of RUSA Standards to the Virtual Reference Interview." *Reference & User Services Quarterly* 54, no. 1: 8–11.

Sheffield, K. Megan, Susan L. Silver, and Lily Todorinova. 2013. "Merging Library Service Desks: Less Is More." *Advances in Librarianship* 37, July: 155–174.

Stevens, Christy R. 2013. "Reference Reviewed and Re-Envisioned: Revamping Librarian and Desk-Centric Services with LibStARs and LibAnswers." *Journal of Academic Librarianship* 39, no. 2: 202–214.

Ward, David, and Eric Phetteplace. 2012. "Staffing by Design: A Methodology for Staffing Reference." *Public Services Quarterly* 8, no. 3: 193–207.

Weak, Emily, and Lili Luo. 2013. "Collaborative Virtual Reference Service: Lessons from the Past Decade." *Advances in Librarianship* 37: 81–112.

Wilkins Jordan, Mary. 2014. "Reference Desks in Public Libraries: What Happens and What to Know." *Reference Librarian* 55, no. 3: 196–211.

Zhang, Jie, and Nevin Mayer. 2014. "Proactive Chat Reference." *College & Research Libraries News* 75, no. 4: 202–205.

**Chapter** **4**

Instruction

Information literacy, in an information age, is the true basis of knowing.
—*William Badke, 2013*

In today's tech-driven environment, students often appear more focused on Facebook and texting than engaged in their learning environments. . . . Perpetual commentary on the tech-savviness of today's students creates a misperception that they also possess high information fluency competencies to function in today's information environment.
—*Jennifer Sharkey and Lisa O'Connor, 2013*

Because of the seemingly infinite amount of information accessible online, including free sites and material provided at a cost through databases, it seems it would be easier to locate and identify pertinent information. It isn't.
—*Cheryl Youse, 2013*

There is considerable evidence to demonstrate that, in recent years, the evaluation of source material has come to be regarded as a mainstream skill that should be promoted . . . by librarians in the context of IL [information literacy] instruction.
—*Alison J. Pickard, Andrew K. Shenton, and Andrew Johnson, 2014*

Librarians know the power of information, and the need to be able to locate it, evaluate it, and apply it to meet a research need. It takes time, practice, and patience to become proficient at research. Librarians also understand it is also not enough to be able to locate an item to answer a specific information need—but that it is essential to be able to assess the quality and relevance of that item to see if it truly meets a stated need. Being able to effectively locate, evaluate, and apply information to meet a need is the foundation of lifelong learning. It allows individuals to not only answer a current need, but it also enables them to use the same skills and techniques to address future information needs. In addition, such abilities—deemed information literacy skills—can have a wide-ranging impact, far beyond enabling a student to complete a class project. As noted by Horton (2013) in a study sponsored by the United Nations Educational, Scientific and Cultural Organization (UNESCO), "Information literacy empowers citizens to better make critical decisions to achieve their full potential, and it enables countries to sustain their political, economic and social development" (p. 7).

Check This Out

The Overview of Information Literacy Resources Worldwide by Forest Woody Horton (Paris: United Nations Educational, Scientific and Cultural Organization, 2013, http://unesdoc.unesco.org/images/0021/002196/219667e. pdf) referenced earlier includes selected information literacy resources available in over 45 languages, showing that literacy efforts are truly a global phenomenon. The work was updated in mid-2014 and available via the author's Web site (http://albertkb.nl/extra.html).

THE NATURE OF LIBRARY INSTRUCTION

Information literacy instruction is a key library service performed by staff on a daily basis. Previous labels for the concept include *bibliographic instruction, library use instruction,* or *user education.* Regardless of the name, instructional activities help users accomplish the goals of effectively locating, evaluating, and applying information. These activities fall into two categories—informal (normally considered "point-of-use" or impromptu instruction) and formal (courses, workshops, guides, and similar resources).

As noted in one of our opening quotations by Sharkey and O'Connor, many times users feel that the availability of online resources should somehow equate to an innate ease in searching and locating information—and that the information found will be current and accurate. We know this is not the case—and have encountered a number of users (students, instructors, and general public alike) who are truly mystified when they find out that the answer to their question is "not all online" and requires one or more print-based resources or those on the "invisible Web" (i.e., content accessible only through subscription databases). Further, the ability of just about anyone to create an online presence means that online resources located may not be the most credible, current, or applicable to an information need—something inexperienced researchers may not realize.

Oftentimes, instruction is designed to meet a specific need—usually a short-term project limited to a specific course or work assignment and it does not have long-term impact. However, that does not mean that research activities cannot have wide-ranging implications. As noted by Secker and Coonan (2013), "Libraries have a fundamental role in providing access to information and knowledge, to enable it to be used and communicated to others. In essence, libraries—whether they are public or academic libraries, school libraries or in the workplace—facilitate learning. Learning enables research and research brings about transformation and progress" (p. xvii). This is something to keep in mind.

INFORMATION LITERACY DEFINED

The concept of literacy—the ability to read and understand—is well recognized as a critical skill. What, then, is information literacy? One of the most commonly used definitions was provided by the American Library Association's Presidential Committee on Information Literacy (ALA, 1989), which defined an information literate individual as one who: "must be able to recognize when information is needed and have the ability to locate, evaluate, and use effectively the needed information." While that definition is very concise and to the point, it is also very dense in scope, in that a great number of skills need to come together in order for a person to be considered information literate. Scott Lanning's definition (2012) of information literacy includes many of the same components as the ALA definition, but adds an additional component that we like, that of being able to use information retrieved in a search "ethically to answer an information need" (p. 2).

In addition to the traditional concept of information literacy is the newer concept of *transliteracy*. As described by Thomas and her colleagues (2007), "Transliteracy is the ability to read, write and interact across a range of platforms, tools and media from signing and orality through handwriting, print, TV, radio and film, to digital social networks." Akin to the concept of digital literacy, the concept of transliteracy will likely become more prevalent as more and more resources migrate to digital and electronic platforms.

Check This Out

DigitalLearn.Org is a Web site launched in mid-2013 by the Public Library Association as a part of an Institute of Museum and Library Services grant project. The goal of the site is to "create an online hub for digital literacy support and training . . . and is intended to build upon and foster the work of libraries and community organizations as they work to increase digital literacy across the nation" (http://digitallearn.org/about).

Jane Secker and Emma Coonan (2013) have an interesting view of the information literacy landscape. They view it as being comprised of five interlocking spheres composed of academic literacies, new literacies, media literacy, and digital literacy, with information literacy at the center. This central or core circle includes elements of transliteracy, study skills, critical analysis, and search skills (p. xxii). Their image is one that may be helpful in conceptualizing how a number of components interact in the area of information literacy.

Even with a clear definition of information literacy in hand—one is left with the question of how to apply it in research or studies. For academic libraries, the Association of College and Research Libraries has been working on developing some "standards" in terms of information literacy since 2000. At the time this volume was being prepared, an ACRL Information Literacy Task Force (http://www.ala.org/acrl/aboutacrl/directoryofleadership/task-forces/acr-tfilcshe) was at work examining and revising the standards, and had released a draft *Framework for Information Literacy in Higher Education* (http://acrl.ala.org/ilstandards/). In the revised framework, the original competencies are replaced by a series of threshold concepts, including "Scholarship is a Conversation; Research as Inquiry; and Format as a Process" (Gibson and Jacobson, 2014, p. 252). A third draft of the framework was slated to be released in November 2014 for comment and feedback, and was voted on by the ACRL board of directors in early 2015 (http://connect.ala.org/node/227725).

Check These Out

Two articles reviewing the ACRL *Standards* revision are:

Gloria Creed-Dikeogu's "Exploring the Revision of the ACRL Information Literacy Standards" in *Kansas Library Association College & University Libraries Section Proceedings* (2014, 4, no. 2: 41–46); and

Craig Gibson and Trudi E. Jacobson's "Informing and Extending the Draft ACRL Information Literacy Framework for Higher Education: An Overview and Avenues for Research" in *College & Research Libraries* (2014, 75, no. 3: 250–253).

At the K-12 level, a series of similar guidelines were created by the American Association of School Librarians via the *Standards for the 21st Century Learner* (http://www.ala.org/aasl/standards). The *Standards* identify four ways learners use resources and skills:

- Inquire, think critically, and gain knowledge
- Draw conclusions, make informed decisions, apply knowledge to new situations, and create new knowledge
- Share knowledge and participate ethically and productively as members of our democratic society
- Pursue personal and aesthetic growth

Still another way to look at the concept of information literacy is the Big6™ system developed by Michael Eisenberg and Robert Berkowitz (2000). The system, which has been adopted by a number of K-12 institutions, revolves around six key concepts for literacy:

1. Task definition
2. Information-seeking strategies
3. Location and access
4. Use of information
5. Synthesis
6. Evaluation. (p. 15)

In addition to the models in place in the United States, A New Curriculum for Information Literacy (the ANCIL model), introduced in the UK in 2011, utilizes 10 steps or "strands" which encompass:

1. Transition from school to higher education
2. Becoming an independent learner
3. Developing academic literacies
4. Mapping and evaluating the information landscape
5. Resource delivery in your discipline
6. Managing information
7. The ethical dimension of information
8. Presenting and communicating knowledge
9. Synthesizing information and creating new knowledge
10. The social dimension of information. (Secker and Coonan, 2013, p. xxiii)

Through each strand of information literacy, the learner develops through four broad levels or bands:

- Key skills
- Subject-specific competencies
- Advanced information handling
- Learning to learn (Secker and Coonan, 2013, p. xxvi)

Although each of these standards differs in its wording and emphasis, several common themes do exist. These include the need to use critical thinking skills to evaluate information resources and use information resources effectively and ethically. These are all areas public services librarians can address in instructional activities—in both formal and informal settings.

Check These Out

Scott Lanning's book, *Concise Guide to Information Literacy* (Santa Barbara, CA: Libraries Unlimited, 2012) is designed to assist the student researcher down the path toward information literacy. The work begins with an overview of the concept of information literacy and its significance, and then takes the research on a journey from identifying an information need through methods of finding information, through evaluating the research process and information retrieved. Worksheets are incorporated throughout the text. It is well worth reviewing.

For a more complete discussion of the ANCIL model, see Jane Secker and Emma Coonan's *Rethinking Information Literacy* (London: Facet, 2013). In addition to providing an overview of the model, the text contains chapters devoted to each of the 10 ANCIL "strands"—with real-life examples of learning outcomes and lesson plans for each area.

Beth Anne Burke gives an overview of the Common Core State Standards (CCSS) movement in her 2013 article "A Librarian's Tour of the Common Care" (*Library Sparks* 11, no. 2: 17–20). As noted by Burke, the CCSS "describe what students should know and be able to demonstrate to be prepared for college and the workforce" (p. 17). The article is well worth reviewing.

THE NEED FOR INFORMATION LITERACY INSTRUCTION

As echoed in our opening quotation by Cheryl Youse (2013), just because information is available online, it does not necessarily mean it is any easier to obtain. While librarians are aware of this fact, many students and faculty are surprised to find this to be the case. New databases and upgrades are regularly added to library Web sites and guides. Administrators and teachers, like students, face the confusing torrent of information on the Web. These challenges have made the need for information literacy even more evident. The nature of what has to be taught changes with time and technology. Unmediated self-instruction, especially with online tools, is possible, but total software standardization, both library and non-library, has not yet arrived. Even though commercial information providers have begun to move toward more standardization, someone still has to show people, including those who know how to use computers, how to use the technology *effectively*—whether it is taking advantage of controlled vocabulary, or using Boolean operators.

Few things make the need for critical thinking more obvious than the unevenness of quality in what is found on the Web. Any 12-year-old can learn how to create an impressively graphic Web page. So can anyone promoting a personal agenda. There are organizations and people who contribute a lot of time and expense to put objective information, or clearly labeled opinion, where the world can reach it. However, the Web also contains a lot of inaccurate information, disguised personal opinion, pseudo-research, promotional, one-sided advocacy material, and even outright deception. We have seen more than one bogus site that masquerades as a real organization's "official" home page via wording, design, language, and/or similar Web address. As with media advertising, people may eventually learn not to believe everything they see as being accurate. At this point, however, many people think any information that is important is online and that all online information is accurate information. Teaching users how to judge a reliable source and how to recognize questionable sites may be as much help as teaching them how to select the best database for a particular task.

The accrediting agencies of both schools and colleges and universities recognize the importance of information literacy instruction by including it in their accreditation standards. Regional accrediting agencies (like the Western Association of Schools and Colleges [WASC]), states, and counties have incorporated information literacy as a required learning outcome, and this has gone far to assist libraries in persuading administrators and teachers about the importance of information literacy instruction.

TYPES OF INFORMATION LITERACY INSTRUCTION

Libraries provide users with a variety of aids to access library resources, including explanatory signage, printed handouts, audiovisual and online aids, and reference help in general. While all these may include elements of information literacy, our focus here is on two methods most specifically identified with the discipline of library instruction, namely *informal (or point-of-use) instruction* and *formal instruction.*

Informal Instruction

Every interaction with a patron, whether in person or virtually via phone, e-mail, chat, or Skype™, has the potential to be a "teachable moment." In their interactions with patrons, many times librarians and public services staff go beyond simply answering the question at hand by offering advice as to how to answer a similar question in the future. When that occurs, information literacy instruction is in practice.

Point-of-use instruction includes such things as explaining how to use an online catalog, or the scale of a map, or how to locate the online version of a periodical, or a certain statistic in a particular reference database or Web site. Of course, not every transaction lends itself to being a "teachable moment"—sometimes a patron simply wants to locate a specific book or DVD, without wanting to know how to perform an advanced search of the catalog or research databases. However, reference staff should be ready and able to "do" informal information literacy instruction at the drop of a hat—especially in school and academic libraries.

Formal Instruction

Formal instruction includes library tours and orientations for groups, formal classroom instruction within a school or academic institution, and workshops or tutorials for groups or individuals. Formal instruction can range from teaching children how to check out a book to teaching an advanced graduate-level research seminar, and everything in between. The simplest way to distinguish between formal and point-of-use instruction is to look at two factors, taken together:

1. The component of advance preparation by the instructor; and
2. The nature of the encounter with the audience.

In many school libraries and special libraries, support staff may be responsible for at least some formal instruction. Indeed, there are many school and special libraries in which the library technician is the sole library staff and must do everything. On the other hand, in most academic institutions librarians typically conduct the formal library instruction activities, although support staff may provide general library orientations.

INSTRUCTIONAL METHODS

The most basic types of "formal" instruction are orientations and library tours. *Orientations* consist of presenting information regarding the library's layout and location of basic services and types of library materials. They also usually include procedural information about such things as obtaining borrowing privileges, checking out types of material, loan periods, fines, connecting to the network connections, and so forth. *Tours* add the dimension of actually walking around the service areas, book stacks, and other parts of the library. Tours and orientations provide a good opportunity to introduce people to the usefulness of public services personnel, and are the most likely kind of formal instruction that support staff engage in.

Classroom Presentations

Classroom presentations, generally delivered by librarians, go into more depth about library procedures and the research process than orientations and tours. Presentations can be either course-integrated or stand alone.

Course-Integrated Instruction

The process of teaching of information literacy skills over a school term, where the instructor works up a series of individual class units and programmatically interweaves these into the curriculum of a particular class, is known as *course-integrated instruction*. There may be separate units on different aspects of information literacy and/or on information-gathering activities in general. Each unit may have a pretest followed by a posttest to determine the effectiveness of the learning and how to improve the program. In this kind of programmatic teaching, the library instructor gets to know a group of students, resulting in better interaction with them and more effective assistance. As found by Van Epps and Nelson (2013), this type of regular contact can have a positive impact on instructional outcomes. They found in their study that "students who were exposed to . . . just-in-time sessions performed in a way that indicates . . . improve[d] knowledge transfer of information literacy skills" (p. 11).

In course-integrated instruction, a library instructor collaborates closely with the regular class instructor over an extended period of time (weeks or even months). They may share or take responsibility for creating assignments and/or quizzes involving information literacy. An interesting chapter related to such extensive collaboration (often referred to as *embedded librarianship*) is Matthew Browers's (2011) "A Recent History of Embedded Librarianship." Over a semester or school term, there are more chances to help faculty further students' ability to engage in critical thinking regarding print materials, media, and the Internet. The library instructor collaborates with the classroom teacher by reinforcing mutually set instructional goals. In such an atmosphere of cooperation, the classroom teacher and library staff member can use their combined gifts of imagination, creativity, and pedagogical excellence to create an effective and exciting program for their students. The experience can be quite enriching for the staff member because, unlike some duties, you can see the results of your efforts as the students grow in knowledge.

On the other hand, it is the lot of most academic library instructors (and, sadly, many school library staff) to have to "do it all" in the space of one class session. This has come to be known as the *one-shot lecture* or "the 50-minute stand."

Check This Out

Course-integrated instruction is not limited to higher education. For example, a series of exercises that can be incorporated into elementary school educational programming (grades 3–6) may be found in *Big6, Large and In Charge* by Danielle Du Puis and Annette C. H. Nelson (Santa Barbara, CA: Linworth, 2013).

One-Shot Lectures

While course-integrated instruction is an ideal, two factors can prohibit it from occurring. First, course time in academic sessions may not allow for multiple visits. Second, librarians are admittedly human, and may not be able to realistically plan for multiple visits to multiple courses over the length of a term or semester and still accomplish other job responsibilities such as reference, collection management, or committee assignments. (Case in point, one of the authors teaches instructional sessions to an average of 25 individual courses per semester. If a significant number of those instructors required multiple course sessions, there would not be time to meet other job responsibilities.)

As a result, many times librarians need to "make do" with a one-time presentation (so called one shot) lectures. While these sessions can be useful in putting a "face" to the library—one drawback of so-called one shot sessions is the tendency to try to use the "firehose" approach, and use the time to insert (or cram) as much information as time will allow. Even if all of the information presented at the session is essential, it can lead to information overload on the part of the participants. A wiser course is to choose a limited number of objectives to cover within the one session (between one and three) and provide additional resources in the form of tutorials, guides, or handouts, for supplemental material.

Even in the one-shot environment, students can be given relatively simple tasks that can boost their confidence as researchers. For example, after a review of the basic features of the catalog, students can be asked to locate one item (book, article, electronic resource) that matches their topic (or a predetermined topic) and e-mail it to themselves and their instructor to prove they understood the process of doing so and were also able to address their own research needs. If the session is held within the library or information center environment, and timing allows, students can be asked to locate and bring back a title from within the collection—thereby reinforcing their skills at not only identifying available resources but also retrieving them from the collection. Students can also be asked to add contact information for the libraries to their mobile devices—so that they have that information available in the future as needed.

From the Advisory Board

Advisory board member Jenny Shanker (Arlington, VA Public Schools) gives her perspective on information literacy instruction in the K-12 environment. She notes: Instruction in the K-12 environment can differ greatly from that of academia. In elementary schools, students usually see the librarian for a short lesson every week for years. Learning about all the resources available in the library can take years rather than minutes or hours. The youngest patrons of a school library have just graduated from preschool, so the focus is on listening to stories, learning how to choose reading materials, and borrowing materials responsibly. As students grow in maturity, librarians will focus on more complex information literacy skills and help students learn how to do their own research and more independently manage their own information needs.

Unlike academic libraries, time in the school library is commonly expected and scheduled on a regular basis, at least in the elementary level. Library schedules can be "fixed" (occurring at the same time and for the same duration every week) or "flexible" (scheduled by the classroom teacher in order to address a particular project or information need). Some schedules are a hybrid of both. A fixed library schedule is less common for older students. Instructional time in a middle school or high school library is generally scheduled by the content teacher for a particular research project or other information need.

A flexible schedule is often more highly valued by many librarians because it gives the librarian and classroom/content teacher time to plan the timing of instruction and collaborate on learning goals, strategies, and assessments. Information skills are learned not in a vacuum but within the context of the classroom curriculum.

CLASSROOM PEDAGOGY

There is an old adage associated with teaching: first, explain what you're going to tell them; then tell them; then tell them what you told them. While repetition may still be the mother of learning, today's students dislike being patronized. They also do not appreciate having preexisting skills ignored. This means that instructors must repeat without seeming to repeat, to make the information easily digestible without making it appear to be baby food. Involving the students in the session is the key to reaching them. Younger students have short attention spans—and that goes for college students at all levels as well. The formal lecture format used by college faculty for generations just doesn't work anymore. Students expect more interactive learning experiences to discover material as they work with other students to understand the curriculum. Younger students have come to expect visually exciting material, participative learning activities, and up-to-date technology. As a result, many librarians incorporate active learning techniques to the classroom. These techniques include role-playing, hands-on projects, audience response systems (e.g., clickers), and group activities and discussion (e.g., small group feedback).

Active learning techniques have been shown to be very effective in student learning and retention of what is learned. One key is that the activity chosen should be something meaningful in the context of the class; examples can be having students create keywords or subject headings for a topic under discussion, creating a set of search terms using Boolean logic for a database search, deciding which databases would best serve a particular topic, and so forth. Follow-up discussion and a demonstration using the results presented by the students will help keep their interest.

One alternative to the standard one-shot library session that relies heavily on active learning strategies is the *flipped classroom*—where students are given information to read or instructional videos to watch prior to coming to the library, leaving a bulk of the time at the session itself for activities designed to reinforce skills introduced. Such in-class activities can include those listed earlier, and building a session around the premise that students have done their "prework" enables librarians to spend time with students honing their skills, rather than delivering material in the standard lecture format. As noted by Datig and Ruswick (2013), "Running a flipped classroom means developing a whole new skill set and way of being in the classroom. It requires the librarian to relinquish control and authority over the classroom, which can be difficult. But the rewards are worth the risk" (p.257).

Check These Out

Flipped classrooms are appearing throughout all levels of instruction. Shannon Betts describes her experiences with flipping instruction with fifth graders in "Flipping the Library Classroom for Information Literacy" (2013; http://connectlearningtoday.com/students-research-in-science-fair-collaboration/).

For an example of how a flipped classroom environment was applied and assessed at the college level, see Sara Arnold-Garza's "The Flipped Classroom: Assessing an Innovative Teaching Model for Effective and Engaging Library Instruction" in *College & Research Libraries* (2014, 75, no. 1: 10–13).

Whether or not the session is taught in a standard or "flipped" format, knowing your audience is an important part of reaching them. Certainly the approach to the young and inexperienced will be different from the approach to a class of returning adults or graduate students. In general, younger audiences may need less explanation about technology and more explanation about basic library and information resources, as well as basic definitions. Mature audiences are usually less reluctant to ask questions, while you may have to read the expression on the faces of a younger audience for clues about what they don't understand. However, even in a group of like-aged people, you will find a wide variety of library experience. Most academic classes will be a mixed bag of students with high, low, and no library experience.

Communicating with the regular instructor—even sitting in on a class or two if there is time—is a good start for getting to know a class. For other audiences, some kind of quick survey, whether written, online, or done orally at the start or during the session, may help gauge their needs.

A positive outlook, respect for your audience, the use of good analogies that your audience relates to and understands, and some good graphic material are almost essential for a successful library session. Personal energy, good voice projection and eye contact, and the other things one learns in speech class are just as necessary with a class of five students as they are for a large auditorium audience.

Factors outside the instructor's control can have an effect on the relative success or failure of a particular session. The day of the week, time of day, room temperature, lighting, presence/absence of the regular teacher, quality of visuals or network connection, and the prevailing psychology of the individual class are some of these. The presenter should be well prepared so that whatever the obstacle, at least the main points of the session "come across" to the audience, using whatever good examples, analogies, diagrams, graphics, and explanations that are necessary to make things clearer.

Check These Out

Bloom's Taxonomy—developed in the 1950s by Benjamin Bloom, David R. Krathwohl, and Bertram B. Masia (*Taxonomy of Educational Objectives: The Classification of Educational Goals.* New York: D. McKay, 1956)—is frequently referred to as a way of conceptualizing the learning process from lower order to higher-order thinking skills. The taxonomy takes into account the knowledge, skills, and attitudes of learners, and can be useful to understand in instructional settings.

As noted by Saunders (2011), "The goal of such an education is to produce students who do not simply absorb and regurgitate information but apply their knowledge, abilities, and skills across diverse situations and experiences" (p. 1).

Three sites worth visiting that update and revise Bloom's work are:

- Churches, Andrew. 2008. "Bloom's Taxonomy Blooms Digitally." *Tech & Learning.* Shows the original taxonomy as well as a revised format introduced in 2001: http://www.techlearning.com/studies-in-ed-tech/0020/blooms-taxonomy-blooms-digitally/44988.
- "A Model of Learning Objectives," from Iowa State University, is an interactive site that allows you to see examples of learning objectives that match the dimensions of Bloom's Taxonomy: http://www.celt.iastate.edu/teaching/RevisedBlooms1.html.
- Another interactive tool for understanding Bloom's Taxonomy is from Eductechalogy.org: http://eductechalogy.org/swfapp/blooms/wheel/engage.swf.

INSTRUCTION: MOVING THEORY INTO PRACTICE

As noted by Sobel (2012), "Library instruction is intended to help real people develop real skills to meet real needs" (p. x). Keeping this in mind, there are a number of factors to consider as you embark on instructional activities. These range from learning to teach, to understanding various factors associated with instruction—from scheduling through assessment.

Learning to Teach

First and foremost, it is important to remember that learning to teach is a process. If you were born with the innate ability to condense complex information retrieval and literacy concepts into manageable and understandable lessons and effectively relay that information to one or more individuals, you are definitely in luck. That is a wonderful skill to nurture! If you were not born with this skill (which is most of us), you can develop it through experience, continuing education classes, workshops or seminars, personal reading in the literature, and/or discussion with and observation of practitioners. Of these methods, we have found that observing the instructional sessions of colleagues is one of the best ways to gain perspective and ideas for instruction. Another method is to offer to team teach or co-teach instructional sessions with your colleagues. Often the best ideas can be generated through collaboration.

Check These Out

The skills and abilities you have as you embark on your teaching activities will no doubt evolve as you become more accomplished and as tools, resources, and even the individuals you will be teaching change. To assist you on that journey, here are several resources to consult:

ALA has a site devoted to information literacy resources that is worth a look: http://www.ala.org/tools/atoz/profresourcesinfolit/infor mation_literacy.

Another resource of note is Patrick Ragains's (ed) 2013 title *Information Literacy Instruction That Works: A Guide to Teaching by Discipline and Student Population* (2nd ed., Chicago: ALA-Neal Schuman). This work includes chapters devoted to subject-specific instruction in such areas as business, English literature, music, and engineering. An online supplemental Web site is also available.

The ALSC (Association for Library Service to Children) section of ALA offers online courses in information literacy, including one on "Information Literacy—From Preschool to High School"—http://www.ala.org/alsc /edcareeers/profdevelopment/alscweb/courses/infolit.

Additional Web resources to consult include:

ILI-L Discussion list
http://lists.ala.org/wws/info/ili-l
A moderated discussion list hosted by ALA, and a great source of resources, suggestions, and ideas.

Info-Mational
http://infomational.wordpress.com/about/
(Note: The spelling of informational without an "r.") Char Booth's (@charbooth) blog on technology and media literacy.

LOEX (Library Orientation Exchange)
http://www.loex.org (@loex_library)
Nonprofit clearinghouse for library instruction, founded in 1971. Hosts an annual conference on information literacy.

One thing to keep in mind about teaching is the individuals you will be working with are just that. They are individuals—each one being from a different cookie cutter. You should expect to encounter a variety of learning styles in a group of students—even when it appears that the students may have similar backgrounds or experiences. You may also encounter individuals with special needs—slow learners, seniors, people with reading or learning disabilities, nonnative speakers of English, underprepared entering students—who need a slightly different approach in explanations, or may require additional resources—such as guides or handouts. Reading a few articles on this subject will allow you to take advantage of the differing modalities of presentation and to more consciously design both what is said and what is shown to classes to reach all major types of learners (see, for example, Sanderson, 2011; Woods, 2012).

Check This Out

One book worth checking out is Karen Sobel's *Information Basics for College Students* (Santa Barbara, CA: Libraries Unlimited, 2012). In it, she includes a discussion of how to work with special student populations—including nontraditional students and international students. She also devotes two chapters to assessment activities to apply before, during, and after instructional programs.

Content Considerations

As mentioned in the section on one-shot presentations, it is tempting to insert as much content as possible within a session, as you have a "captive audience." Our advice: don't do this! Good planning includes deciding exactly what *basic messages* you want to get across, and then being sure to focus on those messages. Consider the assignment parameters and needs of the students at the time of the session. For example, if their immediate need is to locate a topic, focus on that and allow supplemental materials to address other aspects. (Online guides, discussed later in this chapter, are one way to provide such reinforcement to an in-class presentation.) When possible, collaboration with the teacher can help assure mutual agreement on these basic goals. Observing your colleagues doing instruction can also suggest various ways to structure information for an audience. Using these structures to shape a talk can help give it form, and make the main points more memorable. Keep in mind that there is no "one size fits all" in instruction—and what works in one setting may not be successful in a different situation.

As mentioned previously, you will need to be aware of the diversity of the students you instruct in terms of background, learning styles, and experiences. One way to address this is through Universal Design for Learning or UDL. An outgrowth of the theory of Universal Design seen in architecture—UDL is a fairly recent construct developed since the 1980s as a means of addressing the diverse needs of learners. Three primary principles of UDL are that the instructor provides multiple means of:

- Representation (how the information is presented—whether it is visual, graphic, auditory, or a combination thereof);
- Action and expression (giving students opportunities to practice what they learned and react to what they heard or saw); and
- Engagement (providing a variety of ways to involve students in learning—whether it is by a physical activity such as locating an item, or performing a task) (Zhong, 2012, p. 36).

UDL thus incorporates elements of active learning (mentioned earlier) as well as means of acknowledging the unique needs of student learners.

Check This Out

The Center for Applied Special Technology (CAST; http://www.cast.org/) is credited with its work on the concept of Universal Design for Learning (UDL). CAST has a number of UDL-related materials available on its Web site, which is well worth a look. Included is a UDL Exchange (http://udlex change.cast.org/home), designed as a clearinghouse for materials on the topic.

Another aspect to consider as you develop the content for your session is what learning objectives you wish to address and whether or not you want to formally assess them.

Learning Outcomes

As noted in the chapter on assessment, higher education institutions have adopted the assessment of student learning outcomes as a means of improving teaching and learning. It is also a key component that is evaluated by higher education accrediting agencies. As noted by Saunders (2011), "Information literacy is included with other outcomes such as critical thinking, written and oral communication skills, and quantitative reasoning as an essential learning outcome applicable to all students across all disciplines" (p. 8). Gilchrist and Oakleaf (2012) outlined four levels to which these outcomes can be applied: institution, program, course, and individual session (p. 5). At the University of Maryland, College Park (UMD), for example, learning outcomes assessment occurs at both the undergraduate and graduate level (http://www.provost .umd.edu/pcloa/index.cfm), with the university libraries playing an active role on the campus-wide committee for undergraduate assessment. In the case of UMD, each unit is free to identify its own program-level goals and measurements. The university libraries, for example, chose to align their outcomes with the ACRL *Standards* discussed earlier (https://www.irpa.umd .edu/Assessment/Goals/GoalsLibr.html). Outcomes are then applied to either the course or individual session, at the discretion of subject librarians. These outcomes will likely shift as the revised ACRL *Information Literacy Framework* is adopted.

One of the challenges in incorporating learning outcomes assessment into instructional activities is that the process is ideally suited to semester-long classes, where there are multiple opportunities to interact with students and assess their progress. As noted earlier, many instructional activities are in the form of "one-shot" sessions—thereby making it difficult to assess student progress over time. This does not mean that learning outcomes assessment is not possible in the one-shot session—but it does mean that care should be taken to identify which outcomes are best to assess.

From the Advisory Board

Jenny Shanker notes that it is far easier to assess learning in a K-12 environment where interactions between librarians and students occur on a much more frequent basis. Assessments can be as informal as making sure students know where to find books on the shelf and as formal as grading student work on a long-term research project. Given these longer and more regular interactions, it's even possible to do formative assessments in K-12 schools, to assess if material is being learned before any final projects are due and graded. Formative assessments give librarians the opportunity to change midcourse if necessary and redirect their instruction in light of the needs of their students.

It is important to realize that learning outcomes assessment is not the same as conducting a course/session evaluation. The goal of the former type of assessment is to determine what the students learned—not what they thought about you as an instructor (or your handouts, or the room temperature/facilities). While it is possible to include such survey/evaluation questions in a learning outcomes assessment, the goal of the assessment questions should be to assess the learning level achieved. Questions are thus tied to objectives, such as being able to tell the difference between a Boolean AND and OR in a search strategy, being able to select the appropriate database to search, or knowing where to go or whom to contact for assistance with research questions. Questions themselves can be formatted in a number of means—fill in the blank, short answer, multiple choice, and the assessment itself can be conducted either in the traditional paper-and-pencil format or via an online survey. Two resources worth consulting if you are considering implementing learning outcomes assessment in your instruction are by Whitlock and Nanavati (2013) and Saunders (2011). Other assessment issues are discussed later in the chapter.

From the Authors' Experience

While learning outcomes can be developed and applied to any instructional session, Saponaro found it was easier to develop and assess courses which had multiple sections. As a starting point, she targeted one of the "core" classes in her discipline that had multiple sections, and worked to refine that assessment before adding additional course assessments.

Since the use of learning outcomes was encouraged at the parent institution, it was easy to gain the support of the subject department's assessment coordinator—who in turn assisted in gaining the support of instructors for each course.

Feedback is a key component of the learning outcomes assessment process, and Saponaro continues to make it a point to meet with the assessment coordinator in the discipline once a semester to review results of the assessment activity. The meetings gave her an opportunity to work with the coordinator to identify what changes should be made to instruction as well as the assessment tool, and reinforces the relationship between the library and academic unit.

Online Instructional Support

Course-specific pages and guides can benefit both students who attended an instructional session and those who did not by serving as a "home base" for useful resources for a course. Such resources may be located both within and outside of a library Web site (e.g., links to both proprietary databases and free resources). One advantage of these support materials is that they can be updated quickly to add additional resources after the instructional session, and provide live links to e-mail or chat widgets—something that is not simple to do with paper handouts. They can be useful places for reference staff to refer students to when they appear, call, or e-mail (inevitably) the day before the assignment is due. They can also serve as a means of supporting the needs of students with different learning styles by providing materials in a different format (visual) than presented in an in-person session. Guides can also include feedback and survey components, as well as links to video tutorials either created in-house or by vendors.

Web Guides and Course Management Systems

Options available for online support include creating individual Web pages, integrating content within Course Management Systems (CMS) such as Blackboard™, or using guide management systems such as LibGuides, LibGuides CMS, or Guide on the Side. LibGuides and LibGuides CMS are products of SpringShare (http://springshare.com/libguides/) and are widely used in a variety of library settings. One advantage of the SpringShare platform is that it is compatible with most mobile devices. Another is that it is fairly intuitive to use—although extensive help is available both via SpringShare and via a Web

search of similar institutions using the platform. Guide on the Side (http://code
.library.arizona.edu/) is an open source online guide system developed by the
University of Arizona. The difference between Guide on the Side and a standard library guide or LibGuide is that it mimics in-person instruction by allowing users to perform their own searches alongside instructions provided by
the library. (For a complete discussion of Guide on the Side, see Sult, Mery,
Blakiston, and Kline's 2013 article on the topic.) One thing to keep in mind as
you develop Web pages or guides (particularly if they are going to be used for
longer than one semester) is that they are of use only if they are kept up-to-
date. This means at the outset you may want to decide whether or not you
want to maintain multiple individual course-specific guides or create more
general discipline-specific guides. No matter which route you take, as wisely
noted by Sobel (2012), guides and Web pages can be useful only if they can be
found—so it is important to be sure that the URL is accessible to students and
instructors alike (p. 20).

Course Management Systems (CMS) such as Blackboard™ or Canvas were
once utilized primarily for distance-learning programming. However, that is no
longer the case, and many institutions are incorporating the use of a CMS into
traditional courses, as well as in "blended" courses, where some course content is presented in a traditional lecture-style environment and other material
is presented either synchronously or asynchronously via a CMS site for the
course. CMSs, by their nature, offer a wide variety of options for libraries to
collaborate with faculty and incorporate instructional material and links to
library resources ranging from the catalog to course reserves.

Some institutions have chosen to create modules for library resources
that appear in every CMS course. Others offer information literacy modules
that can be inserted by faculty into individual courses (examples include
Old Dominion University—http://guides.lib.odu.edu/modules, and College
of DuPage—http://codlrc.org/IL/modules). Other institutions, such as the
University of Maryland, College Park, have both course-specific modules created by subject librarians inserted into courses in addition to having modules
available for more general library resources such as course reserves. One key
advantage of incorporating materials into a CMS is that it "reduces the frustration that users experience when required to consecutively log in to multiple systems" (Foley, 2012, p. 175). An additional advantage of CMSs is that
instructors can choose to provide librarians access to their course sites so
that they can monitor and participate in discussion boards and comment on
assignments students may have and suggest additional resources to enhance
their research.

Check These Out

Training materials for creating online guides are widely available. Two
resources of note include the SpringShare LibGuides help center—http://help
.springshare.com/libguides and the Guide on the Side discussion
group—https://groups.google.com/forum/#!forum/gots-discuss.

Working with Massive Open Online Courses (MOOCs)

Massive Open Online Courses (MOOCs) were just beginning to come onto their own as a method of instruction in higher education at the time we prepared this chapter. Three major players in the MOOC arena as of late 2013 (Finder, 2013, B10) were EdX® (https://www.edx.org/; a nonprofit created by Harvard and MIT in May 2012), Udacity (https://www.udacity.com/; a for-profit founded by former Stanford professor Sebastian Thrun in January 2012), and Coursera® (https://www.coursera.org/, a for-profit founded by two computer science professors from Stanford in April 2012).

In a MOOC environment, students enroll in free virtual classes available on a variety of topics. As noted by Wu (2013), "A MOOC is not the online version of a face-to-face (F2F) class. It is not a collection of 'recorded classroom lectures' and lecture notes. It is a 'born digital' class, even if it's adapted from an existing F2F class" (pp. 576–577). The courses can incorporate such elements as video lectures, interactive quizzes, and peer graded assessments. Courses are designed to allow the opportunity for students to interact live with their classmates and teachers. In some cases, students located in the same geographic area create informal study groups or "meet ups." Students who complete the coursework receive an electronic certificate of completion. At the time this volume was being prepared, very few universities in the United States had yet accepted a MOOC course for credit, although many institutions were contemplating the long-term impact of MOOC courses (Weiner, 2013, p. 20).

Working in the MOOC environment, from the library instruction point of view, is not without its challenges. One challenge is the sheer size of the enrollment in classes themselves. Enrollments can be in the tens of thousands. While librarians have successfully "embedded" themselves in virtual or blended courses at a campus level, these generally have manageable enrollment sizes that allow librarians to respond to individual student questions. In addition, as noted by Wright (2013) "because MOOCs use their own platform to host course content, the work done by librarians within their university's course management system, such as embedding lesson plans or offering an 'Ask a Librarian' feature, would not easily transfer to outside MOOC platforms. This means librarians would have to create research assignments for multiple online environments if they want to be involved with MOOCs to the same extent that they are involved with their university's online courses" (p. 10).

Another challenge encountered is that students in the courses may not be enrolled in a particular university or have access to licensed library resources that may be applicable to that course. One innovative way around this challenge was employed by San Jose State University (SJSU) which attached an enrollment fee to its MOOC courses offered through Udacity. Although SJSU-enrolled students still have access to library materials, non-SJSU students do not, a reminder that librarians must work with professors designing MOOCs to "ensure that the resources such as reading materials would originate from open-access journals or websites rather than subscription databases" (Becker, 2013, p. 135). One possible remedy is for libraries to "begin developing a collection of open-access journals and sites as recommended sources for MOOCs. The *Directory of Open Access Journals* (DOAJ;

http://doaj.org) is one such resource that indexes and links to nearly 9,000 open access journals" (Becker, 2013, p. 137). These resources can then be shared with instructors as they develop courses in the MOOC environment. How successful MOOCs remain as an instructional method and how much involvement individual librarians may have with MOOC courses remain to be seen, but this is definitely a trend worth following.

Check This Out

For a discussion of the impact of MOOCs in the school library setting, see Audrey Watters's 2013 article "Got MOOC?" in *School Library Journal* (59, no. 4: 29).

Scheduling

Library instruction requires time, planning, scheduling, and energy. Giving general library tours and orientation talks becomes second nature after a while; it often can be done by the experienced with minimal preparation. However, almost every subject session or workshop requires additional time for preparation. Lists of appropriate resources, subject-related exercises, online guides or tutorials, and handouts take time and care to produce. Even when the same faculty member asks for the same library session year after year, handouts and visuals must be updated with the newest reference sources, indexes, Web sites, and database interfaces and strategies reviewed. A change in the interface of a key database for a discipline or the nature of a research assignment may necessitate additional preparation, or even a completely different approach. Instructors are constantly updating their knowledge because technological products and interfaces are always in flux.

At the University of Maryland, a faculty member cannot schedule an instructional session specifically on a day the faculty member is unable to attend (such as going to a conference or other meeting). This way, the librarian is not forced to become the de facto substitute for the faculty member. There are certainly exceptions to this policy, but for the most part faculty members understand that their presence in an instructional session underscores its importance in the content covered for that particular class. Based on personal experience we can state with confidence that students tend to pay more attention when the faculty member or instructor is present than when they are not.

From the Advisory Board

Jenny Shanker notes that in many school districts, library instruction is not planning time for a classroom teacher but an opportunity for a classroom teacher and the librarian to co-teach a lesson integrating both content and information literacy skills. Similar to an academic-level course, K-12 students often pay more attention and behave more appropriately when their regular teacher is present.

Even when faculty are available, sometimes scheduling options are limited to the space available. Many times, instructional labs within libraries are in high demand, necessitating sessions to be held off-site in the home classroom of the instructor. When that classroom is also a lab setting and students can participate more actively with hands-on activities, or they are able to follow along with their own computers/tablets, that is generally more successful. However, you need to be prepared for situations where you will only be able to demonstrate resources using a projector system. This is where online guides (covered elsewhere in this chapter) and handouts are useful.

Another consideration in scheduling is the timing of the session with regards to the class goals or assignments. If an instructional session is held weeks or months before the skills taught at that session are actually needed, they will often have been forgotten by the students. If at all possible, it is better to negotiate upfront with the teacher or professor to schedule the session close to when the assignment (or a key component of the assignment—such as topic selection) is due.

From the Authors' Experience

While it is true that some sessions are scheduled too early within a semester or term to be effective, the opposite can also occur. Saponaro worked at an institution where she taught between 25 and 30 instructional sessions a semester. Many were "repeat" sessions, where she was working with the same instructors semester after semester. Over time, many instructors came to realize the importance of scheduling sessions at the time most needed in the semester, rather than to "fill" an open slot in their syllabus. One fall semester, however, Saponaro had an instructor who was truly last-minute and called upon her to teach a session the week before Thanksgiving. The research paper students were expected to produce as a result of the session (6–8 pages) was due the following week. This was hardly enough time between the session and due date for students to adequately research their topics. The instructor realized this during the session and promised to hold sessions earlier in the semester in the future.

Assessing Learning

Throughout time, libraries and library instruction activities have been afforded a special status—considered essential or a "given," so to speak. However, with shortfalls in funding, educational institutions and libraries that operate within them are finding themselves needing to prove their impact, and this extends to the impact of instructional activities. One of the ways this is being done is through outcomes-based evaluation, mentioned earlier. As noted by Gilchrist and Oakleaf (2012), in an academic setting, learning outcomes become a key component in an assessment program as librarians "routinely state specific instructional goals, explain rationales for teaching methods, identify ways they expect students to be impacted by information literacy instruction, and detail the effect of library instruction, facilities, resources, and services on student success" (p. 5).

It is important to consider assessment as part of an ongoing cycle, not a stand-alone activity that occurs once in a while. Oakleaf (2009) developed a model for assessment named the Information Literacy Instruction Assessment Cycle (ILIAC). The original cycle included seven stages starting with reviewing learning goals through interpreting data and enacting decisions for future activities (pp. 543–544). A more streamlined approach of ILIAC method includes the following steps:

- Identify learning outcomes—creating a specific set of actionable outcomes for the session
- Create and enact learning activities
- Gather data to check for learning—to see if identified outcomes were met
- Interpret data
- Enact decisions to increase learning (Gilchrist and Oakleaf, 2012, p. 17)

Once the final stage concludes, the cycle begins again with a new review of learning goals. It is at this point where it is important to, as Sobel stated, "use whatever happened to make the next class better" (2012, p. 53).

Check This Out

Standards can be useful in targeting instruction and measuring its impact. In addition to the broader ACRL *Standards* discussed earlier, ACRL has created a set of discipline-specific standards that can be useful for specific fields such as journalism, political science, or education—http://www.ala .org/acrl/issues/infolit/ilcc/ilcc-standards.

There are a number of ways to gather assessment data in instructional activities. Ideally, assessment would occur both before and after the instructional session (in a pretest/posttest environment) in order to more effectively measure the impact of the instructional effort. However, it is not always possible to conduct both a pre- and posttest of the students. In those cases where a pretest is not possible, posttest data can still be extremely useful in determining if learning outcomes were achieved. The timing of posttests can also be variable—and be offered during the session, immediately afterward, or at some point later in the semester. (One caution of offering assessment once you have lost the "captive audience" present in an instructional session; once they have left the library, students are unlikely to take the time to fill out a survey or assessment form, no matter how short or simple it is to complete.)

The assessment instrument itself can take many forms, from a paper-and-pencil survey to completion of a "one-minute paper" e-mailed to the librarian, to an online form constructed using a survey tool such as SurveyMonkey® or Google Forms. Walsh (2009, p. 21) performed an analysis of nine assessment methods reported in the literature and found that the top three methods of assessment were multiple-choice questionnaires, used in 34.1 percent of instances, followed by analysis of bibliographies compiled by students (18.7%) and quizzes/tests (15.4%). Beyond these, and the tools mentioned in chapter 6, rubrics can also be an effective form of assessment, and provide a further opportunity for faculty/librarian collaboration (see Hoffmann and LaBonte, 2012, for an example of the use of rubrics). Assessment can also be incorporated into online guides and CMS systems—either through surveys embedded in the guide or quizzes or review modules incorporated into the CMS. Another tactic separate from assessing the students is to survey the faculty (either formally or informally) both after the session and later in the term to determine whether or not the skills taught in the session were indeed those needed, and if they were applied by the students.

Check These Out

A number of resources exist for developing assessment tools. Two worth checking out are:

Instruction Clearinghouse Initiative: Assessment Tools
http://www.lib.vt.edu/instruct/clearinghouse/assessments.html
From Virginia Tech University Libraries; and

RAILS: Rubric Assessment of Information Literacy Skills
http://railsontrack.info/
Funded by the Institute of Museum and Library Services (IMLS).

In addition, a variety of assessment tools, including ones that are commercially administered as well as examples of ones that were institutionally developed, are reviewed in "Catching Up with Information Literacy: Resources for Program Evaluation" by Cheryl Blevens (*College & Research Libraries News*, 2012, 73, no. 4: 202–206). It is well worth a look.

Regardless of what method is used for assessment, it is important to maintain statistics so that they can be reported as needed.

Statistics

As with other services, keeping statistics is useful for evaluating, improving, and promoting an information literacy program. The number of tours and orientations, subject sessions, term paper clinics delivered, Web guides accessed, the number of attendees, and even the number of new handouts or online resources designed are raw material for the departmental annual report. These data will also allow better planning for future years, and enable better targeting of groups and more effective use of time and resources. Taking this information into account, instructional goals and objectives can be defined more realistically, and the program made more effective. If good statistics are maintained at the reference desk, changes in the number or quality of inquiries can reflect well on the information literacy program. For example, if a sharp rise in the number of reference questions follows a new high in orientation attendees, a correlation might be drawn. If the proportion of reference or research questions to merely directional questions increases dramatically after a hard-fought campaign to reach all entering students, this may well be an indication of a success story. Of course, things may not always progress smoothly, but evidence is important in planning and gaining administrative support.

Statistics can be collected automatically from instructional modules used in CMSs and also from Web guides or guide management systems. Statistics from instructional sessions can be kept in a variety of formats—from maintaining a simple spreadsheet/workbook to creating online reporting forms for library-wide use. Although online forms can be made publicly available—it may be more secure to house such a form on an intranet or other secure/password protected site, so as to minimize "false" entries. LibAnalytics (http://springshare .com/libanalytics/) is one fee-based instructional management system available to libraries. LibAnalytics is offered by SpringShare (the same company responsible for LibGuides, mentioned earlier). An advantage of such a system is that it automates the collection process and facilitates the reporting process. Regardless of how statistics are collected, they should be kept for several years, since they are often requested during regional accreditations.

Check This Out

For a concise overview of instructional management systems (e.g., LibAnalytics), see the Summer 2012 issue of the ACRL Instruction Section's *Tips and Trends* series, entitled "Instruction and Assessment Management" by Amanda Izenstark and Jackie Belanger (http://tinyurl.com/ppep8zy).

CLOSING THOUGHTS

Although librarians may be fighting a seemingly losing battle against the use of Google and Wikipedia as "sole sources" for research, there is progress being made in terms of teachers and faculty understanding the importance of information literacy. Partnerships between librarians and educators are growing and will continue to play a key role in information literacy activities in the future. As noted by Secker and Cloonan (2013), "We must recognize that librarians are not islands in the education sphere. Neither are they owners of 'information literacy.' That may be seen by some as revolutionary, but if we are truly committed to information literacy we will recognize that it is too important to remain the preserve of the library. We must seek out partnerships to work interprofessionally in our schools, colleges and universities" (p. XVIII).

Chapter Review Material

1. Define information literacy.
2. List three alternative terms used in the past for information literacy instruction.

3. Define transliteracy. Why is this skill important for researchers at all levels?
4. Discuss how standards can be helpful in designing instructional programming.
5. Describe the difference between informal and formal instruction.
6. Define active learning. What is one activity you could ask students to perform in a classroom setting that would incorporate active learning techniques?
7. What are MOOCs? What challenges and opportunities do they present in terms of instructional support?
8. List three factors to consider when scheduling instructional sessions.
9. What are the steps of the assessment cycle? Why is it important to continually assess instructional activities?
10. List three types of assessment tools that could be used to evaluate an instructional session.

REFERENCES

American Library Association. 1989. *Presidential Committee on Information Literacy: Final Report.* Chicago: American Library Association. http://www.ala.org/acrl/publications/whitepapers/presidential.

Association of College and Research Libraries. 2000. *Information Literacy Competency Standards for Higher Education.* Chicago: American Library Association. http://www.ala.org/acrl/sites/ala.org.acrl/files/content/standards/standards.pdf

Badke, William. 2013. "Teaching Research Processes for the Long Haul." *Online Searcher* 37, no. 3: 68–70.

Becker, Bernd W. 2013. "Connecting MOOCs and Library Services." *Behavioral & Social Sciences Librarian* 32, no. 2: 135–138.

Brower, Matthew. 2011. "A Recent History of Embedded Librarianship: Collaboration and Partnership Building with Academics in Learning and Research Environments." In *Embedded Librarians: Moving Beyond One-Shot Instruction*, ed. Cassandra Kvenild and Kaijsa Calkins, 3–16. Chicago: American Library Association.

Datig, Ilka, and Claire Ruswick. 2013. "Four Quick Flips." *College & Research Libraries News* 74, no. 5: 249–257.

Eisenberg, Michael, and Robert E. Berkowitz. 2000. *Teaching Information & Technology Skills: The Big6 in Secondary Schools.* Worthington, OH: Linworth Pub.

Finder, Alan. 2013. "A Surge in Growth for a New Kind of Online Course." *New York Times*, Sep 26: B10.

Foley, Marianne. 2012. "Putting the Library at Students' Fingertips." *Journal of Electronic Resources Librarianship* 24, no. 3: 167–176.

Gibson, Craig, and Trudi E. Jacobson. 2014. "Informing and Extending the Draft ACRL Information Literacy Framework for Higher Education: An Overview and Avenues for Research." *College & Research Libraries* 75, no. 3: 250–253.

Gilchrist, Debra, and Megan Oakleaf. 2012. *An Essential Partner: The Librarian's Role in Student Learning Assessment.* Champaign, IL: National Institute

for Learning Outcomes Assessment: Occasional Paper #14. http://www
.learningoutcomeassessment.org/documents/LibraryLO_000.pdf.

Hoffmann, Debra, and Kristen LaBonte. 2012. "Meeting Information Literacy Outcomes: Partnering with Faculty to Create Effective Information Literacy
Assessment." *Journal of Information Literacy* 6, no. 2: 70–85.

Horton, Jr., Forest Woody. 2013. *Overview of Information Literacy Resources Worldwide.* Paris: United Nations Educational, Scientific and Cultural Organization. http://unesdoc.unesco.org/images/0021/002196/219667e.pdf.

Lanning, Scott. 2012. *Concise Guide to Information Literacy.* Santa Barbara, CA:
Libraries Unlimited.

Oakleaf, Megan. 2009. "The Information Literacy Instruction Assessment Cycle:
A Guide for Increasing Student Learning and Improving Librarian Instructional Skills." *Journal of Documentation* 65, no. 4: 539–560.

Pickard, Alison J., Andrew K. Shenton, and Andrew Johnson. 2014. "Young People
and the Evaluation of Information on the World Wide Web: Principles, Practice and Beliefs." *Journal of Librarianship & Information Science* 46, no. 1:
3–20.

Sanderson, Heather. 2011. "Using Learning Styles in Information Literacy: Critical
Considerations for Librarians." *Journal of Academic Librarianship* 37, no. 5:
376–385.

Saunders, Laura. 2011. *Information Literacy as a Student Learning Outcome:
The Perspective of Institutional Accreditation.* Santa Barbara, CA: Libraries
Unlimited.

Secker, Jane, and Emma Coonan. 2013. *Rethinking Information Literacy: A Practical Framework for Supporting Learning.* London: Facet Publishing.

Sharkey, Jennifer, and Lisa O'Connor. 2013. "Establishing Twenty-First-Century
Information Fluency." *Reference & User Services Quarterly* 53, no. 1: 33–39.

Sobel, Karen. 2012. *Information Basics for College Students.* Santa Barbara, CA:
Libraries Unlimited.

Sult, Leslie, Yvonne Mery, Rebecca Blakiston, and Elizabeth Kline. 2013. "A New
Approach to Online Database Instruction: Developing the Guide on the
Side." *Reference Services Review* 41, no. 1: 125–133.

Thomas, Sue, Chris Joseph, Jess Laccetti, Bruce Mason, Simon Mills, Simon Per-
ril, and Kate Pullinger. 2007. "Transliteracy: Crossing Divides." *First Mon-
day* 12, no. 12. Online. http://firstmonday.org/ojs/index.php/fm/article
/view/2060.

Van Epps, Amy, and Megan Sapp Nelson. 2013. "One-Shot or Embedded? Assessing Different Delivery Timing for Information Resources Relevant to Assignments." *Evidence Based Library & Information Practice* 8, no. 1: 4–18.

Walsh, Andrew. 2009. "Information Literacy Assessment: Where Do We Start?"
Journal of Librarianship & Information Science 41, no. 1: 19–28.

Weiner, Jon. 2013. "Inside the Coursera Hype Machine." *Nation* 297, no. 12: 17–21.

Whitlock, Brandy, and Julie Nanavati. 2013. "A Systematic Approach to Performa-
tive and Authentic Assessment." *Reference Services Review* 41, no. 1: 32–48.

Woods, Helen Buckley, 2012. "Know Your RO from Your AE? Learning Styles in
Practice." *Health Information & Libraries Journal* 29, no. 2: 172–176.

Wright, Forrest. 2013. "What Do Librarians Need to Know about MOOCs?" *D-Lib
Magazine* 19, no. 3/4: 10.

Wu, Kerry. 2013. "Academic Libraries in the Age of MOOCs." *Reference Services Review* 41, no. 3: 576–587.

Youse, Cheryl. 2013. "Trillions of Resources Provide New Opportunities." *Library Media Connection* 32, no. 2: 40–41.

Zhong, Ying. 2012. "Universal Design for Learning (UDL) in Library Instruction." *College & Undergraduate Libraries* 19, no. 1: 33–45.

SUGGESTED READINGS

Andreae, Jennifer, and Erin L. Anderson. 2011. "Re-Conceptualizing Access." *Communications in Information Literacy* 5, no. 2: 74–81.

Badke, William. 2010. "Why Information Literacy Is Invisible." *Communications in Information Literacy* 4, no. 2: 129–141.

Bernnard, Deborah, Greg Bobish, Daryl Bullis, Jenna Hecker, Irina Holden, Allison Hosier, Trudi Jacobson, and Tor Loney. 2014. *The Information Literacy User's Guide: An Open, Online Textbook*. Geneseo, NY: Open SUNY Textbooks, Milne Library. http://opensuny.org/omp/index.php/SUNYOpenTextbooks/catalog/book/170

Booth, Char. 2011. *Reflective Teaching, Effective Learning: Instructional Literacy for Library Educators*. Chicago: American Library Association.

Bottorff, Tim, and Andrew Todd. 2012. "Making Online Instruction Count: Statistical Reporting of Web-Based Library Instruction Activities." *College & Research Libraries* 73, no. 1: 33–46.

Broussard, Mary Snyder, Rachel Hickoff-Cresko, and Jessica Urick Oberlin. 2014. *Snapshots of Reality: A Practical Guide to Formative Assessment in Library Instruction*. Chicago: American Library Association.

Calhoun, Cate. 2014. "Using Wikipedia in Information Literacy Instruction: Tips for Developing Research Skills." *College & Research Libraries News* 75, no. 1: 32–33.

Calkins, Kaijsa, and Cassandra Kvenild, eds. 2014. *The Embedded Librarian's Cookbook*. Chicago: Association of College and Research Libraries.

Canino-Fluit, Ana. 2013. "Flying High with the Information Fluency Continuum." *Knowledge Quest* 41, no. 5: 46–50.

Catts, Ralph. 2012. "Indicators of Adult Information Literacy." *Journal Of Information Literacy* 6, no. 2: 4–18.

Christensen, Joanne, Fawn Morgan, and Janae Kinikin. 2013. "An Online Information Skills Tutorial." *School Library Monthly* 29, no. 5: 8–10.

Coonan, Emma, Jane Seker, Katy Wrathall, and Helen Webster. 2012. "ANCIL in Action: Progress Updates on a New Curriculum for Information Literacy." *SCONUL Focus* no. 55: 4–8. http://www.sconul.ac.uk/sites/default/files/documents/2.pdf.

De Abreu, Belinha S., and Paul Mihailidis. 2014. *Media Literacy Education in Action: Theoretical and Pedagogical Perspectives*. New York: Routledge/Taylor & Francis Group.

Detlor, Brian, Lorne Booker, Alexander Serenko, and Heidi Julien. 2012. "Student Perceptions of Information Literacy Instruction: The Importance of Active Learning." *Education for Information* 29, no. 2: 147–161.

Dewan, Pauline, and Michael Steeleworthy. 2013. "Incorporating Online Instruction in Academic Libraries: Getting Ahead of the Curve." *Journal of Library & Information Services in Distance Learning* 7, no. 3: 278–296.

Farkas, Meredith. 2012. "Participatory Technologies, Pedagogy 2.0 and Information Literacy." *Library Hi Tech* 30, no. 1: 82–94.

Francis, Mary. 2012. "Using Fun to Teach Rigorous Content." *Communications in Information Literacy* 6, no. 2: 151–159.

Gore, Hannah. 2014. "Massive Open Online Courses (MOOCs) and Their Impact on Academic Library Services: Exploring the Issues and Challenges." *New Review of Academic Librarianship* 20, no. 1: 4–28.

Gray, Andrew. 2013. "Wikipedia and Information Literacy: A Springboard for Research." *School Librarian* 61, no. 1: 8–10.

Greenwalt, R. Toby. 2013. "Small Steps, Big Steps." *Public Libraries* 52, no. 1: 23–53.

Hanz, Katherine, and Jessica Lange. 2013. "Using Student Questions to Direct Information Literacy Workshops." *Reference Services Review* 41, no. 3: 532–546.

Havelka, Stefanie, and Alevtina Verbovetskaya. 2012. "Mobile Information Literacy." *College & Research Libraries News* 73, no. 1: 22–23.

Julian, Suzanne. 2013. "Reinventing Classroom Space to Re-Energise Information Literacy Instruction." *Journal of Information Literacy* 7, no: 1: 69–82.

Koltay, Tibor. 2011. "Information Literacy for Amateurs and Professionals: The Potential of Academic, Special and Public Libraries." *Library Review* 60, no. 3: 246–257.

Lanning, Scott. 2014. *Reference and Instructional Services for Information Literacy Skills in School Libraries.* 3rd ed. Santa Barbara, CA: Libraries Unlimited.

Lohmiller, Darcy, 2012. "Teach and Assess Library Skills in 30 Minutes (or Less)." *Library Media Connection* 30, no. 4: 52–53.

Margino, Megan. 2013. "Revitalizing Traditional Information Literacy Instruction: Exploring Games in Academic Libraries." *Public Services Quarterly* 9, no. 4: 333–341.

Miller, Carl, and Jamie Bartlett. 2012. "'Digital Fluency': Towards Young People's Critical Use of the Internet." *Journal of Information Literacy* 6, no. 2: 35–55.

Oakleaf, Megan, Jackie Belanger, and Carlie Graham. 2013. "Choosing and Using Assessment Management Systems: What Librarians Need to Know." *Proceedings of the ACRL 2013 Conference, Indianapolis, Indiana.* Chicago: Association of College and Research Libraries. http://www.ala.org/acrl/sites/ala.org.acrl/files/content/conferences/confsandpreconfs/2013/papers/OakleafBelangerGraham_Choosing.pdf.

Oakleaf, Megan, and Patricia L. Owen. 2010. "Closing the 12–13 Gap Together: School and College Librarians Supporting 21st Century Learners." *Teacher Librarian* 37, no. 3: 52–58.

Purcell, Kristen, Lee Rainie, Alan Heaps, Judy Buchanan, Linda Friedrich, Amanda Jacklin, Clara Chen, and Kathryn Zickuhr. 2012. *How Teens Do Research in the Digital World.* Washington, D.C.: Pew Research Center's Internet & American Life Project. http://www.pewinternet.org/2012/11/01/how-teens-do-research-in-the-digital-world/.

Rempel, Jennifer, and Danielle M. Cossarini. 2013. "Communicating the Relevance of the Library in the Age of Google: Improving Undergraduate Research Skills and Information Literacy though New Models of Library Instruction." *Nordic Journal of Information Literacy in Higher Education* 5, no. 1: 49–53.

Ritterbush, Jon. 2014. "Assessing Academic Library Services to Distance Learners: A Literature Review of Perspectives from Librarians, Students, and Faculty." *The Reference Librarian* 55, no. 1: 26–36.

Russell, Becky. 2012. "Colorado Library Program Assessment." *School Library Monthly* 28, no. 8: 5–7.

Travis, Tiffini. 2011. "From the Classroom to the Boardroom: The Impact of Information Literacy Instruction on Workplace Research Skills." *Education Libraries* 34, no. 2: 19–31.

Walker, Kevin W., and Michael Pearce. 2014. "Student Engagement in One-Shot Library Instruction." *Journal of Academic Librarianship* 40, no. 3: 281–290.

Wiener, Jon. 2013. "Inside the Coursera Hype Machine." *Nation* 297, no. 12: 17–21.

Chapter **5**

Document Delivery

We forbid those who belong to a religious order to formulate any vow against lending their books to those who are in need of them, seeing that to lend is enumerated among the principal works of mercy.

—*Decree of the Church Council, Paris, 1212* CE

The key principle of resource sharing centers on enabling libraries to provide access for their patrons to materials beyond their immediate local collections.

—*Marshall Breeding, 2013*

The prevalence of Google and other search engines has led library users to expect easy searching, immediate results, and free access to most resources.

—*Colleen Kenefick and Jennifer A. DeVito, 2013*

The largest group of libraries in the United States, K-12 school libraries and media centers, however, seem to rarely participate in interlibrary loan, even though these libraries are perhaps the least well-funded libraries in the country.

—*C. William Gee, 2011*

One recurring theme in this book, as well as one mentioned in many other library publications, is that the level of library funding is almost always too low to allow libraries to do as much as they would like. When it comes to adding materials to library collections, there are always many more items that would be of high interest to some members of the service community than there are funds to purchase the titles. No library, even the very largest such as the Library of Congress, can secure copies of everything that would be desirable to have. Certainly the giants of the library world come very close to achieving such a goal, but even they reach out to other libraries for a needed item occasionally.

101

Our first two opening quotations identify the standing solution that libraries have and do employ to expand their users' access to the full range of information resources—resource sharing. Breeding's quotation provides a concise definition of library resource sharing. There are several ways in which libraries go about expanding access beyond the local collection. Interlibrary loan, reciprocal borrowing agreements, mediated document delivery, and unmediated document delivery are the broad categories that libraries employ; we should note that there are variations within some of the categories.

Interlibrary loan is a system of loaning items between libraries and has been employed for a very long time. *Reciprocal borrowing* is based on signed agreements between local libraries that allow a registered borrower at one library to borrow (in person) items from the participating libraries. *Mediated document delivery* is often based on some form of access to remotely stored material (located either in the library's storage unit or in a cooperative unit). There are a number of unmediated systems in operation that allow users to directly request items from an online union catalog (OhioLINK and UBorrow are two such examples). We will discuss each of these broad categories in this chapter.

When it was just a world of physical collections that a library might potentially share with other libraries, the process was involved but not filled with too many legal concerns. Katie J. Birch, Matt Goldner, and Kendra N. Parson (2013) suggested that in the digital world the process is more challenging, noting: "With new developments in resource sharing, both borrowing and lending have been impacted in recent years. . . . Libraries are finding it harder to share resources, especially e-resources, when there are: difficulties in delivering the resource to the patrons, copyright and licensing problems, and a variety of systems that e-resources can be delivered through such as Ariel, Odyssey and Article Exchange to name a few" (p. 13). This is the first of several chapters that will raise the issues of copyright, licensing, technology, libraries, and the law. Our primary discussion of legal considerations and libraries is in chapter 13.

INTERLIBRARY LOAN

We will start with the oldest of the resource sharing methods—interlibrary loan (ILL). ILL is the most common label for the concept; however, you will encounter terms such as interlibrary borrowing, interlibrary lending, interlibrary services, and sometimes document supply. As noted earlier, it is the process through which a library borrows an item from another library for one of its users. At its simplest, a branch library user requests a book, article, or video from the central library. A more complex transaction might be a researcher requesting a film or paper copy of a medieval manuscript from an overseas library. In either case, aside from the number of steps in each procedure and the needed expertise of the parties involved, the procedure is basically the same.

U.S. libraries began using ILL in the early 1900s. It was first codified by the profession in 1917. Borrowing activity remained low until the 1950s when a standardized request form was adopted by the American Library Association. The development of union catalogs and serials lists in the 1960s containing the holdings of multiple libraries greatly aided the ability to locate wanted materials, and the introduction of the OCLC interlibrary loan subsystem in the 1970s allowed the electronic transmission of requests. ILL continues to evolve today through the Internet, resulting in speedier fulfillment of requests, providing more user control over the process as well as generating greater satisfaction with the outcomes of the process.

Users have mixed views regarding ILL. They are glad that the service exists, but view it as the last resort for gaining access to needed materials. Most people employ the "law of least effort" when it comes to satisfying their information needs. That is, they seek the desired material from as close at hand as possible—first looking around the office, then their bookshelves and files, next comes a search of the Internet (today that may be the most common first step), followed by asking friends and colleagues, moving still further from home checking the holding of the local libraries, and, when all else fails, "do an ILL request." A major factor in why it is the last choice is time. As you will learn later in this chapter, the request undergoes a number of steps for both borrowing and lending libraries. Without a doubt, technology has made the process faster than it was in the pre-Internet days; nevertheless, it still takes time—often more than patrons who are used to instant results are willing to wait. The title of a 2013 article by Colleen Kenefick and Jennifer A. DeVito—"Google Expectations and Interlibrary Loan: Can We Ever Be Fast Enough?" rather concisely sums up the speed factor.

An active ILL program is a significant commitment of library resources. Costs for providing ILL service, or for that matter any resource sharing activity, vary from library to library depending upon how the library structures the activity. Two examples of the cost variations for ILL, in this case academic libraries, are $28 at George Mason University (http://library.gmu.edu/use /ill/faqs#fines) and $45 at James Madison University (http://www.lib.jmu .edu/info/faqsitem.aspx?id=109). Approximately two-thirds of ILL costs relate to staffing (Jackson, 2004). The variations arise from the service's activity level and the staffing levels and commitment to the activity.

There are a few libraries that offer very limited ILL services because they lack the staffing as well as on their assessment of the potential demand. Some libraries resolve the issue by borrowing from others while limiting their lending or not lending at all. ILL is a good faith activity between libraries; borrowing but limiting one's own lending is acceptable, especially in the case of true financial problems. ILL requires staff time with users, verification, searching, communicating, expediting, record-keeping, retrieval, and returning materials; all of these factors translate into costs. There are also costs involving forms, shipping, automation hardware and software, database licensing, packaging, furniture and space, and postage (see Figure 5.1 for a flow chart of the process).

Borrowers initiate the typical ILL request at the circulation or reference desk or via a Web form when a person cannot satisfy his or her particular informational need from the local collection. The requestor typically completes a form, digital or paper, which the ILL staff reviews for completeness. Today, some user-initiated systems send the request directly to a lending library, initially bypassing the borrowing library. (This approach is typical of consortium document delivery systems—see later.) Web forms for ILL requests allow

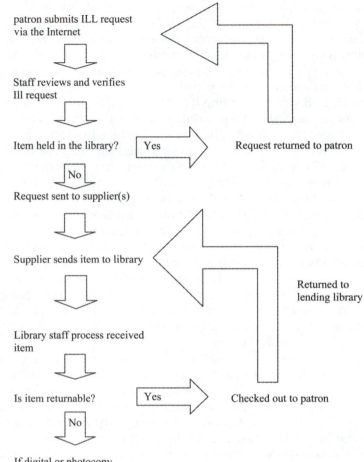

patron submits ILL request
via the Internet

Staff reviews and verifies
Ill request

Item held in the library?   Yes   Request returned to patron

No

Request sent to supplier(s)

Supplier sends item to library

Returned to
lending library

Library staff process received
item

Is item returnable?   Yes   Checked out to patron

No

If digital or photocopy,
patron retains

Figure 5.1 ILL Procedures

borrowers to request materials any time, day or night, from any location, and represent the majority of ILL requests. The more information the borrower supplies, the more accurate and more timely the loan is likely to be. Securing the borrower's e-mail or telephone number at the outset is a useful policy. The ability to clarify verification problems by contacting the borrower before transmitting the loan request saves time and trouble for all concerned.

Before initiating an ILL request, the borrowing library must determine if it already owns or has electronic access to the requested item by checking its OPAC. Some unmediated systems automatically check ownership information and, if owned, it notifies the requestor and cancels the request. If the desired item is missing (something automatic checking is likely to miss), a staff member conducts a search before placing the request. (See the following chapter for a discussion of searching for missing collection items.) Occasionally a desired item is part of the local collection, but if it is mutilated or defaced in some manner, the library may initiate an order for replacement pages or a new copy (when available and desirable) in addition to carrying out the ILL transaction.

With non-local items, ILL staff members verify the actual existence of the item (bibliographic verification). Frequently what looks like a complete citation contains incorrect data; sending the request off in that state will only delay the delivery of the desired material. Typographical errors do exist in databases and Web sites, and researchers' tired eyes can blur when looking at long lists of citations. There are even spurious references by a pseudo scholar. Typically, one verifies the information by consulting an online bibliographic utility such as WorldCat, or DOCLINE (for medical libraries), or an index or abstracting source. Such verification is an integral part of the preparation for ILL; if nothing more it saves time in the long run for all the parties involved in the transaction.

Once the staff confirms the existence of the item the actual borrowing process begins, usually through electronic transmission of requests to a potential lending library or document supplier. Knowing who owns the desired material is, of course, essential for an effective fast ILL service. Using WorldCat supplies both verification and possible lending libraries. "Possible" because OCLC holdings data does not indicate if a particular holding library will actually lend the item (e.g., some libraries have non-circulating collections but the records are still in the OCLC database). There is also a question of which potential lenders will provide the item for free or with a fee for the borrowing institution.

Many ILL services select a number of potential lenders in priority order (e.g., by geographical proximity, best service, or lowest fee). Some user-initiated systems automatically select potential lenders based on pre-programmed selection parameters. In a consortium, the system may employ a "load balancing" algorithm that tries to achieve a balance of lending and borrowing workloads for the member libraries. In either case, the process involves contacting the potential lenders in priority order until a library accepts the request. Such an arrangement increases the probability that the requested item becomes available as quickly as possible. ILL management systems (IMS), like OCLC's Illiad (http://www.oclc.org/illiad.en.html), are central to high-performing operations. Automated procedures are crucial to improving performance measures like fill rate, turnaround time, and user satisfaction.

Some libraries have to charge for some ILL expenses, such as photocopy charges. Some individuals are willing to pay total service charges, direct and indirect, to maintain highly desired services. In such situations, libraries might find it in their interest to make the possibilities evident to the community, and let their public decide whether or not such service can be supported.

Only a few libraries still use non-automated ILL procedures. Because there are a variety of non-automated procedures of varying complexity we cannot do more than mention that such ILL service still exists. In smaller libraries, a simple phone call to another branch or the public library in the next community might be all that is possible. Larger institutions and longer distances require more formal procedures. The ILL form developed by the American Library Association continues to be the standard, and is used by many hundreds of libraries around the United States (http://www.ala.org/tools/libfactsheets/alalibrary factsheet08#illform). Many libraries also follow the *Interlibrary Loan Code for the United States*, first prepared in 1994, and revised in 2001 and 2008 (http://www .ala.org/rusa/resources/guidelines/interlibrary). ILL staff should be familiar with this code and with the state and local practices which may govern ILL locally, regionally, or within networks. Most other countries have their own ILL codes and the International Federation of Library Associations and Institutions (IFLA) developed guidelines for best practices for ILL and document delivery to assist ILL staff in all countries (http://www.ifla.org/publications/guidelines-for-best-practice-in-interlibrary-loan-and-document-delivery).

Check This Out

If you are interested in the topic of interlibrary lending, you may wish to explore the STARS Interlibrary Loan Committee (http://www.ala.org/rusa/contact/rosters/stars/rus-mouill). The committee is a subgroup of the Sharing and Transforming Access to Resources (STARS) section of the Reference and User Services Association (RUSA) in ALA.

DOCUMENT DELIVERY

Mediated document delivery is another resource sharing activity and takes several forms, especially for special libraries. One variation involves purchasing information (especially periodical articles) from commercial document suppliers when access from other libraries is either unavailable or too slow. It is a fee-based system that is less complicated than traditional ILL—you know you will get the desired material from the company, your verification process is generally less complex, and you can, for an extra fee, get very fast delivery. People, especially in the special library setting, often prefer this form of document delivery because of its speed. Some commercial suppliers can deliver requested items within 24 hours or less. However, a number of studies have shown that average turnaround time for some document suppliers is not statistically faster than the average ILL turnaround time (e.g., see Kurosman and Durniak, 1994; Pedersen and Gregory, 1994).

Some examples of commercial services are AccessInformation (http://www.access-information.com/), Documents Delivered (http://www.documentsdelivered.com/), Information Express (http://www.ieonline.com/docdel.html), and Reprints Desk (http://www2.reprintsdesk.com/). Many of the Web sites provide general pricing information with fees ranging between $15 and $30 per item; some vendors charge a copyright fee that ranges from $10 and $20. Such services can help libraries stretch their material budgets by purchasing information for their service community in lieu of subscribing to low use or expensive periodicals. Another plus is that long runs of low-use journals eat into collection storage space; this is a major problem for many libraries (not just special libraries). You might ask, isn't this different in the digital world? As we discuss in later chapters, especially in chapter 9, a very large percentage of reliable/accurate information is digitized but in "bundled" commercial databases. That is, a library cannot pick and choose which titles it accesses in a database; it is all or nothing. And, while there is some duplication between databases in terms of titles, it is not all that large a percentage. This can mean a library may have to lease a number of databases to gain coverage of desired titles. Journal databases are also fairly expensive, especially those in the STEM (science, technology, engineering, and medical) fields.

Another version of document delivery is delivering library-owned materials, via mail or the Internet, directly to library clientele. Libraries do this to assist users who live at a distance or are otherwise unable to come to the library. It may also be offered as a service enhancement, for example, by academic libraries for faculty (see, e.g., Yang, Hahn, and Thornton, 2012). Some academic libraries provide such service to faculty members' offices, as part of a public relations program (see http://www.lib.umd.edu/access/department_delivery for an example of one such service).

A growing form of this service is delivering library-owned materials stored in remote facilities. Staff members usually retrieve, or act as intermediaries to, remote storage items. It is rare that users are given access to such areas, even when the facility is within walking distance of the library. The reasons relate to collection growth, facility costs, and storage arrangements. Collections in many libraries do grow, especially in academic libraries, and eventually fill all available shelving space. There are options for handling this but all are expensive. For example, expanding a building, much less constructing a new and larger facility, is a costly undertaking. There is a significant difference in cost of traditional open stack space and "closed stack" (no user access and less costly) space. Although less costly to build, closed stacks, to be cost effective, generally employ shelving methods that maximize shelf storage space (such as by size or double shelving). We explore this issue in more detail in chapter 19.

An interesting variation on this approach is the Center for Research Libraries (CRL) which is a mix of remote storage, purchasing agents, and document delivery service. This "cooperative," to which a library pays an annual membership fee, came into existence in 1949 under the name Midwest Inter-Library Center. It has morphed from a storage facility of low-use materials for a small group of Midwestern academic libraries into an international organization with over 250 members (as of late 2014). Its purpose is:

> To establish and maintain an educational, literary, scientific, charitable and research interlibrary center; to provide and promote cooperative, auxiliary services for one or more non-profit educational, charitable and scientific institutions; to establish, conduct and maintain a place or places for the deposit, storage, care, delivery and exchange of books . . . and other articles containing written, printed, or recorded matter. (http://www.crl .edu/about/history)

Today CRL continues its role as an important resource of scarce low-use scholarly resources such as newspapers from around the world, doctoral dissertations, both domestic and international, and even children's literature. It supplies copies or the physical item to member libraries.

A third variation definition is when libraries offer fee-based document delivery, and sometimes research service, to the general public or businesses (e.g., see Luzius and King, 2006; Brooks, 2010). Libraries generally charge for this service, a document fee (whether the material is in the collection or acquired from a commercial agency) and a handling charge. Although not all that common today, its usage may expand as libraries are expected to generate a larger portion of their annual operating budgets. Today, the most common "income streams" for a library are photocopy fees and various fines.

COOPERATIVE RESOURCE SHARING

It is true that traditional ILL is dependent upon libraries cooperating with one another; however, it is still a voluntary activity and the who, what, and how of the process is highly variable. Today there is an ever-growing number of resource sharing groups (consortia) where the lending terms are a matter of a formal agreement. Such formality reduces the workload for libraries through statements that spell out the whos, whats, and hows for the group. Also, many of the groups have a common "union catalog" and a user-initiated request system. Many libraries belong to networks formed for the purpose of facilitating interlibrary lending.

Access to information becomes a matter of not only what one library can purchase, but also what subject strengths all participating libraries can provide. Rarely used expensive volumes, sets, or specialized periodical subscriptions may be bought only by the most appropriate library, but access is maintained for the patrons of all cooperating libraries. Indeed, there are specific institutions that have as their mission the lending of materials to other libraries, just as others have as their mission the preservation of last or only copies. Examples of each of these are the British Lending Library and the Center for Research Libraries, respectively.

Such schemes might lead you to believe that large university research libraries or large public libraries might be drained by many smaller libraries nibbling away at their collections. In fact, when the lending vs. borrowing transactions is tallied, many of the smaller college and public libraries are net lenders rather than borrowers. People often need to borrow from the specialized materials and collections in smaller libraries, and smaller institutions often have a faster turnaround time, making them preferred lenders.

Check This Out

One title that includes a section on cooperative resource sharing is Corinne Nyquist's *Resource Sharing Today: A Practical Guide to Interlibrary Loan, Consortial Circulation, and Global Cooperation* (Lanham, MD: Rowman & Littlefield, 2014). It is well worth the read.

OTHER RESOURCE SHARING SYSTEMS

In order to improve service by speeding up the borrowing process, libraries and vendors have developed systems permitting borrowers to gain access to materials directly from lending institutions; this is sometimes referred to as user-initiated ILL. User-initiated requests are a relatively recent enhancement to resource sharing.

The second oldest sharing method, after traditional ILL, is reciprocal borrowing. Libraries base reciprocal borrowing on an agreement between a group of libraries to allow any registered borrower, in good standing, to go to any member library and check out materials. In the past, the libraries were relatively close to one another; that is less the case today thanks to technology. The idea of such a system is simple in concept but surprisingly complex to implement.

Complexities arise in several areas. The first issue is relatively straightforward. In most cases, the libraries involved are part of different political or administrative agencies (city, school district, county, etc.). Most jurisdictions have very specific policies and rules regarding where their funds may be expended. What is often required is a legal document that permits use of funds outside the jurisdiction for a specific purpose—intergovernmental agreement is one term for such an arrangement. Another approach to formalizing the agreement is to employ an MOU (memorandum of understanding). No matter what type of document the libraries employ, it almost always requires the approval of governing boards—city councils, boards of supervisors, and others. The approval process can consume a surprising amount of time, even when everyone involved has favorable views of the concept.

Check These Out

The following provide some examples of reciprocal borrowing policies:

Bemidji State University (Minnesota) Reciprocal Borrowing Policies—
http://www.bemidjistate.edu/library/about/policies/reciprocal.cfm

Pierce County Library System Reciprocal Borrowing Agreements—
https://www.piercecountylibrary.org/about-us/policies/reciprocal-borrowing-agreements.htm

Springfield City Library (Massachusetts) Policy on Reciprocal Borrowing—
http://www.springfieldlibrary.org/library/about/policy-on-reciprocal-borrowing/

Virtual Academic Library Environment (VALE NJ) Reciprocal Borrowing Program and Agreement—
http://www.valenj.org/services-resources/reciprocal-borrowing-program
VALE NJ is a consortium of academic libraries and the New Jersey State Library that has good description of how such programs operate.

Tampa Bay Library Consortium Reciprocal Borrowing—
http://tblc.org/programs-and-services/reciprocal-borrowing
An example of a multitype library service that includes school and special libraries in the agreement.

During the pre-technology days of reciprocal borrowing, complexities came about on the implementation side. There were, and still remain, a variety of policy differences between libraries to resolve in a cost-effective manner. Lending materials to individuals is a process that involves a number of steps, as we will discuss in chapter 6. Libraries do have a variety of loan periods for different materials and those periods are not the same from library to library. Then there is the question of renewals; again there is little consistency regarding if they're allowed and how many times. Equally different are the policies regarding the handling of overdue materials. A term sometimes used to label gaining commonalities on issues that involve several independent organizations is *harmonization*. Gaining harmonization on lending policies is not as easy as you might think. One reason there are policy differences relates to organizational structure and staffing patterns as well as funding levels. Thus, gaining uniformity for reciprocal borrowing may require some libraries to make substantial changes or even drop out of the project.

Perhaps the most challenging aspect, during the early days of such services, was two words we mentioned earlier—good standing. Almost all libraries that lend materials have policies covering what constitutes "good standing." Frequently, a person's status relates to paid or unpaid fees or fines. Certainly there may be other things that limit or even revoke borrowing privileges, but outstanding fines/fees are the common issue. Prior to online library systems it was almost impossible for a library to easily determine if a person presenting a card from a member library was, in fact, in good standing.

Consortial Borrowing and Delivery Services

With evolving technology and the Internet, in-person reciprocal borrowing changed. It has not disappeared, but has rather decreased in volume. Now it is a user-initiated request system with the added feature of document delivery. Current systems enable borrowers to initiate their own requests for items and receive materials from the lending organization at their home library. In some systems, a person may even specify a third library as the pick-up location. This is most common in consortia involving academic libraries where the thought is such an arrangement may be beneficial for students or faculty who are away from their home campus (distance education students or students and faculty at home during a vacation period). Such systems track the progress of the loan requests when users log on to their account. A key component of the system is the online union catalog—sometimes that of a consortia or the WorldCat database.

Some consortia are single library types. Perhaps the best known single library type is OhioLINK (https://www.ohiolink.edu/), which is comprised of 90 academic libraries and the State Library in Ohio. It was the first organization (created in 1992) that was statewide and provided a quick method of delivery of items users requested from other libraries using a courier service. It was not too long before other library consortia organized similar programs.

Check This Out

Anita Cook and Dennis J. Smith provided an excellent discussion of OhioLINK and how it operates in their 2011 article "The Ohio Library and

Information Network: Resource Sharing at Its Best" (*Journal of Interlibrary Loan, Document Delivery & Electronic Reserve* 21, no. 5: 219–225).

An example of an academic and public library consortia, modeled after OhioLINK, is California and Nevada's LINK+ (https://csul.iii.com/). Originally LINK+ was a small group of California academic libraries (public and private) and since expanded first to California public libraries and then to libraries in Nevada. Like other such groups, the basis of the service is a union catalog of contributed holdings from participating libraries in California and Nevada. Users at member libraries are able to input online requests for titles that are unavailable at their library. Firsthand experience by one of the authors showed that some requests were for items in the requestor's home library collection but were currently on loan to another local user. While not part of the original planning for the service, the governing board decided that the volume of such requests was low and did provide a user with the desired material and should remain an option. Delivery time is between two and four days, depending on the requestor's location and the library loaning the item. Even a request from a Reno library for an item in a San Diego library averaged 3.4 days for delivery.

TexShare is a consortium of Texas libraries joining together to share print and electronic materials and purchase online resources. The consortium was founded in 1994, with customer service as its goal: "At the heart of TexShare is the synergy that occurs when librarians work together to serve customers better" (https://www.tsl.texas.gov/texshare/history.html). One feature of the program is a TexShare borrower's card (similar in concept to reciprocal borrowing except it requires a special card) that allows in-person borrowing from any member library (https://www.tsl.texas.gov/texshare/cardpage.html).

There are hundreds of such consortia, far too many for us to cover in all their various forms and services. Consortia have become a mainstay in resource sharing activities. Users especially like the speedy delivery of documents that often took weeks or months to secure through a standard ILL service. We should note that not all such consortia succeed in difficult economic times. One example is Nylink (New York), which told its 300+ members in mid-2010 that it was closing its operations due to financial shortfalls. It ceased operating in May 2011 (see Penniman, 2011, for a description of the service and its demise). Such announcements serve to remind people that while everyone loves resource sharing and the other benefits of collaborative/consortia programs, there is *no* "free lunch." It takes people, time, effort, and a good amount of money to make these projects work.

PRESERVATION AND RESOURCE SHARING

Library materials on loan, regardless if to a local user or a person hundreds of miles away, are subject to misuse, damage, or even non-return. The difference is that materials loaned to other libraries must face the additional potential dangers of getting from point A to point B and back again, as well as the rigors of local usage. Whether sent through the rain, sleet, snow or heat of snail mail or through a network vehicle, damage is a very real possibility. Sometimes they just go missing, never to be seen again in a library. Therefore, proper packing for shipment is important.

Books sent in padded mailing envelopes are not in too much danger; it is other physical formats that face a significant risk of damage. Some materials should be not only wrapped, but also boxed or even crated. A few items should not be loaned at all and while lending policies will usually specify classes of such items, there will be times when you encounter a loanable item in poor condition and likely to become more damaged if it is loaned. It is best to ask the supervisor before proceeding with the loan. Similarly, photocopying or digitizing items may be restricted due to the condition of the paper or binding or copyright/license issues. Magnetic media such as audio and video tapes must be conspicuously labeled as such on the outside of packaging, lest they be accidentally erased. General criteria and guidelines can be set by the supervising librarian, but the judgment and good sense of staff members is often the difference between a successful transaction and damage or loss of library materials.

Check These Out

Two sources of guidance for shipping special materials are from the Association for Library Collections & Technical Services (ALCTS) division of ALA:

Guidelines for Packaging and Shipping Magnetic Tape Recording and Optical Discs (CD-ROM and CD-R) Carrying Audio, Video, and/or Data— http://www.ala.org/alcts/resources/preserv/pstapediscs

and

Guidelines for Packaging and Shipping Microforms—http://www.ala.org /alcts/resources/preserv/psmicroforms.

Some books are artifactually valuable: that is, the book itself in its present physical form is important. This may be because of bibliographic details of the particular printing or edition, the binding or its decoration, an autograph or inscription, or other physical features which are significant to scholars. Some libraries loan artifactually valuable materials for exhibits. If so, there should be a thoroughly documented procedure, from the receipt of request to the final physical examination of returned materials by the appropriate staff member. This might be the special collections librarian or conservator or the chief administrator. In cases of truly unique items of scholarly or historical importance, a library might consider digitization or other reproduction before lending the item, to prevent the item's damage or loss.

Every library that lends artifactually valuable materials should include special instructions as part of the loan agreement. Such things as financial responsibility and insurance, as well as acceptable levels of heat, lighting, length of loan, exhibition mounting procedures, security, and repackaging for transport, should all be part of an agreement reached and signed by both sides before the loan is approved or begun. The ACRL/RBMS *Guidelines for*

Interlibrary and Exhibition Loan of Special Collections Materials (http://www
.ala.org/acrl/standards/specialcollections) provides useful guidelines.

The best course of action is to consult with the appropriate librarian if there
is even the suspicion that any material is of artifactual or historic value, or
too fragile for loan. The loan may be offered conditionally, with explanation
and explicit use limitations, for example, to be used only in the library, or in
the presence of a librarian, or with photocopying disallowed. Loans of microform often have "in-house use only" as a condition of loan. Unless there are
duplicate copies, original, unique bound paper copies of masters' theses and
doctoral dissertations are often unavailable for ILL.

WORKING SPACE CONSIDERATIONS

Resource sharing activities, no matter what form they take, require a surprising amount of work space. In busy libraries engaged in resource sharing,
there is likely to be a number of transactions underway at the same time.
Incoming and outgoing items need their separate spaces. Shipping materials
takes space as do the computers and associated equipment, such as scanning
and copying equipment. Needless to say, large tables for packing and sorting
purposes also eat up floor space.

Something you might think of as a necessity for document delivery purposes
is a high-quality scale. Having an accurate record of weight goes beyond calculating the correct postage. Current consortia systems often employ a "courier"
service to move the requested items from library to library. For example, the
LINK+ system employs such a service with a contract addressing, among other
things, shipping fees. The service employs fairly large canvas bags for ship-
ments. There is charge for each bag picked up. You can add several items to a
bag going to the same library; however, there is a limit on the weight of the bag
(7 pounds) without additional fees being charged. Based on firsthand experience, keeping a careful record of the bags sent and their weight is important as
the vendor's and your records for the month may be rather different. There are
substantial costs involved, both for staffing and for delivery fees. Large tables
or work surfaces for packing/unpacking work, at an ergonomically comfortable height, are essential.

It is the authors' experience that once a consortial resource sharing service
begins it grows quickly. What was adequate space when it began soon spills
over into other work areas and, in time, requires rethinking what to place
where as well as storage options.

LEGAL CONCERNS

Maintaining data on titles borrowed provides some useful information for staff
engaged in collection development activities. However, there are also legal
reasons for maintaining such records. Copyright concerns did, can, and do
impact resource sharing activities. Although we address copyright in several
places in this book, it is necessary to look at one area of the law that most
affects how or if documents may be shared.

Copyright holders have the exclusive right to do and authorize others to, among other things:

- *Reproduce* and *distribute* the copyrighted work;
- *Sell* copies of the copyrighted work:
- *Perform* or *display* the copyrighted work publicly. (Hilyer, 2006, p. 54)

The first point regarding copying and distributing copyrighted works does have implications for resource sharing. A recent (2013) Supreme Court decision (*Kirtsaeng v. John Wiley & Sons, Inc.*, 133 S. Ct. 1351) related to the so called first sale doctrine (copyright holders' control over the initial sale) may become another factor for resource sharing. Some lawyers have suggested the decision may limit any type of library loaning of covered materials, even to the local service population (see Ferretti, 2013 for an overview of the case and its impact; we also explore the topic of first sale in more depth in chapter 13).

The granted rights are not unlimited. Section 108 of Title 17 of the *Copyright Revision Act of 1976* (17 *USC* §108) and the interpretive guidelines provided by the National Commission on New Technological Uses of Copyrighted Works (CONTU) provide for "fair use" duplication of copyrighted material for ILL, provided two conditions are met: the requested copy becomes the property of the user, and a copyright notice is displayed where requests are made and on the order form and the copy itself (CONTU, 1979).

Section 108 also prohibits reproduction of "aggregate quantities" of a work that might affect sales. Because the law is vague as to just what aggregate quantities means, the CONTU guidelines also address this issue. The Commission developed the "Guideline of Five:" during one calendar year, no more than five copies may be received from any one work whose publication date is within five years of the date of the user's request without obtaining copyright permission (Hilyer, 2006, p. 58). This requires borrowing libraries to maintain detailed records of copies requested from specific periodical titles. Libraries with an IMS have this information automatically tracked. When a library receives a request that would exceed fair use or CONTU guidelines, there are several possible options: refusing the request, requesting permission from the copyright holder, sending the user to another library which holds the title, or paying the appropriate royalty for permission to copy. An organization that helps expedite such permissions exists: the Copyright Clearance Center (CCC, http://www.copyright.com/). The American Association of Publishers created the organization at the suggestion of the U.S. Congress. It serves as a publisher-supported collector and distributor of fees payable to copyright holders. Libraries, especially for-profit corporate libraries and large academic libraries, often have formal legal agreements with the Center that creates a depository account, at a discounted rate, to cover annual royalty charges. Although contacting the individual publishers may seem burdensome, it can be worthwhile. (It is one author's experience that some publishers grant permission without a fee or at a rate lower than CCC's.) Again it is matter of keeping resource sharing costs as low as possible—it is not free.

Check This Out

The Copyright Clearance Center provides a number of training and professional development opportunities on its Web site (http://www.copyright.com) including online certificate programs in copyright basics. The American Library Association also has a number of copyright resources available, including a "Public Domain Slider" designed to assist in determining the copyright status of a work published in the United States (http://www.ala.org/advocacy/copyright-tools).

Another challenge for resource sharing resides with the e-materials. Katharine Lareese Hales (2012) clearly outlined the challenge, noting: "One of the problems is that many libraries do not actually own most of their electronic resources, but rather, they hold a license for the limited use of the material. This creates an issue because licenses fall under contract law, not copyright law, and the library is only allowed to use the material as dictated in the terms of the license" (p. 129). Most such lease agreements either severely limit or prohibit making copies for those not affiliated with the contracting institution. With multiple suppliers of e-materials, as you might expect, there are a variety of contractual terms that impact if and how you might honor an incoming request.

Libraries try to have license agreements that specifically permit the use of digital articles and books for ILL. Libraries must be careful not to voluntarily sign away their fair use rights to duplicate material for educational purposes when negotiating contracts for electronic products. We address the concept of licensing in chapter 9.

A final legal issue relates to user confidentiality (user privacy). User records are covered in most states by confidentially laws. Such laws apply to all usage records, including document delivery usage. We look at this topic in more detail in chapter 6 as well as in chapter 13.

CLOSING THOUGHTS

Despite the amount of information available on the Web, resource sharing remains an important library service. An increasingly technology savvy population and advances in user-initiated ILL and document delivery have greatly increased the speed of delivery and user satisfaction.

Although local procedures differ, established protocols for resource sharing transactions help provide the necessary qualities of consistency, accountability, and efficiency which make the services practicable. The typical borrowing process for the physical loan of materials includes the following steps:

- User request, confirmation of non-ownership, verification of the item's existence, identification of institutions holding the item, transmission of request by borrowing library, usually by an electronic system. (OCLC is the most commonly used ILL system in the United States.)

- Loaning library's reception of request, verification of ownership, confirmation of availability, any necessary clearances for loan, check-out, proper packaging and labeling and shipment, and possible notification of borrowing library regarding overdue materials.
- Borrowing library's reception of material, notification of customer, and communication to customer of any special conditions including due date, possible follow-up notification of customer if return is late, possible collection of fee and/or fine, repackaging, and shipment with insurance.
- Loaning library's reception of material, examination of condition, check-in, and return to shelves.
- Both sides file and retain appropriate paperwork and records.

Some libraries utilize commercial document delivery suppliers to supplement traditional resource sharing functions because of their speedy response time. Despite the popularity of digital resources, there are thousands of non-digitized titles from which articles are still available only through traditional means. As noted by de Jong and Nance (2014) "ILL departments are tapping into free online resources available to us, but balancing traditional workflows and free resources to save money and time is still an art, an art that is in early development" (p. 48).

Chapter Review Material

1. What are the most common library resource sharing methods?
2. Discuss the value of resource sharing.
3. What are the factors that make traditional ILL less popular than some other resource sharing modalities?
4. What are the advantages of user-initiated document delivery over mediated delivery? Are there any disadvantages?
5. Describe the steps involved in most of the current consortia-based resource sharing services.
6. What are three of the most significant legal issues related to library resource sharing services?

REFERENCES

Birch, Katie J., Matt Goldner, and Kendra N. Parson. 2013. "Seven Degrees of Interlibrary Lending." *Interlending & Document Supply* 41, no. 1: 12–17.

Breeding, Marshall. 2013. "Introduction to Resource Sharing." *Library Technology Reports* 49, no. 1: 5–11. (Note: This entire issue of *Library Technology Reports* is devoted to the topic of resource sharing.)

Brooks, Andrea Wilcox. 2010. "Library Research on Campus: Examining a Fee-Based Library Service within University Walls." *Journal of Academic Librarianship* 36, no. 4: 347–350.

CONTU (National Commission on New Technological Uses of Copyright Works). 1979. *CONTU Guidelines for Photocopying under Interlibrary Loan Arrangements*. Washington, D.C.: Library of Congress.

de Jong C.J., and Heidi Nance. 2014. "In a World of Amazon, Is It Time to Rethink ILL?" *Interlending and Document Supply* 42, nos.2/3: 42–50.

Ferretti, Jennifer A. 2013. "First Sale Decided: The Road to the Kirtsaeng v. Wiley Decision and What It Means for Libraries." *Serials Librarian* 65, nos. 3/4: 261–276.

Gee, C. William. 2011. "Connecting K-12 School Media Centers to University Library Resources through Interlibrary Loan: A Case Study from Eastern North Carolina." *Journal of Interlibrary Loan, Document Supply & Electronic Reserve* 21, no. 3: 101–116.

Hales, Katharine Lareese. 2012. "Rebuilding Walls to Access and Service: The Impact of Electronic Resources on Resource Sharing." *Journal of Interlibrary Loan, Document Delivery & Electronic Reserve* 22, nos. 3/4: 123–136.

Hilyer, Lee Andrew. 2006. *Interlibrary Loan and Document Delivery: Best Practices for Operating and Managing Interlibrary Loan Services in All Libraries.* Binghamton, NY: Haworth.

Jackson, Mary E., with Bruce Kingma and Tom Delaney. 2004. *Assessing ILL/DD Services: New Cost-Effective Alternatives.* Washington, D.C.: Association of Research Libraries.

Kenefick, Colleen, and Jennifer A. DeVito. 2013. "Google Expectations and Interlibrary Loan: Can We Ever Be Fast Enough?" *Journal of Interlibrary Loan, Document Delivery & Electronic Reserve* 23, no. 3: 157–163.

Kurosman, Katheen, and Barbara Durniak. 1994. "Document Delivery: A Comparison of Commercial Document Suppliers and Interlibrary Loan Services." *College & Research Libraries* 55, no. 2: 129–139.

Luzius, Jeff, and Pambanisha King. 2006. "Fee-Based Document Delivery: Who's Buying?" *Journal of Interlibrary Loan, Document Delivery & Electronic Reserve* 16, no. 3: 67–73.

Pedersen, Wayne, and David Gregory. 1994. "Interlibrary Loan and Commercial Document Delivery." *Journal of Academic Librarianship* 20, no. 5/6: 263–272.

Penniman, W. David. 2011. "Changing Organizations: Three Case Studies." *Advances In Librarianship* 34: 97–111.

Yang, Zheng Ye, Douglas Hahn, and Elaine Thornton. 2012. "Meeting Our Customers' Expectations: A Follow-Up Customer Satisfaction Survey after 10 Years of Free Document Delivery and Interlibrary Loan Services at Texas A&M University Libraries." *Journal of Interlibrary Loan, Document Delivery & Electronic Reserve* 22, no. 2 (2012): 95–110.

SUGGESTED READINGS

Bailey-Hainer, Brenda, Anne Beaubien, Beth Posner, and Evan Simpson. 2014. "Rethinking Library Resource Sharing: New Models for Collaboration." *Interlending & Document Supply* 42, no. 1: 7–12.

De Jong, Mark, and Ryan Shepard. 2012. "The DocumentExpress Model: Proposals for Improving Interlibrary Loan and Document Delivery Services." *Journal of Access Services* 9, no. 4: 187–199.

Frederiksen, Linda, Margaret Bean, and Heidi Nance. 2011. *Global Resource Sharing.* Burlington: Elsevier Science.

Harris-Keith, Colleen. 2014. "Evaluating the Staffing of an Interlibrary Loan Unit: An Exercise in Data-Driven Decision Making and Debunking 'Anecdata.'" *Journal of Access Services* 11, no. 3: 150–158.

Herrera, Gail, and Judy Greenwood. 2011. "Patron-Initiated Purchasing: Evaluating Criteria and Workflows." *Journal of Interlibrary Loan, Document Delivery & Electronic Reserve* 21, nos. 1/2: 9–24.

Kochan, Carol, and Lars Leon. 2013. "Revisiting Interlibrary Loan Best Practices: Still Viable?" *Interlibrary Lending & Document Supply* 41, no. 4: 113–119.

Leykam, Andrew. 2014. "The Devil Is in the Details: Exploring Individual Interlibrary Loan." *Journal of Access Services* 11, no. 1: 30–43.

Litsey, Ryan, and Kaley Daniel. 2013. "Resources—Anytime, Anywhere: Branding Library Services, A Case Study of Texas Tech's Document Delivery Department." *Journal of Interlibrary Loan, Document Delivery & Electronic Reserve* 23, no. 1: 19–34.

Müller, Harald. 2012. "Legal Aspects of E-Books and Interlibrary Loan." *Interlending & Document Supply* 40, no. 3: 150–155.

Munson, Kurt. 2012. "Herding Cats: Challenges in Interlibrary Loan Lending of E-Journal Articles." *Journal of Interlibrary Loan, Document Delivery & Electronic Reserve* 22, nos. 3/4: 163–173.

OCLC. 2013. *Meeting the Delivery Challenge: A Cooperative Solution to Put Resources—Digital, Electronic and Physical—In the Hands of Library Users, Quickly, Efficiently, Effectively around the World.* Dublin, OH: OCLC. http://cdm15003.contentdm.oclc.org/cdm/ref/collection/p267701coll5/id/364.

Okamoto, Karen. 2012. "Licensed to Share: How Libraries Are Handling Electronic Journal Article Requests." *Journal of Interlibrary Loan, Document Delivery & Electronic Reserve* 22, nos. 3/4: 137–154.

Percy, Joanne. 2013. "E-Book Lending: The Challenges Facing Interlibrary Loan." *Interlending & Document Supply* 41, no. 2: 43–47.

Posner, Beth. 2013. "The Ethics of Library Resource Sharing in the Digital Age." *Interlending & Document Supply* 40, no. 2: 119–124.

Posner, Beth. 2014. "The View from Interlibrary Loan Services: Catalyst for a Better Research Process." *College & Research Libraries News* 75, no. 7: 378–381.

Suhr, Karl F. 2013. "Get It Now: One Library's Experience with Implementing and Using the Unmediated Version of the Copyright Clearance Center's Document Delivery Service." *Journal of Electronic Resources Librarianship* 25, no. 4: 321–325.

Weible, Cherié L., and Karen L. Janke, eds. 2011. *Interlibrary Loan Practices Handbook.* 3rd ed. Chicago: ALA Editions.

Xu, Anne, and Margarita Moreno. 2014. "Journey of Discovery: Challenges of E-Book Lending in a Digital World." *Interlending & Document Supply* 42, nos. 2/3: 51–56.

Circulation

One may view the circulation department as the heart of the library.
—Michael Krasulski and Trevor Dawes, 2013

Teachers shared with me daily about how excited their students were to come to the LMC—and many students simply couldn't believe that there was no longer a checkout limit for books!
—Christine Bentheim, 2013

Fair use and electronic course reserves are back in court. . . . Librarians who track copyright and intellectual-property issues are paying close attention.
—Newsletter on Intellectual Freedom, 2013

In any e-reserve system, there are three major components that must be balanced: usability, labor, and copyright.
—Steven J. Schmidt, 2014

All libraries develop some method through which people may use their resources for limited periods of time. How long and where such usage may occur varies from library to library. Linda Johnson and Jean Danham (2012) highlighted one of the challenges all libraries face and address in some manner—balancing stewardship of its resources and providing equitable access to those resources. (Note: like all policies, those related to lending activities require periodic review and revision.) Circulation and reserve services reflect the usual method libraries utilize to handle what can be, at times, a difficult choice. Some libraries that preserve rare and specialized information resources employ very limited control access. On the other side of the spectrum, public and school libraries have very limited preservation goals and their access method is more open, with only modest controls in place.

Circulation and reserve services are two of the most frequently utilized library services in academic and school libraries. Public and special libraries rarely have any form of reserve services; the only time they might is when they are supporting an educational program. (There are instances of joint public and school library facilities that combine circulation and reserve functions into a single service point due to the overlapping functions and to maximize its staffing pattern.) There are some large corporations that offer advanced education/training programs and their libraries might employ the "course reserve" concept. Circulation and reserve services share many common functions; it is for that reason we have combined them into a single chapter for this edition while still addressing their differences where appropriate.

COMMONALITIES BETWEEN CIRCULATION AND RESERVES

One of the commonalities between circulation and reserves is that both provide access to library resources while trying to assure all users have an opportunity to use the material within a reasonable timeframe. Both units face some serious legal concerns—privacy for circulation and copyright for reserves, for example. Staff members in both units must have an understanding of the current status of such laws as interpreted by the courts. There are ongoing legal challenges regarding such services, as suggested by our opening quotation from the *Newsletter on Intellectual Freedom*.

Another commonalty is staff members of both units are the true "front line" of the library as they are the staff members most likely to be directly contacted by users to deliver services or answer questions. Indeed, they are often the only staff members with whom the public interacts. Their service desks are also the point at which the library's customer service philosophy is most apparent and where a person's first and most important impressions of the library take place. First impressions tend to be long lasting and thus are difficult to change when a person's experience is negative. That fact means staff in these units may require constant training in customer service.

Both services are points from which a person gains the necessary clearance to use library resources (e.g., borrower registration for circulation, or checking borrower status for both reserves and circulation). Yet another commonality is they both impose some time limits on how long person may have an item "checked-out" or borrowed, thus increasing resource sharing. One aspect of user sharing is the role of fines should the person borrowing the item(s) not return them when he or she should, or worse—damage or lose the item. Both staffs face some challenging situations with their "publics," especially with individuals who may be unhappy about something such as a fine. Both have long service hours—generally all the time the library is open—which can result in night and weekend shifts that may add to staff stress.

It has been the authors' experience that the personnel in both units tend to believe they are at least underappreciated, if not in fact unappreciated, and are misunderstood by both the public and their work colleagues. Many of the circulation unit staff members are unaware of the valuable information their work provides the library, when properly performed, for planning library services and activities. Often understanding the value of their activities makes

TABLE 6.1 Circulation and Reserve Services: Similarities and Differences

Similarities	Differences

• Checking borrowers' status
• Loaning all collection formats
• Monitoring loan periods
• Handling returned loans
• Resolving loan period violations
• Taking item reservation requests
• Complying with legal constraints
• Providing valuable library planning data
• Creating and maintaining library's customer service image
	• Registering borrowers (C)
	• Maintaining open collection order (C)
	• Searching for missing items (C)
	• Working with teaching faculty (R)
	• Obtaining copyright clearances (R)
	• Creating e-reserve material (R)
	  C = Circulation
	  R = Reserves

all the difference between quality and lackluster service as well as creating stronger staff morale.

Borrowing (or circulation) data has value for other library staff and even service community members such as teaching faculty. For example, data about what topics are receiving heavy borrowing interest aids collection development personnel in their selection duties (additional titles on the topic or extra copies of heavily loaned items). Another planning activity aided by borrower data is demographic; that is, having information about the people with borrowing privileges can assist in planning marketing and promotional activities and perhaps new service locations. When it comes to thinking through borrowing policies, data about overdue materials and fines may indicate that loan periods ought to be reevaluated. Knowing their work is not just a basic service, but also one that generates valuable planning operational data for the entire library, can boost morale for circulation personnel as well as generate greater care in work performance. We explore all these issues on the following pages, while Table 6.1 summarizes some of the commonalities and differences between circulation and reserve services.

ACCESS CONTROL

A key issue for libraries, as noted earlier, is providing access to their resources while protecting stakeholders' investments in these resources. Balancing stewardship and allowing access are challenging goals for all libraries. The key to resolving that challenge is controlling access in an equitable and appropriate manner. Circulation and reserve services are, at their most fundamental level, controlling activities. They represent the library's effort to assure its users effectively share its resources in the fairest way possible, including determining who may use the resources and for how long, if a person may remove an item from the library, and assuring the material is returned on time (or at least returned).

In pre-computer–based library systems (ILS, integrated library systems) days, the manual systems then in place allowed the services to operate but were prone to human errors. The process was dependent upon the accurate filing of cards and other paper records. Such systems generated a fair amount of unhappiness for both the staff and the individuals making use of the services. Human error can still cause problems in an ILS, but are much less common.

The vast majority of today's libraries have some type of computer-based operation such as the ILS. Such systems have components (modules) that cover most of the fundamental library activities. Typical components of such systems include acquisitions, cataloging, public catalog (OPAC, online public access catalog), circulation, reserves, and serials control. Libraries might not even exist today if not for such systems, as increasing demands for libraries to do more, perform better, and be faster, and to do so with small, if any, increases in resources would have overwhelmed manual systems.

Circulation and reserve services are still rather labor intensive, as users require assistance. In the case of reserves, a staff member almost always retrieves the item a user wishes to have. That means some interaction regarding what the person wants before the staff member can retrieve the item; all of which means staff time. There is also the fact the service demand fluctuates: at times there is very high demand and other times little or none. Achieving a cost-effective service-oriented staffing pattern is a challenge. Unlike reserves, circulation services at least have the option of utilizing self-checkout units to assist with high volume periods. Such units are not inexpensive to acquire but do provide long-term saving—primarily in salaries.

CHARACTERISTICS OF LOAN SYSTEMS

In theory, a loan control system allows staff to determine the current location of each collection item and, if on loan, who has it. The features discussed here are typical of most ILS modules that address user loans. Most ILS systems have both a circulation and reserves module that address the special features noted in Table 6.1. They are separate features, as not all libraries need the reserves capabilities.

Obviously, loan systems must be easy for both borrowers and library personnel to use. A cumbersome system often creates poor service and worse user relations, especially when borrowers view it as an obstacle rather than an aid. Simplicity and ease of use might be the most important qualities of any circulation control system.

Naturally, there must be system reliability; that is, the system must almost always be "up." It must accurately record transactions with little opportunity for user or staff error. Further, the system must allow library staff and borrowers to identify the material on loan, any fines owed or other restrictions on borrowing, and the date items are due back. All integrated library systems (ILSs) provide this information upon checkout and is easily retrievable when necessary. Many modules have a "my account" feature that allows individuals to easily determine what they currently have charged out, when the items are due, and any outstanding fines/fees owed remotely, at any time.

Given a library's goal to offer equitable resource sharing, an important feature of loan modules is how it handles monitoring loans, due dates, and borrower notification functions. Staff members use such information to send overdue notices, provide a record for fines, and develop a list of materials for possible replacement. Related to set due dates, there are times in almost every type of library when there is very high demand for a certain item and the item(s) are on loan to someone. An individual seeking such an item may request a notification when the item is available to borrow. This process is called reserving a book, or a *hold* request. (Some of the typical instances where reserving an item is common is for popular best sellers in the case of public libraries and examination times for reserves materials in academic and school libraries.) In some instances, materials can be requested from a patron who currently is using it—known as a *recall*. As discussed later in this chapter, in a recall situation, the patron is required to return the loaned material by a set due date (generally shorter than the original loan period). If the material is not returned by the new due date, a fine can be assessed. Hold/recalls can be used in conjunction with one another. The ILS system should check returned materials against hold requests so that items can be held for the next borrower.

A critical feature of loan systems is the ability to automatically delete the link between item and borrower on return of the item. This is a privacy issue and in many states a legal obligation. Most systems can generate a wealth of data related to collection usage that is a key element in library planning. The following is a list of tasks most automated circulation systems automatically perform:

1. Identifying delinquent borrowers who have overdue materials and/or owe fines.
2. Displaying the reason for the delinquency.
3. Alerting staff to lost or stolen identification cards when one is presented.
4. Displaying all items currently checked out to a borrower, and eliminating any record of past circulation activity upon check in, thereby preserving borrowers' confidentiality.
5. Allowing placement and notification of reserves (holds) and indicating when a reserve has been placed on an item.
6. Calculating fines and fees for overdue items.
7. Printing and sending (or sending via text message or e-mail) recall, hold, and fine notices.
8. Automatically issuing overdue and fee statements to be sent by print, text, or e-mail.
9. Indicating whether a particular item is already checked out or is temporarily unavailable; for example, at the bindery or lost.
10. Recording and printing a variety of statistical information concerning collection use and circulation activities.

Check These Out

Although most people think of books as the primary items circulated by libraries, other types of materials are almost always included in the circulating collection. These formats may require special loan policies and circulation procedures. Some examples include:

Becker, Bernd. 2014. "Circulating Laptops in Academic Libraries." *Behavioral & Social Sciences Librarian* 33, no. 2: 125–129.

Musser, Linda. 2014. "Power to the Patron: Loaning Batteries to Users." *Pennsylvania Library Association Bulletin* 69, no. 3: 10–11.

"Unusual Stuff to Borrow"—From the Ann Arbor District Library. Their list includes art tools, home tools, and telescopes, among other circulating items (http://www.aadl.org/catalog/browse/unusual).

A key element in an ILS, regardless of the module you consider, is a relatively small printed object—a barcode label, sometimes referred to as the "zebra number" or OCR (optical character recognition) label. Barcodes serve as the linking mechanism in ILS systems. They uniquely identify each item in the collection as well as doing the same for each authorized borrower—each collection item and eligible borrower has a unique barcode. When an item and borrower's barcodes are linked in the system, the borrower is, almost always, in possession to the item. There can be occasions where the link was not broken when the item had in fact been returned. When that occurs, it often creates a situation with an unhappy person who received an overdue notice and "knows" he or she has in fact returned the item in question. During a loan transaction, a staff member scans the borrower's barcode number and that of the item the person wishes to borrow.

A recent alternative to barcodes is radio frequency identification (RFID) tags. The RFID tag is on each item in the library's collection and serves the same function as the barcode, but has some additional features that assist in collection maintenance. We look at those features later in this chapter. We also examine some concerns related to RFID tags and privacy in the chapter on legal concerns.

BORROWERS

All loan activities (circulation or reserves) start with verifying that the individual wishing to borrow some library resource has the right to do so. Authorized borrowers normally have some form of library identification card that provides the requisite information—as a minimum, the person's name, valid borrowing dates, and a barcode or other machine readable data that identifies the person in the system. Often there is a picture on the card, especially in educational libraries, where the card serves a number of functions at the institution in addition to using the library.

Part of the process may involve "registering" a person as an eligible borrower. Public library circulation departments usually handle borrower registration. In the case of academic and school libraries, the authorization process is handled by some administration office such as the registrar at an academic institution. The following are the key elements that must be part of the registration, from a library perspective, regardless of which unit handles the process:

1. Identifying persons who have the right to borrow materials, or in some cases the right to use a library;
2. Providing a borrower with some form of identification to show in order to check out material/use the library;
3. Securing contact information so library staff can communicate with the person regarding holds, overdues, and other matters;
4. Obtaining data of a demographic nature regarding borrowers that assist the library in planning activities such a service locations and;
5. Providing borrowers access to information (in print or online) outlining the person's responsibilities regarding borrowed items such as fines for overdue materials, fees for lost or damaged items, and any other fees associated with the lending services.

From the Authors' Experience

Borrower registration varies from library to library. Some of the processes are easy and quick, while others can be involved and a little complex. Often public libraries require proof of residency such as driver's license or perhaps, lacking a license, a municipal service bill might be sufficient (water, trash pick-up, or the like). For children, often the parent must come with the child; in almost all cases a parent signature is required. Essentially the registrant process sets the tone for the person's perception of the library's service philosophy.

Evans spent a substantial amount of time engaging in research and teaching in the Nordic countries; many of the stays were months in duration. No matter which country he was in, he easily obtained a public library borrower's card for no cost. The only time there was a "borrowing cost" was in Iceland. Even there, his fee was the same as anyone else wishing to borrow items—100 kroner to borrow 50 items (we mentioned the clip card concept in chapter 2). When you used up the card, you paid another fee good for a further 50 items. The fees went into the library's acquisition budget to purchase additional resources.

Another interesting feature of Scandinavian public libraries, beyond the ease with which anyone can secure borrowing privileges, is their approach to "resource sharing." Yes, there are due dates, but no fines are assessed for failing to return the item on time. Even lost items are treated rather differently than in the United States. Evans once left a borrowed book on the night train between Copenhagen to Oslo. When he reported the loss to the Oslo public library, he was told not to worry, the railroad people would turn it in. When Evans asked, What if they don't? The response was, "Well, that would mean someone needed the book more than we do." As we will discuss later in this chapter, the use of fines, especially for overdues, is a matter of debate in the profession.

Normally some type of library identification card is all that is required to provide the eligibility verification. The ILS barcode scanning capability can quickly handle this process by "reading" both the borrower's barcode and the one attached to the desired material. A simple and straightforward process most of the time.

"Most of the time" is true, but there are situations that arise that can present some challenges. Perhaps the most common "other time," at least in academic and school libraries, is the person's borrowing privileges are restricted or "on hold" because of unpaid fines, fees, or other issues. Some libraries set an upper limit on how high unpaid fines may become before the loan privileges are blocked. Normally the upper limit is a matter of governing board approval as is the policy outlining the method for reestablishing the privileges. Thus, service point staff may be limited in what they can do. Removing the hold from the system is likely to require "administrative" access to the ILS and that is something that most frontline staff will not have. You can probably imagine what confrontations may arise when a hold is encountered and the item is needed for an upcoming exam and there is no one available who may override the hold.

Another common "no borrowing" issue is where the desired material is not "loanable" by library policy. The two most common categories of such non-circulating items are reference resources and current issues of periodicals. In some libraries, neither current nor bound volumes of periodicals circulate. Having readily available and modestly priced photocopying or free scanning equipment can help alleviate an all-too-common issue regarding non-circulating materials—mutilation and/or theft. Certainly e-serials have reduced, but not completely eliminated, the problem of users cutting out articles from periodicals. While inexpensive photocopying services and e-resources do not completely eliminate the challenge of having key articles disappear from print journals, the service is still necessary and is one aspect of good stewardship. (We look at theft and other security issues in more detail in chapter 16.)

From the Authors' Experience

Evans had a particularly memorable mutilation incident some years ago. A young man, exiting the library, set off the security alarm. (Many libraries employ security tags to their collection items, similar to those encountered in retail stores, to help reduce theft. See chapter 16 for more information about such systems.)

A "tag" attached to a journal article in his backpack had set off the alarm. What made this incident memorable was what the young man said when confronted with evidence, "Oh, I didn't take that from your library, it's from another library." As it turned out that was not true. Sometimes all you can do is shake your head in wonderment.

A third common and rather challenging "other time" is a person's borrowing status—child, young adult, "outside" borrower, and others—that may limit what or how many items may be borrowed. Many libraries—academic and public in particular—allow individuals who are not part of their primary service population to acquire limited access to their resources, including borrowing. A common limit in such instances is on how many items the person may have at one time. Some academic libraries may restrict access to the open collection—that is, no access to items from the open collection that are currently on course reserve.

Children's borrowing privileges also can be one of those "other times." There are issues regarding how much parental control is possible when it comes to borrowing library materials while still maintaining a reasonably easy to use system. (We cover the topic of children and Internet access in later chapters.) Often it is a matter of what collection(s) a child may borrow from—the children's, young adult (if there is one), and/or adult. One published example of at least a partial solution is from the Charlotte-Mecklenburg public library system. As noted by Margolis (2001), in 2002, the library system was slated to start issuing or reissuing children's borrowing cards for those patrons 12 years old and younger and requiring the parent to select to either prohibit the child from checking out items from the adult collection or allow full access to the resources. Currently, the checkout restrictions also extend to items within the DVD collection—where parents indicate if their child can have access to the entire collection of DVDs—provided they were given "standard" check out privileges for books, just the children's collection, or no access to DVDs (http://www.cmlibrary.org/catalog/jcardapp.pdf). Other libraries employ variations on that concept, such as restricting access to certain classes of material—videos with certain motion picture ratings (we discuss rating systems in chapter 8) are one example.

For the school library, a more complicated situation can arise when it is only a few students involved. That is, parents can and do request an alternative assignment when they have an objection, on some grounds, to a teacher's assigned topic. Although having to do a report about a particular book or a paper dealing with evolution is objectionable for only one or two children, coordinating who can and cannot use what material can be a challenge. The issue is further complicated by the fact that most LMCs are very dependent upon parent volunteers for their operations. Communication about the "who and what" may not always be as clear as it might be. There is also the possibility that the volunteer's personal values may further complicate the situation (see chapter 14 for a discussion of personal values).

Many systems today also allow self-charging by users. Permitting borrowers to check out their own items frees staff to perform other service functions. When there is an issue regarding either the borrower's or item's loan eligibility, staff must assist in the transaction. Borrowers generally like these systems as they often allow them to bypass a line at the circulation desk, thus speeding up their transactions. It may also improve productivity and efficiency, reduce expenses, and allow libraries to handle increasing circulation activity without increasing staff while affording users an option for self-service resulting in increased user satisfaction. The borrower places a library card in the system and if the card is approved, instructions appear on how to position the item and scan the barcode or read the tag. The system then verifies the circulation status of the item, checks it out, and desensitizes the item. Date due slips are sometimes printed, and if there is a problem the system prompts the user to inquire at the circulation desk.

Librarians say that self-service options generally improve service overall and staff have more time to assist patrons or answer questions with these tools in place (Enis, 2012, p. 32). Kiosks, such as 3-M™'s Cloud Library Discovery Terminals, and discovery centers such as Media Stations by OverDrive, promise to raise the awareness of e-books. Tech Logic, which has a background in RFID checkout/check-in systems, introduced a stand-alone kiosk that securely locks away iPads and then dispenses them when patrons swipe a valid credit card and a library card. The system automatically compares this information with the library's user database to ensure that the patron is in good standing and is authorized to check these items out.

Some benefits of self-service kiosks are:

- Meets needs of users who require a "click and go" experience.
- Increases foot traffic, better enabling the library to become a focal point of the community it sits in.
- Offers 24/7 access to books, e-books, CDs, DVDs, and tablets.
- Self-check-in streamlines and expedites updating of library holdings and patron records.
- Systems can be "device agnostic," allowing for a mix/match of device models (Dell, Apple, HP, etc.).
- Frees up valuable and limited floor space in libraries.

Check These Out

Two recent articles worth reviewing on developments in access services technology are:

American Libraries. 2014. "Tech for Speedy Services." 45, nos. 1/2: 76–77.

Dempsey, Kathy, 2014. "Machinery That Can Transform Your Lending Services." *Computers in Libraries* 34, no. 6: 19–22.

LOAN CONTROL

Libraries establish limits on the length of time a borrower may keep library materials. The limits ensure that borrowers will return items within a reasonable time, making them available to others. The length of the loan period depends on the size of the collection, amount of circulation, purpose of lending materials, the clientele served, and sometimes the nature of the material loaned. For most items, loan periods are typically from one to four weeks. Certain materials (e.g., periodicals, CDs, or DVDs) are usually lent for shorter periods of one to seven days. In some libraries, certain categories of borrowers are permitted longer loan periods than others. Academic libraries, for example, usually permit faculty and graduate students, because of their research needs, to check out materials for longer periods than undergraduates. In this case, items with extended loan periods usually are subject to "recall" after the standard loan period is over. This process allows undergraduates and others to gain access to items that may have loan periods of up to a year (in the case of faculty). These periods vary depending on the library.

Reserves loan periods are more complex and generally have very short time periods in comparison with items from the general collection. This is due to the primary function of reserves—providing access for a number of individuals to limited resources within a narrow time frame, that is, a journal article or book with only a single copy available for a class assignment which may never be repeated. Reserves loan periods may be just an hour or two to perhaps three days outside of the library. Short loan periods, as you might expect, can lead to overdues, fines, and public relations challenges.

When items come back, the staff member engages the system's discharge/check-in mode. The system reads the barcode or tag on the item and clears the record from the circulation database unless the item is overdue, in which case the system automatically generates a fine notice. The borrower's record is either cleared or attached to the overdue information. If another borrower has a reservation (hold) on the item, the system displays this on the monitor and the staff member takes appropriate action to notify the requesting borrower.

As staff members discharge material, they inspect it for wear or damage and, in the case of multipart items, if all pieces were returned. This is the time to identify damage that will require repair and reimbursement from the borrower. Repairing torn pages or loose bindings is a must before the material circulates again, or the item may be damaged beyond repair and perhaps the wrong person will be charged for the damage. This is a serious problem because many items may be out of print (i.e., the publisher has no copies available for purchase) and replacements are available only at great cost. It is rare for the circulation staff to make repairs. Usually they send the damaged material to the bindery unit, which decides how to handle the repair—in-house or using the services of a commercial bindery or restoration service. When the item goes to the bindery/repair unit, the circulation department updates the item's location in the OPAC.

Search and Hold Procedures

Loan systems are essentially inventory control systems. The goal of an inventory control system is to be able to locate any item in the system at any time. Users often ask circulation staff to find material that the library owns but is not on the shelf. One of the measures of a good control system is how well it allows staff to locate misfiled materials. Procedures for locating requested materials and notifying the requester that materials are available are often called "search and hold" procedures.

To initiate the procedure, the user or staff member usually fills out a search request form (either manually or online). Staff members employ the same search procedure when a borrower states he or she has returned an item that the system indicates is still on loan. Sometimes, most often in public libraries, there is a small fee for placing a hold. The requester or staff member fills out the call number, author, and title on the search form, as well as the requester's name and address, so a notification can go out when the item is again available. Staff members begin the search by checking the circulation records and the shelves. (It is the authors' experience that approximately 50% of the "searched" items are actually in their proper location.)

If the material is not on the shelf, an extended and standard search procedure follows. The search expands to all possible locations—book carts, sorting shelves, missing files, mending areas, the tops of dust canopies in the stacks (some tall individuals or someone using a stepstool may forget they laid an item up there), and other locations materials might be found. Many academic libraries maintain remote storage facilities for seldom-used material, and if the item is found there, it is retrieved for the requester, typically within a few days. Because of the library's emphasis on providing access to information, this is an important service, and libraries make every effort to locate missing items for their users.

Another characteristic of a good circulation system is its ability to identify holds, also known as reserve requests, when material is returned. Many online systems allow the public to place holds in the OPAC. The system links the requestors' data with the desired item and notifies staff when a requested item is checked in and a notice of availability goes to the requestor. The library holds the material for only a limited time, usually a matter of days. If the person does not check out the item, a staff member notifies the next person in the hold queue or it goes to the reshelving area. Some libraries mail the material directly to the borrower who requested it instead of requiring the individual to come to the library.

Overdues, Fines, and Billing

Overdue materials present some service issues for both the public and staff because late items are unavailable to others. As a result, most libraries charge fines for past-due items. Both of these facts create potential PR concerns. The latter especially can cause tension and require conflict resolution. Libraries levy fines hoping that economic incentives will encourage borrowers to return materials on time.

Through the years there have been trends to lower or eliminate fines in some libraries, while others raised fines in the hope that increased costs would improve the timely return of materials. Some have tried alternate methods of collecting fines to make the process less onerous, for example, accepting credit card payments. A few accept food donations for the needy in lieu of cash, especially around holidays.

Check This Out

Two recent examples of institutions that opted to revise their loan and/or fines policies are:

Duane Wilson's "Why Can't They Keep the Book Longer and Do We Really Need to Charge Fines? Assessing Circulation Policies at the Harold B. Lee

Library: A Case Study" in *Journal Of Access Services* (2014, 11, no. 3: 135–149); and

Kathleen Reed, Jean Blackburn, and Daniel Sifton's "Putting a Sacred Cow Out to Pasture: Assessing the Removal of Fines and Reduction of Barriers at a Small Academic Library" in *Journal of Academic Librarianship* (2014, 40, nos. 3/4: 275–280).

While there is a lack of confirming evidence in the literature, most libraries believe some form of fines/billing system is an effective means for convincing borrowers to return books on time. Some library parent organizations even assume a certain level of fine/fee income from the library when establishing the library's annual budget.

As part of the registration process, the new borrower should receive information either in print or online of the basic loan policies and information about fines and fees. Some libraries print the fine schedule on the transaction card inserted in the book pocket, on the pocket itself, and on their Web site. A few post a sign at the circulation desk listing rates and fees. Few libraries have complete freedom to set the fine policy; instead, they must conform to the desires of their governing bodies. In a public library, the director may make recommendations on a fine policy, but the library board of trustees has legal authority to establish the policy. In a college or university, the director makes recommendations first to the advisory board (usually comprised of faculty and students) and then to the senior campus administrators.

Fine rates vary for different types of loans; for example, fines for short-term loans (such as those encountered in reserves loans) are often higher than for long-term loans. Fine amounts may also vary according to type of item; for example, there may be higher fines for high-demand items like popular DVDs or books. There may be a different fine schedule for children and/or juvenile borrowers (usually lower than the adult rate). Some libraries do not charge children overdue fines at all, believing it is more important to encourage reading as a positive experience. The Columbus Metropolitan Library in Ohio allows children to write off fines by reading with staff members or volunteers (Futty, 2003). Colleges and universities often do not fine faculty or staff, although they often bill for lost items.

Many libraries have tried moratoriums to encourage the return of overdue material. If a borrower returns the overdue material within the specified period, the staff cancels the fine. The rationale for such amnesty programs is that the purpose of fines is not to punish borrowers or to make money for the library; rather fines are levied as an incentive to encourage the timely return of material.

Most ILS systems automatically produce overdue notices to send to the delinquent borrowers (by either snail or e-mail). Some libraries use telephone calls to remind borrowers items are past due. If the borrower does not respond to the first notice, systems usually generate second, third, or more notices at predetermined intervals. The number of notices is a matter of library policy. A library usually bills a delinquent borrower for the amount of the fine, plus a service charge to cover processing costs. If the fine remains unpaid or the material unreturned, libraries generally suspend further borrowing privileges until the individual resolves the outstanding loans/fines.

Libraries may resort to using collection agencies for very long-term delinquent borrowers. In some extreme instances, libraries may take legal action in small-claims court. Decisions to employ collection agencies or initiate legal proceedings are of major significance and go far beyond possible bad PR. As such, it is a matter for senior managers and almost always the library's governing board. Academic libraries work with the university registrar or business office to withhold transcripts or degrees from students with unpaid library fines. School libraries usually contact parents to take care of rule violations.

Borrowers do contest fines rather frequently. The most common position is that the items were, in fact, returned on time and library records are in error. A wise step is to state the library will make a search and, if the item is found, will cancel the fine. A somewhat more challenging situation is when the person is holding the overdue material and stating he or she found it on the shelf where it belonged. Again a good practice is to accept the statement as fact and cancel the fine. (Occasionally, there will be an individual who repeatedly does this, making harder and harder to believe the staff has made the same error with the same person over and over.) We suggest that flexibility in fine collecting does much to preserve good PR while obtaining the return of overdue materials. That goal is not to generate income for the library, or to enforce a moral code.

An important note—many borrowers assume fine monies go to the library. This is not the case for a great many libraries, both public and private. What most often occurs is the monies must be deposited into a parent body's (school district, city, county, state, etc.) general fund. Some people are upset when they learn, at least in the case of fees for lost books, that the money allowed for a replacement of the lost or damaged item will not go directly back to the library.

Many library jurisdictions do take into account the amount collected from lost or damaged items. Most often this takes the form of some percentage of the prior year's collections being allocated to the library's operating budget. Sometimes, especially when the budgeting process includes an expected amount of fees the library will collect during the coming fiscal year, a percentage of that amount is also added to the library's budget.

PRIVACY OF LOAN DATA

In 1971, the ALA adopted a *Policy on Confidentiality of Library Records*, the current version of which was revised in 1986 (http://www.ala.org/advocacy/int freedom/statementspols/otherpolicies/policyconfidentiality).   Organizations within ALA, such as the American Association of School Librarians (AASL), also adopted their own statements based upon this policy (2012, http://www .ala.org/aasl/advocacy/resources/statements/library-records).

Although there are no federal laws protecting the confidentiality of library records, as of this writing, 48 states and the District of Columbia have confidentiality laws. Such statutes attempt to strike a balance between access and privacy. Each law permits some access, in particular to court orders or subpoenas. Thirty-five states provide that libraries need not disclose circulation records under the state open-records law. Common exceptions include that records may be disclosed to permit the performance of library routines, if the user consents, and pursuant to a subpoena, court order, or otherwise required by law (Bowers, 2006).

The current status of confidentiality laws leaves several issues unclear. Under current legislation, libraries may be liable for civil or criminal liability for wrongful disclosure of records. (Note: the USA PATRIOT Act overrides state statutes. We explore this and many other legal issues related to library services in chapter 13.)

All library staff must be familiar with privacy policies because chances are high that someday a citizen or government authority will request that the library disclose information on the reading habits or other library practices of a particular user. Staff members who receive requests of this type should refuse to comply and immediately report the request to their supervisor or otherwise follow their library's policy.

Check This Out

Privacy issues are surprisingly complex, and keeping staff well informed about those complexities, especially newly hired staff, is a challenge. An interesting work about one technique for handling such training is Ann Mackay Snowman's 2013 article "Privacy and Confidentiality: Using Scenarios to Teach Your Staff about Patron's Rights" (*Journal of Access Services* 10, no. 2: 120–132).

STACK MAINTENANCE

Stack management encompasses a wide range of tasks associated with storing, retrieving, and maintaining the physical collections of a library. Core elements of stacks management include:

- Shelving library materials using a classification system
- Shelf reading to maintain call number order
- Shifting collections to create space for collection growth

Maintaining an orderly arrangement of library materials is an important function generally assigned to the circulation unit. Probably 90 percent or more of U.S. libraries have "open stacks," which means that the public can look for materials of interest in storage areas. As you might expect, that can mean the area is in a constant state of change or, perhaps a better word, disorder. Common issues are materials left on a table or shelf and not where they would be appropriately shelved. Another factor is some people try to "help" the staff by reshelving items but misplace them because they do not understand the ins and outs of the library's classification system.

Unlike the general collection, reserve units are "closed stack" operations. That is, a borrower requests an item and a staff member retrieves the item from a non-public storage area. Reserves units generally employ the system used by the general collection, although some units find it effective to arrange the material by the course or instructor. It is not uncommon for reserves units to place all the materials for a course together, regardless of format. Doing so speeds delivery to the requester. The reason for closed access policy is due to the primary function of the reserves—providing short-term loans to a large number of users of items that may only be available in a single copy. Maintaining the proper storage arrangement is even more critical for reserves due to the nature if its loan demands. For this service there is a predictable pattern of moving materials by putting items into the collection prior to and during the first days of a new term and removing the items at the end of term.

Shelving of materials accurately, quickly, and efficiently makes life easier for both users and staff—both spend less time trying to find items that are officially "in the library" but not where they are normally located. You might not realize how many places an item can be and yet not be where it "belongs." If you've worked in a circulation department, the following list will be rather familiar:

- In a "returned" item bin or box
- On a cart waiting to be checked in
- On a "sorting" shelf
- On a book cart ready to be re-shelved
- In the technical service area awaiting a minor repair
- On a shelf to go a repair service or decision regarding its replacement
- On a table or chair in the public area where a person left it after looking at it
- On a shelf where a person left it
- Mis-shelved by a well-meaning person
- Misplaced by a person who wishes to maintain sole access (generally only an academic library issue)

The preceding list covers only some of the more common reasons why quick and accurate shelving will save everyone's time. Some of these are also issues for reserves.

Returned items and, in most cases, new acquisitions require scanning into the ILS database before shelving the items. Initial sorting of items, either onto "sorting shelves" or "book trucks" (heavy-duty carts with wheels), may be arranged based on format—print or media—and then destination. This is done for two reasons. First, different formats are often arranged differently; for example, books are filed by classification number, while periodicals are often organized by title. Another factor is that some formats, due to shape or size, require special storage units. Books and periodicals are housed on "standard shelving," pamphlets in file cabinets, microfilm in specially designed cabinets, and maps generally laid flat in map cases. Some libraries shelve media (or their empty cases) in the stacks along with books and periodicals but more commonly, media formats require special shelving.

Backlogs of un-shelved materials cause delays in service and require staff time to locate material. Mis-shelved items are essentially lost until they are noticed and re-shelved correctly. When closed stacks were the rule with only library staff having access, maintaining an accurate arrangement was fairly easy. Today's open stacks are challenging to maintain.

Classification Systems

Libraries employ some type of classification system to arrange their collections. The system's purpose is to group collections into categories that bring like subjects together in a manner that best meets the needs of both the public and the library. In actuality, the arrangements are better suited to the need of the library than they are for the public. One reason for that fact, and one not too often mentioned when people criticize existing systems, is the public's interests are so highly varied that any system based solely on user preferences would satisfy a relatively small percentage of the total service population. There are some "homegrown" systems that exist that are designed just for a small homogenous service population. There are also specialized systems such as the National Library of Medicine that many U.S. medical libraries employ. Such systems are far beyond the scope of this book.

There are two popular and generally employed classification systems used in the United States—the Dewey decimal classification (DDC, used primarily in school and public libraries) and the Library of Congress system (LC, generally used only in academic libraries). DDC uses decimal numbers to classify knowledge, while the LC system employs a combination of letters and whole numbers. The DDC system may present more problems in shelving because of the numbers to the right of the decimal point. It is important for shelvers to remember that, because these numbers are decimal fractions, a number like .16 is smaller than .9 and will file before the latter. As an example, the DDC numbers that follow are given in the order in which they would appear on the shelves:

581.21	581.21	581.31	581.4	581.498	581.5
D4	E73	A4	A47	R3	J6

Notice that .498 files before .5 because it is the smaller decimal. The second line is a combination of both letter and number, also a decimal, used to group items by the same author together (and sometimes called the author number). For example:

512	512	512
A37	A4	D26

The LC classification is arranged first by letters and then by numbers. The third line is the number that, like the second line of the DDC, serves to keep material in alphabetical order by author. Notice that the author number in the following examples is treated like a decimal:

L	L	LA
LB	LC	LC
7	7	96
3063	4701	4701
D47	D5	G5
R71	R19	R2

Shelvers *must* understand the classification system the library uses in order to properly shelve materials. While it may be nice for the public to understand, it is not essential as a savvy library user rather quickly learns where the topics of personal interest are located without an understanding of why they are where they are.

Shelf-Reading

Shelf-reading (checking that each item is in its proper call number place) is an important aspect of stacks management. This is particularly true of open stacks, where browsing may be heavy. Mis-shelved items are as inaccessible to users as if they were permanently lost or damaged beyond repair. Technology has come to the aid of shelf-readers. By scanning books using an ILS inventory control module or electronic shelf list, items can be checked not only for proper call number order, but also for whether they have been properly checked in, have been declared missing, and so on.

As you might surmise, shelf-reading is a tedious work. Shelf-readers can maintain the concentration needed for accuracy for only about one or two hours at a time. When scheduling personnel for this work, the supervisor should consider these limitations.

Check This Out

One article on the topic of shelf-reading is Kevin Brown and Wendi Arant's 2007 piece "Shelf Reading as a Collaborative Service Model" in *Journal of Access Services* (4, no. 3/4: 93–105), which describes a model for shelf-reading developed at Texas A&M University.

Collection Growth and Shifting

Collections of physical items tend to grow over time while shelving space is finite. There are two primary types of shifting—small and large scale. Small shifts are almost a daily occurrence for the staff shelving materials. Subject areas do not grow at the same rate. And, although the staff may be able to plan for an average annual growth rate, there is no predicating how subject interests and the resulting availability of items on that topic may change. Thus, shelvers will encounter, from time to time, a shelf that is completely filled and have one or two items in hand that must be fit in. With luck the person may only have to shift items on two or three shelves to gain the necessary space. At other times it may involve shifting the contents of several "sections" (a traditional shelving section is 3 by 7+ inches with seven shelves) before the space is available where needed. Eventually a large-scale shift (involving many stack ranges, a range is a group of sections with an aisle(s) at the end) becomes necessary; the goal is to open up space in many growth areas and reduce the amount of staff time devoted to small-scale shifts.

Shifting materials is time-consuming, is physically tiring, and requires a high degree of concentration. Measuring the space for a collection must be precise. Accurately calculating fill rates becomes even more pressing when one takes into account the fact that the commonly accepted definition for the maximum working capacity of bookstacks is 85 percent. Fill rates above 85 percent will cause problems for staff shelving materials, users in finding materials, and even staff attempting to preserve collections for future generations. A crowded shelf is much more likely to cause damage to its books than one with a few precious inches of empty space.

Libraries have limited options for dealing with such growth in collections. One option, generally unacceptable, is to stop acquiring additional resources. Another option, that is more often than not difficult to implement, is to have the library expanded or a new larger one built (we explore physical facility issues in chapter 19). A third option is to withdraw items from the collection at roughly the same rate as new ones are acquired. Again this is a difficult option to effectively implement, as "weeding" items from the collections tend to be labor intensive—and labor is a resource that is scarce in most libraries. Another possibility is to squeeze more storage space into the exiting square footage (installing compact shelving can reduce the number aisles), or shelving material in a different manner such as by size.

Many libraries respond to the lack of collection space by building or renting high-volume storage spaces and filling them with the lesser-used portions of their collections. This is particularly true in academic libraries as they have a significant long-term preservation responsibility and thus are less able to discard materials. A number of newer academic library facilities include automated storage and retrieval systems (ASRS). These allow for high-density storage of items in close proximity, often adjacent to the library. Generally the storage area is a return to the "closed stack" concept with only library personnel having access. Borrowers wanting an item in storage request it via the catalog terminal. The request activates the automated retrieval system and the item is delivered via conveyer belt to the circulation desk, usually in just a few minutes.

Remote storage facilities usually involve the shipping of items to a warehouse-like facility contracted by the library. Items in off-site storage are indicated in the OPAC and are retrievable via a request, with delivery usually taking a few days. Needless to say, such delays can create some PR issues. However, when the person realizes the relatively short delay is in place of some of the document delivery options we discussed in chapter 5, which generally take longer, he or she agrees the remote storage approach is acceptable.

PUBLIC RELATIONS

Almost everything done in a library is an act of public relations. Anything that affects the user's attitude toward the library, negatively or positively, is part of public relations (PR). How long it takes to process items for use, how employees answer the telephone, the accuracy of the reshelving process, the inflection in one's voice in answering a question, the presence and quality of signage, and the "warmth" or atmosphere of a library are only a few examples that have an impact on PR.

There is a practical reason to address PR issues. Good PR stems from the delivery of quality service. Conversely, bad PR is a sign that the library's service is defective in vision, execution, or both. Many libraries make formal attempts to assess user satisfaction in order to determine how well they are meeting and exceeding the needs of their users. (See chapter 2, "Customer Service," for more information on this.) From a practical standpoint, good user relations are vital for the stability of a library's financial base. Whether public, academic, special, or school, a library depends on a parent agency for funding. Libraries are expensive yet low-profile institutions and in times of financial exigency (i.e., most of the time) they are easy targets for budget slashing unless they can rally supporters. Good PR is essential in building this corps of advocates and thus helps to guarantee that a library will continue to have the resources it needs to fulfill its mission and goals.

Because of their central role in providing service to library users, a large share of the responsibility for good PR rests on the circulation and reserves staff. There is a growing need to understand cultural differences and the needs of non-English speakers in order to provide good quality service. If staff members apply rules and regulations with fairness and flexibility, if each user receives individualized treatment in the sense that the person's needs are important, and if routines aimed at providing efficient service are accurately performed, positive user feelings about the library are likely to follow.

It is important that circulation staff members do not get into the habit of considering all library users with problems as "problem users." Users often have valid criticisms and to treat them all as problem users is to reflect a negative service attitude on the part of staff. (See chapter 16 for a more thorough discussion of dealing with problem users.) What sorts of problems are brought to the attention of a circulation staff member? A review of the literature through the years reveals some common themes. Inability to find cataloged materials on the shelves and insufficient numbers of desired titles are common complaints. Circulation limits on reserve items and restrictions on renewals are other problems, as well as dissatisfaction with strict application of circulation rules. Short loan periods and not being notified about their overdue materials, or about materials they believed they had returned, are also common user problems.

The staff should be aware of the most frequent user complaints and pass that information on to supervisors. Many libraries have manual or online "suggestion boxes" and complaint forms available for the public to document problem areas. Some libraries post responses, in writing or online, to user questions or complaints.

Check This Out

A number of articles, books, and other resources are available on the topic of library public relations. One Web-based resource worth reviewing is the Public Relations and Media Relations Toolkit (PR Rx) from the Texas Library Association: http://www.txla.org/PR-toolkit.

LOAN DATA FOR PLANNING PURPOSES

Statistics measuring loan activities are necessary to satisfy governing boards, city, state, and federal authorities, academic administrators, and school boards when those bodies judge how many library services are delivered. The data is also important for internal library purposes. Some of the questions, which require regular compilation of statistics to answer, are:

- To what extent are people using the library, and is its use increasing or decreasing?
- What portions of the collection receive the greatest use, and is this changing?
- What is the level of in-house use of library materials?
- What amount of money in fines and fees is collected?

In order to answer these and other questions, the following kinds of statistics are generally calculated by automated circulation systems, or recorded by circulation staff:

- The number of items circulated, recorded by type of material (book, video, government document, etc.) and by status of user (adult, juvenile, student, faculty, and so forth), and by time of day
- The number of items circulated by subject (usually determined by classification number)
- The amount of fine money received
- The number of questions answered at the circulation desk
- The number of items used within the library
- The number of items requested and either supplied or not supplied
- The number of ILL and document delivery requests filled and not filled
- The number of people who come into the library (using automated door counters)
- The number of materials lost or missing
- The number of items taken from the shelves for library use

In addition to providing information for governing authorities, the analysis of statistics can provide library managers with valuable planning information. For example, assessing current levels of performance and comparing them with past and desired levels; diagnosing problem areas; monitoring progress toward the library's goals and objectives; planning for the future; justifying, internally and externally, resource allocations; and documenting service improvements. Statistics collected serve as the basis of reports required at regular intervals by the library administration. The monthly or annual report of the circulation section forms a unit in the report of all library activities, showing the relation of circulation work to that of the library as a whole.

SPECIAL ASPECTS OF RESERVE SERVICES

Reserve services are a service found primarily in libraries serving educational institutions, especially colleges and universities. Teachers frequently want to supplement their required books and classroom resources with additional resources from the library and perhaps personal items. What makes reserves loaning different from that of the general library collection is, generally, the number of students who need access to a limited number of items for brief time. Further, that demand may never occur again, making it impractical to acquire duplicate copies of those items. Originally the class reserves system was created to handle short-term, infrequent need for a number of potential users to the physical material (books, articles, media of various types, etc.). While there is still such a need, the main major focus of today's reserve services is focused on remote electronic access to such materials.

Instructors assign various types of material, for example, copies of journal articles, teachers' personal copies of books or other instructional materials, videos, and copies of quizzes and answers. Libraries support this instructional endeavor by establishing policies and procedures to make these "reserved" materials available to students. Reserve service guarantees (well, almost always) that assigned material will be available, on a first come, first served basis, for students to use as needed.

The role of a reserve service is to enhance the teaching and learning process by enabling instructors to temporarily control access to general collection items that will support their course(s). Today's very typical electronic reserve systems involve the scanning of documents into a database and allowing remote retrieval by students at any time. These systems are popular as a more effective and labor-saving means (up to a point) of distributing reserve readings in comparison to paper-based systems.

Today's reserve room or desk operates like a mini-library within the larger institution. Staff members accept reserve requests from teachers and faculty, remove books and periodicals from the general collection (in the case of paper-based materials), and photocopy or scan the items (with the exception of books). Digitized documents become files in the reserve module for each instructor and course. Regardless of format, paper or electronic, there are copyright compliance issues associated with reserves that are more complex than for other library service areas. The only area that comes as close to that complexity is library programming that involves the use of library-owned media (see chapter 13 for a discussion of performance rights).

Some educators question the value of reserve services. Writers have commented on the low use of some reserve items, along with the high cost of administration (see, e.g., Bradley, 2007; De Jager, 2001; Self, 1987). Students, faculty, and staff are sometimes critical about various aspects of traditional reserve service. Students complain that material is not put on reserve fast enough, that service is poor, and that waiting times are too long. Teachers sometimes also protest about the time it takes to process assigned material, about the amount of work they must do before material goes on reserve, and about copyright limitations. Library staff complain about the amount of time it takes to process materials, that faculty do not give them sufficient time to process reserve items before assigning them, do not appreciate or adhere to copyright restrictions, place excess quantities of material on reserve that students never look at, and are slow to remove items when they are no longer assigned.

In addition to these complaints, there are pedagogic arguments against reserve services. There is evidence that using assigned reserve materials has no significant influence on academic performance. A study at the University of Virginia measured the correlation between over 8,000 students' use of reserve materials and the grades they received in their courses. The study revealed only a weak connection between reserve use and grades. The study also revealed that depending on reserve readings may even obstruct the educational process. Relying on reserve services to provide library materials may discourage students from using the rest of the library and learning necessary library use skills. It also prevents the serendipitous discovery of information that occurs through normal library use (Self, 1987).

Such concerns notwithstanding, reserve operations are present in many libraries. Today's students' preference is for digital information and the spread of electronic reserve services has increased the popularity of reserve systems. Studies of electronic reserve systems reveal that reducing the limitations related to traditional library resources and employing digitized resources results in greater use of digital reserves and greater satisfaction with the service (Ji, Michaels, and Waterman, 2014; Isenberg, 2006; Jacoby and Laskowski, 2004; Pilston and Hart, 2002).

E-Reserve Services

Traditional reserves was/is a labor-intensive activity, and e-reserve has not reduced staff efforts in handling the service. In fact, if anything, it has made the work more complex and demanding. Certainly there is reduction in staff time devoted to "fetching, filing, and refiling" traditional materials. However, those savings are eaten up in a variety of technology-related activities, such as scanning and assuring a number of "compliance" concerns—in particular copyright. This involves where the library secures the electronic copy to place on reserve—by scanning a paper-based item or leasing the item through a database, for example. Another concern is what happens in the case of a system crash? Having backup material can involve further legal/copyright issues.

There are a number of technology issues and a growing number of legal/copyright concerns (see the following section). While it is true most ILS products have a reserves module, as of this writing, they do not always integrate well with the campus "course management" systems that more and more academic institutions employ. To achieve integration requires the library to work with campus IT, faculty, and vendors other than its ILS vendor. Such multiple systems and units can lead to finger pointing when things do not work as hoped. LeEtta Schmidt (2013) discussed this issue when she wrote, "More than a decade ago, course reserves faced the revolution of electronic delivery. Many libraries cobbled together solutions using systems at hand to provide protected access to online course material. . . . Shopping for new solutions, however, is not easy when integration is the name of the game. The rise of course management systems for holding and delivering content to both distance and in-person students has made it necessary for libraries to connect course materials to course management systems" (pp. 47–48). Krista Clumpner, Michael Burgmeier, and Thomas Gillespie (2011) provide further insight into the complexities in their article and noted, "In the 2010 fall semester, we worked together to integrate course reserves into the course management system so that students could seamlessly access materials on reserve for a particular course. It took the cooperation of the library systems staff, the web services librarian, and the instructional technologist to piece together the necessary systems and services into a puzzle with a complete picture of embedded course reserves as the end result" (p. 11).

The complexity related to e-reserves, especially the legalities involved, suggests that much of the work ought to be in the hands of full-time staff who have extensive training in dealing with those complexities. How big an issue are they? Looking at just currently available journal titles, there are roughly 50,000, including a combination of paper-based (many of which are also in digital form) and digital-only titles, that libraries may draw upon for e-reserves. The challenge is that different vendors/publishers will have a variety of limitations on what they allow as fair use. When you add chapters from books, Web links, audio and video files—again with varying conditions—the challenges are substantial.

A relatively recent example (2013) and one still not fully resolved is that of a lawsuit filed against Georgia State University (GSU) by Cambridge University Press et al. (the Association of American University Presses has filed an amicus brief on support of the plaintiffs) for copyright infringement with the e-reserve service at the University. (For a good brief overview of the case see, Jennifer Howard's *Chronicle of Higher Education* online post "Publishers and Library Groups Spar in Appeal to Ruling on Electronic Course Reserves:" http://chronicle.com/article/PublishersLibrary-Groups/136995/?cid= wc&utm_source=wc&utm_medium=en). The comments about the foregoing article are also interesting as they suggest additional aspects of the current environment and the cost of higher education. Although the publisher lost on most of its charges in 2012, it decided to appeal the decision and as of late 2015 the case is still in the courts.

Some years ago, publishers sued a national photocopy service (Kinkos) for producing "course packs" (collections of journal articles and book chapters a professor supplied). The "packs" were sold to students rather than purchasing a textbook or utilizing library reserve services. In that instance the publishers won their infringement case (758 F. Supp. 1522). In the GSU case, the publishers are making the claim that e-reserves is just a variation of the paper-based course packs and thus are also an infringement.

Another issue related to fair use and higher education costs are textbooks. Until relatively recently academic libraries had polices that more or less excluded adding "textbooks" to their collections. Naturally there were questions as to just what made a title a textbook. A great many books in an academic library could be a textbook for some professor in some course. However, the ever-increasing cost of textbooks in the campus bookstore (prices have increased between 5 and 7% per year since the early 1990s, a rate far higher than the CPI) has led students to pressure libraries to purchase textbooks. The University of Oklahoma created a Textbook on Reserve program in 2007 (Murphy, 2013) that remains operational (see "Got Textbooks?" at http://libraries.ou.edu/cms/default.aspx?id=3). A few other libraries/institutions have started similar programs. Any such program must be a campus effort as the bookstore is likely to see this as a serious threat to its revenue.

From the Authors' Experience

Evans had two approaches to some of the issues discussed earlier when he wished to use a textbook he had authored. One approach was to work with the library's reserve department and personally buy copies of the book. The number of copies and loan period(s) were worked out jointly. This was a good approach when the book would be required again and again.

The second approach was to have the students buy an unused copy of the book (note—neither the publisher nor author receives anything from the campus bookstore's reselling used copies) and he reimbursed the students the royalty amount he would get as a result of such sales.

Check These Out

The following provide further insights into the issues related to e-reserves:

Adams, Carolyn, and Erin Silva Fisher. 2012. "Optimizing Electronic Reserves with Ares." *Journal of Interlibrary Loan, Document Delivery & Electronic Reserves* 22, no. 1: 1–8.

Brown, Jennifer Everson, and Bethany B. Sewell. 2013. "Assessing Electronic Reserves at the University of Denver: A Faculty Satisfaction Survey." *Journal of Access Services* 10, no. 1: 28–42.

Poe, Jodi, and Bethany Skaggs. 2007. "Course Reserves: Using Blackboard for E-Reserves Delivery." *Journal of Interlibrary Loan, Document Delivery & Electronic Reserves* 18, no. 1: 79–91.

One particularly challenging format for reserves units is video. An interesting article looking at issues related to video and in particularly streaming video is Rue McKenzie and LeEtta M. Smith's 2012 article "Isn't Everything Online Yet? Streaming Media and Electronic Reserves" in *Journal of Interlibrary Loan, Document Delivery& Electronic Reserves* (22, nos. 3/4: 175–180).

An older, but still useful title addressing e-reserves in depth is *Managing Electronic Reserves*, edited by Jeff Rosedale (Chicago: American Library Association, 2001).

Copyright Compliance

Copyright has been a long-standing issue for libraries, starting about the time that photocopy machines came on the scene at a relatively affordable price in terms of both equipment and cost per copy. Not long after that, reserves usage of multiple copies on an owned item, almost always journal articles, became a concern. Perhaps an even more complex issue is the items the instructor brings to the library—as personal items—to put on reserve for his or her course. The most problematic are, or were, video recordings ("home use only"). Essentially, it is as Andrew R. Albanese (2007) wrote, "For now, in today's world, managing e-reserves is about managing risk" (p. 36). Although his comment was about e-reserves, the paper-based concerns have not gone away. They may have become background issues but they have not disappeared.

We noted earlier that there may be different legal implications depending upon where the library secures the e-copy for reserve usage. For example, the library may have a dozen or more databases containing journal articles. Each database vendor will have its standard lease agreement. (Note: libraries almost never "own" the content of such databases, unlike the paper issues of journals they have in their collections.) Thus, unless the library has been able to get identical terms into the lease agreements, it may be possible that it would be illegal to place any article from a particular database on e-reserve. (A lease is a legal document, see chapter 13 for a more detailed discussion of contracts and leases.) Another complicating factor is some journals are part of different vendors' databases. Thus it may be legal to use an article from a journal in database A but not from database B.

The legality of scanning of an article from a journal that library subscribes to may also have more than one answer. There may also be different issues related to scanning a chapter from a book in the collection. This becomes even more important if the instructor wishes to place poetry on reserves—a short poem is the entire "work" and copyright has strict restrictions regarding copying entire works, much less changing its format. Does it matter if the poem is in a collection? The answer varies. As you might expect, putting music and video clips on reserve presents further challenges in terms of copyright and fair use.

Although the current (2015) copyright laws do acknowledge the concept of fair use, just what is "fair" resides in the minds of the various interested parties (copyright holders, publishers, libraries, instructors, and users, to name the major players). To date, the courts, which are called upon to resolve ambiguities in a law, have struggled to clearly define the concept. The concept was complex in a paper-based environment; the digital era has created even more complications. We discuss copyright further in chapter 13.

Teacher and Faculty Relations

Diplomacy with regard to teacher and faculty relations is important in all aspects of public services, but especially so in the reserves function. Teachers and faculty probably take a greater personal interest in the reserve service than in any other service, except perhaps ILL. This is because they believe reserve services play an important role in supporting their day-to-day classroom instruction. Teachers and faculty will often have the majority of their contact with library personnel at the reserves desk. Consequently, they will form their opinion of the importance and value of the library from the quality of these interactions and the service they receive.

The nature of many of these encounters between reserves staff and instructors, however, is sensitive. They sometimes involve requests to change policy or procedures to meet the desires of a particular instructor. The exceptions teachers typically request include processing their items ahead of others, placing more items on reserve than normally allowed, substituting different loan periods than those offered, leaving items on reserve for extended periods (sometimes called "permanent reserve"), and overlooking copyright restrictions on photocopying. Communicating with faculty on these and other points requires finesse and staff must have good interpersonal skills in order to negotiate effectively.

Staff must be both sympathetic to a teacher's particular needs and able to make exceptions to policy when appropriate. There may be nothing wrong with placing materials on reserve after the normal deadline or accepting more material than policy allows if doing so will benefit the students in a particular course, and if the decision does not create problems for others. Some requests, however, would compromise the efficient operations of the service or perhaps be illegal under copyright law. Staff must be able to refuse courteously and explain the reason for the denial and, if possible, offer alternative solutions. Administrators responsible for reserve services should carefully select personnel who possess good interpersonal skills and train them to negotiate effectively with faculty and other users.

Making reserve readings accessible requires several steps. The first step is to persuade instructors to submit their reserve lists or materials in a timely manner. The greatest amount of processing work, which is time consuming, comes at the beginning of the semester or academic term. To help guarantee that staff will have enough time to prepare materials for circulation or scan them into a database and index them, nearly all libraries request that faculty place material on reserve at least two weeks before classes begin. Nevertheless, many teachers do not submit materials until just before or even after they have assigned them. Once staff process reserve materials, access depends on students knowing what items are on reserve. All students and instructors must be able to tell which materials are removed from public access to reserves, and students need to know what materials are placed on reserve by their instructors. Libraries with ILSs have an answer to many of these problems. A message can be attached to any record in the online catalog indicating that the item is "on reserve." The most popular ILSs have reserve modules integrated with the library's OPAC, and there are commercial stand-alone alternatives as well, which can be integrated into the library Web site. Some course management systems also allow for a direct link to reserves materials. Reserve modules permit staff to list all items, including non-library and scanned materials, kept on reserve.

Loaning E-Books

Andrew Albanese (2013) quoted Joe James, from an interview with James asking about e-books and libraries, as saying, "For your average user in your average library, why does it take up to 37 steps to download freaking e-books when you can go to Amazon and do it in four? That piece I think is particularly important; if we lose people now, because it is too hard for them to download a library e-book, then we will have lost them forever" (p. 36). The current systems that are available for libraries do tend to be cumbersome. We have not addressed loaning of e-books in this chapter because, as of 2014, there are so many unresolved issues surrounding if, and/or how often, libraries will be granted the right to loan e-books. Certainly by the time of the next edition most of these concerns will, we hope, be sorted out in a manner that allows the practice to take place and on a fair economic basis. (See chapter 9 for more detail about e-books.)

CLOSING THOUGHTS

The circulation and reserve unit staff are the frontline of library services. As such they will define, to a great extent, user satisfaction with the entire library and its programs. Staff members work a greater variety of hours and, due to fines, have to handle upset users with diplomacy, tact, and with a gentle firmness. E-reserves, something the students and faculty like, do present some serious challenges for the library, both technological and legal. One way to keep current regarding issues in circulation and access services is through the Circulation/Access Services Committee—part of ALA's Library Leadership & Management Association (LLAMA) division/Systems and Services Section (SASS) (http://www.ala.org/llama/sections/sass/sass_committees /circulation-access-services).

Chapter Review Material

1. Name some characteristics of successful loan control systems.
2. Other than checking out materials and checking them in, what are some other functions performed by circulation/reserves staff in terms of loan activities?
3. What is the primary purpose of charging fines? Are there other purposes?
4. What can staff do to lessen the negative impact of fines?
5. Why are user relations an important concern?
6. Discuss the issue of confidentiality of loan records.
7. What is the conceptual basis of both the Dewey decimal and Library of Congress classification systems?
8. What three operations are most commonly identified with stack maintenance?
9. What sorts of statistics are commonly maintained by circulation staff? How are they used?
10. What is the special role of reserve services in terms of library loaning activities?
11. Why is attention to teacher/faculty relations especially important for reserves staff?
12. Describe the processing necessary to prepare physical and digital reserve items for circulation.
13. What is the most important legal consideration for reserve staff?
14. What are some advantages of electronic reserve systems? Disadvantages?
15. What are the current issues surrounding the loaning of e-books?

REFERENCES

Albanese, Andrew Richard. 2007. "Down with E-Reserves." *Library Journal* 132, no. 16: 36–38.

Albanese, Andrew Richard. 2013. "The Library of 2020 Will Be . . ." *Publishers Weekly* 260, no. 23: 34–38.

Bentheim, Christine. 2013. "Continuing the Transition Work from Traditional Library to Learning Commons." *Teacher Librarian* 41, no. 2: 29–36.

Bowers, Stacey L. 2006. "Privacy and Library Records." *The Journal of Academic Librarianship* 32, no. 4: 377–383.

Bradley, Karen. 2007. "Reading Noncompliance: A Case Study and Reflection." *Mountainrise: The International Journal of the Scholarship of Teaching and Learning* 4, no. 1: 1–16.

Clumpner, Krista E., Michael Burgmeier, and Thomas J. Gillespie, 2011. "Embedded Course Reserves: Piecing the Puzzle Together." *Computers in Libraries* 31, no. 4: 11–14.

De Jager, Karin. 2001. "Impacts and Outcomes: Searching for the Most Elusive Indicators of Academic Library Performance." In *Meaningful Measures for Emerging Realities, Proceedings of the 4th Northumbria International Conference on Performance Measurement in Libraries and Information Services*, ed. Joan Stein, Martha Kyrillidou, and Denise Davis, 291–297. Washington, D.C.: Association of Research Libraries.

Enis, Matt. 2012. "Helping Users Help Themselves." *Library Journal* 137, no. 14: 32–34.

Futty, John. 2003. "An Incentive to Read: Library System Lets Children Pay off Fines by Hitting the Books." *The Columbus Dispatch*, July 14: 1C.

Isenberg, Laurie. 2006. "Online Course Reserves and Graduate Student Satisfaction." *Journal of Academic Librarianship* 32, no.2: 166–172.

Jacoby, JoAnn, and Mary S. Laskowski. 2004. "Measurement and Analysis of Electronic Reserve Usage." *Libraries and the Academy* 4, no. 2: 219–232.

Ji, Sung Wook, Sherri Michaels, and David Waterman. 2014. "Print vs. Electronic Readings in College Courses: Cost-Efficiency and Perceived Learning." *The Internet and Higher Education* 21, April: 17–24.

Johnson, Linda, and Jean Danham. 2012. "Reading by Grade Three: How Well Do School Library Circulation Policies Support Early Reading?" *Teacher Librarian* 20, no. 2: 8–12.

Krasulski, Michael J. andTrevor A. Dawes, eds. 2013. *Twenty-First Century Access Services: On the Front Line of Academic Librarianship*. Chicago: American Library Association.

Margolis, Rick. 2001. "NC Library to Give Parents More Say." *School Library Journal* 47, no. 12: 17.

Murphy. Molly. 2013. "Textbooks on Reserve: A Case Study." *Journal of Access Services* 10, no. 3: 145–152.

Newsletter on Intellectual Freedom. 2013. "Is It Legal?" 62, no. 2: 67–68.

Pilston, Anna Klump, and Richard L. Hart. 2002. "Student Response to a New Electronic Reserves System." *Journal of Academic Librarianship* 28, no. 3: 147–151.

Schmidt, LeEtta M. 2013. "Planned Flexibility for Course Reserves." *Journal of Interlibrary Loan, Document Delivery & Electronic Reserve* 23, no. 2: 47–56.

Schmidt, Steven J. 2014. "Course Reserves, E-Reserves and Serving the Remote User." *Indiana Libraries* 19, no. 1: 24–27.

Self, James. 1987. "Reserve Readings and Student Grades: Analysis of a Case Study." *Library and Information Science Reports* 9, no. 1: 29–40.

SUGGESTED READINGS

American Libraries. 2013. "Case Study: Innovative Materials Handling." 44, nos. 1/2: 85.

Austin, Brice. 2012. *Reserves Electronic Reserves and Copyright: The Past and the Future*. Hoboken, NJ: Taylor and Francis.

Chakraborty, Mou, Michael English, and Sharon Payne. 2013. "Restructuring to Promote Collaboration and Exceed User Needs: The Blackwell Library Access Services Experience." *Journal of Access Services* 10, no. 2: 90–101.

Eschenfelder, Kristin, Tien-l Tsai, Xiaohua Zhu, and Brenton Stewart, 2013. "How Institutionalized Are Model License Use Terms? An Analysis of E-journal License Use Rights Clauses from 2000 to 2009." *College & Research Libraries* 74, no. 4: 326–355.

Goodson, Kymberly Anne, and Linda Frederiksen. 2011. "E-Reserves in Transition: Exploring New Possibilities in E-Reserve Service Delivery." *Journal of Interlibrary Loan, Document Delivery & Electronic Reserve* 21, nos. 1–2: 33–56.

Hansen, David R., William M. Cross, and Phillip M. Edwards. 2013. "Copyright Policy and Practice in Electronic Reserves among ARL Libraries." *College & Research Libraries* 74, no. 1: 69–84.

Leung, Yau-Ching. 2010. "Effective Access Management of Reserve and Normal Loan Materials." *Journal of Access Services* 7, no. 1: 1–14.

Long, Dallas. 2012. "'Check This Out': Assessing Customer Service at the Circulation Desk." *Journal of Access Services* 9, no. 3: 154–168.

Massis, Bruce E. 2013. "From iPads to Fishing Rods: Checking Out Library Materials." *New Library World* 114, nos. 1/2: 80–83.

McMenemy, David. 2010. "On Library Fines: Ensuring Civic Responsibility or an Easy Income Stream?" *Library Review* 59, no. 2: 78–81.

Middlemas, Julie, Patricia Morrison, and Nadra Farina-Hess. 2012. "Reserve Textbooks: To Buy, or Not to Buy?" *Library Philosophy and Practice*, 796. http://digital commons.unl.edu/libphilprac/796.

Pollitz, John, Anne Christie, and Cheryl Middleton. 2009. "Management of Library Course Reserves and the Textbook Affordability Crisis." *Journal of Access Services* 6, no. 4: 459–484.

Sanders, Eugene R. 2014. "How Our Library Employs a Collection Agency." *Indiana Libraries* 4, no. 4: 156–159.

Sung, Jan S., and Bradley P. Tolppanen. 2013. "Do Library Fines Work? Analysis of the Effectiveness of Fines on Patron's Return Behavior at Two Mid-sized Academic Libraries." *Journal of Academic Librarianship* 39, no. 6: 506–511.

Sutherland, Kerry. 2014. "Library Cards." *Voice of Youth Advocates* 36, no. 6: 32–33.

Troy, Sarah, and Nicole Lawson. 2012. "Change Is the New Normal: Access Services in a New Public Services Paradigm." *Journal of Access Services* 9, no. 4: 173–186.

Weare, Jr. William H., and Matthew W. Stevenson. 2012. "Circulation Policies for External Users: A Comparative Study of Public Urban research Institutions." *Journal of Access Services* 9, no. 3: 111–133.

Print Collections

About 11,000 items are added to the LC collections daily.
—Information Today, *2013*

As library budgets continued to shrink and demands of library resources increased, acquisitions managers became more creative in obtaining materials.
—*Jeanne Harrell, 2012*

The main questions at this point are: Can we afford to cancel a major print multivolume set, such as a case reporter, and instead utilize free online services? Is it viable to cancel our library's subscription to our existing print case reporter volumes?
—*Paul Galfano, 2013*

Secondary sources are a cornerstone of undergraduate education. But where do secondary sources come from?
—*Shan Sutton and Lorrie Knight, 2006*

Libraries still have large collections of print material and other physical formats. Some of the people predicting the demise of libraries and paper-based resources sometimes refer to these materials as "traditional" or legacy formats. Perhaps traditional is a reasonable label, assuming it is not used as a pejorative. Paper-based materials have been a core component of library service for a very long time and remain so today. Although circulation statistics for paper-based collections continue to trend downward as the usage of e-books and e-journals increases exponentially, we see no evidence suggesting paper-based resources will disappear from libraries during the lifetime of this edition. Do keep in mind this chapter is about paper-based resources, and the two following chapters address other physical formats and e-resources.

We don't know what percentage of the Library of Congress's (LC) daily intake of 11,000 items daily is in terms of paper, other media based, or digital. We are very confident that a significant percentage is paper and that other libraries in the United States are also adding print items on a daily basis. Academic libraries, however, spend a growing percentage of the collection budget on e-books, e-journals, and other digital materials if for no other reason than the costs of adding these high-demand collections leave an ever-decreasing percentage of funds for paper-based print collections. More compelling arguments for electronic resources often take priority over print, and space within libraries is often at a premium.

It may come as something as a surprise, given the growing popularity of e-books and digital materials, that print material does have advantages. As noted by Jabr (2013): "Despite all the increasingly user-friendly and popular technology, most studies published since the early 1990s confirm earlier conclusions: paper still has advantages over screens as a reading medium. Together laboratory experiments, polls and consumer reports indicate that digital devices prevent people from efficiently navigating long texts, which may subtly inhibit reading comprehension. Compared with paper, screens may also drain more of mental resources while we are reading and make it a little harder to remember what we read when we are done" (p. 50). This is something to bear in mind when reading about how print is dead. Further consider the practical realities Grobart (2011) identified when comparing books to their electronic counterparts: "It has a terrific high-resolution display. It is pretty durable; you could get it a little wet and all would not be lost. It has tremendous battery life. It is often inexpensive enough that, if you misplaced it, you would not be too upset" (p. 8).

Check These Out

Two books that discuss many of the experiments and studies Jabr mentioned in his article are Abigail Sellen and Richard H. R. Harper's 2001 *The Myth of the Paperless Office* (Cambridge, MA: MIT Press) and Maryanne Wolf and Catherine Stoodley's 2007 *Proust and the Squid* (New York: Harper Collins).

An article that discusses the issue is Julia Parish-Morris, Neha Mahajan, Kathy Hirsh-Pasek, Roberta Michnick Golinkoff, and Molly Fuller Collins's 2013 "Once Upon a Time: Parent–Child Dialogue and Storybook Reading in the Electronic Era." (*Mind, Brain, and Education* 7, no. 3: 201–211).

What are the traditional collection resources? They are surprisingly varied, from printed books to games to realia (e.g., science models). The following is a partial list of materials that you can and do find in some libraries:

Books (hardcover, paperbacks, large print, etc.)
Serials (popular magazines, scholarly journals, newspapers, etc.)
Audio recordings (music, books, etc.—see chapter 8 for coverage)
Video recordings (cassettes, DVDs, etc.—see chapter 8 for coverage)

Maps (topographic, soils, geologic, etc.)
Graphic materials (photographs, posters, slides, etc.—see chapter 8 for coverage)
Government publications
Manuscripts (personal papers, historic material, etc.)
Microforms (reels, sheets, etc.—see chapter 8 for coverage)
Games and realia
Etc.

The "etc." in the preceding list is significant as many libraries, large academic and public libraries in particular, have "legacy formats, that is, a format no longer produced but retained for content reasons. Three examples of such legacy items are filmstrips, 33⅓ vinyl long-playing recordings, and Beta videocassettes. Whether a library elects to retain any materials, regardless of format, for historical purposes only rests with the mission of the library and the priorities and criteria set out in the library's collection development policy.

Each format has some implications for public service staff. All require some storage space and ongoing maintenance. Some require equipment to access content either within the library or at home by borrowers (see chapter 8 for coverage). Often the content exists in several formats such as in the case of plays (e.g., books, audio and video recordings). Many titles are now available in both physical and virtual form and sometimes with different legal usages. As you might expect, all the variations can present challenges for staff learning and training.

COLLECTION FORMATS

Some sense of the staying power of print is found in sources such as Bowker®, which records the publishing industry statistics. Evidence of that staying power appeared in the 2014 press release. In 2012, the industry's output of new titles was 309, 957 and by 2013 (the latest available data in late 2014) it was projected at 304, 912 (http://www.bowker.com/assets/downloads/products/isbn_output_2002_2013.pdf). Although this is a slight decline over production in the prior year, it is still an impressive figure.

A major reason for the staying power of books is that paper copies still provide the least expensive means of distributing large quantities of timely information to a large number of people in the format they read and use.

HOW PUBLISHING WORKS

Traditional publishers supply the capital and editorial assistance required to transform an author's manuscript/ideas into books and other information products. Generally, publishers perform six functions regardless of what format they work with:

1. Tap sources of materials (concepts).
2. Raise/supply the capital to produce salable products.

3. Aid in the development of the material.
4. Contract for the manufacturing (duplication, packaging, etc.) of the product.
5. Distribute materials, including promoting and advertising.
6. Maintain records of sales, contracts, and correspondence relating to the production and sale of the materials.

These functional areas are basically the same for any type of publishing activity (physical or virtual).

Book Publisher Types

We turn now to a discussion of some of the most common variations in publishing:

- Trade
- Mass market/paperback
- Serials
- Specialty
- Self-publishing
- Small press
- University presses
- El-hi/college textbooks

Trade publishers produce a wide range of titles, both fiction and nonfiction, that have wide sales potential for the so called general reader. Harper-Collins; Alfred A. Knopf; Doubleday; Macmillan Publishers; Little, Brown and Company; Thames & Hudson; and Penguin Random House are typical trade publishers. Many trade publishers have multiple, even hundreds of, divisions that produce specialty titles, such as children's, college textbooks, paperback, and reference. Trade publishers have three primary markets: bookstores, wholesalers, and libraries, but with the diminished number of brick-and-mortar bookstores, including large chain bookstores such as Borders Bookstore which closed its doors in 2011, online retailers such as Amazon.com have taken the place of traditional bookstores for many consumers of books.

Paperback publishers produce two types of work: quality trade paperbacks and mass-market paperbacks. A trade publisher may have a quality paperback division or may issue the paperbound version of a book through the same division that issued the hardcover edition. The publisher may publish original paperbacks, that is, a first edition in paperback. Distribution of quality paperbacks is the same as for hardcover books. Mass-market paperback publishers issue many reprints of titles as well as original titles of authors they know have a mass-market following. Their distribution differs from other book distribution. Their low price is based, in part, on the concept of mass sales. Another cost reduction factor is when the title is a reprint—editorial costs are much, much lower. Sales occur anywhere the publisher can get someone to handle them. The paperback books on sale in train and bus stations, airline terminals, corner stores, and kiosks are mass-market paperbacks. These books have a short shelf life compared to hard covers.

Contrary to popular belief, using a paper cover rather than a hard cover only reduces the unit cost of a book by between 40 to 50 cents. Original paperbacks incur the same costs, except for the cover material, as a hardcover title, which is why their cost is so much higher than reprint paperbacks.

Specialty publishers share some of the characteristics of textbook houses. Many have narrow markets that are easy to identify. Focusing marketing efforts on a limited number of buyers allows specialty publishers to achieve a reasonable return with less risk than a trade publisher takes on a nonfiction title. Specialty houses exist for a variety of fields; examples include art (Harry N. Abrams, Inc.), music (E. C. Schirmer), scientific (Academic Press), technical (American Technical Publishers), law (West Publishing), and medical (W. B. Saunders). Many specialty books require expensive graphic preparation or presswork. Such presswork increases production costs, which is one of the reasons art, music, and science and technology titles are so costly. Another factor in their cost is the smaller market as compared to the market for a trade title. A smaller market means that the publisher must recover production costs from fewer books.

Textbook publishers, especially those that target the primary and secondary schools (el-hi), occupy one of the highest-risk areas of publishing. Most publishers in this area develop a line of textbooks for several grades, for example, a social studies series. Preparation of such texts requires large amounts of time, energy, and money. Printing costs are high because most school texts feature expensive color plates and other specialized presswork. Such projects require large upfront investments that must be recouped before a profit can be realized. If enough school districts adopt a text, profits can be substantial, but failure to secure adoption can mean tremendous loss. Textbook firms, such as Prentice Hall School, Key Curriculum Press, and McGraw-Hill School Division, produce several series to help ensure a profit or to cushion against loss. College textbook publishers have a higher risk than do trade publishers but lower than El-Hi (elementary-high school) publishers as their markets are more individual/instructor driven rather than by selection committees that decide for all the schools in a district. Also, they are able to issue new editions more quickly and, generally, with less costly illustrative material.

From the Advisory Board

Ruth Kifer noted that many academic libraries are supporting efforts at universities nationwide to cut the exorbitant cost of buying textbooks for college students. Kifer notes, "At San Jose State University (SJSU), this is done in two ways: 1) In collaboration with the university bookstore, the library posts on the library website all required textbooks for a given semester that happen to be available in the library's e-book collection and thus available freely to students. The library does not systematically purchase textbooks in any format and only acquires e-books with multiple use licenses. For the 2012/2013 academic year, this initiative saved SJSU students close to $250,000. 2) SJSU librarians work one-on-one with faculty in academic departments to assist them in finding free or low cost open educational resources (OER) for use in lieu of requiring students to purchase costly print textbooks. These resources can be embedded in the learning management system course shells for face-to-face classes or online classes. See http://als.csuprojects.org/course_content for more information about affordable learning solutions and the use of OER within the California State University system."

University/scholarly publishers, as part of not-for-profit organizations, receive subsidies in one form or another and thus reduce their risks. Most are part of an academic institution (University of California Press), a museum (Museum of Northern Arizona), a research institution (Getty Institute), or a learned society (American Philosophical Society). Such presses exist to produce scholarly books that would not be acceptable (profitable) to commercial publishers. These publishers rely on the community of scholars to assist with peer-reviewed materials. Most scholarly books have limited sales appeal. A commercial, or for-profit, publisher considering a scholarly manuscript has three choices: (1) publish it and try to sell it at a price that ensures cost recovery; (2) publish it, sell it at a price comparable to commercial titles, and lose money; or (3) do not publish the item. Because of economic factors and a need to disseminate scholarly information regardless of cost (i.e., even if it will lose money), the subsidized (by tax exemption, if nothing else), not-for-profit presses exist.

Self-publishing and vanity press services differ from other publishing houses in that they receive most of their operating funds from the authors whose works they publish. Self-publishing requires all the basic functions of any publishing operation; what changes is who carries the financial risk for the activity—the author. There are a host of firms that offer services to an author that may improve the quality of the publication; examples are AuthorHouse® (http://www.authorhouse.com/) and Lulu.Com™ (http://www.lulu.com/). Such firms offer assistance in editing and design as well as formatting items, both print and/or digital. Some handle marketing and distribution functions as well. With the Internet, self-publishing has skyrocketed as our earlier quotation from Kelly Gallagher noted. How many authors actually recover their full investment is unknown. The service firms, of course, describe the successes. Some individuals have indeed done well underwriting their writing efforts. We suspect the vast majority of self-publishers are fortunate to cover their upfront costs.

In the past, there was a major difference between self- publishing and small presses. Some of the differences still remain but the lines are blurring. *Small presses* differ in that they take the publisher's financial risk when they publish a title; the author's risk lies in how well he or she wrote the material and how well the publisher presents it to the reading public. Some people, including librarians, think of small presses as literary presses. The reality is that small presses can be as diverse as the international publishing conglomerates. Size is the only real difference; in functions and interests small presses are no different from large trade publishers. Many such presses publish no more than four titles per year. However, often it is only through the small press that one can find information on less popular topics. A small press like Algonquin boasts writers such as Julia Alvarez (*How the Garcia Girls Lost Their Accents* and *In the Time of the Butterflies*) and Sara Gruen (*Water for Elephants*), as well as surprise commercial successes like Amy Stewart (*The Drunken Botanist*).

Another factor that sets small presses apart from their larger counterparts is economics. Large publishers have high costs and need substantial sales to recover their costs, but small presses can produce a book for a limited market at a reasonable cost and still expect some profit. Small presses also can produce books more quickly than their larger counterparts.

Costs and risks have been mentioned several times in the previous material. How often have you heard, "The book prices are outrageous!" or some variation? There are times when they may well be so, but the reality is the public's notion of profitability far exceeds the actual situation. The following is broad generalization of the costs and profit on a $25 trade book:

Suggested list price	$25.00	
Editorial and overhead	–2.00 23.00	
Manufacturing	–2.00 21.00	
Discount to retailer	12.50 8.50	
Royalty	1.25 7.25	(most are paid on net income)
Marketing/fulfillment	4.50	
Profit	**3.35**	

(The example as noted is a broad generalization; however, the percentages do work for most titles.) The actual costs obviously vary; however, the return on investment is generally not much better than putting money into a tax-free municipal bond fund.

Check These Out

For more information on commercial publishing, see:

Richard Guthrie's 2011 *Publishing: Principles & Practice* (Thousand Oaks, CA: Sage Publications) which provides a solid overview of both print and digital publishing of today.

Giles N. Clark and Angus Phillips's 2008 *Inside Book Publishing* (4th ed., New York: Routledge) which has some excellent sections on the history of publishing.

Titles providing more background on the self-publishing industry are:

Eric Kampmann and Margot Atwell's 2012 *The Insider's Guide to Book Publishing Success* (New York: Beaufort Books). They present detailed information about both commercial and self-publishing.

Ellen Lupton's 2008 *Indie Publishing: How to Design and Produce Your Own Book* (New York: Princeton Architectural Press) focuses solely on the ins and outs of being your own publisher.

Serials

Serials normally contain the most current information about a topic, although some professional society/association publications are slow to appear, even in digital form. There are some people today, perhaps many, who believe that the paper-based serial is ready to become a museum object at best. As we noted earlier, paper serials are still with us and likely to remain so during the lifetime of this edition.

From the Advisory Board

Ruth Kifer noted that academic libraries in many public teaching universities (not necessarily large research-intensive libraries) have been systematically, but selectively, canceling and withdrawing back issues of portions of their print journal collections which are duplicated in electronic journals and databases. This is possible because of consortial collection sharing organizations such as WEST—The Western Regional Storage Trust. WEST is a "distributed retrospective print journal repository program serving research libraries, college and university libraries, and library consortia in the Western Region of the United States. Under the WEST program, participating libraries consolidate and validate print journal backfiles at major library storage facilities and at selected campus locations. The resulting shared print archives ensure access to the scholarly print record and allow member institutions to optimize campus library space. This collaborative regional approach to managing library collections represents an important step, when joined with other initiatives, toward development of a network-level shared print archive" (http://www.cdlib.org/west/). Comprehensive databases such as JSTOR also serve to make this possible (http://about.jstor.org/10Things).

From a public service point of view, currency is the most important factor for individuals who use serials, except for those engaged in historical research. (As we will note in chapter-resources, e-journals are not always the most current format.) A very common question from users is, "Is the latest issue of ____ in yet?" Providing an accurate answer can take some time as you must determine what the latest issue is that the library has and if it is the current issue. A frequent follow-up question, in terms of paper-based serials, is, "Where is it? I looked on the shelves and it's not there." Answering that question will take even more time.

Related to currency is the frequency with which information is updated. For books that do go into new editions, and only a small percentage do so, the updating interval is a number of years. However, for serials, the update interval can be very short, daily in the case of many newspapers. Articles in a serial are usually short and focus on a fairly narrow subject. Readers with very specific information needs frequently find that serials provide the desired data more quickly than books. Finally, serials are often the first printed source of information about a new subject or development. People use serials as a source for learning about new things while using books to gain a broader or deeper knowledge of a subject they may have first encountered in a serial. Also, the sheer volume of "new" information appearing in serials far exceeds that of books.

Just what is a "serial"? Librarianship has its share of jargon and serials contribute more than its share to that pool. The public may use the term *magazines* or *periodicals*. A few people will ask for *journals*. In the library world, all three terms are labels for publications that fall into the broad class of materials called *serials* and each has a slightly different meaning. Serial is an all-inclusive term encompassing many publication variations in form, content, and purpose. The *Online Dictionary for Library and Information Science* provides the following definitions:

> *Serial*—A publication in any medium issued under the same title in a succession of discrete parts, usually numbered (or dated) and appearing at regular or irregular intervals with no predetermined conclusion. In AACR2 2002, serials are classified as a type of continuing resource.
>
> Serial publications include print periodicals and newspapers, electronic magazines and journals, annuals (reports, yearbooks, etc.), continuing directories, proceedings and transactions, and numbered monographic series cataloged separately. When serials split, merge, or are absorbed, a title change may occur. Most libraries purchase serials on subscription or continuation order. (http://www.abc-clio.com/ODLIS/odlis_s.aspx)

As you can see, the definition contains many of the labels we mentioned earlier and are also defined in the *Dictionary*. General dictionaries, however, have even greater overlap and frequently use phrases such as "a journal is a magazine" or "a magazine is a periodical." Thus, it is not surprising that users, and sometimes library staff, use these terms interchangeably.

Types of Serials

Serial librarians usually divide the materials they work within several broad categories. We will briefly describe seven common categories.

Institutional Reports

This category covers annuals, semi-annuals, quarterlies, and occasional reports of organizations. Within this group are the financial reports of corporations and financial institutions: a format widely collected by academic and corporate libraries as well as larger public libraries. In today's electronic world this is not nearly the challenge it once was; however, libraries still must get on the distribution list. A further issue is following up to verify if the e-version has arrived.

Yearbooks and Proceedings

Annuals, biennials, and occasional publications of societies and associations constitute another common serial found in libraries. These yearbooks, almanacs, proceedings, transactions, memoirs, directories, and reports are usually already bound or stapled. Most of the publications in this category are substantial in length and size, and many libraries normally treat them as books.

Superseding Serials

In the past, the most problematic serial category was the superseding serial service. This was and occasionally still is a publication in which each new issue or part supersedes the previous issue/part and the library discards the older material. Included in this category are telephone directories, airline and other travel-related schedules, catalogs, as well as loose-leaf data services (e.g., Commerce Clearing House publications—http://www.cch.com/about/).

Newspapers

This category can cause some problems for public service personnel. Keeping the newspapers in good order, with all the sections for a given date intact and in place, can be a frustrating activity. Especially frustrating is keeping track, whenever possible, of who has or had today's copy of the *Times* or where they left it. Availability of online versions of major newspapers provides alternative access to these dailies and makes it possible for librarians to subscribe to a limited number of paper titles and to keep back issues for a limited period of time.

Newsletters

One serial category that a surprising number of libraries collect is newsletters, leaflets, and news releases. For many special/business libraries, they are the primary collecting area. Due to their small size and assumptions about the worth of small-sized, short-length formats, they present some challenges for staff. With the ubiquitous nature of the Internet and libraries now recognized as an access point to it, many libraries no longer maintain newsletter collections in paper format.

Magazines

Within this category there are several subtypes of mass-market publications:

- Mass-market serials, weekly or monthly newsmagazines (e.g., *Time*).
- Popular magazines dealing with fiction, pictures, sports, travel, fashion, sex, humor, and comics (e.g., *ESPN: The Magazine*).

- Magazines that popularize science, social, political, and cultural affairs (e.g., *National Geographic*).
- Magazines focusing on opinion and criticism, especially social, political, literary, artistic, aesthetic, or religious (e.g., *National Review*).

Journals

Journals have more specialized markets and four widely accepted subcategories:

- Nonspecialized journals for the intelligentsia are for persons well informed on topics such as literature, art, social affairs, science, or politics. (*Scientific American* would be an example.)
- Learned journals for specialists, both primary and secondary, are major components in academic and large public libraries' serials collections—*American Indian Culture and Research Journal*, for example.
- Practical professional journals in fields such as medicine, law, agriculture, management, and librarianship (e.g., *School Library Monthly*) are also common in all libraries.
- Parochial journals are of interest to a local or regional audience. (*Rock Art* is an example.) Local history groups often publish a small journal for members. While most issues are only of local interest, some large research libraries collect such publications in support of their mission of collecting and preserving research and potential research materials.

These variations help make it clear why there is confusion about terms relating to these publications. Each type fills a niche in the information dissemination system. While they did (in paper) and sometimes still do (when online) create special handling procedures and problems, they are a necessary part of any library's collection, and the public service staff must deal with them.

Check This Out

Vincent Larivière, Cassidy R. Sugimoto, and Blaise Cronin's 2012 "A Bibliometric Chronicling of Library and Information Science's First Hundred Years" (*Journal of the American Society for Information Science & Technology* 63, no. 5: 997–1016) provides a look at how bibliometric methods are employed to assist in evaluations of collections as well as a review of the profession's history.

Maps

Maps are a form of pictorial material, and most libraries have traditionally held at least a small collection, in addition to atlases in the reference collection. Internet map sites, such as MapQuest, Google Maps, or Multimap, have significantly reduced the demand for roadmaps in libraries. Information found on such sites provides what the majority of people were seeking when they came to the library "looking for a map"—that is, street/highway information.

Maps actually come in a variety of forms and content. Large public libraries, academic libraries, and many business and industrial libraries have extensive collections. Maps take the form of graphic representations of such things as geological structures, physical features, economic data, and population distributions. They may be folded, sheets, raised relief, globes, and even aerial/satellite images.

Depending on the collection's purpose, maps may be organized in a simple geographic location sequence or by some more complex system. "Do you have a map of X?" may (and usually does) mean a map showing streets, roads, and other cultural features. It could mean a topographic (topo) map, which provides elevation information in addition to cultural features. Or the individual may really want a soil map to get information for agricultural or construction purposes. Most map users who want a contour map will ask for "the topo map of X." Normally the person with specialized map needs is knowledgeable about maps and will be precise in his or her request. In a large collection, it is common to keep types of maps together, for example, topographic, cultural, political, and geologic maps. In addition to content, factors such as projection and scale may be important in the organization and storage of maps. Staff working with large map collections will need special training to handle this format properly. As with many serials, maintaining maps in an established order can be staff and labor intensive and is thus extremely expensive. Many academic libraries provide access to GIS data through individual instruction or in collaboration with other campus organizations. A geographic information system, or GIS, is a system designed to capture, store, manipulate, analyze, manage, and present geographically referenced data. A GIS includes both hardware and software components.

PAPER-BASED COLLECTION ISSUES FOR PUBLIC SERVICE STAFF

Paper-based collections do present a few ongoing issues for public service staff. Maintaining the storage space for the collections has several aspects—such as, shelving and reshelving items, keeping the items in their proper order, and searching for items that should be "on the shelf" but are not. The dual nature (e.g., print, large print, and digital formats for some items) of some items can cause some confusion for users and staff alike.

Shifting collections, regardless of physical format, is something every type of library will have to deal with from time to time. However, it is the academic library where the shifting challenge is greatest as it has a responsibility to preserve information long term. Libraries in comprehensive teaching institutions have a different mission than research-intensive institutions where historical treatment of a subject area may be more important. Thus, collection growth is a given.

Public and school libraries face a somewhat different challenge—finite space with little prospect of gaining additional space. At times it is almost a matter of a new item is added an existing item must be removed (the process of removing collection items is often labeled "weeding"). Weeding may not be as physically challenging as moving print volumes for an hour or so, but can be mentally stressful as you have to decide to discard an item that has been in the collection for some time. There may also be a problem if the administration doesn't understand the value of the process. Some school principals may question why you want to buy new books when you are throwing away so many other perfectly fine books. Academic libraries are now learning from public libraries that more streamlined collections allow library users more success in finding what they need on the shelves and thus create a much more highly used print collection than one where weeding is not viewed as an integral part of collection development.

From the Advisory Board

Jean Wallace, a school librarian, reported having the following experience with regards to weeding collections: "I worked in one school library where in my first days there the principal proudly showed me all the books they had rebound. They included a large number of titles by Zane Grey and Gene Stratton Porter—worthy authors in their day, but not in demand by high school students in the 1970s. But he was so proud of them that I didn't dare weed any of them."

Check These Out

An example of a weeding guide for a type in library is Donna J. Baumbach and Linda L. Miller's *Less Is More: A Practical Guide to Weeding School Library Collections* (Chicago: American Library Association, 2006).

The long-standing guide to weeding library collections is Stanley J. Slote's classic *Weeding Library Collections: Library Weeding Methods* (4th ed., Englewood, CO: Libraries Unlimited, 1997).

Print serials (magazines/journals) can be especially physically challenging to shift, as the bound volumes can be heavy. School libraries may store issues in boxes—the Princeton type with tops to keep the dust out. Handling those boxes, for shifting or simple retrieving a single issue, is a challenge. Boxes can spill, which then takes time to get the issues back in order. We heard of one school library that stored its boxes by size, digests in small boxes up to *Life Magazine* in the large boxes.

How the library organizes and provides access to paper-based magazine/journals can cause public service staff to have more or less shifting work. There are three basic ways to organize paper journals and magazines for the public: alphabetically by title, alphabetically by title within broad topical groupings—also known as reader's interest, depending on type of library, for example, public libraries may have gardening, cooking, travel; school libraries may have nature, science, literature; academic may have philosophy, STEM, literary criticism; special libraries may have accounting, biological sciences, marketing—and in classified order, using the same classification system as used for the books in the collection.

What are the implications of these options? It is important to seek input from users. Each type of library and its users may have a different need. It is assumed the fewer places a person has to look to locate materials, the better. Thus, the classified approach, with the current issues shelved next to the backfiles and books with the same classification number, may be the preferred arrangement. Unfortunately, from the staff's point of view this option generates the greatest amount of work as they have to shift a high volume of material as both new books and serials arrive. It is possible to make this less onerous, if you have ample empty shelf space and lots of data about the growth rates for serials and books by call number. How many libraries have empty shelf space? There would probably be weeks of shifting materials to start with as you opened up shelves in the right amount in the right area, but then there should only be minor shifts for some time. One given for print serials is their constant growth; this necessitates shifting them to make room for new materials, no matter what approach the library takes to housing them. Some large research libraries use off-site storage or compressed shelving, or rely on microfilm for backfiles. Public, school, and special libraries, with their very finite space, often pull back issues once a year. Shifting serials is an ongoing challenge for the public service staff. Of course, with serials increasingly available online, many libraries have opted for this alternative, as it eliminates storage and shifting issues.

Users approve of the classified approach only as long as *all* of their most frequently used titles are together. Very few publications truly have a single focus; almost all can and do have multiple subject headings. Classification schemes only provide one location for a single concept. What is to be done with a serial about criminal sociology? When the library receives only one copy of the journal, the staff must select a single location, whether it is the sociology, law, criminology, or perhaps the criminal sociology section, and some users may be unhappy with the choice. All you can do is base the decision on a judgment about the content of the work *and* the most frequent potential user of the title in question. Be prepared to change your decision if the most frequent users turn out to be different than you anticipated.

No system, increased use of signs, or added bibliographic instruction, will eliminate all problems. The way a library decides to organize its serials depends on the type of titles in the collection, collection size, and the needs of library users. Popular magazines seem to change names less often than their scholarly cousins, the journals. If most of the users are individuals who use the library regularly and over time, the system which makes the most efficient use of the library staff is the most reasonable approach. The library must also decide if it wants integrated or separate backfiles and current issues. Often the deciding factors are the budget and availability of staff.

From the Authors' Experience

As we noted earlier, academic libraries tend to have a substantial amount of "collection shifting" work due to their long-term preservation responsibilities. And, as we will discuss in more detail in the final chapter of this book (chapter 19), they have difficulty gaining approval to expand their physical facilities. Evans was head of medium-size university library for over 17 years. From his first day on the job to the day he retired, one of the major challenges was collection growth, finding storage space, and almost constant collection shifting. (Final planning and fund raising for a new building was almost complete when he retired.)

Every time the library found a way to add some additional stack space (such as removing user spaces or installing movable stacks) there were significant collection shifts. One major effort, conducted over the winter break period, involved moving over 500,000 items. From the staff's point of view, that shift was done by a moving company—actually four of the authors were also involved in supervising the move.

Eventually many large libraries can find no more "tricks" to pull out more storage space in the existing facility. When that happens and the library must continue to grow, remote storage comes in to play. Although planning for a new building was ongoing for more than 12 of the 17+ years, storage space, both actual and potential, ran out long before the new building came into existence. Evans and his staff used the three most common remote storage options available to libraries—cooperative, warehouse, and commercial storage firms. Regardless of the option chosen, there will be an increase in public service staff workloads and some amount of dissatisfaction among users because of inherent delays in having materials remotely stored.

Another ongoing task in terms of physical collections is "shelf-reading," discussed in chapter 6. In part, this activity arises from shifting activities as well as other factors. Physical collection volumes are arranged on their storage shelves in a fixed order so that staff and users know where to look for a particular item. What that arrangement is will vary in terms of local needs; however, most U.S. libraries employ some variation of the Dewey Decimal System or the Library of Congress system.

You should keep in mind, even if at first it seems unlikely, that both shifting and shelf-reading play an important role in how the public perceive the quality of library service. Neither process is intellectually stimulating, both can be tiresome, shifting can make your back ache, and, in a sense, neither is ever finished. Nevertheless, failure to perform either process accurately and regularly will have a negative impact on the library's reputation.

A major frustration for library users is not finding something that the library owns and should be, according to the OPAC, available (not checked out to someone) and not where it should be on the shelf. There are number of reasons for this to occur. Inaccurate reshelving is often the culprit. There are times when the item has been stolen. Another possibility, that is difficult to establish, is that someone is using the item somewhere in the library. Other possibilities are the item is being repaired/at the bindery and has been checked in (OPAC status changed to available) but still in the circulation area or on a book truck awaiting reshelving. In school libraries, shelving is done by students so quality of work may vary widely with different students. Both the reshelving and shifting processes can cause items to get out of their proper order.

Most major shifting projects should end with a careful shelf-reading of the shifted materials. When there is a new staff person/volunteer doing reshelving, a supervisor should check that person's work until there is confidence the person understands the classification system, as locally employed. Long decimal numbers—perhaps seven or eight behind the decimal point—can get confusing, especially when a person is under pressure to get the work done quickly.

Even other users can create shelving issues. Many libraries post signs asking users *not* to return items to shelf—but instead to leave them on the table or on specially labeled "sorting shelves." Nevertheless, well-meaning users reshelve items, sometimes correctly and sometimes not. Libraries making such requests usually have two reasons for doing so. The first is to avoid the problems of inaccurate shelving. A second reason, and often of more importance, is to assess the use of items within the library. One outcome measure is, of course, service usage. Just using checkout data may well underestimate the actual usage of the collections.

From the Authors' Experience

Evans began his library career by working as a "page" in a public library while in high school. He worked in a branch where the head of the branch had *very* strong views of what people should read—nonfiction or classic literature. (That fact may well suggest how long ago his first experience was.) In the librarian's view, reading popular fiction was a waste of time.

In those days, circulation systems depended upon cards (located in a "book pocket" in each book) that the borrower filled out and the library retained. The check cards were filed by call number or author name in the case of fiction. Each Friday afternoon, the librarian would tally the week's circulation of fiction and nonfiction. If fiction led the way, pity the poor user who next checked out a work of fiction. They would be on the receiving end of a lecture about wasting time.

The staff kept a running total they shared so they knew what the data would show. They all found something to do away from the desk on Fridays when fiction came out ahead. Evans could always depend upon having shelf-reading to do those afternoons—it never does end.

From the Advisory Board

Jean Wallace wrote that Evans's experience reminded her of "when I first became a school librarian and started attending conferences, there was an ongoing debate on whether a school library should include 'sub-standard' literature. After all, we were supposed to be a school and should introduce and encourage our students to read quality literature, not fluff like Nancy

Drew. I remember that I finally came down on the side of all reading, quality or not when I talked to some of our English teachers about what they were reading on their own time. These were intelligent people who did read quality stuff, but they also regularly read lightweight pop fiction. I figured if they could read Mary Higgins Clark and Danielle Steele, the students could read Nancy Drew. And that's a decision that I never regretted."

GOVERNMENT INFORMATION

In the not-too-distant past, government documents were a common element in many library collections. There are still "legacy" copies of such items in collections; however, all levels of government have shifted their efforts to disseminate information from print to digital formats. (Note: government information did and still does exist in a variety of formats—print, videos, graphic, and microforms as well as digital.) Not only are their communication efforts more and more based on the Internet and Web, but so are their services. One result is that libraries acquire fewer and fewer hard copies of government information while playing a greater role in providing access to such information and services.

When it was just a print world, FDLP (Federal Depository Library Program) libraries were the primary source for government information (many of the depositories were and still are academic libraries), and a person had to visit the library to gain access. Today, Web searches provide government information alongside other sources of information. What has changed is that public libraries are now the most active in providing people with access to government information and services. Almost by default, public libraries, because of the open access to their facilities and services, have become a major interface between citizens and government information. In fact, some public librarians actually teach or coach patrons on accessing and using government information, a trend that will likely continue to grow.

Because government information is a product of many branches and agencies of government, it has no special subject focus and usually reflects the concerns of the agency that produced it. Predictably, a document produced by the U.S. Department of Agriculture (USDA) probably deals with a subject related to agriculture, such as livestock statistics, horticulture, or irrigation. However, the relationship may be less direct, because the USDA also publishes information about nutrition, forestry, and home economics. As remote as the connection may seem, most government information has some connection to the issuing agencies' purpose.

Currently, what is perhaps the most user-friendly site for accessing U.S. federal government information is the portal USA.gov—Government Made Easy, which is called the "The U.S. Government's Official Web Portal" (http://www.usa.gov). In addition to the expected search box at the top of the page, the home page offers a set of broad topical selections (e.g., "Benefits, Grants and Loans" and "Health Insurance, Nutrition and Food Safety") that provide links to government information on the topic from any agency. There is also a "Government Agencies and Elected Officials" tab that has links to the three main branches of government and their agencies, to online sites for the states and U.S. territories, local jurisdictions, and tribal governments. The state, local, and tribal pages also offer more search options.

Access to, and identification of, state and local government information was difficult in the past, but sites such as GovENGINE.com (http://www .govengine.com) provides links to such information, which has greatly enhanced access. Yet another service is the STATE & LOCAL GOVERNMENT on the Net Web site (http://www.statelocalgov.net/). We explore digital government information in chapter 11 ("Public Computer Access").

ARCHIVES—SPECIAL COLLECTIONS

Archives and special collections play unusual and special roles in public services. They are sources of pride, image, and value to both the library and the service community. Even small public libraries that open only a few hours a week often have one shelf, in a secure area, where one or two books of special value reside. The value is not always monetary; it can be informational or even psychological in nature. Like the old family Bible, retained because of age and its record of the family, communities and organizations frequently have materials that carry special meaning for them and that may exist in only one copy. And, unlike the old family Bible that is coming apart from too much handling and mishandling, communities and organizations make a significant effort to properly preserve and protect such items.

Our last opening quotation for this chapter mentioned primary and secondary sources. Archives and special collections are usual places researchers and others find primary resources. Genealogical collections are found in many public libraries. Government organizations, for example, the Smithsonian Institution, have special library collections in their various buildings.

Primary sources are contemporary accounts of an event, written by someone who experienced or witnessed the event in question. These original documents (i.e., they are not about another document or account) are often diaries, letters, memoirs, journals, speeches, manuscripts, interviews, and other such unpublished works. They may also include published pieces such as newspaper or magazine articles (as long as they are written soon after the fact and not as historical accounts), photographs, audio or video recordings, research reports in the natural or social sciences, or original literary. As such they allow researchers to get as close to original ideas, events, and empirical studies as possible.

Secondary sources interpret primary sources. They are at least one step away from the event described and draw conclusions about the events covered in primary materials. Typical secondary materials take the form of journal articles or books or radio or television documentaries, and conference proceedings.

Some people add a third layer to the degree of closeness to an event or fact—*tertiary sources*. Such resources provide overviews of topics by synthesizing information gathered from other resources. Common types of such resources are encyclopedias, chronologies, almanacs, and textbooks.

Joan Reitz's *Online Dictionary for Library Science* uses the following definitions to categorize the topic of this section:

Archives—An organized collection of the noncurrent records of the activities of a business, government, organization, institution, or other corporate body, or the personal papers of one or more individuals, families, or
groups, retained permanently (or for a designated or indeterminate period
of time) by their originator or a successor for their permanent historical,
informational, evidential, legal, administrative, or monetary value, usually
in a repository managed and maintained by a trained archivist. Also refers
to the office or organization responsible for appraising, selecting, preserving, and providing access to archival materials. (http://www.abc-clio.com
/ODLIS/odlis_a.aspx)

Special Collections—Some libraries segregate from the general collection
rare books, manuscripts, papers, and other items that are (1) of a certain
form, (2) on a certain subject, (3) of a certain time period or geographic area,
(4) in fragile or poor condition, or (5) especially valuable. Such materials are
not allowed to circulate and access to them may be restricted. (http://www
.abc-clio.com/ODLIS/odlis_s.aspx)

You can probably see that there is some overlap in the definitions for these
collections. From a practical point of view, based on an examination of the
types of materials held, archives and special collections are very similar. Both
may have collections of printed material, photographs, digital material, handwritten material, art works, audio and video recordings, and objects. Both
have the same primary purpose—preserve their collection of original materials
indefinitely. Both limit access and handling of these materials. Both do not
allow users to "browse" materials in the sense normally thought of in terms
of libraries—staff members bring to the user specifically requested files one or
two at a time. Users are *not* allowed access to the storage areas, except on a
guided tour. Both have similar environmental control issues related to their
preservation mission (see chapter 16). They may organize the materials in
different ways depending upon the person's training/background—archivist
or librarian.

While much of the material housed in or acquired by archives/special collections is old, age alone is not the deciding factor for housing material in this
department. Something may be more than 100 years old and yet not be appropriate for the collection, while something produced yesterday may be most
appropriate. The two basic factors for inclusion are, first, the item's suitability
for the library's collection (which should, of course, reflect the parent institution's mission) and, second, its need for special handling to assure long-term
preservation. If an item fits both criteria, it should be in special collections.
Staff members who work in special collections are custodians in the same
sense as that conveyed by the very old phrase for a librarian, "keeper of the
books."

Regulating access to the collections is a very important issue and ranges
from no restrictions to requiring a written request in advance of a visit (sometimes with personal references) explaining why it is necessary to use the

collection. Although costly, the more screening carried out before a person gains access to the collection, the less likely the library is to have problems with misuse. However, for "libraries of record," (holding primary materials) the extra procedures make perfect sense. Library-of-record materials do not circulate outside the library except for exhibits, and so are almost always available.

The complex issue of access via duplication of special collections materials is too broad to address in detail in this book. A good quality copy (paper or electronic), however, may provide a satisfactory and cost-effective solution to the problem of access, supervision, and preservation. In such a situation, the library makes a paper, microform, or digitized copy of the item, which the reader may take away to use at his or her leisure. Thus, the material is not handled unnecessarily and the staff need not engage in all the activities required when the reader uses the physical item in special collections. Obviously, copyright restrictions apply and often donors impose additional restrictions upon both the use and duplication of their gifts.

Once a prospective user becomes an approved user, other conditions regarding use apply. The *ACRL/RBMS Guidelines Regarding Security and Theft in Special Collections* (ACRL/RBMS, 2009) outline the major areas of concern in terms of monitoring researchers:

> Staff should observe researchers at all times and not allow them to work unobserved behind bookcases, book trucks, stacks of books or other obstacles that restrict staff view. Researchers should be limited at any one time to having access only to those books, manuscripts or other items which are needed to perform the research at hand. . . . Researchers should not be allowed to exchange materials or have access to materials brought into the room for use by another researcher. (http://www.ala.org/acrl/standards/security_theft)

These relatively few words have significant implications for staffing and operational procedures in special collections. Providing adequate, secure storage space for the users' personal property may present a problem if there is a lot of it, but is essential if one is to maintain collection security. Checking each item before and after each use for "condition, content, and completeness" will add a significant element to the workload. Not doing the checking, however, can result in the loss of plates, charts, maps, pages from books, or important pages from manuscript collections. Having a staff member present in the reading room when researchers are present is mandatory, even if that means some other tasks may not be completed.

Few departments have the luxury of staffing such that the reading room monitor can do nothing else. However, the physical presence of a staff member who clearly is monitoring user activities does increase security. Closed-circuit television cameras and recorders provide even more security, but cannot replace the presence of a staff person. Limiting the number of items a reader may have at one time certainly adds to the workload. The proctor, however, helps assure that users cannot build up visual barriers that impede monitoring their activities and use of the materials. Carefully planned placement of user stations can help staff monitor use of the materials. Maintaining check-out records indefinitely presents few problems, except in large, heavily used collections where eventually storage space may become a problem.

Why maintain usage records? Few, if any, special collections have enough staff to literally check every page of every item after every use. When a user reports something missing, having past use records may allow the library to recover the missing material. Occasionally, these records also help identify and convict a thief. One such case occurred in Norway many years ago (Thompson, 1984). In that instance, a high government official had been stealing rare plates and maps from special collections around the country. The records of his use of rare items, which had missing plates and maps, helped convict the man.

CLOSING THOUGHTS

Paper-based collections (books and serials) are still a significant component of any library's service program. Whether they remain so for the lifetime of this edition and thereafter is a matter of opinion; however, given the relatively short lifespans of most editions, they are unlikely to totally disappear. In any case, maintenance of these legacy or traditional collections contributes to the library staff's workload. Although not as large as other print-based materials, the content of a library's archive/special collections is important to society as it preserves unique cultural patrimony and contributes to historical research.

Chapter Review Material

1. List 10 of the most common types of legacy or traditional physical format collections found in libraries.
2. What are the basic functions a publisher performs when producing information resources?
3. Describe five common types of publishers.
4. What are two of the characteristics of serials that make them of high interest for library users?
5. List and describe the major types of serials.
6. Discuss the types of maps that libraries still collect.
7. What are two of the most common challenges public service staff have in terms of physical collections?
8. Discuss the changes in how a person now typically accesses government information.
9. What makes archival and special collections important to libraries and their service communities?
10. Discuss the differences between primary, secondary, and tertiary resources.
11. Describe some of the more unique aspects of providing access to archives and special collection resources.

REFERENCES

Galfano, Paul. 2013. "Can I Cancel My Print Case Reports Collection? A Look at the Merits of Free Online Resources as a Substitute." *AALL Spectrum* 17, no. 6: 24–25.

Grobart, Sam. 2011. "Gadgets You Should Get Rid Of (or Not)." *New York Times*, March 24: B8.

Harrell, Jeanne. 2012. "Literature of Acquisitions in Review: 2008–2009." *Library Resources and Technical Services* 56, no.1: 4–13.

Information Today. 2013. "Test Your Knowledge." 30, no. 5: 10.

Jabr, Ferris. 2013. "Why the Brain Prefers Paper." *Scientific American* 309, no. 5: 48–53.

Sutton, Shan, and Lorrie Knight. 2006. "Beyond the Reading Room: Integrating Primary and Secondary Sources in the Library Classroom." *Journal of Academic Librarianship* 32, no. 3: 320–325.

Thompson, L.S. 1984. "Biblioclasm in Norway." *Library & Archival Security* 6, no. 4:13–16.

SUGGESTED READINGS

Arbeeny, Pamela, and Lloyd Chittenden. 2014. "An Ugly Weed: Innovative Deselection to Address a Shelf Space Crisis." *Journal of Library Innovation* 5, no. 1: 78–90.

Brown, Christopher C. 2011. "Knowing Where They Went: Six Years of Online Access Statistics via the Online Catalog for Federal Government Information."*College & Research Libraries* 72, no. 1: 43–61.

Chadwick, Cynthia, Renée Di Pilato, Monique le Conge, Rachel Rubin, and Gary Shaffer. 2013. "The Future of the FDLP in Public Libraries." *Public Libraries* 52, no. 4: 40–46.

Cheney, Debora. 2010. "Dinosaurs in a Jetson World: A Dozen Ways to Revitalize Your Microforms Collection." *Library Collections, Acquisitions, &Technical Services* 34, nos. 2/3: 66–73.

Danet, Pierre. 2014. "The Future of Book Publishing: Seven Technology Trends and Three Industry Goals." *Publishing Research Quarterly* 30, no. 3: 275–281.

Faran, Ellen W. 2011. "Sustaining Scholarly Publishing: University Presses and Emerging Business Models." *College & Research Libraries News* 72, no. 5: 284–287.

Gray, David J., and Andrea J. Copeland. 2012. "E-Book versus Print." *Reference & User Services Quarterly* 51, no. 4: 334–339.

Haynes, Elizabeth. 2009. "Getting Started with Graphic Novels in School Libraries." *Library Media Connection* 27, no. 4: 10–12.

Hoy, Susan. 2009. "What Talking Books Have to Say: Issues and Options for Public Libraries." *APLIS* 22, no. 4: 164–180.

Kirch, Claire. 2014. "Regional Publishing Takes Its Place." *Publishers Weekly* 261, no. 39: 48–49.

Lewis, David W. 2013. "From Stacks to the Web: The Transformation of Academic Library Collecting." *College & Research Libraries* 74, no. 2: 159–176.

Love, Mark. 2011. "Marketing Government Information Resources to the K-12 Community." *DttP: A Quarterly Journal of Government Information Practice & Perspective* 39, no. 2: 14–16.

Mitchell, Nicole, and Elizabeth R. Lorbeer. 2009. "Building Relevant and Sustainable Collections." *Serials Librarian* 57, no. 4: 327–333.

Mulholland, James. 2014. "What I've Learned about Publishing a Book." *Journal of Scholarly Publishing* 45, no. 3: 211–236.

Overholt, John. 2013. "Five Theses on the Future of Special Collections." *RBM: A Journal of Rare Books, Manuscripts, & Cultural Heritage* 14, no. 1:15–20.

Searing, Susan E. 2012. "'The Special Collection in Librarianship': Researching the History of Library Science Libraries." *Journal of Education for Library & Information Science* 53, no. 4: 225–238.

Smith, Debbi A. 2009. "'Format Overlap of the 'New York Times': A Collection Management Case Study." *Collection Management* 34, no. 2: 94–111.

Staenberg, Linda, and Susan Vanneman. 2013. "How Special Is That Special Collection?" *School Library Monthly* 29, no. 5: 28–40.

Way, Doug, and Julie Garrison. 2013. "Developing and Implementing a Disapproval Plan; One University's Experience." *College & Research Libraries News* 74, no. 6: 284–287.

West, Marsha. 2013. "Classified Information Policy, Government Transparency, and WikiLeaks." *Dttp: A Quarterly Journal Of Government Information Practice & Perspective* 41, no. 2: 13–17.

Withey, Lynne, Steve Cohn, Ellen Faran, Michael Jensen, Garrett Kiely, Will Underwood, Bruce Wilcox, Richard Brown, Peter Givler, Alex Holzman, and Kathleen Keane. 2011. "Sustaining Scholarly Publishing: New Business Models for University Presses." *Journal of Scholarly Publishing* 42, no. 4: 397–441.

Media Collections

For many years, educators have been a little suspicious about using audio versions of books with readers. . . . Recent research in the use of audio-books is finally placing this misconception to rest.

—*Teri Lesesne, 2013*

Like VHS recorders before them, DVD and Blu-ray players will eventually vanish from U.S. households, as people transition toward options such as cloud storage for content that they own and streaming services for content they want to rent.

—*Matt Enis, 2012*

City youths looking to hone their "Call of Duty" video game skills can't do it at the Paterson's [New Jersey] libraries anymore. The library's board voted in January to ban playing direct-shooter video games on the computer at its facilities.

—*Joe Malinconico, 2013*

Emerging technologies present new challenges for librarians while stretch-ing the limits of copyright law.

—*Jud Copeland, 2012*

Media formats found in library collections do not have as long a history as paper resources; however, they have been a part of most library collections for some time. In the case of sound recordings, they have been in libraries for close to 100 years. A few formats, such as DVDs or Blu-rays, are more recent additions to library collections. Like paper resources they are still acquired and are heavily used components of almost all library collections in spite of our being in the digital age. Certainly over the coming years the media technol-ogy will evolve—past history of media in libraries provides many examples of formats that came and went. We believe that pattern will continue. The major challenge is to have the resources to phase out the older forms and replace them with the new.

Media formats are both a boon and bane for public services and the library. In 2012, Will Manley, librarian and part-time humorist, wrote about a major issue with media formats and libraries:

> Age among librarians used to be fairly easy to determine, but no longer in our era of nips, tucks, Botox, and hair coloring. And you can't just come out and ask someone his or her age; such a question today is not only impolite but possibly discriminatory.
>
> If you are really curious about how old a librarian is, the safest and most effective approach is to start talking about an obsolete library format. Here is a good icebreaker, 'Weren't phonograph records the biggest pain to process and maintain? No patron ever [admitted to] scratch[ing] an LP'. . . . If the librarian replies, 'What is an LP?' he or she is not nearly as old as you thought. (p. 64)

LPs (long playing recordings) are just one of several music recording formats libraries have had to deal with over the past 60 plus years. Just about every media format has gone through several incarnations. A few, such as microforms and filmstrips, had several variations at the same time. We come back to this issue later in this chapter.

In the not-too-distant past, many libraries treated media as marginal, if they stocked them at all. They were viewed as a way to get people into the library and then getting them "hooked on books." Many libraries, with the notable exceptions of media centers in schools and community colleges, only saw recreational or entertainment value in media materials. Primary, secondary school, and community college libraries led the way in incorporating all formats into their service programs. These institutions used media for instruction and recognized that many ideas are best expressed using a form other than the printed word. Schools regularly use media in what is called *resource-based education.* Further, the media are integrated into the library's collection. Undoubtedly one reason for this, at least in the case of schools, is the relatively limited floor space and the need to keep things simple from an administrative point of view. Why have two units, one for print and one for media, when one unit could handle the workload for both? Use of media in classrooms has been a long-standing tradition in these institutions, unlike four-year colleges and universities. All levels of education are more cognizant of the different learning styles; thus, the use of media is valued as a way to engage audio/visual learners. And, it is important to include closed captioned media for the hearing impaired population.

Academic institutions tended to view media, essentially films, as solely classroom material; even then there were doubts about its real instructional value on the part of some professors who believed, and a few still do, that use of media in the classroom was the lazy person's way of not "doing" the teaching himself or herself. Beyond that there are legal issues to consider—we address those in chapter 13. Certainly, art, film, music, and theater programs were exceptions, but they often created departmental collections, independent of the library, and only available to staff and departmental majors. Community colleges have incorporated mixed media, for example, recorded book sets that include both an audio and print version of a story. This format is popular with ESL and/or developmental language students. Sets like this are also helpful for standardized test preparation (TESOL, SAT, GED, etc.).

Public libraries were early collectors of sound recordings, and a number also developed film collections. Sound recordings circulated and over time expanded from just classical music to all forms of music and the spoken word. Motion picture films attracted groups for in-house showings and were also available for loan to groups such as scouts, churches, and occasionally schools. There are relatively few libraries today that do not have at least a few videos or DVDs in their collections.

From the Advisory Board

Jean Wallace noted that public libraries are now more apt to have collections of movies, TV shows, and so on, because more people have the capacity to play those movies in their own homes. It used to be necessary to have a 16mm projector to show a film, and that pretty much excluded the average home. The advent of VCRs and DVD players changed all that.

Media play an important role in meeting the educational and recreational needs of the service community. Some people are print-oriented, while others prefer audio or graphic presentations of information. For many types of information, a print format is inappropriate. There have been studies of the brain and how people learn, and while most are visual learners, who benefit from reading and taking notes, and so on, a fair number are primarily auditory learners. They need to hear something, and if they try to write it down, they cannot absorb the materials as well as if they just listen. Films and recordings are great for those people. Limiting a collection to one or two formats seldom provides the range of services appropriate to the service community's needs.

From the Authors' Experience

Sinwell had the following experience: When I started at my community college, we still had 16mm films. I suggested we migrate to VHS tapes, (i.e., replace the existing titles with this new format). Was I surprised at the resistance from the faculty and the media resource person! They loved their films. While we moved ahead with purchasing VHS, the media resource person *hid* the 16mm films (along with a projector) for use by his friends (the faculty). When the media person retired he took the 'hidden collection' of 16mm films with him. (Maybe they're worth money today?)

Then, as DVDs became the favored format, and IT staff was removing VHS players from classrooms, the collection librarian moved aggressively to weed the VHS collection and replace them with DVDs. Again, there was push back from faculty who wanted their VHS tapes, but they have adjusted. Two lessons were learned in this recent shift: library staff did not communicate well enough in advance with faculty before weeding VHS tapes and Blu-ray DVD's were purchased without realizing they wouldn't play in standard DVD players.

AUDIO

Few libraries are actively collecting audio recordings today other than audio books. However, in the past these were a major component of many libraries' collections. As a result, there are a variety of legacy audio formats in many collections—including CDs, cassette tapes, and phonograph records. Music recordings were among the first non-print formats collected by libraries. In public libraries, the recordings were usually part of the circulating collection. For educational libraries the purpose is usually instructional, with limited, if any, use outside the library. This is a media category that most clearly reflects the long-term influence of a changing technology on a library collection.

Some of the major music collections have older formats because the content has not yet migrated to a digital format and may never do so. Usually someone interested in hearing such material has some familiarity with the equipment, so assisting him or her is not a great problem. A few libraries are purchasing relatively low-cost equipment and software that allows one to convert phonograph records to an MP3 format. Naturally, the library must be careful to do this in compliance with copyright laws.

The LP, mentioned in the Manley quotation previously, was somewhere near the middle of the history of evolving audio recording technologies—the turn of the twentieth century there were wax cylinder recordings, LPs came along mid-twentieth century, and now it is streaming audio on the Internet. There are some archives and special collections that have wax cylinder recordings (a form of primary resources mentioned in chapter 7). You hear more scratching than music or voices on those early recordings. From a listener's point-of-view, each new generation of recording technology was an improvement in sound quality. From the library point-of-view, each change represented a potential and often realized cost factor and service challenge. The move went roughly from wax cylinders to disks that played on a turntable at various revolutions per minute (rpm, 78, 45, 33⅓). Then came cassettes of various types (single, dual, and eight track, etc.) along with several reel-to-reel formats. Those were followed by a return to disc format (CDs, they are still around). And, today, music is available primarily through digital downloads or streaming audio.

Each of the changes, assuming the library wished to stay current with the public's listening preferences, meant new equipment, and new recordings of material already in the collection but the in old(er) format. Library operating budgets have never been "generous" and having to acquire Beethoven's Fifth for the fifth time because of changing technology drained limited acquisition funds.

From the Authors' Experience

Evans once had the following experience with a new head of the music department at a university. The department head made an appointment to come to "discuss the library's music collections." Just what that discussion might entail was not made clear before the meeting. Two possibilities were that he wanted to have a larger allocation for purchasing music materials or perhaps how to achieve a music library (all materials—books, recordings, scores, etc. in one location), which was a recent recommendation of the music education accreditation agency.

His objective, it turned out, was neither of these. Rather, he wanted the library to remove all the "dinosaurs" from the collection—all but a few of the existing newest recordings. "I don't want my students listening to anything but the best quality recordings. You can sell the older material to collectors to help raise money to buy the replacements."

Evans decided it was pointless to suggest that, if collectors would be interested, perhaps the university library had some responsibility to preserve the material. He tried the notion that some of the "best" recording of certain pieces had not yet migrated to the new format and perhaps there should be a more nuanced approach to upgrading to the newest format.

At the "end of the day," after a dean, academic vice president, and even the president supported the library position of moving less hastily, many of the dinosaurs stayed. There was a three-year supplement to the music department acquisition budget to speed the process of adding the newest format.

Audiobooks

Ben Malczewski (2012) noted, "Audiobooks have endured for more than 30 years, achieving a growing success and acquiring a wider audience of print converts. . . . Libraries persist as the stronghold for audiobooks, but the medium's reach is growing—slowly" (p. 26). Audiobooks are today's most common audio recording purchase in libraries. (Note: audiobooks have migrated from cassettes to CDs.)

For public libraries, audiobooks have become almost as important as the video collection. DVD players and portable handhelds have created a major market for audiobooks. Even reading a small paperback on a crowded subway or bus can be difficult. Listening to a player that fits in one's pocket with a headset allows one to close out the noise, to some degree, and enjoy a favorite piece of music or listen to a best seller. The same is true for those commuting in their cars or just out for their "power walk." Another value of audiobooks is providing those with vision impairments additional opportunities to enjoy "print" material that goes beyond those available through the National Library Service for the Blind and Physically Handicapped (NLS, http://www.loc.gov/nls/index.html) a service offered by the Library of Congress.

Books on tape cassettes, CDs, and DABs (digital audio books) are very popular. Many libraries have formed or are forming collaborative DAB services.

Midwest Collaborative Library Services (http://mcls.org/eresources-products /vendors/recorded-books/) is one such service.

Unlike the digital music field, DAB is much more stable and does not face the copyright issues of music. There are several major vendors offering DAB products—Audible (http://www.audible.com), OverDrive© (http://www.over drive.com), and TumbleBooks™ (http://www.tumblebooks.com). There are other smaller services, offering very few titles, but as they grow they may well become significant market players. Many classical titles are freely available from Librivox (https://librivox.org/), Loyal Books (http://www.loyalbooks. com/), Lit2Go (http://etc.usf.edu/lit2go/), and Open Culture (http://www .openculture.com/freeaudiobooks) among others, but the recording quality of the selections from major vendors or other vendors such as OneClickdigi- tal (http://www.oneclickdigital.com/) will be better than what may be found when using one of the free sites mentioned earlier.

Check These Out

One source of current information on all aspects of audiobooks is Mary Bur- key and Francisca Goldsmith's Audiobooker blog, through "The Booklist Reader:" http://www.thebooklistreader.com/category/audiobooks/.

Burkey also created an audiobook lexicon, which is appeared originally on the Audiobooker blog, and also appears as an appendix to her 2013 title *Audiobooks for Youth: A Practical Guide to Sound Literature* (Chicago: ALA Editions). The lexicon is also available online: http://www.alastore .ala.org/pdf/appendix_A.pdf.

For public service staff, there may be a learning process in order to assist users who are unfamiliar or uncomfortable with downloading these titles. Many libraries offer two options for accessing their DAB service—a link from the title's MARC record or a link on the library's Web site. Almost all impose a "loan period" and a limit on the number of titles a person may have at any one time. At the time we prepared this chapter, the major issue was DAB incom- patibility with the iPod. For libraries using Overdrive (http://help.overdrive. com/#devices), this is not a problem.

There are major advantages to having DABs as part of a library's audio ser- vice program. Most notably, DABs:

- Are available 24/7
- Are never lost or damaged (at least for the library)
- Require no processing
- Require no shelf space
- Never require overdue notices or fines (files automatically get deleted at the end of the loan period)
- Provide the visually impaired another means of access to popular titles
- Allow for simple weeding
- Allow for easy collaboration
- Vendors provide usage data

In the past, academic libraries rarely offered audiobooks. DABs may change that fact. If nothing more, the fact that there is no storage space required may make the format attractive. Robert Fox (2004) explored the question of offering audiobooks in academic libraries. He found a few libraries had small collections, more through donations than an active collecting plan, but none viewed them as central to their service goals. His concluding statement was, "audiotapes *do* have a place in academic libraries" (p. 11).

Perhaps the lack of audiobooks in educational libraries will change, in part due to the research alluded to in our opening quotation from Teri Lesesne. Her article (2013) briefly discusses some of the advantages of using such materials with young people and teens. Some of those pluses are—hearing new words in a meaningful context, hearing words being properly pronounced, and assisting in meeting the listening component in the Common Core State Standards.

Check This Out

A good book to read, if you are interested in the research on and use of audiobooks with young people, is Sharon Grover and Lizette D. Hannegan's *Listening to Learn: Audiobooks Supporting Literacy* (Chicago: American Library Association, 2012).

One of the drawbacks of audio recordings (spoken word or music) is that they have a relatively short life span, five to six years, even under optimal usage conditions. They are also usually housed in small containers that have few places upon which to attach a security strip/device. Thus, their loss rate ("shrinkage" in retail terms) can be rather high. Nor, for that matter, is there much room to apply bar codes or other property markings. Replacing lost items can be costly. From both the public's and the staff's point of view, the fact that an unabridged audiobook can have as many as four to six discs means that keeping everything sorted in its proper order can be a problem. Certainly the staff must check each title that has multiple discs each time it is returned. If in fact a person is listening to, say, discs in the car and there is more than one title, there is a very good chance a title/disc will end up in the wrong container. No one wants to have the ending of a "whodunit" delayed because the last disc is for Shakti Gawin's *Creative Visualization Meditations* (New World Library).

MICROFORMS

Are microforms still a part of a library's growing collections? Surprisingly, in many instances the answer is yes. You might think that in this digital era microforms would be a legacy collection, if retained at all. This is not the case, yet. In late 2014, a check of the useful Web site, AqcWeb (http://www.acqweb.org/pubr/micro.html) indicated there are 20 firms producing and selling microforms to libraries. Some are rather well known such as Bell & Howell Information and Learning Company (probably best remembered when it operated under the name University Microfilms) and NewsBank. Some are less well known, but are significant sources for useful material, especially backfiles of newspapers. A Web search for microform equipment and supplies generates hundreds of hits, such as The Microfilm Shop (http://microfilm.com/).

From the Advisory Board

Jean Wallace shared the following example of the continued use of micro-formats: "The public library in Clinton has a collection of old newspapers on microfilm. In fact the Friends of Warner Library recently contributed a substantial sum of money to buy a gadget which would enhance the search process in very old newspapers on microfilm. They anticipate that the genealogy people will be the primary users. Also, the State of Illinois has an extensive collection of newspapers from all over the state on microfilm."

There are three primary reasons libraries did and do acquire microforms:

- To increase collection storage capacity
- To preserve delicate materials or replace items too fragile for general use
- To acquire rare/unique/special materials that exist in only one or two libraries

Check This Out

A brief, but informative outline of the history of microfilm is available at the HeritageMicrofilm.Com Web site: http://www.heritagearchives.org /History.aspx.

As we noted in chapter 7, physical collections do grow, especially serials, and there is a finite amount of storage room available in libraries. Microforms can reduce hundreds of feet of physical volumes to just a few inches. Many paper-based items in collection can become "brittle" (the paper breaks very easily). The problem was/is the acidic paper that was commonly used in books and serials through the late nineteenth century and most of the twentieth century. Microform copies can reduce handling of such items and provide access to the content while preserving the item. Commercial firms offer sets of hundreds of rare items that address a limited topic such as early publications of the sixteenth- and seventeenth-century U.S. colonies or files of early national or international newspapers.

From the Authors' Experience

An additional reason to consider maintaining microfilm holdings, particularly of newspapers, is that online equivalents may or may not be "complete." Saponaro worked at a library where the public services staff were tasked to reduce the size of the microfilm collection by half. She and a colleague had earmarked several major newspaper collections for withdrawal as they supposedly had a "complete" online equivalent. It was later discovered that the online version omitted certain photographs due to copyright. These photographs turned out to be more in demand by researchers than Saponaro and her colleague anticipated. This made it necessary to "reverse" the withdrawal order and retain the microfilmed material. Luckily, the film had not been withdrawn from the collection. The alternative would have been to fill the orders via interlibrary loan. Although this would have been a feasible alternative, it would have added a time component to the research process.

Microformats are something of a challenge for the public service staff. There are two very common microform formats in libraries—reels and fiche. Reel formats are the older of the two and were widely used for newspapers and serial collections. Reel microfilms are long strips of film on the appropriate size reel and have traditionally been available in several sizes: 16 mm, 35 mm, and 70 mm. The film can be positive (clear with black text) or negative (dark with white text). Public service staff need to know about these different types because microfilm reader/scanners are high maintenance and require adjustment for different film sizes and types. Failure to use the correct size take-up reel can damage film. Failure to adjust the reader for positive or negative film will make it difficult to produce a readable paper copy on a reader-printer machine. Most people make paper copies of microfilm items, and thus the print feature on the reader is another service need.

Most libraries try to confine their microfilm collection to one or two sizes (35 mm and 70 mm) and one type (positive). With any large-scale collection, however, more variety is inevitable, because the information needed by the library was available only in a particular size and type of microfilm. The choice is either to accept yet another variation or forego having the information. Individuals who regularly use microforms are aware of many of the problems and can make the proper machine adjustments without staff assistance, unless they spin the film off the reel or film breaks. Most individuals, however, will avoid microforms and use them only as a last resort; these people will need assistance.

Microfiche are sheets of film with the images of the original document arranged in columns and rows. Fiche were primarily employed for materials that might have a number of simultaneous users of the collection/title, such as college catalogs or telephone directories. Fiche can be a great space-saving device while providing much greater access by breaking up the file into smaller units, somewhat like drawers in a card catalog—the forerunner of today's OPAC.

Like other media, microfiche came in a variety of sizes as well as reduction ratios. Common sizes are 3 by 5 inches, 3 by 6 inches, and 6 by 7 inches, while reduction ratios range from 12 to over 200. The greater the reduction ratio, the more information the producer could fit on a single fiche. Many commercial publications were "48x" (the "x" equals "reduction ratio"), but the other relatively common ratio is "16x." The reduction ratio is an issue for public service staff because the reading machines seldom come with a single lens capable of handling all the reductions. Some of the most expensive readers have a lens capable of "zooming" from 10x to 75x. Such units were very costly, in the tens of thousands of dollars. When they break, you need to wait for repair service. If you have just one machine and it's broken, service complaints will arise.

Most libraries must get along with readers that have interchangeable lenses, that is, one lens for each of the common reduction ratios. These lenses need to be available at a public service desk and the staff need to know how to change them. Using the wrong lens with the wrong type fiche will not damage the equipment or the fiche, but it will increase user resistance to microforms. While a 16x lens with a 48x fiche will produce a very fuzzy image that, with effort, a determined individual can read, that person will be certain that microforms are a form of library torture. A 48x lens with a 16x fiche will produce a very sharp image of a very small part of the text. Reading the text will tax the patience of the most friendly user, as very small shifts of the fiche carrier result in substantial shifts in the text. One unfortunate characteristic of fiche is that they do not indicate on the eye-legible header what the reduction ratio is. If they did, it would be a great help to the library staff assisting the public. Lacking accepted standards, commercial vendors selected the size and ratio most convenient for them, perhaps to maximize their income if they produced enough material that libraries believe they must own.

Public service staff may not have to handle any of the other media formats discussed in this chapter, but it will be the exceptional library that does not have at least one type of microformat. Microforms, like serials, require substantial staff time in assisting users, who often require help with the equipment, from loading the film/fiche to focusing and getting the image "right-side up," to making a paper copy of the image needed. The staff must also refile the microforms, because allowing users to do this only creates problems later.

VIDEO

As with most other media, video has had several formats and as long as libraries have made video a component of their service program, they will present some issues for the staff. If you take into consideration the motion picture formats libraries acquired (16 and 35mm, sound and silent, etc.), the variations are almost as numerous as that of audio recordings.

Format battles in the video field have been ongoing for some years now. Perhaps the battle between Beta and VHS is best known. A more recent contest was between cassettes and DVDs. And, even more recently, the struggle for market share between Blu-ray and DVD. Libraries may once again be caught in the middle of a commercial battle where they must bet on a winning side or spend limited funds duplicating the same content in competing formats.

From the Advisory Board

Advisory board member George Oberle (George Mason University) noted that like other media formats, DVD is not a single format. DVDs come in several variations, DVD+R, DVD+RW, DVD-RAM, DVD-R, DVD-RW, DVD-ROM. These variations do have equipment implications, but rarely arise in most library settings.

Notwithstanding the Blu-ray/DVD issue, most libraries still have substantial collections of VHS tapes and DVDs. This is, in part, due to the fact that some of the general public, like libraries, invested heavily in that format and still have players. And, again like libraries, those users find it difficult to justify the money to buy the new format, even if there is a significant difference in picture quality. Another factor is that Blu-ray players will play both DVDs and Blu-ray discs; however, a DVD player will not play a Blu-ray disc. Given the discs look alike and often the library owns copies of both, mix ups can occur. Finally, there is the factor Matt Enis (2012) noted in his quote at the beginning of this chapter: still more changes are on the visible horizon. We cannot ignore continuing changes—most notably, streaming video and Internet access to feature movies and documentaries.

DVDs do present two different and significant service challenges for libraries—damage and security. Damage to DVDs is very high. One librarian, in responding to Norman Oder's 2005 survey, said that staff at their library joke that DVDs "are used for coasters and Frisbees" (p. 39). One obvious factor in the damage is that, unlike a cassette, the operating surface is fully exposed during handling of the disk. Scratches, chips, even warping are problem areas. Thus, the expected circulation life of a popular DVD is low. Many libraries think if they get 15 to 20 circulations, they are lucky.

Additionally, because of their small size, theft is a much greater problem for DVDs than is true of the VHS cassette. How to display available titles is also a challenge. Some libraries just put out empty cases. Others have tried locking display cases similar to those used in commercial outlets. A few display color photocopies of the cases and keep everything behind a service desk. (All these options clearly have staffing implications.) Libraries that try employing security strips usually drop that approach as thieves merely take the disk and leave the empty case. (We explore the use of security strips/systems in the chapter on security [chapter 16].) So far, the use of RFID (radio frequency identification) tags has not proven any more effective. Oder (2005) reported that one library indicated it had experienced losses in excess of $90,000 in less than five years of offering DVDs (p. 39). Until someone comes up with a real solution, public service staff will find they spend a significant amount dealing with DVD security matters.

Check This Out

The Video Round Table (VRT; http://www.ala.org/vrt) of the American Library Association addresses all issues related to video collections, services, and programs for video material in all formats. VRT maintains a "Professional Resources for Video Librarians" site (http://www.ala.org/vrt/professionalresources/vrtresources/resources) that includes links to published guidelines for media materials, sources for video reviews, and links to various e-mail lists for media librarians. VRT also releases an annual "notable videos" list.

DVD collections, given the quick release after its theatrical release, generate some of the same issues as the best-seller book. Everyone wants it *now*, not next month after all the talk has faded. In terms of circulation, feature film videos beat nonfiction hands down; theatricals represent roughly 68 percent of the collections, 72 percent of the expenditures, and 80 percent of the circulations (Oder, 2005, p. 40). Fortunately, there is a DVD equivalent of the McNaughton book rental plan for DVDs, where a library can lease multiple copies of a popular title for a short time and return all or some of the copies after the demand has died off (see: http://www.brodartbooks.com /mcnaughton-library-subscription-services/dvd/page.aspx?id=273). The plan supports both DVD and Blu-ray formats, and includes foreign-language titles. Some libraries opting not to establish a McNaughton plan attempt to establish a ratio of copies to requests (holds). The problem with purchased multiple copies is they occupy valuable storage space after the demand has died off and scarce money has been expended on the same content. However, not having the material available when the demand is high can have negative consequences in the form of unhappy users.

Streaming Media

One of the educational usage issues with video is that frequently an instructor only wants access to a segment from several videos in a single presentation. While it is possible to have several video players available, having all the equipment present and having all the videos properly queued is a nuisance and distraction. With streaming video it is possible to select the desired segments and put them together in the desired sequence. An example might be demonstrating how different actors/directors interpret a scene in a Shakespeare play. Redden (2005) suggested that with video streaming it is possible:

- To select segments for an entire class or an individual student
- For teachers or students to select segments for presentations
- To bookmark segments for future use
- To control the video the same as on a player (play, pause, rewind, and fast forward)
- To use selected elements in student assignments (p. 15)

Video streaming is reaching all levels of education from kindergarten to Harvard Business School. Some educational video content providers offer streaming video services and occasionally material from other producers who are not yet offering such service. Generally the charge for the streaming service is an annual fee based on enrollment.

As Matt Enis's (2012) quote at the beginning of the chapter revealed, there is currently a transition in video access from traditional formats such as VHS, DVD, and Blu-ray to cloud-based storage and retrieval options. Enis's statement alerts us to the reality that like every media format transition before, the shifts pose challenges for libraries as they attempt to serve their existing patrons and plan for the future.

Library users are migrating toward streaming services for both music and movies. Libraries dealing with transition from DVDs to streaming media formats have many video file formats to choose from; at the time of publication, the most common formats are:

- Windows Media
- RealMedia
- Quicktime
- MPEG (in particular MPEG-4)
- Adobe® Flash®

This is a very dynamic environment, so expect advancements most of which are likely to occur quickly. With change come challenges for libraries to "keep current" in the field. Some challenges include:

- Need to deal with vendors to secure/purchase streaming access
- Need to understand various formats
- Need to understand copyright issues
- Need to know how to help end user access streaming formats
- Where library provides media development centers, need to know how to produce in-house media to stream

Check This Out

One way to keep current in the area of media is the VIDEONEWS e-mail reflector from the ALA Video Round Table. VIDEONEWS is open to all individuals, and is designed to serve as a "clearinghouse for information about new services, products, resources, and programs of interest to video librarians and archivists, educators, and others involved in the selection, acquisition, programming, and preservation of video materials in non-profit settings" (http://www.lib.berkeley.edu/MRC/vrtlists.html). To subscribe to VIDEONEWS, see https://calmail.berkeley.edu/manage/list/listinfo/videonews@lists.berkeley.edu.

Access to streaming media on the Internet (video, audio, animations, etc.) is via *downloading* and *streaming*. When you *download* a file, the entire file is saved on your computer (usually in a temporary folder), which you then open and view. This has some advantages (e.g., quicker access to different parts of the file) but has the big disadvantage of having to wait for the whole file to download before any of it can be viewed. If the file is quite small, this may not be too much of an inconvenience, but for large files and long presentations it can be very off-putting.

The easiest way to provide downloadable video files is to use a simple hyperlink to the file. A slightly more advanced method is to *embed* the file in a Webpage using special HTML code. Delivering video files this way is known as HTTP streaming or HTTP delivery. *HTTP* means *hyper text transfer protocol*, and is the same protocol used to deliver Webpages. For this reason it is easy to set up and use on almost any Web site, without requiring additional software or special hosting plans.

Streaming media works a bit differently—the end user can start watching the file almost as soon as it begins downloading. In effect, the file is sent to the user in a (more or less) constant stream, and the user watches it as it arrives. The obvious advantage with this method is that no waiting is involved. Streaming media has additional advantages such as being able to broadcast live events (sometimes referred to as a *webcast* or *netcast*). True streaming video must be delivered from a specialized streaming server.

There is also a hybrid method known as *progressive download*. In this method the video clip is downloaded but begins playing as soon as a portion of the file has been received. This simulates true streaming, but doesn't have all the advantages. The method you choose will depend on your situation, but most people will opt for HTTP streaming (download or progressive download). This is the easiest and cheapest way to get started.

From the Advisory Board

George Oberle suggests that streaming is where the media business is going, but the licensing is challenging at best. He notes that libraries will be forced more and more to rely on subscription content models instead of ownership.

George noted he bought the rights to digitize materials about five years ago and it "took me lots of money to buy a media server and to host it properly once it was transformed into a web-based codex."

From the Authors' Experience

Sinwell experienced one of the "nightmares" mentioned in George's comment. She notes: My colleague and I asked for streaming video rights to a particular title, which we needed for online course we were preparing. It took the university 6 months to negotiate the rights to it.

She also has had issues with multiple students accessing a streaming video at the same time. This could be a result of multiple factors, including the wireless connection at the university or the source site.

MEDIA RATINGS AND LIBRARIES

Ratings, in terms of the appropriate viewer/user age group, are something of an issue for public service staff and libraries. The two main formats where they may be of concern are videos and computer games. Schools and public libraries are most vulnerable to getting complaints about an inappropriate-aged person getting access to the wrong rating or even for the library to have a certain rating in their collection. (We explore the issue of challenges later in chapter 14; here we need to note the issues of movie ratings and how they may impact public services.)

Certainly the reason for the ratings is for "parental guidance;" however, they do come into play when the library decides to add videos or computer games to its service activities. Even with such ratings there are differences of opinion regarding whether or not the rating on a particular item is correct (parents often have very different assessments of what is appropriate for their child and occasionally try to impose that standard on other children). It is important to keep in mind that ratings are set by the industries involved, not a group of parents or panel of child psychiatrists.

The Motion Picture Association of America (MPAA) has a rating system for its releases—the familiar G, PG, PG-13, R, and NC-17 one sees in the movie section of the newspaper and television. The Classification and Rating Administration (CARA, http://www.filmratings.com) within the MPAA handles the establishment of each film's rating. While these ratings have no legal force and, in fact, are based on the somewhat subjective opinion of the CARA rating board, the general public usually accepts them as appropriate. The key is the content of each film in terms of its suitability for children.

Although the ALA has issued a statement opposing labeling (see http://www .ala.org/advocacy/intfreedom/librarybill/interpretations/labelingrat ing), the majority of public libraries do consider the MPAA/CARA ratings when making acquisition decisions. The fact is that even a collection of G and PG rated titles does not ensure there will be no complaints. One possible way to handle the situation, although not always easy to accomplish, is to create two sections for video, one in the children's/young adult area and another in the adult area. Again, this will not forestall all complaints, but it could help. You might want to check the video policies of some other libraries (such as the Brookston—Prairie Township Public Library (IN) http://www.brookstonlibrary.org/html/videos.html, Pawtucket (R.I.) Public Library—http://www.pawtucketlibrary.org/circulationpolicies.htm, or Baltimore County (MD) Public Library—http://www.bcpl.info/services-policies /policies-procedures). From the staffing point of view, making certain that the videos are in the proper section will be something of a challenge, unless the storage boxes are clearly color-coded or marked in some way that makes sorting easy.

Like motion pictures, games have a rating system. Most video games released in North America carry a rating from the Entertainment Software Rating Board (ESRB®; http://www.esrb.org/index-js.jsp), which according to its Web site is a "nonprofit, self-regulatory, third-party entity formed in 1994 by what is now the Entertainment Software Association. ESRB® ratings consist of three parts: a rating symbol on the front of the box addressing age appropriateness, one of more than 30 different content descriptors (e.g., alcohol reference, blood and gore) elaborating on elements that may be of interest or concern to users and their guardians," and an assessment of the interactive elements of the game—such as "the ability of users to interact, the sharing of users' location with other users, or the fact that personal information may be shared with third parties" (http://www.esrb.org/ratings/ratings_guide.jsp#- descriptors). The seven ratings are EC, early childhood; E, everyone six and up; E10, everyone 10 and up; T, teen 13 and up; M, mature 17 and up; AO, adults only 18 and up; and RP, rating pending. The rating system complexity and the need to provide information about system requirements exemplify the types of challenges that face libraries that are collecting games. Games also raise some serious policy issues as noted in our opening quotation about "Call of Duty." And, of course, there is the question of how the staff are to monitor who uses what rating.

Computer games also have their equipment platform variations. There are at least 10 platforms for electronic games. Although the platforms compete for market share, the competition has not focused on whose standards or technology will win; rather, it is whose games attract and hold players' attention longest and the money spent on products for a given platform. Following are several of the most popular game platforms that were still in use in 2014:

- Amazon Fire TV
- Nintendo DS™
- PC/MAC-based games
- Nintendo GameCube™
- Xbox®
- Playstation 3™
- Xbox 360®
- Playstation 4™
- PSP® (PlayStation portable)
- Game Boy Advance®
- Wii U™

Like videocassettes, some people as well as libraries have early versions of the platforms and the games for them.

Check This Out

A good discussion of the whys of having nonbook collections is Meghan Harper's 2009 article "H. W. Wilson *Nonbook Materials Core Collection*" in *School Library Monthly* (26, no. 2: 35–37).

CLOSING THOUGHTS

Media collections play an important role in any type of library service program. Some individuals prefer to do their learning and recreational activities through media rather than paper-based resources. Media formats present several challenges for public service staff members. Some formats generate complaints about content or who gets to use what; handling such matters is usually somewhat stressful. Most of the formats involve the use of equipment, either library or user owned; in either case there are issues of repair and damage to monitor. Then there is the fact that most formats have migrated through several technological variations and many library collections contain one or more of the earlier variations. Finally, there are some legal (copyright) concerns that don't exist for print materials, adding further to staff challenges. Nevertheless, few libraries would think of foregoing one or more of these formats—users want and expect them. Librarians need to stay abreast of new formats and the eventual impact technological upgrades have on media services.

Chapter Review Material

1. What role do media play in public service programs?
2. What is the current most commonly circulated type of audio recording? What are some of the drivers of this usage?
3. Discuss the issues of evolving media formats for libraries regardless of type.
4. What are the common problems for media use?
5. Videos present some special problems for the staff. What are these problems?
6. Discuss the issue of "rating" systems in terms of library public services.

REFERENCES

Copeland, Jud. 2012. "Emerging Technologies and Copyright: A Librarian's Guide to Fair Use and Copyright." *Arkansas Libraries* 69, no. 1: 8–10.

Enis, Matt. 2012. "DVD Circ Holds Steady." *Library Journal* 137, no. 19: 38.

Fox, Robert. 2004. "Do Audiobooks Belong in Academic Libraries?" *Georgia Library Quarterly* 40, no. 4: 9–11.

Lesesne, Teri. 2013. "Reading with Our Ears: An Odyssey for All." *Young Adult Library Services* 11, no. 3: 30–32.

Malczewski, Ben. 2012. "Multitasker's Dream." *Library Journal* 137, no. 6: 24–28.

Malinconico, Joe. 2013. "Paterson Libraries Ban Playing of Violent Video Games." *PatersonPress.com.* January 27. Online. http://thealternativepress.com /towns/paterson/articles/paterson-libraries-ban-playing-of-violent-video-g.

Manley, Will. 2012. "Will's World. The Coolness Factor." *American Libraries* 43, nos. 3/4: 64.

Oder, Norman. 2005. "The DVD Predicament." *Library Journal* 130, no. 19: 38–40.

Redden, Linda. 2005. "Videostreaming in K-12 Classrooms." *Media & Methods* 42, no. 1:14–15.

SUGGESTED READINGS

Alexander, Bryan, and Paula Sullenger. 2014. "Libraries, Mobile Devices, and the Visible College." *Serials Librarian* 66, no. 1–4: 31–43.

Brandon, Robbins M. 2013. "Games and Violence." *Library Journal* 138, no. 5: 88.

Caudle, Dana M., Cecilia M. Schmitz, and Elizabeth J. Weisbrod. 2013. "Microform— Not Extinct Yet: Results of a Long-Term Microform Use Study in the Digital Age." *Library Collections, Acquisitions, and Technical Services* 37, no. 1: 2–12.

Cho, Allan. 2013. "YouTube and Academic Libraries: Building a Digital Collection." *Journal of Electronic Resources Librarianship* 25, no. 1: 39–50.

DeCesare, Julie A. 2014. "Patron-Driven Access to Streaming Video: Profile of Kanopy Streaming." *Against the Grain* 26, no. 4: 28–30.

Handman, Gary. 2010. "License to Look: Evolving Models for Library Video Acquisition and Access." *Library Trends* 58, no. 3: 324–334.

Harris, Christopher. 2013. "Gaming the Common Core." *School Library Journal* 59, no. 10: 1.

King, David Lee. 2009. "Video on the Web: The Basics." *Multimedia and Internet @ Schools* 16, no. 1: 14–16.

Linden, Julie. 2010. "Do We Need All These Microforms . . . Right Here?" *DttP: A Quarterly of Government Information* 38, no. 3: 27–30.

Ludwig, Herard. 2012. "Brown v. Entertainment Merchants Association, 131 S. Ct. 2729." *Journal of Art, Technology Intellectual Property Law* 22, no. 2: 515–526.

Malczewski, Ben. 2013. "Generation Access." *Public Libraries* 52, no. 6: 10–12.

Mariner, Matthew C. 2014. *Managing Digital Audiovisual Resources: A Practical Guide for Librarians.* Lanham, MD: Rowman & Littlefield.

Miller, Sandra L. 2013. "Innovating to Meet the Demand for Streaming Video." *Journal of Library Innovation* 4, no. 1: 29–43.

Salmon, Stephen R. 2013. "User Resistance to Microforms in the Research Library." *Preservation, Digital Technology & Culture* 42, no. 4: 209–214.

Sayward, Jacob. 2012. "Law Library Collections Post-Microform: Future Implications for the Newest Legacy Format." *AALL Spectrum* 17, no. 2: 4–5. Special section.

Schroeder, Rebecca, and Julie Williamsen. 2011. "Streaming Video: The Collaborative Convergence of Technical Services, Collection Development, and Information Technology in the Academic Library." *Collection Management* 36, no. 2: 89–106.

Scordato, Julie, and Ellen Forsyth. 2014. *Teen Games Rule! A Librarian's Guide to Platforms and Programs.* Santa Barbara, CA: Libraries Unlimited.

Chapter 9

E-Resources

What role will libraries have when patrons no longer need to go to them to consult or to borrow books? This question has already spurred massive commentary and discussion. But in the past year, as large-scale controversies have developed around several libraries, it has become pressing and unavoidable.

—David A. Bell, 2012

Ok, it's time for a little tough love for public library leaders. We haven't been as visionary, vigilant, or assertive as we need to be when it comes to mapping our future in the e-book world.

—Patrick Losinski, 2012

Digital content and libraries, and most urgently the issue of e-books, continues to be a focus (of the library community).

—ALA executive director Keith Michael Fiels, 2013

Under copyright law, anyone who buys a printed book can lend or rent it, but the same does not apply to digital works.

—The Economist, 2013

Digital formats are an important component of a library's collection. They are becoming an ever larger segment of that collection. In time they may be more than 90 percent of a collection, and in fact, many academic libraries allocate 90 percent of their current materials budget to electronic formats and only 10 percent to print collections. Digital formats play a significant role in how libraries approach public services and access to collections and content.

The opening quotations by David Bell and Patrick Losinski highlight facts that make library public service work both interesting and challenging. Radical changes are taking place and will be continuous for the library of the future, especially in terms of library public services. First, and perhaps fore-most, is the fact that today's library users expect and demand 24/7 access to library services. What makes such service a possibility has been the tech-nological developments in the Internet and e-resources. As Sarah Pritchard (2008) wrote, "In the digital environment, we still have resources, staff, and facilities that combine in various ways to acquire and provide information. These recombinations challenge traditional definitions of library organiza-tion. . . . All parts of a library are involved, not just some pieces that we can conveniently segregate as a special type of content or a special service" (pp. 219–220). In her article, she explored in some detail what those recom-binations are and how they will possibly change in the near future. It is true that it is not just e-resources that allow libraries to provide 24/7 services. However, digital resources enabled by technology do represent a major por-tion, if not the majority, of transactions and use of collections that occur when the physical library is closed.

During the early days of 24/7 service, individuals accessed the Internet from PCs or laptops and some form of hardwired connection. Then wireless access and laptops became the typical approach for surfing the Web and remains a common approach today. However, today's "mobile world" of smart phones, tablets, and the like are capable of providing Web access for people to access all manner of library resources 24/7 from a wide variety of platforms any time and any place. For example, in mid-2012, the Pew Research Center's Internet & American Life Project reported that 70 percent of all U.S adult cell phones were used to secure a piece of information, some of which was from a library resource (Rainie and Fox, 2012, p. 2). The Pew Center also noted that as of early 2014, 90 percent of the entire U.S. adult population had cell phones of some type, with 58 percent of the total population owning smartphones (*Device Ownership over Time*, 2014).

The increasing variety of platforms that people employ to access library resources means public service staff must become increasingly conversant with the library's technology and the various modes of access. Compatibility among the technologies is less than ideal; proprietary concerns can lead to finger pointing as to whose technology may be the "problem." The users really don't care about whose fault it is; they just want things to work when they want them to. As a result, when there is an issue with accessing something from the library, they call the library and expect the matter to be quickly resolved. Staff members must understand and realize they cannot handle every technical access issue; however, they also must understand that too many failures to resolve problems will reflect badly on the library. This is yet another area where staff training is critical and why budget allocations must reflect the priority of having the latest technology and a staff who is well trained in its use. Devin Crawley (2013) rather clearly highlighted the con-cern when he wrote, "For library staff on the front lines, the subtleties of user experience have been largely overshadowed by the priority of keeping up with the proliferation of new devices and demands for support. . . . Public libraries across Canada have had to jury-rig training programs both for the public and staff and encourage information desks to morph, at least partly, into techni-cal help desks" (p. 22).

From the Authors' Experience

In the spring of 2010, the director of public services at the University of Maryland Libraries identified a need to expand library employee knowledge related to mobile technologies. In increasing numbers, library patrons were using such devices, yet library staff had little experience with mobile devices or mobilized content. At that time, the campus was in the midst of a mobility initiative (http://mobility.umd.edu) to study whether incorporating mobile technology enhanced the student educational experience. Capitalizing on that campus initiative, the Libraries partnered with the campus Office of Information Technology to receive a number of iPod Touches during two months in the summer of 2010. With those devices as a base, a Mobile Technologies Pilot was developed to provide Library employees with needed experience. Saponaro served on the steering committee for this project.

Between the loaner devices and participation of employees that already owned an iPod Touch or an iPhone, about a third of the Libraries staff participated, including all of the subject liaisons. An outgrowth of the project is the "Emerging Technologies Discussion Group," which continues to meet monthly to give Library staff an opportunity to discuss technology-related services and explore new technologies. The pilot is described in: "Mobilizing Staff with Mobile Technologies" by Nevenka Zdravkovska, Maggie Z. Saponaro, and Tanner Wray (*Information Outlook*, 2011, 15, no. 8: 21–24).

When it comes to digital material that the library does in fact own (much of it, including e-books and databases, is simply leased), who will preserve those items? It costs money to retain things long term. Certainly it would/will be the most unusual commercial firm that keeps digital material that is not generating at least some income. Web sites come and go, URLs change, and so forth, making tracking down a site that is several years old something of a challenge. One library that is exploring undertaking such a monumental task such as preserving "online pages" is the British Library. Just as the Library of Congress (LC) has compiled an archive of all public tweets from Twitter and continues to preserve public tweets (Osterberg, 2013), the British Library announced in 2013 that it was going to try "an automated Web harvester [that] will scan and record 4.8 million sites, a total of 1 billion pages. Most will be captured once a year, but hundreds of thousands of fast-changing sites such as those of newspapers and magazines will be archived as often as once a day" (Lawless, 2013, p. A22). We will explore other library efforts to archive such materials later in this chapter.

A second fact, that we have not commented on before when discussing the library as a social construct, is how libraries underwrite the dissemination of information and knowledge. Libraries, especially public and school, since at least the nineteenth century have been engaging in such underwriting efforts. We believe the world would be a very different place were it not for libraries providing free access to information and knowledge. At least in the past, public libraries were often referred to as the "university of the people"—you don't hear that often any more, if at all, in this digital world. School libraries provide free access to needed curriculum support resources that only some parents could afford to buy. Even most private academic libraries allow non-affiliated individuals to consult their resources—perhaps not check out anything—but they can spend as much time they like using resources and taking notes or making photocopies. The information divide would be very much larger if libraries did not exist.

Some claim the Web has taken that role over such as the above. What is overlooked by those making such a claim is that most of the best information and knowledge of value is not freely available on the Internet; for-profit companies sell access to the information. For example, newspapers and serial publishers usually offer subscribers full online access to their publication(s) and allow others a limited number of free "page views" (in the hope some of those will become subscribers). Another example, one that we admit is almost unique, is the *Harvard Business Review* (*HBR*). If you want access to that journal, you have two options: become a personal subscriber or find a library that has an EBSCO database that contains the title. Unlike most other magazine/journals that have their full-text material in several databases, *HBR* has an exclusive agreement with EBSCO. So much for "everything of importance" being freely available on the Web.

Check This Out

Efforts to assess the usage of e-resources can be time-consuming and complicated. One resource available to assist libraries in this effort is Usus— http://www.usus.org.uk/—a joint U.S./UK project. As the site notes, Usus is intended to serve as "a medium to discuss all aspects of usage in general and ways of measuring usage in particular. Usus is designed to serve librarians, library consortium administrators, publishers, aggregators, repository managers, as well as individual scholars."

DIFFERENCES BETWEEN E-RESOURCES AND OTHER RESOURCES

There are several important aspects to keep in mind about the differences between print and digital resources. The most significant aspect is that a library rarely *owns* the electronic materials; rather, the library pays for *access* to the material and there is no physical product. As long as the library pays the appropriate fees and usage of the material complies with the license/contract, access remains available. Failure to pay will result in the vendor "pulling the plug." In today's tight economic environment, libraries are often faced with very hard choices of what resources they can maintain.

In the days when libraries did receive a physical product (e.g., CD-ROMs) containing digital content such as an indexing service, the library agreed to either return or destroy the CD-ROM upon receipt of an updated version. And, should the library not be able to re-subscribe, often the library could retain the last CD it paid for. That is a rare event in today's e-environment.

A license or contract governs the terms of access for library users. Most such documents contain the vendor's "standard agreement" clauses outlining to whom and how to provide access to the e-material. Libraries can, should, and do negotiate changes in that standard agreement. However, some vendors are more flexible than others in such matters. What that means for the public service staff is they should be very aware of what is the e-resource use agreements contain. There is a high probability of important variations in those agreements, assuming the library does negotiate changes. Often the standard limitations go against the library's service philosophy, such as being open to all or sharing resources. Some of the more common limitations are restrictions that limit or forbid the use of the content for interlibrary lending, limits on the number of individuals who may access the material at the same time (simultaneous users), restrictions on the use of the material by non-cardholders (or any user group not identified in the license), remote access availability (proxy server issues and in-library usage), and even restrictions that attempt to make the library liable for how an individual makes use of the information gathered after it has been accessed either in the building or remotely.

How the library acquires access to an e-resource can complicate matters later. Very often e-resources are acquired through a consortia arrangement. As such purchases are group based, decision making tends to be complex (many voices, many opinions) and drawn out. More often than not, the library's cost to take part in "the deal" is unknown until almost the last minute. The final cost is almost always a function of the number of libraries taking part. That means a last-minute dropout or joiner can impact the price, which in turn may influence other libraries' decision to participate resulting in a change to the cost per library. The latter factor relates to the agreement renewal period. Especially in difficult economic times, libraries have to make difficult decisions regarding what they can and cannot fund. In the case of consortia, the chances are a few members will fall on very hard times and have to pull out of the renewal agreement(s). If enough libraries have to drop out, "the deal" may become too costly for the remaining members, resulting in a lost e-resource.

Lack of permanence of e-resources, as just mentioned, actually has three aspects. First, and foremost, the library does not own the product or service. When it becomes necessary to cancel a service, it may be possible to retain access to the material that was available during the time the library paid for access. That, however, is something the library must address at the time of purchase. A second issue is that what is there today may not be there tomorrow, even though the library is fully paid up. Vendors can and do pull material from their product without notifying the library. Finally, there is the issue of long-term preservation of electronic resources in general—they are actually less permanent than traditional formats.

So the questions become, what happens if a library must drop an e-product or service? What if the vendor drops material that is of high value to many of the library's users? What if the e-vendor goes out of business? What if the e-vendor merges with another firm? The first "what if" unfortunately is a fairly common occurrence today. The second "what if" is a major conundrum; what recourse is available for the library? It is something to think about when negotiating the initial agreement. The last two, while not all that common, do take place from time to time. Later in this chapter we address preservation issues for digital materials.

In the past, when the library possessed and owned a book, journal, recording, and so forth, it retained something for the monies spent when one of the aforementioned scenarios occurred. With e-products, unless the library is careful during the initial acquisition process, the likely outcome of any of these situations is that you may be left with nothing. The money is gone, and with it, so is the information. Robert Wolf (2009) summed up the situation as follows: "We have spent the last decade building our electronic journal subscriptions without seriously considering the real obstacles to perpetual access. We know publishers offer perpetual access [at least some do], and that is good; however, we have not taken steps necessary to ensure that it is in a format we can actually use" (p. 34).

From the Authors' Experience

Saponaro can speak from experience as to another aspect of e- versus print title purchases: that of cost. She and her colleagues have noted on more than one occasion that the cost of an e-book can be two to three times that of its print counterpart. Restrictions on simultaneous users and total usage, as well as the duration of the e-book license, also must be taken into account—something that is not necessary in the print world. While selection decisions are beyond the scope of this book—it does become a public services issue when an institution is not able to purchase as many desired titles due to their combined cost.

Two articles of interest on the topic are Stanley M. Besen and Sheila Nataraj Kirby's "Library Demand for E-Books and E-Book Pricing: An Economic Analysis" (*Journal of Scholarly Publishing*, 2014, vol. 45, no. 2: 128–141) and "E-Book versus Print" by David J. Gray and Andrea J. Copeland (*Reference & User Services Quarterly*, 2012, vol. 51, no. 4: 334–339).

Saponaro has also seen from experience that faculty from certain academic disciplines (social sciences, business, STEM) are more receptive to having titles purchased in the e-book format, while those in the humanities disciplines still prefer print.

Sinwell has observed that the topic of e-book costs and purchase options is not limited to academic institutions, as this was a topic of discussion for a public library e-mail discussion list in mid-2014.

There are several aspects to the "what if" situations mentioned earlier—legal, technical, and long-term preservation. The "what ifs" apply to almost all e-products and services; however, e-serials and e-books, given their popularity with users, are the most often addressed in the literature. The technical issues are the same for e-books, music, serials, and video.

Although they may be seen as an alternative in such a situation, archival services such as LOCKSS (*Lots Of Copies Keep Stuff Safe*, based at Stanford University Libraries) and Portico (a digital preservation service) are of limited value in the aforementioned circumstances. In the case of LOCKSS, the library must have an active subscription for the title or service. That does not help in cancellation times, which are likely to continue well into the future. Portico services are also not useful for cancellation access.

At the time this volume was being prepared, few good options existed to protect the library's investment in e-resources when the library falls on hard economic times and must start canceling titles and services. There are better protections, if far from ideal, available to cover circumstances that are vendor or publisher related. Giving serious thought to the "what if the library has to cancel" question during the selection phase is rather important.

E-RESOURCE TYPES

What do we mean by e-resources? Materials, whether converted to or "born" digital, fall under the e-resources umbrella. Current usage of born digital relates to material first published or disseminated in a digital format. Some such items may later be issued in a paper format, but the initial release was electronic. We address the following in this chapter:

- Databases
- E-Books
- Streaming media (digital video and music)
- Web resource links
- Institutional repositories
- Other e-resources (e.g., Gutenberg project and Google Books)

Databases

There are several types of databases that may be found in some libraries; however, the most common are some version of an aggregator database of journal articles (e-serials). There are databases such as those offered by EBSCO in which many different publishers are represented, while others, such as Emerald, are databases of all the titles published by the firm. Each vendor has a slightly different approach to searching its product(s), which translates into keeping public service staff conversant with the variations and any changes the vendor makes to its search engine.

Check This Out

Online database searching has become an essential skill for many librarians, especially those in reference and information services. An excellent professional guide is Suzanne Bell's *Librarian's Guide to Online Searching*. The fourth edition is scheduled for publication in January 2015.

Everyone thinks e-serials are a wonderful concept, assuming they are available 24/7. They are frequently the go-to source for articles by many users. They are much more searchable than their print cousins. Journal database search engines generate more useful information in a shorter time than was ever possible for a single user in a print-only environment and provide robust search engines for precision searching. Those of us who know e-serials in greater depth recognize that the foregoing statements are more or less correct. However, we are also aware that there are some e-serial "warts," many of which users are unaware of or ignore.

Most users have a belief that print and e-journals are identical. They also believe that e-journals are superior to print titles. Funding authorities did, and some still do, believe e-journals will save money in comparison to print subscriptions. Both users and funding agencies probably rarely, if ever, think about long-term access; they believe the information will always be there. As we noted earlier, none of that is necessarily true, especially the long-term access.

Even the notion that e-resources are available 24/7 is not completely accurate. Certainly their availability is far superior to print journals given few libraries are open 24/7. However, anyone who engages in almost daily searching of journal databases has occasionally seen the "server not found" error message. Such messages are generally the result of overloaded server demands somewhere in the system. Another "service disruption" is that all servers require some maintenance, which means eventually there must be some down time.

Some publishers allow free online access when a library or an individual places an order for a print subscription. An example is the *Economist*, which allows for online access to back issues, additional material for a story in the print issue, and access to additional news stories. (As of late 2014, the *Economist* also offered a mobile version of its Web site and free mobile device apps for subscribers to access content online. Free iPod audio was also available, with professional newscasters reading the articles.) One reason for providing the access for libraries is that it appears to maintain a subscriber base, which is a factor in how the publication is able to charge advertisers—more subscribers equal a higher advertising fee. The extra material available online becomes a bonus for the library users.

One significant wart of e-serials is the "embargo." A common belief of users of such material is that the e-version is the most current. While that is often true, it is by no means always the case. Some publishers embargo some or all of their titles. That is they do not release the e-version for a period of time after the paper-based version is out. The time period varies from a month to as many as six months. Part of the publisher's reasoning is embargo will help drive sales of paper-based subscriptions.

E-Books

E-books have become a very popular format from a circulation point of view, especially in public libraries. On the other hand they have and do present some challenges for libraries and public service staff. Their popularity in public libraries primarily is in terms of recreational reading and travel material. Even if we haven't done it ourselves, most of us have heard friends talk about loading up their e-readers with books and travel guides before heading off on vacation. Erin Kelsey, Mandy Knapp, and Meredith Richards (2012) noted, "In the past year our library system has seen a dramatic increase in the use of e-books and e-readers. Circulation of e-books is 131 percent higher now than it was in 2010, with the most notable increase occurring when Amazon's Kindle was made compatible with OverDrive, our e-book vendor" (p. 42). So far the e-book has not become commonplace for classroom required texts, but more for technical issues than anything else. In time, those issues will be resolved, but as of 2014 the issues remain.

Check This Out

Library Journal conducts regular surveys on e-book usage, purchases, and trends in the K-12, public, and academic arenas—and all are available for download from its DigitalShift site: http://www.thedigitalshift.com /research/.

The typical approach, in early 2011, was for a public library to "subscribe" to individual titles from an e-book vendor, such as OverDrive©. Libraries treated an e-book like any other book in their collection—allowing ongoing circulation although they did not "own" the title. In the spring of 2011, HarperCollins announced a plan to place a "cap" on the number of circulations for e-books purchased from it; new titles licensed from library e-book vendors would be limited to 26 circulations before the license would have to be renewed (in many cases, the cost of which would be equivalent to purchasing the title again). Earlier in this chapter we raised several "what if" questions related to e-resources. In some ways, e-books are a prime example of the "what ifs" coming to pass.

In addition to limiting the number of usages for a title, the "Big Five" publishers (Hachette, HarperCollins, Macmillan, Penguin Random House, and Simon & Schuster) also have contracts that allow them to revoke and cease to offer material without prior notice. (See Charles Hamaker's 2011 "E-Books on Fire: Controversies Surrounding E-Books in Libraries," *Information Today* 19, no. 10, pp. 20–28, for a discussion of such restrictions/imitations.)

Try This

Go to each of the "Big Five" publishers' Web sites and review their e-book terms. What are the commonalities and differences? Can you see any possibility for finding common ground that would allow libraries to offer e-books in basically the same way they offer print titles?

In December 2012, David Vinjamuri made the point, "Libraries and Big Six publishers are at war over e-books: how much they should cost, how they can be lent and who owns them. If you don't use your public library and assume this doesn't affect you, you're wrong" (http://www.forbes.com/sites/davidvin jamuri/2012/12/11/the-wrong-war-over-ebooks-publishers-vs-libraries/).

As of late 2014, that war was still going on; however, there were some signs that some type of peace was being actively discussed by the two parties. One factor in leading to at least a truce is the fact that as of 2013, 76 percent of libraries surveyed by ALA reported offering e-books (ALA, 2013, p. 8). Each side has a major position—librarians believe their offering e-books increases overall sales of e-titles. Publishers believe library usage "cannibalizes" sales of e-books. It is important to note that on both sides it is a "belief" rather than a fact driving the dispute.

Perhaps some serious fact-finding would help find a reasonable solution for both sides. We can think of two possibilities that could resolve the differences, both of which have worked in libraries. Neither idea is totally desirable from the library perspective, but either would allow libraries to offer the full range of e-titles. One concept that was and still is employed with scholarly journals is a dual pricing scheme—one price for the individual and a higher price for the library—perhaps some sliding scale based on circulation (100, 200, etc.). The other idea has not been employed in the United States, but has a rather long history in many English-speaking countries—PLR, public lending right. In the countries with PLR, it is the author of a circulated work who receives compensation, but not the publisher. Also, the fees generated by PLR are paid from a general government fund. To make such a system work in the United States it would probably be necessary for the fee to be paid to the publisher and leave it to author/publisher contracts to sort out who gets how much. Perhaps the funding for such fees could come something like the Icelandic system we mentioned in chapter 1. Users wanting to "borrow" e-books would pay an annual fee for x number of books and pay extra transaction-based fees beyond the basic allowance. (This is not all that outlandish; Amazon's Kindle Owner's Lending Library is available to Amazon Prime members with their annual Prime membership fee of $99, allowing them a "free" book a month with a fee for anything accessed beyond that number.)

Check This Out

The issue of not being able to share e-books among libraries via interlibrary loan functions was the focus of a statement made in early 2014 by the Oberlin Group—"On E-Books & Libraries" (http://www.oberlingroup.org /node/14801). The statement includes a number of suggested principles to follow in the acquisition of e-book content.

As the statement notes, "Our intent . . . is to suggest that libraries and presses work together to make material available to all who need it. . . . We expect in return that publishers work with us to realize our shared mission: making good scholarly literature available to everybody who needs it." The statement is well worth a look.

No matter how the library/publisher e-books issue is resolved, assuming it is something that allows for some form of library lending, there are public service challenges to address. One major challenge is the number of platforms available (over 50) for e-books. See Mirela Roncevic's "E-Book Platforms for Libraries" (2013) for a brief discussion of each of the 51 e-book platforms. The good news is not all of the platforms are U.S. based; however, most are. Each description indicates what type of market is the focus for the firm and what broad categories of e-material it offers. Earlier in this chapter we quoted from an article by Kelsey, Knapp, and Richards. In that piece they commented on the technological challenges of e-books, noting: "Helping patrons with e-books and e-readers can be intimidating for staff. To provide the best customer service staff must be comfortable with technology and have up-to-date information to use as a reference" (2012, p. 43).

Streaming Media

As noted by James Careless (2012), "Libraries have many reasons for streaming content across the Web. Not surprisingly, these reasons often fall into line with each institution's particular mission and core audience" (p. 18). Some of those reasons reflect long-time library collection formats—music and motion pictures—while others are a combination of outreach and marketing. In the latter vain, libraries, such as the New York Public Library, stream video content from events they sponsor. Other libraries stream staff development programs. Some may post videos of their events on YouTube so people can view the material anytime they wish. Some academic and school libraries offer streaming video of commercial educational films.

One streaming educational video program is the Arizona Universities Library Consortium (AULC, the University of Arizona, Arizona State University, and Northern Arizona University libraries) that offers on-demand streaming video service (Farrelly, 2008). In 2008, the group partnered with Films Media Group, an outgrowth of the long-standing educational film company Films for the Humanities, to allow students and faculty access to all 5,500 educational videos available from the company. (The company's program, Films on Demand, is available at http://ffh.films.com/digitallanding.aspx). The AULC hosts the files on its server (Farrelly, 2008, p. 67). The arrangement is a mix of lease and purchase—AULC purchases a video that is accessed more than x number of times.

Many libraries now provide links to both audio and video material. Some of the sites offer free usage, while others charge a fee that the library collects and sends, directly or indirectly, to the appropriate copyright holder.

What are the options for libraries wishing to provide access to digital music files for their users? As of 2015, there are only a few choices available beyond securing downloads from recording companies that do not have end user–only licenses. One of the firms offering both music and video packages is Alexander Street Press. In terms of music, its collections cover classical, jazz, contemporary world music, the *Smithsonian Global Sound*® package, and a product called "American Song" that covers a variety of American music genres. The video products are primarily education oriented, but there is a variety of publicly supported television programs as well (http://alexanderstreet.com/)

Another music resource is Naxos Music Library (http://www.naxosmusiclibrary.com). It is a service specifically designed for music education and libraries. As of late 2014, its Web site indicated it had over 100,000 CD-length recordings consisting of over 1.4 million individual files, including classical, jazz, classic rock, nostalgia, and world music. In addition to the files themselves, Naxos provides access to liner notes, original cover artwork, and other production data. Other features include a pronunciation guide for composer and artist names, a glossary and guide to musical terms and work analyses, interactive music courses for Australia, Canada, South Korea, the United Kingdom, and the United States, graded music-exam playlists, and a "junior" section. Subscriber fees are based on the number of simultaneous users the library requires.

A not-for-profit "aggregator" is DRAM, which focuses on the educational community's interest in streaming music (http://www.dramonline.org/page/about). Its focus is on U.S. music. The service is available to member libraries (academic and public) and allows both in-library and remote access to its files.

Libraries offering video access must think about bandwidth. In the past, any data packet on the Internet was and, as of the time we prepared this section, still is, treated the same (net neutrality). That is, no packet has a higher or lower priority for transmission. What some bandwidth service providers (e.g., telephone and cable companies) propose is a system of preferential service for those who pay a fee. What that would mean, if it happens, is any organization paying a fee could deliver faster, better quality material (especially image-rich files such as video) than those not paying the fee. Those proposing the change argue that packets that take up more bandwidth should pay a higher fee and the current system penalizes everyone with having slower service. Opponents suggest such a system would allow those with "deep pockets" to dominate service. As of 2014, how the disagreement will play out was up in the air, although the U.S. Supreme Court, in a different case, ruled in mid-2013 that government agencies could set rules. That decision will support the FCC's (Federal Communications Commission) net neutrality stance (Wyatt, 2013, n.p.).

Check This Out

For more information on the network neutrality issue, see the American Library Association's Network Neutrality advocacy page—http://www.ala.org/advocacy/telecom/netneutrality.

Our point to consider when discussing bandwidth is that libraries must carefully consider how capable their technological infrastructure is before moving into online video activities. Available bandwidth matters for both the sending and receiving parties.

There are two aspects to online video and libraries—access to content produced by others and access to library-generated content. Both are likely to increase in importance over time as it is obvious people like visual materials. Just looking at the growth of YouTube makes it clear how attractive video material is for many people.

Library-generated content is a topic beyond the scope of this book, but is something that some libraries are currently doing, as we noted earlier. It is an area that is likely to grow quickly and become part of many libraries' service programming. Although commercial video production company quality may be desirable, it is clear that anything even slightly above the average YouTube quality is acceptable to most people. Thus, with even modest equipment and some planning, time, and effort on the library's part, a library can produce acceptable online video content. What are some of the possibilities?

- On demand "how-to-use" instruction for library services/databases
- On demand information literacy sessions.
- On demand library tours
- On demand reviews of collection resources by staff and/or users
- On demand staff training sessions
- On demand on "how-to-do" pieces on some activity (not necessarily library related—fixing a leaky faucet—with perhaps a connection to existing library resources)
- Public relations material, coverage of library events, storytelling, and so forth

The list is limited only by your imagination and, of course, the time to do it.

We have already mentioned two sources of online video—Alexander Street Press and Films Media Group. A third player in this arena is OverDrive©. OverDrive© (http://www.overdrive.com/) is the only one of these three vendors that offers popular movies, television series, and children's programs. We also mentioned Naxos in the section on online music; that firm also provides online video of musical performances and is strong in the area of ballet. Another specialized source of online video is IndieFlix (http://www.indieflix.com), a service providing access to independent films and licensed to libraries by Recorded Books (Klose, 2014, n.p.).

Web Resource Links

As any well-informed Web user knows, there is "stuff" and "good stuff" on the Internet. Libraries make serious efforts to help others learn how to assess Web sites and other e-resources through programs such as information literacy sessions or courses. Another approach is to post links to the "good stuff" that are believed to be accurate, informative, and useful on library Web sites.

Unlike other resources, a value of Web sites is that they are dynamic. One great advantage of Web pages is they are relatively easy to update, delete material, or even take down. They also have a habit of changing URLs with no notice. Thus, unlike other resources that do not change in location or content once they are in the collection, Web sites are constantly evolving. That in turn means someone must monitor the sites that the library provides links to on a regular schedule.

Surfing the Internet can be enjoyable, but is not all that efficient for identifying potential appropriate sites for linking from the library's Web pages. Seeking out online Webliographies (often prepared by librarians) is a quicker approach. Another method is to look at links that other libraries have in place. Most libraries have a formal or informal list of libraries they consider their peers which they employ from time to time for comparative purposes. Starting with those libraries' links is a good way to monitor what may be of interest to library users. Discussion lists are yet another source for identifying possible additions for your links.

One long-standing online resource, at least in Internet terms, for learning about Web sites that have been "reviewed" by information professionals is the Internet Scout Project (http://scout.wisc.edu). The service has been operational since 1994. It describes itself as follows: "Scout's acclaimed reports and resource archives provide educators, students, researchers, and librarians with fast, convenient ways of staying informed about the most valuable online resources. Our most popular publication, the Scout Report, is one of the Web's oldest and most respected current awareness services. Published every Friday since 1994, it is received by more than 50,000 readers every week" (http://scout .wisc.edu/about). Another resource that can be particularly useful in school and public library settings is "Great Websites for Kids," sponsored by the American Library Association's Association for Library Service for Children (http://gws.ala.org/).

Professional journals that review library materials generally also review potential Web resources—for example, *Booklist*'s "Reference on the Web" section. *College and Research Library News* has an "Internet Resources" section in most of its issues that are topical in character. Although many of the topics are oriented toward higher education, many others are not. A few examples of subjects that could be of interest to any type of library are:

- Online biographical resources (July 2014)
- Finding government statistics on the Internet (March 2014)
- Learn computer programming and Web design (November 2013)
- Resources for locating international publications (May 2013)
- SK8 zines—The craze and menace of skateboards (March 2013)
- Learning languages on the Web (February 2013)

Past issues are available online (http://crln.acrl.org/) and are worth an occasional review.

Institutional Repositories

There is no doubt that scholars and researchers, regardless of their discipline, have added new approaches to their collaborative activities over the past 20 to 25 years as the Internet became ever more reliable. It took a long time, more than 100 years, for librarians to begin to get a handle on what has been called the "invisible college" and associated "gray literature." New methods of communication and the ease of collaborating with scholars around the world have made the challenge for information professionals greater than ever. One method for meeting the challenge is by creating an institutional repository (IR).

IRs are an effort to capture and make available as much of the gray literature as possible. The IR concept itself is relatively new, with the term first being introduced post-2000. Clifford Lynch (2003), a proponent of information technology and of expanding its scope in libraries, defined IRs as:

> a set of services that a university offers to the members of its community for the management and dissemination of digital materials created by the institution and its community members. It is most essentially an organizational commitment to the stewardship of these digital materials, including long-term preservation where appropriate, as well as organization and access or distribution. (p. 328)

What is gray literature included in IRs? Gray literature was and is the text and data that result from the sharing between scholars. Only a small proportion of a researcher's work ever appears in the "open" or published literature (books and journals). Close colleagues often share drafts of potential open literature material. Feedback often leads to changes and deletions, with the published version being very different from the early drafts. It was and is a vetting process that takes place prior to the traditional prepublication vetting. Some of the material that does not make "the final cut" can provide useful clues to further work for others, if they learn about the material. Conference papers and presentations were and still are of value to people long after the program is over. Only a small percentage of such papers ever appear in the open literature. In the past, exchanging copies of such presentations was common. Today such exchanges still take place, but in electronic form. For a library serving researchers, tracking down hard copies of such presentations was difficult at best. That difficulty is compounded today.

During its early days IRs were and remain primarily academic library based. In our view, the concept is useful in almost any type of library setting. Why not have a school or school district develop an IR? It could contain a variety of special papers, projects, even recordings of special events. Public libraries could greatly enhance their local history collections by employing an IR. Perhaps they could create partnerships with local free newspapers, which might not be preserved, to add the material to an IR. In a very real sense, IRs are institutional archives that are readily available through the Web.

From the Advisory Board

Jean Wallace noted that local genealogical societies might want to contribute to such IR activities as well: The Dewitt County Genealogical Society had a project to record tombstone data of every cemetery in the county, no matter how small. Some of them are now unreadable so the pamphlet the society printed is the only source for that data.

Creating an IR for such material enhances preservation as well as increasing accessibility.

A major open source repository software program is DSpace (http://www.dspace.org). Other options for institutions interested in creating IRs include the Digital Commons® from bepress (http://digitalcommons.bepress.com/), Eprints' (http://www.eprints.org) Open Access and IR services, and ExLibris's Rosetta (http://www.exlibrisgroup.com/category/RosettaOverview). A library must decide which option will work best for its planned application.

Check These Out

For more information on IRs, check out the following:

The Institutional Repository: Benefits and Challenges, by Pamela Bluh, Cindy Hepfer, and Marisa L. Ramírez (Chicago: Association for Library Collections & Technical Services, American Library Association, 2013).

Lasting Impact Sustainability of Disciplinary Repositories, by Ricky Erway (Dublin, Ohio: OCLC Research, 2012). http://www.oclc.org/research/publications/library/2012/2012–03.pdf.

"Beyond the Repository: Rethinking Data Services at the University of Maryland" by Robin Dasler, Trevor Muñoz, and Karl Nilsen (*Contributed Papers, SLA Annual Conference 2013*. http://hdl.handle.net/1903/14743).

"Have Digital Repositories Come of Age? The Views of Library Directors" by David Nicholas, Ian Rowlands, Anthony Watkinson, David Brown, Bill Russell, and Hamid Jamali (*Webology*, December 2013, 10, no. 2: 1–16).

Older, but still useful publications on the topic included the fall 2008 issue of *Library Trends*, which included "Introduction: Institutional Repositories: Current State and Future," by Sarah L. Shreeves and Melissa Cragin (57, no. 2, pp: 89–97) and Nancy L. Marin and K. Kirby Smith's *Current Models of Digital Scholarly Communication* (Washington, D.C.: Association of Research Libraries, 2008).

Digitized Printed Books

Every discussion of e-resources must address another type of e-book—printed books that are converted to a digital format. A host of questions arise from such efforts and the primary issues arise around copyright law. Beyond the legal questions there is a question about how to handle the costs involved in doing such projects—there is more than one such effort. The one project that almost everyone involved in information work knows something about is the Google Books Library Project (GBP). However, GBP is neither the first nor the most recent effort to digitize existing books that are not in an electronic form. Two other endeavors are Project Gutenberg and HathiTrust—both are not-for-profit (unlike GBP). Project Gutenberg pre-dates GBP by a great many years, while Hathitrust is more recent and, in a sense, came about due to the "what if" scenarios we have mentioned more than once in the chapter. Before discussing those two activities we will start with GBP in order to provide some context for understanding what the major issues are.

To say GBP has mixed reviews from many people is an understatement. Probably the only people completely happy with the concept are the attorneys who represent the various parties involved in the litigation regarding GBP. Lawsuits have been a part of the project almost from day one and may occur in the future. Many more years are likely to pass before everything is sorted out by the courts. What the ultimate arrangement will be is impossible to predict. While it seems highly likely to be different from what currently exists; however, it will exist in some form.

The goal of the GBP, in a nutshell, is to digitize all the books in major U.S. and foreign libraries and make them available to anyone. Of course there are some advertisements associated with what a person views. Access varies due to various factors, principally copyright. End users who search the system see "basic bibliographic information about the book, and in many cases, a few snippets—a few sentences showing your search term in context. If the book is out of copyright, you'll be able to view and download the entire book. There are links to online bookstores where a person may buy the book as well as libraries from which it can be borrowed" (http://books.google.com/googlebooks /library.html).

Currently, the project scans all items in a participating library's collection, not just those in the public domain—and does so without gaining permission from copyright holders. Despite the fact that currently only selected portions of copyrighted texts are visible in search results, this approach, as you might imagine, upsets a number of authors and publishers, thus the legal wrangles.

Check These Out

The American Library Association maintains a Google Books Settlement site: http://www.ala.org/advocacy/copyright/googlebooks.

In addition, Charles W. Bailey has created a "Google Books Bibliography," which provides background to the GBS affairs (http://www.digital-scholarship.org/gbsb/gbsb.htm).

It is unclear what the drafters of the 2005 agreement had in mind by the phrase "not commercially available." Are books for sale by out-of-print dealers "commercially available"? It seems likely that the dealers would say so as many of the titles in their stock are not yet in the public domain and are available for purchase. There is no indication there was anyone from that field at the table when the proposed settlement was reached in 2005. Today, the future is slightly clearer—but is not completely settled. In mid-November 2013, federal circuit court judge Denny Chin dismissed a lawsuit (*Authors Guild v. Google*), which questioned the legality of Google's work to scan articles. Libraries considered the ruling a win (Chant, 2013, p. 14). Not surprisingly, the Authors Guild did file an appeal (Chant, 2014, n.p.). Thus, it will still be some time before we can realistically assess the impact of the project on library services and library budgets.

Turning to not-for-profit endeavors, we look first at HathiTrust as it is most similar to GBP in scope and purpose. The program began in 2008 by a group of academic libraries; as of mid-2014, it had 90 member institutions collaborating in its digitization program (http://www.hathitrust.org/). Most of the members are large research university libraries, but it also includes a few colleges, two consortia, and several non-U.S. universities.

In many ways, the effort is a reaction to GBP and those pesky "what if" questions related to long-term access to digitized materials. Some of the original founding members were involved in the GBP program. As such, the library received a database of all its digitized materials as part of the agreement to allow Google access to its collections. These databases became the starting point of the ongoing effort. Three of the endeavor's major goals are:

- To build a reliable and increasingly comprehensive digital archive of library materials converted from print that is co-owned and managed by a number of academic institutions
- To help preserve these important human records by creating reliable and accessible electronic representations
- To create a technical framework that is simultaneously responsive to members through the centralized creation of functionality and sufficiently open to the creation of tools and services not created by the central organization. (http://www.hathitrust.org/mission_goals)

As of late 2014, the collection contained 6.3 million book titles and 4.47 million volumes (roughly one-third of which are in the public domain) and 323,000 serial titles (http://www.hathitrust.org/about).

Steven Seidenberg (2013) summed up current thinking about the project's importance by noting, "HathiTrust will likely strengthen libraries' willingness to digitize their collections and to use their digitized copies in new ways" (p. 21). It seems likely that whatever those new ways are, lawsuits from copyright holders will follow. The concept of fair use must be resolved as a whole and not in snippets in various court decisions: decisions which often appear to be in conflict with one another.

The longest-standing book digitization project is Project Gutenberg. This project started in 1971, long before Google was a glimmer in someone's mind or libraries thought seriously about digitizing print material. It is a volunteer effort to digitize works in the public domain (no longer covered by copyright). Although the number of titles available is not nearly as large as the collections of GBP or HathiThrust, each of its titles is fully available at no cost. In addition to the U.S.-based projects there are similar undertakings in other countries such as Australia and Canada. Thus, the number of titles available from "sister projects" makes the total available larger than you might expect. The organization makes an important point—"all our books were previously published by *bona fide* publishers" (http://www.gutenberg.org/wiki/Main_Page). In our opinion, Gutenberg efforts are an overlooked valuable library resource and one well worth promoting and providing as a link for users.

Our final project is a library collaborative effort related to digitized collections. While it is slowly getting off the ground, it may well become something like OCLC that started small and grew to be an international giant in the information field. We are referring to the Digital Public Library of America (DPLA) undertaking. Founded in late 2011, DPLA's interest is in any type of digitized cultural patrimony, not just print resources. The organization does not engage directly in digitization work; rather it facilitates access to material that has been digitized. Thus, "the Digital Public Library of America brings together the riches of America's libraries, archives, and museums, and makes them freely available to the world" (http://www.dp.la/info). This is done by providing:

1. A *portal* that delivers students, teachers, scholars, and the public to incredible resources, wherever or not they may be in America.
2. A *platform* that enables new and transformative uses of our digitized cultural heritage.
3. An advocate for a strong *public option* in the twenty-first century. (http://www.dp.la/info)

In time, as more and more organizations become partners, this may well become *the* place to go for top quality digital information.

DIGITAL PERMANENCE

Some believe that being digital means longevity far beyond anything paper can accomplish. Unfortunately that is a misconception. If anything, digital material is trickier to deal with than paper. This is due in large measure to the rate of change in technology. Preserving digital resources is a very complex issue.

Why is it complex? There are a number of technical issues for starters. There are ownership issues that are no longer straightforward. For example, freelance writers may retain all rights beyond first publication; this fact is important when their material becomes part of a digital package from a publisher or aggregator who also has rights (see *New York Times Co. v. Tasini*, 533 U.S. 483 [2001] for an example). Finally, there are issues relating to who realistically has an interest in and the resources available to preserve the material in the long term. Ingrid Mason (2007) made the point that "technological innovation per se is unpredictable and volatile, and, in itself, poses feasibility issues for collecting organizations and their fitness to respond proactively to develop the means to acquire and preserve digital material" (p. 200).

Let's start with the technology aspect of long-term preservation. One way to approach the challenges is to split the issues into two broad categories— storage and access. How and where digital material is stored is a factor (e.g., floppy disks, zip drives, tape drives, CDs, and the cloud). Some readers may not know much about, or even know of, some of these formats. That is our point. Digital storage devices change rapidly, as does the rest of technology.

How long the stored data will last and remain error free long term is unknown. Some years ago, it was reported that despite NASA following best practices, up to 20 percent of the digital data it had from the 1976 Viking mission to Mars was gone or unreadable (Stepanek, 1998, p. 128). Thirty-five plus years does not seem long term to us. Scholars today can read the Dead Sea Scrolls written thousands of years ago as well as provide interpretations of their meaning. Yet it is difficult—and at times impossible—to read digital data we stored not all that long ago.

Check This Out

An interesting assessment of digital longevity is Roger Pogue's 2011 commentary "Seeing Forever: Digital Photos and Videos Are Great, but Don't Expect Your Grandkids to See Them," in *Scientific American* (304, no. 4: 34).

From the Authors' Experience

Another of the many hats Evans wore at Loyola Marymount University was that of campus archaeologist and liaison with the local Native American group (Tongva nation). In the early 1980s, the university acquired property for a campus expansion that contained two archaeological sites. A firm was hired to excavate portions of the sites and prepare a report for the university (1984 and 1986).

Between 1994 and 1997, the university expansion took place. In 1998, the Tongvas requested that the university create a campus memorial for the two village sites that were destroyed by the expansion activities. The university president asked Evans to handle the matter. As a starting point, Evans read the report about the 1980s fieldwork that was in the library archives department. Much to Evans's surprise, the second chapter of the report indicated that it was a two-volume document; however, no one at the university indicated they had ever seen volume 2. Volume 2 would be essential for any further analysis of the literally tons of excavated material housed at the university. Without that information, the material was just so much junk. The plan was to rebury the material under the memorial site, if the provenance information (volume 2) was not recovered.

The archaeological firm did not have a paper copy. All it had from all of its work in the 1980s were floppy disks for a Tandy (RadioShack) computer. Archaeologists did not want the material reburied, especially by the firm that did the work. It took the company 29 months and a considerable amount of money to recover the data. (It also started converting all its old Tandy disks to the then current standards.)

This incident makes the clear point that both storage and access are linked in ways that present long-term preservation of information a challenge.

Access is the second technological issue that relates to hardware, operating systems, and software capable of retrieving the stored information or data. All of these elements change over time, and not an insignificant number disappear from the marketplace. The storage device may have uncorrupted data, but are the hardware, operating system, and application available as functional entities? Where do you find, in 2015 and beyond, XyWrite or WordStar applications? You can, for a fee and for free if you have enough time to do the work, get files converted. Check out the various options on the Web.

Libraries have serious concerns around such issues. Many academic libraries house a special collections department and perhaps also the institutional archives. In addition, libraries have to wonder about the long-term commitment of commercial vendors of databases after the older materials cease to provide an adequate income stream. Who will indefinitely archive such material and at what cost? As more academic libraries create IRs, thoughtful consideration needs to be given to long-term preservation and how to maintain document integrity. Yaniv Levi (2008) stated:

> While many libraries and information centers have digital asset management systems or digital repositories for managing and storing digital objects, these systems are not designed with the preservation of the digital knowledge in mind. Rather they focus on access management, or facilitating the day-to-day use of digital content by users. On the other hand, digital preservation is about guaranteeing the future usability of and accessibility to digital content. (p. 22)

Answering the question about who should be responsible for digital preservation is not easy. Four main players have an interest in doing so as well as some responsibility. The originators (authors) of the content have a vested interest, but few of them have resources to do much beyond making backup copies of their work and rarely have time to migrate the material from platform to platform.

Publishers and the vendors who package and sell access to the information have the greatest resources, both technologically and financially, to address the preservation issue. However, given that most of them are for-profit entities, their focus is on revenue generation (and even not-for-profits generally have to break even financially), and they have little incentive to retain material that fails to produce income. The reality is that long-term storage of very low-use material will do almost nothing positive for the bottom line of such organizations.

Individual libraries and cooperative library efforts are the other two groups with a strong interest in long-term preservation. In the past, these two groups handled preservation activities and neither originators nor sellers took much notice; but today, information and intellectual property have taken on a significant financial value. As a result, publishers and vendors generally no longer sell the material, but rather lease it to libraries and place limits on what a library can and cannot do with material—including long-term preservation.

For digital serials that are purchased via individual subscriptions—that is, not as a part of a publisher or vendor package of serial titles—a library might be allowed to create a "dim" or "dark" archive on its server for material for which it paid the subscription price. (A digital *dark archive* is one that allows no public access to the stored information except under the most exceptional circumstance—a trigger event—such as the publisher going out of business. A *dim archive* allows some limited public access under less drastic circumstances—such as an extended period where online access is otherwise unavailable.) As noted by Kenney and her colleagues (2006), "What librarians really want, in short, is at least a dim archive—though the level of dimness can vary" (p. 55). If the activity falls to individual libraries, there will likely be costly duplication and probably great holes in the coverage.

Four of the more established cooperative efforts are:

JSTOR (http://www.jstor.org): Today, over 8,400 organizations worldwide participate in JSTOR, which was founded in 1995 and archives scholarly high-quality academic journals in the humanities, social sciences, and sciences, as well as monographs and other materials valuable for academic work. The archives are expanded continuously to add international publications.

In 2009, JSTOR merged with and became a service of ITHAKA (http://www.ithaka.org/), a not-for-profit organization to help the academic community use digital technologies to preserve the scholarly record and to advance scholarship and teaching in sustainable ways. Libraries pay a rather substantial annual fee—tens of thousands of dollars—to participate in the program. See http://about.jstor.org/10things for more details.

LOCKSS (Lots Of Copies Keep Stuff Safe, http://www.lockss.org/): Based in Stanford University Libraries, LOCKSS is an international community initiative that provides libraries with digital preservation tools and support so they can easily and inexpensively collect and preserve their own copies of authorized e-content (http://www.lockss.org/lockss/How_It_Works). In addition to numerous libraries participating in the program, as of mid-2014, over 530 publishers had elected to use LOCKSS as their digital preservation and post cancellation partner.

OCLC Digital Archive™ (http://www.oclc.org/digital-archive.en.html): One of many services and products offered by OCLC. It is also a local library digital preservation system with an integrated monitoring and reporting mechanism.

PubMed Central® (PMC; http://www.ncbi.nlm.nih.gov/pmc/): The National Library of Medicine/National Institutes of Health provides a free digital archive of biomedical and life science journal literature through PubMed (http://www.ncbi.nlm.nih.gov/pmc/about/intro/).

As we enter the second decade of the twenty-first century, there are two relatively new collaborations emerging as leaders in the field: HathiTrust (mentioned previously) and the Library of Congress's National Digital Stewardship Alliance (http://www.digitalpreservation.gov/ndsa/). In late 2010, the Library of Congress announced the formation of the Stewardship Alliance as a "partnership of institutions and organizations dedicated to preserving and providing access to selected databases, web pages, video, and audio and other digital content with enduring value" (http://www.loc.gov/today/pr/2010/10–178.html). As of late 2014, there were 320 partner institutions in the Alliance, including United States and international members from the academic and commercial sectors, as well as the state and national levels.

CLOSING THOUGHTS

Libraries rarely own e-resources; they are licensed *access* to the material. This fact creates some significant issues regarding long-term preservation and access. As of 2015, there is little progress toward reaching some long-term resolution to the "what if" questions.

With traditional print materials, you do not have many "people issues" to think about. Perhaps the only real concern might be whether a title selected will cause complaints about its inclusion in the collection. Such is not the case with e-resources. There are both end user and staff factors to take into account.

Ease of use is a major consideration regarding almost all e-resources. How easy is it for the public to use? how much staff assistance will be required? Each e-vendor will try to differentiate its search capability/product(s) from other vendors by employing a proprietary search engine and features. Each new vendor, for the library, is likely to have something different regarding access methods for its material. Clearly, the more intuitive the search processes are, the better for both the user and staff.

Products or services that involve downloading activities often call for staff involvement. First-time users of the product or service are likely to require some assistance even when the person has experience with downloading materials, as the vendor is likely to have some special requirements. There are some services that require creation of a user account or individualized password by the library staff. In addition, there may be fees associated with the service that the library is responsible for collecting. All of these activities add to the staff workload, which seems to grow exponentially with little prospect of adding new staff. Another related matter is, given extended library service hours and the fact that most users assume anyone working in a library is a "librarian," more public service staff will need detailed training for the new product. It is no longer just the reference librarians who must know more than a little about each e-product or service.

We conclude this chapter with a news note from January 2014. Bexar County (Texas) public library opened what it labeled the BiblioTech library in fall of 2013 with a digital-only hub that has 10,000 e-books, 600 e-readers, and close to 100 computer stations. Through the BiblioTech, library patrons can access digital works on their personal devices by linking their cards to a 3M Cloud Library app. The organization's mission is to "provide residents the opportunity to access technology and its applications . . . equipping residents of our community with necessary tools to thrive as citizens of the 21st century" (http://bexarbibliotech.org/about.html). It appears to be the first public library to attempt a paperless collection.

How well this will play out is an open question as of the time we prepared this chapter. We know of several academic libraries as well as one school library tried to do this and after much fanfare began to acquire paper-based and media formats for their collections. There may well be a difference between libraries that must support educational programs and one for the general public. Such a shift is likely to successfully take place down the road, but not likely during the lifetime of this edition. There are also issues regarding how much true access to the wealth of digital information people and libraries actual can afford under current economic conditions. We explore the "digital divides" that exist in some detail in chapter 11.

Chapter Review Material

1. Discuss the most significant difference between "traditional" collection materials and most e-materials.
2. There are several "what if" questions that can arise in relation to e-products and services. Discuss those questions and their possible answers. Are the questions different for different types of libraries: public, academic, school, special?
3. Both traditional and e-formats will likely coexist for some time to come. Each has something to offer libraries and their users. What are those factors?
4. Technological considerations can be critical to a library's decision to offer or not offer an e-service. Discuss those considerations.
5. E-books are here. Do you see use increasing? What factors would support or hinder an increase?
6. For libraries, the proprietary aspect of the current devices creates substantial challenges and cost considerations. What are those challenges?
7. Streaming video is a challenge for some libraries where bandwidth is limited; why is that, and how can libraries address the issue?
8. Institutional repositories, while currently used to increase access to and use of scholarly information, have long-term potential for all libraries as technologies become easier to implement and maintain. Discuss several of the advantages of establishing an institutional repository.
9. Discuss the pros and cons of the current efforts to digitize libraries "traditional" collections.

REFERENCES

American Library Association. 2013. *The State of America's Libraries 2013.* Chicago: ALA. http://tinyurl.com/salr2013.

Bell, David A. 2012. "The Bookless Library: Don't Deny the Change, Direct It Wisely." *The New Republic* 243, no. 12: 31–36.

Careless, James. 2012. "Libraries Harness the Power of Streaming Media." *Searcher* 20, no. 9: 18–24.

Chant, Ian. 2013. "Lawsuit against Google Books Dismissed." *Library Journal* 138, no. 21: 14.

Chant, Ian. 2014. "Authors Guild Appeals Dismissal of Google Books Lawsuit." *LibraryJournal.Com.* April 16. Online. http://lj.libraryjournal.com/2014/04/litigation/authors-guild-appeals-dismissal-of-google-books-lawsuit/#_.

Crawley, Devin. 2013. "Public Libraries and E-Books: After a Tumultuous Honeymoon, Seeking a Stable Marriage." *Feliciter* 59, no. 1: 21–23.

Economist. 2013. "Electronic Lending and Public Libraries: Folding Shelves." 406, no. 8828: 65–66.

Farrelly, Deg. 2008. "Use-Determined Streaming Video Acquisition: The Arizona Model for FMG on Demand." *College and University Media Review* 14, no. 1: 65–78.

Fiels, Keith Michael. 2013. "Executive Director's Message. Reenvisioning ALA." *American Libraries* 44, nos. 1/2: 6.

Kelsey, Erin, Mandy Knapp, and Meredith Richards. 2012. "A Practical, Public-Service Approach to E-Books." *Public Libraries* 51, no. 1: 42–45.

Kenney, Anne R., Richard Entlich, Peter B. Hirtle, Nancy Y. McGovern, and Ellie L. Buckley. 2006. *E-Journal Archiving Metes and Bounds: A Survey of the Landscape.* Washington, D.C.: Council on Library and Information Resources. http://www.clir.org/pubs/reports/pub138/pub138.pdf.

Klose, Stephanie. 2014. "Stepping into the Stream: Bringing Netflix-Style Video to Libraries. *Library Journal Reviews.* April 7. Online. http://reviews .libraryjournal.com/2014/04/media/video/stepping-into-the-stream-bringing-netflix-style-video-to-libraries/.

Lawless, Jill. 2013. "UK: British Library Works to Archive All Online Pages." *Arizona Republic* Sunday, April 2: A22 (an Associate Press report.)

Levi, Yaniv. 2008. "Digital Preservation: An Ever Growing Challenge." *Information Today* 25, no. 8: 22.

Losinski, Patrick. 2012. "A Call for Vigilance on the E-Book Front." *Library Journal* 137, no. 14: 26–28.

Lynch, Clifford. 2003. "Institutional Repositories: Essential Infrastructure for Scholarship in the Digital Age." *ARL Bimonthly Report,* no. 226. Washington, D.C.: Association of Research Libraries.

Mason, Ingrid. 2007. "Virtual Preservation: How Has Digital Culture Influenced Our Ideas about Permanence?" *Library Trends* 56, no. 1: 198–215.

Osterberg, Gayle. 2013. *Update on the Twitter Archive at the Library of Congress.* Library of Congress Blog. January 4. Online. http://blogs.loc.gov /loc/2013/01/update-on-the-twitter-archive-at-the-library-of-congress/.

Pew Research Internet Project. 2014. *Device Ownership over Time.* January. Washington, D.C.: Pew Research Center. http://www.pewinternet.org /data-trend/mobile/device-ownership/.

Pritchard, Sarah. 2008. "Deconstructing the Library: Reconceptualizing Collections, Space, and Services." *Journal of Library Administration* 48, no. 2: 219–233.

Rainie, Lee, and Susannah Fox. 2012. *Just-in-Time Information through Mobile Connections.* Washington, D.C.: Pew Research Center's Internet & American Life Project. http://www.pewinternet.org/2012/05/07 /just-in-time-information-through-mobile-connections/.

Roncevic, Mirela. 2013. "E-Book Platforms for Libraries." *Library Technology Reports* 49, no. 3: 33–42.

Seidenberg, Steven. 2013. "Searching the Stacks: Legal Questions Surrounding Google Books Lead to Infringement Suit against Libraries." *Inside Counsel* 24, no. 252: 20–21.

Stepanek, Marcia. 1998. "From Digits to Dust." *Businessweek* April 20, no. 3574: 128–130.

Vinjamuri, David. 2012. "The Wrong War over E-books: Publishers Vs. Libraries." *Forbes Blog.* December 11. Online. http://www.forbes.com/sites /davidvinjamuri/2012/12/11/the-wrong-war-over-ebooks-publishers-vs-libraries/.

Wolf, Robert. 2009. "Budget Crisis: A Review of Perpetual Access." *North Carolina Libraries* 67, no. 1:34

Wyatt, Edward. 2013. "A Ruling Could Support F.C.C.'s New Neutrality Defense" *New York Times Bits Blog.* May 20. Online. http://bits.blogs.nytimes .com/2013/05/20/aid-for-f-c-c-in-defending-its-net-neutrality-rules/?_ php=true&_type=blogs&_php=true&_type=blogs&ref=netneutrality&_r=2.

SUGGESTED READINGS

Bishop, Chanitra, and Marijke Visser. 2013. "E-Books? So What's the Big Deal?" *Young Adult Library Services* 11, no. 3: 4–8.

Bobay, Julie. 2008. "Institutional Repositories: Why Go There?" *Indiana Libraries* 27, no. 1: 7–9.

Breeding. Marshall. 2011. "E-Book Lending: Asserting the Value of Libraries as the Future of Books Unfolds." *Computers in Libraries* 31, no. 9: 24–27.

Byrne, Richard. 2012. "Summertime and the Reading Is Easy." *School Library Journal* 58, no. 7: 13.

Colvin, Jenny. 2010. "For Your Consideration: Models for Digital Music Distribution in Libraries." *Music Reference Services Quarterly* 13, nos. 1/2: 35–38.

Enis, Matt. 2013. "Mobile Evolution." *Library Journal* 138, no. 2: 34–36.

Enis, Matt, and Meredith Schwartz. 2012. "HathiTrust Digitization Project Ruled Fair Use." *Library Journal* 137, 18: 18–20.

Frederiksen, Linda, Joel Cummings, Lara Cummings, and Diane Carroll. 2011. "E-Books and Interlibrary Loan: Licensed to Fill?" *Journal of Interlibrary Loan, Document Delivery & Electronic Reserves* 21, no. 3: 117–131.

Hoseth, Amy, and Merinda McLure. 2012. "Perspectives on E-Books from Instructors and Students in the Social Sciences." *Reference & User Services Quarterly* 51, no 3: 278–88.

Katz, Linda S. 2013. *Managing Digital Resources in Libraries.* Hoboken: Taylor and Francis.

Kirk, Shana. 2013. "Random Access: The 21st Century Audio Library—Dusty Shelves Be Gone!" *American Music Teacher* 62, no. 5: 60–63.

Leary, Heather, Kacy Lundstrom, and Pamela Martin. 2012. "Copyright Solutions for Institutional Repositories: A Collaboration with Subject Librarians." *Journal of Library Innovation* 3, no. 1: 101–110.

Matarazzo, James & Pearlstein, Toby. 2013. "E-Books in Corporate/Special Libraries." *Online Searcher* 37, no. 3: 41–48.

Mattson, Ingrid, and Linda-Jean Schneider. 2013. "Negotiating and Complying with Electronic Database Agreements: Why Understanding Your Users' Expectations Can Make All the Difference." *AALL Spectrum* 17, no. 4: 9–12.

Mehrpour, Saeed, and Yaser Khajavi. 2014. "How to Spot Fake Open Access Journals." *Learned Publishing* 27, no. 4: 269–274.

Nichols, Jane. 2011. "Perusing Google E-Bookstore." *Collection Management* 36, no. 2: 131–136.

O'Brien, David, Urs Gasser, and John G. Palfrey, Jr. 2012. *E-Books in Libraries: A Briefing Document Developed in Preparation for a Workshop on E-Lending in Libraries.* Harvard University, Berkman Center Research Publication No. 2012–15. http://ssrn.com/abstract=2111396.

O'Leary, Mick. 2011. "HathiTrust Shapes Libraries' Digital Future." *Information Today* 28, no. 10: 20–21.

Percy, Joanne. 2013. "E-Book Lending: The Challenges Facing Interlibrary Loan." *Interlending & Document Supply* 41, no. 2: 43–47.

Piper, Paul S. 2013. "The Library's Future Is Digital: HathiTrust and the Digital Public Library of America." *Online Searcher* 37, no. 2: 22–26.

Pogue, David. 2010. "The Trouble with E-Readers: Electronic Books Are Still Too Crude to Replace Ink and Paper." *Scientific American* 303, no. 5: 36.

Polanka, Sue. 2012. *No Shelf Required 2: Use and Management of Electronic Books.* Chicago: American Library Association.

Rainie, Lee, Kathryn Zickuhr, and Maeve Duggan. 2012. *Mobile Connections to Libraries.* Washington, D.C.: Pew Research Center's Internet & American Life Project. http://libraries.pewinternet.org/2012/12/31/mobile-connections-to-libraries/.

Samples, Jacquie, and Ciara Healy. 2014. "Making It Look Easy: Maintaining the Magic of Access." *Serials Review* 40, no. 2: 105–117.

Sanders, Martha Rice, Bob McQuillan, and Amy Carlson. 2012. "On Beyond E-journals: Integrating E-books, Streaming Video, and Digital Collections at the HELIN Library Consortium." *Serials Librarian* 62, nos. 1/4: 189–195.

Shamel, Cynthis A. 2012 "The Future Is Now!" *Searcher* 20, no 9: 32–45.

Thatcher, Sanford G., 2014. "Legally Speaking—What Does the HathiTrust Decision Mean for Scholarly Publishers?" *Against the Grain* 26, no. 4: 46–49.

"Unlocking the Riches of HathiTrust." *American Libraries* 2013, 44, nos. 1/2: 40–43.

Walters, William H. 2014. "E-Books in Academic Libraries: Challenges for Sharing and Use." *Journal of Librarianship & Information Science* 46, no. 2: 85–95.

Weiss, Andrew. 2014. *Using Massive Digital Libraries: A LITA Guide.* Chicago: ALA TechSource.

Wolf, Robert. 2009. "Budget Crisis: A Review of Perpetual Access." *North Carolina Libraries* 67, nos. 1/2: 34.

Zickuhr, Kathryn, Lee Rainie, and Kristen Purcell. 2013. *Younger Americans' Library Habits and Expectations.* Washington, D.C.: Pew Research Center's Internet & American Life Project. http://libraries.pewinternet.org/2013/06/25/younger-americans-library-services.

Zickuhr, Kathryn,, Mary Madden, and Joanna Brenner. 2012. *Libraries, Patrons, and E-Books.* Washington, D.C.: Pew Research Center's Internet & American Life Project. http://libraries.pewinternet.org/2012/06/22/libraries-patrons-and-e-books/.

Part III

Specialized Programs and Services

Chapter 10

Variations in Programs and Services

To effectively serve 21st century library users, librarians must strongly challenge their current assumptions about patron needs, service programming, and about their own roles as information professionals.

—*Daryl Youngman, 2002*

It is clear that the library's success is about more than the circulation of books, magazines, audiotapes, videos and other content it contains. What really makes it worth the millions to build it is the library's staff's ability to transform it into a true community meeting place. The library now hosts an average of 45 public events per month. It has a children's area, work space, meeting rooms, Wi-Fi access, and a coffee shop. It is not your grandmother's library—library staff is there to help, not shush, you. Each visit is a community experience.

—Steamboat Today *(Steamboat Springs, Colorado) editorial, 2013*

The library is fulfilling a "shadow mandate," addressing the social service needs of patrons in addition to checking out books. . . . city libraries have become multipurpose community centers, offering business services, tax assistance, safe havens for children after school, and places where immigrants can learn English.

—*Irene McDermott, 2012*

The emphasis on addressing community needs created an atmosphere that inspired staff members to reexamine their roles.

—*Julie Cruise, 2013*

"What makes your library special?" is a question to which you will hear a variety of answers reflecting local conditions. However, almost all of those answers will contain elements of three themes—great staff, outstanding service to our community, and interesting programming. In this chapter, we look at the programs and services libraries make available to their communities that go beyond the basics of circulation, document delivery, instruction, and reference. Some of the services and programs we discuss in this chapter are variations on one or more of the foregoing activities while many go far beyond that.

As all of the opening quotations suggest, a library's primary focus must be on its service community. Essentially no two service communities are identical. Cruise, author of one of the opening quotations of the chapter, wisely noted that "traditional, one-size-fits-all libraries ignore the needs of those who rely on the institution for personal growth and assistance" (2013, p. 33). Since each service community is slightly different, there is no guarantee someone else's program will translate effectively to your library. Many services or programs will translate across libraries but most will require a tweak or two to provide the best fit for your community. (We suggest reviewing the section on "What Users Want" in chapter 2 for a discussion of understanding your community.)

As our opening quotation by Daryl Youngman states, today's libraries must rethink their assumptions about user needs, wants, and desires. Youngman (2002) went on to suggest: "As fewer patrons avail themselves of traditional desk-based reference services, increasing numbers of users are taking advantage of remote-access library services that are often served with no option to seek librarian help. Libraries must be positioned to deliver services to this new generation of academic library users whose expectations and use patterns differ markedly from their predecessors" (p. 1). The fact is, all types of libraries, not just academic, face the same situation.

From the Authors' Experience

Evans, when teaching in library school, worked with a student on a master's degree paper that looked into the issue of creating new services or programs for a public library. With the assistance of 16 library directors, a literature review, and Evans, the student developed a list of potential programs and services. The student surveyed the library staff (librarians, support, and part-time) about what programs or services they thought the community might want. The same survey was later mailed to all the residents of the community.

A somewhat surprising result was the fact that the part-time staff (pages, volunteers, etc.) most accurately reflected what the residents stated they would like to see offered. The librarians' assessments were the furthest removed from the residents' thoughts on the matter. The study emphasized the importance of conducting a community assessment whenever thinking about expanding one's services—guessing or just going by press releases about the newest and best new activities in other libraries is not a good idea.

We wish to stress that rethinking does *not* mean that all the standby services are relegated to the dustbin. Far from it; most if not all services are still highly regarded by users. Some services, such as reference, are morphing into more virtual forms, but the basic reference procedures remain at the heart of the process regardless of the delivery mechanism. We touch on a variety of old and new services in this chapter. We cannot predict what new services will become the "new standbys," even in the very near future; public service staff members just have too active imaginations to make any accurate predictions.

Although the *Steamboat Today* editorial and Irene McDermott quotations are public library focused, their basic message applies to all types of libraries—today they are *not* your grandmother's library in service or philosophy. Public libraries have had a major advocate for their importance to society for more than 40 years—Urban Libraries Council (ULC). In 2011, ULC identified five key leadership roles for public libraries:

- Civic educator
- Conversation starter
- Community visionary
- Community bridge
- Center for democracy in action. (Becker, 2012, p. 21)

The Becker article provides several examples from existing library programs for each of the roles. We believe the roles, with a little tweaking in phrasing, apply to any type of library.

Check These Out

The following are some articles that further delineate the expectations that many people, including funding authorities, have for today's libraries:

Dowd, Nancy. 2013. "If You Don't Have Time for Partnerships, Chances Are Your Community Won't Have Time for You." *Library Journal Online.* August 5. http://tinyurl.com/lg3kldk.

Edwards, Julie Biando, Melissa S. Rauseo, and Kelley Rae Unger. 2011. "Community Centered: 23 Reasons Why Your Library Is the Most Important Place in Town." *Public Libraries* 50, no. 5: 42–47.

Herrera, Kevin. 2013. "Tough Decisions: Phasing Out a Popular Option to Maintain Overall Service Viability." *Bottom Line: Managing Library Finances* 26, no. 3: 109–115.

Simmons, Keith, and Kent Oliver. 2012. "Library Trustees as Community Connectors." *National Civic Review* 101, no. 4: 24–26.

Yelton, Andromeda. 2012. "Expanding Access to Devices, Collections, and Services." *Library Technology Reports* 48, no. 1: 19–24.

Young, Rashad. 2012. "More Than Just Books: The Role of Public Libraries in Building Community and Promoting Civic Engagement." *National Civic Review* 101, no. 4: 30–31.

People often employ the terms service and programs, in relationship to libraries, as one and the same. They are, in fact, rather different. Joan Rietz's

Online Dictionary for Library and Information Science employs the phrases access services and library programs to differentiate between the concepts:

> *Access services*: The provision of access to a library's resources and collections, which includes the circulation of materials (general circulation, reserves, interlibrary loan, document delivery), reshelving, stack maintenance, security, and signage. (http://www.abc-clio.com/ODLIS/odlis_A.aspx)
>
> *Library program*: An activity or event (or series of events) scheduled by a library for the benefit of its patrons. Examples include book talks, read-a-thons, and summer reading programs for children and young adults. (http://www.abc-clio.com/ODLIS/odlis_l.aspx)

The following are some of the more common programs and services that libraries of various types offer. We discuss most of them in this chapter.

Programs	*Services*
Book clubs/discussion	Consumer information
Summer reading	Job assistance
Story hours	Outreach (home/institutional bound)
Lecture/presentations	Small business support
Literacy (language/technological)	Laptop/equipment loans
Exhibitions	Meeting rooms/study spaces
Homework assistance	Mobile circulation service
Gaming/role playing	College access information
Life Long Learning	Genealogical assistance
Puppet shows/craft programs	English as a Second Language resources
Music recitals/concerts	Research consultations

It should go without saying, but we will emphasize the point, that whatever programs are offered should be closely linked to the library's mission, goals, and objectives. Sometimes program ideas get ahead of the library's formal documentation. This rarely causes a serious problem, but it is always wise to check your idea(s) against the stated library purposes before going too far into the planning process.

Obviously, the library's environment plays the dominant role in the selection of what to offer. What is desirable in a school media library setting is unlikely to be appropriate for an academic library. However, you should not dismiss out of hand a service just because you've only read about it being offered in another type of library. The underlying concept may well become suitable, if one thinks about it and "tweaks" it a little.

We have organized the remainder of this chapter into two sections—programming and services. Both categories are far too broad to describe all their components. However, we do cover the most common activities in each category as well as note some less common ones. A few are library type specific, such as story hours, while others, such as presentations, apply to almost all types of libraries. Table 10.1 identifies the programs and services of a public library, while table 10.2 lists the programs and services at a school library.

TABLE 10.1 Programs and Services Offered by the Flagstaff City—Coconino County Public Library (Spring 2014)

Programs	Services
Storytimes/Dial a story	Reference (in person/telephone/ online)
Computer and Device (i.e., iPads and Kindles) Tutoring and Classes	Circulation (including e-books and Downloadable audio
Job Assistance	Bookmobile
Flagstaff Reads and the Big Read	Palsmobile (Preschoolers Acquiring Literacy Skills)
Lego Club	Talking Books
Anime Club	Public computers
Author Visits and Book Signings	Large type books
Star Wars Day	Interlibrary loan
Holiday Celebrations (Halloween Harvest, Winter Wonderland)	Meeting room
Movies	Microfilm reader and scanner
Book clubs for adults and kids	Scanner
Stories to Life	Photocopier
Summer Reading Program for adults and kids	Kurzweil Reading Edge
Teddy Bear Picnic	CCTV
Learning Lectures	Book Club Kits
	MonoMouse and Shoppa
	Laptop Loans

TABLE 10.2 Programs and Services Offered by the Arlington County Public Schools (Spring 2014)

Programs	Services
Book Clubs	Circulation
Summer Reading programs	Readers advisory
Reading incentive programs	Information literacy instruction
Author visits	Maker space (3D printing)
Book fairs	Audiovisual equipment
Family library night	Laptop and other technology loans
Teen Advisory Boards	Homework help
Other programs	Interlibrary loan
	Gathering resources for teachers
	Other services

TABLE 10.3 Programs and Services Offered by the University of Maryland College Park Libraries (Spring 2014)

Programs	Services
Future of the Research Library Speaker Series: The Evolution of Open Access	Terrapin Learning Commons
Edible Book Festival	Finals Week Extended Hours
Speaking of Books . . . Campus Authors Series - Emily Landau, Dept. of English— Spectacular Wickedness Sex, Race, and Memory in Storyville, New Orleans - Howard Norman, Dept. of History— I Hate to Leave This Beautiful Place	Information literacy instruction
Love Our Gadgets	3D and poster printing
Library Award for Undergraduate Research	Group study rooms
GIS Workshops	Laptop and other technology loans
WUMC Symposium: Saving College Radio	Writing centers—graduate and undergraduate
Google Glass	Interlibrary loan/UBorrow (CIC)
Online exhibits, including: - How We Might Live: The Vision of William Morris - Women on the Border: Maryland Perspectives of the Civil War - Nancy Drew and Friends: Girl's Series Books Rediscovered - Taking a Leading Role: Women in Broadcasting History	Circulation/course reserves
	Adaptive Technology Lab
	Article Express (Desktop Article Delivery)

TABLE 10.4 Programs and Services Offered by the Northern Virginia Community College, Annandale Campus Library (Spring 2014)

Programs	Services
Faculty Author Celebration—faculty spoke about being writers/writing process/their books	Circulation/course reserves
Plagiarism—programs offered each fall for faculty/students	Audiovisual equipment
Writing Across Curriculum—faculty and library staff offered three-part series on "how to write papers for different disciplines"	Laptop and other technology loans

Programs	Services
Writing style guides tips—programs offered each fall	Group study rooms
	Media center
National Library Week Activities	Information literacy instruction
- an International Poetry Reading where students and faculty from various countries gathered to read poems in their native languages, with English translations projected behind them for the audience to follow along	Blogs
- a Student Poetry Contest co-sponsored with the writing center with a reception where students could read their poems and get recognized for their work	
- an Edible Book Contest	
- a book reading by distinguished Prof. Terry Alford from his upcoming work about John Wilkes Booth—to be published by Oxford Press	
- a panel discussion with faculty and staff about how libraries were important for them growing up and how they can be very important to seniors as well	

Tables 10.3 and 10.4 list the services and programs offered by a university and community college library.

PROGRAMMING

We noted earlier in the Rietz definitions; programs are activities that benefit users. It is important to clarify such activities may well draw aspects of a library's service program. In fact many do so; however, that element is not the driving factor in having the program. In this section of the chapter, we discuss some of the most common programs offered by libraries. We start with a basic goal of almost every library—lifelong learning.

Lifelong Learning

Lifelong learning is a good example of the mix of "user benefit" and access to library resources. In a sense, all library activities foster lifelong learning whether or not people view them that way. Every library item, borrowed or used, has the potential of furthering a person's learning—yes, even reading popular genre items such as mysteries, romances, and westerns.

What people mean when using the term lifelong learning varies widely. There are dozens of definitions; however, there appear to be three core elements on which most people agree. One element is that it is often informal; the individual decides what and how to learn about something. A second aspect is that it is often sporadic in nature; the individual can start and stop at will and there can be long and short pauses between those activities. Finally, it is personally driven; no outside agency or person directs the process. The underlying key is it is open to anyone willing to make the effort, not just those matriculated in an educational program, nor does it require any level of attainment.

Lifelong learning, to be effective, requires collaboration between educators and libraries. Sara Gillis and Julie Totten (2006) describe a highly successful collaborative program in the Halifax Public Library and the school district, while Lighthart and Spreder (2014) detail a successful long-term partnership between Creeds Elementary School and the Pungo-Blackwater Public Library in Virginia Beach, Virginia. On the other hand, Alan Bundy (2006) suggested that educators often seem more concerned with teaching a curriculum rather than lifelong learning. (There are some significant reasons for that focus, at least in the United States. One of the reasons is that schools can lose funding when their students don't achieve certain levels on standardized tests.) Perhaps curriculum focus is an opportunity for libraries where they can, with educator input, take on some of the broader aspects of lifelong learning. Bundy went on to say: "So what is meant by education? Is it learning the three Rs? Is it learning physics, chemistry, and math? Is it learning languages or about a country's history and politics, geography and economy? Is it about value development?" (p. 128). No matter which of his questions, or the host of others, one focuses on, libraries are one of the places where independent learning can occur. One of the roles the public service staff can and must play in the process is to assist the individual in identifying the most appropriate resources for what he or she wishes to learn about. Bundy ended his article with a plea for greater cooperation and coordination between educators and libraries.

Literacy Programs

One significant educational issue is just how much concern society should have about the level of reading literacy. Certainly the Urban Libraries Council's "civic educator" role suggests it is a significant concern for some national groups. Computers and related technologies may be what today's youth focus on and understand and those technologies are likely to increase as factors in our daily lives. However, people who never read a book and only use computers still must be able to read and understand the written words that appear on the screen. In 2007, the National Assessment of Adult Literacy (NAAL) issued a report on adult literacy in the United States. The study looked at three types of literacy (Kutner et al., 2007, p. iii):

- Prose (the knowledge and skills needed to search, comprehend, and use information from continuous text),
- Document (the knowledge and skills needed to search, comprehend, and use information from noncontinuous text, such as labels on medicines, job applications, and tables), and
- Quantitative (the knowledge and skills needed to identify and perform computations using numbers that are embedded in printed materials, such as calculating discounts and handling a checking account).

The report compared data collected in 1992 with data from 2003. Overall, the results were rather disappointing, if not surprising. "White and Asian/ Pacific Islanders adults had higher average prose, document and quantitative literacy than Black and Hispanic adults. Black adults had higher prose and document literacy than Hispanic adults. . . . A higher percentage of adults with below basic prose, document and quantitative literacy lived in households with income below $10,000 than adults with higher levels of literacy" (Kutner et al., 2007, p. v). The proficiency levels measured were "Below Basic," "Basic," "Intermediate," and "Proficient."

Nicole Whitehead (2004) noted "that frequent reading is directly related to higher performance in reading" (p. 165). She focused on the school library environment. One of her findings was that "groups that visited the library eight to twelve times within the six month study period had higher averages in most of the areas measured (5 out of 7) in comparison to the group that did not go the library as a class" (p. 172). She examined six areas—reading performance, attitudes toward reading, time spent reading at home, number of books in the home, family and class visits to the community library, and the child's "ownership" of a library card. At least in this study, the public library did help improve classroom performance in reading, especially when the child had a library card and the family and class visited the library. We look at early literacy in the Story Hour section of this chapter.

An interesting program that involves both parents and children is the Boulder Public Library's "Reading Buddies" (Sherry, 2004, http://www .boulderreads.org/services/buddies.html). The idea grew out of the fact that many of the adults who took part in the library's adult literacy program had child care issues. The library and the local university's school of education developed a program where a student teacher became a "buddy" to one of the children with a parent in the literacy class. The service, while encouraging the children to read with their buddies, also wished to help the children with their homework. Mentors helped the children find material in the library, played word games with them; a few even wrote a "book" with their buddy. Because the student teachers receive service-learning credit they proved reliable and motivated. Their buddies were very enthusiastic and regular in their attendance as well. The program continues today as part of a larger BoulderReads! literacy initiative.

An article about reading buddies appeared in the November/December issue of *American Libraries*—dog buddies. "The concept is simple: students read aloud to animals—usually dogs—instead of their peers, and the fear of making a mistake will subside, allowing them to achieve their full reading potential" (p. 30). An interesting idea positive and negative potential; both of which the article explores.

ESL Programs

Related to lifelong learning and literacy is ESL (English as a Second Language) programs. In part, these services arise from the fact that most schools, of all types, have full ESL courses as well as waiting lists. Many libraries employ technology to provide a structured, but self-paced, means of learning English. There are downloadable programs for learning English based on the native

language of the learner—for example, Pimsleur Language Program (http://www
.pimsleur.com/) and Rosetta Stone (http://www.rosettastone.com/). There
are, of course, the PC-based programs in many libraries that offer the learner/
user the opportunity to get assistance from the library staff. This does of
course require the public staff members to be familiar with the programs, or
at least the basics of using them. To date, we are not aware of any challenges
to offering such programs, unlike some of the concerns about print materials.

Check These Out

In addition to the BoulderReads! literacy program at the Boulder Public
Library, other notable ESL/literacy programs are:

Austin Public Library's New Immigrants Program—which provides
access to study centers, multilingual materials, software programs, as well
as sponsors "Talk Time" conversational programs in seven APL locations
(http://www.austinlibrary.com/newip/).

Los Angeles Public Library Adult Literacy Services Programs—include
tutor programs for adult literacy, as well as offer for limited English proficiency and family literacy (http://www.lapl.org/adult-literacy).

Jones Library (Amherst, MA) E.S.L. Center—considered a "model for
civic integration efforts at community libraries" provides tutors, study
materials, classes, and referral services (http://www.joneslibrary.org/esl
/index.html).

Queens Library Adult Literacy-ESOL Program—literacy classes enroll
over 3,000 students per year from over 80 countries, while the English practice program includes access to learning activities and educational field trips (http://www.queenslibrary.org/services/adult-literacy
/learn-english).

Story Hours

Many public libraries have story hours for preschoolers to encourage reading.
Are story hours an element in lifelong learning and literacy? We believe they
are. A successful story hour program will instill in many, if not most, listeners
a love for a well-written and presented story and encourage them to explore
other stories on their own.

Although early reading efforts have a long history in public libraries, recently
(early in this century) ALA, the Public Library Association, and Association for
Library Service to Children have strongly promoted the concept. Every Child
Ready to Read (ECRR) (http://www.everychildreadytoread.org/) is a major
imitative that started in 2004 which focuses on parents. Library story hours
have always been to some extent models for parents to follow at home with
their children. ECRR formalizes such models and offers libraries several "tool
kits" to promote the concept as well as assist parents in their efforts to have
their children become literate as soon as possible.

Books for Babies (http://www.ala.org/united/products_services/booksfor
babies/) is another early literacy project of the profession's. This effort provides

parents of new borns with ideas for getting the child's lifelong learning off to a fast start, at least in terms of literacy. Two other initiatives in this area are Born to Read (http://www.ala.org/alsc/issuesadv/borntoread) and Striving Reader's (http://www.ala.org/advocacy/sites/ala.org.advocacy/files/content/literacy/earlyliteracy/ec_striving_readers_fy2010.pdf).

Most libraries with such a program offer different groupings for their story hours, such as babies, toddlers, preschoolers and families. Many libraries are also offering special story times for children with different challenges, like autism. (Two examples are the offerings of the Seattle Public Library—http://www.spl.org/audiences/children/chi-for-parents-and-caregivers/sensory-story-times and Scotch Plains Public Library—http://www.scotlib.org/2014/06/sensory-storytime-for-children-of-all-abilities-10/). The time is usually divided into the telling of the story and other activities to engage the listeners' attention. Not all of us are good story time presenters, even with book in hand. Good presenters go well beyond a few voice changes for characters and tonal qualities. They draw in the listeners by getting the audience to engage in the story with a variety of techniques such as pointing something in an illustration, or asking a question what do they think? Essentially the presenter expands the listeners' awareness that the story has messages beyond the words on the page. Presenters also often suggest other titles; "if you liked this story try these stories." Such methods help develop an interest in exploring other materials and thinking about meaning, both of which are keys to lifelong learning and increasing literacy.

Three interesting free online storytelling sites of note are "Story Time for Me" (http://storytimeforme.com/stories/1http://www.stoylineonline.com/), Starfall (http://www.starfall.com), and Storyline Online (http://www.storylineonline.net/). "Story Time for Me" offers a variety of stories that change over time. Starfall is a site that helps children with reading or reading more effectively, and the books are animated with audio. Perhaps the most interesting of the three is Storyline Online. It offers stories read by members of the Screen Actors Guild. There are also a variety of online storytelling sites that require a payment/subscription; a good starting point is Elizabeth Figa's "Storytelling Websites and Resources (http://www.courses.unt.edu/efiga/STORYTELLING/StorytellingWebsites.htm). The ALA also offers the Every Child Ready to Read® initiative, which is specifically designed to teach parents, caregivers, and anyone who works with young children skills to improve a child's literacy through story hours (http://tinyurl.com/ndy6flb).

Check These Out

Two resources of note for individuals interested in storytelling are Nina Schatzkamer Miller's *The Storytime Handbook: A Full Year of Themed Programs, with Crafts and Snacks* (Jefferson, NC: McFarland, 2014)—which includes 52 weekly themes, and Susan Anderson-Newham's *Cooking Up A Storytime: Mix-and-Match Menus for Easy Programming* (Chicago: American Library Association, 2014).

Summer Reading Programs

Summer reading programs have been a public library staple for a very long time. An equally long-standing question is which goal is most important in summer reading programs—promoting lifelong reading, providing children with an enjoyable summer activity, or maintaining, if not increasing, reading skills during the summer, or all of the foregoing? We believe the answer is all are equally important; however, achieving all three is very challenging for single activity.

A key method for accomplishing these goals, as well as helping to reinforce reading gains of the past school term, is to work with the local schools. Walter Minkel (2003) acknowledged it requires real effort to develop a sound relationship with the various schools; however, the children are the long-term beneficiaries of the effort. In some school districts, librarians from the public library visit every elementary school to do "book talks," give information, and generate enthusiasm for their summer reading program. A factor in a successful summer program is getting the word out to parents. If one can get the schools to distribute a flyer about the program near the end of the school year, participation increases substantially. These programs also increase circulation during what can be otherwise slow times.

Something to ponder is, how do you measure the success of a summer reading program? Does it matter who is doing the assessment—public library or school district? Is it a matter of how many children sign up? The number of children who complete the program? The number of titles read? Can you measure changes in reading skills? What are the long-term outcomes, if any, of the program? These are just a few of the possibilities.

Aimee Meuchel (2013) raised some interesting points about summer reading success. She suggested that a library is unlikely to see 50 percent of those signing up actually complete the program. In addition, she suggested that a program based on incentives/rewards sends the wrong message. Further, that motivation research indicates that an intrinsic reward will motivate a desired behavior in an unmotivated person, but—it is a big but—only for as long as there are rewards.

A motivated child is very likely to enjoy being rewarded for doing something that is already enjoyable. What about the unmotivated child? The child may engage in the desired behavior, if the reward/bribe is attractive enough. However, when the reward is gone or deemed unattractive the child goes back to what he or she enjoys doing.

Check This Out

A book that fully explores the issue of using rewards to promote desired behavior is Alfie Kohn's 1993 *Punishment by Rewards: The Trouble with Gold Stars, Incentive Plans, A's, Praise and Other Bribes* (Boston, MA: Houghton Mifflin).

Some answers to the earlier questions, if not the issue of rewards, may be found in the article by Natalie Cole, Virginia Walter, and Eva Mitnick (2013). They wrote, "The value of outcomes–based programming is well documented. . . . However, despite this, summer reading programs are not commonly planned or evaluated according to outcome-based principles. Consequently, the impact of summer reading programs is undocumented, although we suspect they are not fulfilling their potential" (p. 38). The authors go on to describe two statewide (California) outcomes intended to document actual success of summer reading activities. You can view the two outcomes at http://www.cla-net.org/?81.

Many libraries now make the summer program a family affair rather than solely child-focused. With parents involved, children realize reading is important, and it may motivate parents to read more often with their children. One method some libraries employ to keep families active in the program is to have the family "write a book" about their summer experiences and offer some modest prizes for the best stories. Whatever you do it should be fun, first and foremost. While there are innumerable guides and Web sites on the topic of summer reading programs, the Association for Library Services for Children (ALSC), a division of the ALA, has a Web page devoted to the topic that is well worth reviewing from time to time: http://www.ala.org/alsc/compubs/booklists/summerreadinglist.

Book Discussion Programs

Library-based book discussion groups have almost as long a history as story hours. Sara Stevenson (2005), a middle school librarian, wrote, "My favorite time of day is after lunch when I host our book clubs" (p. 48). She offers four clubs—horror, fantasy, mystery, and "girls' time out." Stevenson's ultimate goal is to make the children better students while making reading and thinking about what is read fun. Her article outlines a number of activities that are fun and, at the same time, moving toward her long-term goal.

Book clubs, book discussion groups, or whatever term one employs for the activity more often than not have several common characteristics—they are informal, have no rules/bylaws, have little structure, and have people dropping in and out without notice. Sessions may be informative or even enlightening, but first and foremost they are to be enjoyable. Many public libraries offer several types of groups—genre based (like Stevenson's), literature of a country or author, and nonfiction topics such as politics or history. The process also varies from group to group—some have everyone read the same book; another approach is to have each member read a different book and lead a discussion; still others use a mixed approach. A library staff member often acts as a group facilitator. Occasionally a library is fortunate to secure the volunteer services of a scholar to handle a group.

From the Advisory Board

Advisory board member Jackie Gropman, retired regional children's manager of Fairfax County Public Libraries (FCPL), noted that in the early 90s librarians in the D.C. metro area recognized the need to create programs designed specifically for teens. The Metropolitan Area Young Adult Librarians Interest Group (MAYALIG) was created to bring like-minded librarians together to brainstorm and share ideas (http://mayalig.info/).

Gropman noted that one branch in initiated a successful book discussion program for 13–18 year olds. Members were guided by a librarian but the teens themselves provided all the planning and leadership for meetings, and trained the next generation of group leaders. The success of this program led to interest in a mother/daughter book discussion group, which continued for over 10 years. *Calling All Girls* was designed for girls 9–12 accompanied by adult women. A comparable book group for "males only," known as *Calling All Guys* (CAGS), started and was facilitated by a male English teacher.

In several FCPL branches and surrounding counties, teens were able to accompany librarians to ALA, present their views about new books to the YALSA panel of Best Books, meet their favorite authors as well as teens from other states. The local teens also attended MAYALIG conferences.

Book discussions have both an intellectual and a social aspect (chatting over coffee and biscotti). People have an opportunity to exchange/share their views with others, meet new people with similar interests (especially reading), have a chance to explore new ideas, think about what they read in a new manner, and perhaps gain new insights.

From the Advisory Board

Jenny Shanker notes that some libraries make use of teen advisory boards—groups of teens, usually in middle school—who meet monthly with the school librarian and/or public librarian and discuss books, programming, and other issues.

Some resources we recommend on such advisory boards are Sarah Bean Thompson's 2013 article "Don't Forget the Tweens" in *Public Libraries* (52, no. 6: 29–30) and Lindsey Tomsu's 2012 "Tips for Successful TABs" in *Voice Of Youth Advocates* (35, no. 5: 430–431). *Teen-Centered Library Service* (Libraries Unlimited, 2010) by Diane Tuccillo and *The Teen-Centered Book Club* (Libraries Unlimited, 2006), by Bonnie Kunzel and Constance Hardy.

One Book, One Community

The One Book, One Community (OBOC) concept came into existence in 1998. It originated at the Seattle Public Library's "Washington Center for the Book." During its early years it was a public library program, but it has since caught on in many types of libraries. Essentially, OBOC is an expansion of the book discussion group. The difference is it goes beyond the book club and tries to become a community-wide activity of reading and discussing issues raised by the title. A "community" can be a single town or city, a cohort of entering students, or an entire state (e.g., Maryland's

"One Maryland, One Book" program—http://www.mdhc.org/programs /one-maryland-one-book/).

Academic institutions that employ OBOC usually do so with their incoming freshmen cohort (e.g., the University of Maryland's "First Year Book" program—http://www.firstyearbook.umd.edu). Sometimes they select a title in collaboration with the local public library. Such collaborative efforts expand the opportunities for interaction between "town and gown," a relationship that can generate tensions (one example is Fall for the Book—a collaboration between George Mason University and the city of Fairfax, Virginia: http://fall forthebook.org/). Such collaborations often make it easier to add features to the process such as inviting the book's author to the community to perhaps give a lecture and always to have group discussions with the readers. State libraries, as well as local libraries, have been employing some aspects of such a program for a number of years.

Check This Out

The July/August 2012 issue of *Public Libraries* (51, no 4: 17–21) included a special section in which several libraries described their approach to OBOC activities. An important factor in success was identified by Elizabeth Davis in her essay ("Scranton Reads," p. 21), "A key portion of any community reads program is promotion. . . . Overall, the driving force should be the book."

Homework Assistance

One popular public library program is homework assistance. To be most effective the schools and public libraries must work cooperatively. One very valuable approach is to add a third organization to the collaborative mix—local schools of education.

Pamela Warton (2001) suggested that homework, for parents, teachers, and students, is "a source of considerable difficulty and conflict at home and school" (p. 155). Public libraries are well positioned to help reduce the stress of homework. Often there are partnerships with after-school programs with assistance being available both in the library and at a learning center. Many programs are tiered—elementary, middle, and high school. A few not only actively partner with a school district but also gain the involvement of a local academic institution (Brookes and Ryan, 2007). The St. Paul (Minnesota) Public Library developed a program that offered both homework centers with volunteer tutors and online tutoring. At the onset of the program, many of the volunteers came from Metropolitan State University's Urban Teachers Program. The Web service came into being through the support of the mayor, the president of Metropolitan State, and the director of the library. Both the mayor and the university president were so impressed with the quality and effectiveness of the face-to-face program that they provided funding to launch the online program. A follow-on article about the service describes some of the government support it received, such as additional funding earmarked for the homework program and enhancing the technical capabilities of the Web site (Cofer et al., 2007). The program continues today, but with online tutoring offered via a professional service (Brainfuse), and through the use of volunteer tutors (http://www.sppl.org/homeworkhttp://www.stpaul.lib.mn.us/home work/thezone.html).

College Access Programs

Some libraries have a program that helps high school graduates gain access to and be ready for a postsecondary educational experience. One interesting article, both for its content and because its author went to work for a college after being a school librarian, is Ellysa Cahoy's (2002) "Will Your Students Be Ready for College?" She suggests that the best way to improve students' chances of "being ready" is for school and academic librarians to work together at the high school level "to start learning about students' potential needs in the local high schools as well as what the high school library(ies) are capable of offering" (p. 15). Her main focus in the article was on ACRLs' *Information Literacy Competency Standards for Higher Education* and how school and academic librarians need to work together in developing realistic expectations for what school libraries are capable of doing in terms of information literacy competencies given their limited resources. (Note: the original ACRL *Standards* and the proposed update—the *Framework for Information Literacy for Higher Education*—are discussed in chapter 4.)

College access programs help spark students' interest in higher education as well as assist parents in negotiating the issues of financing and supporting the student once admitted. June Eiselstein (2003) described Boston Public Library's "Higher Education Information Center" (30-plus institutions took part in the program), which gave insight into student higher education life. The center provided advising and referral services and identified scholarship opportunities, as well as offered guidance into the application process and educational requirement information. Her article explores the issues related to college access programs, and she notes that collaboration is the key to the success of any such endeavor.

The Higher Education Information Center Eiselstein described has evolved since the time of her article. As of 2014 it was called the ASA College Planning Center, managed by American Student Assistance (ASA). Nonetheless, it continues to offer the same basic services as the earlier iteration (http://www .asa.org/for-students/college-planning/), and continues to be housed at Boston Public Library.

Check These Out

Two recent examples of school/library collaborations for college access are detailed in the following articles, which are well worth the read:

Angell, Katelyn, and Eamon Tewell. 2013. "Collaborating for Academic Success: A Tri-Institutional Information Literacy Program for High School Students." *Public Services Quarterly* 9, no. 1: 1–19.

Martin, Coleen Meyers, Eric P. Garcia, and Marc McPhee. 2012. "Information Literacy Outreach: Building a High School Program at California
State University Northridge." *Education Libraries* 35, no. 1/2: 34–47.

Many academic libraries provide a related service for some high school students along the lines of "advanced placement (AP) student access." Most of
the libraries offering such services enter into an agreement with each high
school wishing to have their AP students have access to the library's resources.
In turn, the participating high school agrees to be responsible for any fines
/fees generated by the students—they have an easier means for recovering the
costs than do the libraries. The school then supplies a list of the eligible AP
students. Generally the agreement allows AP students access to all resources
in the library and offers limited borrowing privileges, not including document
delivery services (ILL) or other remote access that generates individual use fees.
A few even offer special instructional classes for the AP students; generally
they do so because they believe in the long run, it will save staff time when
working with such students. High school students are different from freshmen,
even if they are enrolled in "college prep" classes; thus anyone teaching library
instructional classes for AP students needs an understanding of teenage development and interests. To be effective, AP library programs require close cooperation between the two parties; the most successful are when the high school
principal and library director meet once or twice a year to discuss the program.

A good essay that covers one such program is Debra Pearson and Beth
McNeil's (2002) "From High School Users College Students Grow." Pearson
and McNeil reviewed the University of Nebraska, Lincoln library's AP program, which was a part of its outreach program since 1980. From the outset
it had been a collaborative program with local school librarians teaching high
school students about research and how to use a university library system
in that process. Not long before they published their article, the university
library modified its lending rules for the AP students; the student had to get a
receipt for each item returned. The change substantially reduced the "I know
I returned it"/missing rate for the program. Other changes focused on the
changing formats the library made available to the students. The authors concluded by stating, "Regardless of whether or not participants decide to attend
the University of Nebraska, the librarians have helped prepare young Nebras-
kans for their college experience and their future information needs" (p. 26).
Currently, the University of Nebraska, Lincoln, offers a broader High School
Users Program, available during the academic year. All students over 16 years
of age are eligible to participate, provided both they and their media specialist
or teacher sign a consent form (http://libraries.unl.edu/highschool).

Lectures, Concerts, and Film Showings

These are other long-standing programming activities, found most frequently
in academic and public libraries. In most cases, the events are sponsored by
the library, although sometimes the library only supplies the space gratis or

for a small fee. When the library puts on an event, there must be a surprising amount of planning in order to achieve success. A few factors that require thought are:

- Budget
- Topic
- Timing

- Audience
- Location
- Marketing

If a library is fortunate, it may have an endowment or Friends of the Library group to underwrite some of the event costs. Even when that is the case, the available funds are rarely adequate to cover the total costs of the program. Speakers/performers of any merit usually charge a fee, often very large, although sometimes there may be a local connection (e.g., personal friend/ family) that will secure a discounted fee. Speaker fee(s) alone make it challenging to put on a meaningful program at a reasonable cost. Collaborative efforts sometimes work well, as long as the library's role is not lost in the process; for example, joint grant requests for program support.

Just because you think a topic is interesting does not mean it will attract a good audience. Having a group involved in topic selection is often the best means for identifying suitable topics and presenters. This is a place where marketing data can be useful in the planning process. Having some "extra" events such as small group meeting(s) with the presenter can help ensure a good turnout for the main event. It may also be useful to provide a brief survey to attendees of current programs to see what type of additional programs they'd like to see offered at the library.

Topics and approaches vary, from single speakers (Robertson, 2007, book collecting) to panel discussions (Howie and Yochelson, 2006, mystery writers; Evans, 2013, global hunger and sustainability). Sometimes the theme is established and the goal is to identify a speaker who can provide new insights on the topic (e.g., Cline Library's [Northern Arizona University] Grand Canyon Country Lecture series, or the University of Maryland's "Speaking of Books . . . Conversations with Campus Authors" series—http://www.lib.umd.edu /speakingofbooks).

Film programs raise additional issues such as performance rights, even if the producer or director is participating in the program. Certainly film series are also more likely to generate a complaint or two (Goldberg, 2004b). There may be pressure to screen only "family friendly" films (Caldwell-Stone, 2004). All in all, film showings require even more thought and planning than traditional lectures.

One academic library (Kansas State University) offers "movies on the grass" (http://www.k-state.edu/mog/). The showings, on a plaza next to the library (or inside the library in case of rain), include a post-showing discussion with several faculty members. The program is a collaborative activity, with the library playing the central coordinating role (Peairs, Urton and Schenck-Hamlin, 2007).

One public library's film series focuses on group discussions (Bence, 2006). The underlying premise of the program was to create "an opportunity for people to connect with one another with the main purpose of fostering meaningful relationships" (p. 4). Bence's program addressed this by focusing on the issue of diversity. According to Bence, the diversity goal was even reflected in the attendees in terms of age, gender, and cultural and economic backgrounds. A slight twist on the theme is from the Paul Sawyer Public Library (Frankfort, Kentucky), where library patrons sign up to receive a copy of the movie to view on their own at home, and then come together as a group to discuss the film (http://www.pspl.org/filmdiscussiongroup0).

Our last example is one that focuses on an age group (teens) and film type (anime). Jane Halsall (2004) wrote an article focusing on "How I learned to love Japanese animation and changed our teen video collection forever" (p. 6). She became exposed to teenagers' interest in the film type through her daughter, who made her mother watch several anime videos and tried to explain what teens like about the genre. As a result, Halsall's library acquired a large collection of such videos. The library continues to have an active anime and manga club (http://mchenrylibrary.org/index.php/my-library/teens-page /anime-manga-club). As a result, Jane Halsall coauthored with R. William Edminster a book, *Visual Media for Teens: Creating and Using a Teen-Centered Film Collection* (Libraries Unlimited, 2009).

Check This Out

Alan Jacobson (2011) provides sound advice for libraries considering offering a film program in his article "How to Offer More Than a Movie" (*American Libraries* 42, nos. 7/8: 42–45). He suggests partnering the film showing with a discussion series. While there are a number of factors to consider, such as managing the audience and discussion, Jacobson has found the experience to be worthwhile.

Exhibitions

Libraries have probably been creating exhibits for most of their history. Certainly most of these are not an exhibition in the museum sense; many are nothing more than displaying dust jackets of newly arrived books or a few themed posters on the wall, or pieces of replica sculptures. (Regarding book dust jackets, many libraries are adding the dust jacket image to the record in their OPACs. Essentially the libraries are taking a page out of the online book sellers' and bookstores' playbook, to catch the attention of readers.)

School media centers often have their walls covered with posters intended to encourage reading. Anyone visiting the exhibits area of an ALA convention quickly learns that publishers give away posters that promote some of their publications. Naturally the children's book posters are the most colorful and useful in promoting reading in a school or public library. Thus, there is an annual stream of useful colorful material available at no cost. The ALA also sells a variety of posters promoting reading, many of which feature celebrities.

Research, academic, and larger public libraries are the most likely to mount exhibitions approaching museum quality. Frequently the special collections unit is responsible for planning and executing such shows. A good show is not inexpensive in terms of staff time as well as for the proper materials and security. It may also require substantial planning, sometimes over several years. The person responsible, or curator to use the formal label, picks a topic and begins identifying potential material. Sometimes the exhibition draws on materials from sources outside the exhibiting library. In those cases, the issues of item security become paramount and there are often costs for proper shipping as well as special insurance. In some cases, online exhibitions accompany the physical exhibition, such as those prepared by Special Collections and University Archives at the University of Maryland Libraries (http://www.lib.umd.edu/special/exhibits/home). One advantage of an online exhibit is that it can make the material available to a far wider group of individuals than those able to travel to view an exhibit in person.

Susan Swisher (2007) described the Hammond (Indiana) Public Library's annual Senior Art Exhibition. Their show had been operational for 16 years at the time she wrote the article and grew in size from a small local exhibition to a regional juried event. The library partnered with the Northern Indiana Art Association, and significant awards were given to category winners. A not unexpected outcome of the event was an increase in the library's reputation as a major contributor to the region's social programs.

Northern Virginia Community College Alexandria Campus Library mounted a different type of art exhibit (Rortvedt, 2007). It was a collaborative show between the library and the art department. Two art faculty members created a class project "based upon an interpretation of the text using the physical elements of the book as catalyst and structure" (p. 27). Unneeded library donations and withdrawn books furnished the raw material for the students to create their "altered book" art. The event was so successful that it was repeated over several years. In addition, the Library used Friends of the Library funds to purchase selected pieces from the students to remain as a permanent exhibit in the Library.

Some academic libraries use their exhibitions to introduce school children to research. A good article discussing this concept is Timothy Young's (2007) "The Young Visitors." Young provides the rationale for such programs and the issues involved in creating a beneficial experience for young people. Further, he discusses 18 lessons learned from the program at Beinecke Library (Yale). His "lessons" included:

- Plan ahead
- Work with campus liaisons
- Advertise early and in different venues
- Host previews for teachers
- Think about sightlines and obstructions for young viewers
- Develop alternative storylines when planning for tours
- Have something to give away (flyers, postcards, etc.)
- Keep the group size manageable (p. 237)

As is true of many library services, exhibitions can lead to complaints as well as praise. Although art shows have the greatest potential for offending someone, even a "Banned Book" exhibit can cause and has caused problems for a library. The factors we discussed in the section on censorship apply to exhibits as well. *American Libraries* (2008) covered a story about an exhibit in the Kennebunk Free Library and its problems. An artist, G. Bud Swenson, had created a series of collages using pieces of discarded U.S. flags or artwork symbolizing the flag ("American Portraits in a Time of War"). Included in these pieces were images of President Bush and Vice President Cheney. Some users complained on political grounds. First the library cancelled the show, but then reversed its decision after the board met with the artist. The director was quoted as saying, "It's easy to have pat answers, but finding the area in the middle requires courage" (p. 26).

Exhibitions are a good public relations tool and generally are appreciated by the service community. From a public service staff point of view, exhibitions generate many viewer questions and they expect informed answers. A useful activity is to have those who planned the show meet with the staff to discuss the material and address the most likely questions.

From the Authors' Experience

Evans' last full-time duty was at a library that had a long-term planning process for exhibitions—three plus years. There was space for both permanent exhibits and those of shorter term (2–3 month maximums). The permanent exhibits never generated any issues. However, it was a different matter for the short-term efforts.

The library always put together the opening exhibitions that were up the entire fall semester. These were two to three years in the planning and generally involved museum quality efforts. The library handled the scheduling of all the other exhibitions almost always for some academic department or program. The library also had several short-term possibilities ready in case the department or program had difficulties getting an exhibition off the ground, which happened from time to time.

Departments/programs were responsible with organizing their shows and it was a rare occasion that anyone in the library saw the content until it was up. Most of such exhibitions started with an opening reception. Certainly the most memorable such exhibition in Evans's memory was one the women's study program mounted—"Feminine Artists View the World." To say the opening reception was filled with drama is an understatement. Many of the artworks were very graphic to the point that many of the attendees (nuns and priests) became very vocal that the works be removed immediately. The library and Evans got their share of "blame" for the nature of some of the material. The resolution of the issue took some time (intellectual freedom and censorship were, of course, main issues). Thereafter, the library was to review a detailed plan for all items to be displayed; concerns were to be reviewed by senior campus administrators (such issues arose several times).

The bottom line: have clear policies as to what and what may not be exhibited.

Gaming

Where to place "games" in this text caused a small debate among the authors due to the variety of physical formats games may take. Most board games are made of paper or cardboard; many games also have pieces/counters or are played on cloth/plastic sheeting on the floor. The reality today is children and young people are much more interested in electronic games (discussed in chapter 8). The result has been an ongoing increase in libraries making e-games available in the library. ALA held its first ever library symposium on gaming in mid-2007 ("Gaming, Learning, and Libraries") with follow-up events held since that time. There is an ALA Games and Gaming Round Table (GameRT, http://www.ala.org/gamert/) that you can join to learn more about such programs.

From the Advisory Board

Jean Wallace, a school librarian, provides an example of the preferences. She noted that once she suggested playing Twenty Questions with students but the students protested saying they couldn't play because no computers were available. The idea of playing with paper and pencil did not seem feasible to them.

You may be surprised by the fact that many libraries, regardless of type, have game collections. Needless to say, school library media centers have such collections. Many academic libraries, at institutions with teacher education programs, have games in their curriculum collections. Public libraries have also found that having some games is useful in attracting users (see http://www.bowker.com/en-US/aboutus/press_room/2013/pr_08082013.shtml for information about methods for making games accessible through OPACS). As noted by Stubbs (2014), "Gaming is a fun learning experience. And it is another tool or approach to engage people with what libraries can do for them" (p. 67).

Check This Out

Stubbs's chapter cited earlier is part of a larger work *Teen Games Rule! A Librarian's Guide to Platforms and Programs*, edited by Julie Scordato and Ellen Forsyth (Santa Barbara, CA: Libraries Unlimited, 2014). The volume is divided into two parts: library examples of gaming and suggested games to implement. It includes a chapter on professional development and new ideas. It is well worth a look.

The loaning of board games often proves to be a problem for the circulation department, because staff need to go through the returned game to be sure all the pieces are still there. Naturally, it also means there must be some easily available record of what should be there. All this takes time and effort away from other activities. When the staff view the process as getting in the way of their "real" work, check-in becomes perfunctory. That view usually results in games with missing pieces and a service that is no longer a service. School library media centers collect educational games for use in the classroom or in the media center. While the checking for missing parts must still take place, the losses are usually minimal and the learning value of the game far outweighs the cost of staff time for checking the returned games.

Rebecca Moore (2006) discussed how she combined teaching research skills with middle school students' desire to play and compete. (Note: in her school, all the students belonged to either a Blue or Gold team that competed throughout the year for points and year-end rewards. Thus, she had existing teams with which to work.) She used a form of *Jeopardy* in her orientation sessions. In all, she describes 12 games that combine a contest and learning objective.

Can video games support learning objectives such as media literacy? Eli Neiburger (2007) believes they can. He makes the point, which many of us may not recognize, that success in video games, at least initially, requires comprehending both text and game conventions (p. 28). Kurt Squire and Constance Steinkuehler (2005) noted, "Game cultures promote various types of information literacy, develop information seeking habits and production practices (like writing), and require good old-fashioned research skills, albeit using a wide spectrum of content. In short, libraries can't afford to ignore gamers" (p. 38). Academics who studied both stand-alone and multiplayer online games, Squire and Steinkuehler, explored the social practices associated with gaming. Some of their concluding recommendations were for libraries to carry games, host game nights, have gaming contests, and stock game-related materials.

Our last gaming topic relates to "cosplay" (costume and play). In a sense, it is an extension of the Halloween costume contest that some libraries sponsor. Brehm-Heeger and colleagues (2007), young adult staff members of the Cincinnati-Hamilton Library, discuss how they employ this concept with their teen anime club. Each year the club puts on a cosplay event in which members dress in anime costumes for judging by non-costumed members. They are asked questions about the costume, the character represented, and the reason for the choice. In addition, there are two-/three-minute skits by the costumed members. They are again questioned about their knowledge of the anime and manga elements in the skit. Through this type of program, members have fun while engaging in research. (For details on the current program, see: http://teenspace .cincinnatilibrary.org/programs/cosplay2014.)

SERVICES

In this section of the chapter, we discuss some of the most common services that are most often found in a single type of library. Even within given library types the service may not be present. Nevertheless, they are rather common and play a role in providing access to library resources.

Meeting Rooms

Public libraries often include one or more meeting rooms that may be reserved by groups that are not affiliated with the library. Academic libraries almost always have individual study rooms as well as group study rooms. Some libraries (both academic and public) even have an auditorium/lecture hall facility. In either case, the library must have clearly stated polices regarding room usage, if the public service staff is to avoid some unpleasant situations. You might wonder how something like having rooms available could generate unpleasant situations on occasions. Our following discussion will highlight some of the issues.

For academic libraries, individual and group study space is not too great a problem for the staff during much of the academic term. Issues, when they arise, are most often during major term paper writing and examination periods. There have even been instances when examinations that are unrelated to campus exam times (bar and medical examinations for example) generate difficulties. Many individuals want reasonably noise-free study space and library study rooms can offer such an environment. It is not unheard of for a person in an individual study room coming to the library staff asking that he or she goes quiet down nearby students in a group study room. The first issue for the library to address is, will it have a method for people to reserve a space? If so, will there be time limits? How long will the reservation be held? What library unit will be responsible for operating the system? These are examples of questions that require careful thought. With or without such a system there are times when stressed-out users can become physically confrontational with one another. Having clear staff guidelines for handling those rather rare, but difficult situations, is important for everyone's well-being. We discuss handling disruptive behavior in chapter 16.

In the case of public libraries, events may be library sponsored or held by outside groups. Community service clubs and interest groups are often the beneficiaries of such room use (charity groups, garden club, chess club, etc.) Libraries have learned, from sometimes bitter experience, that there must be a clearly stated and governing board-approved policies and procedures for the use of the space. Lacking such documentation is likely to cause problems, with the public service staff often caught in the middle. Perhaps in the past there were few issues arising from having a meeting room available. Today, the issue of who may make use of the space could end up at the U.S. Supreme Court, even with a policy/procedure in place. The following three examples provide some perspective on the complexity of having a meeting room available to the public.

Our first example of a public library facing a meeting room challenge took place in Colorado Springs (*American Libraries*, 2005). The Rampart Library District had a board-approved policy that stated if the rooms were used by religious or political groups, the meeting must provide a balanced view. Early in 2005, a religious group asked to use a room and the request was turned down because it would be a religious service. Shortly after the use denial occurred the library received a lawsuit notice that was filed by Liberty Counsel (a religious rights defense organization located in Florida) for denying use of the room for a religious program. The Rampart District decided to modify their use policy because they did not have the funds to engage in a legal battle. (Liberty Counsel has filed at least seven such suits since 2000. It won some of them for the same reason that Rampart conceded—lack of funds to engage in a legal battle.)

Early in 2006, the Montana State Library cancelled an ACLU film screening that was critical of the USA PATRIOT Act due to some complaints that the program did not list a speaker who would support the act. Rather than file a lawsuit, the ACLU booked a room in the Lewis and Clark Library (the local public library). The difference between the two libraries, according to *American Libraries* (Goldberg, 2006), was the presence and absence of room usage policies. Lewis and Clark had a policy that stated as long as a program dealing with a controversial topic provided most, if not all, points of view on the topic, the meeting room could be booked. The State Library had no policy and reacted to several telephone calls complaining about the program. The article did note that the ACLU had invited a representative from U.S. Attorney General's Office to speak by the time they applied to Lewis and Clark. However, no such representative came to the meeting.

Our last example took several years to resolve (2004–2007). It started in 2004 when the Antioch branch of the Contra Costa County (California) Library system rejected a room request from the Faith Center Church Evangelistic Ministries. The denial led to a lawsuit (Goldberg, 2004a). The denial was based on the library board's policy that stated that rooms cannot be used for religious services based on separation of church and state grounds. Library staff stated the denial was based on the fact that the group indicated it would hold prayer services as part of its program. (The group had distributed flyers throughout the area inviting people to attend a worship service at the library.) Interestingly enough, the U.S. Department of Justice took the position that Contra Costa County had to allow the group to use the library room for their service: a somewhat strange twist on the separation of church and state concept. Contra Costa County pushed the case forward, as it viewed this more than a matter of library room use. It had no problem with the group using the space for non-worship service purposes, but not for a religious service. Each side appealed the case; each side won and lost in the lower courts. On the first day of the 2007–2008 term, the Supreme Court refused to hear the appeal of the Ninth Circuit Court of Appeals, ruling that the library and county had acted properly. (Note: the ruling only applies to those libraries in the Ninth Circuit Court's jurisdiction.) Kniffel (2007) reported in *American Libraries* that the religious group said they would revisit the case in lower courts using a new set of arguments. As of mid-2014, we have not seen any indication the issue was pursued further. Who would guess having a library meeting room could cause so most stress and expense for everyone?

Outreach

Turning to outreach, a term with a variety of meanings and thus services, we explore a few of the most common activities. For some people, library outreach just goes back to the 1960s. Actually, one can trace the concept much further back when it was called "library extension." In its early days, library extension focused on providing library service to rural populations. It quickly expanded to urban dwellers lacking transportation. Today's bookmobiles are the direct descendants of the extension service concept. By the late twentieth century, outreach expanded further to providing service to groups with special needs of some type or who were/are underserved.

Determining the appropriate special service(s), like all other activities, requires a sound understanding of the service community composition, needs, and wants. Looking to other community service agencies may provide unexpected partnership opportunities as well as a way to stretch limited funds. Satia Orange and Robin Osborne (2004) suggested, "If we reframe what we know as 'outreach' so that it is based upon equality rather than underserved populations, we can open a new window to information access and, more importantly, service delivery" (p. 47). We agree, outreach is not dead, but rather will be richer if libraries broaden the concept to equality of access for all. Also, as we will discuss in chapter 11, technology has changed how and when outreach activities take place.

Mobile Services

Essentially, mobile services are branches that move. They are a way to address the "Law of Least Effort." That is, people tend to expend the least possible effort to secure information, even when it is reasonably important to them. Is it in arm's reach? In my office/home? How far away is the most likely source? If not right here, is it worth the effort? These are questions we all ask ourselves—whether we are aware of it or not. The greater the effort required the less likely we are to make it. Thus, reducing the effort, especially for remote users, makes sense for libraries.

Today's mobile rigs are a far cry from those of 30 years ago. It has been a long time since all they carried were books and magazines. Now they may include computer access and employ satellite technology. Many draw on travel trailer concepts such as pull-out sections that provide extra space once they open for business. More information on bookmobile services, National Bookmobile Day activities, may be found on the ALA's Office for Literacy and Outreach Services Web page (http://www.ala.org/advocacy/diversity/outreachtounderserved populations/bookmobiles), while information on National Bookmobile Day is available at http://www.ala.org/offices/olos/nbdhome.

The Flagstaff City-Coconino County Public Library has a "PALSmobile," (*Preschoolers Acquiring Literacy Skills*), a small-scale bookmobile. The service visits preschools, day care, and Head Start centers throughout the county (http://flagstaffpubliclibrary.org/services/youth_services/parents_and_edu cators/palsmobile.html).

Not all "mobile" services are confined to wheeled vehicles. For many years, some libraries offered "books by mail;" academic libraries employed this approach in the early days of distance education programs. In the case of public libraries, users received lists of available books; they filled out a form, mailed it to the library, and the library mailed the book(s). A few libraries now use the Internet as the means of communication, but still use "snail" mail for books that are not in an e-format. In remote coastal areas, book boats provide the service, often also serving as the postal service. A few countries with large merchant marines, Norway, for example, have libraries assemble "book boxes"—today they include all formats—that go to outgoing merchant ships. Ship captains exchange the boxes; the boxes may be at sea for a very long time and sometimes never return to Norway.

While some libraries have experimented with mobile libraries via bicycle (Lapides, 2014), perhaps the most unique mobile service we are aware of is the "camel-mobile." (It would seem mobile service is only limited by the staff's imagination.) The Kenyan National Library operates a camel book service (Hoffert, 2007; Kaplan, 2013) to its remote northeastern areas. The service has even inspired a novel (*Camel Bookmobile*, HarperCollins, 2007) by Marsha Hamilton; it explores the tension between people with deep traditional values and those who believe the modern world and its books are essential to long-term survival.

Check These Out

If camel mobiles sound intriguing, you can read more about this service at http://www.geolib.org/camel.html, in Margriet Ruurs's 2005 "Books by Boat, Camel, and Elephant! (*Reading Today* 23, no. 1: 24), and Richard Masaranga Atuti and J.R. Ikoja-Odongo's 1999 "Private Camel Library Brings Hope to Pastoralists: The Kenyan Experience." (*Library Review* 48, no 1: 36–42).

The most recent iteration of mobile libraries is the "pop-up" library, which is a temporary outpost for the library—not necessarily on wheels.

One example is Seattle Public Library's Open Air library: http://www.spl.org/using-the-library/library-on-the-go/open-air see also: http://www.dnainfo.com/new-york/20140523/long-island-city/pop-up-mobile-libraries-bring-books-hunters-point-this-summer

Note: some pop-up libraries are hosted by individuals, but libraries are definitely in on the act.

Services to Special Populations

A great many books and articles exist about this topic; thus we will touch only on a few areas. For years libraries provided books in their original languages as a service to those who either spoke the language originally or who had learned it later. There was also the goal of aiding immigrants in becoming assimilated into the dominant society.

Edwin Clay (2006) raised the question of what is today's goal: integration, assimilation, or multiculturalism. How one answers that question has significant service implications. He made the point that the dialog has gone from "melting-pot" to "mosaic" to, perhaps, "co-existence." Further, he suggested that a new goal might be better thought of as to "foster positive attitudes toward multiculturalism" (p. 12), such as becoming aware of how backgrounds and experience act to form views about cultural diversity and beginning to understand how others view the concept. Essentially he suggested that by understanding how others view diversity there is better chance of having less stressful relations, even in the absence of full acceptance of the differing views.

Whatever the label, libraries did and do attempt to provide appropriate services to a host of people of differing cultural backgrounds as well as classes of people (seniors, youth, institutionalized, and partially sighted to mention but a few). In 2012, the Association of College and Research Libraries (ACRL) issued *Diversity Standards: Cultural Competency for Academic Libraries*. The statement reads in part "diversity is an essential component of any civil society. It is more than a moral imperative; it is a global necessity. Everyone can benefit from diversity, and diverse populations need to be supported so they can reach their full potential for themselves and their communities." The standards outlined in the document recognize the need to provide culturally diverse services to library clientele. A good start for developing a useful model for approaching cultural diversity is Geert Hofstede's *Cultures and Organizations: Software of the Mind*, 2nd ed. (New York: McGraw-Hill, 2005). It will provide very useful insights for both thinking about the service community as well as workplace colleagues.

A major social issue in the United States is illegal immigration, with a particular focus on Hispanic people. Such was the concern that the October 2007 issue of *American Libraries* published two articles offering different points of view regarding library service to illegal immigrants. Julia Stephens took the position that "by creating bilingual collections, librarians are contributing to a divided America" (p. 41). Todd Quesada's position was, "Eliminating Spanish-language fiction undermines the validity of public libraries" (p. 40). Stephens also stated, "Our founding principles of a unified nation with one language are being cast aside" (p. 43). Letters in the "to the editor section" of the two following issues suggested this was indeed a "hot topic." Although the overwhelming majority of the letter writers were against Stephens's position, not everyone disagreed with it. If nothing else, the articles and the reaction to them demonstrated just how complex outreach can be.

Surprisingly, the issue of providing non-English language materials is not cut and dry, as exemplified by another 2007 article about such services that caused no ripples. Yelena Nedlina (2007) described service to Russian speakers and the pros and cons of creating separate sections for different language materials. Libraries have almost always had material in other languages in their collections. Often this was because the item is/was considered a classic in its original language and knowledgeable individuals know that something is always "lost in translation" and they want to read/see it in its original form. Also, there was/is the desire to provide recent arrivals with the opportunity to continue using their mother tongue. There is a question, which Nedlina explores, as to the effectiveness of separating materials by their language. What seems to be the current driving force behind the Spanish language debate is illegal immigration and national security rather than the desirability of providing non-English materials.

Academic libraries have long recognized that their international students, as well as those with different cultural backgrounds, have values/expectations that may call for specialized assistance when it comes to library services. Very often they partner with ethnic studies centers and the international students' office to develop such services—one of this book's authors developed and taught such a program for Native American students at the University of California, Los Angeles. The goal of such services is to assure there are appropriate resources and support for the students. Emily Love's (2007) article provides a good overview of the issues involved in such services. Her major points were the importance of:

- Identifying potential campus partners
- Identifying the needs of student service groups
- Establishing meaningful relationship with such groups
- Actively cultivating those relationships
- Ensuring long-term partnerships
- Engaging in effective publicity that reflects existing partnerships
- Evaluating and assessing the partnerships on a regular basis. (pp. 15–16)

Check This Out

One title worth consulting on developing services designed for patrons with multicultural backgrounds is Carol Smallwood and Kim Becnel's *Library Services for Multicultural Patrons: Strategies to Encourage Library Use* (Lanham, MD: Scarecrow Press, 2013). This work includes sections on developing partnerships with organizations outside the libraries, using technology effectively in a multicultural setting and provides examples of sample programming and events.

A good, well-balanced article about developing multicultural collections in a school library setting is by Denise Agosto (2007). She covers the benefits of such collections and what factors to take into account. Such collections do reach out, in a meaningful way, to children with different cultural backgrounds. Agosto suggested student learning benefits from creating such collections included the following:

- A sense of belonging
- A facilitation of student learning
- An appreciation of differences
- An increased knowledge of the world (pp. 27–28)

Her suggestions for evaluating the quality of multicultural materials are not that different from those you would employ for any item—accuracy, expertise, purpose, format, quality, and, most importantly, respectful treatment. Judi Moreillon (2013) suggests creating opportunities where students are not only exposed to the literature of another culture via materials in the library collection, but also have firsthand experience via programming. She notes, "Outstanding programs may include guest speakers who are immigrants from other cultures and travelers who recently returned from the country or culture depicted in the literature to share information or their experiences" (p. 37).

Specialized service to seniors is common in public libraries, if nothing more than large-print materials. Who are seniors? People who are retired? People of a certain age? If so, what age? People who have visual and/or physical limitations? Perhaps the best answer was Alan Bundy's (2005): "The one thing that seniors have in common is they are all different" (p. 158). The problem in defining the group more specifically is that various agencies define it differently. The U.S. Social Security office allows a person to start collecting retirement payments at age 62 and the individual may continue to work. The American Association of Retired Persons starts membership at age 55, whether one is retired or not. Perhaps it would be best to drop the term and just have the services available to anyone who needs them, essentially what happens in any case. In addition to large-print materials, there are "assistive" technologies (text readers and monitor enhancers, for example), homebound services, and basic computer literacy courses. Although a higher percentage of "older" users may benefit from the services, they are clearly not the only group that can benefit.

Check These Out

Many public libraries include links to senior services Web sites on their Web pages. In addition, some additional resources libraries provide to their older clientele include:

Fairfax County Public Library has a number of resources available including audio-described DVDs, braille awareness kits, and nostalgia kits (multimedia programming for a group of older adults)—http://www.fairfaxcounty.gov/library/branches/as/specialcollections.htm.

Santa Monica Public Library has had a Shut-In service available since the early 70s. In it, a patron who is unable to come to a library to check out materials can work with a Shut-In Service Volunteer to select materials and have them delivered in-person—http://smpl.org/Senior_Services.aspx.

In addition to a homebound delivery service, Normal (IL) Public Library offers fine free library cards to anyone over 60 years old as well as provides deposit collections at local nursing homes and retirement communities: http://www.normalpl.org/seniors/services/.

One resource site available for libraries wanting to further develop resources for older adults is the Transforming Life after 50 (TLA50) site, maintained by the California State Library. The site provides links to training presentations, tools, and program models: http://www.transforminglifeafter50.org/.

Some other outreach services are to institutionalized individuals (long-term care, prisoners, ex-convicts [e.g., see Dowling, 2007; MacCreaigh, 2010]). Services to government agencies (Davidsson, 2006) are not all that common, but also do exist. Providing consumer health information calls for careful planning and some training as there can be some legal issues. Roma Harris and colleagues (2010) provide a good review of the issues involved in such a service. Our Suggested Readings section offers many other articles on topics we covered, as well as some we didn't have room for.

CLOSING THOUGHTS

Knowing the community is the key to offering effective programming and services. Once you have that information you can begin to explore possible new or modified activities. Naturally, another important factor to consider is what skills currently exist in the staff that would allow the activity to be effective. Sometimes, it is necessary to wait until a new position is authorized or a resignation occurs so you can develop a new job description.

Many of the activities we covered in this chapter call for some special skills or knowledge in addition to the basics of library public service. Not everyone is comfortable or effective working with one or more of the groups or activities covered. However, Karen Hake (2000) makes a key point. When discussing service to children, she noted: "To provide good service, the staff must be friendly, committed, enthusiastic, knowledgeable, and reliable" (p. 7).

The ALA's Association for Library Service to Children (ALSC) developed a set of competencies for those going into this area on a more or less full-time basis (ALSC 2009, http://www.ala.org/alsc/edcareeers/alsccorecomps). The set covers such concepts as having an understanding of the theories of infant, child, and adolescent development, the special needs of various cultural groups, and the social development of children. The basic competencies appear to apply to public service work in all library settings. The nine competency areas are:

- Knowledge of client group
- Administrative and management skills
- Communication skills
- Knowledge of materials
- User and reference services
- Programming skills
- Advocacy, public relations, and networking skills
- Professionalism and professional development
- Technology

Language and communication skills are essential in any area; however, when it comes to outreach to special populations, one may need bilingual skills or at least cultural awareness/understanding abilities as well. When it comes to teaching a class, having the ability to "pitch" the presentation at the proper level for an audience is critical for success, and is a talent that not everyone possesses. Even the availability of staff members who are able to handle a large mobile unit may not be as widespread as one would like.

Chapter Review Material

1. In what ways do the services covered in this chapter differ from those we addressed in other chapters?
2. How do programs differ from services?
3. Discuss the concept of lifelong learning and the role libraries can play in that process.
4. In what way do One Book programs differ from other book discussion programs?
5. What are some of the keys to having successful library programs?
6. What are some of the likely causes of problems related to usage of library meeting rooms?

7. What are the goals/purposes of outreach programs?
8. Discuss the controversy regarding services for illegal immigrants.
9. What are some other specialized skills/knowledge one might need to be effective in one or more of the services discussed in this chapter?

REFERENCES

Agosto, Denise E. 2007. "Building a Multicultural School Library." *Teacher Librarian* 34, no. 3: 27–31.

American Libraries. 2005. "Colorado Gets Meeting-Room Religion." 36, no. 9: 28–29.

American Libraries. 2008. "Bush, Cheney Images Reelected to Exhibit." 39, nos. 1/2: 26.

Association of College and Research Libraries. 2012. *Diversity Standards: Cultural Competency for Academic Libraries*. Online. http://www.ala.org/acrl /standards/diversity.

Becker, Christine. 2012. "Engaged Libraries Leading the Way." *National Civic Review* 101, no. 4: 21–23.

Bence, Tamara. 2006. "Fostering Friendship through Film Discussions." *Kentucky Librarian Association* 70, no. 4: 4–5.

Brehm-Heeger, Paula, Ann Conway, and Carrie Vale. 2007. "Cosplay, Gaming, and Conventions." *Young Adult Library Services* 5, no. 2: 14–16.

Brookes, Joanna, and Rebecca Ryan. 2007. "A Tale of Two Libraries." *Public Libraries* 46, no. 4: 9–12.

Bundy, Alan. 2005. "Community Critical: Australian Public Libraries Serving Seniors." *Australasian Public Library Information Services* 18, no. 4: 158–169.

Bundy, Alan. 2006. "Supporting Students." *Australasian Public Library Information Services* 19, no. 3: 126–136.

Cahoy, Ellysa. 2002. "Will Your Students Be Ready for College?" *Knowledge Quest* 30, no. 4: 12–15.

Caldwell-Stone, Deborah. 2004. "Movie Ratings Are Private, Not Public Policy." *Illinois Library Association Reporter* 22, no. 2: 10–13.

Clay, Edwin S. 2006. "They Don't Look Like Me." *Virginia Libraries* 53, no. 4: 10–14.

Cofer, Sarah, Janet Ingraham Dwyer, and Suzanne Harold. 2007. "Homework Help Is a Click Away." *Young Adult Library Services* 5, no. 2: 17–20.

Cole, Natalie, Virginia Walter, and Eva Mitnick. 2013. "Outcomes + Outreach: The California Summer Reading Outcomes Initiative." *Public Libraries* 52, no. 2: 38–43.

Cruise, Julie. 2013. "Tailored to Succeed: Meeting Community Needs Also Helped the Library." *Public Libraries* 52, no. 2: 30–33.

Davidsson, Robert. 2006. "Serving Government Clients Using Library Electronic Resources." *Florida Libraries* 49, no. 1: 10–12.

Dowling, Brendan. 2007. "Public Libraries and Ex-Offenders." *Public Libraries* 46, no. 6: 44–48.

Eiselstein, June. 2003. "College Access Programs and Services." *Public Libraries* 42, no. 3: 184–187.

Evans, Cathy. 2013. "One Book, One School, One Great Impact!" *Library Media Connection* 32, no. 1: 18–19.

Gillis, Sara, and Julie Totten. 2006. "Creating Lifelong Learning Opportunities through Partnership." *Feliciter* 52, no. 6: 244–246.

Goldberg, Beverly. 2004a. "Censorship Watch." *American Libraries* 35, no. 8: 17.

Goldberg, Beverly. 2004b. "Libraries Nix Flicks as Patrons Cry Partisanship." *American Libraries* 35, no. 11: 18.

Goldberg, Beverly. 2006. "Montana State Library Pulls ACLU Film Screening." *American Libraries* 37, no. 4: 12.

Hake, Karen. 2000. "Programming and Children's Services." *Bookmobiles and Outreach Services* 3, no. 2: 7–10.

Halsall, Jane. 2004. "The Anime Revolution." *School Library Journal* 50, no. 8: 4–13.

Harris, Roma, Flis Henwood, Audrey Marshall, and Samantha Burdett. 2010. "I'm Not Sure if That's What Their Job Is." *Reference & User Services Quarterly* 49, no. 3: 239–252.

Hoffert, Barbara. 2007. "Books by Camel." *Library Journal* 132, no. 5: 6.

Howie, Emily, and Abby Yochelson. 2006. "Deft, Daring, Delightful: Popular Mystery Writers Discuss Their Craft." *Library of Congress Information Bulletin* 65, no. 6: 150–151.

Kaplan, Eva. 2013. "Library Services in Kenya: A Process of Reinvention." *International Leads* 27, no. 1: 1–3.

Kniffel, Leonard. 2007. "Supreme Court Won't Hear Meeting Room Appeal." *American Libraries* 38, no. 10: 18.

Kutner, Mark, Elizabeth Greenberg, Ying Jin, Bridget Boyle, Yung-chen Hsu, and Eric Dunleavy. 2007. *Literacy in Everyday Life* (NCES 2007–480). U.S. Department of Education. Washington, D.C.: National Center for Education Statistics.

Lapides, Sam. 2014. "Pedal Power." *Public Libraries* 53, no. 1: 12–14.

Lighthart, Matthew, and Creedence Spreder. 2014. "Partners in Lifelong Learning." *Knowledge Quest* 42, no. 4: 32–37.

Love, Emily. 2007. "Building Bridges: Cultivating Partnerships between Libraries and Minority Student Services." *Education Libraries* 30, no. 1: 13–19.

MacCreaigh, Erica. 2010. "Tough Times after Hard Time: How Public Libraries Can Ease the Reentry Process for Ex-offenders." *Interface* 32, no. 1: 11.

McDermott, Irene. 2012. "Web Help for Low-Income Patrons." *Searcher* 20, no.6: 7–11.

Meuchel, Aimee. 2013. "I Prefer to Count on Success: A Summer Reading Program That Supports Lifelong Reading." *OLA Quarterly*, 29, no. 1: 14–16.

Minkel, Walter. 2003. "Making a Splash with Summer Reading." *School Library Journal* 49, no. 1: 54–56.

Moore, Rebecca. 2006. "From Jeopardy to Microfiction Mprovs." *Voice of Youth Advocates* 29, no. 3: 219–223.

Moreillon, Judi. 2013. "Building Bridges for Global Understanding." *Children & Libraries: The Journal of the Association for Library Service to Children* 11, no. 2: 35–38.

Nedlina, Yelena. 2007. "Public Services to Russian-Speaking Patrons." *Bookmobile Outreach* 10, no. 1: 25–31.

Neiburger, Eli. 2007. "Games . . . in the Library?" *School Library Journal* 53, no. 7: 28–29.

Orange, Satia Marshall, and Robin Osborne. 2004. "From Outreach to Equity." *American Libraries* 35, no. 6: 46–51.

Peairs, Rhondalyn, Ellen Urton, and Donna Schenck-Hamlin. 2007. "Movies on the Grass." *College & Research Libraries News* 68, no. 7: 444–457.

Pearson, Debra, and Beth McNeil. 2002. "From High School Users College Students Grow." *Knowledge Quest* 30, no. 4: 24–28.

Quesada, Todd Douglas. 2007. "Spanish Spoken Here." *American Libraries* 38, no. 10: 40, 42, 44.

Robertson, Guy. 2007. "One for the Books." *Feliciter* 53, no. 2: 89–91.

Rortvedt, Sylvia. 2007. "Text, Image, and Form: The Altered Book Project." *Virginia Libraries* 53, no. 3: 27–28.

Sherry, Diana. 2004. "Providing Reading Buddies for the Children of Adult Literacy Students: One Way to Provide Onsite Child Care While Also Addressing Intergenerational Illiteracy." *Colorado Libraries* 31, no. 1: 40–42.

Squire, Kurt, and Constance Steinkuehler. 2005. "Meet the Gamers." *Library Journal* 130, no. 7: 38–41.

Steamboat Today. 2013. "Our View: Library Delivers on Public Promise." April 14. http://www.steamboattoday.com/news/2013/apr/14/our-view-library-delivers-public-promise/

Stephens, Julia. 2007. "English Spoken Here." *American Libraries* 38, no. 10: 41, 43–44.

Stevenson, Sara. 2005. "When Bad Libraries Go Good." *School Library Journal* 51, no. 12: 46–48.

Stubbs, James. 2014. "Traditional Board Games: From Ameritrash to Eurogames." In *Teen Games Rule! A Librarian's Guide to Platforms and Programs*, ed. by Julie Scordato and Ellen Forsyth, 65–88. Santa Barbara, CA: Libraries Unlimited.

Swisher, Susan H. 2007. "'A' Is for Art, Not Age." *Indiana Libraries* 26, no. 2: 38–39.

Warton, Pamela. 2001. "The Forgotten Voice in Homework." *Educational Psychologist* 36, no. 3: 155–165.

Whitehead, Nicole. 2004. "The Effects of Increased Access to Books on Student Reading Using the Public Library." *Reading Improvement* 41, no. 3: 165–178.

Young, Timothy G. 2007. "The Young Visitors." *College & Research Libraries News* 68, no. 4: 235–238.

Youngman, Daryl C. 2002. "Re-Shaping Library Service Programming for the New Millennium." *IATUAL Proceedings* no. 12: 1–5.

SUGGESTED READINGS

Alicea, Zaira R. Arvelo, and Ileana Cortés Santiago. 2014. "Witty Latina Grandmas, Silly Skeletons, and Birthday Cakes: A Library Program Focused on Bilingual Literacy." *Indiana Libraries* 33, no. 1: 16–18.

American Libraries. 2012. "New Americans and the Digital Literacy Gap." 43, nos. 11/12: 20–21.

Britton, Lauren. 2012. "The Makings of Maker Spaces." *Library Journal* 137, no. 16: 20–23.

Burhanna, Kenneth J. 2013. *Informed Transitions: Libraries Supporting the High School to College Transition.* Santa Barbara, CA: Libraries Unlimited.

Bush, Gail. 2006. "Walking the Road between Libraries: Best Practices in School and Public Library Cooperative Activities." *School Library Media Activities Monthly* 22, no. 6: 25–28.

Farkas, Meredith. 2014. "Just a Game?" *American Libraries* 45, nos. 1/2: 26.

Ferguson, Stuart. 2012. "Are Public Libraries Developers of Social Capital? A Review of Their Contribution and Attempts to Demonstrate It." *Australian Library Journal* 61, no. 1: 22–33.

Gauquier, Erica, and Jessica Schneider. 2013. "Minecraft Programs in the Library: If You Build It They Will Come." *Young Adult Library Services* 11, no. 2: 17–19.

Gee, James Paul. 2003. *What Video Games Have to Teach Us about Learning and Literacy*. New York: Palgrave MacMillan. (Note: This is a classic work on the topic.)

Jacobson, Alan. 2011. "How to Offer More Than a Movie: Producing Film Discussions That Are Serious Cultural Events." *American Libraries* 40, nos. 7/8: 42–45.

Hands, Africa S., and Amy Johnson. 2012. "Lighting the Way." *Children & Libraries* 10, no. 2: 56–57. (Note: Discusses the Ready to Read Corps from Columbus Metropolitan Library.)

Harrod, Kerol, and Carol Smallwood, eds. 2014. *Library Youth Outreach: 26 Ways to Connect with Children, Young Adults and Their Families*. Jefferson, NC: McFarland.

Hill, Nanci Milone. 2012. "One Book/One Community Programs." *Public Libraries* 51, no. 4: 17–21.

Intner, Carol F. 2011. *Homework Help from the Library: In Person and Online*. Chicago: American Library Association.

Knott, Dana, and Kristine Szabo. 2013. "Bigfoot Hunting: Academic Library Outreach to Elementary School Students." *College & Research Libraries News* 74, no. 7: 346–348.

Lilienthal, Stephen M. 2013. "Prison and Public Libraries." *Library Journal* 138, no. 2: 26–32.

Mars, Amy. 2012. "Library Services to the Homeless." *Public Libraries* 51, no. 2: 32–35.

Morris, Carla. 2013. "Tea for Two Hundred? Having a Fairy Tea Party at Your Library." *Children & Libraries* 11, no. 2: 39–42.

Oravet, Cate Calhoun. 2014. "Humans vs. Zombies at the Library: Gauging the Impact of a Live Action Gaming Event on Students' Library Use and Perceptions." *Journal of Library Innovation* 5, no. 1: 127–138.

Pender, Wendy, and José M. Garcia, Jr. 2013. "With Literacy for All." *Public Libraries* 52, no. 1: 8–10.

Phillips, Susan P. 2012. *Displays! Dynamic Design Ideas for Your Library Step by Step*. Jefferson, NC: McFarland.

Poland, Matthew, and Homa Naficy. 2012. "The American Place at Hartford Public Library: Tackling Digital Citizenship." *National Civic Review* 101, no. 4: 27–29.

Powell, Annmarie. 2013. "Get in the Game: Encouraging Play and Game Creation to Develop New Literacies in the Library." *Library Trends* 61, no. 4: 836–848.

Preddy, Leslie. 2012. "New Books Club." *School Library Monthly* 28, no. 7: 36–37.

Rockefeller, Elsworth. 2008. "Striving to Serve Diverse Youth: Mainstreaming Teens with Special Needs through Public Library Programming." *Public Libraries* 47, no. 1: 50–55.

Rovito, Jessica. 2012. "Crossing the Threshold into the Private Space: The TD Summer Reading Club Outreach to Shelters Project." *Feliciter* 58, no. 2: 59–61.

Rzepczynski, Mary. 2013. "Winter Reading Programs." *Public Libraries* 52, no. 6: 14–15.

Sanchez, Victoria. 2014. "More than Just 'Hanging Out.'" *Children & Libraries: The Journal of the Association for Library Service to Children* 12, no. 2: 16–20. (Note: Discusses Reading Lounges at Milwaukee [WI] Public Library and reading programs the library offers.)

Silverman, Karyn N. 2013. "Connecting Authors to Readers through the School Library." *Knowledge Quest* 41, no. 5: 26–29.

Spina. Carli. 2013. "Gamification: Is It Right for Your Library?" *AALL Spectrum* 17, no. 6: 7–9, 25.

Sullivan, Megan. 2013. "Welcoming Children and Families Affected by Incarceration into Public Libraries." *Public Libraries* 52, no. 4: 41–43.

Weinberger, David. 2012. "Library as Platform." *Library Journal* 137, no. 18: 34–36.

Computer Access

For more than thirty years, it has been standard practice in libraries to provide some type of computer facility to assist students in their research. . . . However, times are changing and the ready access to mobile technology has brought into question whether libraries need to or should continue to provide dedicated desktop computers. Do students still use and value access to computers in the library?

—*Susan Thompson, 2012*

Public librarians know that public access terminals and wireless Internet access are an increasingly popular resource among their patrons. But most only have an impression of how patrons use the library's technology from their over-the-shoulder glimpses of patrons' screens and basic statistics about the number of sessions they host.

—*Samantha Becker, 2013*

The continued growth of e-government information, communication, and services raises many fundamental questions about the nature of government information, as well as its management, dissemination, access and preservation.

—*Paul Jaeger, John Carlo Bertot, John Shuler, and Jessica McGilvray, 2012*

The three-week United States federal government shutdown in late 2013 received a great deal of attention among the public and the media. . . . But the shutdown also manifested something unexpected: the loss of e-government information, communication, services, and transactions. As it turns out, for e-government to function, you actually need a government that functions.

—*John Shuler, Paul Jaeger, and John Carlo Bertot, 2014*

In this chapter, we focus on programs and services that are technology based and are sometimes a mix of programs and services—public access to computers and e-government. Access to computers is considered a service when the computers provide access to library resources (traditional and electronic/owned or leased). It is defined as a program when it provides access to the Internet.

Information communication technology (ICT) has become a part of daily life for the vast majority of people in the United States, whether they recognize that fact or not. Young people who have known nothing but such a world find it hard to imagine a time when that was not the case. The fact is that time is not all that long ago—less than 30 years. As we will discuss later in the chapter, in the 1990s there was concern about the growing "digital divide." Libraries have and continue to play a significant role in addressing the "digital divide" and providing individuals with free access to computers and the Internet, as we will discuss later.

Samantha Becker and her colleagues (2010) in an Institute of Museum and Library Services (IMLS) report entitled *Opportunity for All* focused on how the American public currently benefits from Internet access at libraries. The report notes: "Internet access is now one of the most sought after public library services and used by nearly half of all visitors" (p. 1). Although the report's focus was primarily on public libraries, much of the material can apply to any type of library. The percentage of users making use of public access computers is not likely to have fallen since 2010. In fact, according to results of a study conducted by the ALA Office for Research & Statistics and the Information Policy & Access Center at the University of Maryland, use of public computers and Wi-Fi actually increased 60 percent over the course of one year in libraries studied (Hoffman et al., 2012, p. 6). Computer access in any type of library program or service is almost a given today, at least in the United States. A person is most likely to begin his or her library usage by employing some form of computing power. Likewise, library operations are highly dependent on technology. Only the smallest of today's libraries are not dependent on computers for at least some aspect of their activities.

There are individuals who firmly believe libraries have not changed since their grandmother's, perhaps even their great grandmother's, day. Their belief is libraries consist of dusty old unused books and magazines. There is also a belief among some that library staff members have no conception of modern technology. A 2011 example of such a misconception appeared in an "op-ed" piece on the *Los Angeles Times* "Opinion L.A." blog in November 2011. The entry "Saving Libraries but Not Librarians" (http://opinion.latimes.com/opinionla/2011/11/saving-libraries-but-not-librarians-blowback.html) spelled out Dan Terzian's belief that librarians and many libraries were no longer necessary. (Terzian is an attorney with no identified background in librarianship.) Some of his comments were: "The digital revolution has made many librarians obsolete;" "All but the most heady research can be performed by a Google, Google Books, or Google Scholar search;" and "Libraries should embrace the digital revolution, even though it entails the loss of librarians." Feedback to his opinions was swift and negative; apparently many librarians and library supporters have at least embraced some aspects of the digital revolution and know how to post comments on the Web.

There are several components to libraries and technology; however, there are two broad aspects. From a library's daily work point of view, ICT has been fully integrated into library operations for some time. Service to the users is equally dependent upon ICT. Almost every library, from schools to the Library of Congress, employs technology for daily work activities and service and has been doing so for some time.

We included Terzian's op-ed piece because we believe it makes an important, if unintended, point. We, librarians, still have significant work to do in getting the message out—that libraries have indeed embraced technology and librarians and libraries have a positive impact (intellectually and economically) on society. For example, libraries are creating digital archives (e.g., local history, institutional archives, and rare book/special materials)—something that no for-profit organization would ever consider.

LIBRARIES AND TECHNOLOGY

Libraries first employed "dumb terminals" (essentially monitors and keyboards connected to a remote mainframe computer) in public service many years ago to give the users access to the library's electronic database (OPACs) of its collections. Libraries have employed computers for cataloging purposes since at least the 1960s. (When OCLC started in 1967, its original purpose was to provide a cooperative cataloging system for academic libraries in Ohio.) As ILSs became more sophisticated, the public access equipment became less and less dumb, up to the point we are today—mobile access. Over the years, more and more digital material became available to libraries, first in the form of CD-ROMS and now through the Internet.

In the late 1980s and early 1990s, with the growing use of the Internet, libraries and the general public became concerned with what was called the "digital divide." That is, there was a recognition that there were individuals and families who were unable to gain the advantages to the digital revolution. Public libraries started to offer free public access to computers to assist in bridging the divide.

You might think that after almost 25 years that the divide would have disappeared. That is not the case, nor is it likely to be so in the near future. Poverty/economic issues are not likely to vanish. When it becomes a matter of food and shelter versus paying for "connectivity" at home, the winner is almost always the former.

There are several divides; most of which have money at their base, but not necessarily poverty. Location is a factor, for those living in rural areas (access is difficult or very costly). Equipment capability is another issue that creates a divide. Bandwidth is also an issue in terms of gaining the full advantages of the digital world. Certainly there are a substantial number of people who do not have the requisite skills to make effective use of what is available digitally. Perhaps an upcoming divide may be the mobile technologies that may impact those less financially well off.

Libraries can bridge many of the gaps, at least in part, for the less affluent in our communities. Our opening quotation from Susan Thompson may be more or less accurate for today's higher education students and, at some point in time, for everyone. However, what is unlikely to change is the necessity of connectivity, regardless of equipment employed, and costs that are out of reach for a substantial number of service community members.

PUBLIC ACCESS TO COMPUTERS

Becker and her colleagues, quoted earlier, noted that "computer technology has become ubiquitous in American society. Without access to computers and the Internet, people are excluded from many jobs, government services, educational opportunities, and social networks. To help ensure all Americans can participate in digital culture, public libraries have been at the forefront of mobilizing resources to support free public access to technology" (2010, p. 12). We would add that academic and school libraries also provide free access. While there are some private academic libraries that restrict access to their buildings, most academic libraries allow anyone access to their OPAC and the Internet. Most do not allow access to their e-databases, except under certain conditions that vary from library to library. As we will discuss in chapter 12, school libraries allow free Internet access, but not to everything on the Net (filtered access).

Certainly the slow economic recovery of recent years has not helped libraries to fully address the challenge of a growing demand for more computer access and assistance to online material. People have expectations of having current technological capability at the library even as they have had to reduce their personal spending on such technology. Prior to the Great Recession, the average number of public library public access computers rose from 6 in 2000 to 12 in 2006 (Becker et al., 2010, p. 18). The *Public Libraries in the United States Survey: Fiscal Year 2011* from the IMLS (the latest available data when we prepared this chapter) reported that there was a 6 percent increase in Internet-ready computer terminals over the prior year (Swan et al., 2014, p. 44). This is not a very large increase given the increased pressures for more access, but the increase was indicative of an upward trend since 2008. One reason for the small reported increase may be due to libraries providing wireless access and loaning laptops for in-library usage—for example, not "computer terminals."

Another statistic in the survey was that the national average of PC usage was 223.9 per 1,000 visits, representing a one-year decrease of 4.4 percent (Swan et al., 2014, p. 25). The survey employed a five-level breakdown of the usage—national, city, suburb, town, and rural. Not too surprisingly, city and rural usage were almost identical (two significant areas in the digital divide)—city 230.7 and rural 246.4, respectively. Notably, "compared to the previous year, each locality saw a decline in public access computer usage per capita (Swan et al., 2014, p. 24). This data suggests that the divide is still present and libraries have significant challenges for helping people have access to the online resources. The survey provided a related statistic that highlights availability—the national ratio of public access computers was 4.4 per 5,000 people, with 42 out of 50 states seeing an increase in computers over the prior year (p. 44).

Do these statistics have any social significance? We believe they do. There is evidence that there is some social gain from having access to computers and information technology skills. In particular, such access and skill assists in educational advancement, community evolvement/participation, and in accessing government services, and health and safety information. There are economic benefits such as developing marketable technology skills, of course, through e-commerce activities.

Check These Out

The following are a few good starting points for gaining more insight into the societal benefits of having access to technology and the digital world:

Abrahamson, Jennie A., Karen E. Fisher, Anne G. Turner, Joan C. Durrance, and Tammara Combs Turner. 2008. "Lay Information Mediary Behavior Uncovered: Exploring How Non-Professionals Seek Health Information for Themselves and Others Online." *Journal of the Medical Library Association* 96, no. 4: 310–323.

Bertot, John C., Charles R. McClure, and Paul T. Jaeger. 2008. "The Impacts of Free Public Internet Access on Public Library Patrons and Communities." *Library Quarterly* 78, no. 3: 285–301.

Case, Donald Owen. 2012. *Looking for Information: A Survey of Research on Information Seeking, Needs, and Behavior.* 3rd ed. Bingley, UK: Emerald Group Publishing.

Horrigan, John. 2008. *Online Shopping: Frictions, Frustrations, and Fixes.* Washington, D.C.: Pew Internet & American Life Project. http://www.pewinternet.org/Presentations/2008/Online-Shopping-Frictions-Frustrations-and-Fixes.aspx.

Kinney, Bo. 2010. "The Internet, Public Libraries, and the Digital Divide." *Public Library Quarterly* 29, no. 2: 104–161.

Real, Brian, John Carlo Bertot, and Paul T. Jaeger. 2013. "Rural Public Libraries and Digital Inclusion: Issues and Challenges." *Information Technology and Libraries* 33, no. 1: 6–24.

Computer Access Policies

Libraries have policies for a variety of public service activities; few are more important than the one addressing public access to library computers and connections to the digital world. There are the usual reasons for having such a policy; however, there are legal implications as well as staff training concerns that magnify its importance. (We look at the legal issues in more depth in chapter 13.) Staff training involves not only an understanding of the policy—the usual issue—but also training related to the software associated with computer access.

Broadly thinking, the obvious elements the policy will address are for whom, what, how, under what terms, and for how long access is allowed. One critical aspect of the policy is infrastructure security—networks, equipment, and so forth. Topics such as passwords (if required, who and how to handle passwording, etc.), hacking, unauthorized copying, and viewing usage logs are also significant issues for inclusion in the policy. It is also important to review any conditions on the use of personal computers/mobile devices on the library's wireless network. This is a very small sample of many technical issues to discuss and decide to or not to include in the final policy.

From the Authors' Experience

Saponaro provided one example of hardware/infrastructure security and public access to library computers issues. The event took place in late February 2013 in the University of Maryland Libraries.

There is a trick that a few unscrupulous individuals employ to steal other people's private information while using a computer—keystroke logging. (Such logging is a means of recording and saving information about every keystroke a person makes while using a computer.)

Library IT personnel, while engaging in routine servicing of public access computers, discovered such logging devices attached to the computers, out of sight, on two machines. There was no way to know how long the devices had been in place. Students and faculty were advised of the problem, and it was strongly suggested they should change passwords and check their financial records.

This is a good example of why part of a library's public computer access policy should clearly spell out both the users' and library's liability for issues arising from using the public machines.

There is an issue that falls into both the technical and user side of the policy. That is the issue of filtering what users may access. The main area of concern is CIPA (Children's Internet Protection Act). We discuss CIPA in more detail in the chapter on legal issues (chapter 13). However, the policy must address whether or not the library will filter Internet access. Also, since CIPA filtering does allow for an adult to request the filter be turned off while he or she is using the machine, the policymakers should think about how to handle such requests and how clearly that right is made known.

Access concerns are also varied. Perhaps foremost among them is who will have access—registered borrowers, anyone coming into the library, and others. Will there be some type of user priority system during peak usage periods, such as for the primary service population? Will there be time limits for those not part of the major service groups? Will there be a system to reserve a time for having access? User privacy is a concern that must be addressed in the policy.

An equally important question to answer is what will be acceptable usages of the computers? People have a number of reasons for wanting access to library technology. A sound policy addresses all or most of the usages. The *Opportunity for All* (Becker et al., 2010) report employed eight broad usage categories—in rank order, social connection, education, employment, health and wellness, government and legal, community engagement, managing finances, and entrepreneurship (p. 5). Sixty percent of the users in the study reported they used their access for social connection purposes. Educational and employment reasons were almost the same—42 percent for learning activities and 40 percent for seeking or investigating job opportunities. The next three were in the 30–40 percent range. A somewhat surprising 25 percent engaged in some type of financial activity. It is surprising in the sense that the users should be aware the public machines are *not* secure and thereby they are taking substantial risks that someone may learn how to access their credit cards/bank accounts, and so on. Entrepreneurial reasons only represented 7 percent of the usage.

All of these categories can and do take place on library computers. (We might add to this list a ninth category—entertainment and recreation—as some libraries do allow for online game playing.) We believe, when developing a policy, you ought to at least think about each of the categories, even if you do not in the end include all of them in the final version.

Other policy and programming considerations surround offering free Wi-Fi. If you do, will users be given the option of having access to a secure network? What about loaning laptops and if so, on what basis? Then there is the issue of how much remote access to allow to library resources and how to control it. Those issues may have legal/cost implications as many database vendors price their products on the basis of number of potential users. There are also issues of controlling access—authentication and so forth. Will people be allowed to use personal media (flash drives, etc.) on library equipment? If so, is there a need for a statement regarding both the person's and library's liability for problems (loss of data, viruses, etc.)?

For academic and public libraries, careful thought should be given to how much "technical" support the staff should give to users. There will be occasions when a person is trying to gain access to online library resources and is having a problem doing so. Some of the time the problem is equipment-related, and not with a database or e-resource. Remote access is an area where this most often arises, and, not infrequently, takes place during periods when there is no IT person available to ask to help sort out the issue. From users' perspective, it does not really matter why there is a problem—they just want a resolution. It becomes a PR issue when the library cannot solve the issue. The question of just how much knowledge about networks, CPUs, proxy servers, and so forth is it realistic for the library staff to have is an important one. There is also a question of how they would gain such information. Thinking the matter through in advance is a sound idea.

It is almost expected that the public service staff, including librarians, are able to assist users resolve most, if not all, issues related to accessing the library's technology. Certainly this is not realistic in solving some infrastructure or network problems; however, even in such cases the staff should try to provide information as to when things will hopefully return to normal. It would be a rare library offering download services that did not have at least one staff member capable of answering almost any user's question about downloading a file.

The preceding one is a small sample of the issues to think about, discuss, and have approved by the library's governing board. An excellent article that details the many issues of such policymaking is Jason Vaughan's 2004 "Policies Governing Use of Computing Technology in Academic Libraries" (*Information Technology and Libraries* 23, no. 4: 151–167). Although his focus is on academic libraries, the topics he covers apply to all types of library environments.

A number of library Internet access policies are available online. One example of a current policy developed and implemented by a public library is that of the Flagstaff City-Conocino (AZ) County Public Library System:

Public Internet Access Fair Use Policy

Computers are available to LIBRARY CARDHOLDERS free of charge, on a first-come, first-served basis. FOR LIBRARY CARDHOLDERS, FREE USE IS LIMITED TO 2 HOURS PER PERSON PER DAY, WITH MULTIPLE SESSIONS. FOR NON-CARDHOLDERS, FREE USE IS LIMITED TO A SINGLE ONE-HOUR SESSION PER PERSON PER DAY. Additional Internet sessions can be purchased for a fee.

VISITORS AND NON-LIBRARY CARDHOLDERS need to check at the Information desk for a reservation.

The library relies on the cooperation of its patrons to efficiently and effectively provide shared resources, and to ensure community access to the Internet. Please observe the posted usage for computers. Up to two people can use a computer at any one time; two people working together are counted as ONE session.

Violations of computer system security, circumvention of the computer use reservation program, unauthorized alteration of software configurations, attempts to damage computer hardware or software, or use of a workstation for illegal or criminal purpose, will result in losing Internet privileges permanently. Illegal acts involving library resources, including violation of U.S. Copyright Law (Title 17 U.S. Code), may be subject to prosecution by local, state, or federal officials.

IT IS UNLAWFUL FOR ANY PERSON TO KNOWINGLY DISPLAY MATERIALS CONSIDERED OBSCENE AS DEFINED BY THE (CHILDREN'S INTERNET PROTECTION ACT, Pub. L. 106–554), and (ARIZONA REVISED STATUTES 13–3501 TO 13–3512). IT IS ALSO UNLAWFUL TO GAMBLE ON THE INTERNET in a public place (ARS 13–3304, AND FCC 6–01–001–0012). Patrons violating these statutes will be told to cease and desist. If they refuse, they will be told to leave the library and will permanently lose Internet privileges.

The Internet provides access to adult subjects. Current library policy does not allow our staff to determine what ideas or information may be presented to any patron. Individual users must determine the appropriateness of materials for their needs. Parents and/or legal guardians are responsible for their child's exposure to ideas and information while in the library.

In general, electronic communication is not secure and networks are susceptible to outside intervention. Therefore, the library cannot guarantee patron privacy when using our machines to access the Internet. Also, public computers may not have the same options as those available on a home computer. Use of any PERIPHERALS, such as digital cameras and storage devices, are not supported by staff or computer equipment.

Library staff is NOT available to answer detailed questions about navigating on the Internet, nor use of Microsoft products. There are numerous books available for checkout from the library that can assist you. Also, consider taking a computer class at the library or elsewhere.

PRINTED COPIES: Each page printed costs 15 cents, and must be paid for in advance at the appropriate print station.

To view full text of the Flagstaff City-Coconino Public Library Electronic Resources Policy go to the library website and look at Policies under the category About Us. (http://www.flagstaffpubliclibrary.org/about/e-resources.html)

GOVERNMENT INFORMATION AND SERVICES IN THE DIGITAL AGE

This section addresses two aspects of providing public access to government agencies and their resources, at all levels of jurisdiction. In the chapter on print collections, we noted many libraries have legacy collections of government documents and publications. (We suggest that there is a difference between documents and publications: documents are records of agency activities—such as draft legislation—while publications are of general interest to the public dealing with topics related to the agency's mission—for example, a *Smokey the Bear* coloring book issued by the Forest Service.) Although agencies still issue some information in print and media formats, more and more is available in digital format only.

Check This Out

An interesting research report that addresses this topic as well as others is Kathryn Zickuhr, Lee Rainie, and Kristen Purcell's 2013 study *Library Services in the Digital Age* (Pew Internet Project, Pew Research Center, http://libraries.pewinternet.org/2013/01/22/library-services/).

Digital Government Information

The shift to a digital information environment for government information has been under way for some time. The transition has meant that libraries of all types are involved in providing access to the full range to government information; it is no longer just the libraries involved in the depository program operated by the Government Printing Office and similar agencies at the state and local levels.

Citizens, if they are to participate meaningfully in their governance, must have some free access to information about government activities and processes. In the not-too-distant past, print documents provided that critical information and libraries filled the role of both as acquirer of government material and as provider of assistance in accessing the information. Today there is a vast universe of digital government information available through the Internet. A significant difference exists between print and digital access.

Michael White (1996) suggested that society's right to government information, at least in the English-speaking world, has its origin in the English *Magna Carta* of 1215. Expanding on this right, the *Constitution of the United States* (Article 1, Section 5) contains the requirement that Congress shall "keep a journal of its proceedings, and from time to time publish same, excepting such parts as may in their judgment require secrecy; and the yeas and nays of the members of either house on any question shall, at the desire of one-fifth of those present, be entered on the journal." James Madison (1822) wrote about the need for an informed citizenry, "A popular government without popular information, or the means of acquiring it, is but a prologue to a farce or a tragedy; or perhaps both. . . . And a people who mean to be their own governors, must arm themselves with the power that knowledge gives."

As you might expect, there is a slight problem in reconciling these quotations in terms of balancing access and security. Although this has always been a challenge, it is a much greater issue now than in the past. The *Constitution* specifically indicates that some government information may require secrecy. How does society achieve a balance between the access Madison believed in and the much-needed security in today's very different world?

We all know that September 11, 2001, brought about significant changes for many people and organizations in the United States. Government information also experienced changes: some large, some small. Initially, librarians thought they observed a significant tightening in the information government agencies made available. One factor in that perception was the ongoing move to a digital format. This process had been under way for some time, but when some materials were pulled by the federal government the sense was the changes were greater than they actually were. It is also true that there was some tightening in what was released; which is not an unreasonable reaction to what had happened. Today, some of the concern has abated, but lingering questions (security vs. access) still remain the subject of strong debate during the time we prepared this chapter.

With print you may not have the most current information, but you know what you are looking at has not been modified by some unknown, perhaps third party. Also, it is not likely to vanish in the blink of an eye. Neither is true of the digital format. Kathy Dempsey's (2004) editorial "The Info Was There, Then—Poof" sums up the issue of permanence and digital information. Her editorial prefaced a themed issue dealing with government information, in which she highlighted a key concern: "Where do you draw the line between which data should be public and which should be kept private?" (p. 4). We might add, "Who should make that critical call?" Dempsey related how one of the articles intended for that issue went "poof" when the White House requested a final review. (The authors of the article in question worked in a federal information center and their piece was to describe the factors and process that determine what information is deemed classified.)

Bonnie Klein and Sandy Schwal (2005) also discussed the delicate balance society must achieve between maintaining free access to information and security. Klein and Schwal (who are federal government employees) in their concluding section made the following points: "Newly generated government information will be evaluated against established criteria for review for public release, the same as always. There is no core group making these decisions, although there may be a tendency on the part of those responsible to err on the side of caution" (p. 23).

Check This Out

An interesting article chronicling how government information is created and shared and how classified information in particular is made available via conventional (governmental) and unconventional methods (e.g., WikiLeaks) is Marsha West's 2013 piece "Classified Information Policy, Government Transparency, and WikiLeaks" in *Dttp: A Quarterly Journal Of Government Information Practice & Perspective* (41, no. 2: 13–17).

Something that is frequently overlooked in the debate about security and access is the fact that depository libraries (the largest holders of print government publications) do not *own* the material. Although they invest significant sums of money in the long-term storage of the material and in staff effort to service the collections, they do not have ownership. The government can and has at various times withdrawn material from depository collections—that process is not just a post-9/11 phenomenon. Further, the federal government can do so without consultation and libraries have no recourse.

Defining what government information is can be a challenge. Are reports prepared by nongovernmental agencies, but required by a government agency, "government" information? What about short- and long-term multijurisdictional groups that produce reports? Government information comes from local, state, federal, and international bodies. In today's digital world, there is undoubtedly more government information, regardless of source, available to more people than in the past—if you know how to get at it. Almost all government material is "born digital," which allows jurisdictions to make it inexpensively available on the Web, if they wish to do so.

We noted earlier that the shift to the digital world has been ongoing for some years. By the time the Reagan administration began in 1981, there were over 1,300 full and partial depository libraries of U.S. government documents. (Today the number is 1,250.) During President Reagan's first term, the Office of Management and Budget (OMB) received authorization to develop a federal information policy as the result of the passage of Public Law 96–511 (Paperwork Reduction Act [PRA] of 1980). OMB had the responsibility to minimize the cost of collecting, maintaining, using, and disseminating information. One of OMB's initiatives supported the concept of disseminating federal information as raw data in an electronic format, often without software for using or searching for desired data. Despite this drawback in providing the mechanism for access, certainly OMB's role in shifting the emphasis from paper to electronic means of dissemination has been significant.

A major problem with the implementation of the PRA was that the necessary national, much less local, technological infrastructure that would make the concept viable did not yet exist. Another significant issue was the lack of government-wide standards for making information available electronically. Only a few individuals who could benefit from government information have the skills to locate and retrieve what might be useful without some assistance. Realistically, until there is a true single standard, most people will have to depend on either their place of employment or libraries to provide the needed assistance.

From a public service point of view, providing such assistance for all the variations in U.S. government databases is a challenge that few libraries can fully meet. We do agree with Gail Golderman and Bruce Connolly's (2002) statement that "whether you are inspired by the dynamic expression of democracy at work in Washington or believe that our politicians must be closely watched at all times, keeping track of how our officials carry out their constitutionally mandated mission has been made easier thanks to online resources" (p. 50). However, we have a long way to go before it is truly easy. Finding your way through the various options to identify the desired information requires patience and persistence. Users will need all the assistance you can provide when they are seeking government information.

As a result of congressional consideration of the Government Printing Reform Act of 1996, various library associations (e.g., the ALA, the American Association of Law Libraries, and the Association of Research Libraries) became active in attempting to influence the final form of the legislation. One of their efforts was to create a list of basic principles:

- The public has a right of access to government information.
- The government has an obligation to guarantee the authenticity and integrity of its information.
- The government has an obligation to disseminate and provide broad public access to its information.
- The government has an obligation to preserve its information (ALA, AALL, and ARL, 1996, n.p.).

In sum, government information created or compiled by government employees or at government expense should remain in the public domain ("Statement on H.R. 4280, the Government Printing Reform Act of 1996," 1996, p. 1). Current federal policy essentially has been to maximize the usefulness of information, within limits of security concerns, while both minimizing costs and recovering some of the costs of developing the information. How the issues are resolved will have implications for public services staff.

Reference service in the era of electronic government information presents some challenges for the staff. There is much to learn about the idiosyncrasies of the various agency databases and Web sites, even in terms of such basics as how to search, display, and print/download. Also, some agencies provide different or more information in the electronic format than they did/do in the print version. The result is that the public services staff and users alike must remember which version supplies this or that type of information.

It is important to note that just because a government Web site or service exists, there are no guarantees its support will be ongoing. As a result, public services staff must remain alert to changes in services and resources. At the time we were preparing this volume, two fairly significant events occurred. The first was the demise of World News Connection (WNC) in late 2013. WNC was a foreign news service for translated and English-language news provided by the U.S. Department of Commerce/National Technical Information Service (NTIS). The reasons for its demise included "increasing costs, increased competition from alternate sources, and incompatibility with mission limitations" (https://web.archive.org/web/20140327173133/http://www.ntis.gov/products/wnc.aspx). One article detailing the demise of WNC is Elizabeth Murray's "US Shutting Down a Key News Source" in *ConsortiumNews.Com*— http://consortiumnews.com/2013/12/03/us-shutting-down-a-key-news-source/.

Another example occurred in mid-2014. In an NPR blog post, S.V. Date (2014) reported on a bill Senator Tom Coburn introduced to Congress entitled the "Let Me Google That for You Act of 2014" (U.S. Senate. 113th Congress, 2nd Session. S.2206). The bill, if successful, would abolish the NTIS entirely. NTIS was originally created to collect, categorize, and disseminate government information. Two programs administered by the NTIS are the National Technical Reports Library (NTRL, http://www.ntis.gov/products/ntrl.aspx) and the Selected Research Service (NTIS-SRS, http://www.ntis.gov/products/srs/).

NTIS was also responsible for the now-defunct World News Connection service, mentioned earlier. The future of the bill was uncertain as of late 2014, but it appeared to have some traction. Even if the current iteration was not successful, as noted by Date "there's probably a good chance of a Let Me Google That for You Act of 2015." We may add to that statement "or beyond."

E-Government Programs

For a number of years the idea of an "electronic democracy" has been discussed and debated—long before there was a World Wide Web. The idea is that it would enable citizens to participate more efficiently in civic life, as well as make the public bureaucracy more "business-like" in the delivery of its programs and services. Certainly most government bodies have a Web presence. Just how that presence has or has not modified programs and services is an open question. "E-government" is a term you see and often appears to have a number of meanings depending on who is talking about the concept. At its most basic level, the term relates to a government's employment of technology to provide information and services to its citizens. You can gain a sense of the variations in meanings when some people view it as a means of emergency communication (e.g., wild fire, flood warning, hurricane), while others see it as a way of gaining access to reports and minutes of meetings. The latter view makes it clear that libraries, especially public libraries, could/ should have a significant role to play, as not everyone has Internet access in their homes.

In 2002, Congress passed the E-Government Act (P.L. 107–347, 112 Stat. 2681–749). The law mandates federal agencies to reduce the scope of their former public services functions, especially those that call for interaction with citizens and thus staffing, and replacing them with digital services. As Robert Davidsson (2008) noted, "One of the goals of the E-Government Act is to offer an electronic alternative to paper-based and direct agency-provided services requiring additional staff" (p. 16). State and local governments have been quick to follow suit in practice, if not with legislation. Thus, government agencies, at all levels, have been making ever greater use of the Internet to carry out their responsibilities. Fewer and fewer documents are printed; rather they are posted on the Web. Some agencies require a person to go to the Web to make an appointment to see an agency employee. This is an example of where the digital divide can be a significant problem for some people. Libraries, especially public libraries, have been active in helping people bridge that divide. Needless to say, the free public access computers are a key factor in an e-government program.

The Economist (February 16, 2008) published an 18-page supplement entitled "The Electronic Bureaucrat: A Special Report on Technology and Government." The introductory essay to the supplement ends with: "Although hopes have been high and the investment huge, so far the results have mostly been disappointing. That reflects a big difficulty in e-government (and in writing about it): it touches on so many other things. What exactly is it that public organisations are trying to maximize, and how can it be measured?" (p. 4). This has been and still remains an issue: what is the role/purpose of government information and e-government? And that in turn raises the question of what role libraries can and should play.

Public libraries, like or not, are becoming e-government service centers. Becoming such a center brings additional work and demands on limited resources: more often than not without additional support from the agencies benefiting from what libraries do for them. Small and rural libraries are particularly hard hit by having to perform activities that are essentially thrust upon them by outside agencies. Further, providing users with assistance in their e-government activities may open up additional areas of legal liability (we look at legal issues later in chapter 13).

Public libraries, assuming they have public access computers (which essentially all of them do), and provide Internet access, will be involved in e-government activities to some extent. Thus, the issue to resolve is what form that activity will take. At the minimum level is a passive approach: doing nothing more for a user trying to access some e-government service than any other person using the library's computers. On the opposite end of the spectrum is an e-government program with a variety of assistance available specifically for such access. (Note: when we say e-government, we don't just mean federal government, but also state and local governments.)

A halfway approach between a passive or full program is to seek out and make available printed forms; many libraries have made tax forms available for a long time, although some have suspended the practice as a means of conserving paper. Adding in a page on the library's Web site that links users to e-government sites is also relatively easy to do and benefits users without adding too much to the staff's workload. Another middle ground technique is to make meeting rooms available to any agency wishing to hold a meeting/ training opportunity for end users of its services. Sometimes an agency will provide an "information kiosk" that spells out its e-services, if the library is willing to provide the floor space.

Is there a difference between having public access computers, even with links to government agencies and forms, and having an e-government program? The answer is a very definite "yes." The former is a passive approach and the second is proactive. Whatever approaches a library takes, some people will use the computers for accessing government services. An e-government program generally involves one-on-one assistance from a person who has training in what the agencies expect and require. (With the passive approach, the library staff is still likely to be asked for help but the staff will have little or no background in what the agency in question may require.) Library e-government programs also offer classes specifically tailored to e-government agency needs, often with agencies support in the form of materials or content suggestions. Programs that public librarians can and do offer cover topics ranging from health (e.g., navigating the Affordable Care Act, Medicare, Medicaid), jobs and retirement (e.g., Social Security), citizenship, financial literacy, and beyond. We will even go so far as to suggest that in the not-too-distant future public libraries with such programs will begin to have positions with titles such as "e-government specialist."

What are some of the more common e-government program elements that may lead to job titles similar to the above? Certainly there would be one-on-one assistance, but with a significant difference. The library staff member would have training in e-government activities. In addition, there may the opportunity for users to make appointments for such assistance. Many libraries offering an e-government program offer group sessions that focus on e-government service, not just on computer skills. The best of such offerings are developed in conjunction with the government agencies covered in the class. Sometimes they even include an agency staff member as one of the presenters. Certainly an important element in a full program is having a staff person designated as the liaison with those agencies that are most heavily accessed by the service community. That in turn may result in true collaborative efforts between the library and an agency—it is not the same as having financial support but is likely to reduce staff stress when e-government services expand. Some libraries create Web 2.0 tools that focus solely on e-government services; one example is from Pasco County Libraries (Florida)—http://www.pascolibraries.org/. The Florida Department of State's Division of Library & Information Services also has a resource site for Florida libraries detailing e-government projects, as well as providing links to recent newsletters and Webinars on the topic (http://www.egovflorida.org/).

Nancy Fredericks (2011) reported that the top two challenges for public library e-government programs related to staffing (p. 33). Neither of the two is too surprising: not enough staff to handle the new workload and serious issues related to knowing enough about what is required to effectively assist users. The first challenge is not likely to change any time soon. It has never been easy for libraries to secure additional FTEs and certainly it is even harder to accomplish during economic downturns. There may be some approaches that might work in some situations, but even in the best of circumstances the odds for success are long indeed. Perhaps the most hopeful technique is doing an ROI (return on investment) study related to the library's e-government activities. (We discuss ROI in some detail in chapter 18.) Even when there is success, a fair amount of time, perhaps several years, will pass before there is an additional position.

As for the second challenge identified by Fredericks, there are a variety of training options that will improve the effectiveness of the library's service if doing nothing to decrease the workload. Training in e-government activities, services, expectations, and so forth is the key. The basic objective, even for libraries that do not plan on offering an e-government program, is to gain an understanding of what current federal, state, and local government e-government activities exist.

Another aspect of the training is learning which of those activities are important and/or needed by the service community. Again, public service staff in libraries that do not have a proactive program of assistance still need some understanding of what users are doing and probably will be asking for help to accomplish. For libraries with a proactive program, there is a need to master the skills to navigate e-government sites and what the agency requires. An essential element in training is to have an understanding of how far staff assistance may go without creating potential liability concerns for the library. From a long-term perspective, proactive programs may explore what e-government services might be useful to but not currently accessed by the service community.

Libraries do not have to be "Lone Rangers" when it comes to learning about e-government services. The ALA offers an e-government toolkit created by the

ALA Committee on Legislation as a means to assist librarians in "planning, managing, funding and promoting E-Government services" (http://www.ala .org/advocacy/advleg/federallegislation/govinfo/egovernment/egovtoolkit). We recommend starting with the "Library E-Government Services" section of the toolkit, which provides a sound overview of what is involved in starting a program (http://www.ala.org/advocacy/advleg/federallegislation/govinfo /egovernment/egovtoolkit/libgov). The federal and state e-government sections include a number of useful links to additional information. There are also brief pages discussing e-government approaches for academic, public, and school environments which assist staff new to such activities with a sense of what is involved.

A follow-up resource within the same ALA toolkit is the "Service Level Policies" section (http://www.ala.org/advocacy/advleg/federallegislation /govinfo/egovernment/egovtoolkit/servicelevel). This site provides more in-depth coverage of what policy issues a library must consider when thinking about offering a proactive program. It is particularly strong in the areas of liability and security.

There are, of course, non-ALA sites available as well. One we particularly like is LibEGov (http://www.libegov.org/). This site has a section on "E-Gov Basics" which is another good introduction to the topic for people new to the concept. Another section offers links to a number of government agencies and information about their e-services. Yet another section provides ideas for implementing a program from classes to creating Web pages. OCLC WebJunction® offers an "Introduction to E-Government" (http://www.webjunction.org /partners/arizona/gi21/gi21-egov.html) that is also well worth checking out.

E-Government Policies

It is essential to develop a set of e-government policies when undertaking a proactive program. All public libraries regardless of what they decide to do about e-government should at least discuss the legal aspects with their governing boards; there may be some liability no matter what the decision may be regarding offering a program.

Like any other library policy, it takes time to get to a final document in place. E-government assistance policies may take a little more time, as it is vitally important that key stakeholders, especially legal counsel, fully understand what the policy covers and the issues involved in having such a policy. Those staff members who already interact with users who are accessing the library's computers may be the best group to begin the work of drafting the document. They will have some familiarity with what users are currently attempting to do and what issues are raised by those interactions. Further, they will have knowledge of how sophisticated users are when it comes to accessing and evaluating Web resources.

An obvious starting point is to see what other libraries have done in this area. Doing so also helps the group focus on the major topics to cover in the draft document as well as getting started on defining what the library thinks it might do in a program of e-government assistance. A major question is, what does the library mean when employing the term e-government assistance?

Will it cover just federal, state, or local government agencies? Will it cover some or all? Will it be a matter of first come first served or will there be an opportunity to make an appointment? If appointments will be available, what will there be a time limit for the session? Will there be a grace period for keeping the appointment? How will the library handle latecomers and are all the staff members assisting other individuals? Such issues may not be in the policy, but they certainly are factors in the library's service reputation and should be thought through before the first incident takes place in the public area of the library.

Some of the other topics to ponder are, will the program focus solely on government agencies or will it include not-for-profit organizations that offer services similar to what a government agency offers? How might the policy impact existing library policies, such as computer access? Will there need to be a change in the mobile phone usage policy? There may be times when a phone call to the agency in question is necessary to resolve a user's question.

Without question, the policy will require some clear-cut disclaimers, if not crafted by then at least approved by the library's attorney(s). Typical disclaimers cover staff members' assistance limitations and liability; library and its staff are not representatives of any government agency other than its parent organization; the library is not liable for failures in electronic transmission (missing a deadline, missing information, etc.); and the library has no responsibility for the outcome of the person's interaction with a government agency. Many libraries have a paper or electronic ("click-through" agreement) form that spells out the disclaimers.

The list of issues is broader than the discussion covered earlier. A good, reasonably comprehensive, site to visit for more detailed information is ALA's "Service Level Policies" in the E-Government toolkit mentioned previously.

Check These Out

An early and widely used starting point for such documents is the e-government assistance policy from Pasco County (Florida) Library System (http://www.pascolibraries.org/about-us/policies/e-government-service-assistance-policy/). A number of libraries have more or less copied that policy with minor adjustments.

A very different approach was taken by the Beauregard Parish Library (Louisiana) governing board (http://library.beau.org/policies/egovt_policy.pdf), which created a very succinct statement covering e-government and computer use simultaneously.

CLOSING THOUGHTS

We conclude this chapter with a brief discussion of social trust and libraries. We do this as the public has come to have less and less trust of government and to raise the questions if users accessing government information through the library have greater trust in that information than they might otherwise have.

A short but concise definition of this complex concept is the belief in the honesty, dependability, and integrity of others (people and organizations). Libraries appear to be a trusted organization in the United States (which, it seems, is not all that trusting a society). The Pew Research Center survey in 2007 found that 50 percent of those surveyed agreed with the statement "You can't be too careful in dealing with people" (Taylor, Funk, and Clark, 2007, p. 1). Many people are even less trustful of government agencies. Those facts have implications for those of us working in library public services. In the following discussion, we shorten the term social trust to just trust.

In a later chapter, we look at the notions related to beliefs, principles, values, and ethics in some depth. Here the important point is that perhaps 50 percent of the people we attempt to assist may not fully trust us, even if we work in a trusted organization. Then there is the fact that we may be part of the 50 percent that believe a person "can't be too careful in dealing with people." If we are, how will that impact our interactions with users?

There would seem to be some serious issues if a trusted organization offers assistance in using services of another organization that may not be viewed as completely trustworthy. That is what libraries do when they passively or actively provide access to e-government. A related question, when a library provides access to the unfiltered Web with its good, bad, indifferent, and wrong information, is there a trust issue? Do people trust whatever they find on the Web when doing so in the library?

Something to Ponder

David Pogue (2014) wrote an essay that discussed lack of organizational trust. The organization lacking in peoples' trust that he wrote about might surprise some readers—technology companies. His thought is, "Our tech companies have a trust problem. Over the years they've brought [it?] on themselves. Google tested privacy tolerance when it introduced Gmail—with ads relating to the content of your message" (p. 28).

An editorial in the *Arizona Daily Sun* also addressed trust and the passing of 2013, noting: "The Associated Press has catalogued a year of what it calls 'dysfunction, discord, and misplaced trust' not just in government but in multiple institutions and private industries" (2013b, A4).

Libraries must be cautious in what they do in order not to reduce the public's trust of the idea of free, reliable, service that is open to all.

By this point, some readers are correctly questioning our statement that libraries are a trusted organization—a person can't be too careful when reading another person's writings. There is a fair amount of indirect evidence to support the idea that libraries are trusted. A great many surveys indicate that people generally view libraries as good for society and provide positive benefits. A recent example (*Arizona Daily Sun*, 2013a) is when the Flagstaff City—Coconino County Public Library System was voted by the public the best public service organization in the community. It is difficult to imagine any organization being viewed in such a fashion and not being trusted at the same time. Beyond the indirect evidence there are some survey results that directly look at trust and libraries.

On the issue of trust, OCLC issued a report in 2011 entitled *Perceptions of Libraries, 2010: Context and Community*, which was an update of a similar study conducted in 2005. The 2010 report noted that libraries and Web search engines were equally trusted (Gauder, p. 40). That outcome may not be all that pleasing for those who worry about the future of libraries in a digital world; however, it does support the notion that libraries are trusted. An earlier report (2006) from Public Agenda, a nonprofit, nonpartisan organization that assists people in navigating divisive, complex issues and work to find solutions, suggested that at least public libraries were almost immune to the distrust people had for other organizations, noting "indeed public libraries seem almost immune to the distrust that is associated with so many other organizations. People have high expectations of their libraries. Topping their list of priorities is that the basic services they come to expect from libraries remain free of charge to the public" (p. 11).

People's trust of libraries arises from a variety of sources. Certainly one of those factors was identified in the preceding quotation—free service. There must be other factors as some other organizations give away some or all of their services and yet lack the level of trust that people have for libraries. We suggest the following are some of the more significant factors leading to trusting the library:

- Open to all
- Free
- Unbiased
- Service focused
- User-centered

We close out this chapter with the thoughts of Aaron Schmidt, who noted that with regards to trust, "Libraries benefit in all sorts of ways when they're trusted institutions. Trust breeds loyalty, and loyal library users are more likely to take advantage of the library. What's more, loyal patrons will also be more apt to sing the praises of the library to neighbors and colleagues" (2013, p. 28).

Chapter Review Material

1. Discuss some of the most significant digital divides and how libraries may bridge such gaps.
2. What are the major components of a library's computer access policy?
3. Describe the major challenges for the staff when public access is provided to computers and the Internet.
4. What role do public service staff members play in helping citizens understand their government?
5. What role do the public service staff have in maintaining the delicate balance between security and access?

6. How has the Internet changed access to government information?
7. What the key components in an e-government assistance policy?
8. In what ways is social trust an issue for libraries, especially in terms of public technological access?

REFERENCES

American Library Association, American Association of Law Libraries, Association of Research Libraries. 1996. *Statement on H.R. 4280, The "Government Printing Reform Act of 1996."* Chicago: American Association of Law Libraries. http://www.aallnet.org/Archived/Government-Relations /Formal-Statements/1996/st121896.html.

Arizona Daily Sun. 2013a. "2013 Best of Flag Winners." December 10, AZDailySun. com. http://tinyurl.com/lfehenc.

Arizona Daily Sun. 2013b. "Let's Build Forward in 2014 on Trust, Solutions." Sunday, December 29, A4.

Becker, Samantha. 2013. "Understanding Your Library's Public Access Technology Users." *Public Libraries* 52, no. 5: 7–9.

Becker, Samantha, Michael D. Crandall, Karen E. Fisher, Bo Kinney, Carol Landry, and Anita Rocha. 2010. *Opportunity for All: How the American Public Benefits from Internet Access at U.S. Libraries.* Washington, D.C.: Institute of Museum and Library Services.

Davidsson, Robert. 2008. "Welcome to the E-Government Library of the Future—Today." *Public Management* 90, no. 3: 16–18.

Dempsey, Kathy. 2004. "The Info Was There, Then—Poof." *Computers in Libraries* 24, no. 4: 4.

The Economist. 2008. "The Electronic Bureaucrat: A Special Report on Technology and Government." 386, no. 8567 (supplement): 1–18.

Fredericks, Nancy. 2011. "E-Government and Employment Support Services." *Library Technology Reports* 47, no. 6: 33–37.

Gauder, Brad, ed. 2011. *Perceptions of Libraries 2010: Context and Community.* Dublin, OH: OCLC. http://oclc.org/content/dam/oclc/reports/2010perceptions /2010perceptions_all_singlepage.pdf.

Golderman, Gail, and Bruce Connolly. 2002. "Government Information Online: Tools for Democracy." *Netconnect* (a *School Library Journal* supplement) 5, no. 2: 50–55.

Hoffman, Judy, John Carlo Bertot, and Denise M. Davis. 2012. "Libraries Connect Communities: Public Library Funding & Technology Access Study 2011–2012." Digital supplement of *American Libraries.* June. http://viewer. zmags.com/publication/4673a369.

Jaeger, Paul T., John Carlo Bertot, John A. Shuler, and Jessica McGilvray. 2012. "A New Frontier for LIS Programs: E-government Education, Library/Government Partnerships, and the Preparation of Future Information Professionals." *Education for Information* 29, no. 1: 39–52.

Klein, Bonnie, and Sandy Schwal. 2005. "A Delicate Balance: National Security vs. Public Access." *Computers in Libraries* 25, no. 3: 16–23.

Madison, James. 1822. "Letter to W.T. Barry, August 4, 1822." In *The Writings of James Madison*, ed. Gaillard Hunt, vol. 9, 103. (New York: G.P. Putnam's Sons: 1910).

Pogue, David. 2014. "In Tech We Don't Trust." *Scientific American* 310, no. 1: 28.

Public Agenda. 2006. *Long Overdue: A Fresh Look at Public and Leadership Attitudes about Libraries in the 21st Century*. New York: Public Agenda. http://www.publicagenda.org/files/Long_Overdue.pdf.

Schmidt, Aaron. 2013. "Earning Trust." *Library Journal* 138, no. 18: 28.

Shuler, John A., Paul T. Jaeger, and John Carlo Bertot. 2014. "Editorial: E-government without Government." *Government Information Quarterly* 31, no. 1: 1–3.

Swan, Deanne W., Justin Grimes, Timothy Owens, Kim Miller, Andrea J. Arroyo, Terri Craig, Suzanne Dorinski, Michael Freeman, Natasha Isaac, Patrick O'Shea, Regina Padgett, Peter Schilling, and Jennifer Scotto. 2014. *Public Libraries in the United States Survey: Fiscal Year 2011* (IMLS-2014–PLS-01). Washington, D.C.: Institute of Museum and Library Services. http://www.imls.gov/assets/1/AssetManager/PLS2011.pdf.

Taylor, Paul, Cary Funk, and April Clark. 2007. *Americans and Social Trust: Who, Where, and Why*. Washington, D.C.: Pew Research Center. http://www.pewsocialtrends.org/files/2010/10/SocialTrust.pdf.

Thompson, Susan. 2012. "Student Use of Library Computers: Are Desktop Computers Still Relevant in Today's Libraries?" *Information Technology and Libraries* 31, no. 4: 20–33.

White, Michael. 1996. "The Federal Register: A Link to Democratic Values." *The Record* 23, no. 4: 6–11.

SUGGESTED READINGS

Axelsson, Karin, Ulf Merlin, and Ida Lindgren. 2013. "Public E-Services for Agency Efficiency and Citizen Benefit—Findings from a Stakeholder Centered Analysis." *Government Information Quarterly* 30, no. 1: 10–22.

Balas, Janet. 2002. "Useful Resources for Writing Library Policies." *Information Today* 22, no. 6: 30–33. (Note: Although slightly dated, this is still an excellent overview of resources to consult when preparing a policy statement.)

Becker, Samantha. 2011. "10 Tips for Improving the Impact of Public Access Technology in Your Library." *ALKI* 27, no. 2: 14–15.

Bertot, John Carlo, Paul T. Jaeger, Ursula Gorham, Natalie Greene Taylor, and Ruth Lincoln. 2013. "Delivering E-Government Services and Transforming Communities through Innovative Partnerships: Public Libraries, Government Agencies, and Community Organizations." *Information Polity: The International Journal of Government & Democracy in the Information Age* 18, no. 2: 127–138.

Bishop, Bradley Wade, Charles R. McClure, and Lauren H. Mandel. 2011. "E-Government Service Roles for Public Libraries." *Public Libraries* 50, no. 3: 32–37.

Caruso, Sloane. 2014. *Creating Digital Communities: A Resource to Digital Inclusion*. New York: Nova Publishers.

Chadwick, Cynthia, Renée Di Pilato, Monique le Conge, Rachel Rubin, and Gary Shaffer. 2012. "The Future of the FDLP in Public Libraries." *Public Libraries* 51, no. 4: 40–46.

DeMaagd, Kurt, Han Ei Chew, Guanxiong Huang, M. Laeeq Khan, Akshaya Sreenivasan, and Robert LaRose. 2012. "The Use of Public Computing Facilities by Library Patrons: Demography, Motivations, and Barriers." *Government Information Quarterly* 30, no. 1: 110–118.

Detlor, Brian, Maureen E. Hupfer, Umar Ruhi, and Li Zhao. 2013. "Information Quality and Community Municipal Portal Use." *Government Information Quarterly* 30, no. 1: 23–32.

Hernon, Peter, and Laura Saunders. 2009. "The Federal Depository Library Program in 2023: One Perspective on the Transition and Future." *College & Research Libraries* 70, no. 4: 351–370.

Jaeger, Paul, John Carlo Bertot, Kim M. Thompson, Sarah M. Katz, and Elizabeth J. DeCoster. 2012. "The Intersection of Public Policy and Public Access: Digital Divides, Digital Literacy, Digital Inclusion, and Public Libraries." *Public Library Quarterly* 31, no. 1: 1–20.

Jaeger, Paul, Natalie N. Greene, John Carlo Bertot, Natalie Perkins, and Emily Ward. 2012. "The Co-Evolution of E-Government and Public Libraries: Technologies, Access, Education, and Partnerships." *Library & Information Science Research* 34, no.4: 271–281.

Jaeger, Paul, Ursula Gorham, John Carlo Bertot, and Lindsay C. Sarin. 2014. *Public Libraries, Public Policies, and Political Processes: Serving and Transforming Communities in Times of Economic and Political Constraint.* Lanham, MD: Rowman & Littlefield.

Leblanc, Evalyn. 2014. *Access for All: The Impact and Role of Computers and the Internet in Public Libraries.* New York: Nova Publishers.

Nam, Taewoo. 2014. "Determining the Type of E-Government Use." *Government Information Quarterly* 31, no. 2: 211–220.

Shin-Yuan, Hung, Chang Chia-Ming, and Kuo Shao-Rong. 2013. "User Acceptance of Mobile E-Government Services: An Empirical Study." *Government Information Quarterly* 30, no. 1: 33–44.

Wilson-Roberts, Shelley. 2012. "E-Government and Public Libraries in the United States and Canada: Challenges Facing the Public Libraries of Today." In *Government Information Management in the 21st Century*, ed. Peggy Garvin, 23–38. Burlington, VT: Ashgate.

12

Social Media and Library Programs and Services

There are probably some local businesses you know that use social media to attempt to connect with you (and increase your business at their store). Librarians and libraries can also use these social media tools to connect with customers.

—David Lee King, 2012b

Although I've been in the profession only a decade, I've seen plenty of hyped-up ideas cycle through over the years. In 2006, every library had to have a blog. By 2008 every library had to have a Facebook page and gaming program or collection. Right now, makerspaces are all the rage. And by 2014 it'll be something else.

—Meredith Farkas, 2013

It is essential to have a plan for the social media presence at your library for several reasons. Social media is easy to start but hard to maintain, and even harder to measure.

—Lynette Schimpf, 2014

Libraries on social networks reach into their communities, talking to patrons where they spend their time and ideally carrying out actual conversations, not just tossing out announcements.

—Walt Crawford, 2013

Social media is almost ubiquitous in today's world. It seems there are "apps" for just about everything people do and think about. As our opening quotation from David King states, organizations of all types, including libraries, make use of social media to "connect" with their users/clients/customers and to strengthen their "brand." Although any use of social media carries some risk, when it is a matter of organization to individual usage the organization carries the larger burden in terms of ethics and impact. As Jotham Wasike (2013) stated: "Social media involves relations amongst people who have some type of relationship or affiliation. . . . It may be conceptualized as socio-technical arrangements incorporating technologies that support such activities. Social media ethical concerns include identity, privacy, surveillance, friending, and user exploitation" (p. 8). Mistakes on the part of organizations can have some significant consequences for them and those with whom they "connect."

It is hard to imagine a person who does not know about the explosive growth and global scope of social media in the twenty-first century. There are ample examples of how such media have influenced people and societies. Facebook, Twitter, blogs, and the like have played significant roles in recent political events around the world. Organizations cannot and have not ignored that impact.

Certainly government agencies, for a number of reasons, have taken an interest in such media as have nonprofit groups. Your library is likely to employ some social media. If you include having a Web site as at least the beginning point of using social media, there are few, if any, libraries that do not have a Web presence. It is as Noa Aharony (2012) noted, "As the social networking phenomenon becomes more widespread in our information world, its presence in the library landscape becomes challenging and intriguing" (p. 358). A great many libraries are far beyond mere OPACs as a Web presence and are employing a variety of diverse social media tools. The major question is how effective that usage is in terms of the library's service community.

Frank Boateng and Yan Quan Liu (2014) looked at the Web sites of the top 100 academic libraries as represented in *US News and World Report*'s 2013 list of 100 best colleges, looking for technologies such as "RSS [real simple syndication] feeds, blogs, IM [instant messaging], podcasts, Vodcast, SNS [social networking sites], and text messaging alerts" (p. 124). They found that SNS (Facebook and Twitter) were the most popular applications, with 100 percent participation rate among libraries studied. Following closely behind were blogs, RSS, and IM services (p. 126). The reasons for a library's utilization of social media are highly varied, as we will note later in this chapter. However, there are several broad underlying reasons for doing so. One obvious reason is to "connect" with people who have or may have an interest in what the library does. Another basic reason is to provide information to people about the organization and, in the case of libraries, some transparency to what and how it does what it does. A third factor is to create a participatory/collaborative environment with people outside the organization and who are interested in its activities. A fourth reason is to reach segments of the population who may not have previously used the library and to educate them on modern library services and programs. Some people in the community may be surprised to discover their local library has a social media presence, thinking of libraries as merely book repositories.

Walt Crawford (2013) stated something every librarian knows but may not think too much about in terms of social media: "Even as every library is different, so is every community. . . . As I write this, it's probably true that Facebook has users in nearly every community. I'm less convinced that every community has a large number of users who want their library to be on Facebook and will interact with it there. . . . Once you get past Facebook, the odds of reaching the people in your community drop rapidly" (p. xi).

In terms of person-to-person social media usage, the basic goals are much the same as for organizations—connecting, sharing, participating, and community building. Something to keep in mind is what initially draws a person to social media is the desire to stay connected with friends and family and to share personal experiences/thoughts with those individuals as well as have a sense of participation in their lives even from a distance. Research has shown that, with the exception of dating sites, people do not think of it as a means of meeting strangers (see, e.g., Danah M. Boyd and Nicole B. Ellison's 2007 article [13, no. 1: 210–230] "Social Network Sites: Definition, History, and Scholarship" in the *Journal of Computer Mediated Communication*).

Thus, as Crawford suggested, organizations hoping to connect with users, share information, gain participation, and create a supportive community that extends beyond their current user base through the employment of social media may well be disappointed. It is possible, but it is not as easy as you might believe and hope. Before exploring how an organization can effectively utilize it, we need to define what we mean by "social media."

Media options are in a constant state of change. The changing landscape creates challenges for libraries that are generally in a low staffing and budget situation. Keeping up-to-date with the latest developments and gaining a sense of which of those people are adopting can be a full-time job, something that few libraries can afford, unless they change the duties of an existing staff member. Once having learned of something that might be useful for the library, there is the time to understand how to employ the option effectively. Finally, just as the library is able to utilize the media effectively, it, or peoples' preferences, may change.

DEFINING SOCIAL MEDIA

Social media is wide-ranging term and people employ it in various ways. Variations involve what types of technology a person includes in his or her mind when employing the phrase as well as what the purpose of those technologies might be. Heidi Cohen (2011) wrote about how 30 of her colleagues viewed social media and how they the defined the concept. A somewhat surprising result of her survey was each of the 30 people had somewhat different views about how to define social media (http://heidicohen.com/social-media-definition/). It is perhaps noteworthy that all her respondents were active social media users.

We have paraphrased and added some connecting words to the eight characteristics that Cohen pulled from her colleagues' definitions:

> Social media consists of a variety of formats—text, video, audio, etc.—that allows for a range of options that facilitate the dissemination of information /views. The social media options allow interaction/communication across various digital platforms on a one-on-one, one-to-many, and many-to-many basis. It allows real time interactions to take place.

That definition does not address the purpose of the interactions, which is as variable as there are people in the world.

Another phrase that is currently associated with social media is *social networking*. Social networking, a.k.a. networking theory, has a long history of use as a research technique in anthropology, organizational research, and sociology. It is a method for mapping/charting the relationships and interactions between people or organizations. It has become a tool for those engaged in data mining and for some commercial organizations that find value in such information.

Some individuals refer to social networks as "social hubs." They suggest that there are a number of such hubs, including Facebook and Twitter. They make an important point: in some cases, social media is too often thought of as a single-function application. For example, Facebook has several functionalities:

- Profiles—personal engagement/connection function
- Pages—business/organization function focusing on marketing
- Groups—"communities" with shared interests/goals/ values
- Events—a method for organizing and inviting people to an "event"
- Applications—allows account holders to add applications—such as text/ image sharing, contests, and opinion sharing

LinkedIn is another such multifunction social platform (SlideShare and Presentations are two examples) that is often viewed a single function media. Our point is that just knowing that someone has an account on such a hub may not be adequate enough information for the library to effectively reach out to the person.

Social media presents libraries with opportunities to increase their ability to reach, understand, provide services, and build relationships with their communities. Such media can enhance "listening," communicating (sharing), and responding to user concerns and questions.

CHALLENGES TO THE EMPLOYMENT OF SOCIAL MEDIA

At first glance, it appears as though the employment of social media tools for the library is a no-brainer: they present a low-cost way to market the library, promote resources, and connect with the local community. As briefly mentioned in the opening paragraphs, however, these tools do not come devoid of potential complications. Failing to update social media accounts frequently and having no clear policies in place to handle controversial responses by outside users are just a couple of the potential issues that can arise when libraries adopt these tools. An interesting article regarding online reputation appeared in an issue of the *Harvard Business Review* (Simonson and Rosen, 2014) that discussed how "opinions" of others, a common feature that is part of some social media tools, impact an individual's behavior in relation to an organization. The authors proposed a continuum of impact from no impact (habitual behavior such as grocery shopping or borrowing books from the library) to a limited impact (already having an idea about the organization's quality—already used and evaluated it personally—reference assistance, for example) to very high impact (digital services/electronics). If the authors are correct, it would seem likely the library's concern should focus on its digital reputation. Perhaps it is better not to get into social media rather than doing it poorly.

After the initial excitement of creating and using any social media tool wanes, the upkeep of the site or tool can deteriorate, resulting in untimely or inconsistent posts. It is also important for libraries to have a dedicated staff person, or team of persons, assigned to the site's upkeep. A large part of social media's appeal is the ability of followers to receive information immediately and to be "in the know." An unattended site "loses its social qualities and, instead of cultivating interaction, becomes just another media channel to infrequently promote services and events" (Burclaff and Johnson, 2014, p. 366). Failing to maintain a consistent relationship with your followers can result in disengagement.

Another challenge to the use of social media is figuring out how to respond to potentially controversial comments or remarks from users that appear on the library's site/account. It is impossible to foresee what reaction a seemingly benign post or tweet may garner from followers. How should a library respond to a highly political or simply aggressive statement? Again, a thorough social media policy can help alleviate this issue, and having a well-trained staff manage social media accounts is a must.

There is another characteristic of social media that is a challenge and something of a small irritation for people and organizations with limited financial and/or staff resources. That is the never-ending environment of change. Laura Solomon (2013) stated the challenge:

It's not hard to understand that *all* of the current social media tools are, at best, ephemeral. Accepting the idea of constant and immediate change may be hard for libraries, which historically act to preserve information . . . the popularity of MySpace has long been in serious decline, Facebook is considered the standard of social networks, and Google has introduced its own Google+. What's popular today may be irrelevant tomorrow. Twitter may be replaced by something completely different a year from now. In order to be successful in online communities, libraries need to accept this fast pace of change and begin to move with it. (p. 1)

Recently libraries have adopted and, in some cases, abandoned a variety of social media. Pinterest, YouTube, Myspace, blogs, Second Life, and others were all at one time touted to be essential for libraries in order to reach a diverse, and often youthful, population and yet did not live up to expectations. In some instances, libraries begin utilizing one of these tools only to find out that maintenance and/or upkeep involved too much staff time or that the response did not warrant the effort. In other cases, libraries dedicated staff resources to a seemingly successful social media platform only to find users abandoning the site for another, newer and flashier, social media bandwagon. The very nature of modern society's relationship to technology makes it nearly impossible for libraries to keep up.

These considerations are echoed by Crawford (2014), who noted four very simple, yet key issues for libraries considering a social media presence:

- Can staff time be devoted to create and manage the account/s?
- Can the library sustain activity—in terms of both posting and responding to comments?

- Does the community you are intending to reach use the same social media tool you are using?
- Do your patrons expect or want to see you in this arena? (pp. 2–3)

WHO IS USING WHAT?

We noted earlier that individual social media applications gain and lose popularity with users as time passes. Thus, what follows reflects information available in 2014 and may be different by the time you read this section. As of late 2014, a great many academic and public libraries in the United States employed Facebook pages. Boateng and Liu's (2014) research on academic libraries, noted earlier, indicated Facebook was the most widely utilized social media tool for those libraries, while Nancy Dowd (2013) indicated the same holds true for public libraries as well. School library media centers have had an added challenge when it comes to using social media—the Children's Internet Protection Act, or CIPA (see chapter 13 for a discussion of CIPA). Until late summer 2011 it was unclear if social media fell under CIPA's filtering requirements. In August of that year, the Federal Communications Commission (FCC) issued a statement indicating that school districts did not have to filter Facebook and Myspace (FCC, 2011, p. 8). Just because it was possible to add such a presence for the library media center did not always translate in the school board agreeing to allow such a presence. Judi Moreillon (2014) noted that "in many school districts, filtering extends to social media such as Facebook, Twitter, YouTube, blogs, wikis, and more. . . . How can educators use participatory culture tools and involve students in knowledge creation if the filter gets in the way?" (p. 30). The best we can say is the usage of social media is spotty and varied in school settings, but does appear to be slowly increasing.

Variability of tool popularity is a concern, in terms of what resource/s a library selects and uses to achieve its social media goals. Jamie Helgren and Zeth Lietzau (2011) reported on a survey of public libraries and noted that in 2008 MySpace and Flickr were both employed by 30 percent of the respondents. By 2010, library "presence" had grown; Myspace usage was at 52 percent, and Flickr usage was at 63 percent. During that same timeframe, Facebook usage went from 11 percent to 80 percent (p. 15). A 2013 survey of public libraries by Meghan Wanucha and Linda Hofschire showed how Flickr usage had both increased and decreased over a four-year period. For example, in 2008, 30 percent of libraries serving populations of 500,000 or greater employed Flickr; by 2010 that rate had risen to 63 percent; however, by 2012, it had dropped to 42 percent (p. 6).

Academic libraries reflected a similar rise and fall of one or more social media applications. Gary Collins and Anabel Quan-Haase (2014) found that, at least in Canadian academic libraries between 2010 and 2012, Facebook, Twitter, YouTube, and Flickr were the most commonly used applications. An interesting pattern was that all but Flickr usage percentages increased during that time (p. 55). While there are several surveys of academic library statistics, such as those produced by the National Center for Education Statistics, only few, as of 2014, report on the type of social media employed and changes over time. Rather they indicate there is social media in use. Our sense, from the literature, is that Facebook, Twitter, and blogs are the top three applications in academic libraries (this is also the picture you gain from articles by authors such as Iris Xie and Jennifer Stevenson [2014] and Samuel Kai-Wah Chu and Helen S. Du [2013]). However, the range of applications covers just about every platform available, at least in some library somewhere.

In many ways, our opening quotation from Meredith Farkas (2013) suggests there seems to be an ever-changing "flavor of the year." We will explore some of the most frequently used platforms that libraries employ in a later section of this chapter.

DEVELOPING A SOCIAL MEDIA POLICY AND PLAN

Many of the obstacles discussed earlier can be lessened or even avoided with the adoption of a well-developed social media policy as well as a carefully thought-out implementation plan. For libraries, as is true of most public agencies, it is not a matter of if they should become involved in using social media; it is matter of how to do so most effectively. Deciding such matters ought to begin, as is true of any library program or service, with looking at the library's mission and goals and be based on a sound understanding of the service community.

Plans and policy are intrinsically linked. If they are not linked, confusion and problems almost always arise. Generally people think of policy coming first in the process, at least in terms of detailed planning. However, very often, it is the idea about engaging in a type of activity that triggers policy development for that activity. When a library starts thinking about employing some, social media is a good example of such a case.

There are probably very few libraries operating today that have not at least thought about being involved in social media usage. However, as Natalie Burclaff and Catherine Johnson (2014) noted in terms of social media planning, we would also add policy to their thought: "After the initial thrill of creating an account or the rush of seeing your follower count tick upward, social media can lose its excitement. As a result, many libraries, especially when seemingly more pressing demands or staffing shortages arise, social media becomes an afterthought. . . . We've found it is important to step back and think carefully about your purpose for using social media" (p. 366). Both a policy and plan based on that policy are critical to thinking through what the purpose may be.

It is also important to have a good policy in place to provide guidance analyzing social media and to protect both staff and the public; the policy should provide guidelines on how to respond to inappropriate remarks made by others in the larger social media realm. It is also not unheard of for employees to be reprimanded or even fired for posting comments about their employer on their personal social media page (e.g., see Russell and Stutz, 2014). It is obvious that there are many considerations to adopting a sound social media policy.

Policy Considerations

The following are some areas to consider when developing a social media policy:

1. What aspects of the library' mission and goals are likely to be advanced as a result of effective use of social media?
2. How will the library assess the success of such usage?
3. Who is the target population(s) for such usage? If more than one target group, should there be different media employed for each group?
4. What content will be appropriate for the usage? How will copyright compliance be ensured?
5. Who will be able to create content?
6. Will there be a vetting process for content prior to going "live"?
7. Will there be a fixed schedule of updating social media content?
8. Is there a need of governing board oversight of social media and if so, at what point?
9. What will be considered acceptable online conduct?
10. Who decides to employ what media when?
11. If the public can create content, should the content be reviewed? If so, by whom?
12. In the case of negative comments, how they should be responded and who should respond?

A library might consider embarking upon a social media SWOT (strengths, weaknesses, opportunities, and threats) analysis to guide it in its policy writing and before adopting any social media tool. The authors have found that taking the time to do a SWOT analysis, at the start of most planning processes, is well worth the effort. We fully agree with Joe Fernandez's view that "a SWOT analysis of social media in libraries will give libraries the opportunity to use such media to develop a dynamic relationship between themselves and their users" (2009, p. 36). Lynette Schimpf, who we quoted at the start of this chapter, has a brief discussion of employing a SWOT analysis in a school library media center context in her piece. In addition to a SWOT analysis, policy writers must have a solid understanding of what social media tools the library's current users employ and what tools nonusers favor or most often utilize.

Despite the many considerations involved in developing a policy, it does not have to be an overly extensive document. Like most well-written policies, it should state simply and concisely why the policy is needed, and provide a clear set of principles that the library supports. It is also important the policy writers understand that the changing nature of social media may require future edits; in this way, the policy should be thought of as a "living" document, enabling it to be better suited to address any issues that may arise from future social media trends.

Check These Out

A very good article on social media policy is Lisa P. Nathan, Alice MacGougan, and Elizabeth Shaffer's 2014 piece "If Not Us, Who? Social Media

Policy and the ISchool Classroom" in *Journal of Education for Library and Information Science* (55, no. 2: 112–132).

One example of a social media plan in action is that of the Montana State University Library (http://www.lib.montana.edu/about/social-media/). In addition, Montana State University Library staff members Mary Anne Hansen, Doralyn Rossmann, Angela Tate, and Scott Young presented a Webinar in 2013 for the Library and Information Technology Association (LITA) on the issue of creating a social media guide. The PowerPoint from this presentation entitled "All Aboard! The Party's Starting: Setting a Course for Social Media Success" is available from the MSU Scholarworks site: http://scholarworks.montana.edu/xmlui/handle/1/2818.

SOCIAL MEDIA IN LIBRARIES

It is difficult to write about trends in the social media arena in a book since they change so rapidly, making this printed document almost obsolete even before publication. What is a valued mode of online communication at the time of this writing may be outdated by the publication date. That said, there are a number of social media platforms currently in use by libraries around the country.

How to present the following material was a tad challenging to the authors. There is a surprising amount of overlap among the social media platforms that libraries employ, at least in terms of what they can do and their content. We decided to categorize and discuss the platforms in four broad groups—social networking, text distribution, image distribution, and audio/video distribution. We discuss some of the library usage of the following fairly common platforms:

Social Networks	Text	Image	Audio/Video
Facebook	Twitter	Flickr	Podcasting
LinkedIn	Blogs	Instagram	YouTube
	SlideShare	Pinterest	

As you can see from this list, the format for social engagement varies greatly, whether it is through unlimited text, character-limited text, single images, videos, audio files, or a combination of all of them. What a library chooses to use must reflect what the members of its community use and are comfortable using.

Libraries may want to explore the use of "social hubs" when focusing on gaining participation/engagement with the library. Such hubs allow for real-time bidirectional exchanges as well as content creation. One such example is the Flagstaff Public Library's involvement with http://visionflagstaff .com/, where residents can post ideas for civic projects, comment on posted projects, and "like" a proposed project.

Facebook

Facebook is a prime example of a social network and is currently arguably the most popular social media outlet for libraries. It allows a person to connect with and share information/photos with family and friends. Connecting and sharing with people and at low dollar cost seems to be just what most libraries hope to accomplish in terms of its service community. There is little doubt that Facebook is the most frequently employed application in terms of libraries.

Check This Out

One of the first research articles to explore the concept of Facebook and its possible use in libraries is Mark-Shane Scale's 2008 piece "Facebook as a Social Search Engine and the Implications for Libraries in the Twenty-First Century" (*Library Hi Tech* 26, no. 4: 540–556). It is well worth the read.

The company claims to have a billion plus members as of late 2014. However, when it comes to the library interacting with some of those members, there are at least three questions for the library to consider. How many individuals in the service community are members? Of that number, how many are regular users? And finally, and perhaps most significant, of the active users how many *want* to interact with the library through Facebook? Certainly it is difficult to determine the answers to such questions and realistically the best approach is to "test the water" by creating a Facebook page. The idea is to test the application and if the there is little response, cease using the page. To be effective, social media calls for constant updating/new material. All of this takes time and effort that tend to be stretched to the limit in most libraries.

Organizations create a Facebook presence using "pages" for their profiles. It is important that the library's pages not be identical with the personal profile of the individual creating the library's presence. You can accomplish this objective by going to the account menu and selecting "Use Facebook as Page." Not taking this approach will result in mixing personal and library postings which can lead to some surprising results, not all of them good.

Noa Aharony reported on an analysis of how 20 U.S. libraries (10 academic and 10 public) used Facebook (2012, p. 361). Two of her interesting findings were that both types of libraries tended to focus on the "information" section of application and posting to the "wall." Another finding was the libraries studied made little use of other Facebook functionalities. The authors wonder if that situation has changed since she did her research or if the apparent decline in Facebook usage has required libraries to reallocate the social media resources to other applications.

There is an important question that was not answerable as of 2014. Is Facebook truly falling out of favor with one of its significant demographic user groups? One of many publications raising some variation of that question was the *Economist*. It had a short piece about "Unfriending Mum and Dad" in its January 4, 2014, issue. The article concluded that while there may be some defections on the part of young people, it is not of the magnitude similar to that of Myspace. A piece of advice from the article was that "the teenagers on Facebook may not be rebelling, but keep an eye on them" (p. 50).

From the Authors' Experience

Christie offers the following thoughts about library utilization of Facebook pages based on several years of handling the pages for her library:

Lessons Learned from Facebook

- Post regularly: we post at least three times per week.
- Use eye-catching graphics and make sure you have copyright clearance for any pictures you use!
- Be relevant: local interest stories receive the most interest (translated in "likes"). We post library programs (of course), but we also will post programs from other local educational and recreational organizations that support our mission, and we'll link to local news articles that may interest our followers.
- Be ready for the unexpected: we've received political comments on a post about computer classes, and advertising links in the comments for programs. Have a policy that's flexible enough to handle the unexpected.
- Most importantly: have fun and experiment! We love receiving feedback via Facebook surveys, and have asked for feedback on everything from our Summer Reading Program to favorite books. Enjoy interacting with your community!

LinkedIn

Although libraries report using LinkedIn, this social media platform is more about employment and professional connections for staff than it is for promoting library activities and services. Basically, it is a social network for professionals. (We should note that in 2014, the site allowed anyone to create a profile.) Organizations may also develop a page. LinkedIn has found a niche as a means of developing relationships, seeking employment opportunities, and HR departments using individual's profiles to identify potential recruits.

Marc Whitt (2014) wrote about the connection and relationship aspect when he stated, "I am a huge fan of Linkedin. . . . I see it as a platform that can build relationship effectively. . . . Once I have established a connection with someone, on Linkedin, I typically will contact them via Skype or invite them to the campus for a one-on-one meeting so our business relationship can mature" (p. 48). Librarians and others also find it to be a useful tool in terms of professional development, as a number of organizations, including the American Library Association and Special Libraries Association, allow for discussions to be generated from members that "follow" the group page.

One of the additional features of LinkedIn is the integration of SlideShare, which can prove useful of sharing information related to work activities. The site states that "SlideShare began with a simple goal: To share knowledge online. Since then, SlideShare has grown to become the world's largest community for sharing presentations and other professional content" (http://tinyurl .com/oonooap).

Blogs

Blogging is one of the earliest online activities that are now labeled social media. A blog is essentially a means of publishing your thoughts, ideas, activities, and so forth on the Web. Engaging in effective blogging takes thought, time, and effort. The last two factors are not usually in abundance in a library when it comes to maintaining quality basic programs and services. A blog is an added extra. As we discuss later, many libraries that did blog have shifted to Twitter because it takes less time and effort. Another likely factor causing the switch is young people who used to blog as a means of maintaining contact with friends, no longer do so. They have moved on to other social media platforms.

Certainly blogs have one advantage over micro-blogs (e.g., Twitter): there is no limit on how much text you post. That means you can provide details that you could not provide in a single micro-blog. There are several blogging platforms to choose from such as Blogger (owned by Google), WordPress, and Tumblr. Many of the services are free, while some charge a subscription fee. Subscription platforms do offer more functionality, especially in terms of making your blog site distinctive.

One measure of a blog's success is the number of "followers." Gaining and maintaining followers rests to a large degree on whether your blog comes up on the list of "hits" from a search engine result for a specific topic. Most blogging platforms allow account holders to add metadata and some offer SEO (search engine optimization) features. Using those capabilities improves your blog's ranking in search result lists.

Many libraries that are blogging use the WordPress platform. Liz Rea (2011) reported on a major Kansas public library implementation of WordPress. In writing about the planned training program for librarians, she noted: "As it turned out, the librarians had almost no trouble understanding how to use WordPress after only one day of training" (p. 59). David Mitchell (2013) wrote about the effectiveness of blogs in teaching literacy, noting: "In my view, the main reasons that blogging is effective in causing an evolution in children's' love of literacy are two-fold. It is about children's love of anything to do with technology and the fact that they can attract feedback from their peers or people thousands of miles away, rather than just their teacher" (p. 130).

Check These Out

Blogs are useful for a variety of reasons, such as knowing what your friends and colleagues are thinking, learning about what successes and missteps libraries are encountering, and professional development. One source of locating library-related blogs is Salem Press's Blog Search site (http://www2

.salempress.com/blogs/blog-search). Listed blogs are indexed/categorized into 32 subject or "focus" areas and are classified by audience including academic, public, school, and special libraries.

For professional development purposes, there are a number of association blogs from which to choose, such as:

ACRLog—Blogging by and for Academic Research Librarians—http://acrlog .org/

ALSC Blog—The Official Blog of the Association for Library Service for Children—http://www.alsc.ala.org/blog/

The PLA Blog—Official Blog of the Public Library Association—http://pla-blog.org/

YALSABlog—For the Young Adult Library Services Association—http://yalsa .ala.org/blog/.

Twitter

A second commonly employed application by libraries is Twitter. Twitter is a micro-blogging application. That is, you may post text, images, and links so long as you stay with the rather short character limitations of Twitter. The application is very widely used, and in a sense Twitter has become the first "source" of breaking news. This fact may well explain why the Library of Congress (LC) has acquired all the tweets since Twitter went "live" in 2010 and continues to do so (Allen and Osterberg, 2013). LC is in the process of making all the tweets searchable; that thought may be a bit scary or embarrassing for some people.

Undoubtedly one factor for its widespread use by libraries is that it is easy to create an account. Darcy Del Bosque, Sam Leif, and Susie Skarl (2012) outlined some of the significant pluses of Twitter for libraries, noting: "Twitter is free, removing any cost barriers for use. Since Twitter relies upon microblogging, it does not require a significant of staff time to create and maintain an account. In fact, there are numerous plug-ins that allow pre-scheduling of tweets, meaning that librarians can establish a weekly or even monthly schedule, further reducing daily staff time needed. Furthermore, many patrons already use Twitter, making it an ideal place for a library to forge connections with them" (p. 200). Susan Jennings's (2012) advice regarding libraries' use of Twitter is short and to the point, "If you Tweet it, they will come" (p. 216).

Laura Solomon (2013) suggested there are several differences between Facebook and Twitter in terms of library goals. One major difference is between connecting with individuals the library already "knows" and those it does not. She suggests the Facebook is best for the known, while Twitter is best for the unknown. Further, Twitter is best for posting time-sensitive information, while Facebook is better at developing "deep" connections. Another, obvious difference, is the length of what you can post—Twitter's 140 character restriction truly limits what you post with the use of too many abbreviations that may not be widely understood. Her list of differences (p. 37) goes on at some length; however, these are among the most important points to keep in mind.

> **Check This Out**
>
> One recent overview of how to establish and maintain a library Twitter presence is provided by Laura Carscaddon and Kimberly Chapman in "Twitter as a Marketing Tool for Libraries," chapter ten (pp. 147–163) in *Marketing with Social Media: A LITA Guide*, edited by Beth C. Thomsett-Scott (Chicago: American Library Association, 2014).

Tumblr

June L. Power (2014) suggested that Tumblr "is blogging-meets-Facebook/Twitter. . . . Tumblr is a mishmash of thematic blogs revolving around every topic imaginable" (p. 91). Tumblr was launched in 2007, and its user base consists of mostly younger bloggers. As noted by McArdle, "What makes library Tumblrs different from your run-of-the-mill library blogs is that they can take advantage of a built-in community with built-in readers. If a WordPress or Blogspot blog is an island, Tumblr blogs are a city" (June 25, 2013). If nothing else, some Tumblr sites can provide a smile or two, if not laughs, on a bad day at work, and some are based on library topics. One such site is "Librarian Problems" (http://librarianproblems.com), which has regular posts from both its creators and its followers.

Given library budget woes, a site worth "pushing" to the library service community is "Libraries Changed My Life" (http://librarieschangedmylife.Tumblr.com). As Power stated, "Too often we hear only negative comments, and hearing the positive ones is a welcome change" (p. 92). Yet another somewhat similar site is "Library Facts" (http://librarianfacts.tumblr.com/), which is a mix of facts, videos, laughs, and quotations.

> **Check This Out**
>
> Amber Welch provides a case study in the use of Tumblr from Mount Holyoke College in her September 2014 article "Tumblr: Extending the Reach of Library Websites" (*Computers in Libraries* 34, no. 7: 6–10). Her article also includes a set of suggested best practices in the use of Tumblr, and is well worth the read.

Flickr

Flickr is the other commonly employed social media from the library point of view. As we noted earlier, this application was adopted early and then plateaued after a few years. Where Facebook is a networking platform and Twitter is form of blogging, Flickr is an image-sharing tool. Flickr allows account holders to post and organize photos and videos. You can have "sets" (two or more images) and collections (two or more related sets). You can tag single images/video sets and collections. Library usage has focused primarily on images of its hosted events. Perhaps the reason for the diminishing use of this platform by libraries is they have not found it to be a good promotional tool.

Ellen Forsyth and Leanne Perry (2010) found that most public libraries use Flickr as an adjunct to providing access to their programs and services. Perhaps this lack of centrality is another reason for the platform's stagnate growth among libraries. The authors reported the top two usages of the platform were for recording events and promoting services (p. 7).

In addition to the main Flickr service, an additional resource—the Flickr Commons—was launched in 2008 in partnership with the LC. The goal of the Commons "is to share hidden treasures from the world's public photography archives" (https://www.flickr.com/commons). At the time this chapter was being prepared, there were over 90 participating institutions from around the world taking part in the Flickr Commons, ranging from the British Library to the Preus Museum to the Library Company of Philadelphia. Images from the Commons are considered copyright-free, and provide one source of visual information for researchers.

Pinterest

Pinterest is yet another example of a mixed social media platform. We see it as a mix of blogging and image sharing. Many view it as a "social discovery tool" which is a variation of what the firm calls itself (http://www.pinterest. com). Pinterest allows for both personal and organizational accounts. There is some evidence that commercial account holders find that such accounts help drive their sales. (See, for example, "How Pinterest Drives E-Commerce Sales"—http://www.shopify.com/infographics/pinterest, and Haley Silver, Eileen Tan, and Cory Mitchell's "Pinterest vs. Facebook: Which Social Sharing Site Wins at Shopping Engagement?"- 2012, http://www.bizrateinsights .com/blog/2012/10/15/online-consumer-pulse-pinterest-vs-facebook-which-social-sharing-site-wins-at-shopping-engagement/). Unfortunately there is little evidence that it is equally effective in "driving" nonprofit organizational goals.

Mark Baggett and Rabia Gibbs (2014) did analyze the impact of two social media image platforms—Historypin and Pinterest—regarding their value as discovery and access tools. They suggested that:

> Digital production and content are not the concern; it is the reformatting of delivery that challenges digital libraries. . . . Even if institutions follow the Open Archive Imitative (OAI) model, which allows for discovery of digital objects through traditional search engines, many digital collections are buried underneath the technical hierarchy of an institution's online presence. . . . The question is whether uploading archival images to image-focused social media platforms enhances access and discovery of digital collections. (p. 12)

For their study, Baggett and Gibbs selected a sample of images from large digital collections. Overall their research indicated that although both platforms (Historypin and Pinterest) increased discovery, they did not drive people to the more comprehensive library Web-based digital collections (less than 1% went on to the larger collection) (p. 20). Perhaps the lack of driving/pushing people to more comprehensive collections is one factor why some libraries do not make more use of such image-focused platforms.

Check This Out

A good review of Pinterest use in libraries is provided by Zara Wilkinson, in her 2013 article "Oh, How Pinteresting! An Introduction to Pinterest" in *Library Hi Tech News* (30, no. 1: 1–4.

Podcasting

Podcasting is a general term used to describe an audio distribution platform, and some authors on social media do not include it as a social media technology. Others, who view it as a marketing tool, do cover it. Jay Conrad Levinson and Shane Gibson (2010) describe podcasts as "a series of audio episodes on a certain topic. These episodes are accessible via a Web browser and often can be played right on the website that hosts them" (p. 81).

From a library perspective, podcasting can be useful in promoting and sharing programs that are primarily audio files (e.g., book discussions). School library media centers have found it useful in teaching literacy. Marina Brodsky and Diane Vahab (2014) wrote about employing podcasts in teaching history and social science, where "the librarian and teacher create an example of the podcast the students can follow. . . . When the podcast is done, the students drag it into his/her iBook" (p. 52). The authors found that podcasts helped make the project at hand more engaging for the students. Melissa Purcell (2014) described an assignment where students created a podcast as part of an assignment to summarize a book (p. 55). Purcell had earlier (2011) created a rubric for grading podcasts based on such elements as technical production, purpose, and content.

YouTube

YouTube is a video-sharing platform that is free to use. It is a good promotional tool for library collections, events, services, and resources, and is regularly used at one of the authors' institutions as a way of promoting services (see: https://www.youtube.com/user/UMDLibraries1). Although some "standard" videos are posted on that account (e.g., the ribbon-cutting ceremony for the new library makerspace, or videos from the "Speaking of Books" lecture series), one of the most popular videos was a nod to services offered during final exams. That one video alone received over 270,000 views ("Carol of Final Exams"—https://www.youtube.com/watch?v=F1uWSxpJB-I&feature=youtu.be&list=UUm_2UwfuhScuvEzFnRn), showing how one short video can have a large impact.

Although there has been little literature about public and school library usage of YouTube since 2012, other academic institutions have created their own YouTube "channels" to make content available. This includes the "Library

Minute" instructional series produced by the Arizona State University Libraries (http://www.youtube.com/user/librarychannel). Allan Cho (2013) outlined how YouTube was explored for use as a tool for the digital collections at
British Columbia University Libraries. As he noted, "Although YouTube is still
in its embryonic stages as a new addition to the digital services of academic
libraries, it is very powerful tool for online learning and as part of a digital
collections, allowing academic libraries to leverage it as a communication platform to interact with faculty, staff, and students in new and exciting ways"
(p. 47). Further, as Katie Buehner states (2014), "Even if your library is unable
to make its own videos, you can still participate in online video communities
through sharing. Try establishing a channel on YouTube and creating playlists
of videos on relevant topics" (p. 52).

Instagram

Instagram is a mix of blogging, social networking, images, and video sharing. First started in 2010, the service has steadily grown. As of October 2014,
Instagram boasted over 200 million monthly active users and over 60 million
average photos shared per day (http://instagram.com/press/). One special
feature is that posts can be shared with Facebook, Twitter, Tumblr, and other
social media platforms. Danielle Salomon (2013) opened her article on Instagram by asking, "Is Instagram worth the additional effort from a library to
support another social network?" (p. 408). Her short answer was "possibly."
She went on to say, "If your library is targeting a young, diverse, urban demographic you might have more success with Instagram than other social media
outlets" (p. 409). In that article, she also discusses how her library has found
Instagram to be an effective outreach tool.

Another study in Instagram use is provided by Wendy Abbott and her
colleagues (2013), who reported on how Bond University Library (AU) has
engaged its users by hosting photo-sharing competitions and two so-called
Insta walks in which "students were invited to share photos of the library to
win prizes" (p. 1). Other uses of Instagram are suggested by Jennifer Birch
(2014) who notes that Instagram can be used in more formalized interactive
learning activities and tutorials, and through such uses it can be "a powerful
tool to reinforce library operations. . . . It's more than just snapping photos—it
can also improve education mobility" (p. 32).

Check This Out

One way to locate Instagram items of note is to check out the YALSA
(Young Adult Library Services Association) blog's "Instagram of the Week"
feature—http://yalsa.ala.org/blog/tag/instagram/.

Other Social Media

There are a great many other social media platforms that various libraries can
employ—far too many for a single chapter to cover. However, the platforms

mentioned earlier were the most frequently discussed in the professional literature at the time we prepared this chapter. As we noted earlier, it can be a full-time occupation keeping up with new platforms, not to mention staying abreast with changes in existing ones. Libraries have to evaluate how they can dedicate staff FTE (full-time equivalent) or part-time hours to monitoring social media developments. Since social media is a vital part of libraries' means to communicate and connect with users, current positions may need to be adjusted to include these tasks to include perusing the professional literature to learn how other libraries utilize the plethora of social media resources available.

MEASURABILITY: THE IMPACT OF SOCIAL MEDIA IN THE LIBRARY

Successful utilization of social marketing tools will yield a greater awareness of the library's programs and services by the public. As such, it is important to assess the library's usage of these tools on a continual basis in order to ensure that not only are limited resources used to their best advantage (i.e., staff time is not being unwisely utilized), but that the tools in use are not obsolete. Again, it is important to develop a social media policy that reflects the library's mission statement and goals; doing this will also support the evaluation of the effectiveness of the use of social media.

According to authors Koontz and Mon (2014) in their book, *Marketing and Social Media*, an important outcome of any assessment exercise is the ability to clearly state the benefits resulting from interaction with the organization via social media. According to them, "the development of relationships between customers and the organization is of utmost value. Measuring the results of these relationships is the key to quantifying success in social media" (p. 251). In fact, measuring impact can result in somewhat surprising findings and can dramatically impact how the library chooses to proceed.

David Lee King (2012a) outlined six of the most important reasons for measuring the effectiveness of the library's usage of social media:

- Reporting purposes—such as funding agencies and governing boards,
- Demonstrating the level of interest and engagement of the service population,
- Checking on the usage in terms of library mission and goals,
- Resolving problems and issues related to the usage,
- Assessing what users do and don't like, and
- Identifying user demographics. (pp. 19–20)

In an article on measuring student responses to social media, Jin Wu and her colleagues (2014) provided statistics they gathered indicating students had "clearly little interest in using social media with the library, but [they did have] significant interest in using devices to communicate with the library to obtain information about hours, availability of materials, due dates and interest in accessing materials licensed by the library, such as e-books and apps" (pp. 127–128). This study illustrates a common question posed by library administrators when considering the adoption of social media tools in an effort to reach their communities: does it really make a difference? While their survey does seem to indicate that embarking upon the use of new social media platforms may not be worth the time investment, it is also important to consider that future studies may show a growing appreciation and use of these tools. If a library does decide to proceed, it is important to continually evaluate the social media outlets it utilizes in order to measure if there has been any change in users over time. While initial participation may be low and somewhat discouraging, monitoring growth can provide evidence of a successful program.

Check These Out

The following are some recent examples of how libraries have and do measure their social media activities:

Colburn, Selene and Laura Haines, 2012. "Measuring Libraries' Use of YouTube as a Promotional Tool: An Exploratory Study and Proposed Best Practices." *Journal of Web Librarianship* 6, no. 1: 5–31.

Glazer, Harry. 2012. "'Likes' Are Lovely, But Do They Lead to More Logins?" *College & Research Libraries News* 73, no. 1: 18–21.

Griffin, Melanie, and Tomaro I. Taylor. 2013. "Of Fans, Friends, and Followers: Methods for Assessing Social Media Outreach in Special Collections Repositories." *Journal of Web Librarianship* 7, no. 3: 255–271.

King, David Lee. 2012. "Use and Engagement on the Digital Branch." *Library Technology Reports* 48, no. 6: 12–15.

Yep, Jewelry, and Jason Shulman. 2014. "Analyzing the Library's Twitter Network: Using NodeXL to Visualize Impact." *College & Research Libraries News* 75, no. 4: 177–186.

Creating a Social Media Participatory Community

Sandy Placzek (2013) noted with regards to social media that "it is important to realize the role relationships play in the work of all law librarians and understand how establishing, evaluating and nourishing those relationships positively—or negatively—impacts our jobs" (p. 28). Although she was referring to law librarians when she made the statement, Placzek's comment applies to all libraries and, indirectly, to library social media. We have mentioned building relationships several times in this chapter. Creating relationships/connections with people is one of the major functions of almost all social media platforms.

Certainly libraries and their service communities have had relationships since the very first libraries were created. The nature of these relationships has changed over time, just as society and libraries have evolved. In the not-too-distant past, when libraries were primarily paper-based with rather modest audio and video resources, the libraries were providers of resources and services to a service community. Library staff identified resources, organized them, and provided access during set operating hours. In the last century, there was a gradual shift on how libraries selected resources and delivered their services. Early on in the twentieth century, the focus was on selecting "good" materials for users. That is, libraries housed items that people "ought" to read and had little regard for what people wanted and perhaps needed in their daily lives. During the latter half of that century there was a recognition that libraries ought to find out what the service population was interested in, liked, and wanted in terms of resources as well as services offered. The involvement of the user community in processes was limited but growing in importance.

This century has seen an ever-increasing recognition of the need for a truly participatory relationship between the library and its service community. Essentially we are looking at developing partnership relations rather than provider-customer. For example, access to library resources was limited at first to a physical location and service hours. Technology has now allowed libraries to make many services accessible 24/7. Reference/research assistance is also available 24/7 (at least in some libraries). Social media makes it easier to gain feedback, ideas, and suggestions for changes, services, resources, and the like from the community. We believe that Linh Nguyen, Helen Partridge, and Sylvia Edwards (2012) were correct when they noted, "Openness and participation are the expected and predicated as the hallmark of future libraries" (p. 342). Libraries have been moving toward the participatory library, and as Nguyen, Partridge and Edwards concluded, "The changing relationship between the library and users is observable" (p. 344).

Laura Solomon uses the concept of "social capital" in her publication about libraries and social media (2013, p. 26). *Social capital* is the source for being able to successfully gain support for something through the active assistance of social media connections. Organization and individuals gain such capital only when they are viewed by their connections as trustworthy. It also arises from being open to participation. Neither of these factors "just" happens. They are earned through careful, thoughtful use of social media. The connections must see there is a willingness to listen and respond to their thoughts, comments, suggestions, and so forth.

Libraries have had both physical and digital "suggestion/comment boxes" for years. The question is, how does the library respond? When was the last time the physical box was opened or the online version checked? A few libraries actively respond to the input and find there is real interaction and growing feedback. Many libraries are rather sporadic in their responses and begin to question the value of the "box." A few do nothing and, over time, find less and less input—the service community has found their feedback falling into something like a black hole. What we are suggesting is that just getting feedback is not enough; there must be acknowledgment and other responses to the comments.

Check This Out

At the time we prepared this chapter, probably the most comprehensive book related to libraries and social media was Laura Solomon's *The*

Librarian's Nitty-Gritty Guide to Social Media (Chicago: American Library Association, 2013).

You can read a very short version of the ideas she covers in her book in a 2013 article she authored, "Understanding Social Capital" (*American Libraries* 44, no. 5: 34–37).

Ethical and Legal Issues in Social Media Usage

It probably comes as no surprise that there are legal and ethical issues related to libraries using social media. As always, copyright comes up as an issue. When using a quotation, keep it to 100 words or less or get the copyright holder's permission to use more. Even that 100-word limit has the proviso—unless. A short poem may be fewer words but is the entire "work"—meaning permission is required! Who holds the copyright may be unclear when wanting to use something from the Web. When it is not clear, starting with the Web site owner is a good bet.

Linking or framing material on a library Web site or its social media can raise issues as well. Generally linking is not a copyright problem as the link takes the person to another Web site and that change of "location" is clear. Framing a Web site differs and most Web sites do not permit the practice (if they discover it took place). The difference is that framing essentially imports the content into the framer's site. Although the material is "framed," many people do not know that the material in the frame is from some other Web site. (To read more about the differences and their legal implications see "Connecting to Other Websites" http://fairuse.stanford.edu/overview/website-permissions /linking/.) Needless to say, in the virtual global world of librarianship there may be times when material from another country, especially English-speaking ones, may seem useful for your Web site. Keep in mind that each country has its version of copyright and often has stricter "fair use" standards.

We have mentioned that libraries sometimes employ visual social media to distribute and make some of their programs accessible. In a legal sense, each person presenting material is a "performer." It is a wise idea not only to have a verbal okay but a signed document that states each that presenter is willing to have his or her presentation and image distributed. This also applies to promotional activities such as posting a picture of the presenter.

Beyond the usual legal concerns there may be some that surprise you. One such issue relates to states' "Open Meeting" regulations. Julie Tappendorfnd and Ancel Glink (2013) reported that at least one state attorney ruled that posting library board members' comments on Facebook is subject to open meeting requirements. They also noted that at least three states have ruled that content posted on government agency-operated Web sites is subject to retention and archiving regulations (p. 16). Yet another open question for publicly supported libraries is whether social media platforms are a public forum and thus the removal of material of "objectionable" material is subject to a due process before they may be removed. Legal concerns and social media are in a constant state of flux, making it an ongoing challenge to stay legal.

Ethical concerns are also changing when it comes to social media. At the time we prepared this chapter there was a growing concern about privacy and organizational use of the data collected and used by an organization (e.g., data mining). As noted at the beginning of this chapter, Jotham Wasike (2013, p. 8) outlined the major areas of library ethical issues with regards to social media, including privacy and user exploitation. He went on to indicate: "Social media ethics are informed by normative theories that aim to develop a set of best practices governing human conduct" (p. 8). One small example is questioning how easy is it for a library follower to find the security setting for the Web site. Most people are only vaguely aware that there are settings that can protect their privacy. Should the library "friend" users? That simple question has raised debate in the professional literature (see Nedda Ahmed and Adriana Edwards-Johnson's 2013 article—"Should Librarians Friend Their Patrons?" *Reference & User Services Quarterly* 53, no. 1: 9–12). Some view the issue as creating stronger relationships, while others see it as an inappropriate connection that confuses professional and personal issues. We touch on a range of ethical issues in chapter 14. We also touched on privacy and "surveillance" of usage by database vendors in chapter 9. There are some ethical issues about the library's gathering of data about usage and incorporating that data into its planning and assessment activities. All of these factors must be taken into account when establishing and assessing a social media presence.

CLOSING THOUGHTS

Social media is the new word of mouth, and it behooves libraries to have a place in these communities to dialogue with their constituents. Social media is all about people and relationships with them. Make it meaningful, and pique people's curiosity.

Some may say social networking has brought huge potential (and some headaches) to librarians nationwide. Can libraries keep up with the rapid growth of technology and social networking? Walt Crawford (2013, p. x) has observed that libraries have been technology leaders for decades—not in being first adaptors, but in being early users of effective technologies. While communications and marketing rely on social media, libraries need to stay in touch with all aspects of their communities and they have done this well in the past, and will do so as they continue to incorporate new technologies and networks.

Regardless of the specific tool, it is obvious that social media in one form or another will continue to influence how individuals interact with their communities, organizations, and each other. The low-cost nature and relative ease of use of these tools create unique opportunities for libraries to market their resources and promote their brand.

The growth of social media as a means to communicate with not only close friends and family but to also connect with the community has created a shift in how organizations approach marketing in this arena. In their article "Brand Presence in Digital Space," Jennifer Rowley and David Edmundson-Bird (2013) note the important role social media plays in cultivating relationships with users. These relationships are an integral part of staying relevant in today's rapidly changing technological world. Additionally, Rowley and

Edmundson-Bird suggest that "social media have given customers a voice, or perhaps, more appropriately a megaphone" (p. 65), thereby putting organizations at risk if they choose to ignore suggestions or complaints or if they fail to adequately engage and gain trust with their customers. They also pointed out that while social media also facilitates conversations with customers, these conversations "will be two-way, not one-way. Organizations will need to ask permission to participate in these conversations, prove that they can be trusted, and show evidence that they have something of value to offer" (p. 75).

Chapter Review Material

1. Discuss the reasons organizations utilize social media:
   a. How do you convince your administration that social media is important (not a passing fad)?
   b. How do you convince your administration that media-competent staff are essential to success of your social media efforts?
2. What is a social network? Give two examples.
3. What are four major challenges for libraries in their employment of social media?
4. Describe eight topics that a library ought to consider when developing a social media policy.
5. What is an example of a behavior on social media that the library may want to regulate or ban through its social media policy?
6. What are some common social media tools libraries currently employ?
7. What is a significant challenge for school libraries hoping to employ social media?
8. Why is assessing the library's social media activities important? Discuss the reasons.
9. What are some ideas for evaluating social media sites to determine what to maintain, add, or delete?
10. In what ways does the implementation of the "participatory library" concept benefit a library?
11. What is social capital?
12. Discuss how copyright issues relate to a library's use of social media.
13. What are the major ethical concerns for libraries in terms of social media?

REFERENCES

Abbott, Wendy, Jessie Donaghey, Joanna Hare, and Peta Hopkins. 2013. "An Instagram Is Worth a Thousand Words: An Industry Panel and Audience Q&A." *Library Hi Tech News* 30, no. 7: 1–6.

Aharony, Noa. 2012. "Facebook Use in Libraries: An Exploratory Analysis." *Aslib Proceedings* 64, no. 4: 358–372.

Allen, Erin, and Gayle Osterberg. 2013. "Update on the Twitter Archive at the Library of Congress." *Library of Congress Blog.* January 4. Online.

http://blogs.loc.gov/loc/2013/01/update-on-the-twitter-archive-at-the-library-of-congress/.

Baggett, Mark, and Rabia Gibbs. 2014. "Historypin and Pinterest for Digital Collections: Measuring the Impact of Image-Based Social Tools on Discovery and Access." *Journal of Library Administration* 52, no. 1: 11–22.

Birch, Jennifer. 2014. "Five Ideas for Using Instagram in the Library." *Voice of Youth Advocates* 37, no. 3: 32.

Boateng, Frank, and Yan Quan Liu. 2014. "Web 2.0 Applications' Usage and Trends in Top US Academic Libraries." *Library Hi Tech* 32, no. 1: 120–138.

Brodsky, Marina, and Diane Vahab. 2014. "ELL History/Social Studies: Teaching Literacy Through iBooks and Podcasts." *School Library Monthly* 30, no. 5: 51–52.

Buehner, Katie. 2014. "Using Video-Sharing Sites to Market Your Library." In *Marketing with Social Media: A LITA Guide*, ed. Beth C. Thomsett-Scott, 51–66. Chicago: American Library Association.

Burclaff, Natalie, and Catherine Johnson. 2014. "Developing a Social Media Strategy." *College & Research Libraries News* 75, no. 7: 366–369.

Cho, Allan. 2013. "YouTube and Academic Libraries: Building a Digital Collection." *Journal of Electronic Resources Librarianship* 25, no. 1: 39–50.

Cohen, Heidi. 2013. "30 Social Media Definitions." http://heidicohen.com/social-media-definitions.

Collins, Gary, and Anabel Quan-Haase. 2014. "Are Social Media Ubiquitous in Academic Libraries? A Longitudinal Study of Adoption and Usage Patterns." *Journal of Web Librarianship* 8, no. 1: 48–68.

Crawford, Walt. 2013. "Introduction." In *Using Social Media in Libraries: Best Practices*, ed. Charles Harmon and Michael Messina, ix–xii. Lanham, MD: Scarecrow Press.

Crawford, Walt. 2014. *Successful Social Networking in Public Libraries*. Chicago: American Library Association.

Del Bosque, Darcy, Sam A. Leif, and Susie Skarl. 2012. "Libraries Atwitter: Trends in Academic Library Tweeting." *Reference Service Review* 40, no. 2: 199–213.

Dowd, Nancy. 2013. "Social Media: Libraries Are Posting, but Is Anyone Listening?" *Library Journal.Com*. May 7. Online. http://lj.libraryjournal.com/2013/05/marketing/social-media-libraries-are-posting-but-is-anyone-listening/.

Economist. 2014. "Unfriending Mum and Dad." 410, no. 8868: 49–50.

Farkas, Meredith. 2013. "Spare Me the Hype Cycle." *American Libraries* 44, no. 5: 23.

Federal Communications Commission. 2011. *Regulation Update: FCC 11–125*. Washington, D.C.: Federal Communications Commission. August 11. https://apps.fcc.gov/edocs_public/attachmatch/FCC-11–125A1.pdf.

Fernandez, Joe. 2009. "A SWOT Analysis for Social Media in Libraries." *Online* 33, no. 5: 35–37.

Forsyth, Ellen, and Leanne Perry. 2010. "Picturing Your Community: Flickr Use in Public Libraries." *Library Hi Tech News* 27, no. 1: 6–9.

Helgren, Jamie E., and Zeth Lietzau. 2011. "U.S. Public and Web Technologies: What Is Happening Now?" *Computers in Libraries* 31, no. 7: 12–16.

Jennings, Susan. 2012. "To Tweet, or Not to Tweet?' *Reference Services Review* 40, no. 2: 214–216.

Kai-Wah Chu, Samuel, and Helen S. Du. 2013. "Social Networking Tools for Academic Libraries." *Journal of Librarianship and Information Science* 45, no. 1: 64–75.

King, David Lee. 2012a. "Statistics." *Library Technology Reports* 48, no. 6: 19–22.

King, David Lee. 2012b. "Social Media." *Library Technology Reports* 48, no. 6: 23–27.

Koontz, Christie, and Lorri M. Mon. 2014. *Marketing and Social Media*. Lanham, MD: Rowman and Littlefield.

Levinson, Jay Conrad, and Shane Gibson. 2010. *Guerilla Social Media Marketing*. Irvine, CA: Entrepreneur Press.

McArdle, Molly. 2013. "The Library Is Open: A Look at Librarians and Tumblr." *Library Journal.com*. June 25. Online. http://reviews.libraryjournal.com/2013/06/in-the-bookroom/post/the-library-is-open-a-look-at-librarians-and-tumblr/.

Mitchell, David. 2013. "Blogging to Improve Literacy: At Key Stage 2." *School Librarian* 61, no. 3: 129–131.

Moreillon, Judi. 2014. "Leadership: Filtering and Social Media." *School Library Monthly* 30, no. 4: 29–30.

Nguyen, Linh Cuong, Helen Partridge, and Sylvia L. Edwards. 2012. "Towards an Understanding of the Participatory Library." *Library Hi Tech* 30, no. 2: 335–346.

Placzek, Sandy. 2013. "The Importance of Relationships: Our Relationships with Various Constituents Define What We Do and Who We Are." *AALL Spectrum* 17, no. 9: 28–29.

Power, June L. 2014. "Access the Web: Tumblr." *Journal of Access Services* 11, no. 2: 91–96.

Purcell, Melissa. 2011. "Podcast Rubric." *Library Media Connection* 29, no. 4: 56.

Purcell, Melissa. 2014. "English: A Podcast Book Summary on a Wiki." *School Library Monthly* 20, no. 7: 55–57.

Rea, Liz. 2011. "Kansas Libraries on the Web." *Library Technology Reports*. 47, no. 3: 58–60.

Rowley, Jennifer, and David Edmundson-Bird. 2013. "Brand Presence in Digital Space." *Journal of Electronic Commerce in Organizations* 11, no. 1: 63–78.

Russell, Reinier, and Michèle Stutz. 2014. "Social Media: What Employers Need To Know." *Journal of Internet Law* 17, no. 8: 3–6.

Salomon, Danielle. 2013. "Moving on from Facebook: Using Instagram to Connect With Undergraduates and Engaging in Teaching and Learning." *College & Research Libraries News* 44, no. 8: 408–412.

Schimpf, Lynette. 2014. "Creating a Social Media Strategy at Your Library." *Florida Libraries* 57, no. 2: 13–16.

Simonson, Itamar, and Emanuel Rosen. 2014. "What Marketers Misunderstand about Online Reviews." *Harvard Business Review* 92, nos.1/2: 23–25.

Solomon, Laura. 2013. *The Librarian's Nitty-Gritty Guide to Social Media*. Chicago: American Library Association.

Tappendorfnd, Julie, and Ancel Glink. 2013. "Legal Issues Relating to Online Social Networking." *ILA Reporter* 31, no. 1: 16–19.

Wanucha, Meghan, and Linda Hofschire. 2013. *U.S. Public Libraries and the Use of Web Technologies*. Denver, CO: Library Research Service. http://www.lrs.org/wp-content/uploads/2013/11/WebTech2012_CloserLook.pdf.

Wasike, Jotham. 2013. "Social Media Ethical Issues: Role of a Librarian." *Library Hi Tech* 30, no. 1: 8–16.

Whitt, Marc. 2014. "The Relationship-Building Business." *University Business* 17, no. 4: 48.

Wu, Jin, Amy J. Chatfield, Annie M. Hughes, Lynn Kysh, and Megan Rosenbloom. 2014. "Measuring Patrons' Technology Habits: An Evidence-Based Approach to Tailoring Library Services." *Journal of the Medical Library Association* 102, no. 2: 125–129.

Xie, Iris, and Jennifer Stevenson. 2014. "Social Media Application in Digital Libraries." *Online Information Review* 38, no. 4: 502–523.

SUGGESTED READINGS

Anwyll, Rebecca, and Brenda Chawner. 2013. "Social Media and Readers' Advisory: A Win-Win Combination?" *Reference & User Services Quarterly* 53, no. 1: 18–22.

Barber, Peggy. 2014. "Contagious Marketing: How Libraries Can Get More Word-of-Mouth Buzz." *American Libraries* 45, nos. 1/2: 32–35.

Barlow, Amy, Heather Love Beverley, Carrie Dunham-LaGree, Sarah Elichko, amd Emily Hamstra. 2013. "Chasing Reference: Librarians and Collaborative Blogging." *Reference & User Services Quarterly* 52, no. 4: 283–286.

Becker, Samantha. 2011. "10 Tips for Improving the Impact of Public Access Technology in Your Library." *ALKI* 27, no. 2: 14–15.

Bell, Steven. 2012. "Students Tweet the Darndest Things about Your Library—And Why You Need to Listen." *Reference Services Review* 40, no. 2: 217–220.

Coleman, Sarah, Terzah Becker, Josie Brockmann, and Christine Kreger. 2013. "CALCON 2012 — Standing Out Socially: Making Your Public Library Shine on Facebook and Other Social Media Sites." *Colorado Libraries* 36, no. 4: 1–6.

Dankowski, Terra. 2013. "How Libraries Are Using Social Media." *American Libraries* 44, no. 5: 38–41.

DeCesare, Julie A. 2014. "User Uploads and YouTube One Channels for Teaching, Learning and Research." *Library Technology Reports* 50, no. 2: 12–20.

Dougan, Kristin. 2014. "'YouTube Has Changed Everything?' Music Faculty, Librarians and Their Use and Perceptions of YouTube." *College & Research Libraries* 75, no. 4: 575–589.

Fredrick, Kathy. 2012. "Sharing Your Library with Facebook Pages." *School Library Monthly* 28, no. 5: 24–26.

Fredrick, Kathy. 2014. "Using Social Media for Career and College Readiness." *School Library Monthly* 30, no. 4: 27–28.

Gantt, John T., and J. Randal Woodland. 2013. "Libraries in Second Life: Linking Collections, Clients, and Communities in a Virtual World." *Journal of Web Librarianship* 7, no. 2: 123–141.

Gunton, Lyndelle, and Kate Davis. 2012. "Beyond Broadcasting: Customer Service, Community and Information Experience in the Twittersphere." *Reference Services Review* 40, no. 2: 226–227.

Hanson, Alida. 2013. "Can We Talk? How School Librarians Discuss Social Media with Stakeholders." *Young Adult Library Services* 11, no. 2: 35–37.

Kim, Kyung-Sun, Sei-Ching Joanna Sin, and Eun Young Yoo-Lee. 2014. "Undergraduates' Use of Social Media as Information Sources." *College & Research Libraries* 75, no. 4: 442–457.

Kwanya, Tom, Christine Stilwell, and Peter G. Underwood. 2011. "Library 2.0 versus Other Library Service Models: A Critical Analysis." *Journal of Librarianship and Information Science* 44, no. 3: 145–162.

Lammers, Deborah. 2012. "Still Facing Obstacles to Web 2.0 Use by Your Library? Try Henrico's Approach." *Virginia Libraries* 58, no. 1: 26–28.

Massis, Bruce. 2014. "Library Marketing: Moving between Traditional and Digital Strategies. *New Library World* 115m, nos. 7/8: 405–408.

McPhee, Jessica. 2014. "10 Ways to Rock on Social Media." *Feliciter* 60, no. 3: 16–17.

Mergel, Ines. 2013. "Social Media Adoption and Resulting Tactics in the U.S. Federal Government." *Government Information Quarterly* 30, no. 2: 132–130.

Mergel, Ines. 2013. *Social Media in the Public Sector: A Guide to Participation, Collaboration, and Transparency in the Networked World.* San Francisco, CA: Jossey-Bass.

Siegel, Daniel J. 2014 "Avoid Social Media Missteps." *Trial* 50, no. 6: 54–55.

Smeaton, Kathleen, and Kate Davis. 2014. "Social Technologies in Public Libraries: Exploring Best Practices." *Library Management* 35, no. 3: 224–238.

Smith, Toby, and Rodney Lambert. 2014. "A Systematic Review Investigating the Use of Twitter and Facebook in University—Based Healthcare Education." *Heath Education* 114, no. 5: 347–366.

Tenopir, Carol, Rachel Volentine, and Donald W. King. 2013. "Social Media and Scholarly Reading." *Online Information Review* 37, no.2: 193–216.

Tidal, Junior. 2011. "Using Web Metric Software to Drive Mobile Website Development." *Computers in Libraries* 31, no. 3: 19–23.

Vassilakaki, Evgenia, and Emmanouel Garfallou. 2014. "The Impact of Facebook on Libraries and Librarians: A Review of the Literature." *Program: Electronic Library and Information Service* 48, no. 3: 226–245.

Witte, Ginna Gautner, 2014. "Content Generation and Social Networks Integration within Academic Library Facebook Pages." *Journal Electronic Resources Librarianship* 26, no. 2: 89–100.

Part IV

Operational Issues in Library Programs and Services

Chapter 13

Legal Aspects

Colorado Library Law (C.R.S. 24–90–101 et seq.) dictates much of what we need to know about how to run our libraries. . . .

—Nina McHale, 2011

Specifically, although we will touch on some of the legal defenses of libraries as institutions, our main concern here is what you, as a practicing professional, can do to keep you and your library from legal difficulties.

—Spencer L. Simons, 2005

The Halstead Public Library Board of trustees debated malpractice insurance for librarians until two o'clock this morning in one of the stormiest sessions in the library's history.

—Allan Angoff, 1976

Over the past ten years libraries . . . have established a presence on websites and other web-based social networking sites. . . . As new forms of web-based social media are introduced, libraries will need to keep up with technology, while ensuring that they do not lose sight of their legal obligations to the public and their patrons in these evolving digital times.

—Julia Tappendorf and Ancil Glink, 2013

On June 27, a diplomatic conference of the World Intellectual Property Organization . . . adopted a treaty . . . to allow a copyright exception on works for the visually impaired readers so they can be sold and distributed outside their countries of origin.

—American Libraries, 2014

We decided that the first chapter in this part of the book had to address legal concerns that may and do influence library programs and services. Although our opening quotation from Nina McHale refers to Colorado library law, every state has some laws that relate to libraries. Such laws and "rules and regulations" do determine much of what and how libraries go about doing their business.

You may be somewhat surprised by just how far reaching such laws go in providing the basic structure of public service activities. Some laws you may know about to at least some degree based on personal experience, for example, copyright and employment laws.

Other laws may be rather surprising, such as laws regarding the handling of lost, missing, and overdue materials borrowed from a collection in a publicly funded library. (As mentioned in chapter 4, often such fine money goes into the parent organization's general fund, rather than into the library's operating budget.) Essentially, laws relate to everything from the creation of a library to its final closure. Would you think that posting, or lack of posting, official library documents on the Web might create legal problems for a library? The opening quotation from Julia Tappendorf and Ancil Glink suggests such could be the case, if the library does not understand a state's law regarding "open meetings."

There are some laws that cause you to shake your head in disbelief. You undoubtedly know that seeing-eye dogs are allowed into any space that their owners may go. Under the law they are considered a "service animal." Until mid-2013, if you worked in an Arizona public library, you would have been in violation of the law that regulated service animals had you tried to exclude a cat, parrot, pot-bellied pig, squirrel, ferret, and many other animals. In 2013, the state legislature passed a law limiting service animals to just dogs and miniature horses (this is no joke: see Alia Rau's article in the *Arizona Republic*, 2013). The law also excluded from the concept of service, such things as providing comfort, companionship, emotional support, or "well-being." (We did not take time to check on what other states have had to say about service animals. However, you must keep in mind there may be federal and local regulations that may come into play. In the case of service animals, they are in fact addressed in the Americans with Disability Act [ADA]).

The Simons article that we quoted at the beginning of this chapter touches upon a wide range of legal concerns that involve the interaction between library staff and the public. His focus is on user behavior and potential liability (tort law) issues for libraries. Tort law applies to all organizations, but is sometimes overlooked by librarians until a problem arises. We look at tort law in more detail later in this chapter.

There are laws at all levels of government (federal, state, and local; sometimes even international treaties) that can come into play in terms of library operations. Our final opening quotation regarding fair use is an example of how even international treaties might have a local impact. In the case cited, what the library might legally provide for a visually impaired person.

The constantly changing legal landscape also means libraries must regularly monitor that landscape, if it hopes to avoid expensive legal processes. Doing so will not guarantee avoidance, but will substantially reduce the probability of it happening. Access to legal counsel is critical even when generating library policies that may limit access to library programs or services.

NOTE: *None* of the following material is intended to be, nor should it be, regarded as legal advice. Our advice is, when a circumstance that *may* have legal implications for the library or its staff arises, seek legal counsel. Failure to do so can have serious consequences for the library as well as its parent body.

CREATING LIBRARIES

All libraries and their parent organizations have a legal basis for their existence (e.g., a charter or articles of incorporation). Some private academic institutions have state charters; others are incorporated as nonprofit organizations. Publicly supported academic institutions are legislatively established and, to a degree, controlled by legislative action. A few such academic institutions are based in the state constitution—for example, the University of California, University of Michigan, and University of Colorado.

Public and school libraries are created through legislative acts as well. A public library law example from Arizona addresses funding levels for library support should a community decide to establish one:

A city or town may levy annually, in addition to all other taxes, a tax not to exceed one and one-half mills on the assessed value of all property in the city or town, exclusive of the valuation of property exempt from taxation, for the purpose of establishing and maintaining therein free public libraries and reading rooms, for purchasing books, journals and other publications, and erecting and maintaining such buildings as may be necessary therefore. (A.R.S. § 9–411[2014]Tax levy for library purposes)

An example of a state law authorizing the creation of school media centers is from the *Virginia Administrative Code*:

A. Each school shall maintain an organized library media center as the resource center of the school and provide a unified program of media services and activities for students and teachers before, during, and after school. The library media center shall contain hard copy, electronic technological resources, materials, and equipment that are sufficient to meet research, inquiry, and reading requirements of the instructional program and general student interest.

B. Each school shall provide a variety of materials and equipment to support the instructional program 8 VAC 20–131–190 (2014).

Special libraries, as is almost always the case, don't have a single, or even two or three patterns for their establishment. Businesses and corporations need no legal basis for creating a library for their employees and do not have to worry too much about library laws or rules and regulations, as long as access is restricted to employees. Should the library allow access to other individuals (which is not too likely), then there can be issues. Even for employees, some laws may come into play such as the "reasonable accommodation" requirement in the ADA and regulations such as building code components that relate to libraries. Special libraries that allow some access, even if there is a vetting/approval process to gain access (e.g., the Huntington Library), must comply with many of the same laws and regulations that concern public libraries.

A given in today's library world is the existence of consortia; some libraries are members of more than one consortium and such groups vary in their goals and purposes. Such groups also have a legal existence. Multitype library consortia are particularly complex legally. A group composed of public and private institutions usually has to have some type of authorization in order for the public institutions to expand funds outside their political jurisdiction. Some cooperative ventures cross state lines which can further complicate the situation. An example of a law allowing cross-state library cooperation is New York State's *Interstate Library Compact.* It also, among many other things, mandates a governing board that would supervise the organization's operations:

> Because the desire for the services provided by the libraries transcends governmental boundaries and can most effectively be satisfied by giving such services to communities and people regardless of jurisdictional lines, it is the policy of the state's party to this compact to cooperate and share their responsibilities; to authorize cooperation and sharing with respect to those types of library facilities and services which can be more economically or efficiently developed and maintained on a cooperative basis, and to authorize cooperation and sharing among localities, states and others in providing joint or cooperative library services in areas where the distribution of population or of existing and potential library resources make the provision of library service on an interstate basis the most effective way of providing adequate and efficient service. . . .

Article IV. Interstate Library Districts, Governing Board

(a) An interstate library district which establishes, maintains or operates any facilities or services in its own right shall have a governing board which shall direct the affairs of the district and act for it in all matters relating to its business. Each participating public library agency in the district shall be represented on the governing board which shall be organized and conduct its business in accordance with provision therefore in the library agreement. But in no event shall a governing board meet less often than twice a year.

(b) Any private library agency or agencies party to a library agreement establishing an interstate library district may be represented on or advise with the governing board of the district in such manner as the library agreement may provide. (NY CLS Unconsol Ch 111-B § 1 (2014))

You might well ask how consortia arise and how they are legally organized might impact a library's programs and services. One of the most obvious impacts is what terms a consortium negotiates for a database. When it comes to group licensing, a vendor does not negotiate terms with individual libraries; it works with the group. Those terms can expand or limit what the individual libraries may do with the database content (e.g., document delivery) as well as what their users do with the material.

USERS AND THE LAW

There are a host of laws, rules, and regulations that come into play when the library is what the courts refer to as a "public forum." Educational libraries (academic and school) often fall into that category even though their focus is on service to students and staff. Private educational institutions may be less public, but most allow some public access and thus face most of the issues as those that are publicly funded. There are issues of access, behavior, privacy, and the like to think about and be ready to handle properly (legally).

Disruptive User Behavior

For staff working in public services, user behavior is an ongoing challenge. Just what behavior the library can put limits on, how much discourteous behavior must a staff member endure, what to do when a user complains about another user, and when to call the police are a small sampling of the issues that can, and do, arise. Proper policies and staff training to keep the inevitable problems to a minimum are keys to handling the situations effectively and legally.

Almost all libraries must address disruptive behavior. Special libraries are the least likely to have such situations arise. For-profit special libraries rarely have non-organization individuals in their space, and the nonprofits usually have limited access—often with pre-visit vetting of the user. Their most likely situation will involve a staff person; nevertheless failure to have procedures in place for handling the event will likely make a bad situation worse. Libraries have to think about the murky area of individual versus group rights under the law.

You might think that school libraries are low on the scale for disruptive behavior. They are certainly lower than libraries open to the general public, but they do have to think about how to handle potential problems. When a kindergarten student brings a loaded gun to school and discharges it (Hassan, 2011), you have to know that there is serious potential for unacceptable behavior even in an elementary school library. Middle and high schools have increasing levels of concern—drug use, bullying, and weapons, for example—for confrontations between students in the library.

Libraries that are open to the public have the greatest number of incidents. It is as Sarah Farrugia (2002) suggested, "Public librarians are more susceptible to patron violence than academic and other special libraries, as their open door policy allows anyone to use the building. This can sometimes invite trouble from asocial citizens who can cause disruption and uneasiness amongst staff and patrons and even lead to acts of extreme violence" (p. 309). It is disconcerting when it is a fellow staff member behaves "strangely;" however, with a colleague you have a baseline for judging what is wrong. With the public, there is almost no basis for knowing what is wrong and what to expect, unless it is one of the regular visitors.

Table 13.1 lists some of the most common unacceptable behaviors library staff encounter. As we stated earlier, successful handling of any of the behaviors, as well as others not on the list, depends upon having sound/legal policies in place and having the staff trained in what to, and what not to, do when the circumstance arises. It is *essential* to work with legal counsel when developing appropriate behavior policies. Legal counsel will be aware of community/state laws, as well as court decisions, all of which will affect the policies.

TABLE 13.1 Common Disruptive Behaviors in Libraries

• Drug/alcohol use (staff or users)	• Drug/alcohol sale
• Verbal abuse toward staff by user	• Verbal abuse between users
• Assault on staff	• Assault between users
• Gang activity	• Indecent exposure
• User viewing/printing pornographic material	• Trespassing
• Arson (especially in book return boxes)	• Disorderly/menacing conduct

When does unusual or strange behavior become disruptive? Every library must decide the answer to that question. Once that is decided, the attorney may not always agree that the behavior may be controlled by the library. You cannot call security every time someone exhibits slightly strange behavior; doing so could lead to a lawsuit against the library. Libraries do face the possibility of litigation over staff action or inaction. Thus, you must have properly formulated policies and staff trained in their application. Workshops conducted by professionals specializing in human behavior/mental health and substance abuse can help prepare the staff to safely handle such potential behavior problems. They also help set reasonable guidelines for when to call for assistance. After training, the policy guidelines should be written down for later consultation when the need arises.

Something to Ponder

An increasing percentage of homeless people in the United States are individuals who, in the past, would have been hospitalized and put on medication. Most of them are harmless, but without their medication their behavior can be erratic and often disruptive. Some users are uncomfortable when homeless people are around them. They may ask you to have such individuals removed from the library. Remember, public buildings are indeed public. How would you handle the situation?

One resource on the topic worth reviewing is "Extending Our Reach: Reducing Homelessness through Library Engagement" from the American Library Association (ALA; http://www.ala.org/offices/extending-our-reach-reducing-homelessness-through-library-engagement-5).

If the library posts reasonable rules regarding access, hours, and behavior, it may, without too much legal concern, remove anyone violating those rules. The two key considerations are reasonable rules and posting. The rules *must* reflect existing laws and should have been reviewed by legal counsel. Both conditions must be present for removal from the library to be legal. Repeat offenders can face legal action, if the library wishes to press charges.

American Libraries (2006a) reported on a problem with the "reasonableness" of library access/behavior polices. In one instance, the Dallas Public Library's plan to ban persons "emitting odors (including bodily odors or perfumes) which interfere with services by others users or work staff" was challenged (p. 11). Homeless advocates questioned the fairness of such a rule. The ACLU filed a lawsuit in Massachusetts (*American Libraries*, 2006b) over a rule that limited a homeless person to checking out only 2 books at any one time when other users could have at least 10 items. These two incidents illustrate the fact that just having written rules regarding access/behavior does not end controversy.

Anyone who has worked in public services for any length of time will have experienced some verbal abuse from a user over some library issue (fines are among the top issues that draw users' ire). How much verbal abuse must one tolerate? Frank DeRosa (1980) commented:

> People in all areas of public service, and librarians in particular, seem resigned to the opinion that abuse from their public is inescapable and there is not much they can do about it. Much of this misconception is due to the fact that many people do not realize the point when disruptive behavior becomes antisocial behavior and when antisocial behavior becomes criminal behavior. (p. 35)

You cannot avoid some verbal abuse if you work in public services. Certainly there are limits to what you have to endure; working with legal counsel can establish some legally sound guidelines for "when enough is enough" (Although this still will not fully ensure there will not be lawsuits from an angry user.) There are some techniques that you can employ during such circumstances that often defuse the anger/abuse. The following extended discussion of handling a situation illustrates how to try to calm down a situation as well as reduce the chances of litigation.

There are times, no matter how carefully handled the circumstance was, the person will go to the media or an attorney. This happens occasionally; however, having proper policies in place and posted and staff trained in conflict control will help keep the "fallout" as small as possible.

One all-too-common problem for libraries (except special libraries and a few specialized research libraries such as the Huntington Library in California) regarding potential liability is unattended children. "Latchkey children" have been a major challenge for public and academic libraries. Some parents expect their child to go to the library (the library being considered a safe place to be) after school and wait for the parent. A few parents even bring the child to the library and leave the building to attend to other activities, leaving the child unsupervised. There is a question of just how much liability a library has for looking after unsupervised children. Can the parent(s) hold the library and its staff liable for an injury or health problem that occurs when the child is alone in the library? We address the issue of latchkey children later and also in chapter 16.

LIBRARY SERVICES AND THE LAW

Many of the services libraries provide are circumscribed by a variety of laws—accessibility to facilities and collections, what our users may do with the resources we make available, and who has access to materials—these are but a few examples.

Access to library resources must comply with ADA, as we noted earlier. Title III of the act states that it is a violation to discriminate "on the basis of disability in the full and equal enjoyment of the goods, services, facilities, privileges, advantages, or accommodations of any place of public accommodation" (42 U.S.C. § 12182(a) 2000). Physical access includes such factors as wheelchair ramps as needed from the front entrance to elsewhere in the building, drinking fountain height, restroom accommodations, and the aisle width in publicly accessible stacks. Many libraries built long before the act passed face substantial remodeling renovation costs to become compliant. For most libraries, the physical access issues have been addressed; however, modifications to ADA, or new legislation, may bring about new requirements and cost. An example of the changing ADA requirements took place in 2004/05 when the agency issued new guidelines (69 Fed. Reg. 44,084, et seq., July 23, 2004, http://blog.librarylaw.com/librarylaw/disability_access/).

On the service side, there were and are compliance concerns. For example, what percentages of your library's collections are accessible to the visually impaired users? Does the collection access meet the "full and equal" provision of ADA? Large print books are one way to meet this need; however, only a small fraction of the total output is available in that format. Mary Anne Epp (2006) noted, "Experts estimate only 5 percent of the world's publishing output is made accessible in alternate formats for people who cannot use print" (p. 411). Her article discusses potential collaborative projects to help address the challenge of providing the visually impaired with access to print-based materials. There are options available to help meet the local need, such as reading machines and volunteers to assist those with vision limitations. Again, there are budget and legal considerations to address.

Then there is the matter of media and e-resources to take into account. Darlene Fichter (2013) provided some sound advice regarding improving accessibility for Web sites. There are solutions available, but you must think about the issues on an ongoing basis. We know from firsthand experience that failure to address these issues for just one user can lead to at least a visit from the user's lawyer and perhaps even a lawsuit.

Filtering the Web

Another example of legislation that circumscribes what resources a library may make available to what users is CIPA (Children's Internet Protection Act). CIPA primarily impacts school and public libraries and to a lesser extent any library hoping to get federal funds for Internet access. The act is the outcome of an earlier effort to protect children from offensive Internet material that was ruled unconstitutional on First Amendment grounds. CIPA got round that issue by using access to federal funding; a library wishing to secure federal E-Rate funding must employ filtering software on its computers. The ALA maintains a page on CIPA that is worth reviewing for more information on the legislation: http://www.ala.org/advocacy/advleg/federallegislation/cipa. ALA also issued an informative policy brief on the impact of CIPA entitled *Fencing Out Knowledge* (Batch, 2014).

Something to Ponder

E-rate (Public Law 106–554) is a shorthand term for Universal Service Rate Discount for Schools and Libraries. The Federal Communications Commission supervises the program, which is administered by the Universal Service Administration Company.

As noted earlier, the program came about as the result of an earlier congressional effort to protect children from questionable Internet material. The program is an element in an effort to completely connect everyone in the country to the Internet. What the program provides are discounts, some as much as 80 percent, on "connectivity" costs, that is, monthly charges for Internet connection, telecommunication costs, and the like. They do not cover equipment, software, and maintenance of such items. The level of discount varies dependent upon such factors as community economic situation, location, (urban, suburban, rural, etc.).

The key factor is only libraries that filter Internet access are eligible for a discount. More information on e-rate is available on the ALA Web site: http://www.ala.org/advocacy/telecom/erate.

Paul Jaeger and Zheng Yan (2009) indicated that by 2005, 100 percent of U.S. public schools had implemented CIPA filtering and "safety policies." In terms of public libraries, by 2008 only 38.2 percent were filtering (pp. 9–10). Adults in public libraries that do filter may request the staff disable the filter while the person uses the computer. That option for adults appears to be a good one; however, Gretchen Kolderup (2013) notes that "even though filters have improved since their initial creation, they still both underblock and overblock content, and practical matters of implementation further deteriorate their value" (p. 26). You have to wonder just how many librarians actually refuse to turn off a filter on the basis of personal values or is it that they are aware of how complicated/time consuming the process is and don't communicate those facts? Also, once the person is finished, the process must be reversed taking yet more staff time, if the computers are not set up to have the filters automatically reapplied after a patron logs off. Other unanswered questions are, for libraries that do filter, do users know when they sit down to use a machine that it has filtering software and that, if it does, they have the right to request that it be turned off ? We know a few public libraries that are filtering all computers that do not have any signage indicating adults may have access to the unfiltered Internet.

Deborah Caldwell-Stone (2013) wrote the following about a major concern regarding filtering and intellectual freedom that should be kept in mind:

In the decade since the Supreme Court upheld the implementation of the Children's Internet Protection Act (CIPA), internet filtering has become a frequent practice in public libraries. It has also become the primary strategy for managing students' internet access in school libraries. . . . Why are we seeing more and more instances where public libraries and schools are actively engaged in censoring online information, despite the library profession's commitment to intellectual freedom, First Amendment rights, and free and open access to information? (p. 58)

Unattended Children

Most people hire a babysitter when they need one. However, there are some people who seem to believe that one of the services libraries offer is free child care. Melissa Higey (2014) noted:

> Children are often left unattended in the library, dropped off by parents for a few hours, or simply "latchkey" children—children that come to the library while parents or guardians are at work or not at home. Most libraries have policies regarding at what age children can be left unattended, how long children can be left unattended, or what areas of the library unattended children can visit. These policies vary from library to library, but most librarians would agree that this is an issue in public libraries today, especially with the increase of working parents and single-parent homes.

Academic libraries also face some challenges in terms of unattended children. In their case, more often than not, it is a staff member that is the parent leaving the child.

Why are unattended children a challenge for libraries? The issues revolve around various laws related to child protection, some state and some local in origination. What are the responsibilities/duties of people who are not the child's parent, guardians, caretaker for children left unattended? As stated on the Connecting Texas Libraries Statewide Web site (http://www.ctls.net/2010/06/faq-unattended-children/), "Have you discussed liability for unattended children with your legal counsel? Although the public library does not have the same provision of care responsibilities that schools and childcare centers have, local laws may set stricter standards."

Essentially, in the absence of a clear, legally vetted, library policy related to such children, the staff are hard pressed as what they ought to do. This is particularly challenging if the child appears to have a medical emergency. Certainly calling the paramedics is a first safe step, but what happens after that while waiting for help to arrive?

Regardless of whatever steps the library takes to address the issue of unattended children, a first step is absolutely necessary to prevent even greater problems: have clear policies and a plan of action reviewed by the legal counsel for the library or parent institution. Some of the options that exist in various jurisdictions are:

- To have libraries bar children without parental supervision
- To offer special programs designed for such children
- To have policies requiring staff to call child welfare services or police to pick up any unattended child at closing time
- To have policies allowing staff to contact police/security when a child is left unattended for a specified period of time during normal school hours

We offer the following Web sites as examples of library policies addressing the issue:

Flagstaff Coconino Public Library System (AZ)
http://www.flagstaffpubliclibrary.org/services/youth_services/parents_
    and_educators/unattended.html

Great Neck Public Library (NY)
http://www.greatnecklibrary.org/libinfo/childpol.php

Messenger Public Library of North Aurora (IL)
http://www.northaurora.lib.il.us/content/board-and-policies/policies-
    and-documents/unattended-children-policy

Prescott Public Library (AZ)
http://www.prescottlibrary.info/about/policies/unattended-child-policy/

Policies need to be posted in prominent locations, especially at public entrances, and provided to parents when a child is given a library card. The library Web site is another location for posting such policies. Another important element is to make it clear that the library assumes no childcare responsibility.

Something to Ponder

A few public libraries in the United States have made arrangements with nearby schools to offer children the opportunity to come to a room in the library where they can get help with homework and/or they can be kept busy with activities until the parent(s) can pick them up. The room is staffed by trained teachers and individuals experienced in summer camp programs.

In the Nordic countries, this type of cooperative activity is very common. There are, of course, some serious legal issues related to such things as who may pick up a child and treatment of health problems.

What do libraries that you know of do about unattended children?

User Privacy

How is library user privacy a legal concern? In most states library user records are legally confidential, for example, California (Cal Civ Code § 1798.3, 2014), Colorado (C.R.S. 24–72–204, 2013), Illinois (75 ILCS 5/1–7, 2014), and New York (NY CLS CPLR § 4509, 2014). Just because there is a legal basis for confidentiality it does not always translate into simple decisions for the library staff. You must release information when there is a court order or subpoena. It is not uncommon for law enforcement officers to request such information without such documentation and to present the request as a means of speeding up the investigation. Once again having a policy in place for handling such requests is important. As we discussed later, how to handle the request depends on what agency is asking—local enforcement or the FBI. Good starting points for policy formulation are the following Web pages from ALA:

> Confidentiality and Coping with Law Enforcement Inquiries: Guidelines for the Library and Its Staff http://www.ala.org/Template.cfm?Section= ifissues&Template=/ContentManagement/ContentDisplay.cfm&Content ID=21654,
>
> Privacy: An Interpretation of the *Library Bill of Rights* http://www.ala.org /ala/issuesadvocacy/intfreedom/librarybill/interpretations/privacy .cfm, and
>
> Privacy Tool Kit http://www.ala.org/advocacy/privacyconfidentiality/tool kitsprivacy/privacy.

From the Authors' Experience

The authors are aware of a situation where at one library, the police showed up asking for the records of a hiker that had gone missing. It was the officer's hope that the missing hiker had checked out books on specific local hiking locations, thereby potentially speeding up the investigation. Unfortunately, the library could not comply with the request without a court order.

There are three broad categories of user information libraries must consider in terms of confidentiality—data collected from a person upon becoming a registered user, data about what a person uses (e.g., items checked out, online services, document delivery service), and finally, user data collected by library vendors as a result of a person using their services. Law enforcement officers are rarely concerned about the first category; however, other people may want that information and can present their requests in seemingly innocent terms (trying to locate a family member—"just need the address"). A library has or should have good control over the data in the first category. It is in the other two categories that control becomes less. A staff member receiving such a request should politely, but firmly, refuse to comply and immediately report the request to their supervisor and otherwise follow the library's confidentiality policy.

Libraries with ILS circulation systems are in a good position to insure collection usage data is handled legally. Today's systems are able to break the link between the borrower and the items upon return and any associated fees that are paid. If the circulation system requires that the name of a borrower appear on a book card or some other traceable record, the staff should render the name illegible as part of the discharging process. Although circulation records are the usage data most often thought of in terms of confidentiality, there may well be other data, such as reserving time to use library computers and document delivery services that should be considered. Many public libraries that are part of city government also have rules regarding when and how to dispose of records that are provided to them by the City Records Technician.

One type of usage data that the library has little control over is database usage. As Angela Maycock (2013) noted, "The ease of communicating in the digital age has changed the way we live, work, and learn—often in wonderfully exciting and positive ways. But the capacity of . . . databases to collect and store personal information presents growing challenges to individuals' privacy" (p. 34). Many library database vendors, like almost all commercial Web organizations, collect data about people using their services. Trina Magi (2010) stated the issue as "the Web 2.0 environment . . . poses new challenges for librarians in their commitment to protect user privacy as vendors of online databases incorporate personalization features into their search-retrieval interfaces, thereby collecting personally identifiable user information not subject to library oversight" (p. 254). Most of the major online library product vendors have prominently placed search options on their opening search page that allows users to personalize their search—some examples are EBSCO's "MyEBSCOhost," Emerald's "Your Profile," and ProQuest's "My Research."

What might vendors collect and do with such data? Even without personalization, many vendors have the option for e-mailing the requested file(s) to the person. That alone provides a vendor with two pieces of marketable information: what the person may be interested in and a means of contacting the person. The personalized profile can generate more marketable data. Magi reported that LexisNexis sells marketing lists such as "Homeowner" and "Relatives and Room Mates" (p. 268).

Is what others do regarding use of library services a concern for libraries and the issue of confidentiality? What can they do about vendor data collection activities? Should users be told that vendors are collecting personal information when they use a database? Do they care? We do not have the answers; however, we do believe that libraries ought to have a serious discussion of the matter and develop a policy regarding how to address a complaint from a user who objects to personal information being collected. Magi (2013) makes a valid point that we agree with: "Don't assume users know anything about how a third-party database works and puts their privacy at risk; tell them" (p. 39).

Check These Out

The following items explore in more detail the issues of privacy, libraries, and digital environment:

Cyrus, John W.W., and Mark P. Baggett. 2012. "Mobile Technology: Implications for Privacy and Librarianship." *Reference Librarian* 53, no. 3: 284–296.

Fernandez, Peter. 2010. "Privacy and Generation Y: Applying Library Values to Social Networking Sites." *Community & Junior College Libraries* 16, no. 2: 100–113.

Park, Yong Jin. 2013. "Digital Literacy and Privacy Behavior Online." *Communication Research* 40, no. 2: 215–236.

Payton, Theresa M. and Ted Claypoole. 2014. *Privacy in the Age of Big Data: Recognizing Threats, Defending Your Rights, and Protecting Your Family.* Lanham, MD: Rowman & Littlefield.

Rubel, Alan. 2014. "Libraries, Electronic Resources, and Privacy: The Case for Positive Intellectual Freedom." *Library Quarterly* 84, no. 2: 183–208.

Rundle, Hugh. 2014. "Who Are You Empowering?" *In the Library with the Lead Pipe*: 1–9.

From the Authors' Experience

Virginia Walter, a long-time colleague of the authors and advocate for children and young adult library services, commented in an e-mail exchange with the authors about confidentiality and children's library records. She noted that there is a somewhat ambiguous nature regarding confidentiality of children's library records. Most libraries routinely allow parents to access their child's borrowing record, usually to see if there are any materials outstanding. However, a few libraries—Santa Clara County (California), for one—restrict access and require that an adult have the child's permission before accessing the record. There are some legal justifications for this; a few city and county attorneys have reasoned that the right to privacy should not be abrogated because of a person's age and that this right carries more weight than a parent's rights. Other child advocates have pointed to more nefarious uses that have been put to a child's library records, particularly in child custody cases.

After 9/11, there was a change regarding access to library records, at least for federal law enforcement officers. The USA PATRIOT Act (Public Law 107–56) authorized warrant-less searches as well as including a requirement that the library not communicate to anyone that such a search occurred or was under way. What data might be available from library records for law enforcement officials that they might more easily access elsewhere? Karl Gruben (2006) wrote, "In actuality, the Department of Justice does not have as much interest in what Johnny is reading as it does in what he is looking at or e-mailing or Instant Messaging on the Internet, particularly since there is suspicion that the 9/11 hijackers communicated through Internet terminals in public libraries" (p. 303).

Section 215 of the act allows the government to secure secret warrants to obtain "business records"—this includes library records and those from library database vendors for named individuals. The act also authorizes the issuance of National Security Letters (NSLs), which do not require a judge's review, that require organizations to secretly provide information. At least one library has been on the receiving end of such a letter. As noted by Pike (2013), a "2008 Justice Department report indicated that nearly 200,000 NSLs had been issued between 2003 and 2006. While the rate has dropped since the 2008 report, the FBI continues to issue NSLs, with nearly 45,000-plus letters issued between 2009 and 2011" (p. 22).

RFID

Some libraries have taken to using RFID technology (Radio Frequency Identification) that may present some challenges in terms of user privacy, at least as it has been presented in the press (for one such discussion see Ayre, 2013). Originally employed as a very effective method for library inventory control, item identification, and self check-out, when, in the unlikely event, its capabilities are extended outside the library building problems might arise.

An embedded RFID chip identifies a specific item and its location unlike the magnetic strips commonly used in libraries in conjunction with their exit control system. The magnetic strip is not item specific and indicates only if the item has or has not been properly checked out. An RFID tag can track locations over a substantial distance—in theory far beyond the library building. Some states have proposed banning or at least greatly limiting the use of RFID chips due to their tracking capabilities. The concern is not particularly directed toward libraries because the typical library RFID is capable of being read only from about 3 feet. The concern is over commercial interests that claim knowing where and when a consumer uses their products. Delivering these products with RFID tabs has implications that extend far beyond library tags.

What the long-term outcome will be is impossible to accurately predict. Used for their original purposes in a library, there should be no major concerns in implementing RFID—beyond the high cost of the chips and the labor required to "embed" one in each item in the collection. The use of tracking capabilities beyond the library proper seems problematic. One easy way to keep up on the topic of RFID in libraries is to monitor sources such as the following from ALA:

RFID: Radio Frequency Identification Technology (Office of Intellectual Freedom)
http://www.ala.org/offices/oif/ifissues/rfid

RFID and Libraries (ALA Library Fact Sheet Number 25)
http://www.ala.org/tools/libfactsheets/alalibraryfactsheet25

Tort Laws and Liability

We have mentioned liability several times. What is involved and what does that mean? Liability is:

A comprehensive legal term that describes the condition of being actually or potentially subject to a legal obligation. Primary liability is an obligation for which a person is directly responsible; it is distinguished from secondary liability which is the responsibility of another if the party directly responsible fails or refuses to satisfy his or her obligation. (http://legal-dictionary.thefreedictionary.com/liability)

Are libraries susceptible to being held liable for some action or failure to act? The answer is yes and no. In the past, those libraries that were tax-supported had some form of governmental immunity from lawsuits and liability. Today many states have greatly reduced the available immunity. One of the most common concerns for library liability is personal injury (tort law). Tort law addresses injuries—physical or emotional—resulting from negligence or intentional causes. Libraries have been involved in litigation arising from both causes. For libraries, it is the negligence category that is most significant.

Broadly thinking, there are three interrelated issues related to negligence, whether a mental, emotional, or physical injury. *Negligence* requires the existence of three conditions: that the cause of the injury must be a person not an act of God; that the person causing the injury has responsibility/duty to the injured party; and that the duty may be one of warning or one of action. An example of possible library negligence would be the failure of the staff to put out signs warning of slippery entryway floors on a rainy or snowy day and a person falling and injuring himself or herself.

Within the concept of personal injury law in the United States and England is a subarea that involves premises, such as the library property. Premises include everything associated with building—sidewalks, grounds, parking lot, and lighting, for example. The courts have divided the "controller" of the premises duties into three broad categories: invitees (users/staff in public areas), licensees (vendors and staff in nonpublic areas such as technical services and administrative offices), and trespassers. There is a descending order of duty to the categories. Beyond these basic categories, there are special duties to children and persons who are mentally or physically challenged.

From the Authors' Experience

Sinwell had an interesting situation with the potential for a liability legal action: One year I had a patron slip on snowy curb outside my public library. She told me she hurt her ankle and wanted to know what we would do regarding her need of medical attention. A mandatory accident form was completed.

Our risk management guidelines are clear in that "we are not to say we are responsible or liable in any way" when talking to a patron.

The patron made a claim to the county and was told the county would be in touch with her about paying medical costs. A county risk management officer interviewed me and staff that worked that day to verify what had been said.

Note: At the time, I had had her sit down and offered some ice for her ankle. As I was returning to the place where she was sitting, she didn't see me, but I saw her walking ably around to help her son with something. When I approached, she started limping and complaining of pain.

Malpractice and Librarians

Our opening quotation from Allen Angoff (1976) is from a fictitious case he created dealing with malpractice. In Angoff's story, the patron was ready to file suit because they claimed they were injured when building a deck at their home after following the steps outlined in a book they checked out from the library. Angoff's antagonist even went so far to state that the library and its "chief reference librarian were grossly negligent in continuing to circulate a long-antiquated volume and in so doing endangered the lives and homes of all library patrons who might consult it" (p. 489). Although the article was not based on an actual incident, in a sense, it was a wakeup call for the profession to start thinking about the possibility that such a case might happen one day. Malpractice is a complex issue with questions about the role of expertise, employee, employer, the person filing the lawsuit, and reasonable expectations. Is it reasonable that public service staff to worry about malpractice?

According to Paul Healey (a holder of JD and MLS), there would be no basis for a successful malpractice case in the situation proposed by Angoff. Healey's point was that both tort and contract laws rely on reasonable expectations (2008, p. 13). Essentially, it is unreasonable to expect a librarian to be an expert in home construction much less deck building (the issue raised in Angoff's fictitious case). It is reasonable to assume a librarian is an expert in locating information about such an activity, but not for the correctness of that information.

Chances are very limited of your being named in a malpractice lawsuit when you are at a service desk at the time an injury occurs. However, it is not totally out of the question that you will be named a defendant as lawyers tend to name every possible person when filing such lawsuits. Also, as you assume more senior management roles, the risk increases. Obviously the library and its parent body will be the lead defendants as they have the "deep pockets;" however, you may also be named. While the parent institution is likely to cover legal fees, there may be instances where the individual's liability is such that the person will need to cover legal costs as well as any legal judgments. As a result, it is prudent to check with one's homeowner/renters insurance to determine if the liability coverage also applies to one's work activities. If not, it may be wise to see what the cost of workplace liability may be. Some library associations offer such coverage to members.

Check This Out

Paul Healey's book mentioned earlier, *Professional Liability Issues for Librarians and Information Professionals* (New York: Neal-Schuman, 2008), covers a host of liability issues for librarians. His background as both a practicing attorney and librarian gives his material credence. The chapters on the legal concepts are straightforward and provide the basis for understanding just how much legal issues can impact on what you do as a manager, at least in terms of liability.

CONTRACTS AND LICENSES

People sign contracts every day. Probably several thousand car rental "agreements" (they are contracts) are signed every few hours. If people had time to read the agreement and understand it, there would probably be many fewer cars rented. Hasty signing usually has no adverse consequences, unless something comes up as simple as a scratch or chip from a stone. That is when you learn just what was in the agreement.

Organizations cannot afford a hasty contract signing. Even when there are days, weeks, or months of work by attorneys for the concerned parties and everyone thought they understood the contract terms, interpretation issues can and do arise. That in turn often results in lawsuits being filed. As we noted in the section on meeting rooms in chapter 10, there are many times when a library simply has no money for fighting a lawsuit, be it for something it wants or to defend itself.

Libraries normally have multiple contracts in force at any time—ILS vendor contracts, book vendors, equipment maintenance, subscriptions, and janitorial services, for example. There are also license agreements for the access/ use of some service/product such as online databases. In the case of a contract, it is likely that the director signed the contract, but they may not be the staff person who implements the terms. The person doing the implementation must have a grasp of what the contract calls for in order to protect the library.

What is the difference, if any, between a contract and license? They are certainly related; however, there are differences and understanding the differences can help the library avoid legal entanglements. A *contract* is a "voluntary, deliberate, and legally enforceable (binding) agreement between two or more competent parties. . . . Each party to a contract acquires rights and duties relative to the rights and duties of the other parties" (http://www.busi nessdictionary.com/definition/contract.html). A *license* is a "revocable written (formal) or implied agreement by an authority or proprietor (the licensor) not to assert his or her right (for a specific period and under specified conditions) to prevent another party (the licensor) from engaging in certain activity that is normally forbidden (such as selling liquor or making copies of a copyrighted work)" (http://www.businessdictionary.com/definition/license.html). Essentially a license is the privilege to use something under certain conditions.

Typical library licensing agreements outline the lessee's (library) responsibility for such things as security, customer service, payment and delivery, limitations and warranties, termination, indemnification, and assignment. All of these factors can affect allowable use. Although adding attorney fees to the cost of creating user-oriented services/collections is unappealing, the fact is that most of the vendors will negotiate changes, and librarians should demand changes that benefit or at least do not create unreasonable demands on the library and its users.

Compliance is a key issue, and the library must do what it can to ensure compliance. Some database licensing agreements contain language that places responsibility on the library (subscriber) to monitor what users do with material after they leave the premises. Such clauses are beyond any library's ability to handle, and librarians should insist that they be deleted from the agreement.

As with computer software, the licensing agreement often comes with the product, that is, after the purchase. It is sealed in a package with a warning message to the effect that opening the package constitutes accepting the terms of the agreement inside the package. When considering a product from a new vendor, ask for a copy of the licensing agreement before making a final decision to purchase. This gives you an opportunity to review the document. It also provides an opportunity to request changes that the vendor may or may not be willing to make. In any event, it will give the library a chance to consider whether it can live with the conditions of the licensing agreement before committing to the purchase.

Check This Out

Because licensing is a major legal issue for libraries, we suggest you look at the "Principles" for licensing electronic resources as proposed by the Association of Research Libraries. Although they were formulated in 1997 and are intended for large research libraries, they remain just as valid today. They can provide useful ideas for all types of libraries when thinking about what you should seek in the way of license changes: http://www. arl.org/storage/documents/publications/licensing-principles-1997.pdf.

COPYRIGHT

Copyright has been a constant library legal issue for a great many years and becomes ever more complex as time goes by. The term copyright originated from the law's original purpose, to protect against unauthorized printing and selling a printed work. Today it is thought of as protecting intellectual property (IP)—a concept that relates to almost all formats that individuals and organizations produce in "hardcopy" or digitally. The complexity is a function of the variety of materials covered, and each new technology is viewed as a potential threat to the copyright holder's rights.

A full discussion of copyright is not possible or appropriate in this book, but some discussion is relevant to this chapter. Please note that what follows *is not legal advice*; it is merely a brief review of the issues and ALA guidelines and position regarding copyright. When in doubt about what is or is not legal, get legal counsel. Copyright holders can and do enforce, and have enforced their rights in court. Institutions and libraries, both public and private, have found this to be true and, more often than not, have lost the lawsuit.

The purpose of copyright is to promote the development and distribution of information while assuring the individual or group developing the idea or information has exclusive rights to profit from that activity. In addition, society, through its copyright laws, reserves for itself the right to use the material developed within limits without violating the copyright holder's right. The labels for the concept vary; in the United States it is "fair use," in the United Kingdom "fair rights." The problem is what is fair?

Section 107 of the U.S. Copyright Law (Public Law 94–553, Title 17 of the *U.S. Code*), while legally establishing the doctrine of fair use, is short and fairly nonspecific. The doctrine relates to copying, reproduction (multiple copies), and actual use. It indicates that use for criticism, comment, news reporting, teaching, scholarship, and research is reasonable. The law specifies four criteria for fair use:

1. The purpose and character of the use, including whether such use is of a commercial nature or is for nonprofit educational purposes;
2. The nature of the copyrighted work;
3. The amount and substantiality of the portion used in relation to the copyrighted work as a whole;
4. The effect of the use upon the potential market for or value of the copyrighted work. (17 USC §107)

Clearly there is room for interpretation and argument based on the criteria. Educators, publishers, and authors have struggled to clarify what is a reasonable definition of the concept. Needless to say, the different perspectives have made it difficult to find a satisfactory approach. As a result, more than a few court cases leave it to the justice system to find a solution. It is important to remember that "copyright protection extends to literary works; dramatic works; pantomimes and choreographic works; pictorial, graphic, and sculptural works; motion pictures and other audiovisual works; and sound recordings" (17 USC § 102).

Is it legal to use a video the library purchased in a program for the public? Is that fair use, especially if the event is free? The answer is, it depends. There is something called *performance rights*. The issue is too complex to explore in this book, but performance rights are part of the mechanism by which all the people involved in the production of the video receive compensation. The easiest way to think about it is in terms of book royalties: each new copy sold means a small payment is due to the author(s). For performance rights each "performance" should mean a small payment is due to each of the participants involved in its production. To cover such costs the producer/distributor of a video may or may not include "performance rights" in the price. (Essentially performance rights pertain when there is a presentation to a number of people at the same time, such as a children's program in the library.) The best approach is to acquire videos with performance rights; this will almost always mean a higher price than listed, unless it is clearly stated that the price includes performance rights.

Check These Out

Two good guides to copyright issues for libraries supporting educational programs are Rebecca P. Butler's *Copyright for Academic Librarians and Professionals* (Chicago: American Library Association, 2014) and Carrie Russell's *Complete Copyright for K-12 Librarians and Educators* (Chicago: American Library Association, 2012).

A very interesting item is Brandon Butler's 2011 "Copyfraud and Classroom Performance Rights: Two Bogus Copyright Claims" (*Research Library Issues* issue 276: 20–28). He makes the case that often both claims are made when, in fact, there is no applicable right. One example he gives is when publishers reprint a title that is in the public domain (no longer covered by copyright). They can claim coverage for any commentary that is new, cover art that is new, and the like but not for the original reprinted material. His basic message is libraries and schools need to have a clear understanding of the copyright laws in order to protect their legal usages of items.

Adding yet more complexity is the fact that most countries have copyright laws, with varying definitions of coverage terms, and others. For the better part of 80 years there has been an international effort to "harmonize" the laws. Today, the major international body trying to bring some standardization to the field is the World Intellectual Property Organization (WIPO). WIPO is a self-funded agency of the United Nations, whose mission is "to lead the development of a balanced and effective international intellectual property (IP) system that enables innovation and creativity for the benefit of all" (http://www.wipo.int/about-wipo/en/what_is_wipo.html).

WIPO was founded in 1967 as a result of the WIPO Convention and consists of 187 member countries as of mid-2014. Earlier we mentioned that IP was a very broad concept in today's digital world. WIPO's definition of IP is reasonably comprehensive:

> Intellectual property (IP) refers to creations of the mind, such as inventions; literary and artistic works; designs; and symbols, names and images used in commerce.
>
> IP is protected in law by, for example, patents, copyright and trademarks, which enable people to earn recognition or financial benefit from what they invent or create. By striking the right balance between the interests of innovators and the wider public interest, the IP system aims to foster an environment in which creativity and innovation can flourish. (http://www.wipo.int/about-ip/en/)

The Web site contains a number of useful explanations of how copyright laws vary around the world as well as a detailed discussion of copyright.

Almost all libraries provide photocopy services to users. There are regulations regarding posting proper signage related to photocopying and copyright. Failure to have such signs could put the library in jeopardy of becoming a defendant in an alleged copyright violation lawsuit.

Interlibrary loan (ILL) has been a staple service for a very long time, as we saw in chapter 5. There are copyright ground rules for how often a library may borrow articles from a single journal title before it risks a lawsuit for using ILL in place of subscribing to the title. Some online database vendors' licenses do not allow for the use of its materials for ILL purposes, unless the library can negotiate that clause be dropped.

The Digital Millennium Copyright Act of 1998 (DMCA, Public Law 105–304) updated U.S. copyright law in terms of the digital world, as well as to conform to the 1996 WIPO treaties. The 1978 copyright law is still in force, but changed dramatically as a result of amendments and DMCA.

One aspect of the DMCA of note to libraries is "Title II: Online Service Provider Liability." The reason for this is that the DMCA defines "online service provider" (OSP) very broadly, and libraries that offer electronic resources or Internet access could be considered OSPs. The law creates some "safe harbors" for specified OSP activities. When an activity is within the safe harbor, the OSP qualifies for an exemption from liability. One should read the most current material available about this title as it is complex, and legal interpretation of it is likely to evolve.

Title IV of DMCA provides some clarification about library and archival digitization activity for preservation purposes. It allows the creation of up to three digital preservation copies of an eligible copyrighted work and the electronic loan of those copies to qualifying institutions. An additional feature is that it permits preservation, including in a digital form, of an item in a format that has become obsolete.

Sometimes a seemingly unrelated court decision can later become a library issue. One example is a U.S. Supreme Court split decision (4 to 4, as the newest justice recused herself due to prior involvement in the case) that occurred in 2010. That decision essentially changed the "first sale doctrine" and potentially impacted library lending. As *Library Journal* (2010) noted at the time, "Why is the Library Copyright Alliance (LCA) interested in a legal battle between watch manufacturer Omega and big box retailer Costco? Because a pending Supreme Court case may threaten the 'first sale doctrine' in the copyright Act, which allows libraries to lend freely copies of all the books it has bought" (p. 13). Omega's position was that its watches are produced outside the United States and thus, Omega had the right to set a U.S. price (higher than elsewhere in the world). Further, Costco could not purchase watches elsewhere in the world (first sale) and resell them in the United States at the lower cost. Certainly there is much more to resolve before we know what, if any, impact there will be. The worst-case scenario was U.S. publishers would use the decision to move all their production activities outside the country.

In 2013, the *Economist* reported that the U.S. Supreme Court ruled that U.S. copyright law does *not* restrict goods produced overseas from being imported and resold in the United States. In the *Economist*'s words regarding first sale doctrine, "With the Supreme Court's ruling, that protection has been swept away" (p.71). From the library point of view, that decision, and the results of the 2013 *Kirtsaeng v. Wiley* decision mentioned in chapter 5, may impact the cost of items for the collection—whether for the better of worse will depend on how producers address the situation.

Related to the doctrine of first sale is another global factor. Some countries (e.g., Australia, Canada, and UK) employ the concept of public lending right (PLR) for authors and the use of their works by library users. It is a system that allows an author to be compensated for the circulated use of his or her copyrighted work from libraries. Given copyright owners' increasing attempts to charge a fee for various types of usage that were free, it may not be too long before the public lending right will come to the United States. Certainly the recent Supreme Court's decision regarding first sale removes one of the issues that clouded the efforts to get a U.S. PLR program in place—what happens after the first sale? Nothing may change as a result of the decision, but it bears watching as a potential threat to free lending.

CLOSING THOUGHTS

Legislation, rules, regulations, and court decisions can and do play a significant role in how libraries go about doing business. A challenge is such legal issues are not static and staying abreast of developments can be challenging. One resource to assist you in tracking legal issues and laws that may impact your library is the LibraryLaw Blog—http://blog.librarylaw.com/librarylaw/ (or @librarylaw on Twitter).

No matter the incident or the event that may have legal issues connected to it, we have three words of advice: document, document, document. Having a record prepared as soon as possible after the "event" is essential in building or defending a case. You might wish that such a step is not necessary, but in today's world when lawsuits seem to be filed at the drop of a hat, it is better to be on the safe side and prepare a record, than not to. Such documentation can range from an e-mail to a supervisor to a form (such as an "incident/accident report")—anything that records what transpired. When in doubt, check with your parent organization's attorney.

Chapter Review Material

1. In what manner can legal issues constrain a library's freedom of action?
2. Why is it important to get legal counsel involved in any potential legal issue?
3. What are some of the common areas where legal counsel is essential?
4. What role does training of staff have in policies such as user access and handling difficult users in avoiding liability issues?
5. Discuss the differences between contracts and licenses.
6. What are some of the areas where liability/negligence lawsuits might arise for a library and some of its staff?
7. How might a library go about keeping current on legal developments that may impact its activities?

REFERENCES

Angoff, Allan. 1976. "Library Malpractices Suit: Could It Happen to You?" *American Libraries* 7, no. 8: 489.

American Libraries. 2006a. "Stir Raised by Dallas Body Odor Rule." 37, no. 2: 11.

American Libraries. 2006b. "Homeless Residents Sue Over Borrowing Restrictions." 37, no. 7: 18.

American Libraries. 2014. "2013 Year in Review." 45, nos. 1/2: 28–31.

Ayre, Lori Bowen. 2013. "RFID, GPS, and 3G: Radio Wave Technologies and Privacy." *Collaborative Librarianship* 5, no. 3: 216–218.

Batch, Kristen R. 2014. *Fencing Out Knowledge: Impacts of the Children's Internet Protection Act 10 Years Later*. Policy Brief No. 5. Chicago: American Library Association, Office for Information Technology Policy and the Office for Intellectual Freedom. http://connect.ala.org/files/cipa_report.pdf.

Caldwell-Stone, Deborah. 2013. "Filtering and the First Amendment: When Is It Okay to Block Speech Online?" *American Libraries* 45, nos. 3/4: 58–61.

DeRosa, Frank J. 1980. "The Disruptive Patron." *Library and Archival Security* 3, nos. 3/4: 29–37.

Economist. 2013. "Reselling Media Content: Seconds to Go." March 23, 406, no. 8828: 71.

Epp, Mary Anne. 2006. "Closing the 95 Percent Gap: Library Resource Sharing for People with Print Disabilities." *Library Trends* 54, no. 3: 411–429.

Farrugia, Sarah. 2002. "A Dangerous Occupation? Violence in Public Libraries." *New Library World* 103, no. 9: 309–319.

Fichter, Darlene. 2013. "Making Your Website Accessible." *Online Searcher* 37, no. 4: 73–76.

Gruben, Karl T. 2006. "What Is Johnny Doing in the Library? Libraries, the U.S.A. Patriot Act, and Its Amendments." *St. Thomas Law Review* 19, no. 2: 297–328.

Hassan, Anita. 2011. "HPD Probing How Kindergartner Brought Gun to School." *Houston Chronicle Online.* April 19. Online. http://www.chron.com/life/mom-houston/article/HPD-probing-how-kindergartner-brought-gun-to-1603519.php.

Healey, Paul D. 2008. *Professional Liability Issues for Librarians and Information Professionals.* New York: Neal-Schuman.

Higey, Melissa. 2014. "Unattended Children in the Public Library: Trends and Issues." Online. http://unattended-children.wikispaces.com/.

Jaeger, Paul T., and Zheng Yan. 2009. "One Law with Two Outcomes: Comparing the Implementation of CIPA in Public Libraries and Schools." *Information Technology and Libraries* 28, no. 1: 6–14.

Kolderup, Gretchen. 2013. "The First Amendment and Internet Filtering in Public Libraries." *Indiana Libraries* 32, no. 1: 26–29.

Library Journal. 2010. "Copyright Case Could Threaten Library Lending." 135, no. 13: 13.

Magi, Trina. 2010. "A Content Analysis of Library Vendor Privacy Policies: Do They Meet Our Standards?" *College & Research Libraries* 71, no. 3: 254–272.

Magi, Trina. 2013. "A Fresh Look at Privacy—Why Does It Matter, Who Cares, and What Should Librarians Do about It?" *Indiana Libraries* 32, no. 1: 37–41.

Maycock, Angela. 2013. "Privacy, Libraries, and Engaging the Public: ALA's Choose Privacy Week Initiative." *Indiana Libraries* 32, no. 1: 34–36.

McHale Nina, 2011. "Who Says I Have to Wear Shoes in the Library?" *Colorado Libraries* 35, no. 4: 1–2.

Pike, George H. 2013. "The Future of National Security Letters." *Information Today* 30, no. 5: 22.

Rau, Alia Beard. 2013. "Reshaping Ariz. Service Animal Laws." *Arizona Republic*, May 5: B1, B3.

Simons, Spencer L. 2005. "Lawsuits and Legal Challenges: Librarians on the Frontline." *Texas Library Journal* 81, no. 1: 18–21.

Tappendorf, Julia, and Ancil Glink, 2013. "Legal Issues Relating to Online Social Networking." *ILA Reporter* 31, no. 1: 16–19.

SUGGESTED READINGS

Adams, Helen R. 2013. *Protecting Intellectual Freedom and Privacy in Your School Library.* Santa Barbara, CA: Libraries Unlimited.

Adams, Helen R. 2014. "Practical Ideas: Protecting Students' Privacy in Your School Library." *School Library Monthly* 30, no. 6: 29–30.

Burkell, Jacquelyn, and Robert Carey. 2011. "Personal Information and the Public Library: Compliance with Fair Information Practice Principles." *Canadian Journal of Information & Library Sciences* 35, no. 1: 1–16.

Copeland, Clayton A. 2011. "Library and Information Center Accessibility: The Differently-able Patron's Perspective." *Technical Services Quarterly* 28, no. 2: 223–241.

Dockens, Elaine B. 2010. "Vendor Pitfalls in Negotiating Large Multi-Year Contracts." *AALL Spectrum* 14, no. 4: 8–12.

Ferretti, Jennifer A. 2013. "First Sale Decided: The Road to the Kirtsaeng v. Wiley Decision and What It Means for Libraries." *Serials Librarian* 65, nos. 3/4: 261–276.

Gressel, Michael. 2014. "Are Libraries Doing Enough to Safeguard Their Patrons' Digital Privacy?" *Serials Librarian* 67, no. 2: 137–142.

Hofman, Darra L., Emily A. Bayma, and Steven Richardson. 2013. "Whose Data Is It Anyway? Legal Risks and Burdens Faced by Librarians in the New Bibliographic Universe." *Journal of Library Metadata* 13, nos. 2/3: 279–289.

Mattson, Ingrid, and Linda jean Schneider. 2013. "Negotiating and Complying with Electronic Database License Agreements." *AALL Spectrum* 17, no. 4: 9–12.

McCord, Gretchen. 2013. *What You Need to Know About Privacy Law: A Guide for Librarians and Educators*. Santa Barbara, CA: ABC-CLIO.

Nasri, William. 2014. *Legal Issues for Library and Information Managers*. Hoboken: Taylor and Francis.

Pautz, Hartwig. 2013. "Managing Access to the Internet in Public Libraries." *New Library World* 114, nos. 7/8: 308–318.

Shaffer, Christopher. 2014. "The Patriot Act a Decade Later: A Literature Review of Librarian Responses and Strategies." *Indiana Libraries* 33, no. 1: 22–25.

Terry, Jenni. 2010. "Access to Copyrighted Works for Those with Disabilities." *College & Research Libraries News* 71, no. 1: 38.

Warwick, Shelly. 2013. "Does Post-9/11 Equal Post-Privacy?" *Bulletin of The Association for Information Science & Technology* 40, no. 2: 32–34.

Weir, Ryan O. 2012. *Managing Electronic Resources: A LITA Guide*. Chicago: ALA TechSource.

Zimmer, Michael. 2014. "Librarians' Attitudes Regarding Information and Internet Privacy." *Library Quarterly* 84, no. 2: 123–151.

Chapter 14

Ethical Aspects

Everyday ethics is about guiding decisions and actions at your library according to principles that ensure that everyone is treated fairly, that governing the library does not happen in secret, that library users have access to all types of information, and that confidentiality is respected.

—*Pat Wagner, 2013*

Yes, I banned a book. I am a seasoned librarian and academic library director and supporter of free speech and democracy, but I banned a book. The term *heresy* quickly comes to mind in the world of librarianship, but the story is much deeper than it first appears.

—*Scott DiMarco, 2013*

Proliferating electronic resources have challenged school librarians—first to keep up with all the new tools that can benefit students, then to analyze their usefulness and select those best suited to the media center, and finally to find ways to make them accessible in school libraries. Intellectual freedom issues emerge at all three levels, but with particular prominence when it comes to access.

—*Angela Maycock, 2011*

It is well documented that people see what they want to see and easily miss contradictory information when it's in their interest to remain ignorant —a psychological phenomenon known as motivational blindness. This bias applies dramatically with respect to unethical behavior.

—*Max Bazerman and Ann Tenbrunsel, 2011*

In this chapter, we focus on factors that help drive the appropriateness and ethical aspects of a library's programs and services. At first glance you might think the topics are so obvious to good library services there is no need to cover them. Unfortunately, that is not always the case. As noted in the last quotation on the opening page of this chapter, people are people and each person has different life experiences that are drivers of their sense of right/wrong, good/bad, appropriate/inappropriate, and so forth.

We begin to form our beliefs and values almost as soon as we develop an awareness of our surrounding. Our parents', guardians', and caregivers' beliefs and values become the basis of our belief and value systems. As we grow and our worldview expands, we begin to notice that not everyone shares our systems. Some of what we see and experience in terms of other beliefs and values are, at times, diametrically opposed to what we hold dear, or thought we should. In such cases, we usually compare the differing ideas to ours and choose the one(s) we think best to serve as our "principles" of behavior. What we must keep in mind is many of the early beliefs and values remain with us even when we think otherwise.

We make "sense" of the world, to a large degree, through the lens of our beliefs and values. Whatever those systems are, they in turn are the basis of our ethical system—our sense of right and wrong, good and bad, appropriate and inappropriate, and so forth. Also, those systems are with us everywhere. We exist in a world of multiple beliefs, values, and ethical systems—personal, societal, workplace, and professional, to name the major ones; there are many others. Even in a very homogenous society there will be some variations in personal systems. U.S. libraries serve very diverse communities; library staff generally reflect such diversity. Everyone working in library public services should, from time to time, assess his or her deeply held values, even those we think we have put aside, in terms of societal and professional ethics.

Jean Preer (2008) made the point, "Ethics relates to 'custom,' the word deriving from ethos, the way things are done. . . . In the years before publicly-funded libraries, librarians had no transcendent obligation to the local community, to the larger society, to their profession, or to the values it embodied" (p. 2). Her book, *Library Ethics*, provides a detailed look at our professional values and the ethics that do, or should, underlie how libraries operate.

ETHICAL CONCEPTS

As Jean Preer stated, "Ethics is about choices. As a system of principles determining right or wrong conduct, ethics defines the parameters of those choices" (2008, p. 1). In other words, ethics guide our actions. What is important? What should be done in this situation? What is appropriate? We have to make such choices almost daily in our workplaces and personal lives. How to make the "right" choice is neither always easy nor straightforward. The basis for making the choices, from an academic point of view, comes from a branch of philosophy called normative ethics. Within this field, there are three groups of theories (utilitarian, Kantian, and social contract) that provide some guidance in making a choice.

Utilitarian theories hold that the outcomes of actions or decisions should be the basis for judgment as to the rightness or wrongness of a choice. John Stuart Mill is perhaps the most notable writer in this area. His idea was that moral choices that produce the greatest good for the greatest number of people are nice, but determining the "good" is a complex and often impossible task. A library example is how much funding to allocate, if any, to services for a group that represents less than 2 percent of the service population. Is it professionally ethical to ignore the group? Certainly, allocating some funds would, to some degree, decrease the "greatest good for the greatest number" suggested by utilitarian ethics. Perhaps it is easier to identify unethical choices; most people would agree that a decision that enhanced only the position of the decision maker at the expense of others is unethical.

Kantian ethics, as the name implies, rest on the ideas of Kant about non-consequential theory. Essentially, and most simply, the idea is to act/decide in a way that people are never the mere means to an end but that they are the end in themselves. Would it be ethical to try to utilize library supporters in an effort to increase library staff salaries? Would there be a slightly different assessment if your salary would also be increased? Will the service community actually receive any "good," if there is a salary increase? Are you employing supporters as a means rather than an end?

Social contract ethics are principles that form the basis of many social contract theories. Two examples are principles of opportunity and justice. Opportunity, as you might guess, relates to equality in access to society's benefits (economic, education, etc.). Justice, in this context, rests on the notion that "goods" are distributed so that even the least advantaged members of society receive some benefit from those goods. A library example that falls into both areas is a public library' efforts to bridge digital divides in its various forms.

Check This Out

John M. Budd provides an in-depth discussion of ethical philosophy and library ethics in his chapter "What Is the Right Thing to Do?" (pp. 111–146) which appears in his book *Self-Examination: The Present and Future of Librarianship* (Westport, CT: Libraries Unlimited, 2008).

WORKPLACE ETHICS AND VALUES

A key to keeping workplace ethical conflict to a minimum is for managers to behave in clearly ethical ways and to recognize that conflicts may exist in the minds of subordinates. A very simple example of how such a conflict could arise would be in a library with a policy that the collection should contain all points of view on subjects. Do the collection-development officers face a possible conflict between personal values and organizational expectations? The answer is often yes, depending upon the subject and an individual's religious, political, and other beliefs.

There is no doubt that people are motivated, in large part, by their personal values. Some people have very, very strong value views (e.g., religious or political) and believe it is a responsibility to convince others that those values are the correct values. If such a person is a senior manager, what are the chances that staff members would act in ways that go against the leader's articulated values? Would they have the courage to at least quietly follow their own or

ALA's ethical guidelines, such as adding items to the collection that they know are contrary to the director's beliefs?

Managers/supervisors may cause staff to behave unethically, often unknowingly. Bennett Tepper (2010) noted, "A compelling body of empirical research evidence suggests that it is disturbingly easy for authority figures to put their direct reports in positions where unethical choices are preferred over ethical choices" (p. 592). Some of the empirical studies that support Tepper's point are Stanley Milgram's *Obedience to Authority* (New York: Harper & Row, 1974), Thomas Blass's *Obedience to Authority: Current Perspectives on the Milgram Paradigm* (Mahwah, NJ: Lawrence Erlbaum Associates, 2000), and Joseph Grenny, Kerry Patterson, David Maxfield, Ron McMillan, and Al Switzer's *Influencer: The New Science of Leading Change* (2nd ed.; New York: McGraw-Hill, 2013).

Thomas Wotruba, Lawrence Chonko, and Terry Loe made the point that "the ethical climate of an organization is a composite of formal and informal policies of that organization as well as the individual ethical values of its managers. In this context, an ethics code as a formal policy would be one building block of the organization's ethical climate, representing a statement of corporate ethical values" (2001, p. 60). The next section of this chapter includes an overview of the ALA *Code of Ethics*, which provides a good starting point for a discussion of professional ethics in librarianship.

PROFESSIONAL ETHICS

Librarians have put forward notions of desirable professional values and ethics for more than 100 years. ALA published its first *Code of Ethics* in 1938, although there was discussion of professional values, responsibilities, and ethical behavior for library staff starting in the late nineteenth century. The latest revision of the *Code* appeared in 2008 (http://www.ala.org/advocacy/proethics/codeofethics/codeethics). The *Code* touches on collections, services, access, intellectual freedom, intellectual property, professional values, and personal interests and user needs. The document is a mix of social responsibility (organizational) and personal behavior (ethics).

Something to keep in mind is there are no sanctions associated with the ALA *Code*, that is, consequences for not following its values. The *Code* is a set of guidelines or principles. It is up to each library to implement the guidelines and decide what to do, if anything, if they see a problem. The reason there are no sanctions is ALA is a voluntary membership organization and does not have a "licensing" function that the fields of law and medicine have. Generally such licensees are required to legally practice in the field of the license. To learn more about why there are no ALA sanctions, see http://www.ala.org/advocacy/proethics/explanatory/enforcementfaq.

You may wonder how a library environment might present a challenge in terms of differing personal, work, and professional values and ethics. When you read the points in ALA's *Code*, they appear reasonable and reflect widespread values that the vast majority of people support, at least in the abstract. One reason there is less than total congruence between what happens "on the floor" as opposed to "on the wall" is most of us in the field have not reviewed the *Code* since our days in the classroom. We have been running so hard to provide services to more and more people and with more and better services while doing so with no new resources, and sometimes with fewer resources, we've had no time to consider ALA's *Code*. Keeping our heads above water has been the most important priority. In such cases it is easy to fall back on our personal beliefs and values.

There are a variety of library standards, guidelines, statements, and codes promulgated by the ALA and other professional organizations that in some way touch upon professional ethics, values, and behavior. We have mentioned standards and guidelines in other chapters in this book. You can check out the wide range of ALA standards and guidelines at http://www.ala.org/tools /guidelines/standardsguidelines. An interesting document on the ALA list is the Association of College and Research Libraries' (ACRL) *Standards for Libraries in Higher Education* (adopted in 2011; http://www.ala.org/acrl/standards /standardslibraries). What makes this document particularly interesting is that it includes a mix of both operational standards (institutional effectiveness) and professional behavior (professional values).

A good example of library values is seen in ALA's *Freedom to Read Statement* (adopted in 1953, last amended in 2004; http://www.ala.org/advocacy /intfreedom/statementspols/freedomreadstatement). Its seven propositions cover many of the long-held values of librarians, publishers, and booksellers. That does not, however, mean there are not challenges to carrying out those values. Likewise the *Library Bill of Rights* (adopted in 1939, last affirmed in 1996; http://www.ala.org/advocacy/intfreedom/librarybill/) is a statement of values that have ethical implications. It is likely you will have more than one occasion during your career when both the *Freedom to Read* and *Library Bill of Rights* statements will come in handy. They may not solve your ethical dilemma, but they will provide you with serious food for thought about what choice to make.

Turning back to ALA's *Code of Ethics* (http://www.ala.org/advocacy/pro-ethics/codeofethics/codeethics), we will look at several of its seven points starting with the first point, access. The *Code* states: "I. We provide the highest level of service to all library users through appropriate and usefully organized resources; equitable service policies; equitable access; and accurate, unbiased, and courteous responses to all requests."

The first point relates to access to library services and programs, while the final clause addresses staff conduct with users. You should not be surprised to learn that in addition to the *Code*, ALA has a number of guidelines about access. One example is "Economic Barriers to Information Access: An Interpretation of the Library Bill of Rights" (adopted in 1993; http://www.ala.org /ala/issuesadvocacy/intfreedom/librarybill/interpretations/economicbarriers.cfm). One outcome of that document and professional concern is seen almost daily across the country as people line up to use computers in public libraries, many of whom cannot afford the equipment or cost of connectivity.

There is a little word in the first point that is loaded—equitable. Just what that means is open to wide-ranging debate. If you look up equitable in a thesaurus, the first synonym listed is "fair." Equitable and equal are not one and the same, although some people would argue they are. More often than not what is viewed as equitable or equal depends on your point of view. The reality is that it is impossible for libraries to provide equal service to its entire service community—the funding simply does not exist to do that. That would require that a user group of 100 would receive an equal amount of support as a group of 1,000. Educational libraries, in particular, face the question of equitable /equal support each year when it comes to allocating funds for subject/teaching department collection development. Would it be equitable to allocate as much funding to an honors program as to a subject area? Would it be equitable to spend less? As you might expect, those little words, *equitable, equal,* and *fair* can generate debates about choices that have to be made.

We use reference work as our example related to access and the *Code.* The performance of reference service has both affirmative and restrictive ethical and legal dimensions. The affirmative dimension includes the responsibilities and duties inherent in reference service regarding confidentiality, quality, and types of service provided. The restrictive dimension includes limitations in such matters as medical, tax, and legal advice or interpretation. The following paragraphs discuss some of the ethical considerations for reference work you should keep in mind.

Information provided to a person should be the most accurate possible, regardless of the type of question or the status of the requester. There is a lot of pressure on reference staff to provide answers. At times, it may be tempting to guess at or speculate about an answer to a question rather than admit that one cannot be found. The proper procedure to follow if one cannot find an answer is to tell the person that a number of sources (and their names, if asked) were consulted and to make a referral to another person or agency.

There should be no differentiation in service because of the person's individual characteristics. Age, ethnic or racial group, height, weight, religious or political affiliation, sexual orientation, personal appearance, or personality type have no bearing on the quality of service provided to eligible users. This is an area where those subconscious beliefs and values may slip into the process.

The ALA's *Code of Ethics* (point III) includes the following relevant statement: "We protect each library user's right to privacy and confidentiality with respect to information sought or received and resources consulted, borrowed, acquired or transmitted" (http://www.ala.org/advocacy/proethics/codeofethics /codeethics). Digital reference services, such as IM, e-mail, and chat, offer additional challenges to protecting user confidentiality. If the digital trails of reference transactions are preserved and if the requesters can be identified, for example by their e-mail addresses or user names, then maintaining user confidentiality is threatened. As noted in chapter 13, the USA PATRIOT Act permits government authorities to confiscate library records and computers without a court order, and if the reference desk computer contains an archive of reference transactions, the user information could be revealed. Reference staff should make sure that digital records of reference questions are erased from hard drives and servers so confidentiality can be maintained.

There are times when an individual seeking help at the reference desk appears uneasy, uncomfortable, or may just be having a difficult time expressing himself or herself. An individual may not want to reveal the exact nature of the question, and only seek the most general kind of assistance. When a user asks a general question about medical dictionaries or self-help books, there may be some resistance when trying to help the user by defining the need more narrowly. Such resistance, or a perception that the user is uncomfortable or embarrassed, even a little angry, is a clue that the person may not want to identify the particular reason the information is desired. Being sensitive enough to recognize such clues about a desire for privacy may be difficult; however, you ought not persist in probing for the actual need. A good approach is simply to show the person the reference area or collection or database/s that most generally address the stated need and say that further assistance is readily available if needed.

"Sharing stories" about such users, tempting as it may be, is, of course, a gross violation of professional ethics. Unless done for a constructive purpose, it works against both the individual library staff member and the professional role of reference staff members.

Because of legal and ethical complexities, there are limitations on the kinds of answers that can be given to users in such areas as law, medicine, and taxes. Staff should always help a user to find *information*, but should never give even a suggestion that the help is *advice* or *interpretation*. This is the case even if the person directly solicits such advice. Doing so opens up a greatly many liability issues for the library—see chapter 13 for a discussion of liability.

Staff members can, in some cases, share personal opinions on social, political, religious, and other matters in a social situation, but *not* as part of a reference transaction or for that matter during any library process. While "on the job," staff members must try to keep an open perspective and promote awareness by giving users a variety of sources that address the information desired, especially on a controversial topic, from differing points of view. When the available sources are heavily opinionated or present a limited viewpoint, staff members ought to at least inform the user that other viewpoints exist, and may suggest additional materials which strive to be balanced, or, when these are not available, materials that present an opposite point of view. If information is dated, the reference person should so inform the user and suggest alternative sources with more current data to supplement or modify the older information. There should be no personal financial gain resulting from the role of the reference staff member as a representative of the library in dealing with the user.

Reference staff members are sometimes caught between their desire to provide information to users and the values of their professional associations, their personal values, and community standards. Internet access means that library users may read, view, or listen to information that may be considered pornographic or otherwise offensive to community standards. This is most likely to occur in public libraries. What should the reference staff member do if asked to help locate information on the Web that may be considered pornographic or otherwise offensive to one's personal or community values? If the staff member has a reason to believe the information may not be protected by the First Amendment, there is good reason for hesitancy. This circumstance would be very rare, however. As with any other request for information, the reference staff's responsibility is to assist the requester to locate the information as efficiently as possible, within the service standards of the particular library. This is true whether the desired information is the Web site for *Playboy* magazine or a site for al-Qaeda. Staff should be aware of and understand the ethical and legal limitations on reference service and be familiar with guidelines as presented in the reference policy of their institution. When questionable or "borderline" inquiries occur, staff should consult with appropriate colleagues for guidance.

INTELLECTUAL FREEDOM

The second topic in the *Code* is intellectual freedom (IF), which has been a long-standing concern for libraries and their staff. It has been a centerpiece in legal actions between members of the service community and libraries. You have undoubtedly read about and discussed this issue in one or more of your LIS classes. IF and censorship are interrelated; however, IF is much broader in scope than censorship. It is closely tied to the First Amendment of the Constitution. This is not the place to explore the complexities of IF. We will, however, briefly look at censorship, ethics, and you.

Challenges to Collection Content

As David McMenemy (2007) noted, "There will undoubtedly be challenges ahead where the ethical neutrality of the librarian is challenged, both positively and negatively. To face such situations we need to know what we stand for as a collective, and ensure it is never forgotten" (p. 181). Anyone who has been in a public services position for any length of time will have had one or more experiences of dealing with someone who objects, often very strongly, to the contents of some item in the collection, or on display, for example. A recent (2013) example regarding problems surrounding a high school art show is reported in the July issue of ALA's *Newsletter on Intellectual Freedom* (62, no. 4, pp. 142–144). You may expect any format to become a target of a complaint—audio recordings, books, Internet access, serials, videos, and anything else the library collects or puts on display.

Check This Out

The *Newsletter on Intellectual Freedom* is a good resource to consult every so often to keep up to date on IF, challenges, and court decisions: http://www .ala.org/offices/oif/oifprograms/ifpubs/nif/newsletterintellectual.

The only type of library that almost never faces this issue is the corporate or special library. School and public libraries experience the highest rates of challenges from users (or parents of users). Surprisingly, academic libraries also are challenged from time to time. Even special collections/archives occasionally have to address the unhappy user.

What may trigger a complaint? The short answer is almost anything. Who would think a biography of actor Steve McQueen could stir controversy? It did so in Flagstaff, Arizona. The Flagstaff City—Coconino County Public Library system had to address such a challenge in 2013 (*Newsletter on Intellectual Freedom* 63, no. 3: p. 123). After a review by the library board, the book was retained in the collection—albeit in the adult section rather than the young adult section.

However, religious or political beliefs are a common source of challenges along with sexual content (or the lifestyle portrayed). Very often the underlying factor is the person's belief that he or she is protecting children from inappropriate material. Even issues of cultural sensitivity can become the focal point of a person's or group's concern. It is often a bigger challenge to handle a formal group's concerns as such groups often have more resources to pursue decisions it does not like.

From a host of possible examples, we have selected a few to illustrate the range of topics that have arisen in various types of libraries. A 2007 case is an interesting and complex situation related to a well-known magazine—*Sports Illustrated*. The problem was related to its swimsuit issue; this annual issue has generated any number of complaints from some library users libraries and, apparently, to the publisher. Many parents have asked that libraries restrict children's access to this issue, sometimes successfully, and sometimes not. As Francine Fialkoff (2007) wrote, "It has long been regarded as soft-core porn and a blatant example of the objectification of women in our society" (p. 8). What made the situation unusual was the publisher decided, without consulting libraries, *not* to send the issue to libraries. This upset librarians as well as others: "One of the first critics of *SI*'s misguided move was Lynne Weaver of Randolph-Macon Women's College" (Fialkoff, 2007, p. 8). The policy was reversed the following year. One suspects the publisher believed it couldn't win no matter what it decided to do about future swimsuit issues. Other serials that generate more than their fair share of complaints are the *Advocate, People, Penthouse, Reader's Digest*, and *Rolling Stone*.

Moving on to books, it probably comes as no surprise that *Harry Potter* has endured more than a few efforts to keep the series out of libraries. Laura Mallory has been a persistent detractor and has fought several legal battles to have the books removed from her local school libraries (Gwinnett County [GA] Public Schools):

> "This is not just fiction or fantasy," Mallory said as part of her one-hour argument before the court. "Witchcraft is real. It's been around for thousands of years, and we were warned of it from God." Arguing that reading the series to schoolchildren is tantamount to indoctrinating them into the Wiccan religion, Mallory asserted. "We don't want our children to be murderers, but we can't teach that in our schools anymore. 'Thou shalt not kill' is out." (*American Libraries*, 2007, p. 22)

She lost her attempt to get the popular series removed in May 2007. However, you might imagine what it was like for the first staff person who had to handle this complaint. Not surprisingly, the *Harry Potter* series tops the 2000–2009 list of "Top 100 Banned/Challenged Books" as reported by the Office for Intellectual Freedom (http://www.ala.org/bbooks/top-100-ban nedchallenged-books-2000-2009).

Check These Out

The ALA's Office for Intellectual Freedom (OIF) receives reports on challenges to books—http://www.ala.org/bbooks/frequentlychallengedbooks. The OIF site also has a number of resources available to encourage intellectual freedom activities, such as the annual Banned Books Week event (http://www.ala.org/bbooks/bannedbooksweek).

The Freedom of Expression Committee of the Book and Periodical Council (Canada) publishes a similar "Challenged Works List" (http://www.freedomtoread.ca/censorship-in-canada/challenged-works-list/) and sponsors an annual Freedom to Read Week (http://www.freedomtoread.ca/freedom-to-read-week/) as well.

Recorded music has had its turn in the censor's spotlight. In 2004, Kansas attorney general Phill Kline opted to refuse over 1,600 music CDs deemed as containing "inappropriate content." The issue arose as "Kline nixed the items from a shipment of 51,000 CDs Kansas libraries were entitled to receive as compensation in a price-fixing suit. . . . He added that the purge of titles by 25 artists was meant to stop libraries from receiving music that promotes gun violence and drug use, which Kline said he wants to discourage since he 'sees the results of [such behavior] every day'" (Goldberg, 2004, p. 15). While the decision was made solely by the Kansas attorney general, KLA (Kansas Library Association) president Patti Butcher noted this was not the preference of libraries in the state. She noted, "It is our hope that in future cases the attorney general's office will work with the library association to ensure that together we can obtain the best materials for Kansas libraries" (Goldberg, 2004, p. 16). Naturally, musicals such as *Jesus Christ Superstar* have also faced a variety of challenges, as a stage performance, audio recording, or motion picture.

Needless to say, video recordings are also prime targets for those wishing to protect others from inappropriate material. Like books, the typical complaints revolve around the level of violence, graphic language, and sexual content.

From the Authors' Experience

Evans worked at a private Catholic university library for some time. During his tenure at the university there were several challenges regarding books and media. In perhaps the most unusual instance, the challenge related to the video collection.

The university had a highly regarded film and television department and, as a result, the library's video collection of motion pictures was very extensive. One day Evans took a phone call from a person who said he was not a student or affiliated with university, but would like to have a meeting with Evans. At the meeting the person said he was spokesperson for a group of concerned neighbors and that he was there to bring to Evans's attention (he was certain Evans was unaware of the situation) that the library video collections contained dozens of blasphemous films that no good Christian could accept. He was *certain* that, although he was not of the Catholic faith, the university would destroy the offensive material once it was brought to Evans's and the university's attention. The meeting did not end with a promise to remove the items. Eventually the person went to the university president and Evans heard the person suggested he and his group would take the matter to the Archdiocese.

The library kept all the titles in question after Evans and the Dean of the School of Film and Television met with the university president. Evans never heard if the matter progressed beyond the university president's office.

Games, both board and computer, have been challenged. The game *Dungeons and Dragons* has generated complaints, usually for allowing the organization of a club that plays in library space. Computer/video games are now the mostly likely to generate complaints.

Even the rating system we described in chapter 8 has been challenged. In that case, the U.S. Supreme Court had to make a decision. As Christopher Clements (2012) wrote:

Violent video games have drawn the ire of parents and commentators alike ever since their inception two decades ago. . . . Most recently, in 2011, the Supreme Court held that California's attempt to legislate in this area would violate of the First Amendment. This Note argues that legislators should tread carefully in the wake of the Supreme Court's unequivocal ruling. Rather than attempt to self-categorize what is or is not appropriate for children, they should instead mandate that video game developers and retailers participate in the ubiquitous Entertainment Software Rating Board rating system. (p. 661)

Our final example comes from special collections/archives and medical libraries. The situation arose in 1996 and concerned the book *Pernkopf Anatomy: Atlas of Topographic and Applied Anatomy*, which was a critically acclaimed anatomical atlas containing more than 800 detailed paintings of dissections that doctors, especially surgeons, used for many years. The first volume was published in Vienna in 1937, part two was printed in 1943, and the final volume appeared in 1952 (Israel and Seidelman, 1996). Urban and Schwarzenberg of Baltimore issued a two-volume set in 1989; later, Wavery Inc. acquired the rights to the title. Both the original and reissue volumes were (and still are) widely held by medical libraries. Reviewers in 1990 used phrases such as "in a class of its own" and "classic among atlases" (Wade, 1996). Anyone thinking about the date and place of the initial publication probably can guess why the controversy arose. Dr. Eduard Pernkopf was a Nazi Party member from 1933 onward, and was named dean of the medical school at the University of Vienna after the Anshluss of 1938. He also spent three postwar years in Allied prisoner-of-war camps, but was never charged with any war crimes. Some doctors in the 1990s wanted medical libraries to withdraw or at least not allow access to the work until there was an investigation into whether concentration camp victims had been used for the dissections upon which the paintings were based. There were differing responses in medical libraries to requests to restrict access, ranging from placing the item on reserve to adding notes to the catalog indicating the nature of the content of the work (Atlas, 2001, p. 55).

Check This Out

A wide range of true stories of censorship in all library settings, some stemming from as seemingly innocuous origins as "suggested reading lists" and displays, are found in *True Stories of Censorship Battles in America's Libraries* edited by Valerie Nye and Kathy Barco (Chicago: American Library Association, 2012). The work also touches upon the concept of self-censorship (discussed later in this chapter). It is well worth the read.

The preceding section gives you a brief picture of the range of topics that may generate a challenge and should make it clear that any type of library can have such problems. You never know when someone will arrive at your desk and present you and, of course, the library, with a situation that requires very careful handling. Sometimes the request is put forward quietly and reasonably, and sometimes not so nicely, but often the person wants the immediate removal of the objectionable item(s). What should you do if you find yourself on the receiving end of such a request? Here again there may be conflicts between your personal beliefs and values and those of the profession.

No matter what, a sound first step, with or without a policy, is to acknowledge the person's right to be concerned. Not doing so can escalate the situation, and you don't want that. Also, an appropriate response is to indicate the issue is of such an importance that the director will need to handle the concern. However, it is critical that you not indicate what the outcome may be or when the decision will take place. (Anything you say along those lines can come back to haunt both the library and you when in the hands of a good lawyer.)

There are some steps to take to prepare for and, to some degree, reduce the chances of a full-blown challenge. Knowing the dangers of censorship and having a commitment to avoid it are not enough in today's world of quick legal action. Librarians should prepare for challenges long before there is a compliant. The first step in preparing for the eventual challenge is to prepare a policy statement about how to handle complaints, and have the policy approved by all the appropriate authorities. There is nothing worse than having no idea of what to do when facing an angry person who is complaining about library materials and is clearly upset. Even with policies and procedures in place, the situation may escalate into physical violence (there have been cases of bruises all the way up to broken bones); without procedures, the odds of violence occurring increase.

After the library develops the policies and procedures and they are approved, everyone working in public services needs to understand the procedure(s) and receive training in implementing the system. Sometimes role-playing is helpful in reinforcing the training. ALA's OIF has a series of materials available with suggestions for what to do before a potential censor arrives (http://www.ala.org/bbooks/challengedmaterials/preparation) and when one occurs (http://www.ala.org/bbooks/challengedmaterials/support/strategies). Three other sources published by ALA are *Protecting Intellectual Freedom in Your Academic Library: Scenarios from the Front Lines* by Barbara M. Jones (2009), *Protecting Intellectual Freedom in Your School Library: Scenarios from the Front Lines* by Pat Scales (2009), and *Protecting Intellectual Freedom in Your Public Library: Scenarios from the Front Lines* by June Pinnell-Stephens (2012).

A typical procedure is to have the individual(s) file a formal complaint by filling out a form that specifies what is at issue. For some individuals, just filling out the form reduces their concern(s), and the prospect of going through a formal process causes them not to go any further. Several organizations, such as the ALA and the National Council of Teachers of English, have recommended forms that are somewhat effective in defusing the immediate anger. As you might expect, some people will react negatively to being asked to fill out "bureaucratic paperwork." You should explain that the reason for the paperwork is because the matter is important and because you must pass the information on to people who can address the concern, and to be certain the individual's request is accurately conveyed to senior managers who may not be immediately available. Make it clear you are not empowered to do more than pass the information forward as quickly as possible. After accepting the written form and passing it on to your supervisor, you should be out of the process. Handling this type of situation can be stressful and is never pleasant, so think about how to handle it before the first time you have to confront it.

From the Authors' Experience

Sinwell notes several challenges to the Fairfax County Public Library (FCPL) Collection Policy. For example, in the mid-1990s, objections were raised about the *Washington Blade*, a weekly newspaper focused on the homosexual community, being available as a handout in the libraries. Although the objection required FCPL to perform a complete examination of its collections, nothing was changed. The decision withstood highly publicized public participation by 200 to 300 people and was upheld by the county attorney. FCPL offered the compromise of placing the newspaper out of the reach of young children.

When FCPL receives challenges from users, such as a recent one by a Muslim group to a specific work of fiction, the challenger is asked if they have read the book; to define what is objectionable about the book; and to state what they wish to have done about the book. These concerns are then addressed through an established book reconsideration process. During this process, the challenged title is evaluated by FCLP librarians, who read the book and any published reviews. The librarians individually submit their written evaluations and their opinions as to how they think the request for reconsideration should be handled to the director of collection development. This input is evaluated and forms a basis for deciding the fate of the book. The complainant is notified in writing of the decision. After completing this process, the book, which the Muslim group had challenged, remained in the library collection. The collection is consistently evaluated and books are removed when they are inaccurate or are no longer current or in poor condition. The library receives 40,000 to 50,000 suggestions (in all forms) each year and averages five or six book challenges a year.

Sam Clay, director of the FCPL, once stated: "If the Library is doing its job of representing all points of view, we have something in our collection to offend everyone" (http://www.lwv-fairfax.org/files/libraryprogram.pdf, 2005, p. R-7).

Major confrontations usually involve an organized group as well as intellectual freedom and free speech issues, which in turn revolve around interpretations of points of law and possible violations of existing law. Therefore, a challenge that gets to the attack level normally involves attorneys and judges rather than librarians and the community. We hear about the cases that reach the courts, but seldom about daily local problems. All cases start as local problems between the library and an individual or group from the community and are usually settled quickly. Depending on the nature of the material, the level of emotional involvement, and the prior administrative actions (i.e., policies), the library may be able to quickly resolve the issue, or the problem may escalate until it reaches the courtroom.

SELF-INTEREST

In today's world of tight library budgets and less than generous staffing, it is rather common for some staff to have some collection development responsibilities in addition to other significant library obligations. When that happens, you may find yourself stressed and knowing you lack the time and energy to do everything as well as you would wish. Extra work, such as a committee assignment or presentation, adds further time demands and perhaps stress.

The following is a hypothetical situation where you have collection management duties that have potential ethical issues. You are reviewing possible collection additions and come across a title that may be of potential interest to a few library users; however, you know from the current professional literature that the title has generated several complaints from users in a few libraries. In at least one case, a lawsuit was filed by a citizen demanding the removal of the title from the collection and the library declined to do so. You are also well aware that challenges are time consuming, stressful, and frustrating regardless of their outcome. To top things off, your annual performance review is due in less than two months, and you have two small, but important projects to get finished in order to accomplish the goals you and your supervisor set a year ago during the last appraisal. What to do?

You can avoid the potential work of dealing with a challenge by not ordering the item. Or, perhaps, just keep it in mind to order later. You can always explain not adding any item on the grounds of a limited budget and/or some better item might be available later. Who will know you made the choice not to add the item for personal reasons, other than yourself? Is that ethical professional behavior? It is easy to say you would never do such a thing sitting in a classroom and quite a different matter when you are in the real work world facing a variety of work pressures and the item does not match your personal values.

As much as the profession might wish otherwise, librarian self-censorship is a very real issue. Debra Lau Whelan (2009) in writing about self-censorship stated, "It's a dirty secret that no one in the profession wants to talk about or admit practicing. Yet everyone knows some librarians bypass good books— those with literary merit or that fill a need in their collections. The reasons range from a book's sexual content and gay themes to its language and violence—and it happens in more public and K-12 libraries than you think" (p. 27). The issue is long standing and the reasons for that occurring go far beyond the topics Whelan mentioned.

Some in the profession have been and are willing to raise the issue. Perhaps the first book on the topic was Marjorie Fiske's 1959 report *Book Selection and Censorship*. Her work was commissioned by the California Library Association in response to heavy pressure from individuals and groups to remove anything that could be considered communistic or socialistic. In her report, she noted librarians often waffle or weasel-worded their view about avoiding adding "potentially objectionable" items to the collection. Fiske illustrated the problem by quoting a librarian in her study: "We haven't been censoring but we have been 'conservative'. After all, this is a conservative community and that is how parents want it to be" (p. 62). You almost always have one or more rational reasons to justify your negative decision regarding an item. The question is, is the decision ethical?

Other Potential Ethical Challenges

We explored the technical and legal aspects of privacy/confidentiality (Point III of the *Code*) in chapter 13. There is an ethical side to that topic as well. Some questions to ponder include whether or not you or the library has an ethical obligation to: (1) inform users that "personalization" of library database sites can provide the vendor with more personal and marketable information than the person might like; and (b) inform, and if necessary stand firm, with database vendors that they must comply with library privacy and ALA confidentiality policies, if they wish to retain your library's business.

There are times when the sections of the *Code* can present you with the dilemma of choosing between competing ethical areas. One example is between privacy (section III) and section IV (intellectual property). Over the years intellectual property laws have become ever broader in scope and more restrictive of what you may freely use without permission (fair use).

Assume you are assisting a student with a class report or term paper. The student wants to find an online image to include in the project and has asked for help. After some time, the two of you find something the student likes and copies it and saves the Web address for the image. Just before closing the page, you notice the image is copyrighted. You decide to take the opportunity to briefly talk about copyright and permissions indicating using the desired image would require such permission. As you see eyes glazing over and a fair degree of restlessness, you wonder if the student will ask for permission.

You know that there is widespread public belief that anything on the Web is free to use as a person wants. Further, you know that the notion that permission might be required is almost nonexistent. So what should you do? Ignore the matter, no one will know the difference and chances of the copyright holder finding out and tracking the use of the image to a library IP is almost nil. (Do remember that in the United States any organization allowing Internet access is considered an Internet Service Provider (ISP) and may have some liability for a proven infringement, if a user accessed the material through that ISP.) Do you have an obligation to follow up with the student regarding getting permission? Do you have a responsibility to check with the student's instructor about the project and image usage? Do you have any obligation to the copyright holder? You face some difficult choices, and the *Code* will provide only a little guidance.

Looking at the two relevant sections of the *Code*, you see they are in conflict as in the previous situation. So, where do you go for guidance? You could check Web sites such as ALA's Copyright Advisory Network (http://librarycopyright .net/). Probably your best option is to go to your mentor, if you have one, or a trusted and experienced colleague for advice or just to talk out the options and issues. They may have had similar experiences and talk about the outcome(s) of their choices.

CLOSING THOUGHTS

Many years ago, Douglas J. Foskett (1962) wrote *The Creed of a Librarian: No Politics, No Religion, No Morals*. In it, he made the case for professional practice that is neutral, noting "The librarian ought virtually to vanish as an individual person, except in so far as his personality sheds light on the working of the library. . . . He must put himself in the reader's shoes" (p. 10). That is what Point VII of the *Code* is saying as ethical professional practice.

That is a simple sounding goal, but one that is very difficult to put into practice day-in and day-out. We mentioned one challenge earlier in this chapter, not selecting an item in order to avoid a possible challenge. The same set of questions we listed then apply to almost any item—I don't like the author's style, the author's philosophy, religion, politics, so forth. It can come up in our other public service activities as well, as seen in the example of homeless individuals in the library in chapter 13 on legal issues. We have included several references in the Suggested Readings section that provide additional examples.

Check This Out

A good article that provides eight ethical situations to think about is Helen R. Adams's 2009 piece "Reflections on Ethics in Practice" (*Knowledge Quest* 37, no. 3: 66–69). The situations depicted in the article are set in a school library media environment; however, it is easy to see how each one could occur in any type of library.

We conclude with two quotations that reflect the challenges involved in professional practice. First, from Renée Jefferson and Sylvia Contreras:

> It is evident that the professional ethics and principles of an organization may often conflict with societal and personal ethics. In fact, professional ethics and principles often have internal conflicts. These conflicts are interwoven into professional responsibilities of information science professionals. (2005, p. 66)

Belle Woodward, Diane Davis, and Flavia Hodis (2007), in paraphrasing Linda Trevino and Stuart Youngblood (1990), wrote:

> Individuals throughout life's experience will struggle with feelings about what is right and what is wrong. More adept individuals at ethical reasoning are more likely to make judgments based on principles they choose as opposed to those gained through peer pressure and other outside influences. Individuals with higher levels of moral development are less likely to engage in unethical behavior. (p. 195)

Chapter Review Material

1. Discuss the types of beliefs, principles, and values that come into play in your work life. Does working in a library raise more issues in terms of ethics than in many other types of workplaces?
2. Organizational ethics rest on what three types of philosophical theories? How do they differ from one another?
3. List and briefly describe the points in ALA's *Code of Ethics* document.
4. Library professional codes of ethics have no sanction powers, so there is no danger of facing penalties should you choose to ignore the code(s).
5. ALA's *Code of Ethics* addresses just about all aspects of library activities that you carry out on a regular, if not daily, basis. What are three areas you believe would create the greatest challenge for you?
6. What are some of the major conflicts in terms of self-interest and ethical choices?
7. There will be times when the ethical choice will not be clear cut and will be difficult to make. What are some of your options for making the final choice?
8. We outlined three possible ethical conflict situations earlier. You can probably think of similar situations. List two additional situations and outline the potential ethical challenges for each. Share your thoughts with some classmates. Do they agree with your assessments?

REFERENCES

American Libraries. 2007. "Harry Potter Foe Loses Challenge." 38, no. 7: 21–22.

Atlas, Michel C. 2001. "Ethics and Access to Teaching Materials in the Medical Library: The Case of the Pernkopf Atlas." *Bulletin of the Medical Library Association* 89, no. 1: 51–58.

Bazerman, Max H., and Ann E. Tenbrunsel. 2011. "Ethical Breakdowns." *Harvard Business Review* 89, no. 4: 58–65.

Clements, Christopher. 2012. "Protecting Protected Speech: Violent Video Game Legislation Post-Brown v. Entertainment Merchants Association." *Boston College Law Review* 53, no. 2: 661–692.

DiMarco, Scott R. 2013. "Why I Banned a Book: How Censorship Can Impact a Learning Community." *College & Research Libraries News* 74, no. 7: 368–369.

Fialkoff, Francine. 2007. "SI vs. Librarians." *Library Journal* 132, no. 6: 8.

Fiske, Marjorie. 1959. *Book Selection and Censorship.* Berkeley: University of California Press.

Foskett, Douglas J. 1962. *The Creed of a Librarian: No Politics, No Religion, No Morals.* Library Association Occasional Papers No. 3. London: Library Association.

Goldberg, Beverly. 2004. "Kansas Librarians Embroiled in CD Flap." *American Libraries* 35, no. 8: 15–16.

Israel, Howard A., and William E. Seidelman. 1996. "Nazi Origins of an Anatomy Text." *Journal of the American Medical Association* 276, no. 11: 1633.

Jefferson, Renée N., and Sylvia Contreras. 2005. "Ethical Perspectives of Library and Information Science Graduate Students in the United States." *New Library World* 106, nos. 1208/1209: 58–66.

Maycock, Angela. 2011. "Issues and Trends in Intellectual Freedom for Teacher Librarians: Where We've Come from and Where We're Going." *Teacher Librarian* 39, no. 1: 8–12.

McMenemy, David. 2007. "Librarians and Ethical Neutrality: Revisiting *The Creed of a Librarian.*" *Library Review* 56, no. 3: 177–181.

Preer, Jean L. 2008. *Library Ethics.* Westport, CT: Libraries Unlimited.

Tepper, Bennett J. 2010. "When Managers Pressure Employees to Behave Badly: Toward a Comprehensive Response." *Business Horizons* 53, no. 6: 591–598.

Trevino, Linda K., and Stuart A. Youngblood. 1990. "Bad Apples in Bad Barrels: A Casual Analysis of Ethical Decision-Making Behavior." *Journal of Applied Psychology* 75, no. 4: 378–385.

Wade, Nicholas. 1996. "Doctors Question Use of Nazi's Medical Atlas." *New York Times,* November 26: C1.

Wagner, Pat. 2013. "Everyday Library Ethics Series." *Pattern Research.* June 23. Online. http://www.sieralearn.com/everyday-library-ethics-series/.

Whelan, Debra Lau. 2009. "A Dirty Little Secret: Self-Censorship Is Rampant and Lethal." *School Library Journal* 55, no. 2: 26–30.

Woodward, Belle, Diane C. Davis, and Flavia A. Hodis. 2007. "The Relationship between Ethical Decision Making and Ethical Reasoning in Information Technology Students." *Journal of Information Systems Education* 18, no. 2: 193–202.

Wotruba, Thomas R., Lawrence B. Chonko, and Terry W. Loe. 2001. "The Impact of Ethics Code Familiarity on Manager Behavior." *Journal of Business Ethics* 33, no. 1: 59–69.

SUGGESTED READINGS

Adams, Helen R. 2013. "Intellectual Freedom 101: Core Principles for School Librarians." *School Library Monthly* 30, no. 2: 33–34.

Adams, Helen R. 2014. "Revisiting the ALA Code of Ethics." *School Library Monthly* 30, no. 4: 33–34.

Ahmed, Nedda H., Adriana Edwards-Johnson, Karen Antell, and Molly Strothmann. 2013. "Should Librarians Friend Their Patrons?" *Reference & User Services Quarterly* 53, no. 1: 9–12.

Beall, Jeffrey. 2011. "Librarians and the Threat to Free Political Speech." *American Libraries* 42, nos. 9/10: 33.

Carnesi, Sabrina. 2014. "Challenging Opportunities: Dealing with Book Challenges." *Library Media Connection* 33, no. 2: 16.

Fletcher-Spear, Kristin, and Kelly Tyler. 2014. *Intellectual Freedom for Teens: A Practical Guide for YA and School Librarians.* Chicago: ALA Editions.

Foster, Catherine, and David McMenemy. 2012. "Do Librarians Have a Shared Set of Values? A Comparative Study of 36 Codes of Ethics Based on Gorman's Enduring Values." *Journal of Librarianship and Information Science* 44, no. 4: 249–262.

Harer, John B. 2012. "The Reasons Why Children's Books Are Censored." *IFRT Report (Intellectual Freedom Round Table)* no. 76: 3–4.

Hill, Rebecca 2010. "The Problem of Self-Censorship." *School Library Monthly* 27, no. 2: 9–12.

Janes, Joseph. 2012. "Data, Data Everywhere: As the Big Data Beast Fattens, Will Privacy and Ethics Get Gobbled Up?" *American Libraries* 43, nos. 5/6: 42.

Jones, Barbara. 2013. "Gun Violence, Videogames and Libraries." *American Libraries* 44, no. 5: 15.

Jones, Barbara M. 2012. "Controversy in Fifty Shades of Grey." *American Libraries* 43, nos. 5/6: 21.

Latham, Joyce M. 2014. *The West Bend Challenges: Open Access and Intellectual Freedom in the Twenty-First Century.* Baltimore, MD: The Johns Hopkins University Press.

Lor, Peter Johan, and Johannes J. Britz. 2011. "New Trends in Content Creation: Changing Responsibilities for Librarians." *Libri: International Journal of Libraries & Information Services* 61, no. 1: 12–22.

Mason, Moya K. 2014. *Ethics of Librarianship: Libraries, Intellectual Freedom, and Censorship in the Age of Technology.* Online. http://www.moyak.com/papers/ethics-librarianship.html.

Moellendick, Cora McAndrews. 2009. "Libraries, Censors, and Self-Censorship." *PNLA Quarterly* 73, no. 4: 68–76.

Perego, Martha. 2011. "Rewind: Taking Steps to Undo the Unintentional Ethical Misstep." *Public Management* 93, no. 10: 2–3.

Posner, Beth. 2012. "The Ethics of Library Resource Sharing in the Digital Age." Interlending & Document Supply 40, no. 2: 119–124.

Reinsfelder, Thomas L. 2014. "E-Books and Ethical Dilemmas for the Academic Reference Librarian." *Reference Librarian* 55, no. 2: 151–162.

Spackman, Andy. 2010. "Our Conservative Ideals: The Profession's Values Are Not Solely Liberal Ones." *American Libraries* 41, no. 4: 25.

Stripling, Barbara K. 2013. "Intellectual Freedom: Moving Beyond Freedom From . . . to Freedom To . . ." *Indiana Libraries* 32, no. 1: 8–12.

Wilkinson, Lane. 2014. "Principlism and the Ethics of Librarianship." *The Reference Librarian* 55, no. 1: 1–25.

Chapter 15

Staffing

The best thing our library has going for it is the staff.

—*Alan Kaye, 2006*

We realized we had a huge hole in our hiring processes. We had never focused on determining a potential employee's soft skills, such as whether a candidate will be friendly and approachable with patrons.

—*Leslie Lea Nord, 2011*

There is an old adage that states, "If you want something done right, do it yourself." Well, this is a nifty saying, but it is outdated. In vibrant organizations today, successful supervisors and managers must learn to delegate.

—*T. L. Stanley, 2012*

Volunteer opportunities within a library benefit both the individual worker and the organization. Baby boomers are untapped resources of knowledge and experience; they could become the qualified volunteers who are desperately needed in all types of libraries.

—*Allison Day, 2014*

Quality service requires adequate funding and reasonable physical facilities; however, even the most generously funded libraries with beautiful new facilities will not be able to provide quality service without staff members who are highly service-oriented. Leslie Nord's opening quotation highlights an important point when it comes to providing quality service—the presence of friendly, approachable, and knowledgeable staff members.

Every library would like to have a staff of the best and brightest people with a strong service orientation. Achieving that goal takes time, effort, and planning. Several key elements in securing the people with that service focus are hiring individuals who are happy, motivated, able to deal with change, and who really do like people. "Hire happy people" may seem trite; however, there is research that shows (*Harvard Business Review*, 2007) that doing so does make a positive difference in customer service and satisfaction: "The bigger the employee's smile, the happier the customer. That is the conclusion of new research from Bowling Green and Penn State Universities. . . . If managers want employees to deliver service with a smile, they can do better than simply mandate it. They should create an environment that encourages genuine smiles" (p. 24). In this chapter, we look at how libraries go about securing the best possible people, retaining those individuals, and assessing their performance. Essentially, this is a chapter on what organizations usually label human resource management (HR or HRM).

Staffing has never been simple, but in the past 25 years it has become even more complex. Increasing government regulations regarding employment practices, from recruitment to dismissal, resignation, and retirement (see, e.g., http://www.dol.gov/opa/aboutdol/lawsprog.htm), have created challenges for anyone involved in HR. Other factors complicating staffing are stagnant or diminishing budgets that often require staff adjustments, changing expectations of staff regarding the workplace, and employees' concerns about compensation and benefits. Recruitment and retention have become major concerns in most organizations, not just libraries. Keep in mind that staffing issues from hiring to dismissal can also be impacted if you are in a union setting, due to the nature of union regulations and policies (see Barriage, 2013; Johnson, 2013). Regardless of the setting, finding and keeping people with the requisite skill sets is a challenge that grows more problematic with time.

Gaining the services of the best and brightest people is a process that requires thoughtful planning. When it comes to hiring people who will provide outstanding service, you must think and plan even more carefully. People are the key to providing successful service—people who are thoughtfully selected, people who are given proper support and ongoing training, and, most importantly, people who really do *like* people. Effective HR programs utilize a series of steps, all of which require a thorough understanding of national and local employment laws and regulations. Once that understanding exists, the staffing procedure normally consists of seven steps:

1. Determining needs
2. Designing each job
3. Recruiting
4. Selecting
5. Providing orientation and training
6. Providing continual feedback and evaluation
7. Coaching

CATEGORIES OF INFORMATION SERVICE PERSONNEL

Like libraries themselves, library staff categories are highly variable. As a general rule, the larger the library, the more complex its structure and the number of staffing categories you encounter. Some very small libraries operate solely on the basis of volunteers; others, such as school libraries, may have one or two people who have had some education in library operations. At the other end of the spectrum are places like the Library of Congress with dozens of different staff categories. In the vast middle ground are libraries with just a few categories. We divide staff into two types—full- or part-time.

Full-time staff in midrange libraries consists of professionals (librarians and perhaps some other personnel such as information technology specialist), support or paraprofessionals, clerical staff, as well as volunteers. All play a vital role in providing high-quality user services. We firmly believe, and practice, that there is no such thing as second-class or less important job category in a library. Everyone's role is important, even when at times you may wonder if what you are asked to do really contributes much, if anything, to the overall service.

Librarians

In today's information world, the differences between a librarian (or information professional, if that is the term you use) and a paraprofessional are probably most apparent in the HR department rather than within the library. The reason for HR's ability to differentiate between the two is that it maintains the job descriptions, position holder's name, and salary classifications. Few, if any, of these attributes are apparent on a daily basis in the library. "On the floor," especially for the users, it is almost impossible to know who holds what job title. For many users, anyone working in the library is a librarian. William Curran (2006) indicated that three-quarters of the libraries in his survey reported that the need for paraprofessionals to perform tasks once done by librarians had increased over the prior five years, and that they also expected the trend would continue for at least five more years. Curran noted, "A redefinition of roles and expectations is needed. The level of competencies in information technology as well as the constant upgrading of equipment create expectations on the part of library users and invite professional and paraprofessional staff into a new routine of duties and responsibilities" (p. 30).

Individuals holding positions designated as "librarian" generally have a master's degree in library science (MLS) or master's in library and information studies (MLIS). "Generally" is an important word in the preceding sentence. School libraries, when they have a librarian, usually require that the individual hold a teaching certificate with some coursework in librarianship. Many large research libraries have bibliographic/subject librarians, archivists, or administrators who may hold a graduate degree in their assigned subject area, but not an MLS. Finally, some librarians may have satisfied a frequent phrase in position advertisements—"MLS or equivalent required." Just what is "equivalent" varies from institution to institution. However, the vast majority of librarians do in fact have an MLS/MLIS degree.

Paraprofessional/Support Staff

If the definition of librarian appears rather vague, deciding on a label and determining the requirements for those holding non-librarian positions in libraries is even fuzzier. Years ago, Elin Christianson (1973) reported on the various labels used to designate non-librarian personnel as well as attitudes about those labels. The list included clerk/clerical, library aide, library associate, library assistant, library clerk, library technician, nonprofessional, paraprofessional, supportive/support staff, and sub-professional. The only label that did not elicit at least a few negative responses from those holding such positions was library technician. The term paraprofessional had only a few negative comments, and today there probably would be none, given the raise of groups such as paralegals. To Christianson's list you can add "Customer Service Associate," shades of Walmart. ALA currently has a list of support staff categories that is over 60 titles (http://www.ala.org/educationcareers /careers/paths/listsupportstaff). One reason for the ALA's lengthy list is it includes series such as information specialist I and library technician II. We use the term support staff throughout this book, unless there is a need to further distinguish a particular job category.

We are firm believers that there are times when everyone, from director to part-time volunteer, needs to "get their hands dirty." As Linda Braun (2013) wrote, "It's probably no surprise to you that sometimes library staffers prefer to work with one age group over another. . . . Still, all staff members in a public library should be ready, willing, able and trained to work with all ages" (p. 64). While her focus was age groups and public libraries, her point about being "ready, willing and able" applies to all types of libraries and public service activities. In today's constricted library world staffers must be able to handle almost any activity.

A long-running journal for support staff was *Library Mosaics*. The journal's editorial staff consistently used the label paraprofessional for their target readers. (We were sad when the journal ceased publication in 2005. It was about the only journal that presented library issues from a non-MLS perspective. You can still find backfiles, with a wealth of information with the support staff point of view in several of the EBSCOhost database packages.) Other support staff organizations such as LSSIRT (the ALA's Library Support Staff Interests Round Table—http://www .ala.org/lssirt/) fill in the void left by the passing of *Library Mosaics*. Another source of information from ALA is its "Resources for Library Support Staff" site http://www.ala.org/offices/hrdr/librarysupportstaff /library_support_staff_resource_center/.

Support staff members are the backbone of library services. Without them, few libraries could offer the variety and quality of services that they do. The U.S. Bureau of Labor Statistics (BLS) indicated that as of 2012 there were 148,400 librarians in the U.S. workforce (http://www.bls .gov/ooh/education-training-and-library/librarians.htm). By comparison, the BLS Occupational Employment Statistics (http://www.bls.gov/oes /current/oes254031.htm) stated that as of May 2013 there were 95,980 employed in the category of "Library Technician." (Note: the 2012 and 2013 data was the latest available on both sites as of late 2014.) Although not stated, that label suggests that a variety of other support staff members are not included in that count—for example, clerks and pages. We believe the number would be at least equal to the number of librarians, if not in excess of that figure.

From the Advisory Board

Jean Wallace agrees with the important role filled by support staff, noting: In my local public library, there are two librarians and about six full time clerks, not counting the part time HS [high school] kids who work evenings and weekends. It's very common to spend several hours at the library without seeing anyone except the clerks.

What type of education and work experience is required to fill support staff positions that now often perform duties and carry responsibilities that were once the sole domain of MLS holders? Like so many questions, the answer is, it depends. Ideally individuals who perform such work would have, and many do have, extensive library education/training, and/or library experience. Without doubt, having a degree from a program that focuses on library and information services, in all their forms, is very valuable. Someone who has demonstrated the ability, interest, and desire to grow and learn on the job can also fill such positions in time. While having a supervisor who encourages and trains people is a wonderful asset, a person can independently gain the requisite knowledge and skills through workshops, online opportunities, and formal classes. (There are some entry-level positions that require no prior library experience or knowledge, that are clerical in nature, and should not carry the label paraprofessional or library technician.)

People usually think of their work in one of two ways—as a job or as a career. *Job-oriented* individuals only focus on the assigned duties. They often perform those responsibilities at an extremely high level and are a very valuable organizational resource. However, when their work shift ends, so does their interest in the organization. They have other interests. *Career-oriented* people, on the other hand, have a strong interest in their organization as well as an interest in the field in general. They are quick to volunteer to take on new tasks, especially those that offer an opportunity to learn a new skill or gain new knowledge. Because of their interest in the organization, they offer suggestions for improvements and accept committee assignments willingly. It is our opinion that the career-oriented individuals form the core of paraprofessional ranks. We also must note that career-oriented individuals, when overworked and under supported, can quickly become job-oriented. This is something that all good supervisors attempt to avoid and try to point out to more senior managers when they observe such mistreatment.

For the career-oriented person, a progression of responsibility (or career ladder) can be useful as a means of keeping these individuals motivated and engaged. One group within the LSSIRT, described earlier, was its Task Force on Career Ladders. The Task Force issued a report that indicated "Career development shifts the responsibility to the individual and away from the organization" (SSIRT, 1999, p. 4). The report continued to point out that libraries have an obligation in this area as well, such as providing opportunities for skill development, promotions, and the chance to put new skills to use.

Another career ladder model is outlined by Jane Fama and Elaine Russo Martin. Their work accomplishes four goals, as it:

1. describes the model for support staff that allows them growth within the library and provides a promotion in place plan,
2. outlines the rationale for implementing the model,
3. explains how the model is different from other models found in the library literature, and
4. makes a case for a competency-based model for support staff development and evaluation." (2009, p. 4)

It is well worth the read for those interested in the topic.

ALA also offers a competency-based service—Library Support Staff Certification (LSSC). The LSSC program is managed by the American Library Association-Allied Professional Association (ALA-APA, http://ala-apa.org /lssc/). The service issues the certificate when an enrolled individual passes 10 of 10 "competency sets" which include Foundations of Library Services, Technology, and Access Services. ALA does not offer coursework in the competency areas; however, it does approve courses offered by such bodies as state libraries, state library associations, regional library cooperatives, and community colleges. As of June 2014, there were 370 active candidates in the program, with 88 individuals completing the certification process (http://ala-apa.org/lssc/files/2014/06/Breaking-News-June-2014.pdf).

Other Full-Time Staff

There are a variety of full-time employees who work in libraries but do not fall into the two categories discussed earlier. The most obvious are clerical staff such as administrative assistants and coordinators. These are job categories that only require general office skills and no prior library experience. Other clerical positions might include processing and mailing notices to users (e.g., overdue and document delivery information) or maintaining order in the current magazine and newspaper area.

Depending on the size of the operation, you may encounter at least one accountant whose only special "library" knowledge is the concept of encumbrance, even that is not unique to the library environment. Someone with a general background in bookkeeping can quickly step into a library administrative office and handle the budget recordkeeping activities. Only if the person is to handle the financial records for the acquisitions department would he or she need to understand the principles of encumbering funds. In larger libraries, there may be some IT staff who handle networking/server maintenance, and the like, and who have no responsibility for specific library technologies. The very largest libraries are likely to have other professional positions, such as fundraising specialists, training officers, marketing and public relations people, or HR personnel who may or may not have an MLS.

Our reason for covering all library staff in our discussion is technology or information communication technology (ICT). Over the years that this book has been available (1971 to the present), there has been a profound shift in staffing patterns, as technology has become an ever more dominant feature in the daily work patterns of library staff. ICT has in fact become so integrated to the work flow that when the system has problems, or "goes down," work almost comes to a complete stop. It has changed work requirements, skills, and who does what. It has also made the case for "cross-training" and/or teamwork crystal clear, thus further blurring job distinctions. Libraries are increasing the use of "empowered teams" that are composed of a variety of job categories. (Empowered teams have decision-making powers.) ICT and other factors have resulted in a flattening of the traditional hierarchy of library organizations.

One impact of a changing economic picture and new technologies is that library staff sizes have remained relatively constant in spite of increased user demands and expectations. Technology allows public service personnel to handle changing and, in a few cases, increased workloads without additional people. Occasionally, it has allowed some libraries to shift positions from technical to public services.

Today's libraries require a much wider variety of skill sets than they did even five years ago. Budget restraints in turn create situations in which public service staff must be able to fill in for one another (cross-training). Technology also brings with it the need for constant training, as it seems to change every day.

Michael Gorman (1987) expressed what he called the "drift down" theory of organization. His theory was:

- No professional should do a task that can be performed by a paraprofessional
- No paraprofessional should do a task that can be performed by a clerical staff member
- No human being should do a task that can be performed by a machine. (p. 158)

Today, few organizations have the personnel (either professional or paraprofessional) available to follow the theory as originally stated. We do, however, agree with his last statement emphasizing the role technology can and does play in the workplace.

THE STAFFING PROCESS

Selecting appropriate staff, regardless of category—full-time, part-time, and even volunteers—requires significant time, planning, and effort. Although few libraries have an HR unit, library staff do become involved in the HR process on an operational level. Because of that fact, we have included a short discussion of the major HR issues. During your career, you are likely to be involved in issues from selection to retirement. Understanding some of the key points of the recruitment and selection process is useful when you are looking for a job as well as when you are asked to serve on a search committee. When you become a supervisor, you will need to have a sense of what goes into a job description, how to orient and train new people, and how to handle the performance appraisal process.

Determining staffing needs is usually the responsibility of senior managers and consists of two lists. One is a wish list of positions that would be wonderful to have, if only funding were available; it is often a long list and it is a special occasion when a new FTE (full-time equivalent) is finally funded. The second and shorter list covers expected vacancies—retirements, promotions, and resignations. It is up to the library to keep HR informed of expected vacancies. Knowing in advance what positions may become vacant and the timing may assist HR in doing some combination recruiting for several units, which should stretch limited advertising dollars and generate a stronger pool of candidates. It also helps if HR will advertise the position before it is vacant so the "vacant" period is kept to minimum. In some cases, HR will let a new employee overlap with exiting staff person so some cross-training can happen.

From the Authors' Experience

Sinwell notes that in addition to planning for current staff needs and roles it is important to engage in the process of succession planning. Library leaders are predicting a leadership crisis in all types of libraries and information centers, with top-level librarians retiring and younger librarians expressing no interest in assuming those top jobs.

While not all professional positions will be maintained due to economic pressures and changes within organizations, there is a great need to develop information professionals at all ranks who will be willing to take on leadership roles.

As noted by Debbie Schachter, "Succession planning helps nurture future library leaders while also addressing skills gaps and ensuring that knowledge is not concentrated in one or two positions" (2013, p. 30).

It almost goes without saying that the job design/description (JD) is the foundation for getting the best and brightest people. The U.S. Department of Labor suggests a process (http://www.careeronestop.org/businesscenter /recruitandhire/recruit-and-hire.aspx) for developing job descriptions and deciding upon the proper selection instruments. The suggested process starts with the library's organizational goals that a particular job is to assist in fulfilling. (Note: every staff member holds a separate "position;" however, several people may hold the same "job"—for example, document delivery assistant.) Designing a job requires answering questions such as "What activities are necessary to accomplish organizational goals?"

Answering this apparently simple question is usually more complex than you might expect. It requires detailed information in order to be useful. Your goal is to be as comprehensive as possible in listing the tasks. Being too brief or broad only creates more work later in the process. For example, a response for a circulation service point should be more than "check out materials." It should cover all aspects of the person's work, such as knowledge of the integrated circulation system including the security system, quality customer service, skills, ability to use technology-based hardware/software, ability to problem-solve users' borrowing issues (lost cards, lost/overdue books, contested fines, confidentiality of record), ability to work in team environment, ability to work independently, and so forth. Such detail is essential for developing sound job descriptions as it helps you identify the necessary skills and knowledge to successfully perform the work.

Another step is establishing job success criterion (JSC). JSCs are the keys to selecting the right person for the right position. This is also the most difficult and subjective of the steps in the model. While the goal of the process is simple to state—"What distinguishes successful from unsuccessful performance in the position?"—it is difficult to carry out. What constitutes success will vary from library to library and from time to time as the work changes. For example, being courteous to users is always important, but what if a person is courteous while providing incorrect information? What about a person who is great with users but is unwilling or unable to work well with other staff members? Thinking through the JSCs for a job makes it much easier to select the right person for the position. JSCs allow you to develop the best questions to ask the candidates, those that most accurately reflect the skills and knowledge needed for success.

Job specifications (JS) are the skills, traits, knowledge, and experience that, when combined, result in successful performance. JSs are what you see in job descriptions and advertisements, such as educational background or degree required, years of experience, and a list of the specific skills sought. From a legal point of view, these items must be BFOQ (bona fide occupational qualifications). Merely saying they are will not satisfy a court, if you are challenged. You must be able to prove that they are the skills, knowledge, and experience a person ought to possess to succeed. You might like to have someone with a high school diploma, but can you prove that it is essential to succeed in the work? If you can't, don't make it a requirement; make it "desirable."

From the Authors' Experience

Evans still recalls the furious debate that arose when he started his professional career over job categories and compensation equivalencies. The statewide personnel system for the library where he worked issued a new set of guidelines grouping jobs into broad equal compensation groups. (This took place not long after the Equal Pay Act was passed by Congress.) Why a furor? Librarians were grouped with hog farm managers. This proves that you just never know when the JS and JSCs will come to the forefront.

Sinwell had a similar experience, noting that at one location, librarians were grouped with positions that didn't require advance degrees (meanwhile accountants and engineers were classified at higher pay scale as they required advanced degrees).

Having completed the steps discussed earlier, you can decide what "instruments" you should use to assist in deciding which applicants to call in for an interview. Some instruments are ones that you know well—application forms, names of references, and letters of interest. Others that are less common are various tests of basic required skills—often handled by HR in order to winnow out individuals who don't possess the skill needed—such as the use of an office software suite. Library skills tests, such as alphabetizing or ordering call numbers, are handled by the library for lower-level clerical staff or student positions. Whatever instruments you select, you must have a clear link back to the JSC and JS in the event that you are challenged in court.

Recruitment

Once you develop the JD, HR can commence the search for suitable applicants. Many large libraries conduct national searches for their librarian and other professional positions while drawing on the local labor market for their paraprofessional and clerical positions. (Note: these searches can take considerable time, so you need to be prepared for a long-term vacancy if the recruitment process is not initiated before the incumbent leaves.) Advertisements for openings ought to provide the basic job description information and indicate where and when a person should apply.

The search often begins as an internal process; that is, an announcement of a vacancy goes to the library's staff. In some organizations, the policy is to interview any internal candidates before going outside. More often, the search is both internal and external—with the internal applicant(s) having the advantage of knowing more about the nature of the open position and being a known quantity to the employer (often, but not always, a good thing). U.S. employers must place advertisements or recruit in places where persons in the "protected categories" are likely to see position announcements.

Selecting the Pool

Most recruiting efforts generate a larger pool of applicants than it is feasible to interview. Deciding who to interview draws on information produced by the selection instruments you identified. The most common place to begin the sorting process is the application form and cover letter (when you apply for a position, keep this fact in mind; how carefully you prepare these documents often decides your chances of getting interviewed). A matrix grid can help facilitate this process, and can be required by HR authorities in some cases. Some of the factors to look for are if the person has the required skills, how carefully their materials are presented, and if the person supplies all of the required information. A "gross" sorting of applicants just using basic issues such as those listed here usually will reduce the pool by a substantial number. A further reduction, if necessary, can be done by asking how many of the "desirable" skills/abilities the applicant possesses. Having a final interview pool of three to six people is likely to produce a person to whom you would like to make an offer. Depending upon the situation, this pool may be further narrowed through a series of telephone (or Skype) interviews, before determining a group of finalists to bring on-site. Because the selection process involves a substantial amount of subjectivity, having developed sound JSCs and JSs and using those to judge applicants against will assist in keeping the process as objective as possible.

Interviewing

We devote some space to the interview process because it will come into play when applying for a position and when you serve on a search committee. In both instances, it requires an understanding of the process as well as a good deal of practice to become effective as an interviewee or interviewer. What follows applies to both sides of the interview table.

A sound interview process has six important elements. First, there is the need to plan the process. Beyond the obvious—such as timing and place—some of the key planning issues are length of the interview, who to involve in the interview, the questions to ask, if there should be a tour of the library, and how much time to devote to answering candidates' questions. As a candidate, you should also plan your questions about the position and institution.

The second element, and perhaps the most critical in a legal sense, is to carefully review the interview questions for their compliance with antidiscrimination laws; this is an area where HR staff can be of great assistance. You also want to have consistency and comparability of information about each candidate. Maintaining consistency in the questions and in the structure of the entire process for all the candidates is critical when it comes time to assess each one and make a final selection. Your questions *must* be job related. If you can't link each question to the job description, don't ask it. Asking open-ended questions gives candidates an opportunity to respond more fully and demonstrate some of their skills. Some suggested questions to consider appear in Table 15.1.

TABLE 15.1 Questions to Consider Regardless of Which Side of the Interview Table You Are On

- What do you think your (current or former) supervisor would tell his or her friend about you?
- What interests you about this position?
- What special skills do you bring to this job?
- Who and what has motivated your work efforts in the past?
- What do you consider to be your strengths?
- What do you consider to be a weakness of yours?
- What things do you like the most about your current position? What do you like the least?
- Tell us about one of the major accomplishments you made in your present position.
- Tell us about the goals you set for yourself in terms of work.
- What does the term "service" mean to you?
- What are some new work skills or knowledge that you believe would improve your performance on the job?
- What are your current career goals? What plans have you made to meet these goals?

The third element is having a segment of time when the candidate is given a clear sense of what the available position actually does and an overview of the library's operation and mission. Also, taking time to explain the relationship of the library to its parent body helps a candidate make an informed decision should an offer be made (if this has not already occurred in any pre-interview contact that may have occurred with the applicant). It is also the time for the candidate to ask the search committee questions.

A fourth element in the process is the "personal impact" of both the candidate and the interviewers on one another. Creating a relaxed and friendly atmosphere at the outset helps candidates become less nervous and thus more effective during the formal interview. Things such as tone of voice, eye contact, personal appearance and grooming, posture, and gestures on the part of both candidate and interviewer influence both parties. Keep in mind, in a culturally diverse community, the meanings of these may be very, very different. For example, lack of eye contact does not always mean the person is the "shifty-eyed character" of English novels.

Related to impact is how the interviewer responds to the applicant (the fifth element). Interviewers must be careful to control any nonverbal behavior that may encourage or discourage the applicant in an inappropriate way. Not showing an interest in what the candidate is saying will discourage the person from expanding on his or her thoughts, and this may well carry over to the remainder of the interview. Anyone with extensive interviewing experience understands just how difficult controlling those two behaviors can be at times. Suggestions for preparing for an interview appear in Table 15.2.

TABLE 15.2 Suggestions for Preparing for an Interview

- Take some time to research the library and its parent organization ahead of time; their Web sites can tell you a great deal about them

- Generate a few questions about the library based on your research and your own interests

- If you did not receive a full position description, ask for one

- Take time to think of questions to ask about the position

- Spend some time thinking about the answers you might give to questions that are likely to be part of the interview (e.g., What interests you about this particular position? What do you consider your strengths and your weaknesses? What does the term "service" mean to you?). Practice your answers with a friend.

- Dress appropriately

- Be on time

- Be certain to have the interviewer's/chairperson's name and its correct pronunciation

- Remember that your "body language" also reflects your interest and attentiveness

- Remember that taking time to think before answering complex questions is appropriate
- When asked a multipart question, be sure to cover all the parts; asking for clarification or for repetition of such questions is appropriate
- If a "personal" question is asked, then ask in a non-confrontational manner how the question is job related; decline to answer if it is not job related
- Thank the interviewer(s) for the opportunity to interview for the position
- Asking about the anticipated timeframe for when the decision of who will be hired will be made is appropriate
- To learn from each interview experience, jot down a few post-interview notes about some of the high and low points of the interview
- Even if you decide during the interview process that this is not the position for you, send a follow-up thank-you note to the chair of the search committee, position supervisor, or head of HR (whichever is most appropriate), thanking them for their time and for giving you an opportunity to meet with them

The final element is to assess the interview data fairly and equitably for all the interviewees. Some of the issues that can cause unfair processing are:

- Stereotyping the "right" person for the position
- Having a search committee whose members disagree on the importance of various attributes
- Overusing visual clues about the candidate that are not job related
- Not recognizing "contrast effects"—that is, when a strong candidate follows a very weak candidate, the contrast makes the stronger applicant look even stronger than he or she may be
- Talking about candidates outside of interview process
- Talking about who was selected before HR confirms the hire action (there are times a candidate is offered a position but declines, so the next candidate will be offered the job, etc.)

We would like to include a few final words about staffing and providing quality service to all. Hall and Grady (2006) made several very significant points about providing library service to a diverse user community and staffing patterns that may or may not reflect diversity:

We have to recognize that the whole process of information access and mediation, especially in the context of public libraries, brings up issues around hierarchy, privilege, and access. The question of who is behind that desk dispensing information and who is in front of it seeking information is in many ways a question of power. . . . Hiring in a manner that reflects this diversity and empowering staff to participate in collection development and create and offer programming is not about truism. . . . It's about seeing the payoff in increased visits, circulation, and funding opportunities. (p. 42)

Check These Out

The following are just four of a great many titles that will provide more in-depth information about the hiring process:

Mary J. Stanley's 2008 work *Managing Library Employees* (New York: Neal-Schuman) is a good starting point to gain an overview of various aspects of working with library staff.

Patricia Tunstall's title *Hiring, Training, and Supervising Library Shelvers* (Chicago: American Library Association, 2010). Although focused on shelvers, Tunstall's work does provide insights into the library hiring practices in general.

Geoff Smart and Randy Street's 2008 work *Who: The A Method for Hiring* (New York: Ballantine Books) is a reasonably comprehensive look at hiring practices.

The United States Merit Systems Protection Board's *Prohibited Personnel Practices: A Study Retrospective* (Washington, D.C.: U.S. Merit Systems Protection Board, 2010) is a review of hiring and other personnel practices you must avoid.

STAFF DEVELOPMENT, TRAINING, AND RETENTION

Once a person has been selected and has accepted the position, you should develop a plan for orienting the individual to both the position and the library. Sometimes people forget that the first few days on the job set a pattern for the new person that can be either negative or positive. Essentially, these first few days are critical to fitting in, retention, and the person's views about the library as well as its long-term training/development program. A well-thought-out orientation, including the training required for the position, will make it more likely that you will retain the person. Too often the first days focus only on the activities of the position; that is natural as in most cases the position has been vacant for a month or more and work has stacked up. If you fall into this trap, you may find yourself having a higher staff turnover than anyone would like.

Generally, the first week should be equally divided between position training and learning about the library and its parent organization. For most people, the first days on a new job are stressful and confusing. The common practice of taking the "new person" around to meet everyone, assuming there are more than a dozen people to meet, leaves the individual with a blur of faces, a few names (rarely connected to the right face), and a vague sense of what others do. Breaking the process up over several days gives the new person a better chance to absorb information and make meaningful connections. Starting with the "home" unit and working out through units that feed into and receive output from the home unit allows the new person to gain a sense of where his or her position fits in the scheme of things and how it is important to library operations. After that you can move on to other units to allow the person to gain an overall picture of operations. Linking new persons to someone at their level in the workgroup (a mentor) provides a personal connection for clarification or for questions that they might be afraid to ask their supervisor, lest they be thought of as silly. It also helps the mentors by giving them recognition and the motivation to check over those points that are often taken for granted.

From the Authors' Experience

Sinwell notes that as a supervisor, she would create a training/orientation sheet for each new employee. Some of items on the list the person could do by themselves (learn the catalog/databases, etc.), some items a colleague did with them (reviewed emergency procedures, opening/closing procedures, etc.), and some items the direct supervisor did with them (customer service policies, HR regulations, etc.).

All of the items were to be completed within 4–6 weeks of the hire date, depending on circumstances. She would ask these new staff to add to list if they saw something left off the list.

Retention

A major concern for today's organizations is retaining their best people. Nora Spinks (2005) offered some interesting thoughts about generational differences and their impact on retention, noting: "If you were a child in the 50s (a Boomer), you saw that working hard was a strategy that led to success. Loyalty was rewarded with long-term employment through to retirement. However, if you were a child in the 70s or 80s, you saw adults working hard and getting laid off, downsized or reengineered out of a job anyway. Employment tenure was out of your control, employers offered you a job as long as they felt you were of value, then let you go" (p. 11).

For many employees, an organization's lack of "loyalty" to long-term staff is coming back to haunt them. "Why should I have any loyalty to the organization if it has none to me?" is a question in the minds of many workers today. For many of them, all it takes is hint of staffing changes—real or imagined—or something perceived to be a threat, and people start looking for other employment and in many cases actually leaving. They have experienced or heard of organizations that announce staff reductions and say in effect to the staff, "We don't need you but fully expect you to give a 100 percent work effort until the day you are terminated." When that happens, the outcome is what you would expect—performance declines and people leaving as quickly as possible. Although the pattern is primarily seen in for-profit organizations, staff reductions in force (RIFs) are not unheard of in libraries.

Training and Development

One key method for gaining and retaining staff loyalty is to have programs that give ample opportunities for staff to grow and develop. Without doubt this will help with the long-term retention of the best and brightest people. You have two basic training/development areas to consider—specific job-related skills and career development competencies and opportunities.

We all know that libraries face a rapidly changing technological environment. Keeping staff current with the changes related to their activities is a major challenge, especially when budgets are static. It is also crystal clear that failing to maintain staff skills will result in users receiving poorer service, which in turn leads to user dissatisfaction. Technology carries with it two financial challenges—acquiring and upgrading requisite technology and funding staff training.

Certainly training and development goes beyond technological issues. Some of the other major areas include training for individuals moving into supervisory positions (as well as ongoing training for those currently in supervisory positions), and keeping staff up to date on changing professional standards and local policies/procedures or tools. Other areas for public service personnel are handling "problem" users, customer service, disaster recovery, emergency procedures, security, and changing legal issues. As noted by Debbie Abilock, Violet Harada, and Kristin Fontichiaro, "Professional development, designed in concert with participants' needs, implemented thoughtfully, and focused on impact over activity, is a powerful way for librarians to leverage their expertise, perspectives, and skills" (2013, p. 13). We feel this sentiment applies to all levels of library employees.

Professional associations can and do provide excellent training opportunities. Annual conventions often have workshops and other continuing education programs as part of their overall program. Unfortunately, there have traditionally been few such opportunities available for support staff. ALA has held a "conference within a conference" for support staff, and state library associations such as the Virginia Library Association have offered similar educational opportunities for paraprofessionals. As more educational institutions and professional bodies extend the range of distance education programs, training opportunities are increasing for support staff—particularly via Webinars and video conferencing. Notable examples of such training opportunities are those provided via OCLC's WebJunction® (http://www.webjunction.org/) or InfoPeople, from the California State Library (https://infopeople.org/).

In addition to concerns about funding, libraries face the problem of limited staffing, at least in most services. When staff are limited, it becomes difficult to have employees away at training programs for any length of time. Some jurisdictions are so short-sighted that they refuse to give time off to attend training programs even when the staff member is willing to pay for the program—this is short-sighted because in time the staff member's services become less and less effective.

Check These Out

A full discussion of staff training and development is beyond the scope of this book. However, there are a number of titles available on the topic. Two worth reviewing are:

Allan, Barbara. 2013. *The No-Nonsense Guide to Training in Libraries*. (London: Facet.) Covers both face-to-face and online training opportunities.

Stewart, Andrea, Carlette Washington-Hoagland, and Carol T. Zsulya. 2013. *Staff Development: A Practical Guide* (4th ed., Chicago: American Library Association.) Addresses all aspects of staff development, including needs assessment, goal setting, core competencies, and program assessment.

PERFORMANCE APPRAISAL

Performance assessment takes two forms—ongoing daily review with occasional corrective action and an annual overall assessment. In terms of corrective action, you should discuss poor performance as situations arise. Trying to avoid unpleasant interactions regarding performance and letting problems "slide" only hurts everyone in the long run. Being told that something was/is amiss during the annual performance review when it is too late to take corrective action causes anger, frustration, and poorer performance down the road. Furthermore, other employees will notice the lack of any corrective action and they are likely to conclude you don't really care about quality performance. When that happens, they are likely to let their work performance slide. By the time that happens, you face a highly complex situation that will be difficult to resolve. Finally, service to users also suffers, and that in turn can lead to a serious lack of user support.

There are some steps you can follow when you need to take corrective action that can help make the process as effective as possible. Start by stating the purpose of the session; even if the situation has the potential for confrontation, speak calmly. Plan on letting the employee talk as much as possible. *Listening* is the key to having a successful session. People can accept criticism if they see that their concerns are being heard and taken seriously. Too often, there is a tendency to start planning one's response rather than listening and trying to *hear* what the person is saying. Silence, even a long one, serves a good purpose—it lets both parties think about what is taking place. Setting a time limit for the session can defeat the purpose of the session; it may take time to get the central issue(s). Expect the employee to be unhappy, upset, and probably argumentative, as well as the possibility that he or she may engage in a personal verbal attack on you. It is important, if difficult, not to take the attack personally, and above all do *not* respond in kind. Total resolution is not the only indication of a successful session. Sometimes it takes a series of sessions to reach a complete resolution. Try to end the session on a positive note and, if appropriate, schedule a follow-up session.

Your goal is to be as consistent as possible in your evaluations. Standards should not shift from one week to the next or, worse yet, vary from one employee to another. Remember you should be evaluating outcomes rather than the process (as long as the process does not cause trouble or problems for others). You shouldn't hold a new employee as closely accountable for an error as an older, experienced person. This does *not* mean that you ignore the newcomer's problem. Naturally, a person lacking the skill to do a task needs additional training rather than criticism. If the training does not work, then other adjustments will be necessary, including the difficult but occasionally necessary step of termination.

Something to consider before taking corrective steps is to think about your personal biases that might color your judgment of people and their performance. If the matter is serious, look at prior annual appraisals before moving ahead. When it is clear something should be done, think about the next appraisal (keeping in mind any and all personal biases), and then begin the counseling process. Keep in mind this may require further action, especially if a person has received a negative review for two years in succession. It is always wise to work collaboratively with HR in these situations.

Annual performance reviews are something that most people endure and almost never look forward to, much less enjoy. Neither the givers nor the recipients have great faith in the process or that much good will come out of what many view as an ordeal.

Probably the biggest challenge, and where the difficulty lies, is in the dual nature of the review process. Although most HR departments attempt to keep it to a single purpose, performance enhancement, the reality that is there is sometimes an unofficial but real link to salary increases. The dual purpose is well documented, but is most clearly articulated by Saul Gellerman (1976). Essentially the single process attempts to handle behavioral issues (work performance) and administrative issues (compensation and occasional promotions). The two purposes are almost diametrically opposed in character. To be effective in improving performance, the process should be open and candid. From an administrative perspective it should be closed and secretive. Trying to accomplish both in a single process is a challenge to say the least. Almost every employee believes the salary aspect is the dominant factor. (See the Suggested Readings section at the end of this chapter for more about this complex and rather unpopular aspect of work life.)

If you give constant honest feedback throughout the year—both praise and correction—the annual review will be as painless and stress-free as possible. In many cases, there is no way to remove the salary component if the parent organization, directly or indirectly, uses reviews as part of its salary deliberations/considerations.

In spite of your best efforts, there will be times when disciplinary action must take place. Needless to say, such action follows only after a number of counseling sessions have failed to resolve the issue. In the United States, HR units label the process "progressive discipline." What the process consists of is a series of steps that become progressively more severe and can end with termination. Most of the time, the process never reaches the termination stage as the parties resolve the issue earlier. The sooner you address performance issues, the less likely it is you will have to go through the stress of a formal grievance procedure.

Part-Time Staff

There is a tendency to pay little attention to part-time staff in the literature. We think this is unfortunate as often the work of part-timers is critical to quality public service—just think about those who reshelve collections materials, most of whom are part-time people, and the impact on quality of service.

Although you will encounter part-time people in almost any job category, there are two very common part-time groups in libraries—student assistants and volunteers. These two groups, especially students in educational settings, may come close to the equivalent of full-time staff in terms of hours worked. For many libraries, quality service would not be possible without the aid of part-time students and volunteers. The work such individuals perform should receive the same attention and thought you give to full-time positions.

Students

Almost all libraries associated with educational institutions make extensive use of student labor. No matter what type of library—college, school, or university—the students have, or should have, the proper handling of their studies as their primary objective. Working in the library, even for pay, is a much lower priority and that fact must be kept in mind when using student labor. Many public libraries also use students for positions such as "pages"/ stack maintenance personnel. At public libraries, unlike at academic institutions, the part-time students are viewed as any other part-time staff members, except that perhaps they are given a little slack during exam periods, which is how educational libraries should handle the situation.

Looking at the early literature about using students as employees, you probably would come away with the view that student workers are too much trouble and not the worth the effort. The focus then was on the limitations/ problems of employing students. Such an emphasis may have been necessary to work out the issues. We believe part of the problem did and can lie in not spending enough time on preplanning and developing true job descriptions for what the students will do, and providing appropriate training and evaluation. What is clear today is that educational libraries are very dependent on such labor.

Beyond the obvious benefit of having valuable work accomplished at a modest cost, students bring several benefits to the library. One benefit, in our view, is that as peers/classmates they are often viewed as more approachable than the full-time staff. This is especially true when the student body's cultural composition and that of the full-time staff is markedly different. Student employees are much more likely to have a sound idea of what technologies students use and how and when they use the technologies. Such information can be of great value when planning a new service or a different approach to an old one. Yet another benefit is that students can assist full-time staff in understanding "where the students are coming from"—they relate more effectively to the primary service population. Finally, they are the pool from which to recruit individuals to our field.

Regardless of how you structure the work, students should be held just as accountable for the quality of their work as full-time staff. (This also applies to volunteer workers.) Having different standards of accountability can and probably will lead to major morale problems and low-quality overall performance for the library.

Sound mentoring is effective in recruiting people to our field. Students tend to be open to mentoring when it focuses on issues they perceive as relevant. If for nothing more than helping them to learn appropriate work behavior and dress, this is useful activity. We have only touched on a few of the benefits of using student workers. We highly recommend you spend some time reviewing Kimberly B. Sweetman's *Managing Student Assistants* (New York: Neal-Schuman, 2007). Although its primary focus is on academic libraries, it has much to offer anyone thinking about or using student employees.

Volunteers

Library volunteers play a growing role in daily operations. They are likely to become even more common as more and more of the boomer generation retires, as alluded to in the opening quote by Allison Day. Many small libraries (rural, school, and church) are totally dependent on volunteers, with perhaps a retired person with library experience taking a lead role. Other libraries may be less dependent on volunteer assistance, but still use such services for important tasks.

During the late 1990s, there was a major effort to increase volunteerism in the United States. Although there is less government emphasis today, volunteer service hours grow steadily. In the previous edition of this book, we mentioned what was then a new youth volunteer program in the St. Paul Public Library. Looking at the library's Web site (http://www.sppl.org/about/volunteers/volunteer-opportunities) it is clear the program was very vigorous as of late 2014.

From the Advisory Board

Jackie Gropman (Fairfax County Public Libraries—FCPL) notes that opportunities for teen volunteers had been available for many years often in conjunction with administering the Summer Reading Game, but it became evident that more creative talents of young adults could be tapped. To this end teens in the Metro area presented original mystery programs, drama and story times. A volunteer fair presented at several branches at FCPL introduced teens to other agencies which recognized teens as a valuable resource.

No matter what value you place on the work, many granting agencies currently allow you to use a $22.14 per hour rate (http://www.volunteeringin america.gov/pressroom/value_states.cfm) for valuing volunteer service, and the annual contribution is in the billions of dollars. While volunteer work is increasing, there is concern about being able to retain volunteers. Daniel Kadlec (2006, p. 76) reported, "Nearly 38 million Americans who had volunteered in a nonprofit in the past didn't show up last year. . . . That is a waste of talent and desire." The "last year" in the quote was 2005, although it is common for one in three volunteers not to return from one year to the next. Organizations cannot waste such potential people power. As boomers retire, they take with them a vast amount of experience and, perhaps more importantly, institutional memory that is very valuable. You will find frequent stories in the professional literature about library staff members retiring and then returning as volunteers. Losing such people because the volunteer activities have not been properly planned is/would be very sad.

With volunteers, you have a vast pool of talented, energetic, and motivated individuals to tap into and, hopefully, retain. Volunteers can become highly committed to a library's organizational goals, given the proper environment, even if they never worked in a library. Part of that environment is thinking about volunteers as just as important to quality service as any paid staff member.

You can begin your thinking and planning for volunteers by considering a few basic questions:

- Should we use volunteers? (A very key question to ponder)
- Where could we use volunteers?
- How would we use them?
- Would the tasks be meaningful for volunteers?
- Who would supervise the volunteers?
- Would we have one person in charge of the overall program?
- Do we have or can we create meaningful volunteer rewards?

Dale Freund (2005) explored the question of whether volunteers should be used in libraries. He believed that when done properly and for the right reasons, the answer is yes. Essentially, success hinges on your thinking through questions such as the ones listed here and creating a plan.

Check These Out

A recent title on the subject of library volunteers is Leslie and Glen Holt's *Success with Library Volunteers* (Santa Barbara, CA: ABC-CLIO, 2013). The work covers all aspects of managing library volunteers, from planning for volunteer positions, to recruitment, benefits and retention issues, to training opportunities and impact analysis.

One Web site worth consulting on the topic is Volunteers @ the Library from the Maine State Library (http://www.maine.gov/msl/libs/admin /vol/index.shtml). The site covers how volunteers can benefit libraries, as well as addresses several "myths" associated with using volunteers (e.g., volunteers can manage themselves). The site also provides a number of resources such as sample policies, codes of ethics, and evaluation forms.

There are three major volunteer categories to think about, at least in the United States. One is the "short-term" volunteer. These are people who will work on special projects or events, but have no interest in a regular commitment, such as coming in one day per week for a few hours. Some library examples are an annual book sale, disaster recovery efforts, or a capital fundraising campaign. A second category is the "commitment" volunteer. These are people who have a strong interest in the area in which they seek volunteer opportunities. They expect to gain gratification, knowledge, and useful skills as well as a sense of accomplishment from the work they perform. For most libraries, these are the people who form the backbone of a successful long-term volunteer program. They are also the group that requires the most careful planning and needs the most meaningful work to perform.

Finally, there are "volunteers" who engage in the activity because of some outside requirement (e.g., community service). You may be able to transform some of these people into committed volunteers, but only through careful planning. There are two significant sources of outside pressure—the workplace and school. Many for-profit organizations, while not making volunteering mandatory, make it very clear they expect employees to engage in some form of volunteer work. Such organizations normally have a very broad definition of what constitutes volunteer work and how that activity counts in the performance review process. A few colleges and universities have gone so far as to make volunteer work a graduation requirement. Most don't go that far, but they do encourage students to volunteer, often through such means as adding it to the student's transcript, offering credit for the approved activities.

Where do you begin your search for volunteers? Your recruiting efforts will not take place in the same venues as for paid staff. There are five major places to explore; each requires a somewhat different approach both in the message and where to place that message. The pools are:

- Retirees
- Students
- Parents/family members
- Employed people
- Unemployed people (most hope to gain marketable skills or perhaps secure a paid position with the organization)

Reaching out to students, the employed, and the unemployed is relatively easy as you have organizations to contact that will assist in getting your message out. Retirees are a little more challenging; however, adult communities and other locations that offer programs for older adults are a good starting point. Parents and family members are the biggest challenge; in this case school libraries can have the inside track on getting great volunteers.

The best way to develop a cadre of committed volunteers is to start with job descriptions, using the same method as you do for paid staff positions. Doing this provides a solid base for everyone about the "whats and hows" of the position(s). Surprises such as "I don't want to make photocopies" are much less likely when the person had an opportunity to review a JD indicating photocopying was part of the job. As with paid positions, the JD should outline duties and experience/skills sought. (Note: after preparing the descriptions it is wise to consult with the HR department to explore any issues such as injury and liability coverage for volunteers.)

When it comes to volunteers, you rarely have a pool of "applicants" to interview—you are happy to have someone interested in the position. That notwithstanding, the interview is just as important for volunteers as it is for paid staff. This is the opportunity to assess skills, motivation, and the nature of the work by both parties.

Just as is the case with paid staff, providing lots of positive feedback is essential for volunteers. However, this does not mean you shouldn't correct problems with volunteer performance. When it does become necessary, do it in as positive a manner as possible. (Volunteers can be quick to leave if they don't think their efforts are appreciated.) Forgetting to thank them each time they come in can be, and often is, viewed as being taken for granted and cause for leaving.

Generally, volunteers require more initial training and development than paid staff. This is particularly true when the volunteer has retired from a somewhat similar paid position—for example, a retired school librarian volunteering in an archive. They need time to unlearn years of past practices and/or modify beliefs about "how things should be done." Too often the supervisor's assumption is that such people have done this before and therefore need very little training. It may be a while before it becomes apparent that that was a poor assumption and work must be redone.

There is no doubt that volunteers provide wonderful assistance to thousands of libraries. As Sue McGown suggests, "Recruiting and working with volunteers requires a time investment, but it pays off in building advocates for the library program" (2007, p. 13). However, there are a few areas in which tension can arise between volunteers and paid staff. One obvious area is a fear/concern about job security, especially where funding is tight or hiring freezes are in place. Paid staff may harbor unstated worries that their jobs may be in jeopardy, especially if some of the volunteers have prior library experience. We are unaware of any documented case where paid staff lost their jobs because of the availability of volunteers. However, we do know of instances where layoffs took place because of funding problems and sometime later the organization restarted a service based on volunteer help. When starting a volunteer program, you should address this concern openly and honestly with the paid staff.

Another challenge is when volunteers and paid staff perform the same task(s), something to avoid whenever possible. When it does happen, performance assessment becomes a significant issue. There may be strong resentment of the volunteers' apparent freedom to come and go with little or no notice and the appearance that they are held to a lower work standard. Paid staff may also think/observe the volunteer(s) receiving encouragement/praise for work they believe is less than standard, or at least a lower standard than they are expected to deliver. Your managerial creativity and ingenuity will face great challenges when you try to provide that extra level of encouragement to volunteers and retain their services, while not undermining staff morale.

CLOSING THOUGHTS

Many years ago John D. Rockefeller is supposed to have said, "the ability to deal with people is as purchasable a commodity as sugar or coffee and I will pay more for that ability than for any other under the sun" (http://www.brainyquote.com/quotes/quotes/j/johndrock147467.html). Whether he said that or not, the sentiment is the key to having quality library services; hire top-notch people and retain their services and loyalty. To be able to do that you need to follow sound people-planning practices and thoughtfully design their work activities.

It may not seem likely right now that you will need much of the information in this chapter; however, we anticipate that many professional positions will need to be filled by qualified, proactive leaders interested in grooming other professionals and paraprofessionals for leadership roles. Paraprofessionals will play an ever-growing role in quality library services in all types of libraries. Both professional and paraprofessional staff will need ongoing training and development in personnel management in order to provide quality supervision of all levels of staffing. We agree with the observations of Meredith Schwartz (2013) who noted, "Modern librarians need to be comfortable and conversant with technology, be willing and able to speak in public, and possess people skills and a commitment to lifelong learning, as the profession and the expertise for success are constantly changing."

Chapter Review Material

1. What are the typical employee categories in most libraries?
2. Which label do you prefer for non-librarian positions in libraries? Explain your preference.
3. Describe the elements of LSSC program.
4. What are the major steps in the staffing process?
5. Why is the job description such an important document?
6. What are some of the legal aspect of the hiring process?
7. Why is training and development so important in providing quality services?
8. Discuss the role of performance appraisal in terms of quality service?
9. In what ways do student workers differ from other library employees?
10. Do you think volunteers are more or less valuable to libraries? Explain your position.

REFERENCES

Abilock, Debbie, Violet H. Harada, and Kristin Fontichiaro. 2013. "Growing Schools: Effective Professional Development." *Teacher Librarian* 41, no. 1: 8–13.

Barriage, Sarah. 2013. "Library Workers Will Not Be Shushed." *Progressive Librarian* no. 41: 86–97.

Braun, Linda. 2013. "The Whole Library Approach." *American Libraries* 44, no. 6: 64.

Christianson, Elin. 1973. *Paraprofessional and Nonprofessional Staff in Special Libraries*. New York: Special Library Association.

Curran, William M. 2006. "The 8R's and Training Needs." *Argus* 35, no. 2: 29–33.

Day, Allison, 2014. "Calling All Baby Boomers." *Kentucky Libraries* 78, no. 3: 18–20.

Fama, Jane, and Elaine Russo Martin. 2009. "One Model for Creating a Career Ladder for Library Support Staff." University of Massachusetts Medical School. *Library Publications and Presentations*. Paper 103. http://escholarship.umassmed.edu/lib_articles/103.

Freund, Dale. 2005. "Do Volunteers Belong in the Library?" *Rural Libraries* 25, no. 1: 19–41.

Gellerman, Saul. 1976. *Management of Human Resources.* New York: Holt Rinehart.

Gorman, Michael. 1987. "The Organization of Academic Libraries in the Light of Automation." *Advances in Library Automation and Networking* 1: 151–168.

Hall, Tracie D., and Jennifer Grady. 2006. "Diversity, Recruitment, and Retention: Going from Lip Service to Foot Patrol." *Public Libraries* 45, no. 1: 39–46.

Harvard Business Review. 2007. "Service with a Very Big Smile." 85, no. 5: 24.

Johnson, Stephon. 2013. "Workers Tell City to 'Save Our Libraries.'" *New York Amsterdam News* 104, no. 11, March 18: p. 10. http://amsterdamnews.com/news/2013/mar/18/workers-tell-city-to-save-our-libraries/.

Kadlec, Daniel. 2006. "The Right Way to Volunteer." *Time* 168, no. 10 (September 4): 76.

Kaye, Alan. 2006. "Library Profile: Roddenbery Memorial Library." *E-news@PLA* 9, no. 8. http://tinyurl.com/ob4wjbd.

McGown, Sue W. 2007. "Valuable Volunteers: How to Find, Use and Keep Them." *Library Media Connection* 26, no. 2: 10–13.

Nord, Leslie Lea. 2011. "How to Hire Delightful Employees: Role-Play Has a Role." *Public Libraries* 50, no. 4: 40–43.

Schachter, Debbie. 2013. "Developing Our Next Generation of Leaders." *Information Outlook* 17, no. 6: 30–31.

Schwartz, Meredith. 2013. "How to become a 21st Century Librarian." *Library Journal.Com*, March 20. Online. http://lj.libraryjournal.com/2013/03/careers/how-to-become-a-21st-century-librarian/.

Spinks, Nora. 2005. "Talking about My Generation." *Canadian Healthcare Manager* 12, no. 7: 11–13.

Stanley, T.L. 2012. "Delegating for Success." *Supervision* 73, no. 4: 7–10.

Support Staff Interest Round Table. 1999. Task Force on Career Ladders—Few Opportunities for Advancement. Chicago: American Library Association. http://www.ala.org/lssirt/sites/ala.org.lssirt/files/content/lssirtstratplan/taskforcereports/career.pdf.

SUGGESTED READINGS

Babcock, Pamela. 2009. "Workplace Stress? Deal with It!" *HR Magazine* 54, no. 5: 67–72.

Bartlett, Jennifer. 2013. "New and Noteworthy: Handle with Care: Benefits and Drawbacks of Volunteers in the Library." *Library Leadership & Management* 27, no. 3: 1–4.

Beach, Karen. 2013. "Volunteer Utilization Report Prepared for Future of the Library Task Force of the Charlotte Mecklenburg Library, 2010." *Public Library Quarterly* 32, no. 2: 150–162. (Includes a discussion of the pros and cons of using volunteers in libraries.)

Bloomquist, Catherine. 2014. "Mentoring Gen-X Librarians." *Public Libraries* 53, no. 3: 30–34.

Boitnott, Kitty. 2012. "Teacher Associations: Extending Our Advocacy Reach." *Library Media Connection* 30, no. 4: 32–33.

Cottrell, Terrance (Terry). 2012."Interviewing Efficiencies or Interviewing Efficiently?" *The Bottom Line: Managing Library Finances* 25, no. 3: 102–106.

Deards, Kiyomi D., and Gene R. Springs. 2014. *Succession Planning and Implementation in Libraries: Practices and Resources*. Hershey, PA: Information Science Reference.

Dickerson, Constance. 2012. "The Preschool Literacy and You (PLAY) Room." *Children & Libraries: The Journal of the Association for Library Service to Children* 10, no. 1: 11–15. (Discusses how volunteers play an active role in the Preschool Literacy and You [PLAY] room at the Noble Neighborhood Library, part of the Cleveland Heights-University Heights Public Libraries, Ohio.)

Driggers, Preston F, and Eileen Dumas. 2011. *Managing Library Volunteers*. 2nd ed. Chicago: American Library Association.

England, Megan. 2014. "Creating Teen Leadership Opportunities." *Young Adult Library Services* 12, no. 3: 8–11.

Grant, Adam M., Jane E. Dutton, and Brent D. Rosso. 2008. "Giving Commitment: Employee Support Programs and Prosocial Sensemaking Process." *Academy of Management Journal* 51, no. 5: 808–918.

Harris, Colleen S. 2011. "Efficiencies and Responsible Staff Stewardship: A Library Manager's Critical Self-Reflection." *Bottom Line: Managing Library Finances* 24, no. 2: 129–137.

Hill, Claire. 2014. "The Professional Divide: Examining Workplace Relationships between Librarians and Library Technicians." *Australian Library Journal* 63, no. 1: 23–34.

Huff-Eibl, Robyn, Jeanne F. Voyles, and Michael M. Brewer. 2011. "Competency-Based Hiring, Job Description, and Performance Goals: The Value of an Integrated System." *Journal of Library Administration* 51, nos. 7/8: 673–691.

Johnson, Cameron A. 2001. "Library Unions: Politics, Power, and the Care of the Library Worker." *Alki* 17, no. 3: 16–19. (Although dated, this article provides a good overview regarding the presence of unions in libraries.)

Lund, James. 2012. "Redefining the Professional in Our Field." *Bottom Line: Managing Library Finances* 25, no. 2: 53–55.

Manley, Laura, and Robert P. Holley. 2014. "Hiring and Training Work-Study Students: A Case Study." *College & Undergraduate Libraries* 21, no. 1: 76–89.

Mitchell, Julie, and Nathalie Soini. 2014. "Student Involvement for Student Success: Student Staff in the Learning Commons." *College & Research Libraries* 75, no. 4: 590–609.

Mosley, Pixey Anne. 2014. "Engaging Leadership: Understanding 'Other Duties as Assigned.'" *Library Leadership & Management* 28, no.3: 1–7.

Owens, Donna M. 2006. "EAPs for a Diverse World: Employers That Provide Culturally Competent Employee Assistance Programs Show Employees They Care." *HR Magazine* 52, no. 10: 91–96.

Rodell, Jessica B. 2013. "Finding Meaning through Volunteering: Why Do Employees Volunteer and What Does It Mean for Their Jobs?" *Academy of Management Journal* 56, no. 5: 1274–1294.

Romaniuk, Elena. 2014. "Losing Staff: The Seven Stages of Loss and Recovery." *Serials Librarian* 66, nos. 1–4: 241–247.

Stewart, Henry. 2012. "How to Have a Happy and Productive Office." *Management Today* February: 38–41.

Chapter 16

Safety Aspects

Court disaster long enough and it will accept your proposal.

—*Mason Cooley, 2000*

Successful library security programs are based on clearly defined and well-communicated behavior policies for public and staff. . . . Today, more than ever, security in your library is every staff member's responsibility

—Library Security Guidelines Document, *2010*

Library collections have always faced the danger of theft, damage, and accidental loss. It's no longer standard to chain books to desks. Instead, many libraries have long relied on electromagnetic security gates that alarm when triggered by sensitized magnetic strips within books.

—*Jonathan H. Harwell, 2014*

While the literature has many articles on transients and mentally ill in the public library setting, there is less to be found that focuses exclusively on these same populations in an academic library setting.

—*Scott E. Muir, 2011*

There is a component of public service work that is an underlying constant, regardless of what activity you are engaging in at the moment. It exists for everyone on duty in public services, from the most senior manager to the newly hired junior page. It is also most unlikely to appear in anyone's position description (see chapter 15 for a discussion of job and position descriptions). What *it* is, as you probably surmise from the chapter's title, is safety and security. Safety and security of both people and things are always concerns for library staff. While senior managers have a fiduciary responsibility for the library building and its content, it is the people "on the floor" who must ensure that the building and contents are safe and secure.

There is a twofold aspect to library safety and security—people and things. It goes without saying, if a choice must be made in terms of safety and security, people are the priority. That said, library things *do* matter both from a safety and security point of view. There is a surprising amount of capital (a.k.a. money) that resides in the collections and equipment found in even modest size libraries. Retail stores have a concept called "shrinkage." That is, merchandise that was not sold, not misplaced, not mislabeled, it has just disappeared. Libraries may not use the term but they do have "shrinkage," as hinted at by our opening quotation by Jonathan Harwell. How to handle this issue without really offending customers or users tests organizational ingenuity. It is also an example of the common library challenge of balancing the safety and security needs of both people and things.

Another example of where people and thing needs are less than congruent is where collections and people are concerned. For libraries with a mission that includes a long-term preservation goal there is a conflict in this area. Although a primary concern for research/academic libraries, a great many public libraries have local history/special collections where there is some expectation of collection longevity. The issue is that the best long-term storage conditions (humidity and temperature) for collection items is rather uncomfortable for people having to spend extended periods in that environment. (We look at issues of humidity, temperature, and other environmental factors in more detail in chapter 19.)

There are also people-to-people concerns. Sarah Farrugia (2002) noted, "Public librarians are more susceptible to patron violence than academic and other special librarians, as their open door policy allows anyone to use the building" (p. 309). Her statement is true; however, the concern about violence goes beyond librarians; it applies to everyone in the public service area—staff and general public. Certainly staff face longer-term exposure to some form of violence as they are not as free to leave the area as are the general public when a problem arises.

It is surprisingly easy for a library to court disaster, as alluded to in the opening quotation by Mason Cooley. One obvious way is not to ever conduct a risk assessment. By not taking the time to think about and assess the potential dangers that do exist, whether one ignores them or not, when one does occur the damage done will be greater than it might need be. Having some plan of action is better than not having one, even if it is far from perfect. In our experience, there are not too many libraries that have not given at least some thought to what to do in case of major natural event such as earthquake or tornado, but it does happen.

Probably the most common library "courting" approach is to think once you completed a risk assessment, developed a plan(s) for handling possible problems, and perhaps even practiced a fire drill evacuation, you are done. That simply is not the case. In today's world of short staffing, low funding, and seemingly limitless demand for more a better services, there is precious little time to do more than the basic activities. You may squeeze out time to do a risk assessment, develop a plan, and perhaps even practice a fire drill, but then it is back to the daily grind with no time to spend thinking about risks. Unfortunately, the environment changes, you have to make small changes in where and how something is done, and rules and regulations regarding public safety are modified. New staff members who may not even be aware there are plans for handling an emergency get hired. All of these "small" changes may, in total, add up to having an almost meaningless plan for handling safety/security issues that arise.

A complete list of the potential dangers would generate pages and pages of text. Some of the broad categories of problem areas we touch on in this chapter are:

- Natural disasters
- Criminal activity
- People health and safety
- Collection health and safety
- Data security

We all know the typical natural disasters—hurricanes, tornadoes, floods, and earthquakes. Some of the others we overlook are wildfires and mud/landslides. The odds are fairly high your library will have to face one of these events sometime during your career. Having a plan to handle the occurrence will help get the library back in operation more quickly. Not having a plan is surely courting disaster.

The topics covered in this chapter are of concern for a great many organizations and as such have generated some standards. For example, the International Information Systems Security Certification Consortium ((ISC)^2®, https://www.isc2.org/) developed "standards" that although focus on information systems, the concepts apply to most organizational safety and security concerns (Yi, 2011). There are three broad areas of concern in the broader concept of security—managerial (e.g., legal and disaster recovery), technology (e.g., network security and access control), and physical (e.g., people, collections, and equipment). Braking down the risk assessment process into three categories reduces the magnitude of conducting the assessment.

RISK ASSESSMENT AND MANAGEMENT

R. Keith Mobley (2011) provided a good definition of risk management:

> Risk management is simply the identification, assessment, and prioritization of risks, followed by coordinated and economical application of resources to minimize or control the probability of occurrence and the impact of negative events. (p. 40)

When engaging in the assessment phase of risk management, you must look at both external and internal possibilities. When it comes to setting priorities, many risk consultants employ a three-level approach—high/probable, moderate/possible, and low/unlikely. Such categories help in your assigning resources to your most serious and likely-to-occur risks. You are most unlikely to have resources to address every identified issue, so having a sense of the importance and likelihood of occurrence is a great help in making decisions.

Security Assessment

Trying to do a risk assessment with just library staff is better than not doing one, but the odds are high that important elements will be missed. Conducting a risk assessment with a risk professional (e.g., someone from the fire/police department or insurance company) will speed the process and provide better data because of the expert's experience in such matters. Another plus is generally the fire and police departments will assist in the process for free, unlike a consultant. One drawback is that although their assistance is often free, it does focus on their area of expertise. That means you will still a lot of assessing to do. One fact is certain: the fire department will tell what issues *must* be addressed, should they identify a problem such as exit lighting or the presence or absence of an audible fire alarm. They can set some top priorities for you; some issues may be matter of legal compliance and without question should be at the top of your list.

Yet another source of free advice/assessment is the library's insurance agents/risk manager. There are governments that self-insure; however, that number has been declining as the cost of losses has escalated. Many insurers have a risk manager(s) who are available to help the insured look at potential risks and even suggest actions to take to mitigate potential problems. Such individuals assess various types of risks for which there is insurance coverage (fire, water damage, personal injury, theft, liability, etc.). They also determine what changes in conditions would reduce the possibilities of a loss or claim. Most risk managers welcome the opportunity to do or review a security audit. There are times when an audit may even reduce the cost of the organization's insurance or lower its deductible. At the same time, a review of the library's insurance coverage may show that the collection and equipment evaluations are too low and an increase would be good, of course at a higher premium. The library or jurisdiction can then make a more informed decision regarding just what risk it is willing to take.

Whoever completes the audit will need some background information about the community, campus, or organization, including demographic data and the physical location and relationship to other buildings and activities. Often, branches of public libraries are in park-like settings and, as a result, are relatively isolated from other activities. Academic libraries, while often located in or near the center of campus, have long service hours and are open long after most other areas have closed for the day. Extended hours result in a form of isolation; no other buildings are open nor are other activities going on at closing time. Isolation and nighttime service hours can add to both staff and user safety concern.

A well-known, prominent, or valuable collection, whether in the open stacks or in special collections, increases certain types of risk. However, keep in mind that most of the books stolen from libraries are not in special collections, but rather in the circulating collection. Finally, there needs to be some evaluation of staff and user attitudes. If either, or both, groups have a negative attitude about the library or the institution the library serves, the risks of theft are greater. Preparing the background paper can be an eye-opener and may point out potential problem areas.

The assessment process consists of two parts: looking for security/risk weaknesses and observing current security procedures. Much of the search for weaknesses involves reviewing the past. Lacking good records makes this a memory exercise that will be selective and subjective. The lack of good security records is itself a weakness. Maintaining a log of incidents and complaints provides better information about the problems and their seriousness and frequency. Some useful questions to explore are:

- What evidence of theft exists?
  - Are there areas that may create problems?
  - Is there a record of user complaints?
- What deferred maintenance exists?
- What key control plan is in operation, if any?
- Are there procedures in place for handling terminations of staff and removal of patrons?
- What happens with regards to:
  - materials checked out;
  - fines owed;
  - keys issued;
  - supervised packing up of personal belongings?
- Does an emergency plan exist?
- Does a disaster plan exist?
- Does a security plan exist?

With the answers to these questions and others like them, one will know how vulnerable the library may be. Some problem areas may be inexpensive to correct; others may be too costly given the frequency or volume of the problem. However, one should base such judgments on information provided by a security audit.

The second phase of the audit involves observing how the existing procedures function. This includes things such as the relationship of service points (places where library staff work) and the building's exits. A number of questions arise in this regard, including:

- Are all of the exits equipped with alarms and/or fully observable from a service point?
- How often is the service desk's view blocked by traffic or people needing assistance?
- Are there guards at the main entrance and exit?
- Do the guards do full, random, or casual searches? Is there a discernible pattern to the searches? With a full search, do guards check purses? Does the frequency of searches vary with the volume of traffic?
- If an electronic security system is in place, is it a bypass unit (materials handed to users after passing through a screening device)?
- What are the characteristics of all doors and locks?
- Who has keys for emergency exit alarms?
- How much visual control is there of loading docks and receiving areas?
- What is the relationship of shelving units used to store recently received, but not yet processed materials, such as the holding area for approval books, to exits?
- What type of ceiling exists? How much crawl space is there? Is the ceiling on the alarm system?

- Are there utility tunnel doors and maintenance areas that are not part of the library key system? If so, who has access to these areas and when?
- How secure is the special collections area?
- If there is a vault or safe, who has a key or knows the lock combination?
- Is there an alarm system tied into the police department, fire department, or security office?
- What security measures exist for the computer room? Are the audiovisual units, computers, and terminals secured to work surfaces in some manner?
- How secure is the after-hours book return?
- How effective is the closing procedure in preventing after-hours concealment?

Clearly a security audit takes time to perform, but the results of the time and effort are important to users and staff. The library can put together a comprehensive security plan with the information gained from the audit. Staff, users, and collections will all be safer as a result of the effort invested, even though staff and users may not even be aware that the audit has been done.

A security plan is actually a combination of plans and activities. The major plans are operational security, a key control procedure, an emergency procedure plan, and a disaster preparedness plan. The operational activities include such things as opening and closing procedures, monitoring library use, and monitoring safety issues. Sometimes an assessment may lead to changing door locks or installing an electronic security system.

Check This Out

The *Library Security Guidelines* (2009) prepared by the Buildings and Equipment Section of the Library Leadership and Management Association (LLAMA), a division of the American Library Association, is a very useful place to begin your thinking about your risk assessment project. There are nine chapters that cover the "Duty to Protect," "Foreseeability of Loss," "Adequacy of Protection," "Fire and Emergency Protection," "Physical Barrier and Lock and Key Security," "Security Duties and Security Staff," "Personal Access and Parcel Control," "Security Alarms and Electronics," and "Crime Prevention through Environmental Design." Although not a complete checklist of issues, it is an excellent starting point for planning an assessment: http://www.ala.org/llama/sites/ala.org.llama/files/content/publications/LibrarySecurityGuide.pdf.

Most libraries have some procedures in place to handle emergencies. Supervisors should train new staff members in the procedures for their area. (When the library has waited for weeks or sometimes months for the new person to start work, it is natural to focus on the main duties the person is to perform. The thinking is, "We will get to the minor areas and things later.") Certainly emergencies are not very common in the library and it is not unreasonable to wait a little while, as long as the subject does get covered. To be a new person on duty alone at the circulation desk for the first time and to have a telephone caller say, "There is a bomb in the library" and then hang up can be a frightening experience. Not knowing whom to call or what to do until help arrives adds to the stress. Knowing the emergency procedure will not eliminate the worry such a call creates, but it does help a staffer get through the situation more effectively.

Key Control

Key control is a chronic problem for any organization. Who has, who must have, who wants this or that key are administrative problems; they are also problems of status and ego. In the absence of a clear and enforced key control plan, the status and ego aspects tend to dominate. "May I borrow key X for a while?" is a common request. If someone does not keep track of who has each key and if the keys are, in fact, returned "in a while," there will be no control over the keys.

To control keys there needs to be single office and person to issue and collect keys or otherwise disable (electronic for example) access for a terminated person. Where that responsibility lies varies; three common units are the HR department, O&M (Operations and Maintenance), or the library administrative office. Having such a single source with the responsibility does not absolve supervisors from knowing which keys are held by which people in his or her unit (or who has swipe card access to what resources). Tom Teper (2003) reported that in a review of supervisors' knowledge of who held what keys, they could only account for 60 percent of the keys issued to their staff (p. 55). He made a crucial point about the problem that arises from poor key control:

> Over time, campus administrators became aware that unauthorized entry and access during non-operational hours and unnecessary access to some spaces affected not only the safety of physical properties and their contents, but also affected the safety of the individuals that worked with the facilities. (p. 54)

The latter point is important. Unfortunately, workplace violence is all too common in the United States and libraries have had their share of such occurrences. Often it is an unhappy ex-employee who has the means of access to the work area who causes the trouble. Being certain all the keys the individual had is only possible when there is a sound key control program in place. (Note: "key control" encompasses all forms of controlled access, not just what we think of as a "key.")

Almost every library has some form of internal key control, even if some other department makes and supplies the keys. A typical model is to have the supervisor submit an "access" request form to the administrative office that spells out the reason(s) the individual needs a key, or other means of access (e.g., pin number, key card, or biometric access). The office reviews the request and, if authorized, orders the appropriate form of access. In the case of a physical key, the person who is to receive the key signs for it and returns the key upon termination of employment or no longer needing such access. The truth of the matter is that the process is seldom as carefully carried out as is necessary for good security.

Check This Out

An example of a policy on key control and access worth reviewing is from the University Library at the University of Illinois at Urbana-Champaign: http://www.library.illinois.edu/administration/services/policies/keycon trol.html. The policy covers eligibility, responsibility for recovery upon separation from employment, and user responsibilities for lost or stolen keys.

One possibility for avoiding a "key" problem, somewhat expensive, but highly effective, is to install electronic locks. These locks allow the institution to issue a code number to each person who needs access to an area. The code number is also put into the lock. When a person needs to enter the area, he or she keys in a personal code number. Individually coded magnetic keycards are also often used as a replacement for physical keys. Today even biometric access (e.g., finger/palm print or eye scan) systems are becoming much less costly and may be worth the extra cost for areas such as special collections or archives.

What is especially good about these locks is that one can, using a special infrared scanner and printer, get a list of code numbers used by date and time. Because some staff members might share their code numbers with others, there is no unequivocal proof that a specific person entered the area, but there is no question about the fact someone did use that number. Locks of this type cost hundreds of dollars, so they are not suitable for all areas. However, they are worth serious consideration for certain areas: staff entrances, rooms with expensive equipment, and special collections.

Opening Routines

Opening and closing procedures for the library have a relationship to key control in the sense that some staff will need to have a number of keys to perform their duties. Also, there are times when other staff will have to substitute for a person who is sick, which can result in "borrowed" keys. Opening procedures are simple, but staff should follow the steps consistently and complete them *before* the public enters the library. While different libraries will have slightly different needs, three basic steps are part of any sound opening procedure.

The first step in the opening process should be turning on lights and checking the equipment. In setting up a regular route to follow when turning on the lights, try to include passing by all the areas where there is equipment. Obviously reporting any missing equipment is normal, but noting any unusual arrangement of furniture and equipment may also forestall a problem. Sometimes only part of a piece of equipment is missing.

Checking any coin-operated equipment is another important part of the opening routine. One of the authors experienced a situation where one of the public service staff discovered during her opening routine that all the photocopy coin boxes and change machines were open and empty. Sometime between midnight and 7:00 A.M. someone came into the library and managed to empty all the coin boxes. Unfortunately, this incident happened before an electronic lock had been purchased for the library. With such a lock, police could have checked on each code number used during the hours we were officially closed. The sooner an investigation starts, the better the chances are it will have a successful outcome. This is one reason why daily checking is so important.

Next, check the after-hours book return. Pick up the returned books, but also check for vandalism. Graffiti is an all-too-common occurrence in public areas of buildings. Book drops and the exterior walls of libraries receive their share of attention from the graffiti artists. As with all vandalism, the quicker the library addresses the issue the more likely vandalism will stop or decline in occurrence. (Many police departments recommend engaging in what they call "the battle of paint cans" to combat graffiti. This means painting over the graffiti as soon as it appears. Continue repainting, washing, or cleaning it up until the "artist" gives up.)

Opening a book drop can be an adventure; you never know what may walk, hop, crawl, or squirm out of the opening. Only the size of the book return's opening and people's (often children's) imagination limits the variety of living things you may encounter. Mice, toads, snakes, turtles, and other living things may startle you when you find them in the return, but they cause no significant harm. It is not living things that create the biggest problems. Liquids like oil, molasses, glues, and just plain water cause serious damage to the items in the return.

The worst form of book return vandalism is arson. Most of the time it is some newspaper or cloth stuck in the return, followed by a few lit matches. Fortunately, such cases usually result in attempted rather than actual arson because the paper or cloth does not catch on fire. The staff member should not simply log the incident, but also report it to the police, fire department, or the library's security service. Unsuccessful attempts frequently result in continued efforts until the arsonist succeeds. Serious arsonists often use a flammable liquid that assures a fire and results in costly repairs and replacements for the library. When the book return is inside the library, such fires can cause major damage. Many building codes now require such inside returns be a small fire rated room (four- or six-hour resistance), which is used solely for book return.

Closing Routines

Many complications exist for the closing routine, and it offers additional challenges for the staff because there are usually fewer staff members on duty and some users can be very reluctant to leave. Once a procedure has been set up, have the security department review it for overall safety. Late service hours and isolation make closing the library a little risky, so a knowledgeable public safety officer's review of the plan can help reduce the risks. Establish a written procedure so that anyone on duty can do the job, not just the regular closer. Unless the library is physically small, have three to four people involved in the closing process. There should be at least one person covering the exit to keep people from coming in and to see that those who leave take only their personal belongings and properly checked-out materials. Working in pairs is safest, but often there are not enough staff members to do this and still finish the process in 15 to 20 minutes. Working in pairs is essential if the library is in a high-crime area and especially where there is gang activity.

Users should get 10 to 15 minutes' notice that it is approaching closing time. At the official closing time library staff *must* go through the building turning off lights, and occasionally moving people out. After-hours conceal-ment is a problem in many libraries, which means the staff closing the library should check all the possible hiding places. The checking process needs to include restrooms, stairways, dark corners, and other places where things can go bump in the night. Staff also must know what to do or not do when they find someone in one of these places. Do they confront the person or call for assistance? One problem for public libraries is finding a child whose parent has not returned or sometimes has "forgotten" a child in the library. After clearing the building, activate any alarms and, if possible, lock the elevators at the main floor. If there are windows that are open, someone must close and lock them for the night.

For staff safety, having at least two people on duty for closing routines is the minimum a library should use. After closing, staff should leave together or call for an escort from the security or police department. Well-lighted walkways and parking areas for users and staff are also part of a sound security plan.

The day's cash receipts can pose a problem. Someone must be responsible for putting away the money. Too often there is no safe in the library, other than the vault in special collections. The result is that the cash box gets "hidden" in a lockable file drawer. Frequently the key to the drawer is in a nearby unlocked desk drawer. When staff start putting things (e.g., cash boxes) away early, the hiding places soon become common knowledge. Having a small safe for public services is a good idea and a reasonably modest investment. (Note: do not write down the combination and leave the information in a "safe place," or there will be no security.) Certainly in high-crime areas the return on invest-ment will be significant; better yet, find a way not to collect cash.

DISASTER PREPAREDNESS PLANNING

There seems to be no limit to what disasters lurk both internally and exter-nally for libraries. "They come in all shapes and sizes, from natural disasters (floods, hurricanes, and earthquakes) to emergencies resulting from an acci-dent (water pipe burst), deferred maintenance (leaking roof), negligence (fire or mold)" (http://www.nedcc.org/free-resources/dplan-the-online-disaster-planning-tool) and surprisingly perhaps, a combination of factors.

Deferred maintenance plays a role in far too many incidents today. We look at deferred maintenance in chapter 19 of the book; however, the concept is, in a very shorthand definition, "we know this should be repaired but there is no funding to do it. We will have to wait and hope nothing bad happens before there is money to correct the problem." That often works, for a while, but it eventually fails if too much time passes. It is, as our opening quota-tion suggests, courting something too long and the invitation will be accepted.

Having a plan for how to handle such situations will make a highly stress-ful event somewhat uncomfortable. One starting point for developing a plan for a disaster is dPlan™ from the Northeast Document Conservation Center (NDCC)—http://www.nedcc.org/free-resources/dplan-the-online-disaster-planning-tool. Unfortunately, there is no easy solution for the deferred main-tenance challenges.

Disaster recovery planning focuses on reducing the losses from a disaster and taking time to prepare. One reason it takes so long is that it must involve every department and ought to have wide staff involvement. In large organi-zations the library's plan must fit into the institution's comprehensive plan; this may require rethinking and rewriting parts of the plan. A small steering committee is essential to keep the work moving, and someone must take on the basically thankless task of writing and rewriting drafts of the plan. Some risk managers/insurance firms require they have a current copy on file. Keys to successful planning are:

- Assessing potential sources of emergencies (fire, bomb threats, floods, water pipes breaking, earthquakes, and occasionally major vandalism)
- Considering the difference in handling just a library disaster from one that is part of a larger local or regional problem
- Setting collection priorities (i.e., what is irreplaceable, what is expensive, but replaceable, what is easy to replace?)
- Determining insurance coverage and access to emergency funds; Does insurance include money for recovery? Can the disaster team leader have authorization to commit money to salvage work? Will cash be readily available?
- Preparing summary posters of the plan's steps and posting them in all staff areas
- Developing an emergency telephone tree and keeping the telephone num-bers up to date (A telephone tree is simply a listing of calls to make and their priority of placement. The tree's design is such that no person makes more than two or three telephone calls.)
- Writing up the plan, reviewing it internally, checking on its agreement with broader-based organization-wide disaster plans, and training the staff in its implementation, which should include a walk-through exercise
- Having floor plans in the document that clearly indicate the first-priority areas for salvage teams
- Collecting supplies for handling the various emergencies
- Having a list of service supply companies and experts that can assist in the recovery work as an appendix to the plan
- Setting up the disaster team, training them, and conducting practices
- Making certain fire and security personnel know where a copy of the plan is and whom to call first
- Having copies of the plan on- and off-site
- Sending team members to workshops and conducting in-house disaster handling programs to keep the staff up to date on developments in the field
- Conducting plan reviews with new employees and yearly plan update sessions for all employees

---

Check This Out

One article that provides the basic outline of a disaster manual and the questions addressed in each section is Sharon Holderman's "Be Prepared: Writing a Practical Disaster Manual" (*Library Leadership & Management* 26, no. 2, 2012: 1–6).

Probably the most common "disaster" in a library is water damage. Storms such as hurricanes and tornadoes can cause structural damage to a library and perhaps damage some of the collection. It is, however, the rain that accompanies these storms that causes the most damage. Most of the time water damage in the library results from an internal library problem. A broken water pipe, a ruptured sprinkler system, clogged toilet, or an air conditioner located on the roof that springs a leak during the one weekend of the year the library is not open (well, it only seems like that is when it happens) are common library water disasters. While such disasters seldom are worth even passing notice in the local newspaper, they still present the same recovery problems a major storm, flood, or fire would cause.

This is not the place to explore in detail the recovery process for water-damaged material. However, the Western Association for Art Conservation produced a brief, but comprehensive set of guidelines, which have been adapted into a Web page, Betty Walsh's "Salvage at a Glance" (http://cool.conservation-us.org/waac/wn/wn19/wn19-2/wn19-207.html).

Check This Out

Conservation OnLine (CoOL) at http://cool.conservation-us.org/ was founded in the late 1980s and is sponsored by the Foundation of the American Institute for Conservation. It is an exceptionally useful site for authoritative and current information on all aspects of disaster planning and recovery, as well as conservation and preservation topics in general.

Fire Protection

Despite their occasional malfunction, sprinklers in the library are the best fire protection. Properly installed and maintained, they provide a quick response to a fire while it is still small. More than 80 percent of all building fires are controllable by three or fewer sprinkler heads, assuming proper installation and maintenance. Yes, there will be water damage, but not as much as when the fire department turns on its fire hose. (A fire hose puts out 2,500 gallons of water per minute, compared to 100 gallons per minute for a typical sprinkler head.) If the sprinkler system is an older zoned type, where perhaps a quarter or a third of all the sprinklers go off at one time whenever one sprinkler responds to a fire, the damage can be much greater. Together, however, they still will not put out as much water as one fire hose.

Everyone working in public service should know how to handle a fire extinguisher and how to determine which extinguisher to use on a specific type of fire. There are extinguishers for combustible materials such as paper and wood (Type A), for electrical fires or flammable liquids (Type B), and for any type of fire (Type C). Comprehensive (Type C) extinguishers are the most expensive, but they eliminate worries about which unit to use. In an emergency, the fewer things the staff must worry about the better they will handle the situation. Most fire departments are willing to come to the library to teach people how to put out a fire with an extinguisher. A half-day fire safety workshop with fire extinguisher training is well worth the time lost from regular duties; annual updates and reviews are very useful.

Building Evacuation

Getting everyone out of the library in an emergency is *the* most important aspect of handling a disaster. Because public service staff members work in areas with or near users, they have the major responsibility for clearing the building of people in an emergency. The type of alarm system the library has (or does not have) will determine how hard or easy it will be to clear the building. Many libraries lack public address systems and must depend solely on a fire alarm system's signal. That signal may work well and be appropriate in a fire emergency, but is it good for a bomb threat or other non-fire situation that requires clearing the building? This becomes even more of a problem if the fire alarm system connects directly to the fire department. Another concern is whether or not one can hear the alarm in every location and office. Individual or group study rooms or audiovisual rooms are special problems. People using such rooms may be concentrating so hard (or have earphones turned up so high) that they do not hear the alarm even when it is audible in the room. What this means is that public service personnel must go through the library, almost like the closing procedure, to be certain everyone leaves.

There are two big differences between the closing routine and evacuating the building. The first obvious difference is that, in the emergency situation, speed is important. If the emergency situation arises during a period when there is full staffing, usually only at peak usage times, the process of clearing can go quickly, because there are enough staff members to go to the key areas at the same time. Problems can arise during low staffing periods (e.g., nights and weekends). Too often when a library conducts a practice evacuation, it is with a full staff. Libraries should plan for and practice both full and minimum staff evacuations.

The second difference from closing routines is that there may be more problems with people. An emergency can occur at any time, but the chances are it will not be just before closing time. This means people may not be ready or willing to leave, especially if they must leave their work behind. Convincing people that there is a problem and that it is important to leave quickly can be difficult. It is particularly difficult when the alarm system is not clearly audible and there is no real indication of a problem, such as the smell of smoke. Knowing how to handle the reluctant individual is a key to quickly clearing the building. Deciding under what circumstances people may or may not pack up their work takes careful planning with the assistance of public safety officials. Another issue that ought to be thought through with public safety officials is what to do about disabled individuals (both staff and users). This can be a challenge in multistory buildings because elevators are generally "off limits" in an emergency.

Earthquakes

Earthquake preparedness presents several special challenges for public services staff. One is in maintaining the collection stacks in a safe manner. As one begins to run out of shelf space, there is a tendency to look at shelving dust canopies (usually a lightweight metal cover) as extra shelving. Although not as strong as regular shelving material, dust canopies are usually capable of carrying the weight of one row of books. The danger comes from the fact that even a moderate earthquake can throw books in any direction because they are freestanding. A bound volume of *Newsweek* simply dropping from a height of eight feet (the usual height of open stack shelving) can cause an injury. Having it thrown off the dust canopy by a 5.5 to 6.5 Richter scale earthquake could cause a serious injury. The potential for injury is high enough in such an earthquake that there is no need to add to it by shelving materials in an unsafe manner. Even book ends can be an issue; "wire" book supports (those that hang from the bottom of a shelf) tend to allow more books to fall than book ends on the shelf, at least the ones with nonskid bases.

In countries and states where earthquakes are common, there are usually special building code requirements for library stack ranges and other storage units. Seismic bracing adds to the cost of installing shelving. Unfortunately, such bracing does not assure that shelving will not fall or twist out of shape; but it does provide better safety for people. This is because the linked ranges do not normally fall to the floor, but rather twist or lean over as a block and never completely collapse. Certainly, whatever is on the shelves will end up on the floor. Study tables or carrels, however, are likely to avoid being crushed by heavy steel or wood shelving. This is important because hiding under a table or desk gives people some protection during an earthquake.

Libraries in areas of high earthquake potential, especially in large urban areas, need to consider what type of supplies they should have on hand when a major quake does strike. Earthquake specialists suggest that any earthquake registering over 7.0 on the Richter scale occurring in an urban area will disrupt community services for about 72 hours. This means being without fire, police, or medical assistance for at least three days. Some libraries in earthquake-prone areas set up storage areas for food, water, basic first aid materials, and rescue equipment. One question facing libraries is whether to have sufficient food and water for three days for the normal work force, for all the staff, or for all staff and an estimated number of users trapped at the library. A second question is, who provides the money to pay for these supplies? For libraries in earthquake zones it is not a question of *if* it will happen, but only *when.*

From the Authors' Experience

There are certain areas of the country with active fault lines and earthquakes or tremors are common or, at the very least, are not completely unexpected. Imagine Saponaro's surprise when she was at the reference desk in College Park, Maryland, when an earthquake struck. As a native Californian, Saponaro had a good idea of what was happening during the event—while most of her coworkers were puzzled. Once the shaking stopped, the library was evacuated as a safety precaution.

The epicenter of the 5.8 quake occurred in central Virginia, roughly 100 miles from the library, in an area not known for seismic activity. However, the main campus library was closed for three days while staff addressed compromised standard and compact shelving units and free-standing bookshelves. Other campus branch libraries, namely Architecture and Art, also sustained damage to their shelving units. Over 27,000 books fell from the shelves from the main library alone, requiring the efforts of a number of library staff (Saponaro included) in sorting and reshelving so that materials could be returned to the shelves. For a review of how the Libraries addressed the event (and pictures), see: http://www.lib.umd.edu/news/2011/earthquake.

FEMA

After a major natural disaster strikes an area in the United States, it is often declared a federal disaster area. When that happens, FEMA teams come to the area. FEMA is the federal agency with the power to provide money to assist local jurisdictions in recovering from a disaster. There are two types of funds: loans to individuals and grants to local government agencies. A FEMA representative or team will assess the damage and prepare a Damage Survey Report (DSR). DSRs are the basis upon which FEMA determines reimbursement. The second step in the process is an "audit" by other FEMA staff, that is, a second survey. The second survey may approve, modify, or disapprove the first DSR. The last step is a later FEMA visit to determine what was done with FEMA funds. The overall objective of DSRs and recovery money is to return the location/person back to the same condition as prior to the disaster as soon as possible. There is considerable room for interpretation as to what constitutes the "same condition" and what it will cost to achieve. (See Oder, 2006, for a review of FEMA activities post Hurricane Katrina.)

FEMA personnel have a responsibility to assure that funds, which are not inexhaustible, go toward warranted recovery efforts. The goal of a representative of a local jurisdiction or "individual" in the case of private institutions is to secure as much of the disaster recovery costs as possible. While these are not mutually exclusive goals, it is clear there is plenty of opportunity for disagreement.

One way to reduce some of the uncertainty and conflict is to have good documentation. As the *Earthquake Preparedness Manual for California Libraries* suggests, "Write it down, log it, or photograph it" (1990, p. 22). Any photographs that are available showing pre- and post-disaster damage will be very useful in *assisting* the FEMA team as they make their determinations. (Note: FEMA does not pay on the basis of photographed damage. However, the library may not be at the top of a long list of sites the inspectors must visit and some clean-up activities are likely to be underway, if not completed, when the inspectors arrive. An example might be picking up and reshelving materials dislocated during the disaster.)

FEMA will reimburse for the cost of books and other collection items lost in a disaster, if they were in the library at the time and the library can provide author, title, or other documentation. If one has an online catalog and backup tapes are available, the documentation should be available. If all else fails, the library may be able to get some useful data from a service such as OCLC.

When it comes to earthquakes, most FEMA inspectors do not know about seismic specifications for shelving. For that matter, they are not familiar with the cost and complexity of library shelving. Having a copy of seismic standards for library shelving and/or a written cost estimate for replacement and repair from a library shelving vendor will help speed the process and reduce some of the conflict between inspector(s) and library staff. Another useful step is to have someone available from the department that maintains the library during the site inspections. As few, if any, staff members are architects or contractors, having a knowledgeable person available who can point out special structural issues is helpful.

TECHNOLOGICAL SECURITY

Technology has become a key component, if not the critical one, in providing quality library service. Libraries have more complex equipment than anytime in the past as well as have users who expect to have 24/7 access to library resources and services. Downloading and e-commerce are becoming "standard" services. All of this raises a variety of security issues for both the library and its users.

Technological security begins with risk analysis, just like all other library security concerns. When thinking about technology, there is sometimes a tendency only to think about equipment, but the library often has as much or more invested in its own databases and software as it does in hardware. (The safety of user information in the library system(s) is an increasing concern. Terrence Huwe [2005] in writing about security breaches, noted: "In the past year, there have been at least three similar incursions on various University of California campuses, some involving library patron records" [p. 31].) Risk analysis should cover at least three issues: value, dangers, and existing safeguards.

One can group library technology security issues into six broad categories—passwords, backups, viruses, hardware, data privacy, and legal. Staff members know that IT personnel seem to push the importance of passwords and the need to change them on a regular basis. However, few of us really appreciate the full significance of keeping passwords secure. Too often we share passwords with colleagues in our department so they are able to "check on" something when we are out of the office. When IT enforces the idea that you should have different passwords for different applications, as they should, there is tendency to create a list of passwords and "hide" it so we can consult it when necessary. The hiding place is also sometimes shared. Another pitfall to avoid is having a "core" element in the various passwords; yes, it helps us remember them, but it also makes it easier for the hacker to gain access to multiple applications. Anyone having authorized access to databases with user information must be very careful about their passwords.

Generally there is little need to worry about backing up the major library databases. Given their critical value to daily operations, the IT personnel make certain backing up is carried out on a regular basis (daily in most cases). The question is what about your files that are just stored on the local hard drive. When was the last time you backed them up? If you are like a lot of us, the answer is probably never. Certainly not every file is worth backing up. Ask yourself, "What would/will I lose if my hard drive crashes?" "Could I really accurately re-create the important files?" Backing up your critical files really is important and, just is the case with library-wide backups, it is a good idea to store the backup outside the workplace or via a cloud storage system.

Another area of concern is virus "infections." When purchasing anti-virus software, be certain it has the approval certification of the National Computer Security Association (NCSA) and provides for frequent updating. Some of the features that one should look for are signature-based scanning, heuristics-based scanning, memory-resident monitoring, and integrity checking. Of course, the best virus protection software is useless if you don't run it on a regular basis. Again, the main concern is for your PC, as there is usually library-wide virus/spyware programs in place that address network security, but as we sometimes learn our computer became infected because we failed to run a regular check.

Not all equipment and software is equally valuable or important. The old PC used by a volunteer to do some word processing is not as important or as vulnerable as a high-end machine located at the reference desk. Knowing the cost and importance helps in setting appropriate levels of security. Another part of determining the appropriate level is an assessment of what dangers exist for the item. (Beyond theft there are disk crashes, power outages, and "hackers" to consider.) Finally, assessing what safeguards already exist (or are possible) determines what more, if anything, needs to take place. (Here one can think in terms of protect, detect, prevent, and recover.)

Installing front-end security involves highly visible elements such as cables and perhaps motion detectors. Another element in front-end security is a secure menu system, which allows users access to features the library deems appropriate and disables those that may create problems. Back-end security protects data and applications. This type of security protects against hackers.

If the library's network is connected to the Internet, it is advisable to use a "firewall" to provide some protection for the library network. In essence, firewall software only allows "authorized" connections between outside systems and the library network. If the firewall is under the control of an agency outside the library (e.g., an academic campus network), there can be delays in getting access to a new Internet-based service. The firewall manager must make the appropriate changes in the firewall to allow the access.

As libraries expand their e-services, they face a number of privacy and legal considerations. Consider the implications when a computer is connected to the Internet and is available for public access. There is also the fact that library collects some data about each registered borrower and stores it in a database. Although no longer the case, in the past, libraries used the person's Social Security number as the identifying number—have all those numbers been deleted for long-time users? Hackers have been able to access user information from library databases (Kennedy, 2006).

Some individuals frequently use library computers for personal activities. Some examples are online shopping, bill paying, online banking, and even paying taxes. If the library has posted policies regarding user confidentially, people may assume they do not have to worry about using the computers. The postings should make it clear the library has no liability when a person uses the public computers for transactions that are not related to library services.

Libraries are engaging in more and more e-commerce which also raises privacy/data security challenges—online book sales (Gerding, 2007), payment for services such as downloads, document delivery, and overdue fines are some examples. All these activities call for staff to provide assistance to users from time to time. More importantly, it means protecting personal information is even more complex and essential.

Anytime a library provides wireless access, additional security/privacy challenges arise. Some libraries checkout wireless security cards to those who wish to use them. This will probably mean public service staff will need some understanding of how to configure the laptop to use the card for those who are unfamiliar with the process. Check out Bill Drew's Wireless Libraries blog (http://wirelesslibraries.blogspot.com/) for an ongoing discussion of wireless issues in libraries.

Library public service staff must understand and be on guard against "social engineering." (Social engineering has come to mean gaining unauthorized access to information or computer systems.) The process works so well because people generally assume others are honest and provide answers to apparently legitimate/harmless questions. Probably the most common ploy is to pretend to be someone needing to verify some personal information. The social engineer first builds a trust relationship and, with data gathered elsewhere, attempts to secure additional information that can help with identity theft. Although, as we noted earlier most ILS systems no longer employ user Social Security numbers; they do have address, telephone numbers, and occasionally e-mail addresses. "I'm calling for my sick mother (or whoever) to verify you have her current address" may or may not be a legitimate call. Samuel Thompson (2006) provided some excellent suggestions for preventing social engineers form succeeding:

- Be suspicious of unsolicited communications asking for people or operational information.
- Never give out passwords no matter who claims to be calling.
- Never provide user information to anyone except when the requestor comes in and presents proper identification.
- Inform supervisors or authorities, if you have any doubts about a request for user information.
- Document and report suspicious communications. (pp. 224–225)

Another factor to keep in mind is one we mentioned in chapter 11, that of a person attaching a device that captures keystroke information.

BUGS AND OTHER NASTY THINGS

Turning to another type of problem, why is it that so many libraries try to prevent people from bringing food and drinks into the building? Perhaps an enlargement of an illustration of a cockroach with a message such as "If you do not want to share your library space with me, leave your food and drinks outside" would reduce the staff's time spent in trying to enforce a no food and drink policy. Unfortunately even with completely successful enforcement of such a rule, insects can still be a problem. Book collections, by themselves, represent a fine gourmet feast for several types of insects (book lice, book-worms, silverfish, firebrats, cockroaches, and termites). These insects account for 95 percent of insect damage to libraries and their collections. Fungus also presents a challenge for public services personnel. Uncontrolled food and drink will, in time, allow insects to share user spaces.

Insects

Book lice love to eat starch in almost any form; library paste is the main source in libraries. These pinhead-sized, gray-white insects prefer dark and somewhat damp conditions. While thousands of lice can reside in a single musty book, overall they really don't do that much damage. Their presence, however, is a clear signal that all is not well with the environmental control system. Of all the problem insects, this is the group most likely to be seen. In fact, anyone who is a frequent book user has seen them. (You may not have known what it was, but that faint quick movement on the page you thought you saw when you opened a book was probably a book-louse trying to scurry to safety in the book's gutter.) Keeping the temperature and humidity at the recommended level (70 degrees Fahrenheit and 55% humidity) is the best method of controlling book lice.

Bookworms are even more destructive. These are actually the larvae of bee-tles; there are over 160 species. Adults burrow through covers or the edge of textblocks and lay their eggs in the pages. The hatched larvae feed on the pages. Their excrement resembles a fine dust that cannot be easily differenti-ated from normal dust. However, if some shelves seem more dusty than nor-mal, especially under the books, open some of the books. If pages are stuck together, there is probably a bookworm problem. When the larvae feed, they secrete a glue-like substance that causes pages to stick together. Good climate control can help prevent the problem, but, once it has arisen, professional help is the best way to resolve an existing problem.

Silverfish and firebrats enjoy late-night dinners or at least eating in the dark. Firebrats prefer hot and dry conditions, while a cool and moist environ-ment is ideal for silverfish. Pages that look like lacework or the work of a Chi-nese papercutter probably are the result of these insects. Seeing one silverfish or firebrat usually means a major infestation because they normally come out only when it is dark. They are long living by insect standards (two to three years) as well as tough, being able to exist four to five months without food or water. Because they attack the inside of books, the first sign of trouble will be small dark lumps (feces) on the shelves, which shelvers may notice when shifting materials.

Cockroaches feed on almost anything: paper, cloth, or leather. Some can even exist inside electronic equipment. A problem with cockroaches requires regular visits from a professional exterminator service. Cockroaches are resilient and seem at times to be immune to insecticides. Like many problem insects, they prefer to move about in the dark unless the population is large, when some risk moving about in the light. Not only are they destructive, but they also can transmit diseases. An early warning sign of cockroach problems is discoloration of shelves, furniture, and cabinets. Cockroaches secrete a dark liquid that discolors surfaces across which they crawl.

Termites attack wood and wood products. Books and other paper materials on steel shelving are fairly safe as long as new additions to the collection, especially gifts, are screened. Naturally, they can be very destructive to the building and furniture. As with most insect damage, termite damage occurs inside the material and the surface offers few clues that a problem exists. Although primarily tropical and subtropical insects, they do exist in areas with extended periods of damp heat. Again, their eradication requires professional services.

What can be done? Circulation staff, especially shelvers, needs training in identifying signs of insect damage. Make it clear that the reason for having no food and drink in the library is to help reduce the possibility or level of cockroach and other insect problems. Emphasize the fact that cockroaches can transmit diseases. Maintaining sanitary conditions is the best insurance against cockroaches and other insects. Naturally, keeping the temperature and humidity in balance and at the recommended levels for libraries creates conditions that discourage insects. When signs of trouble do appear, set some traps, especially glueboards. This will help establish the areas and degree of trouble. While small insect outbreaks may be suitable for in-house treatment, if there is any doubt, call in the experts and do not wait too long to make the call. If the library staff try treatment on its own, it is better to use a bulb applicator rather than spraying. Powders are longer lasting, do not stain materials, provide a more precise application, *and* afford less danger of inhaling the poisons. To be effective the material must be highly toxic, and improper handling can lead to real trouble. Whenever possible leave this work to those trained to do it safely, even if this means waiting a little longer to solve the problem.

When you encounter infected or infested books, isolate them in sealed plastic bags. Freezing the material for a week usually solves the insect problem. A few people suggest that keeping the material 60 seconds in a microwave oven on high will also do the job. Be aware, however, that heat ages paper. If the materials are worth saving, send them for professional treatment rather than attempting in-house cures.

Recently, libraries have had to address another insect that does not actually affect the collections but is very much a "people issue"—bedbugs. Bruce E. Massis and Angel Gondek (2011) published an article on the latest bug issue for libraries. They reported several libraries had to close down for bedbug extermination work. It seems people still like to read in bed and elsewhere that bedbugs reside and the critters decide to travel around community in library collection items. The authors report library staff noted the bugs on chairs in their children's area and called in the exterminator. It is as the authors concluded, "from a library perspective, any sign of bedbugs must be attended to immediately so that the infestation does not spread further" (p. 380).

Check These Out

In December 2012, the *New York Times* ran an article about bed bugs in libraries by Catherine Saint Louis entitled "A Dark and Itchy Night" (December 6: D1)—mentioning an episode that occurred earlier that year at the University of Washington Libraries. The University of Washington Libraries responded to the article via a page on its library Web site, as a means of answering any lingering questions about the bed bug incident: http://www.lib.washington.edu/about/news/announcements/uw-libra ries-and-bed-bugs.

Fungus

Fungus is another problem that increases when environmental control is poor. Damp, warm conditions not only encourage insects but also speed up the growth of molds and mildew. Anyone living in tropical or subtropical areas knows the situation is normal and deals with it on a daily basis. Elsewhere, people often don't worry about the problem, but anytime there are damp conditions the problem can arise. After a fire or water leak, molds and mildews can grow on anything that got wet. Information about this aspect of the fungi problem can be found in many sources about library conservation.

Another concern is for human health (see Rogers, 2001: *American Libraries*, 2006; *ILA Reporter*, 2008). Three basic factors influence the level of health danger. The first factor is the concentration of fungi spores in a specific area; as the concentration raises so do risks to health. The second is that the environmental conditions that lead to increased spore production (warmth and moisture) also enhance the chances of health problems. Finally, there is the level of personal susceptibility, which varies from person to person. For a few unfortunate individuals even small concentrations of fungi spores in a relatively cool environment can cause an illness. At the other end of the susceptibility spectrum are those individuals who never seem to get sick. In between there are the majority of staff members, who can and will get sick if the spore count becomes too high.

Almost all of the health problems resulting from fungi will be of an allergic nature. Some can be mycotic (disabling) and a very few toxic (fatal). Rhinitis (asthma) is a fairly common allergic reaction in workers in libraries: they are allergic to book dust. By itself this reaction is not fatal, but it can cause severe discomfort (dry coughing, wheezing, and shortness of breath) and it will also complicate other pulmonary disease problems. Most of the fatal reactions to fungi are the result of ingesting the spores as food (mushrooms) or with food. It is possible to transfer spores from your hands to your food and then eat them.

We will only mention a few examples of fungi found in libraries that, under *some* circumstances, can cause health problems. *Aspergillus fumagatus* can cause pulmonary aspergillosis. *Aspergillus niger* could cause ear infections. *Geotrichum candidum* may cause geotrichosis, which can take the form of an oral, intestinal, bronchial, or pulmonary infection. Certain strains of *Pricillum* can cause pericillosis, which affects the bronchial and pulmonary functions. It is also a possible cause of some eye, ear, and urinary tract infections.

Good air filtering systems will help control spore levels, but the best control is maintaining proper temperature and humidity. Good housekeeping and sanitary practices further reduce the potential for trouble. We point out these potential health issues not to frighten people or raise undue concern, but rather to emphasize that control of fungi in the library does have implications beyond a little mildew on a few books.

COLLECTION SAFETY

Certainly the topics we covered earlier can affect the safety of the collections. They also are people concerns as well. In this section we look at issues that apply to collection items and that carry no people safety aspects. In chapter 6, we discussed the issues of damage and theft of material, especially in the absence of copying equipment. We briefly mentioned theft detection systems. We explore these systems in more depth in this section.

Electronic theft detection systems have been available since the mid-1960s. Today they are in general use in all types of libraries. The purpose of these systems is to reduce theft and other types of unauthorized removal of library materials, such as the user or library director who innocently forgets to check out material. These systems, which operate on the principles of electromagnetism, or radio frequency, are generally effective, and they are the single best deterrent to library material loss. To determine whether a library has a theft problem, one can use inventorying and sampling techniques. Theft detection systems are available from several commercial vendors.

The systems operate by placing a sensitized element, called a *trigger, tag,* or *target,* in library items. When staff check materials out, they deactivate the target with a special piece of equipment or pass the item around the detection system and the borrower exits through the detection system normally. When a user does not properly check out material, a sensing unit installed near the exit doors detects the sensitized target and an alarm sounds (or a light flashes). The sensing unit can detect sensitized targets even in concealed material.

Libraries with a theft detection system will have a policy outlining the procedures to follow when the system activates. Because the person detected is in a sensitive situation and because of possible legal consequences, circulation staff must be careful not to accuse someone of theft and must strictly follow library policy and routine.

Several problems may result from the presence of a theft detection system. In large collections, there are often not enough human or financial resources to target all materials, so it must be done selectively. Generally, this means the more expensive, hard-to-replace, or most used titles. Even items that are targeted or tagged may not always activate the system, and savvy thieves may remove targets from items. There are some materials that should not be placed in or near a desensitizing or sensitizing unit. Some magnetic detection systems, for example, can damage audiotapes and videotapes if they are placed in or very near the sensitizing unit. To prevent these accidents, staff must be aware of the dangers inherent in the system used by the library. Some libraries report that mutilation of materials increases after the theft detection unit is installed.

While most libraries that have implemented an RFID technology use high frequency (HF), a public library in Michigan was the first to launch ultra-high frequency (UHF) RFID system in 2012. The UHF RFID can automate book returns, check out several books at once, provide a security gate that identifies items, and more (*American Libraries*, 2013.)

Check These Out

Lori Bowen Ayre authored an issue of *Library Technology Reports* devoted to the concept of RFID (2012, 48, no. 5). Two articles in that issue include "RFID Costs, Benefits, and ROI" (pp. 17–19) and "RFID Standards" (pp. 20–26).

Ayre also discussed "The RFID Opportunity" in *American Libraries* (2012, 43, nos. 9/10: 17).

From the Authors' Experience

We all know change is inevitable in personal and work life. There are a few occasions when a change has unexpected consequences and even a substantial dollar cost.

Evans had such an experience in terms of RFID and energy savings. The library's parent organization decided to go green, as much as possible, in its energy consumption. To that end, the facilities department decided to switch out all florescent lighting with new energy efficient "tubes."

It was several months later before staff realized the RFID security system was not actually functioning although it was turned on. More months passed with repeated visits from the RFID company service "rep" trying to determine what the problem was. Eventually, and after a great deal of "finger pointing" between the company and the facilities department, it was determined that the ballasts (the unit that fires up the florescent tubes) and the RFID system operated on the identical radio frequency. As long as the lights over the gate system were off, the system worked. Lights on, the system did not work. Since staff and users really could not work in the dark, some solution was necessary.

At the end of the day a new model RFID system solved the problem, but at a cost of over $30,000, not counting service calls and facilities staff time. Close to a year passed between the new lights and a once again working RFID system. We had no clear idea how much material "walked" during that time. We know users were aware the system was inoperative, as we tried to implement gate monitors who inspected backpacks and large handbags. Gate monitors are not always effective for a variety of reasons.

Good Housekeeping and the Stacks

Public service personnel have the greatest impact on the condition, and often the survival, of library materials. Good handling practice among staff prevents damage by those who most often handle library materials. Staff members also model the handling of books and materials for library users; be that model good or bad. If the staff member checking out a book treats it roughly, borrowers will, consciously or unconsciously, learn to devalue the book and treat it in a similar manner. If shelving is sloppy, with materials stuffed in helter-skelter, with books leaning so loosely they warp, with volumes falling off shelves or off overloaded and unbalanced book carts, the users' attitude toward library materials will reflect what they observe.

Good housekeeping includes the proper (not damaging) removal and replacement of volumes to a shelf—that is, don't pull one off the shelf by its "headband" (the top of the spine). Squeezing "just one more" item into already tightly shelved set of volumes can damage several volumes, not just the one being forced in. Items that are not vertical for long periods will weaken the binding—straightening up shelves is not just about having things look neat. Staff training in the foundations of good book handling habits becomes the basis for a good model. People have a tendency to become sloppy with any repetitive task; setting a good example, good training, and follow-up supervision are the best ways to overcome this tendency. User education is another means to avoid damage to library materials. Besides library staff setting a good example, such things as providing thin, non-harmful bookmarks, signage that informs users of situations dangerous to library materials, and well-publicized information about library problems may all be of help. A CD-ROM or DVD melted in the sun is often used in public libraries for this purpose, sometimes with a lot of creativity.

Check This Out

Among the materials available from the Northeast Document Conservation Center Web site is a series of preservation leaflets. One of particular use in the area of "good housekeeping" is *Storage Methods and Handling Practices* (http://tinyurl.com/pdccnnu).

PEOPLE SAFETY

Libraries are, by their very mission, people welcoming. That was not always the case during the early years of libraries existence, but today most libraries—public or private—allow access to the public. Certainly there are libraries where that access is very limited but possible under certain conditions. Being a welcoming organization does create some challenges in terms of safety and security. We look at several aspects of people safety in this section.

We touched some of the legal aspects of users in the library in chapter 13 (legal issues). Here we look at some other aspects that are legal in a sense and also people's feelings about safety/security when in the library. While there are some differences between publicly and privately funds libraries, they are slight (e.g., privately funded libraries have somewhat more latitude in defining who may enter and under what conditions).

There is an important legal decision from the early 1990s, *Kreimer v. Bureau of Police* (958 F.2d 1242 [1992]) that has set and continues to set the limits regarding public access to libraries. Grayson Barber (2012) began his article recounting the lasting impact of the case with the following that points to the long-term significance of the decision: "A homeless man's lawsuit against a public library went to federal court 20 years ago, leaving a legacy of constitutional law that balances the rights of library customers against the responsibilities of library administrators" (p. 89). You won't be surprised to learn, like many other court decisions, what the Kreimer means for library access is "complicated."

The key facts of the Kreimer decision are: there is now a constitutional right (First Amendment) for individuals to receive information from libraries, and a library may infringe on that right by expelling a person from the library. However, and it is big however, a library may legally remove a person should that person violates publicly posted library behavior policies. Naturally, there are several caveats to that principle—"prominently posted" is an important phrase and having those policies posted just on the library's Web site will seldom pass legal muster. Most importantly, the "rules" must not have intentional or unintentional discriminatory elements. The person being expelled must have the right to appeal the expulsion decision ("due process").

Some facts to keep in mind as part of the legacy and that affect the safety/security atmosphere of a library related to why the library repeatedly expelled Mr. Kreimer. Essentially, although he did use library resources, the library had him removed by the police based on appearance, behavior ("staring at people"), sleeping, and body odor. (We listed a few later cases where lawsuits have been filed based of one or more of those issues in the Suggested Readings at the end of this chapter.) It is a challenge to include such factors in a policy and not discriminate against those who are not fortunate enough to have a regular home. The key is behavior—yes, appearance or status—no. Even that can be tricky—using words such as annoy/annoying in a policy is problematic and it is open to interpretation. What annoys one person may not bother many other people.

The balancing of the needs of all users is challenging as is the enforcement of behavior policies once they are vetted by legal counsel and approved by governing bodies. This is an area where labels should matter. In management speak, a policy serves a "guide" to thinking about what to do or not do in a situation; a rule sets forward what will or will not be done in a situation (no leeway). Thus, it might be best to post the rules of behavior rather than the behavior policies. Variations in staff interpretations and decisions of what should happen are an open invitation for lawsuits.

Children and Library Safety

All types of libraries, except special libraries and a few specialized research libraries (e.g., the Huntington) must expect a greater or smaller percentage of their visitors to be children. As noted in chapter 13, the issue of "latchkey children" has been a major challenge for public and academic libraries. Whatever steps the library takes to control this problem, one step is absolutely necessary to prevent even greater problems: have clear policies and a plan of action reviewed by the legal counsel for the library or parent institution. Some of the options that exist in various jurisdictions are:

- To have academic libraries bar children without parental supervision
- To offer special programs designed for such children
- To have policies of requiring staff to call child welfare services or police to pick up any unattended child at closing time
- To have policies of allowing staff to contact police/security when a child is left unattended for a specified period of time during normal school hours

Rules need to be posted in prominent locations, especially at public entrances, and provided to parents when a child is given a library card. Another important element is not to make it appear that the library assumes any childcare responsibility.

Crime in the Library

Generally libraries are very safe, but as public facilities anyone can come in. Robert Doyle noted that in 2005, public libraries had 1.3 billion visitors and only a tiny fraction of those visitors caused a problem (2006, p. 15). However, from the theft of unattended items to trespassing to assault, libraries can and do experience crime. As a result, public services staff must be ready to react appropriately. Table 16.1 is a list of the most common crimes that occur in the library.

The vast majority of public libraries, as well as others, have written and posted policies regarding access and what is acceptable behavior. They also should have guidelines for when the staff should call the police as well as provide training in handling disruptive situations. Doyle suggested seven situations (2006, p. 16) that should result in a call for assistance:

- When a person threatens to or engages in physical harm to a user or employee
- When a person threatens to or damages physical property whether the library's or a user's
- When a person refuses to leave the library after being asked to do so
- When a person sells, uses, or possesses illegal drugs or is intoxicated
- When a person views or prints pornographic material on a library or personal computer while in the library
- When there is a missing or abandoned child in the library
- When a person engages in public indecent acts

TABLE 16.1 Crimes in the Library

1.	Intentional book damage	11.	Drug use by staff or patron
2.	Book theft	12.	Drug sale by staff or patron
3.	Reference material stolen	13.	Verbal abuse to patron
4.	Equipment stolen	14.	Verbal abuse to staff
5.	Other thefts	15.	Indecent exposure
6.	Vandalism outside the building	16.	Assault on patron
7.	Vandalism inside the building	17.	Assault on staff
8.	Vandalism of patron's car	18.	Arson
9.	Vandalism of staff cars	19.	Trespassing
10.	Vandalism of equipment	20.	Disorderly or menacing conduct

If you think about each of these, you can imagine many variations when assistance might not be needed as well as other situations not listed that could be very serious without assistance. That is why training and guidelines are so important.

Four categories of people commit the majority of library crimes. Regular users are usually the source of most of the deliberate damage done to books and library property. Unfortunately, many of the thefts are done by staff members (anyone who has a work-related reason to enter the library). This includes security staff, maintenance personnel, and even some contract maintenance and repair people. Professional thieves seldom bother with libraries; when they do, they usually steal valuable books, bookplates, and occasionally equipment—although theft of purses, briefcases, and other personal belongings of the staff and public is probably the result of at least semi-professional thieves. Most of the disruptive behavior, vandalism in and outside the library and breaking into cars of users and staff are usually acts of individuals who do not use the library.

One form of crime seldom reported because it is difficult to detect is skimming. Whenever an organization collects cash, the opportunity for theft is present. Coin-operated photocopiers, microform reader-printers, and networked printers are services that can generate significant amounts of money. In moderately busy libraries a single photocopier, at $0.10 per copy, can generate from $22,000 to $28,000 per year. That amount may approach the salary of a full-time staff member. Certainly, there are ways to control or monitor use and income, but they are complex and require checks and balances. If the library collects fines and other fees, using a numbered duplicate receipt system is the first step in monitoring the process. That is, one receipt is for the person paying the fee and the second remains in the library as a record of monies received. With each set of receipts serially numbered, there is a way of checking on missing numbers. Using a cash register or recording receipts in an automated circulation system also provides some control. No system is foolproof, but most staff members are honest and such systems help trustworthy people stay honest.

PROBLEM USERS

As we noted earlier, staff need to have policies/rules regarding acceptable behavior and know when to call for backup help. Disruptive behavior is a problem all public service staff experience at one time or another. It is especially disconcerting when it comes from a fellow staff member. With a colleague, however, one usually has a baseline for judging what is wrong. With the public there is less basis for knowing what is wrong and what to expect. Unfortunately, today the behavior may be drug related; this applies to all types of libraries, even those in middle schools.

When does unusual or strange behavior become disruptive? Every library must decide the answer to that question. (For example, an increasing percentage of homeless or street people in the United States are individuals who, in the past, would have been hospitalized and on medication. Most of them are harmless, but without their medication, their behavior can be erratic and often disruptive.) Certainly, you cannot call security every time someone exhibits slightly different behavior. Like the boy who cried wolf, you might not get help when it is truly necessary. Workshops conducted by professionals specializing in human behavior and substance abuse can help prepare the staff to handle such problems safely. They also help set up reasonable guidelines for when to call for assistance. Also helpful is training from specialists in mental health. After training, the policy guidelines should be written down for later consultation when the need arises.

One type of disruptive behavior is the user who becomes verbally abusive about a library issue, such as a fine or policy. How much verbal abuse must one tolerate? Frank De Rosa (1980) commented:

> People in all areas of public service, and librarians in particular, seem resigned to the opinion that abuse from their public is inescapable and there is not much they can do about it. Much of this misconception is due to the fact that many people do not realize the point when disruptive behavior becomes antisocial behavior and when antisocial behavior becomes criminal behavior. (p. 29)

Defusing Anger

There are three types of abusive users that staff will encounter at some time: upset, angry, and disruptive. Some of the individuals will be focused on a library service concern; others will upset about some non-library issue and directing their feelings toward either or both the staff and other users.

The first level, and most common, is the confused or upset person. With these individuals, as is true for the other levels, attentive listening is the starting point. Asking for additional information is often helpful: "Tell me more," "I do not quite understand, please tell me about . . ." Paraphrasing the person's comments indicates that you are listening to their concern. It is not a good practice to make the response a personal choice (such as "I wish I could . . ."); it is better to respond in terms of library policy and practice. Your focus should be on determining what the situation is and keeping the event from escalating while maintaining library policy so that it does not become a personal matter between the user and staff member.

Level two (anger) is more complex and less common. Angry people can exhibit one of three categories of anger: controlled, expressed, and irrational. Occasionally the person who appears confused is really in a state of controlled anger. A sensible approach is to assume that anyone with a complaint is at a controlled anger level. If you make this assumption and follow the appropriate steps, you have a better chance of keeping the situation under control. The best approach is to:

- Rephrase/paraphrase the person's statement of concern
- Always treat the person with respect and his or her concern as important
- Clearly state the service's position on the concern, once the nature of the concern is fully understood

or

- Present firmly and clearly the possible consequences of action contrary to the position of the service

When you rephrase the person's statement, use your own words; do not "parrot" their comments. Key elements in restating are to treat the user as an equal, not use professional jargon, and mirror the user's vocabulary. By paraphrasing, the person has an opportunity to clarify any misunderstanding. It also indicates you are trying to understand the situation. Using phrases that equate the library as the "authority" and the person as "subordinate" is likely to escalate the situation. Use of jargon and/or complex terms and words may confuse and offend the person.

Another element in displaying respect for the person is to acknowledge the emotion(s) the person feels regarding the situation. This does not mean agreeing with the user regarding what the person wants; rather, it lets the individual know there is respect for the individual and the goal is to find a satisfactory solution.

If the matter is one of library policy, explain it from the library perspective and what the limits are on what can be done immediately. Keep the explanations in the third person. Making it appear as if "I" can in fact do something or as if "I" am responsible for the problem often leads to greater confrontation. In many cases, less explanation is better.

An alternative approach, if the situation appears to be escalating, is to outline the possible consequences if the person persists; however, take care not to threaten. Telling a person what may or will happen is very different from delivering an ultimatum. What this does is allow the person to make a decision with a full awareness of the possible outcomes. While this step may make the person angrier, the demonstration of concern and respect for the person's rational decision-making capability more often than not leads to a successful resolution.

When the person is uncontrollably angry, begin by acknowledging the person's anger while being ready to call for backup help. As with controlled anger, the goal is validation and understanding the anger and feelings.

At the same time, be certain to identify the problem; rephrasing the concern allows the person to verify that there is or is not agreement concerning the nature of the problem. When it is not a library issue, get backup assistance.

If it is a library operation matter, explain how the person's behavior affects you and others in the area. By focusing on the behavior and its affect, the focus is kept off the person. Saying "this behavior . . ." rather than saying "you" may make the person less defensive and consequently easier to handle. When doing this, it is better to avoid sweeping generalities about the behavior's impact. Personalizing the effects leaves little room for the angry person to argue, especially if it has already been acknowledged that the anger is a justifiable feeling.

The first step is to allow the person to vent the emotions. If possible have the "conversation" away from the public area, but not isolated from other staff, you have no way of knowing what might happen. Although it is not enjoyable to listen to someone "rant and rave," there is a better chance of resolving the situation by first letting the person release some of the anger. A person who is irrationally angry will not be very likely to hear anything until he or she has "had his or her say." Being patient and listening for clues as to what is the issue is difficult but essential in such situations. There is little point in a long explanation or in apologizing unless it is clear there was an obvious library error. All too often it is necessary in such situations to use direct confrontation. "Your behavior is disruptive to our work (and perhaps to other people here). If you do not stop, then we must . . ." (call the security office/police for example). Try to present the statement in an unemotional manner. The statement sets clear limits and states what the consequences will be but leaves it to the angry person to decide what to do. To summarize, when dealing with an upset user:

- Listen first, watching for nonverbal clues as to the emotional state of the person.
- Rephrase the person's concern in order to clarify the issue.
- Maintain an unemotional state, if possible.
- Acknowledge the emotions and do not try to calm the person just in order to be comfortable. The goal is to find a solution.
- Being defensive usually does not help resolve the situation.
- State clearly the options and consequences in institutional rather than personal terms and, if possible, allow the user to decide which option to take.

We know dealing with irate people is neither comfortable nor easy. It is something you get better at with training. Having an opportunity to practice conflict-management skills in a workshop environment is very useful for frontline staff as well as supervisors and senior staff. Knowing and using conflict-management skills are two very different things. Staff members, who work shifts that have limited or minimal staffing, should be the first to receive training and practice; they have fewer backup resources available if disruptive behavior arises.

Check These Out

The following are useful books to read as well as being a "recommended reading" assignment for new public service staff members regarding "difficult people:"

Library-Specific

Mark Willis's *Dealing with Difficult People in the Library* (2nd ed., Chicago: American Library Association, 2011).

Mosely, Shelley E., Dennis C. Tucker, and Sandra Van Winkle. *Crash Course in Dealing with Difficult Library Customers* (Santa Barbara, CA: Libraries Unlimited, 2014).

Rhea Joyce Rubin's *Defusing the Angry Patron* (2nd ed., New York: Neal-Schuman Publishers, 2011).

Any Environment

Harvard Business School's *Dealing with Difficult People* (Boston, MA: Harvard Business School Press, 2005).

Karen Mannering's *Dealing with Difficult People* (London: Hodder Education, 2008).

Kevin Fauteux's *Defusing Angry People: Practical Tools for Handling Bullying, Threats, and Violence* (Far Hills, NJ: New Horizon Press, 2011).

Renee Evenson's *Powerful Phrases for Dealing with Difficult People: Over 325 Ready-To-Use Words and Phrases for Working with Challenging Personalities* (New York: AMACOM, 2013).

CLOSING THOUGHTS

Library security is everyone's business. Time, effort, and money spent monitoring the library and replacing lost materials means less money for new materials, services, or equipment. Antisocial behavior can lead to fewer people being willing to come to the library; and that, in turn, could lead to fewer people being willing to fund library programs. Preparing for disasters takes time and practice, but, if that effort pays off in preventing even one injury, it is worthwhile. Knowing how to handle wet library materials properly and quickly can save the library thousands of dollars and perhaps some valuable cultural material. It takes a team effort to plan for such problems, to develop appropriate policies, and to execute the policies and procedures when needed.

When a disaster strikes or a security problem comes up, all staff members should know what to do and know that they do have the authority to act. There should be no hierarchy of decision making at the moment a problem comes up. All staff should be well trained and involved in regular disaster-handling drills and fire safety updates.

Chapter Review Material

1. What are the major elements of a security plan?
2. Who are some of the important constituents or collaborators you should consult when developing a risk assessment plan?
3. Outline the steps in a safe closing routine.
4. What are the key elements in having an effective disaster plan?
5. Why is it important to maintain a no food or drink policy in the public areas of a library?
6. What are some of the security issues associated with library technology?
7. What is social engineering and why is it a critical issue for library staff?
8. What are some the most significant crime problems in libraries?
9. What are the steps in diffusing anger in a disruptive patron?
10. What are some of the guidelines for when to call for assistance when you face disruptive behavior?

REFERENCES

American Libraries. 2006. "Mold-Affected Missouri Library Reopens." 37, no. 9: 11.

American Libraries. 2013. "Case Study: Innovative Materials Handling." 44, nos. 1/2: 85.

Barber, Grayson. 2012. "The Legacy: Kreimer v. Bureau of Police, Twenty Years Later." *Library & Archival Security* 25, no. 1: 89–94.

California Library Association, Earthquake Relief Grant Ad Hoc Committee. 1990. *Earthquake Preparedness Manual for California Libraries.* Sacramento, CA: California Library Association.

Cooley, Mason. 2000. *Aphorisms of the All-too-Human.* New York: Ragged Edge Press.

De Rosa, Frank J. 1980. "The Disruptive Patron." *Library & Archival Security* 3, nos. 3/4: 29–37.

Doyle, Robert P. 2006. "Libraries as Sanctuaries for Criminals?" *ILA Reporter* 24, no. 6: 12–17.

Farrugia, Sarah. 2002. "A Dangerous Occupation? Violence in Public Libraries." *New Library World* 103, no. 9: 309–319.

Gerding, Stephanie. 2007. "Online Book Sales for Libraries." *Public Libraries* 46, no. 1: 32–35.

Harwell, Jonathan H. 2014. "Library Security Gates: Effectiveness and Current Practice." *Journal of Access Services* 11, no. 2: 53–65.

Huwe, Terrence. 2005. "New Technology's Surprising Security Threats," *Computers in Libraries* 25, no. 2: 30–32.

ILA Reporter. 2008. "Mold Hits University of Illinois Rare Book Library." 26, no. 2: 17.

Kennedy, Shirley Duglin. 2006. "I've Been Violated." *Information Today* 23, no. 6: 17–18, 20.

LLAMA BES Safety & Security of Library Buildings Committee. 2010. *Library Security Guidelines Document.* Chicago: American Library Association. http://

www.ala.org/llama/sites/ala.org.llama/files/content/publications/LibrarySecurityGuide.pdf.

Massis, Bruce E., and Angel Gondek. 2011. "What's New in Libraries: Bedbugs in Our US Libraries." *New Library World* 112, nos. 7/8: 377–381.

Mobley, R. Keith. 2011. "What Is Risk Management?" *Uptime* June/July: 40–41.

Muir, Scott E. 2011. "Security Issues with Community Users in an Urban University Library." *Library Leadership & Management* 25, no. 2: 1–12.

Oder, Norman. 2006. "How'd You Come Out?" *Library Journal* 131, no. 10: 38–41.

Rogers, Michael. 2001. "Toxic Mold Forces Library Closure." *Library Journal* 126, no. 17: 16.

Teper, Tom. 2003. "Re-Establishing Key Control as a Security Measure." *Library & Archival Security* 18, no. 1: 53–61.

Thompson, Samuel T. 2006. "Helping the Hacker?" *Information Technology and Libraries* 25, no. 4: 222–225.

Yi, Myongho. 2011. "Balanced Security Controls for 21st Century Libraries." *Libraries & Archival Security* 24, no. 1: 39–45.

SUGGESTED READINGS

Alire, Camila. 2000. *Library Disaster Planning and Recovery*. New York: Neal-Schuman Publishers, Inc. (Note: Although dated, this is still a useful manual on the topic.)

Barstow, Sandra. 2010. "Library Security after the Renovation: How Much Is Enough?" *Library & Archival Security* 23, no. 1: 37–48.

Calzonetti, Jo Ann, and Victor Fleischer. 2011. "Don't Count on Luck, Be Prepared: Ten Lessons Learned from the 'Great Flood' at the University of Akron's Science and Technology Library." *College & Research Libraries News* 72, no. 2: 82–85.

Fansler, Craig, and Ellen Daugman. 2013. "Developing a Continuity of Operations Plan." *North Carolina Libraries* 71, no. 2: 17–26.

Gleason, Diana. 2013. "Can I Bring My Gun? A Fifty-State Survey of Firearm Laws Impacting Policies Prohibiting Handguns in Public Libraries." *Public Library Quarterly* 32, no. 4: 275–301.

Goldberg, Beverly. 2014. "Taking Aim at the Reality of Guns in Libraries." *American Libraries* 45, nos. 1/2: 16–17.

Graham, Warren D. 2012. *The Black Belt Librarian: Real-World Safety & Security*. Chicago: American Library Association.

Halsted, Deborah D., Shari Clifton, and Daniel T. Wilson. 2014. *Library as Safe Haven: Disaster Planning, Response, and Recovery: A How-to-Do-It Manual for Librarians*. Chicago: ALA Neal Schuman.

Harris, Jamey L., and Scott R. DiMarco. 2010. "Locking Down a University Library: How to Keep People Safe in a Crisis: A Mansfield University of Pennsylvania Perspective." *Library & Archival Security* 23, no. 1: 27–36.

Horava, Tony. 2014. "Risk Taking in Academic Libraries: The Implications of Prospect Theory." *Library Leadership & Management* 28, no. 2: 1–13.

Kaaland, Christie. 2011. "Proactive Advocacy: 'Emergency Preparedness' for the School Library." *School Library Monthly* 27, no. 4: 49–51.

Kahn, Miriam B. 2008. *The Library Security and Safety Guide to Prevention, Planning, and Response*. Chicago: American Library Association.

Kahn, Miriam B. 2012. *Disaster Response and Planning for Libraries*. 3rd ed. Chicago: American Library Association.

Kelley, Michael. 2013. "No Guns in the Library." *Library Journal* 138, no. 1: 8.

Levine, Capron Hannay, and Bryan M. Carson. 2012. "Legally Speaking—Loss Prevention and Insurance." *Against the Grain* 24, no. 4: 63–65.

McHale, Nina. 2011. "Who Says I Have to Wear Shoes in the Library?" *Colorado Libraries* 35, no. 4: 1–2.

Murvosh, Marta. 2013. "Don't Let the Book Bugs Bite." *Library Journal* 138, no. 12: 430.

Raffensperger, Thomas Edgar. 2010. "Safety and Security in Urban Academic Libraries: A Risk Assessment Approach to Emergency Preparedness." *Urban Library Journal* 16, no. 1. Online. http://ojs.gc.cuny.edu/index.php/urbanlibrary/article/view/1252.

Rockefeller, Elsworth, and Rollie Welch. 2012. "Seven Nasty Things Guys May Bring to the Library." *Voice of Youth Advocates* 34, no. 6: 574–575.

Sanders, Mark. 2012. "Creating a Safe Haven for University Students: How Are We Doing?" *Journal of Access Services* 9, no. 4: 200–211.

Todaro, Julie Beth. 2009. *Emergency Preparedness for Libraries*. Lanham, MD: Government Institutes.

Weihs, Jean. 2013. "Unusual Security Problems and Plain Greed." *Technicalities* 33, no. 3: 15–17.

Zimerman, Martin. 2009. "The Dangers of Malware in a Library Computing Environment." *The Electronic Library* 29, no. 1: 5–19.

Assessment

The authors love assessment and evaluation, and we believe it should be integrated into all aspects of library programming. There. It's been said. Reaching that point in our relationship with assessment and evaluation has definitely had its ups and downs, and we still struggle with it.
—*Claire Hamasu and Betsy Kelly, 2013*

Most of us may not love accountability, assessment, evaluation, and outcomes, but like it or not we know we must live with them and do them on an ongoing basis.
—*G. Edward Evans, 2014*

Assessment is a cycle; its purpose is improvement; its application is local. The cycle of assessment can be described simply as listening to the patron (collecting information), analyzing the implications of what we hear, and improving based on the input.
—*Jeanne M. Brown, 2010*

Most teacher-librarians know that what they do improves student achievement and research supports this. . . . However, it is easy for an administrator to dismiss these studies by saying, "I need evidence in *my* school."
—*Pamela K. Kramer and Linda Diekman, 2010*

Claire Hamasu and Betsy Kelly's opening quotation, at least the final sentence about ups and downs, probably reflects the thoughts of most library staff members about assessment and evaluation. Although both concepts have a long history in library practice, the situation has changed. What has changed is the importance of both concepts, along with accountability and outcomes, in terms of a library's viability.

Libraries have been evaluating their services for at least 100 years by collecting statistics on the inputs and outputs relating to services delivered. This data includes statistics such as the number of reference questions answered, the number of items checked out, the number of information literacy sessions delivered, and the number of ILLs obtained for library patrons and loaned to other libraries. Essentially the thought was "more is better;" if the numbers increased, all was well. Only when the numbers declined was there a search for what happened. Such efforts were and are useful to a point, but are no longer adequate to address the concerns of funding agencies as well as the general public.

Today, parent organization administrators, federal, state, and local governmental authorities, users, and the general public are demanding that institutions be accountable. They want evidence of value for monies provided ("evidence in *my* school" notion). Libraries are attempting to address the accountability challenge through new and more purposeful assessments that go far beyond quantifying inputs and outputs. For much of the twentieth century, large libraries, and academic libraries in general, were often viewed by funding agencies as "black holes," absorbing ever greater quantities of money and little evidence of positive outcomes. What agencies now want is evidence, or to use a business term, ROI (return on investment).

The trend calling for increased accountability is driven by economic pressures on all funding agencies. That in turn has led to greater concern about the outcomes of all expenditures. The 1993 federal Government Performance and Results Act (P.L. 103–62) required annual progress reports from every government agency toward achieving performance goals and being accountable. This has affected publicly funded state and local libraries. Major foundations are also requiring greater accountability for how their funds are used. Some state libraries, for example, Florida's, expect that libraries submit grant proposals to use outcome assessments as a measure of accountability. The Institute of Museums and Library Services (IMLS, http://www.imls.gov), through grants and awards, also encourages the adoption of outcome-based evaluation in both libraries and museums.

As Virginia Cairns noted, "Librarians sometimes have difficulty quantifying the value of the services and resources we provide our constituencies" (2006, p. 1). A major reason for this chapter is the fact that public service's daily activities are critical in terms of outcomes for the library. That, in turn, has important implications for library support from funding agencies and other interested people. Thus, as a public service staff member you will play a role in many assessment activities, even when you are not aware of that fact.

KEY CONCEPTS

There are several terms to keep in mind when thinking about assessment—accountability, assessment, authority, outcomes, and responsibility. Although each term has a special meaning, in the workplace they are interlinked.

Accountability is a rather complex concept in the work world. Essentially each level of the organization is accountable to some broader/higher/outside body; no one escapes being accountable to one or more people or bodies. Staff members are accountable to their supervisors for what they do, or don't do, as well as how well they do what they do. At the same time the supervisors are accountable to senior library leaders for everything that takes place in their units. By the same token, the senior leaders are accountable to all library stakeholders (governing board, general public, etc.) for everything the library does and doesn't do. The point to keep in mind is that accountability is individual in character, not group based.

Authority and responsibility are linked to accountability in the following manner. All three have an individual basis in a sense. A supervisor may delegate some *authority* to a staff member to do certain activities without checking with the supervisor—in essence the supervisor gives up some of his or her authority to the staff member. In accepting that authority, the staff member tacitly, or openly, accepts *responsibility* for carrying out the activity. He or she is also accountable for how the activity gets carried out. At the same time, that person's supervisor is also responsible and accountable for the person's performance to those higher up the chain of accountability. Essentially, a person may delegate authority but never the final responsibility or accountability.

The manner in which accountability, responsibility, and authority are monitored in organizations is through assessments and outcomes. *Assessment* involves the documenting of observed, reported, or otherwise quantified changes in activities on the basis of outcomes. That is, what were the outcomes of doing the activity—positive or negative? A person, a unit, or a library is accountable for performance results.

Outcomes are the end result of the use of the library's resources (time, money, and effort) in terms of its mission and goals. Library stakeholders want *evidence* that there were positive outcomes as a result of such expenditures (look back at the opening quotation from Kramer and Diekman for an example). For example, a school media center may have provided access to *x* number of databases. The principal is likely to ask for evidence of how the students benefited educationally from that accessibility. One important reason for such requests is the principal will be asked the same question by the school board. Other types of libraries face similar requirements. Coming up with suitable methods for identifying and assessing valid outcomes has been and remains a challenge for libraries.

REASONS FOR DOING ASSESSMENTS

In the preceding discussion, we emphasized the demands of outside library stakeholders as the driving force behind the library's need to demonstrate accountability and positive outcomes. It is certainly true those demands have been important; however, it is equally true that there has always been a need for libraries to be efficient and effective. Evaluation and outcomes are useful in becoming more efficient and effective even without outside pressures to do so. They can be particularly useful in developing library goals and objectives. Thus, it is both a matter of internal and external pressures that are or should be driving library assessment and outcomes.

Initially, libraries undertook evaluation of their services for internal reasons. They wanted to use the information gathered from evaluation to improve library efficiency or effectiveness. Internally, the increasing complexity and cost of library operations, along with increasing demand for services, requires good information for planning and decision-making purposes. Managers need objective, standardized data on which to make decisions. Assessments help managers allocate resources and plan their operations and services, and to make better decisions in general. The data also helps to assess the success of new programs and services. Carol Weiss (1982) described a number of decisions influenced by such internal uses of evaluation data (pp. 244–245):

- *To continue a program.* For example, should a middle school library continue purchasing extensively in the field of mathematics if the material is rarely used?
- *To institute similar programs elsewhere.* Should a public library expand the practice of filtering all public terminals to all its branch libraries, or just to those with no separate children's room?
- *To improve practices and procedures.* How can corporate library staff improve their recall rates for online searching, for example, without overloading company researchers with irrelevant citations?
- *To add, drop, or change specific program strategies and techniques.* Should an academic library expand its evening hours when requested to do so by the sophomore student government?
- *To allocate resources among competing programs.* Should the budget allocation for books be reduced in order to increase the amount spent on online databases?
- *To accept or reject a program approach or theory.* Would students be more likely to read and view reserve materials available in a digital reserve system than they are through the traditional service?

A further reason for libraries to undertake evaluations of their programs is to publicize their worth to the public. Libraries and library staff have generally done a less-than-stellar job of educating their publics about the library's contributions to society. Elliott Shore, executive director of the Association of Research Libraries (ARL), delivered a clarion call in a 2013 assessment conference keynote address, titled "The Role of the Library in the Transformative Higher Education Environment: Or Fitting Our Measures to Our Goals." In it, he challenged the library assessment community to radically change the measures it collects and uses. He proposed that libraries shift their assessment focus from description to prediction, from inputs to outputs, from quantity to quality (Groves, 2013, n.p.). Joan Durrance and Karen Fisher (2005) stated the issue succinctly by noting: "The truth is that librarians have failed to explain to those outside the field what contributions they and their institutions actually make to society at large" (p. 4). Experts, legislators, and decision makers often don't understand the vital role libraries play in supporting learning and developing an informed citizenry.

Valerie Gross, CEO of Howard County Public Library and *Library Journal*'s 2013 Library of the Year, said her library system defines everything about system in what she calls "words that work," concepts that are brief, understandable, clear, and simple for the 282,000 residents of Howard County. "We trade traditional library lingo that tends to minimize our value for powerful, value-enhanced terminology that people outside the profession understand,"

Gross explained, adding, "This instantly conveys our true worth, and requires no further explanation" (Berry, 2013, p. 30).

TOOLS THAT AID IN ASSESSMENT EFFORTS

There are a variety of techniques and tools that help the library gather *evidence* about its services that can help in demonstrating its vital role in supporting its service community's needs and activities. Some are the long-standing input/output data collected by libraries; others involve the users. Many are tailored to the specific library; others are broader in their focus to the state/regional/national levels.

Check These Out

The following are very useful to review when beginning an assessment project:

LLAMA Measurement, Assessment, and Evaluation Section (MAES)
http://www.ala.org/llama/sections/maes
A section of the Library Leadership and Management Association (LLAMA), a division of the American Library Association.

ACRL Value of Academic Libraries
http://www.acrl.ala.org/value/?page_id=39
An initiative from the Association of College and Research Libraries (ACRL), a division of the American Library Association. Includes a link to a listing of related assessment resources.

Library Assessment
http://libraryassessment.info/?p=1122
A blog for and by librarians interested in library assessment, evaluation, and improvement supported by the Association of Research Libraries.

A shift to looking in more detail at user experiences began in the 1980s. Interest went beyond using internal library data alone and involving users in the assessment process. Focusing on the user was hardly a new concept in libraries. Techniques such as user surveys were commonly employed to gain a picture of user satisfaction with service quality. The number of these user studies increased greatly in the 1990s. The increasing use of information technology to compile and share data gave rise to the use of benchmarking as a means to judge quality based on comparison of output data with that of carefully selected institutions.

One definition of outcomes is offered by the IMLS:

Learning represents knowledge, attitudes, skills, and behaviors that support individual success in our complex world—in short, outcomes.

Outcomes allow us to know something about the extent to which we have (or haven't) reached our audiences. Information about outcomes allows us to strengthen our services. Equally important, it communicates the value of museums and libraries to the broadest spectrum of those to whom we account. Without data, it's been said, "you're just another guy with an opinion." (http://www.imls.gov/applicants/outcome_based_evaluations.aspx)

The last sentence in this IMLS definition is important. Libraries continue to measure inputs and outputs, both to assess their programs and services and to benchmark their outputs against peer institutions as a measure of quality, but they now try also to relate these and other measures to user benefits.

Keep in mind that libraries should and do collect both qualitative and quantitative data for internal and external purposes. Most of the following techniques can generate either type of data and often, in the best circumstances, both during one project.

Surveys

Surveys or questionnaires are probably the data-gathering methodologies most familiar to library staff. Although most library staff are not trained in survey methodology, such as instrument design, sample selection, and statistical analysis, it is easy to find examples in the library literature of surveys conducted by all types of libraries. Survey instruments may be administered via the Web, mailed, e-mailed, or distributed in person to library patrons. A survey can reach more people than interviews and focus groups, for example, and provides a more valid and reliable statistical sample. Questionnaires can also be administered on a pretest/posttest basis to measure outcomes. This latter application is often seen as part of Web-based tutorials to measure the effect of information literacy instruction.

Interviews

Data gathering via interviews involves an interviewer asking questions of one or more individuals, usually one participant at a time. The questions are predetermined so as to limit data to the questions or areas being evaluated. Interviewing has gained increased popularity as library staff members have become more familiar with focus group methodology.

Focus Groups

Used since the 1920s, focus groups are a form of group interviewing. They involve open-ended, in-depth discussions with small groups, usually between 6 and 10 individuals. The participants are purposely selected and led (ideally) by a trained facilitator, although resources do not always make this possible. The groups explore a predefined topic in a nonthreatening and semistructured setting, and the goal is to obtain data about a single topic or limited range of topics. The entire group answers questions together (Walden, 2006, p. 222).

Focus groups are often used to determine users' perceptions of library programs and to explore the reasons behind their satisfaction, dissatisfaction, new services, and so forth. While focus groups can provide a rich source of qualitative data about library services, the methodology is labor intensive and that limits its wider use in libraries. Focus groups are frequently used in conjunction with surveys to gather both qualitative and quantitative data about an issue.

Observation

Observation of user and staff behavior has been a popular data-gathering method since at least the 1960s. One popular method, called unobtrusive observation, involves someone (referred to in the business world as a "secret shopper") posing as a user seeking some assistance from the library staff and then judging the quality of the staff's response. Reference question content is carefully prepared and tested to insure consistency and the answers are judged against predetermined answers. Some libraries have used extensive observation programs, including videotaping, to assess service behavior. However, observation is most commonly used informally by managers seeking quick information about library operations.

Citation Analysis

The citations of student papers are sometimes analyzed to assess the use of higher-level references. This is often used to measure the outcomes of information literacy presentations, especially if compared with the papers of students who did not receive information literacy instruction. The papers of students receiving instruction often show more scholarly resources, less reliance on the Web, fewer incomplete citations, and higher grades from instructors.

Transaction Log Analysis

Looking at the records of patron OPAC searches reveals mistakes patrons make in using the catalog, and unsuccessful searches. One of the most common mistakes revealed by transaction log analysis is misspellings. This information can be used to improve the OPAC (such as including spell checkers and "do you mean" prompts) and suggests frequently searched authors, titles, and subjects for purchasing decisions. The library's ILS (Integrated Library System) can generate a wealth of data about usage of library services that will assist in assessment activities.

Logs, Diaries, and Journals

Users are sometimes asked to keep a record of their information-searching practices in order to allow library staff to discover barriers to the search process. Web log analysis also provides valuable assessment information. The results allow staff to design programs to help improve patrons' searching experience. For example, Web sites may be redesigned to allow easier access to resources and services. This process may also ask patrons to reflect on their research experience as it progresses and report on how well they are coping with the process.

Think-Aloud Protocol

Related to logs and diaries, this method asks participants to articulate their experiences into a recorder while accomplishing a particular task. The recordings are later transcribed for analysis.

From the Authors' Experience

Sinwell provided this example of how several assessment methods could be combined in one project:

> In the mid-1990's, just as PC's were becoming prolific in libraries and databases were entering the research world, we did a few studies of student use of databases. We wanted to use the assessment outcomes to improve our instruction, i.e., how to teach students to do the most effective searching.
> One study was observational. With student approval we would watch them search databases as they aimed to find information on their topic. The other study was one-on-one interview with student as he/she did research. (Ruth Kifer, one of our advisory board members, was author of that study.)

> Today, Northern Virginia Community College is querying students about what they learned immediately after an instructional session and using that to improve teaching techniques; they are also partnering with instructors on English assignments to measure whether or not an instructional session had an impact on student success on research paper/assignment.

Standardized Assessment Instruments

General, widely disseminated tests like the National Survey of Student Engagement (NSSE) and the College Senior Survey (CSS) are examples of national assessment tools. Some of the questions asked on these assessments are relevant to library support of student learning. For example, the 2014 Cooperative Institutional Research Program's *Your First College Year Survey* (YFCY), administered to freshmen, included the question: "Please rate your satisfaction with this institution on each of the aspects of college life listed below: Library facilities and services" (http://www.heri.ucla.edu/PDFs/surveyAdmin /YFCY/2014YFCYInstrument.pdf). Library staff can use these test results to see if student satisfaction improves over time, and to see how student ratings of facilities and services compare with those of peer institutions.

Another national library specific tool is LibQUAL⁺® (http://www.libqual .org/). This is an assessment tool developed jointly by the ARL and Texas A&M University to measure user satisfaction in libraries. The assessment is based exclusively on users' opinions of service quality, gathered via a Web-based survey. The survey utilizes "gap analysis" to identify shortfalls that may exist between the level of services received and the level expected. Libraries have found LibQUAL⁺® to be particularly useful in that the results can be used to identify specific changes to make in specific services.

What a library decides to assess should be based on the goals and objectives of the individual library. Many libraries design their own assessments, especially survey instruments, to measure their effectiveness. Staff should design these assessments to inform library personnel, students, institutional members, and external constituents of the strengths and weaknesses of the program and the progress being made toward quality outcomes. Locally developed tests need to be checked for reliability and validity.

From the Advisory Board

Jean Wallace shared the following about assessments: "The above last sentence is important in terms of the school environment. The national achievement tests used by schools used to include some library-type questions, but they were not well constructed. I remember one, in the days of the old card catalog, which asked to student to identify the card pictured as a title card or author card or subject card. Not a good question! I wanted my students to know that all three areas were searchable, but I didn't care if they could identify the cards themselves.

Benchmarking

Benchmarking is an example of an assessment tool that can be local, regional, or national in character. The technique involves assessing one or more organizational operations such as preparing a purchase order. Benchmarking can be regionally done or even nationally depending on the objective of the assessment—best practice, best in class, comparative data, and so on. For example, a parent organization might want to compare the cost of preparing such a document in each of the units within it with an objective of identifying "best practices" and groups of similar organizations might wish to compare data for such an activity. Often a comparison library, or libraries, is chosen based on the perceived high quality of the library's resources and services, which the library doing the benchmarking wishes to aspire to. This allows a library to evaluate its own operations based on the perceived "best practices" of the comparison library or group.

Gathering data to do benchmarking studies used to be a time-consuming task, but for public and academic libraries, Web-based comparison tools make the task much easier. Data from the annual *Public Libraries Survey* is made available at the IMLS Web site (http://www.imls.gov/research/public_libraries_in_the_united_states_survey.aspx). The database allows library staff to choose a comparison library, or libraries, based on one or more variables such as city, state, collection size, or income per capita. Data from more than 9,000 libraries is included in the database. Staff can then compare their own library's inputs and outputs, such as operating revenue, FTE staff, collection size, reference transactions per capita, children's program attendance per 1,000 population, and so forth.

From the Authors' Experience

Evans employed benchmarking to improve resources and services for his library in advance of an impending visit by a regional accrediting agency. He used academic library Web sites for libraries considered "comparable" to his to compare his library's staffing, collection size, and budget per FTE student, and others. The comparisons showed the library's staffing and collections budget to be far below the mean for the other institutions. These data helped convince the college to adopt a multiyear plan to increase staffing and collections budgets to the mean level of the other institutions (and earned a commendation from the accrediting agency).

Check These Out

The following items provide some in-depth looks at some of the assessment methods covered in the main text:

Focus Groups

Hill, Jennifer C., and Christine Patterson. 2013. "Assessment from a Distance: A Case Study Implementing Focus Groups at an Online Library." *College & Undergraduate Libraries* 20, nos. 3/4: 399–413.

Marshall, Joanne Gard, et al. 2013. "The Value of Library and Information Services in Patient Care: Results of a Multisite Study." *Journal of the Medical Library Association* 101, no. 1: 38–46.

Observation

Fox, Robert, and Ameet Doshi. 2013. "Longitudinal Assessment of 'User-Driven' Library Commons Spaces." *Evidence Based Library & Information Practice* 8, no. 2: 85–95.

Long, Dallas. 2014. "Assessment and Evaluation Methods for Access Services." *Journal of Access Services* 11, no. 3: 206–217.

Surveys

Schachter, Debbie. 2014. "Measuring Value Using Research Results and Learning Outcomes." *Information Outlook* 18, no. 2: 26–30.

Stouffer, Christine, and Ertin Umit. 2013. "Survey Savvy." *AALL Spectrum* 17, no. 4: 21–24.

Benchmarking

Blowers, Helene. 2012. "Benchmarking Your Technology Edge." *Computers in Libraries* 32, no. 5: 26–28.

Hill, Rebecca. 2012. "All Aboard!" *School Library Journal* 58, no. 4: 26–30.

National Assessment Tool Report for an Institution

LibQUAL+ Santa Clara University http://www.scu.edu/library/info/assessment/libqual/execsummary.cfm

Voorbij, Henk. 2012. "The Use of LibQUAL+ by European Research Libraries." *Performance Measurement and Metrics* 13, no.3: 154–168.

Additional reports are available on the LibQUAL+® Web site—http://www.libqual.org/publications.

OUTCOMES

Outcomes were defined by the 1998 report of the Task Force on Academic Library Outcomes Assessment as "the ways in which library users are changed as a result of their contact with the library's resources and programs" (ACRL, 1988, n.p.). Satisfaction on the part of a user is an outcome; so is dissatisfaction. The Task Force considered simple satisfaction a facile outcome, however, too often unrelated to more substantial outcomes that hew more closely to the missions of libraries and the institutions they serve. The important outcomes of an academic library program involve the answers to questions like these:

- Is the academic performance of students improved through their contact with the library?
- By using the library, do students improve their chances of having a successful career?
- Are undergraduates who used the library more likely to succeed in graduate school?
- Does the library's bibliographic instruction program result in a high level of "information literacy" among students?
- As a result of collaboration with the library's staff, are faculty members more likely to view use of the library as an integral part of their courses?
- Are students who use the library more likely to lead fuller and more satisfying lives?

Questions like these are difficult to answer. That is to say, empirically rigorous measurement of library outcomes is hard to do. The Task Force firmly posited that it is *changes in library users* such as the ones addressed in these questions that comprise the outcomes with which academic, or other, librarians should be concerned. It may be that these outcomes cannot be demonstrated rigorously, or in a short period of time, or even by many institutions.

The Task Force believed that they can be measured, however, and their relationship to resource inputs and program inputs can be meaningfully determined through careful and lengthy research.

Good outcome measures are based on specific library objectives and help determine if these objectives have been achieved. They are not only concerned with how much library patrons like a particular service or resource, but how much it benefited them. An important part of successfully using outcomes to ascertain the impact of resources and services is planning. Before embarking on outcomes measurement, library staff should develop an assessment plan that identifies what changes in patron skills, values, and perceptions the library wishes to produce. These should then be expressed as outcomes. The plan should also articulate the measures that will be used to determine if the outcomes have been achieved. This assessment plan should not be static, but should evolve and change to reflect modifications based on the extent to which the assessment reveals progress, or lack of it, toward the desired outcomes.

Academic Libraries

For colleges and universities, the primary impetus for assessing outcomes is changes in the criteria regional accrediting agencies employ to evaluate the quality of educational institutions since the early 1990s. The accrediting agencies have incorporated increased accountability into their standards in the form of evidence of the effectiveness of student learning. Before the 1990s accrediting agencies based their evaluations on the assumption that an educational institution's quality of outcomes was directly related to the amount and quality of institutional inputs. Today accrediting associations are more concerned with evidence of a library's effects on its users. For example, the Western Association of Schools and Colleges (WASC), one of the six regional accrediting associations in the United States, revised its accreditation standards in 2012. Questions in some form like the following are now commonplace, "To what extent does the institution provide an environment that is actively conducive to study and learning, where library, information resources, and co-curricular programs actively support student learning?" Coming up with suitable answers to such questions can be a challenge.

External constituencies, including segments of the public such as the business community and funding authorities, have become skeptical of the social model that higher education benefits individuals directly and society indirectly. They are looking for evidence that higher education is adequately preparing students for careers and to participate in society. An economic model that demands evidence of a return on investment is now prevalent. This produces pressure on the institution as a whole, and the library in particular in the case of information literacy, to assess the positive impact they have on student learning.

Public Libraries

Public libraries, too, moved toward outcomes assessment as local governments have demanded accountability from public agencies. Prescriptive national standards have been replaced by locally developed effectiveness plans that focus on user services. Public libraries are increasingly using user surveys to inform planning and to assess the effectiveness of and improve their services.

In the case of public libraries, Sheila Intner and Elizabeth Futas (1994) addressed accountability as follows: "Public money supports public libraries. Members of the public are held accountable in their own lives for their actions, including spending money, so they expect the same from their institutions. And this is right and proper. As citizens we want to know where our money goes, how it gets there, and what it buys. We hold government officials accountable for how tax money is collected, contracted, and consumed. Libraries need to show how their expenditures of tax dollars benefit the public" (p. 410).

The Public Library Association (PLA) addresses outcomes in its *Strategic Planning for Results* (Nelson, 2008). While useful for measuring productivity and the success of efforts to attract users, the outputs do not assess the library's effect on its users. Some of the potential assessment topics are:

Basic literacy
Business and career information
Library commons (A public area for people to meet and interact with others, such as discussing community issues)
Community referral
Consumer information
Cultural awareness
Formal learning support
General reference service
Government information and access
Lifelong learning support
Local history and genealogy

An example of how output measures may be used to assess several of these service responses can be found in the study *Counting on Results: New Tools for Outcome-Based Evaluation of Public Libraries* (Lance et al., 2001).

School Libraries

School libraries and media centers are also feeling pressure to document the value of the library's program to parents, faculty, and administrators. As noted by Debbie Abilock, "Whereas once school librarians would ask *whether* evaluating students was appropriate to their role, now many are intent on learning *how* and *which* evaluations and assessments to use, as well as *what* to assess and *why*, and feeling less satisfied with their final decisions" (2007, p. 9).

From the Advisory Board

Jean Wallace noted that it is difficult to come up with a plan for evaluating a school library program when there is such diversity in the school libraries themselves. In suburban Chicago, there are large, well-funded schools with

> multiple librarians and library clerks. In much of downstate Illinois, there is one librarian who probably started as a classroom teacher, and who may have a clerk, often part-time. The librarian may want to evaluate the program, but the demands of basic services—selection, processing, consulting with classroom teachers and offering classes for their students or coordinating materials for the teachers' projects—take so much time and energy that there's not much time left. At Clinton, Illinois, the four unit librarians presented the administration with reports from magazines about the effectiveness of library programs, but we saw little response in our own situations. The woman who replaced Wallace as junior high librarian was, after three or four years, was given responsibility for both the high school and junior high libraries when the high school librarian retired. Wallace's advice to her was to relax as they had now officially made the job impossible.

In spring of 2013, American Library Association president, Maureen Sullivan expressed concern about current and future challenges facing school libraries. In a blog post, she echoed what had already been stated in ALA's 2013 *State of America's Libraries* report, noting, "I am concerned that school administrators may not fully understand the critical role school libraries and their librarians play in fostering academic achievement and student success in a technology-driven world" (Sullivan, April 15, 2013). She suggests assessment data should provide school officials, who are making decisions about this valuable resource:

- How students are developing skills to find accurate and reliable information to solve problems and make decisions that has been identified as an essential twenty-first century skill
- How librarians demonstrate their vital role in teaching essential skills of inquiry, critical thinking, digital citizenship, and technology
- How librarians help students meet the new Common Core standards

Sullivan concluded her essay by noting, "School librarians make a significant difference in student achievement and their work is a critical component of the success of all of our children." This statement should be the overarching goal all school libraries assessment strive to meet.

Another factor guiding assessment in schools is the No Child Left Behind Act, (NCLB, 2001, P.L. 107–110). NCLB ties federal K–12 educational support to schools meeting national and state content standards. Each state is required to implement a comprehensive accountability system aligned with its curriculum and covering all students in the public schools.

The American Association of School Librarians (AASL) offers several documents that outline services and goals for school library media centers (http://www.ala.org/aasl/standards-guidelines). As of late 2014, some of the tools provided by AASL include:

- *Empowering Learners: Guidelines for School Library Programs*
- *A Planning Guide for Empowering Learners with School Library Program Assessment Rubric*

- *A 21st-Century Approach to School Librarian Evaluation*
- *Library Spaces for 21st-Century Learners: A Planning Guide for Creating New School Library Concepts*

Given the expanding role of school library media centers in student learning, the effectiveness of a school's information literacy instruction in the states' accountability systems assumes increased importance. School library media centers in a number of states are responding to this imperative by evaluating how their programs and services positively affect student learning in their schools. Inputs like staffing levels and budget allocation and outputs such as collection size and currency, the number of hours open, number of networked computers available, and the amount of time spent on information literacy instruction are being correlated with learning measures like students' SAT scores. As you might imagine, positive correlations are being found between student learning measures and stronger library programs. Links to descriptions of a number of these state assessment efforts may be found on the *School Libraries Impact Studies* Web page from Library Research Service (http://www.lrs.org/impact.php).

From the Advisory Board

Advisory board member Sari Warren shared the following thoughts: "Fairfax County Public School librarians are using LRIS to track a number of resources—number of students, teachers and parents that they assist, number of classes they teach, how many people come in for checkout, what types of lessons are being taught and what critical thinking skills are being focused on during lessons, uses of the library for other things. This data is going to be compiled and shared to show the impact that the school librarians have in the school."

She noted it was interesting to read this section and realize that what they are doing was exactly what is mentioned above.

Special Libraries

Special libraries, too, are called on to prove their value to their parent organizations. As with academic, school, and public libraries, special libraries have long relied upon analysis of inputs and outputs to judge their effectiveness and efficiency. With the increasing strain on library resources and increasing demand for specialized levels of service, coupled with competition from other sources (e.g., Google), outcomes assessment as a means for demonstrating a library's value to the parent organization is gaining popularity. Because outcome measures focus on the impact of the library on the parent organization and its members, they are seen as a good way to demonstrate a library's value.

One method of assessment that is more prominent in special libraries than other types of libraries is calculating a return on investment (ROI). (We will discuss ROI in more detail in chapter 18.) This may be especially true in for-profit institutions. The benefits from using the library are identified by the clients, and the costs for providing library services are known from the library's budget. The preparation of the cost-benefit analysis allows the library to prepare an estimate of the library's ROI. Depending on the approach taken, ROI calculations range from 2.5:1 to 28:1 (the value of benefits compared with the costs of the library).

Check These Out

Once it is gathered and analyzed, data needs to be reported. While standard tables and charts are one method of doing so, reports with more visual appeal can have a greater impact. Standard office productivity software (word processing and spreadsheet applications) does present some options for presenting data in a visual manner. However, other data visualization tools available include:

Piktochart—http://piktochart.com/—A free tool to create infographics.
TableauPublic—http://www.tableausoftware.com/public/
A free visualization program to embed charts into Web sites. A gallery of TableauPublic projects is available at http://www.tableausoftware.com/public/gallery.

Visualization options that require more coding experience or resources include:

OpenRefine (originally Google Refine)—http://openrefine.org/

and

Google Code Playground—https://code.google.com/apis/ajax/playground/.

Also of note is Nathan Yau's *Visualize This: The FlowingData Guide to Design, Visualization and Statistics* (Indianapolis: Wiley, 2011), which covers all aspects of presenting data from gathering it through choosing the appropriate visualization tool, to comparing differences and spotting trends.

CLOSING THOUGHTS

Libraries have long collected information on library use in order to measure the amount of work done, improve effectiveness, and demonstrate the value of the library to its parent institution. Originally most of the data collected was statistical, primarily easy-to-count output measures like acquisitions, circulation, and reference statistics.

More recently library users have become the focus of assessment efforts, both in terms of ascertaining patrons' satisfaction (or dissatisfaction) with various aspects of the library and in trying to measure the effect or impact of programs and services on library users. Federal and state government authorities, higher education accrediting agencies, and for-profit businesses are asking for evidence of libraries' contribution to the funding authorities' goals and objectives. As a result, libraries now try to assess outcomes, the ways in which patrons are changed through contact with library resources and programs. These outcomes are difficult to measure accurately, and libraries are struggling to find ways to do so in order to prove their value by supporting their parent institutions' goals and objectives.

Libraries use many quantitative and qualitative measures to assess their outputs and outcomes. Staff often try to combine quantitative and qualitative measures in order to get the most complete and accurate picture of an assessment target. Anyone working in public services will often find themselves assisting in one or more assessment efforts no matter what kind of library they work in.

Chapter Review Material

1. How would you define "assessment"?
2. What are some of the reasons libraries try to assess their performance?
3. Give an example of an "input" and an "output."
4. Discuss the relationship and differences between accountability, assessment, authority, responsibility, and outcomes.
5 What does accountability mean in terms of library performance?
6. How does accountability change the way libraries assess themselves?
7. What are the two primary categories of evidence libraries collect?
8. Give examples of quantitative and qualitative means of collecting data.
9. Give some examples of how outcomes assessment methods have been applied in school, academic, public, and special libraries.

REFERENCES

Abilock, Debbie. 2007. "Choosing Assessments That Matter." *Knowledge Quest* 35, no. 5: 8–12.

American Library Association. 2013. *The State of America's Libraries 2013*. Chicago: ALA. http://tinyurl.com/salr2013.

Association of College and Research Libraries (ACRL). 1998. *Task Force on Academic Library Outcomes Assessment Report*. Chicago: American Library Association. http://www.ala.org/acrl/publications/whitepapers/taskforceacademic.

Berry, John N. 2013. "Pillar of Community Education." *Library Journal* 138, no. 11: 30.

Brown, Jeanne M. 2010. "Informal Assessment for Library Middle Managers." *Library Leadership & Management* 24, no. 1: 18–22.

Cairns, Virginia L. 2006. "Demonstrating Your Worth to Administration." *Tennessee Libraries* 56, no. 2: 1–11.

Durrance, Joan C., and Karen E. Fisher. 2005. *How Libraries and Librarians Help: A Guide to Identifying User-Centered Outcomes*. Chicago: American Library Association.

Groves, Kaylyn. 2013. "Radical Change in Library Assessment Called for by Elliott Shore at Northumbria Conference." *ARL News*. September 17. Online. http://www.arl.org/news/arl-news/2916-radical-change-in-library-assessment-called-for-by-elliott-shore-at-northumbria-conference.

Hamasu, Claire, and Betsy Kelly. 2013. "Assessment and Evaluation Is Not a Gut Feeling: Integrating Assessment and Evaluation into Library Operations." *Journal of the Medical Library Association* 101, no. 2: 85–87.

Intner, Sheila S., and Elizabeth Futas. 1994. "Evaluating Public Library Collections: Why Do It, and How to Use the Results." *American Libraries* 25, no. 5: 410–413.

Kramer, Pamela K., and Linda Diekman. 2010. "Evidence = Assessment = Advocacy." *Teacher Librarian* 37, no. 3: 27–30.

Lance, Keith Curry, Nicolle O. Steffen, Rochelle Logan, Marcia J. Rodney, Suzanne Kaller, Christie M. Koontz, and Dean K. Jue. 2001. *Counting on Results: New Tools for Outcome-Based Evaluation of Public Libraries*. Aurora, CO: Bibliographical Research Center. http://www.lrs.org/documents/cor/CoR_Full FinalReport.pdf.

Nelson, Sandra. 2008. *Strategic Planning for Results*. Chicago: American Library Association.

Sullivan, Maureen. 2013. "State of America's School Libraries." *Huffington Post*. April 15.Online. http://www.huffingtonpost.com/maureen-sullivan/state-of-americas-school-_b_3063055.html.

Walden, Graham R. 2006. "Focus Group Interviewing in the Library Literature." *Reference Services Review* 34, no. 2: 222–241.

Weiss, Carol H. 1982. "Purposes of Evaluation." In *Strategies for Library Administration: Concepts and Approaches*, ed. Charles R. McClure and Alan R. Samuels, 238–252. Littleton, CO: Libraries Unlimited.

SUGGESTED READINGS

Alman, Susan Webreck, Christinger Tomer, and Margaret L. Lincoln. 2012. *Designing Online Learning: A Primer for Librarians*. Santa Barbara, CA: Libraries Unlimited. (Includes a chapter on assessing learning activities.)

Anthony, Carolyn A. 2014. "Moving toward Outcomes." *Public Libraries* 53, no. 3: 5–7.

Applegate, Rachel. 2013. Practical Evaluation Techniques for Librarians. Santa Barbara, CA: Libraries Unlimited.

Baker, Lynda M. 2006. "Observation: A Complex Research Method." *Library Trends* 55, no. 1: 171–189.

Brown, Jeanne M. 2011. "Demonstrating Library Value: Examples and Applications." *Art Documentation* 30, no. 1: 48–53.

Dando, Priscille. 2014. *Say It with Data: A Concise Guide to Making Your Case and Getting Results*. Chicago: American Library Association.

Hernon, Peter, Robert E. Dugan, and Joseph R. Matthews. 2014. *Getting Started with Evaluation*. Chicago: American Library Association.

Krasulski, Michael J., and Trevor A. Dawes, eds. 2013. *Twenty-First Century Access Services: On the Frontline of Academic Librarianship*. Chicago: Association of College and Research Libraries.

Markless, Sharon, and David Streatfield. 2013. *Evaluating the Impact of Your Library*. 2nd ed. London: Facet.

Morriston, Terry. 2007. "Carving a New Assessment Trail." *Knowledge Quest* 35, no. 5: 48–49.

Murphy, Sarah Anne. 2014. *The Quality Infrastructure: Measuring, Analyzing, and Improving Library Services*. Chicago: American Library Association.

Orcutt, Darby, ed. 2010. *Library Data: Empowering Practice and Persuasion*. Santa Barbara, CA: Libraries Unlimited.

Paulus, Amy R. 2014. "Using Data to Assess Staffing and Services: University of Iowa Main Library." *Journal of Access Services* 11, no. 3: 189–205.

Russell, Becky. 2012. "Colorado Library Program Assessment." *School Library Monthly* 28, no. 8: 5–7.

Saunders, E. Stewart. 2007. "The LibQUAL+ Phenomenon: Who Judges Quality?" *Reference & User Services Quarterly* 47, no. 1: 21–24.

Smyth, Joanne B., and James C. MacKenzie. 2006. "Comparing Virtual Reference Exit Survey Results and Transcript Analysis: A Model for Service Evaluation." *Public Services Quarterly* 2, nos. 2/3: 85–99.

St. Clair, Guy, Saadat, Tony, and Maria Phipps. 2014. *Transforming Libraries: Measuring Knowledge Services: Critical Success Factors*. Soutron Global. March 18. http://smr-knowledge.com/wp-content/uploads/2014/03/140 318-Soutron-Measuring-and-Metrics.pdf.

Tatarka, Agnes, Chapa, Kay, Li, Xin, and Jennifer Rutner. 2010. "Library Assessment Plans: Four Case Studies." *Performance Measurement and Metrics*. 11, no. 2: 199–210.

Walter, Scott. 2014. "Assessment Is Everywhere: Sharing Assessment Information and Initiatives at DePaul University." *College & Research Libraries News* 75, no. 9: 502–505.

White, Marilyn Domas, Eileen. G. Abels, and Neal Kaske. 2003. "Evaluation of Chat Reference Service Quality." *D-Lib Magazine* 9, no. 2. http://dlib.org /dlib/february03/white/02white.html. (Although dated, this is a key article on the topic.)

Chapter 18

Fiscal Concerns

Library budgets are tighter now than I've ever seen them during my fifteen years as a librarian, and I don't know anybody who hasn't felt the squeeze.
—*Daniel Chudnov, 2011*

ROI [Return on Investment] is one approach to meeting the challenge of demonstrating value. The basis of ROI studies is to quantify and demonstrate the library's economic value to the institution.
—*Carol Tenopir, 2010*

Fundraising events can be daunting at their worst, or they can be an extremely successful vehicle for raising significant unrestricted dollars for your library.
—*Sue Hall, 2014*

One of the ways we measure the support for public libraries is through the success or failure of local library referenda.
—*Kathy Rosa, 2014*

The funding squeeze that Daniel Chudnov mentioned is perhaps somewhat abated today than it was in 2011, but funding is still an ever-present concern for all types of libraries. We all know that funding is the essential ingredient in every library activity, program, and service. Securing funds that support the library in adequate amounts is a major challenge for library directors. What we sometimes forget is that every staff member can assist, to some degree, in securing those funds. Not directly, but through their job performance. Quality of service is a major factor in a library's funding level. That is a fact often overlooked in the midst of daily work activities.

Funding for libraries is primarily a matter of securing funds from a parent organization (government, school district, academic institution, etc.). It would be a rare situation in which there were not other agencies seeking funding from that larger organization, and all at the same time. It is almost unheard of that an agency willingly does not ask for an increase over the prior year's allocation. Thus, everyone is asking for more money. It is also a "Black Swan" event when the total amount being requested by all the agencies does not far exceed the amount of money available for allocation. Thus, the process of gaining the funds is, more often than not, a political process in which there is competition with other agencies seeking funding.

Staff members do not have to understand the local budgetary politics beyond knowing it exists and does impact an agency's level of funding. They should also keep in mind that what may seem like a rather "weird" action regarding a budget matter taken by senior managers may, in fact, be a political move that will help in securing needed funding. Those who are not adept at "playing the budgetary politics game" are rarely able to do much more than retain existing funding levels.

Check These Out

The classic book about budgetary politics is Aaron Wildavsky and Naomi Caiden's *The New Politics of the Budgetary Process* (5th ed., New York: HarperCollins, 2004).

Another good title on the topic is Carol Lewis's *Budgeting: Politics and Power* (2nd ed., Oxford/New York: Oxford University Press, 2013).

Success in the "budget process" rests on several elements, beyond the personal communication skills of the person making the budget presentation. One important element is having solid data to back up claims of increased workloads, service requests, and so on. Thus, those pesky "stats" you're asked to keep up to date and accurate, and which may seem pointless when doing them, do play a positive role in library funding. Lacking solid evidence, the chances of having a successful budget request outcome drop. Another element relates to what type of support there is from those who use the library. Yet another element is demonstrating, with facts, the "value" of the library's services to the community. Again, both of these elements ultimately rest on the quality of the work the staff perform.

Check This Out

The American Library Association has created a page with several indicators of library value that can be useful in advocacy efforts: http://www .ala.org/advocacy/advocacy-university/value-libraries.

Most of the staff do not need to know the ins and outs of the budget process, although some may be interested; however, there are some budget basics everyone should know. The reason is the budget sets the parameters of what the library can and cannot do in the sense that every activity requires some measure of funding, whether you realize it or not. Therefore, our first section of this chapter covers the most basic aspects of library budgeting. The balance of the chapter looks at specific areas where public service activities do play a part in how well funded the library will be. Some of the ways appear indirect at first thought, but on closer examination you will see they have a greater impact than you may have imagined.

From the Authors' Experience

One year, Evans caused shock and dismay among the library staff, especially those who had collection development responsibilities, when they learned he had voluntarily offered to forego increases in the acquisitions allocation for the upcoming budget cycle. Staff members did not understand that it was a calculated risk. If it worked, the library would gain some goodwill from senior administers and perhaps be better off in the future.

The library had received 10 percent increases for book and media resources, 12 percent for serials, and 15 percent for e-resources for 15 straight years. The next budget cycle was going to be very tight and the dollar amount of the annual acquisitions allocation increase was substantial. Almost everyone on campus had a high regard for the library. Well, there was an exception during the budget cycle when deans and vice presidents, other than the academic vice president, all opposed the acquisition allocations.

The academic vice president, who was an avid library supporter, said upon hearing the offer, "Good move, which will help me with some other touchy budget issues."

As it turned out, the risk paid off. In the following budget cycle the "normal" acquisitions allocations were back in place, with additional "make-up" amounts for the prior year. Could it have been a bad move? Absolutely! Would it have worked again? Probably not. The offer was made knowing there was a risk but was also based on an understanding of the campus budgetary politics.

BUDGET BASICS

A *budget* is a control device for all organizations. Budgets are plans, essentially an estimate of how much money it will take to accomplish planned activities over a period of time. At the broadest level, a budget sets a limit on what an organization does; that is, when the money is used up, all activity—in theory—stops. We know that is not always the case, especially in terms of state-funded agencies. It is a surprisingly common event for state legislatures to fail to approve a new budget prior the fiscal year ending. In theory all state activities should cease as there is no approved funding. What happens in practice is agencies are told to continue to operate, sometimes several weeks before funds are actually approved. At an agency-level overspending, an allocation can in fact shut down operations and even lead to problems for the agency managers. Thus, budgets do have some control over what managers do or don't do—managers are accountable for all expenditures.

Because budgets are estimates, there needs to be flexibility in how the agency expends the funds. Managers do have some latitude in how the monies are spent, even on something not in the original budget request. There is recognition that there are rapid shifts in circumstances, needs, opportunities, and so on; but any major alteration requires careful thought and caution. Managers do not have carte blanche to move funds around. For example, they almost never are allowed to move salary monies to another expenditure category.

Library budgets are almost always one of two types—operating and capital—although there are times when other types may exist to meet a special need such as construction. *Operating budgets/expenses* (OE) identify amounts of money the library expects to expend on basic activities such as collections, postage, salaries, and supplies. OEs cover a specific timeframe—a fiscal year (FY) which is usually 12 months long. Different organizations use different fiscal years (some examples are January 1 to December 31, June 1 to May 31, July 1 to June 30, and October 1 to September 30) as well as budget preparation cycles.

From the Authors' Experience

Sinwell noted that in terms of controlling budget expenditures one organization she worked in began a budget review process that required units to produce monthly statements for the college budget office to ensure they were monitoring their costs/expenditures correctly/responsibly.

You are likely to encounter restricted and unrestricted funds. The OE is *unrestricted*; that is, you may spend OE collection funds for any appropriate item. An example of a *restricted* fund would be a collection-development fund that might require you to only buy children's literature items. It is not uncommon for a donor to restrict the expenditure of the gift to areas in which he or she has a special interest. As experienced fundraisers know, securing an unrestricted gift is difficult, as "no one wants to give money for light bulbs and toilet paper." We will look at restricted funds and fundraising later in this chapter.

Capital budgets are for expenditures on equipment (usually items expected to last two or more years). Expenditures for technology (hardware and infrastructure) usually fall into the capital expense category. The other major expense is for new construction or remodeling projects.

From the Authors' Experience

Sinwell had to deal with capital projects in both public libraries and community college libraries, planning for renovations or new technological advancements.

> In each one of the situations, a great deal of time was spent dialoguing with staff and system administration to determine what was needed. It was important in each case to demonstrate wise planning and good stewardship of funds.

There is a *budget cycle*, and more often than not it consists of at least three FYs—the prior year, the current year, and next year. Some funding authorities go back two as well as forward two years. During the approval process, funding authorities look at current year expenditures, compare that with what occurred in the prior year(s), and the request for the coming FY.

Not surprisingly, the budget cycle lasts for some time when it follows best practices. Normally it starts by senior administrators being informed what the jurisdiction/parent organization guidelines are for the upcoming cycle—overall increase or decrease in funding, role of inflation if allowed, and so on. Senior managers pass that information along with their own perspective about what would be reasonable to their unit heads. Unit heads develop a unit request—sometimes with or without staff input—and pass the information back to senior managers. Almost always the total increase is beyond the guidelines, and meetings follow with unit heads to hammer out a realistic request. Often the library's governing board must also vote on the request and, rather often, they have slightly different fiscal priorities and the need to revised starts the internal process again. Once the request is finalized, the person who will present the request begins to plan how to best present the document and look at the current and prior years' budget expenditures. Some people practice their presentation with two or three people who act as opponents to one or more of the increases. Finally, there is the actual presentation and the wait to learn the results. All of these can cause budget people to be a tad more grumpy and stressful than normal, and that is normal.

BUDGET FORMATS

Libraries rarely have a voice in what type of budget format they will have to employ. The parent organization makes that decision and it is a decision that may change from time to time. There are several formats; some of which, such as zero-base and program budgeting, are very labor intensive to prepare. In such instances, staff may well be asked for a variety of information, data, and ideas that go beyond what they experienced under a different budget format. We will briefly cover four of the most common types of budgeting systems found in libraries—line item, performance, program, and zero-base.

Line-Item Budgets

The *line-item budget* is the most common format. It has a long history of use and allows for easy comparison of expenditure categories from year to year. Line-item budgets focus on classes of expenditures, each class being a "line."

Each major unit in a large organization, such as a library, police department, and so forth, has an identifying budget number. Within the budget number there are numbered "lines." These lines represent various classes of expenditure (office supplies, postage, salaries, etc.) the funding authority wishes to track. Whatever the label used for line items, the purpose is to allow for easy tracking of expenditures across agencies/departments. If the funding body wants to know how much the organization as a whole spent on office supplies, all it needs to do is add up all of the relevant lines in the active account numbers. There is no "standard" numbering systems for the lines. The number of lines employed also varies from organization to organization.

Line budgets are the least complex to manage. A budget request usually starts with last year's allocation and builds from there (incremental). More often than not you will have received some "guidelines" from the parent body about its overall plan for the budget. These will almost always indicate how much, if any, inflation you may add to which lines. You may be encouraged to shift monies from one line to another to better reflect your operating needs (an exception here is you rarely have freedom to shift salary monies).

Performance-Based Budgets

Some researchers/scholars believe the line-item budgets are not as good as other budgeting formats, especially from an efficiency and effectiveness point of view. One obvious reason for such thoughts is line-item budgets tend to be highly incremental. That is critics say, "Once a line always a line, and once a mistake always a mistake." Another issue is that the lines focus on categories of expense, not on effectiveness of the expenditure. Stakeholders have no easy way to relate library expenditures to its mission, goals, or objectives. The other formats do link expenditure and achievements.

Performance budgets focus on tasks rather than on classes of expenditure. A performance budget is an expansion of a line-item budget. The major drawback to the performance budget is that it is of little value in assessing quality. Thus, while closer to relating expenditures to the mission, goals, and objectives it still does not clearly show the relationship to quality. In essence, you give functional department heads their own line-item budget to manage. It will usually result in more realistic budget requests from the department heads as they gain an understanding of budgetary issues.

In a library context, there might be five or more "performance" units such as acquisitions, cataloging, reference, circulation, document delivery, outreach, and administration. Again, it is matter of library choice as to the number of performance areas it wishes to include in its budget. Each area would employ the same types of lines—salaries, supplies, for example. Units can include special expense categories as necessary; examples might be—acquisitions might have individual lines for print resources, media, and e-resources, while cataloging might have a line for OCLC fees.

Program Budgets

A further expansion of a funding agency's budgetary oversight is the *program budget.* Such budgets provide an even tighter link between expenditures and mission, goals, and objectives. One drawback of this process is they require substantially more time to prepare than the previous two we described. A program budget takes more time to prepare because the library must allocate staff time to each activity (e.g., reference, children's story hour, or public access to computers). While some staff may devote 100 percent of their time to a single program, others may have responsibilities in several programs. The question for such individuals is how much time to attribute to each program.

The ultimate objective of the costing and work measurement is to develop a standard cost and performance for various functions, activities, and subactivities. From a library point of view, probably the greatest drawback of such a budget is its emphasis on the quantification of library activities.

Zero-Base Budgets (ZBB)

The chances are you will not encounter a *zero-base budget* (ZBB), at least in its full application. It is also without doubt the most labor intensive to prepare. Supporters claim ZBB is the best possible approach to avoiding incremental budget increase. When taxpayers have major concerns about their tax burden, ZBB has widespread appeal, if not application. Given the current general feeling about governments and their costs, we may see an upswing in requiring agencies to use the ZBB format regardless of how time consuming it may be.

The term zero-base comes from the first step in the process: that is, the submitting agency is to assume that it is just starting from point zero. Thus, the focus in the planning and development phase of the ZBB is on the purpose and what functions the agency should perform in order to meet its mission. In theory, an organization that uses ZBB would become more cost-effective by continuously reviewing its purposes and attempting to remove unneeded activities.

ZBB requires the agency undertake four phases: construction, planning, budgeting, and control. Construction is the most time-consuming part of the process. It is during the construction and planning phases that the budget maker assumes that the unit is starting at zero activity and then identifying all the appropriate activities. Also part of these activities is creating "decision packages," which become the basis for calculating the cost that go into the budget request. The control element is the same as with any budget—it helps managers monitor activities/performance throughout the budget cycle. Clearly, the time necessary to prepare a comprehensive zero-base budget on an annual basis is enormous; few organizations that still employ ZBB revisit the construction phase annually.

FUND ACCOUNTING

If you don't have much experience with financial matters, you might guess there are several types of budgets but that accounting is accounting. That is not the case. Accountants have developed a special approach to handling financial transactions of nonprofit organizations. The system is known as *fund accounting* and exists because of some basic differences that exist between for-profit and not-for-profit organizations. The four most important differences for nonprofits are:

- The focus on social benefits
- The relative absence of profit-motivated behavior on the part of resource contributors (public and private)
- The special government- and constituent-imposed constraints on their activities
- The lack of generating a profit (this is not the same as generating income)

There are several types of funds under this accounting system. One is the *general fund* that handles resources not accounted for in any other group of accounts. General fund operating statements show revenues, expenditures, and encumbrances, as well as changes in fund balances. (Note: an *encumbrance* is a means of setting aside funds to be expended at a later date while removing that amount from the "available" monies. Acquisitions departments make great use of this accounting technique when placing orders. The reason is some items may not be immediately available, most will have some discount off the list price, and the shipping and handling will be unknown until delivery. This helps ensure there is enough funding to pay invoices as well as not overcommit acquisition funds.)

Debit funds track resources segregated for paying interest and principal on a general obligation debt. (Some libraries have outstanding bond obligations that require interest payment to bond holders and do this through a debit fund. Many new libraries facilities are funded all, or in part, by a bond issue—also known as a *general obligation debt.*) *Capital project* funds control resources for the purpose of acquiring major fixed assets such a remodeling effort or the acquisition of a new ILS system.

A *special-revenue fund* accounts for, and reports on, resources that come from special sources—for example, a library foundation—or that carry restrictions on their use. Two common ways of discussing various funds is to refer to them as being unrestricted or restricted. All the funds mentioned in the preceding paragraph are largely unrestricted in a sense while being broadly restricted—debit funds must be employed to pay debit obligations but there may be several obligations that are paid for from that fund. There are also funds that tightly restrict their usage. Many libraries have endowments which would fall into this category, especially in the area of book acquisitions—restricted to the purchase of materials related to a specific subject or format (e.g., Southwestern Native American basketry). Monies in such accounts may go unspent for several years before an appropriate item becomes available. Needless to say, nonprofits seek funds with as few restrictions as possible while still securing the money. Donor wishes, however, tend to override the unrestricted desire of recipients.

Some libraries, public and academic, engage in some limited form of commercial activity. *Enterprise funds* control activities that provide goods or services to the general public (e.g., Friends of the Library merchandise) or user-charges (photocopy charges are common). Library photocopy income would be part of the enterprise fund. Internal library funds are similar, except the "customer" is part of the organization. You may encounter "chargeback" situations in which a non-library unit charges the library a fee for its services; two common chargeback areas are computing and building maintenance.

Check These Out

Here are two titles worth reviewing that cover the concepts of accounting and budgeting in greater depth:

Kirk, Rachel A. 2013. *Balancing the Books: Accounting for Librarians* (Santa Barbara, CA: Libraries Unlimited).

Turner, Anne M. 2007. *Managing Money: A Guide for Librarians* (Jefferson, NC: McFarland & Company).

GARNERING BUDGET SUPPORT

It would be a difficult task to identify a library that receives all the funding it needs to operate in the desired manner from its funding agency. In this section we look at how libraries can enhance the chances of securing additional funds from its primary funding body as well as from other sources.

Developing and maintaining a positive public image is important for all libraries—and is essential for generating support for increased funding. There will be no opportunity for securing funds if the library's image is anything but positive. Having a positive image is not enough. Each time public service staff interacts with users, they are either enhancing or detracting from the library's image.

Quality customer service should be a given, as should be effective and efficient programs and, in a sense, they are rather passive in nature in terms of gaining increased public support for the library. Evidence, hard data relating to the library's effectiveness, efficiency, and value to the service community are critical components to winning budget increases.

There are some simple things public service staff might do to help with collecting hard data for budget request purposes. For example, Evans and Christie gathered data about registered borrowers in the Flagstaff City Coconino County Public Library system for just the city of Flagstaff. The result was rather surprising. The population of the city in 2013/14 was 65,870; of that number, based on circulation department data, there were 58,913 registered borrowers. Without doubt there were a number of inactive borrowers in the data. However, the library has a policy of requiring that a person renew his or her card every three years, thus the "inactive" have become inactive recently. Another factor in the large borrowers' N is there may be individuals who work in Flagstaff but live outside the city limits thus inflating the "borrower" population. Even if you discount the registration figure by 30 percent, the percentage of citizens with a card is impressive. It is also a figure that would likely surprise people, including the funding authorities. This is a small example of something the public service staff can become aware of and communicate to upper management to employ as they think appropriate. Being able to cite figures such as the above is much more effective than saying "most citizens use the library."

Special libraries are frequently called upon to "prove their worth," especially those in a for-profit setting. Regardless of setting, many funding bodies believe libraries are just a cost center, or worse—a bottomless pit, swallowing up more and more money with little or no return. Other types of libraries may not be bluntly asked to prove their value, but that is always an underlying issue when it comes to library budget request time.

The good news is there are some techniques that can help you be proactive in proving the library's worth or at least determine if there is value. We will briefly look at one broad category of approaches to demonstrating value—*cost benefit analysis* (CBA). One of the strengths of the techniques that fall into the category is they are useful in handling several processes that libraries must engage in beyond as a budget request strategy. Cost benefit analysis is very useful in assessing most of the activities libraries employ on a daily basis from workflows to alternative approaches to resolving some issue. Such studies assist in planning activities, decision making, and assessment.

There are several CBA techniques. The most widely used by businesses is IRR, or internal return on investment. Other techniques are net present value (NPV), hurdle rate, payback period, and profitability index to mention a few. The technique that many libraries have used in the recent past is return on investment (ROI). When ROI is employed by nonprofit organization, it is often referred to as social return on investment (SROI).

Check This Out

We recommend Bruce R. Kingma's *The Economics of Information: A Guide to Economics and Cost-Benefit Analysis for Information Professionals* (2nd ed., Englewood, CO: Libraries Unlimited, 2001) for anyone interested in learning more about cost benefit, as well as economic aspects of information activities in the library context.

In 2004, Alison Lingane and Sara Olsen made a comment that applies to any SROI study, although their focus was on the value to a for-profit organization employing one: "Conventional wisdom dictates that financial and social goals are in opposition. . . . The real opportunity, however, is the 'blended value' model articulated by Emerson" (p.116). (The Emerson article they reference is Jed Emerson's *The Nature of Returns: A Social Capital Markets Inquiry into the Elements of Investment and Blended Value Proposition* [Social Enterprise Series, No. 17, Boston: Harvard Business School, 2000.]) Lingane and Olsen also suggest some SROI "guidelines" that can apply to any such study. We have paraphrased their 10 ideas to better fit a library context:

- Include both positive and negative impacts of the metrics employed
- Involve all the stakeholders in the process from start to finish
- Be sure certain impacts of all the metrics are direct rather than indirect
- Do not double count impacts
- Use only those metric impacts that are the result of a single organization

- Use care when monetizing impacts
- Place numeric metrics in a context
- State all underlying assumptions
- Test all assumptions
- Build in impact tracking over time

As you might surmise from the preceding list, two key components of an SROI are metrics and impacts. The metrics are what you measure; for example, some library metrics might be the circulation of a book, the use of a media format, having a book discussion group, and providing free computer access. An impact is the result from a metric taking place, almost always in terms of money. The following is an example of a metric and its impact which the authors have firsthand experience:

Metric: Hardback books
Valuation: $17 per book
Basis for evaluation: A survey of book prices, on Amazon, of fiction, non-fiction, and YA titles/
Financial impact of library's hardback book collection: $7,196,131.00

From the Authors' Experience

Christie and Evans were involved in an SROI study in 2013/14 involving the Flagstaff City—Coconino County Public Library system. The study examined the direct impacts of 26 library programs and services organized under four broad headings—media usage (including print, media, and e-resources), computer usage, community services, and reference services. The study also examined "consequential outcome community benefits" (metrics included literacy-education, economic development, community health cost savings, public safety cost savings, community support, and government services savings).

The final result was a very nice social return on investment for the library system. For every dollar the library spent, including donor support and grants, there was a $4.62 return to the community. These data will be useful in seeking financial support from all sources of funding, not just the government.

It is true that SROIs can be very useful; however, keep in mind that not every such study produces positive results. It might be possible to demonstrate the lack of a positive return is the result of serious underfunding over a period of years. We know of no such undertaking, but we do know of cases where the study produced negative results. You will find several SROI studies listed in the suggested readings section at the end of the chapter. These items will provide ideas for developing your own such study as well as illustrating library outcomes from libraries that have undertaken such projects.

OTHER SOURCES OF FUNDING

Libraries' parent organizations are the primary source of funding; however, the reality is that funding can cover only some, perhaps most in best case situations, of the cost of the library's annual operations. In addition, there may be ideas for doing something new or otherwise not done before that may be part of a budget request, but that were unfunded. Many libraries do not give up in such cases; rather they seek the necessary funds from other sources. Securing "outside" funding may free up general operating funds for important or special activities that are underfunded. Keep in mind that there will be competition from other libraries and other organizations seeking extra funding, and it will require an investment of time and collaboration within the organization if it is to be successful.

Check These Out

Two articles addressing the options for outside funding are:

Eye, John, and Vik Brown. 2013. "Establishing a Friends of the Library Advisory Board." *Bottom Line: Managing Library Finances* 26, no. 1: 25–30.

Cuillier, Cheryl, and Carla J. Stoffle. 2011. "Finding Alternative Sources of Revenue." *Journal of Library Administration* 51, nos. 7/8: 777–809.

Fundraising

It is a rare library that does not engage in some form of fundraising or development work. The effort may be sporadic and limited in scope, but the efforts do play a role in what and how the library operates. Regardless of the size of the effort, there are some notions that apply to all such efforts. Once again the success or failure of those efforts hinges, to some extent, upon how well public service staff perform their daily activities.

Fundraising, while it may have to be a part-time activity, requires planning and leadership. Only the very large libraries have the luxury of a full-time fundraiser. Most must depend on the efforts of several people who devote some of their time to fundraising—a team approach. As with any team, there needs to be a captain in charge to call meetings, set agendas, propose ideas, implement plans, push initiatives forward, and monitor outcomes. Generally, that person is the senior or next-most senior manager of the library. One reason for this is because donors and granting agencies want to know they are working with the decision makers.

Some years ago, Stanley E. Gornish (1998) in writing about fundraising identified six factors in why such efforts may fail. His points, paraphrased here, are as valid today as when he described them:

- Lack of a realistic plan
- Lack of top leadership

- Lack of sufficient cultivation of prospects
- Lack of institutional traditions of giving
- Lack of realism in assessment and objectives, and
- Lack of clear and compelling articulation of the relationship between library's needs and the donor's benefits (p.98).

Although he was focusing on major fundraising activities, his points apply to any such library effort. A Friends group or Foundation (see later) may suffer from some or all of his "lacks." Even volunteer groups can become discouraged when there is a lack of top management involvement in the fundraising efforts.

Regardless of source, income generation is largely a matter of the right person asking the right source for the right amount for the right project at the right time and in the right way. As you might imagine, getting all those "rights" correct takes planning, practice, preparation, and practical experience. Workshops help, but only real-world experience as well as some disappointments along the way, will translate into "money in the library's bank account."

One long-standing internal revenue source for libraries is the sale of duplicate or otherwise unwanted gifts/donations. "Gifts in kind" to libraries are very common; how libraries dispose of such items varies. Publicly supported libraries need to be aware of any regulations regarding the disposal of "public property." Donors may benefit from a tax deduction for donations in cash or kind to charitable or public bodies. In any case, cultivating relationships with donors is an important activity.

From the Authors' Experience

Whether it is one book or $1 million, it is important to acknowledge contributions of all donors. Saponaro has worked at several institutions that have recognized donor contributions in different ways. At one institution, a small afternoon reception was hosted to honor a donor who provided funds for a new circulation counter. (The donor's contribution was also acknowledged via a brass plate placed on the counter.) Whether the recognition made the difference or not is hard to tell, but the donor later provided funding for a new reference desk for the same facility. The same institution used traditional (paper) bookplates to indicate donations to collections. An alternative method used at the University of Maryland Libraries is the "Legacy Bookplate"—which allows a donor to have a digital bookplate assigned to anything from one title to a collection of titles—depending upon the amount donated (see: http://www.lib.umd.edu/bookplate).

Another quasi-internal source is through activities undertaken by nonstaff people on behalf of the library via "Friends of Anywhere Library," "Library Associates," "Supporters of ———," or similar group titles. Such groups may be no more formal than some volunteers who handle an ongoing book sale or may be a formal legal entity (a 501 (c) (3) organization). In some situations, governing board members may be expected to make an annual contribution to the library. There may be special types of "internal" funds such as endowments, wills, trusts, and living trusts. Support groups are two types: those that just raise and distribute funds and those that "manage" library investments.

Check These Out

A dated, but still good source that addresses the processes involved in establishing a foundation is John A. Edie's *First Steps in Starting a Foundation* (5th ed. Washington, D.C.: Council on Foundations, 2002). The Council on Foundations also has information on starting a foundation available from its Web site: http://www.cof.org/resources/starting-foundation.

Two useful publications to read to get more in-depth information are Kenneth E. Dowlin's *Getting the Money: How To Succeed in Fundraising for Public and Nonprofit Libraries* (Westport, CT: Libraries Unlimited, 2009); and *Beyond Book Sales: The Complete Guide to Raising Real Money for Your Library*, edited by Susan Dowd (Chicago: American Library Association, 2014).

The significant difference between a support group and a foundation is the support groups may not have the IRS status 501(c)(3). That means they may not indicate that donations may be tax deductible. Such groups have been raising a great deal of money for libraries over the years. Even though many of their events only raise a small sum, the annual total is impressive.

Check This Out

For U.S. libraries, regardless of type, a good source of information about "friends" groups is the American Library Association's United for Libraries (Association of Library Trustees, Advocates, Friends and Foundations): http://www.ala.org/united/.

Library foundations exist to handle funds that are not totally distributed on an annual basis and that are invested to generate ongoing income for the library. In the early days of a foundation's existence, there is likely to be a limited amount of income generated by the investment(s) and which is reinvested. Eventually the funds do generate some significant income, and the foundation makes decisions about how to handle the income. Generally the decision is to "payout" some of the income and reinvest the balance to, hopefully, generate even more income in the future. A common payout is between 4 and 4.5 percent of the income. The payout rate becomes available for library use.

There are also some rare and, in the past, overlooked opportunities to raise substantial amounts of money locally through wills, trusts, and other planned giving opportunities as well as create endowments. Clearly bequests in a will only become a source of funds at death; however, today many nonprofit groups actively work with people to have the library included in a will. Trusts, on the other hand, come in many shapes and sizes. Some may generate income for the library only during the donor's lifetime; others may generate income for both the donor and library during the donor's lifetime, while others only become effective on the donor's death. These are likely to increase in importance for libraries over the coming years.

Partnerships with business are one of the newer fundraising approaches for libraries. Many libraries prefer to use the term "collaboration," as it seems less profit-oriented. Glen Holt (2006) listed several reasons for seeking "corporate partnerships." His last reason, in our opinion, is the most telling: "Co-funding through sponsorships can be a great way to build and share current and potential audiences between the public and private sector" (p. 35).What you need to do is think broadly or imaginatively to find sponsorship possibilities. Partnerships with business can be extended to acquiring expertise that is not available within the library. For example, local radio and TV stations may provide airtime, local newspaper reporters can brief staff on how to write good copy, and public relations companies may well be prepared to offer their help to nonprofit libraries.

In June 2013, *American Libraries* included a one-page piece dealing with another form of partnership a few libraries are trying, that is, allowing commercial enterprises to advertise their products/services in the library (Goldberg, 2013, p. 17). It may generate more than some additional funding for the libraries trying this. One obvious potential problem is who and how to decide which commercial firms may advertise. You can imagine there could be legal challenges relating to how library handles the selection process. You might also think that some people may not be happy about having commercial ads in the library. It could also present an image problem; will ads diminish the notion the library is a neutral entity and one that is trustworthy?

Given the above, you can perhaps understand why our opening quotation from Sue Hall is important. Her article provides a number of ideas for fundraising events as well as tips for effective fundraising efforts. Emily Silverman (2010) began her article on planned giving with a comment we heartily endorse, "Fundraisers have patience. We take time to get to know potential donors. We share ideas and information with them. We develop relationships" (p. 132). Effective fundraising takes time, planning, patience, optimism, not being too upset when the effort is not as successful as you had hoped, and a keep-on-trying spirit.

Grants

Grants and "gifts" from foundations and government agencies are another funding source. The art of grantsmanship is something you can develop, but like any art it takes practice and then more practice before you have consistent success. Seeking grants is usually project-focused—seed money for a new program, partial support of a facilities project, funds for new or replacement equipment, and so on. As such it requires carefully thought-out plans.

An important step, in fact a key step, is to be certain you know what a foundation's or agency's current funding priorities are. Although their broad interest seldom changes over time, their annual funding priorities within a broad area may in fact vary from year to year. Do your research before making a call or sending a letter of inquiry. Most granting agencies have Web sites where you can do a substantial amount of research about their mission, priorities of the current funding cycle, what the funding cycle is, proposal guidelines, deadlines, and much more. Most grant-giving agencies are willing to talk by phone to explore projects. This can save the time of the agency and the library.

Check These Out

Two good starting places for locating sources of library grants are the *Foundation Directory* from the Foundation Center (online subscriptions available from https://fconline.foundationcenter.org/) and the *ALA Book of Library Grant Money* (Nancy Kaikow Maxwell, ed. 9th ed., Chicago: ALA Editions, 2014). Even if a subscription to the *Foundation Directory* is not feasible, the Foundation Center provides a great deal of information on grantsmanship and funding on its Web site (http://foundationcenter .org/), and is worth a review.

If you have no prior experience in grant/proposal preparation, signing up for a workshop or two is well worth the time and expense. Some grant-giving agencies organize workshops to outline their requirements. Also, when possible seek the assistance of an experienced grant writer. Be prepared to fail to get a grant on your first few efforts; however, keeping trying and you will succeed. The good news is that with many foundations, once you are successful, your chances of receiving later grants go up—assuming you have delivered on the first grant.

Bond Issues—Referenda

Publicly funded agencies may and do issue bonds in order to finance major projects. They may also have referenda related to their funding level (tax levy) or other financial needs. Private organizations, such as colleges and universities, also may issue bonds. There is a major difference between the public and privately issued bonds. A publicly funded library must put any such issuance to a public vote, unlike private organizations.

One aspect of a bond is they carry an interest rate that paid throughout the bond's lifetime (10 or 20 years is common). Thus, a successful bond issue vote obligates the library, or its jurisdiction, to pay the required annual interest rate. What that interest rate will be depends on how the jurisdiction is rated by rating agencies. A high rating normally means a moderate interest rate, while a low rating results in a high interest. Just because the issuance passes do not necessarily translate into library funds. Bond buyers are investors—they expect a reasonable ROI. If the interest rate offered is thought to be too low, the bonds will not sell.

Like any issue requiring a public vote, there are successes and failures. One of our opening quotations was from Kathy Rosa's (2014) article about the 2013 library referenda results. There were 69 such library-related votes that year and 41 of those were successful. She reported there was a successful (66% yes) bond referendum for $59 million for the Richland Library in Columbia, South Carolina. In that instance, taxpayers voted in favor of raising their property tax by more than $12 per $100,000 house evaluation (p. 45). Unfortunately, there were also 28 unsuccessful efforts; one such failure was in New Jersey where the vote was 22 percent yes to change 78 percent against a referenda that would provide $343,437 for the East Greenwich Township library (p. 47). These two results suggest that the money being asked for may be less important than how well the message for passage resonates with the voters.

All referenda vote results rest, in part, on whether or not voters believe there will be value for money should there be a successful outcome. This is an occasion where a positive SROI can play a helpful role during the "campaign" as well as where staff performance may be a critical factor. Other factors are how much money is being asked for, the tax timeframe, and how well the library states its case for the funding.

Referendums can create some interesting and challenging situations for public service staff members. It is very likely there is an ordinance, regulation, law, or governing board policy that has wording along the following lines: public employees shall not actively engage in political activities during such hours as that person is being compensated for the performance of that person's public employee duties. Note: such limits *do not* affect what a public employee does with his or her time when off duty.

What creates the personal challenges is that other political campaigns do not directly involve the library. With a library referendum, every library staff member must expect that a few people using the library will ask about the referenda and perhaps even ask a question such as "what do you think about the importance of the request?" In the first instance, the best advice is to follow the dictum of an old television series where the main character would say, "just the facts ma'am, just the facts." Stating what the referendum is for and other facts covered in the statement or handing the person a copy of the statement of need is not political activity. It is the other direct question about your views that can be difficult to handle, especially when the person asking it is someone with whom you have develop a good working relationship.

From the Authors' Experience

Sinwell provided several examples of successful referenda. Traditionally, all of Fairfax County Public Library's (FCPL) bond referendums have passed. An example from 2012 was a $25 million library bond to pay for renovating three libraries and build a new library. The libraries benefitting from the bond were Pohick Regional Library ($5 million), John Marshall Library ($5 million), Tysons-Pimmit Regional Library ($5 million), and Reston Regional Library ($10 million). The success can be attributed to thorough planning, dedicated library supporters, and a lot of hard work in publicizing the need for the referenda.

> FCPL has a very large and well-organized Friends of the Library consortium (https://www.fairfaxcounty.gov/library/friends/). Each of the 24 branches has its own group, but the George Mason Regional Library (GMRL) group is the largest and is seen as system-wide group. The GMRL Friends group has the support of the county executive in that he approved providing space to store book-sale books and providing "community service" volunteers to help with book sales and other activities.
>
> The county also had a Library Foundation for over 20 years and an active Library Board. Last but not least, the high quality of customer service staff display has generated a high level of community commitment to the library system. All of these factors contribute to the success of the system in garnering community support for funding activities.

When a library referendum is coming up, it is probably a sound idea to have an all-staff meeting, with the library's attorney, to cover how to handle situations such as the ones mentioned earlier. It is not unknown for opponents, to any referendum of a public agency not just a library's, to try to get agency staff to violate the "no political activity while on duty" rule in hopes of creating a "scandal" and perhaps defeating the measure.

Check This Out

Denice Rovira Hazlett wrote an information piece "Homegrown Fundraising" that appeared in *Library Journal* (2014, 139, no. 1: 1). The article described the efforts of the Holmes County, Ohio public library to pass a referendum, and when that proved unsuccessful after three attempts, how they sought out and were awarded an Institute of Museum and Library Services (IMLS) grant. The article highlights the reality that funding efforts may take several attempts (and formats) before success is achieved.

CLOSING THOUGHTS

Money may or may not make the world go round. What is certain is that without money, libraries would not exist as we know them. It is also almost a given that libraries must fight hard during budget approval times to keep last year's funding, let alone secure additional funds.

Public service staff members play an important role in the success of a library in having adequate funding. They may be unaware of that fact, but all of their interactions with the public do add or detract from the library's public image. That in turn plays a role in how funding officials view the library. If anything, their work performance plays an even bigger role in how successful the library is in securing funds from "outside' sources. Staff members do not have to be fully conversant with the ins and outs of budgeting and nonprofit accounting; however, some understanding will be helpful to advancement in a person's career.

Chapter Review Material

1. Why is public service staff so important when it comes to library funding?
2. In what way(s) is budgeting a political process, and why does it require careful monitoring of the library's environment? In what way can public service staff assist in the monitoring process?
3. What are some of the quantitative data libraries need to collect? What would be some qualitative data questions?
4. How does library accounting differ from that in for-profit organizations?
5. What are the most common budget formats, and which is most common in libraries? Discuss the pros and cons for each type.
6. Name at least three main expense categories in a "line-item budget," and at least one subaccount for each.
7. What are the most common sources from which libraries seek additional financial support?
8. What are the major flaws in fundraising efforts?
9. Describe the differences between a library support group (Friends of) and a library foundation.
10. What is the challenge for library staff during a library referendum?

REFERENCES

Chudnov, Daniel. 2011. "Show Me the Budget." *Computers in Libraries* 31, no. 3: 27–28.

Goldberg, Beverly. 2013. "Libraries Weighing Accepting Paid Ads to Keep Afloat." *American Libraries* 44, no. 6: 17.

Gornish, Stanley E. 1998. "How to Apply Fund-Raising Principles in a Competitive Environment." *Library Administration & Management* 12, no. 2: 94–103.

Hall, Sue. 2014. "Taking the Fear Out of Fundraising Events." *Public Libraries* 53, no. 2: 22–23, 50.

Holt, Glen E. 2006. "Economics: Corporate Sponsorships." *Bottom Line* 19, no. 1: 35–39.

Lingane, Alison and Sara Olsen. 2004. "Guidelines for Social Return on Investment." *California Management Review* 46, no. 3: 116–135.

Rosa, Kathy. 2014. "Referenda Roundup." *American Libraries* 45, nos. 1/2: 44–49.

Silverman, Emily. 2010. "Beyond Luck and Money—Planned Giving: Preparing for the Future." *Bottom Line* 23, no. 3:132–134.

Tenopir, Carol. 2010. "Measuring the Value of the Academic Library: Return on Investment and Other Value Measures." *The Serials librarian* 58, nos. 1/4: 39–48.

SUGGESTED READINGS

Bodycomb, Aphrodite, and Megan Del Baglivo. 2012. "Using an Automated Tool to Calculate Return on Investment and Cost Benefit Figures for Resources: The Health Sciences and Human Services Library Experience." *Journal of the Medical Library Association* 100, no. 2: 127–130.

Boyd, Liz, Sue Hall, and Peter Pearson. 2013. "Raising Money and Building Relationships through Your Annual Fund." *Public Libraries* 52, no. 5: 20–122.

Bureau of Business Research IC2 Institute, University of Texas at Austin. 2013. *Texas Public Libraries: Economic Benefits and Return on Investment.* Austin: University of Texas. https://www.tsl.texas.gov/roi.

Casey, Anne Marie, and Michael Lorenzen. 2010. "Untapped Potential: Seeking Library Donors among Alumni of Distance Learning Programs." *Journal of Library Administration* 50, nos. 5/6: 515–529.

Cervone, H. Frank. 2010. "Using Cost Benefit Analysis to Justify Digital Library Projects." *OCLC Systems & Services* 26, no.2: 76–79.

Epstein, Marc J., and Kristi Yuthas. 2014. *Measuring and Improving Social Impacts: A Guide for Nonprofits, Companies, and Impact Investors.* San Francisco: Berrett-Koehler Publishers.

Hammerman, Susan Summerfield. 2014. *Researching Prospective Donors: Get More Funding for Your Library.* Chicago: American Library Association

Hartmann, Meg Klinkow. 2011. "Show Me the Money: Privatization and the Public Library." *Illinois Library Association Reporter* 29, no.1: 4–7.

Huber, John J. 2011. *Lean Library Management: Eleven Strategies for Reducing Costs and Improving Customer Services.* New York: Neal-Schuman.

Kostagiolas, Petros. 2012. *Managing Intellectual Capital in Libraries: Beyond the Balance Sheet.* Oxford, England: Chandos Publishing.

LaRue, James. 2010. "Tough Times and Eight Ways to Deal with Them." *American Libraries* 41, nos. 1/2: 16–17.

Linn, Mott. 2010. "Cost-Benefit Analysis: A Primer." *Bottom Line* 23, no. 1: 31–36.

Linn, Mott. 2011. Cost-Benefit Analysis: Examples." *Bottom Line* 24, no. 1: 68–72.

Lorenzen, Michael. 2010. "Fund Raising for Academic Libraries: What Works, What Doesn't." *Library Philosophy and Practice*, October: 1–21. http://digitalcom mons.unl.edu/libphilprac/487/

Matthews, Joseph R. 2013. "Valuing Information, Information Services, and the Library: Possibilities and Realities." *Portal: Libraries & the Academy* 13, no. 1: 91–112.

Moreillon, Judi, 2014. "Leadership: Grant Writing as a Collaborative Activity." *School Library Monthly* 30, no. 8: 24–25.

Pan, Denise. 2013. "More Than a Number: Unexpected Benefits of Return on Investment Analysis." *Journal of Academic Librarianship* 39, no. 6: 566–572.

Pan, Denise, and Yem Fang. 2010. "Return of Investment for Collaborative Collection Development: A Cost-Benefit Analysis." *Collaborative Librarianship* 2, no.4: 183–192.

Pen Fels Institute of Government. 2010. *The Economic Value of the Free Library in Philadelphia.* Philadelphia: University of Pennsylvania. http://www.freeli brary.org/about/Fels_Report.pdf.

Price, Lee. 2011. "Wanted: High Net Worth Donors." *Public Libraries* 50, no. 3: 28–31.

Price, Lee. 2012. "How to Ask Me for Money." *Public Libraries* 51, no. 6: 17–19.

Roberts, Brent S., and Cheryl L. Hoover. 2014. "Waging a Successful Library Funding Campaign: A Case Study." *Library Management* 35, no. 3: 164–174.

Romero, Nuria Lloret. 2011. "ROI. "Measuring the Social Media Return on Investment in a Library." *Bottom Line* 24, no. 2: 145–151.

Silverman. Emily. 2008. "Building Your Base: Identifying Library Donors." *Bottom Line* 21, no. 4: 138–141.

Steele, Kirstin. 2008. "Are Budget Limitations Real? Perspective, Perceptions, and a Plan." *Bottom Line* 21, no. 3: 86–87.

Steffen, Nicolle, Zeith Lietzau, Keith Curry Lance, Amanda Rybin, and Carla Molliconi. 2009. *Public Libraries- A Wise Investment: A Return on Investment Study of Colorado Libraries.* Denver, CO: Library Research Service. http://www.lrs.org/documents/closer_look/roi.pdf.

Tenopir, Carol. 2013. "Building Evidence of the Value and Impact of Library and Information Services: Methods, Metrics and ROI." *Evidence Based Library & Information Practice* 8, no. 2: 270–274.

Watson, Ann M. 2013. "We Will Get by with a Little Help from Our 'Friends.'" *Bottom Line* 25, no. 3: 107–108.

19

Libraries as Place

Actually, the architectural design needs of libraries are fairly simple. Libraries need to be strong, well-lighted, comfortable, safe and secure, flexible in use, expandable, and have low occupancy costs. The problems lie in the details.

—*Fred Schlipf, 2011*

One of the challenges of managing a public library is dealing with maintenance issues and emergency situations.

—*Kathryn Ames and Greg Heid, 2011*

In today's public libraries, librarians rarely "shush" patrons . . . libraries have become beautifully noisy spaces.

—*Hadi Dudley, 2012*

Many college and universities across the United States have adopted sustainability in their curriculum and operations. Academic libraries need to support the mission of their university and therefore must also play their part in sustainability education and operations.

—*George J. Aulisio, 2013*

One of our objectives for this edition has been, as stated in the Preface, to highlight the changing nature of our field. We believe one of the most profound changes is in terms of library facilities. In various chapters we have touched on the impact of the digital age and how it is changing the way information is generated and disseminated. Some people believe the library, especially as a place, is dead or very near to death's door. By now you know that is not our belief; in fact we hope we've convinced you that we are correct. If not, we hope this chapter will do the job.

Yes, the digital world is changing how we go about our business, including how we make use of building spaces. However, there is nothing new in this; libraries have been evolving for more than 4,000 years along with their societies, technology, and the manner in which people seek and use information.

We believe there will be libraries as place far beyond the lifetime of this edition. Rolf Hapel (2012) wrote an excellent article about library as a physical space and its future. In commenting about those who believe libraries are doomed, he noted: "This negative argument usually proceeds as follows: Gradually, as the Internet penetration in various countries increases, and the new digital net-borne formats gain ground, the need for physical libraries will vanish" (p. 50). Later on he wrote, "That conclusion, however, is erroneous and overlooks certain societal tendencies that need to be considered" (p. 52). Hapel identified five societal challenges that libraries help to address—knowledge sharing and dissemination, literature and linguistic development, innovation and growth, social growth and cohesion, and empowerment and culture. We might add a sixth challenge: a community gathering place and increasing social engagement. He also made the point that libraries are one of the few places a person may enter without being confronted with requests for payments, or feeling out of place because of religious or political beliefs. Libraries attempt to be highly inclusive rather than exclusive.

Libraries continue to evolve as technology and society change. One example of how there is a change in physical space use appeared in a *Hechinger Report* article by Jill Barshay that described meeting library space needs for teenagers. It reported on a joint IMLS (Institute of Museum and Library Services) and MacArthur Foundation funded project focusing on libraries and young people. The article opened with, "Imagine walking into a public library filled with PlayStations, Wii game consoles, and electronic keyboards pumped up to maximum volume. . . . That is exactly how one enormous room on the ground floor of the Chicago Public Library's main branch functions" (November 29, 2011). Initially, according to Amy Eshleman, there was a clash between library staff, designers, and funding agencies over a space for books versus other uses. The library's desire to move its young adult collections into that space prevailed and "book circulation has gone up by about 500 percent since the space opened." The article also indicated that public libraries in Houston, Miami, New York, Philadelphia, San Francisco, and many smaller towns across the country would be designing similar spaces.

Some libraries now design spaces around activities and services, while book stacks become secondary. This allows for greater flexibility. Such libraries can remake their space fairly easily by rearranging shelving. One such library is Anythink Libraries in Colorado (http://www.imls.gov/assets/1/PodCast/Anythink.pdf). As our opening quotation from Hadi Dudley stated, libraries now have spaces for noisy and quiet collaboration. They also have spaces for differing media experiences such as gaming or videos, comfortable seating for individuals and for groups, popular materials and display areas designed for "impulse" borrowing, activity areas for messy work in the children's spaces, craft space, space for preschool-toddler-baby-families, iconic spaces (e.g., tree-houses), bookstore operations, convenient, fast pick-up and check-out, computers and computer labs, program/learning spaces, book club spaces, and so forth. Libraries, especially public libraries, are indeed changing and shushing is becoming rare except in designated quiet areas. There was time, not all that long ago, when "library silence" was the expected norm.

As the percentage of young people in a library's service population grows and grows, you will see more and more space designed to meet interactive needs as well as quieter space for more contemplative activities, including the use of print materials.

A new design concept is for early childhood and family spaces. In fact, Family Place Libraries™ is the name for a national movement that started at the Middle Country Library in New York and has spread throughout the country (http://familyplacelibraries.org/index.html). Participating libraries pay to be trained in the principles of a Family Place Library, which include elements of programming, collection development, and space planning. An early childhood area that is designed for caregivers to spend time with their children ages zero to three is created. It includes age-appropriate toys and games that would not be out of place in a well-equipped nursery school. There is a focus on creative play as critical to early childhood development and to the acquisition of early literacy skills. The goal is for families to come and spend time interacting with their very young children instead of grabbing some picture books and leaving.

There is another aspect to libraries as significant community places—a haven in time of trouble. FEMA (discussed in chapter 16) frequently establishes an office in a local library as it engages in its emergency recovery services. Michael Kimmelmann of the *New York Times* wrote an essay discussing the idea of expanding the number of branch libraries in the city because, as he noted "places that serve us well every day serve us best when disaster strikes. . . . The branches have become our de facto community centers, serving the widest range of citizens—indispensable in countless, especially poorer, more venerable neighborhoods" (October 3, 2013: C1).

LIBRARY AS PLACE

You can find a number of articles about "library as place." Just what does that phrase mean? Marcia A. Mardis (2011) provided a sound definition: library as place "is a place where, cultural, social, and intellectual exchanges occur, often mediated by the resources in the library collection; the library is a space defined by social mood, cultural and civic expression, and intellectual values (like reading) of the larger community" (p. 1).

The notion of libraries as social places has been with us almost as long as libraries. An interesting very early example of libraries and community spaces, documented by both archaeological and textual data, is from Roman times. Some Roman public baths included a library as part of the amenities (http://www.ancient.eu.com/Roman_Baths/). A more contemporary example of incorporating the idea of social space into libraries is found in the Nordic countries' public libraries. They have designed their public libraries as a major cultural/community place since the 1950s. Many of the large public libraries there have included restaurants/cafés as part of their facilities for more than 60 years. Also, many are part of the community's cultural complex—library, meeting halls, museums, sport complexes, and theatres.

The idea of having a café associated with or in a library is becoming more and more common in new and existing U.S. library buildings. As library collections become increasingly digital, there is less and less concern about having a "no food in the library" policy. The underlying reason for such policies was/is concern about insect infestations and their potential health issues for both people and collections. Kimmelmann's *New York Times* article quoted earlier even suggested branches have commercial level kitchens incorporated into the new designs to serve the community in emergencies.

From the Authors' Experience

Sinwell had an experience in which a coffee bar was added to the library where she worked. A coffee bar was thought to be a great idea and plans moved forward with the concept. The campus cafeteria (a Starbucks® vendor) was in charge of it and they hired students to handle the operation. Unfortunately, in the enthusiasm for the idea, no one thought about the fact there was no kitchen facility in the library and no place from which to easily get water for them to brew coffee or to do clean-up work. Thus, they made coffee in cafeteria and carted the thermoses of coffee over to library "coffee stand" in another building. Another problem was they never brought any pastries/food items. Perhaps the other major problem was no vendor management staff member ever came to check on the operation. As a result, Sinwell had to supervise the operation—one handled by students who were not on the library payroll. Supervising bored student staff, who had little to no business due to the lack of anything to offer but coffee was a challenge. The area became a student hangout/party space for the workers and their friends.

The experience was an example of a good idea put into operation without all too necessary detailed planning which ruined the idea. The authors believe a properly planned coffee/snack service has a place in the library. There are thousands of highly successful operations—including full cafeterias—available in many libraries.

We like Terence Huwe's (2010) view about the issue. He noted, "People love to study and commune together. With respect to understanding that basic human need, we have been remarkably effective in the battle for the hearts and minds of our communities. Of course, the digital era has revolutionized society's perception of space. Even so, against this backdrop, the struggle to preserve and enhance library space is a battle for the hearts and minds of our communities. It is ongoing and it will never end" (p. 29).

We sometimes forget with all the talk about digital formats killing the need for libraries as space that technologies can actually enhance the concept of library as place. Marshall Breeding (2011) made the point, "One of the most conspicuous ways that technology plays a role in a library's physical facilities involves the equipment made available to patrons. As you can imagine, many libraries see high demand for public–use computing, In fact, in many areas, libraries provide a lifeline to their patrons who need the computers

for vital tasks such as submitting governmental forms, seeking and applying for jobs, or other activities that require access to an internet-connected
computer" (p. 29).

Susan Montgomery and Jonathan Miller (2011) further emphasized that
technology is part of "new normal" for libraries as place. They argue that "the
core role of the library as place, the new normal for library buildings, is as
a place of collaborative learning and community interaction" (p. 229). They
suggest we operate in a hybrid environment, that is, a mix of traditional and
digital formats and information services.

The above may have seemed overly long since this is a text about library
programs and services. Perhaps it was, however, public service staff members
who are on the frontlines of the changing nature of library operations. They
are in daily contact with the public and are the first to notice changes in user
needs and wants. The vast majority of the interactions take place in the library
building. Some of the changes suggest that the library ought to assess how
its spaces can be used or modified. Public service staff also are, on a practical
daily level, "facility managers."

Check This Out

Hans Pul wrote an interesting essay on library as place: "The Role of Libraries in Communities, The Global Street Concept and Civil Participation in
Society" on the EngagingCities Web site. It is well worth the read: http://
engagingcities.com/article/role-libraries-communities-global-street-con
cept-and-civil-participation-society.

MANAGING THE FACILITY

Our first opening quotation from Fred Schlipf lists several factors that make
for an effective library. For many of those design factors, their success or
failure falls on the public service staff's abilities to handle the design elements. This is not to say that those elements do not make the staff's efforts
more or less difficult; they do. However, the bottom line is once constructed
many of the elements simply cannot change. One example is the placement of
emergency exits. That is a matter of building/fire code regulations. From the
library's point of view, every exit is a potential problem as individuals may exit
with library resources and may not exit during an emergency. Indeed such
exits are alarmed so their unauthorized use is made known; however, the individual is likely to out of sight by the time a staff member gets to the exit. Staff
lines of sight for exits may be good or not very good. The library might be able
to relocate staff, but not the exits.

There are two broad aspects to managing the library as a building. First,
there are the daily issues of keeping the facility safe, healthy, and inviting
for users as well as protecting the community's investments (collections and
equipment). The second is something you may become involved in some time
during your career—renovating or designing a facility.

Housekeeping Matters

Kathryn Ames and Greg Heid (2011) stated, "A safe and clean facility is the responsibility of all staff" (p. 10). Their focus was on public libraries; however, their point applies to any type of library. With the exception of school and corporate libraries, most libraries are standalone facilities.

You rarely hear much about library "housekeeping" in the course of your library studies; an exception might be in terms of proper handling of bound volumes. It is most unlikely that there is a discussion of dripping faucets, overflowing toilets, or water dripping from the ceiling. However, these are among the more common housekeeping issues arising for the public service staff.

Library service hours are generally longer than any one staff member's workday. Often service is provided seven days a week, and sometimes 24 hours per day. Inevitably some facility issues arise when few, if any, senior members of staff are on duty. There need to be plans for handling typical issues—ranging from the leaking faucet to a fire or earthquake.

As a result of long service hours, the library staff have more responsibility for the space. Today it is rare for a library to have full-time maintenance/custodial personnel on duty, much less on staff. Parent organizations usually find that sharing the services of carpenters, electricians, painters, plumbers, and others is more cost effective than assigning full-time FTEs to a single facility.

On a daily basis, basic housekeeping is an issue. Poor housekeeping can affect the health and safety of staff, users, and collections as well as the library's public image. Basic questions, such as who empties wastebaskets, and how frequently, become important for the library and its users. How often are restrooms cleaned and provisioned, especially those for the public? Do custodial staff have responsibility to dust the books and shelves? How often the floor is cleaned and who vacuums/cleans the floors? Does anyone have the responsibility? These may seem like small problems, but there are health issues involved—more for staff than users.

Prolonged exposure to "collection dust" can cause some people to become sick enough to have to go on long-term sick leave. In extreme cases, the person may be unable to return to work. Beyond the health issue, which is serious but not that common, there is collection health to consider. Dust and dirt on the shelves act as a very fine abrasive on materials as users and staff pull them off and replace them on the shelves. Over time, the small damage from each cycle accumulates to the point that the item needs repair or replacement. You have to balance the annual cost of such repairs and replacement against the cost of having shelves dusted. Dust also plays havoc with computers, photocopiers, and other equipment. One fact, which always exists in terms of dusting books and shelves, is dusting them is not part of a standard custodial contract. It is almost always an extra service, and not inexpensive, that has to come out of library operating funds. It is hard to identify a donor who will provide funds for any housekeeping activity.

Other housekeeping issues are light bulb burnout, problems of temperature and sun control, plumbing issues, leaky roofs, cracked sidewalks, wet floors, and others. The list could go on at some length, but you can see the point. The reality is any building component can cause a problem sometime during its lifetime. What happens when a user reports that a water faucet in the restroom will not shut off and water is spilling over the floor late on a Saturday afternoon? Is there someone or someplace to call? Will someone fix it before the start of the next shift? What do the staff do until the problem is resolved? In the chapter on legal issues (chapter 13), we noted the liability concerns regarding the library and users. Staff must understand how to handle facility problems.

Fixing matters related to housekeeping or the building is not the responsibility of the library staff. That is the parent organization's responsibility. Most such entities have facilities managers who arrange contracts and organize the work of specialist maintenance trades such as plumbers and electricians. They, like librarians and libraries, face severe budget problems. Mike Kennedy (2011) wrote, "In the funding climate that schools and universities find themselves, building managers will be fortunate to hang on to the budget they have, let alone receive the resources they need to address short- and long-term maintenance requirements" (p. 32).

Custodial Personnel

As we noted earlier, generally custodial staff members are not library employees. If they are, there is a high probability they are unionized and have a contract clearly delineating the services provided. Whether they are union members or not, there will still likely be a contract spelling out the services provided. Anything not covered or going beyond contractual limits may be available, but only at an additional charge. With tight budgets, extra charges are difficult, if not impossible, to handle. In case of non-library personal, you may be taken aback when you ask such a worker to perform what seems to you to be a minor but related task (e.g., emptying the wastebasket that the person filled with unneeded material) only to be told "It is not my job."

A few libraries are fortunate enough to have on their staff full- or part-time staff members who handle such duties. Why are they fortunate? Part of answer lays in the rather common phenomenon, in good work environments, where staff members think of the work place and its facilities as "theirs." That is, they take pride in how the space looks and operates. Nancy Dolan (2013) wrote about the maintenance staff at her library (two full- and two part-time people). Her brief essay is worth reading, if nothing else just to get a sense of all the maintenance tasks that are common in almost every library. She concluded her piece with the following: "Our maintenance team members are quick to respond and exhibit a positive attitude. They are inventive and creative, and always find a way to make things work. We at OPL definitely want to sing the praises of our 'unsung' maintenance heroes" (p. 12).

Certainly nonstaff maintenance personnel can be, and often are, positive and friendly in their approach to their work for the library. They almost always perform those task(s) appropriately and on time. However, it is rarely the case that they bring inventiveness or creativity to the task at hand. The library asks that a certain type of work be done and they do what was requested. The library is just one of many places they do such work. For the on-staff maintenance individuals, how well all the work is done reflects on them, it is "their building."

From the Authors' Experience

Sinwell noted that both the public and the college libraries where she worked went from on-staff to contract maintenance service in early 1990s and everyone noted the fall off in how the facilities looked and the quality of care taken in the work done.

She also noted several common issues with contract services. One, they almost always work at night so there is little opportunity to interact with them and discuss issues. A second problem, a result of low wages and the nature of the work, is some of them did not speak English, thus leaving them written messages it did not always work. Another issue is, although there is a "crew chief" present most of the time, there can be problems with communication. Owners and overall supervisors rarely are on site to check on work quality.

Check These Out

Two titles worth reviewing for more information on facility management are:

Roper, Kathy O., and Richard P. Paynet. 2014. *The Facility Management Handbook.* 4th ed. New York: American Management Association.

Trotta, Carmine J., and Marcia Trotta. 2001. *The Librarian's Facility Management Handbook.* New York: Neal-Schuman.

Health, Safety, and Security

Health, safety, and security within the library are critical issues for everyone—staff, users, and even collections. A surprising number of hazards can emerge in operating a public facility such as a library. Libraries have a duty to ensure staff, users, and the collections have proper protection (see chapter 16 for more on these topics). Involving all members of staff in identifying risks is a good exercise and makes people aware of potential hazards.

Staff members in public services need to keep an eye on the furniture and equipment. Upholstered couches and chairs are comfortable, generally; they help create a relaxed environment and are well used when available. "Well used" is an important phrase. Upholstery gets worn, dirty, and torn. Any of those factors will detract from the library's image if not corrected. There are some health hazards as well, especially when the fabrics are not cleaned on a regular basis. One reason that much of a library's furniture is un-upholstered is it is much less costly to maintain. However, such furniture also wears out. Chairs do break, hopefully not when someone sits in it. Getting "wobbly" chairs out of public areas is another of those minor duties of being in public service. Tables are less of a problem; however, if not cleaned on a regular basis they too can present health issues. Also, some individuals, for whatever reason, like to carve initials into wood.

Such graffiti, like all other graffiti, attracts more graffiti when left in place. An all-too-common place for graffiti is in restrooms rather than on tables. In the case of restrooms, the graffiti is often crude, demeaning, gang related, and the like; its quick removal is very important. (Another maintenance surprise you will likely find is outside custodial workers do not have responsibility to remove graffiti as part of their normal/contractual duties. They may not even report the graffiti's existence. Instead, you learn of it from an upset person who was offended by what they saw. If graffiti is not quickly removed, there is a tendency to see more and more graffiti. Some individuals refer to the "graffiti battle," they create it, you remove it. When you remove it repeatedly and quickly, the "artist" usually gives up and moves to some other location.)

Lori L. Smith (2013) raised an interesting question in her articled entitled "Is Your Library Plus-Size Friendly?" Having appropriate furniture for users is something that libraries think about when starting up and perhaps when reconfiguring existing space—such as providing children-sized tables and chairs for varying age groups. Another common consideration is ergonomic furniture for computer usage. As far as we could determine, the Smith essay is the only current example of planning for about 33 percent of all adults and the 17 percent of children, as of 2009–2010, who fall into the medically "obese" category (p. 44). All of us have heard and read about the ever-growing concerns of medical professionals regarding overweight or obese individuals.

In her article, Smith provides some insights into how to address the issue. One obvious solution is to replace some or all of the chairs with armrests. She notes that molded plastic chairs are almost as bad as chairs with armrests, because they tend to be less stable than wood chairs. One suggestion for looking into replacement furniture is to do an online search using the phrase "bariatric chairs." Some other "plus size" issues are classroom desks with the writing surface attached to the chair and auditorium chairs that were fixed in place and designed for an "average" size person. Almost all libraries have stepstools and even short ladders. Do you know if there is a weight limit for their safe use? There likely is, and if that information is not clearly displayed on the stool or ladder a safety problem as well as liability issues may well arise.

Environmental Control

An increasing challenge is maintaining a comfortable working environment as we experience the effects of global warming. One constant issue is controlling temperature and humidity levels. Probably every staff member has wondered from time to time, "Why, if they can send people into outer space and not have them freeze or burn to death, can they not design a building heating, ventilating, and air conditioning (HVAC) system for Earth that works?" One reason for the complaints is the variations in people's inner thermostats; some people need cool temperatures, others need warmer. In addition to individual preferences, over time systems break down, need to be taken out of service for maintenance, and simply wear out. As with custodial work, personnel responsible for the HVAC are rarely part of the library staff. This makes issues of response time and level of service matters of discussion and complaints.

A great challenge is balancing concerns for people and the collections. What is good for people is not ideal for the collections and equipment. Once again, two big challenges are temperature and humidity control. Collections and equipment do have one thing going for them; they are not vocal about any environmental problems they experience. You know there was a problem when they break down and have to be replaced. The old saying "silence is golden" applies and does not apply. Silence does not necessarily mean that all is well and is golden in terms of having to spend limited funds on replacements.

For libraries with significant preservation responsibilities, such as archives, research libraries, and national libraries, the balancing act is challenging. Both staff and customers generally prefer a working temperature at or near 72°F (22°C) with 50 to 60 percent humidity. Ideal storage conditions for collections are 60°F (15°C) and 50 percent or less humidity. This means compromise, usually in favor of people and technology, if the goal is to mix people and materials. Separation may or may not be feasible or affordable, as it probably requires two HVAC systems or modification of a single system into the equivalent of two systems.

Security Concerns

User spaces in isolated or remote parts of the building are higher-risk areas than in large open areas which have many user spaces. Poorly lit and remote staircases are also high-risk areas. You have a number of options that range from:

- Doing nothing (this will raise the library's liability risk)
- Devoting some staff time to patrolling the building (which reduces time for other work)
- Hiring security staff or a firm to patrol the building (a costly but effective option)
- Installing a variety of electronic surveillance equipment (costly and could carry unexpected legal consequences, e.g., questions of privacy)

We covered security issues and staff training in the security aspects of public service in some detail in chapter 16.

Check These Out

Several titles on library security worth consulting are:

Cravey, Pamela. 2001. *Protecting Library Staff, Users, Collections, and Facilities: A How-to-Do-It Manual for Librarians*. New York: Neal-Schuman.

Graham, Warren D. 2012. *The Black Belt Librarian: Real-World Safety & Security*. Chicago: American Library Association.

Kahn, Miriam. 2008. *Library Security and Safety Guide to Prevention, Planning, and Response*. Chicago: American Library Association.

Wilkie, Everett C. 2011. *Guide to Security Considerations and Practices for Rare Book, Manuscript, and Special Collection Libraries.* Chicago: Association of College & Research Libraries.

Emergency and Disaster Management

We addressed planning for emergencies and other disasters in chapter 16; here we focus on the staffing aspects. Emergencies happen. For the staff, few events are more stressful than at night or on the weekend when a person comes to the desk and says, "I'm not sure what is wrong, but there is a person on the floor not moving," or "I just saw a man on third floor holding a gun." You may never hear either of those statements; however, there is a very good chance you will hear something equally disquieting.

Perhaps the most common disaster is water damage and not just from major storms or firefighting efforts. Water pipes and radiators break, and this may happen when the library is closed; a day may pass before anyone notices the problem. Even an unremarkable rainfall can cause damage if building maintenance has been deferred for too long.

Having emergency and disaster preparedness plans ready to put into action when necessary will make both the staff and users safer. Consider separating the two documents to make it easier for the staff to find the appropriate information, if they don't already know what to do. Working with local police/institutional security, fire departments, and emergency medical technician groups about what to and not to do gives the staff a greater sense of confidence. Having more confidence and knowing what to do results in less stress and very likely a more positive outcome.

One surprising fact that you might not know and is somewhat counterintuitive relates to mobility handicaps. That is, most fire officials say that in a multistory facility, in an evacuation situation, those who have physical disabilities that make it impossible or very difficult to walk should be left in place where they are, or taken to a shelter area on that floor. Their location is to be *immediately* reported to the emergency professionals who will handle the individual's evacuation. This situation might also arise with an obese person who cannot handle stairs—elevators are off limits to everyone in an evacuation procedure.

From the Authors' Experience

At one of the libraries where Evans worked, practice fire drills and other emergency scenarios requiring building evacuations were held every year. Some were part of a campus drill, while others were just for the library—including night drills when staffing was much lower. There were surprise drills that included having "handicapped" individuals somewhere in the building. The staff's handling of those cases was fully and carefully critiqued by the emergency responders and after a few drills the staff understood what and how to handle the situation—including how to work with a handicapped person pleading not to be left alone.

The practice experience, thankfully, never had to be tested in reality, but the staff were ready and probably would have performed very well.

Wayfinding/Signage

All too often in the excitement and anticipation of having new space available, be it a totally new building, an addition or an existing area that is remodeled/renovated, a small but significant issue gets overlooked or addressed too quickly—directional signage. In the field of architecture and design the concept is known as wayfinding. That is how people go about finding specific areas within complex spaces. Amusement parks sometimes have mazes a person tries to navigate. Although not designed as a maze, many large and medium size libraries are considered such for many first-time and infrequent users. This is due in part to the design itself and/or poor or inadequate signage. Even one-story relatively small (overall square footage) libraries can baffle first-time users. Another factor in creating a library maze is, even when there is good signage when the space "went active," that we often make a small change in space usage here and there. Over time the "small" changes add up to the fact the signage no longer reflects the reality on the floor.

Library space complexity arises from the fact there are a number of different service points, relatively high collection storage units that reduce sightlines, and often several rooms open to the public. Normally the circulation service point is immediately visible on entering a library, and there is usually an open sightline to the reference desk. Even those two service elements are not always readily identifiable due to design elements. (There is a tendency to design a grand library entrance to what some people think of as a cultural monument. Hopefully any grandeur is on the exterior of the building rather than interior.)

Once again, public service personnel will be the first to notice wayfinding issues. Questions such as "Where are the computers?" "Can you tell me where the restrooms are?" "Do you have a children's room?" "I can't seem to find the newspapers; can you help me?" provide insights into where the public is having trouble navigating the library's layout. There are times when additional signs will resolve an issue, but there are also times when signage can't do the job and some rethinking of the furniture and equipment layout is the only solution.

Check These Out

Three good articles related to wayfinding and libraries are:

Dan Schoonover and Kirsten M. Kinsley's 2014 article "Stories from the Stacks: Students Lost in the Labyrinth" (*Journal of Access Services* 11, no. 3: 175–188).

Lauren H. Mandel's 2010 article "Toward Understanding of Patron Wayfinding: Observing Patrons' Entry Routes in a Public Library" in *Library & Information Science Research* (23, no. 2: 116–130).

Rui Li and Alexander Klippel's 2013 piece "Wayfinding in Libraries: Can Problems Be Predicted?" (*Journal of Map and Geography Librarianship* 8, no. 1: 21–38).

DEFERRED MAINTENANCE

What is deferred maintenance (DM), and why is it an issue in public services? You can probably guess that DM relates to putting off some maintenance activities for a time. You would be correct, but you might not guess how long that "some time" might be. Large-scale and expensive maintenance projects are often put off for years, not a matter of a month or two. In some cases, based on the authors' personal experience, the deferral can be decades in length.

Almost every organization has a growing list of DM projects. Mike Kennedy (2011) in writing about maintenance issues in educational institutions noted that for 2010–2011, 52 percent of districts surveyed DM projects and an estimated 60 percent of districts would be doing so in the following year (p. 33). Deferring maintenance projects is something we all do, if nothing more than deciding to vacuum the floor tomorrow. When it comes to significant building repairs, years of delay will mean a greater cost; if nothing else there will be an inflation factor. Almost every library has one or two deferred projects.

One of the more common projects that get deferred for years is roof replacement. Roofs just like other building components have an expected lifespan, after which it must be replaced. Even structural beams do have a finite safe lifespan. Think about the all the discussion about the need to address the deferred interstate highway infrastructure repairs and especially bridges. One factor in DM is that structural components don't usually fail catastrophically; rather it is a slow progress of becoming less and less trustworthy to do its designed function. When it is a slow failing and money is an issue, and when it isn't an immediate issue that must be addressed, it is easy to say "we'll try to get to that next year."

Most roofs don't just collapse one day; there may be times when you wish they would—that would force you to get a new roof now. They fail bit by bit, leaking here and there, then there and here. With each passing DM year, the number and locations of the leaks increase. You can almost hear the drip, drip, drip, splash, splash, splash of rain drops falling, inside the library. Those raindrops in the public service area become hazards for people and things. Injuries to people are always a possibility with wet floors, and wet collection items will impact salvage and preservation skills.

From the Authors' Experience

Evans once worked at library where the public service personnel were experts in handling leaking roofs and public access areas. They had to be; there was little choice as in some cases their workstations would become wet.

Staff members knew just where to place the plastic wastebaskets and even several 50 gallon trash cans (all the metal wastebaskets were gone as they rusted out rather quickly). They knew just where the plastic sheeting would be needed in the collection areas. "Caution Wet Floor" signs were strategically placed. Years of "repairing" leaks never accomplished anything. A researcher probably could have conducted a study of the history of caulks and caulking in the facility and never been criticized for missing some variety.

Sinwell experienced similar roof leaks that became a DM issue. It is the rare library that does not face this problem at some point in time and has to deal with that problem for more time than is good for people, equipment, or collections.

In Evans's case, the leaks did not get resolved until the building was "repurposed" and the library was moved to a new facility.

There are any number of other DM issues; we used roofs because they are rather common. Many of these become public service challenges until the matter is actually resolved. One type of DM project, "tuck pointing," might not seem a likely candidate as a challenge, but it can be. Libraries with brick or stone exterior facades all have to be tuck pointed at some time. That is, the mortar holding the brick/stone in place slowly weathers way and must be removed and new mortar applied. This is a slow and costly process. Why is it a problem? Wind-blown rain can and does seep through to the interior walls. If nothing more, there can be water stained walls—not something that enhances the library's image when the wall is in a public area. A more serious issue is if the interior is dry wall sheets. Dry wall absorbs water easily and also allows for rather rapid development of mold. Mold mitigation is costly, and having the removal team going about in what looks like spacesuits does little to enhance a library's image.

Public service staff is not responsible for correcting DM issues. However, they are the ones who must handle the problem when it does occur. They are also most likely to be the first to notice the problem and realize it is larger in scope or frequency. Passing such information on to the decision makers is their responsibility.

From the Authors' Experience

Sinwell suggests that a library must work long and hard to get the parent institution's facilities department to include the library in their long-range planning process. There are predicable replacement cycles for such things as carpeting/floor coverings, roofs, and painting interior walls.

SUSTAINABILITY

Sustainability is a word seen widely in both the popular and professional press. We placed our discussion of the concept here as it applies to both existing buildings and the design of new facilities. The concern about saving energy is not a new issue. As James Qualk (2010) noted, "The idea that a new or existing building can be capable of using very little, if any, grid energy or water while serving as a healthy place for people to live and work is now commonplace. But this is just one of many ways that buildings still fall short of their true potential" (p. 75). Brian Edwards (2011) in writing about library building design illustrated the overall issues in sustainability, "Concerns over climate change and the consequent drive for energy efficiency is leading to new approaches to the design of libraries and reshaping of existing ones. Greater attention is being paid not just to fossil fuel energy consumption but to a wider range of environmental and ecological issues. In many ways the architectural approach to the twenty-first century library is returning to the roots of the modernist library found in Scandinavia with its emphasis upon high levels of daylight, natural materials, social harmony, and contact with nature" (pp. 190–191).

Facility managers, usually from the parent organization not the library, have been engaging in energy saving efforts for 40+ years. Their efforts and the library's purpose, especially for libraries with major preservation responsibilities, can come into conflict. Earlier we noted that one of your challenges in managing a library building is that peoples' comfort levels in terms of temperature and humidity and what is good for collections are rather different. Items in the collections are made up of a composite of materials (paper, acetate, emulsions, plastic, glues, cloth, cardboard, thread, etc.). Each component expands and contracts at rather different rates as the temperature and humidity change. Every expansion and contraction stresses the item and shortens its useful life. The greater the swing in temperature and humidity is, the greater the stress on the item. When facility managers, as they often did/do, turn off the heating or air conditioning during non-service hours to save energy, the library collections experience "roller-coaster" swings in temperature and humidity.

There are times when some librarians do not like to discuss collections as capital goods (appreciation, depreciation, capitalizations, etc.). However, when it comes to roller-coaster temperature and humidity swings and trying to make the point that a more constant 24/7 environment will protect the parent organization's investment, it is time to start talking about collections as capital goods.

New buildings can be both environmentally appropriate and energy efficient. This is particularly true if there are efforts to have the facility receive a LEED certification. The U.S. Green Building Council (USGBC, http://www.usgbc.org/) developed the LEED (Leadership in Energy and Environmental Design) rating system for buildings. It is a third-party certification process using a point system. The rating system has a maximum of 110 points assigned to the seven categories:

Sustainable sites 21 (emissions)	Water efficiency 11
Energy and atmosphere 37	Materials and resources 14
Indoor environmental quality 17	Innovation in design 6
Regional priority 4 (varies by region of the country)	

Earning 40 points gets a building certified, while earning 80+ points gets a building a platinum rating. There are also silver (50+) and gold (60+) levels. It seems likely this system will become a standard part of the design process over the coming years. It is already being considered in building renovations, as seen in the LEED certifications attained by renovations to the George R. White Law Library at Concordia University School of Law (http://www.cu-portland .edu/about/sustainability) and Seattle University's Lemieux Library & McGoldrick Learning Commons, A *Library Journal* 2012 New Landmark Library (http://www.seattleu.edu/sustainability/what-su-is-doing/buildings/).

From the Authors' Experience

Evans was involved in the design of a collection storage facility for a museum. The archives were to go into the new building; unfortunately there was not enough money to include the library collections. The building earned a platinum level LEED award. The sloped roof has native plants at the top level and rain water is collected to irrigate the plants. Essentially the building is for storage with very limited office space. Researchers use materials in other buildings. The interesting aspect of the project was meeting LEED ratings did not materially increase the cost of the building.

PLANNING FOR RENOVATION OR NEW SPACE

In time, even with the best possible design and layout of library space, collection growth, changing user needs, or added services and programs will force the library to look to renovating/reallocating existing space, adding space, or even seeking a totally new facility to meet the changing library goals. Doing so will raise some issues that go beyond how much more square footage we need or how we can reallocate existing space. These issues include:

- Greater attention being given to environmental factors resulting from global warming and the need for buildings to be energy efficient
- Increasing concerns regarding the health and safety of staff and users
- Increased need for security of people, documents, and electronic data
- Changing impact of technology now and in the near future
- Pressures lower operating and maintenance costs

Regardless of what type of project a library undertakes in terms of space, there are some basic considerations to think about and incorporate in the new design/layout. These include:

- Flexibility
- Expandability
- Compact
- Secure
- Comfortable
- Adaptability
- Accessible
- Stable in climate control
- Attractive
- Economical to operate and maintain

Flexibility is essential since the use of the space changes; for example, the volume of technical services work is declining as a result of outsourcing. Changes in the way reference work is done means that formerly desk-bound staff are frequently moving about the facility (e.g., see, Warnement, 2003; Bugg and Odom, 2009; Miles, 2013). A modular design with few, if any, internal non-weight-bearing walls is typical of a flexible design. Internal walls that are non-weight-bearing can be relocated without causing structural damage or very complicated and costly work.

Check This Out

Donald Beagle's 2010 article "The Emergent Information Commons: Philosophy, Models, and 21st Century Paradigms" (*Journal of Library Administration* 50, no. 1:7–26) provides some idea of the range of issues related to adaptability.

Given the inevitable growth of archives and libraries, having a facility that can be expanded is highly desirable. Funds for an addition or remodeling are easier to raise than those needed for an entirely new building. The designer must consider where the future expansion space might be and how that relates to the existing structure. It is not uncommon for the area labeled "future expansion" on the original plans to turn out to be unsuitable, for various reasons, when the time comes to expand. One challenge public services face when it comes to remodeling and many addition projects is whether or not there should be an attempt to maintain some service while the work is taking place. The authors can attest to the fact that doing so is very challenging for the staff. Perhaps the most common "let's stay open" policy challenge is carpeting/floor covering replacement. The work does proceed in increments which can make such a policy tempting, but there are a variety of physical hazards as well as potential health concern for some individuals who may react to the adhesives used in the project area.

In addition to the desirable design elements for any renovation or expansion plan, there are some elements you should think long and hard about including. Many of these elements are of the type that architects and donors especially like and that are not functional from a library perspective. They also often only cause problems for the staff. The elements apply to almost any new space project:

Any Project	**New or Addition Projects**
Skylights	Atriums
Indoor water features	Courtyards
Nonrectangular interior spaces	"Floating" staircases
Indirect lighting	Open riser stairs

Check These Out

Three interesting articles that address planning new library spaces are:

EunYoung Yoo-Lee, Tae Heon Lee, and LaTesha Velez's 2013 article about how the University of North Carolina central library rethought the use of its spaces, "Planning Library Spaces and Services for Millennials: A Evidenced-Based Approach" (*Library Management* 34, nos. 6/7: 498–511).

Kirstin Steele's 2013 article on community building and communication, "Breaking Walls and Building Hopes" (*Bottom Line* 26, no. 4: 140–141).

Mantra Henderson's 2012 article on a major renovation project at James Herbert White Library at Mississippi Valley State University, "Library Renovation Lessons Learned . . . and Still Learning" (*Mississippi Libraries* 75, no. 2: 47–49).

You might think that library renovation and new building projects, once funded, are popular with the public as well as the staff. Unfortunately, that is not always the case. There are times when a library building is thought to be a community architectural landmark that must be preserved. Carnegie libraries are often viewed this way (Carnegie libraries were built in communities across the United States during the first part of the twentieth century with funds from the Carnegie Foundation.) In 2013, when the New York Public Library (NYPL) began to plan renovations inside the iconic main facility, issues arose. An Associated Press article by Jennifer Peltz published at the time reported, "But plans for a major change within the landmark have kindled an intellectual culture clash over its direction and the future of libraries themselves" (p. A8). In chapter 18, we discussed library referenda, many of which relate to library facility projects; having community-wide discussions well in advance of highly detailed design work can help avoid the type of problems NYPL faced.

MOVING TO A NEW LOCATION

Moving the furniture, equipment, and collections into the new location becomes a staff challenge. Somehow, moving costs, probably because they are the last stage in the "new space" process, never seem to be adequate for the job at hand. It is true that moving gets included in the project costs at the start; however, they are often eaten away through a process commonly referred to as "value engineering." That is a nice name for cutting costs of a project. The result is moving costs are an easy target.

Richard Snow (2004) provided a perspective on such moves that almost anyone who has had the experience fully understands:

> Deans and directors are shrewd. They may scrutinize the smallest details in a library, but supervising a move is something they eagerly delegate. The recipient of the honor of being move coordinator, also known as move director, mover manager, and the patsy, is usually a middle management sort with possible masochistic tendencies. . . . Unless your employment depends on it or you enjoy long hours with great responsibility and little authority, reject this job. (p. 55)

Perhaps that is a little too bleak a point of view, but one that touches on some of the challenges of handling a move. In fact Snow concluded his article by stating "But the move stayed with me, a defining achievement of my professional life, maybe *the* defining achievement" (p. 66). Thus while nerve wracking, physically demanding, early to start/late to finish, and after seemingly never ending work hours, handling a successful move can be rewarding.

From the Authors' Experience

Sinwell had an experience when she started a new library administrative position of handling a construction project. In this case, her director had planned a small remodeling job for the library but he was going on vacation the week she arrived. (Perhaps this is an example of the shrewd directors alluded to in the Snow quotation.)

The director handed her the RFP and told her the workers would be coming on a Friday night after the library closed and would work all weekend on project. She was to take charge and ensure all went according to plans, serving as the onsite project manager. In talking with staff, she discovered some individuals didn't even know details of a project that would affect their work space. She managed to avoid a disaster in terms of the staff by immediately engaging them in discussions about project details, highlighting the benefits of the changes and listening to their suggestions for possible adjustments. Communication skills were also critical in working with the contractor to negotiate minor adjustments to original.

Thus, in space planning, it's not just the design concept that needs careful consideration; it's the conversation with space users that is equally important.

There is always great time pressure to get the move done by a certain date and usually that date is rather sooner than you might desire. "The move" is the last step in a project that almost everyone is eager to see completed and is excited about. Moving the items from point X to point Y and maintaining the proper sequence for collection materials is not as easy a planning task as it might seem. A second challenge is to complete the task with the funds available, often they are not enough to hire all the extra help as is required to do the move properly. (Staff members and volunteers are the usual fallback resource in such cases. Moving is a physically demanding activity and that limits who can do what for how long.). The ideal solution is to employ professional movers who have experience in moving libraries. Options beyond that are many, all the way up to trying to get enough volunteers to do the job for free (or at most, for the cost of food and drink for the day). Moving down the options in cost terms, it is vital to calculate increased staff costs in the supervision of putting things back in order after the move is complete. We strongly recommend finding the funding to hire one of the several moving companies that specialize in handling library moves. They will save time and effort, especially staff time making the cost much more reasonable.

Having completed the move, a post-occupancy evaluation should be carried out, recording the outcomes for both the stakeholders, and the colleagues planning the new premises. Norman Oder (2001) reported the challenges facing the San Francisco Public Library when its post-occupancy evaluation indicated dissatisfaction on the part of users and staff.

JOINT-USE FACILITIES

Joint-use facilities, what are they and why discuss them? A joint-use library is one that combines two or more different types of libraries within a single building. Such facilities have staffing, programming, and service implications that can become rather complex. The two most common combinations are public-school and academic-public libraries. Just briefly thinking about such combinations you quickly see some of the public service staff challenges that might arise.

Such libraries are not a new phenomenon for the field. In fact, the senior author had his first library job in a public-school library facility—and that was indeed sometime in the distant past. There are a variety of reasons for creating such libraries; however, the underlying factor is economic. If nothing more, a shared building may indeed save on construction costs—one HVAC system rather than two, for example. There can be some savings in terms of shared maintenance costs and perhaps energy savings.

Karen Dornseif (2001) in writing about joint-use libraries suggested that there is an integration continuum in terms of the purposes for such facilities. There is no "best" model in terms of integration. Dornseif suggested at one end of the continuum is minimal integration moving to selective, and finally to fully integrated (pp. 107–108). Most of today's joint-use libraries are somewhere in the middle of the continuum.

One obvious reason for the middle ground approach is such facilities bring together organizations that have rather different missions and service clientele. One easy integration possibility, beyond the sharing of a building, is combining technical service functions (e.g., acquisitions and cataloging). Budgetary autonomy is still possible while combining/sharing common activities. (Cooperative cataloging has a long history, the clearest example being OCLC.) When it comes to public service activities and programming, the matter is not as clear cut. A shared circulation service may be possible and desirable; however, policy issues can be complex, for example, loan periods, recalls, and fines.

Services such as reference and information literacy instruction or children's programming are less susceptible to integration. Cross-training staff may allow for greater integration, but there are real challenges in shifting from assisting a graduate student one moment and helping a fourth grader with homework the next. A person who is outstanding in working with children may do a poor job on a general reference desk, and vice versa. Some of the more common issues for academic/public library joint faculties are:

- Children's areas need to be on separate floor or enclosed areas
- Cataloging using Library of Congress (LC) versus Dewey
- Academic staff members who don't want to work with children
- Academic librarians who do not normally do much public service work versus public librarians who spend almost all of their time in public service duties
- Need for quiet study areas
- Combined service desks

> ## Check These Out
>
> A recent title covering all aspects of joint-use facilities—from design to legal considerations—is *Joint Libraries: Models That Work*, by Claire B. Gunnels, Susan E. Green, and Patricia M. Butler (Chicago: American Library Association, 2012).
>
> A good article spelling out the challenges of reference service in a joint-use library is Nora J. Quinlan and Johanna Tuñón's 2004 article "Providing Reference in a Joint-Use Library" (*Internet Reference Services Quarterly* 9, nos. 1/2: 111–128).

Despite their challenges, it appears likely there will be more joint-use libraries developed in the future. It is almost a certainty that library staff will be tested, especially their ingenuity and imagination, when it comes to balancing the varying needs/wants for programs and services of differing service communities. Regardless of the setting, there will be the ever-present requirement to provide top quality services with limited resources.

CLOSING THOUGHTS

Physical space plays a surprisingly big role in how libraries go about providing the programs and services to their particular service community. How the space was/is designed determines how much flexibility the library has when it tries to adjust to changing needs, economic conditions, technology, and the like. It also plays a role in how efficient library operations are or can be.

Jennifer LeGarde summed up our views regarding library physical facilities and services. On July 30, 2014, she posted the following on her blog, "Adventures of Library Girl:"

> Where libraries thrive, students thrive. I've seen this over and over again. Rural, urban, rich, poor, big, small . . . it doesn't matter the school or the system. In places where libraries are thriving, active places where kids do more creating than consuming, those students do better. Period.
>
> First impressions count. . . . Every person who walks through the door is a potential library supporter. We cannot afford for our spaces to make bad first impressions. (http://tinyurl.com/LibraryGirl0714)

Although her focus was on the school library context, her thoughts apply to all types of libraries and their service populations.

The library as place is likely to exist well beyond the life time of this edition. Libraries play a variety of roles that go beyond being a source of information—something that many of those when predicting the physical library's imminent demise generally overlook.

Public service staff members are the most affected by the facilities' design. The good and the bad elements of the design, and few libraries have only good or only bad elements, makes work easier or harder. Deferred maintenance issues almost always exist and those issues frequently add to the staff's workload. The public service staff must be heavily involved in the planning of new or renovated spaces. Without their active input, the new space is unlikely to be as efficient to operate as it might otherwise be.

Chapter Review Material

1. List the factors that strongly suggest libraries will continue as a physical space.
2. Housekeeping does matter. Discuss the reasons why it does and the role of public service personnel in how the work gets handled.
3. Discuss climate control issues that often present staff with challenges.
4. In what ways do emergency/disaster preparedness plans assist public service personnel?
5. Deferred maintenance is a fact of life in many nonprofit organizations. Discuss how that issue impacts public service staff.
6. Sustainability will become an ever-growing factor in library facility operations. In what ways does that issue affect programming and services?
7. New construction and remodeling projects are complex and may require professional assistance. What role should public service staff play in the design process?
8. When it is a matter of a new facility, discuss some of the design elements that may arise that would present long-term service issues.
9. What role do public service staff members play in any library moving/relocation activities?

REFERENCES

Ames, Kathryn, and Greg Heid. 2011. "Building Maintenance and Emergency Preparedness." *Georgia Library Quarterly* 48, no. 1: 10–13.

Aulisio, George J. 2013. "Green Libraries Are More Than Just Buildings." *EGJ, Electronic Green Journal* 1, no. 35. Online. http://escholarship.org/uc/item/3x11862z.

Barshay, Jill. 2011. "Louder Libraries for a Digital Age to Open Across U.S." *Hechinger Report*, November 29. Online. http://hechingerreport.org/content/louder-libraries-for-a-digital-age-to-open-across-u-s_6960/.

Breeding, Marshall. 2011. "Using Technology to Enhance a Library as Place." *Computers in Libraries* 31, no. 3: 29–31.

Bugg, Kimberley L., and Rosaline Y. Odom. 2009. "Extreme Makeover Reference Edition: Restructuring Reference Services at the Robert W. Woodruff Library, Atlanta University Center." *Reference Librarian* 50, no. 2: 193–204.

Dolan, Nancy. 2013. "Maintenance, The Unsung Department That Keeps the Library Humming." *Public Libraries* 52, no. 4: 11–12.

Dornseif, Karen. 2001. "Joint-Use Libraries: Balancing Autonomy and Cooperation." *Resource Sharing & Information Networks* 15, nos. 1/2: 103–115.

Dudley, Hadi S. 2012. "No 'Shushing' in Public Libraries." *Arkansas Libraries* 69, no. 3: 4–5.

Edwards, Brian W. 2011. "Sustainability as a Driving Force in Contemporary Library Design." *Library Trends* 60, no. 1: 190–214.

Hapel, Rolf. 2012. "The Library as a Place." *Public Library Quarterly* 31, no.1: 48–55.

Huwe, Terence K. 2010. "Hearts, Minds, and the Library's Physical Space." *Computers in Libraries* 30, no. 8: 29–31.

Kennedy, Mike. 2011. "Maintaining Perspective in the Maintenance Department." *American School & University* 83, no. 10: 32–35.

Kimmelmann, Michael. 2013. "Next Time, Libraries Could Be Our Shelters from the Storm." *New York Times* Arts & Design, October 3: C1.

Mardis, Marcia A. 2011. "Reflections on School Library as Space, School Library as Place." *School Libraries Worldwide* 17, no. 1: i–iii.

Miles, Dennis B. 2013. "Shall We Get Rid of the Reference Desk?" *Reference & User Services Quarterly* 52, no. 4: 320–333.

Montgomery, Susan E., and Jonathan Miller. 2011. "The Third Place: The Library as Collaborative and Community Space in a Time of Fiscal Restraint." *College & Undergraduate Libraries* 18, nos. 2/3: 228–238.

Oder, Norman. 2001. "SFPL Faces a Host of Challenges." *Library Journal* 126, no. 10: 60–62.

Peltz, Jennifer. 2013. "Renovations at NY Public Library Strike a Nerve." *Daily Sun* Friday, August 2: A8.

Qualk, James D. 2010. "Buildings 'Shall Be Capable Of.'" *Environmental Design & Construction* 13, no. 11: 75–76.

Schlipf, Fred. 2011. "The Dark Side of Library Architecture: The Persistence of Dysfunctional Designs." *Library Trends* 60, no. 1: 227–255.

Smith, Lori L. 2013. "Is Your Library Plus-Size Friendly?" *American Libraries* 44, nos. 9/10: 44–46.

Snow, Richard. 2004. "How Not to Move a Library: Misadventures in Moving." *Collection Management* 29, no. 2: 53–67.

Warnement, Mary. 2003. "Size Matters: The Debate Over Reference Desk Height." *portal: Libraries and the Academy* 3, no. 1: 79–87.

SUGGESTED READINGS

Accardi, Maria T., Memo Cordova, and Kim Leeder. 2010. "Reviewing the Library Learning Commons: History, Models, and Perspectives." *College & Undergraduate Libraries* 17, nos. 2/3: 310–329.

Barclay, Donald, and Eric D. Scott. 2011. *The Library Renovation, Maintenance and Construction Handbook.* New York: Neal-Schuman.

Beagle, Donald Robert. 2006. *The Information Commons Handbook.* New York: Neal-Schuman.

Buschman, John E., and Gloria J. Leckie. 2006 *The Library as Place.* Santa Barbara, CA: Libraries Unlimited.

Carr, Mary M. 2013. *The Green Library Planner: What Every Librarian Needs to Know before Starting to Build or Renovate.* Lanham, MD: Scarecrow Press.

Corbett, Tom. 2011. "The Changing Role of the School Library's Physical Space." *School Library Monthly* 27, no. 7: 5–7.

Council on Library and Information Resources. 2005. *Library as Place: Rethinking Roles, Rethinking Space.* Washington, D.C.: Council on Library and

Information Resources. http://www.clir.org/pubs/reports/pub129/pub 129.pdf.

Eaton, Amy. 2013. "Modern Spaces, Changing Light." *AALL Spectrum* 17, no. 7: 15–17. (Note: The article includes photographs of a reference desk created out of deselected books.)

Erickson, Paul W. 2011. "School Maintenance Needs." *American School & University* 83, no. 8: 26–28.

Harland, Pamela Colburn. 2011. *The Learning Commons: Seven Simple Steps to Transform Your Library.* Santa Barbara, CA: Libraries Unlimited.

Hauke, Petra, and Klaus Ulrich Werner. 2012. "The Second Hand Library Building: Sustainable Thinking through Recycling Old Buildings into New Libraries." *IFLA Journal* 38, no.1: 60–67.

Henderson, Jill. 2007. "Exploring the Combined Public/School Library." *Knowledge Quest* 35, no. 3: 34–37.

Jones, Ashley. 2014. "Sustainability in Library Preservation." *Technical Services Quarterly* 31, no. 1: 31–43.

Jones, Ryan. 2014. "Wired for Learning." *The Penn Stater*, January/February: 37–42. Klipper, Barbara. 2014. "Making Makerspaces Work for Everyone." *Children & Libraries: The Journal of the Association for Library Service to Children* 12, no. 3: 5–6.

Larue, James. 2014. "Why Build Libraries?" *Public Libraries* 53, no. 4: 12–17.

Leuzinger, Julie. 2013. "Reducing Service Points in the Academic Library: How to Provide Quality Customer Service in the Face of Budget Cuts." *College & Research Libraries News* 74, no. 10: 530–533.

Maxymuk, John. 2010. "Library as a Place in Space." *Bottom Line* 23, no. 3: 128–131.

Mueller, Charles G. 2012. "The Once and Future Library." *American Libraries* 43, nos. 3/4: 39–41.

Niegaard, Hellen. 2011. "Library Space and Digital Challenges." *Library Trends* 60, no. 1: 174–189.

Peterson, Richard A., Megan von Isenberg, Barbara Dietsch, and Dawne Lucas. 2014. "Going Green: One Library's Journey toward Sustainability." *Journal of Hospital Librarianship* 14, no. 1: 14–23.

Poggiali, Jennifer, and Madeline Cohen. 2014. "A Low-Hassle, Low-Cost Method to Survey Student Attitudes about Library Space." *Library Leadership & Management* 28, no. 3: 1–8.

Polger, Mark Aaron, and Amy F. Stempler. 2014. "Out with the Old, In with the New: Best Practices for Replacing Library Signage." *Public Services Quarterly* 10, no. 2: 67–95.

Pomerantz, Jeffrey, and Gary Marchionini. 2007. "The Digital Library as Place." *Journal of Documentation* 63, no. 4: 505–533.

Raab, Christopher. 2014. "Visual Management for Libraries." *Library Leadership & Management* 28, no. 3: 1–7.

Robinson, Carla. 2006. "Working at a Joint-Use Library." *Journal of Access Services* 4, nos. 1/2: 75–84.

Sarjeant-Jenkins, Rachel, and Keith Walker. 2014. "Working Together: Joint Use Canadian Academic and Public Libraries." *Collaborative Librarianship* 6, no. 1: 5–19.

Schlak, Tim. 2014. "Why Didn't ANYONE Tell Me? A Dozen Things No One Tells You about Library Building Projects." *American Libraries* 45, nos. 9/10: 42–45.

Shepherd, F. 2002. "Diary of a Move." *Records Management Bulletin*, no. 109: 107–109.

Singh, Rajesh, and Amber Ovsak. 2013. "Library Experience Matters! Touchpoints to Community Engagement." *Journal of Library Administration* 53, no. 5/6: 344–358.

Tarabula, Jill M. 2013. "Reinventing Douglas: How One Library Revamped Its Space." *Computers in Libraries* 33, no. 4: 6–11.

Tooey, Mary Joan. 2010. "Renovated, Repurposed and Still 'One Sweet Library.'" *Journal of the Medical Library Association* 98, no. 1: 40–43.

Williment, Kenneth. 2011. "It Takes a Community to Create a Library." *Public Libraries* 50, no. 2: 30–35.

Worpole, Ken. 2013. *Contemporary Library Architecture: A Planning and Design Guide.* New York: Routledge.

Index

Note: Page numbers followed by *f* indicate a figure on the corresponding page. Page numbers followed by *t* indicate a table on the corresponding page.

About the Authors

G. EDWARD EVANS, PhD, is a semi-retired, award-winning author and Fulbright Scholar. He holds several graduate degrees in anthropology and library and information science. Throughout his career, he has been an administrator, researcher, teacher, and writer. As a researcher, he has published in both anthropology and LIS and held a Fulbright Fellowship and a National Science Foundation Fellowship. His teaching experience has also been in both fields in the United States and the Nordic countries, in particular at the Graduate School of Librarianship and Information Science at the University of California, Los Angeles. Evans has substantial administrative experience at private academic libraries such as Harvard University and Loyola Marymount University. He retired from full-time work as associate academic vice president for libraries and information resources at Loyola Marymount University. Evans consults at the Museum of Northern Arizona library and archives and at the Flagstaff City–Coconino County Library System.

MARGARET ZARNOSKY SAPONARO, MLS, is librarian for journalism and hearing and speech sciences at the University Libraries, University of Maryland, where she is responsible for collection management, reference, and instruction for these disciplines. Her prior work experience includes serving as manager of staff learning and development at the University of Maryland, as associate director of learning resources at the Alexandria Campus of Northern Virginia Community College, and as librarian for the College of Human Resources at Virginia Polytechnic Institute and State University. Saponaro has also served as an adjunct faculty member for the University of Virginia and is currently a member of the American Library Association, ACRL, and the Special Libraries Association. She holds a master's degree in library science from the University of California, Los Angeles, with postgraduate work in the areas of personnel programs and public administration. Her research interests are in the areas of collection management, instruction, and emerging technologies in libraries.

HOLLAND CHRISTIE is the Public Services Manager at the Flagstaff City-Coconino County Public Library where she supervises the Reference, Circulation, and Youth Services departments. She is responsible for collection development, policies and procedures, programming, and a small archive. She has an MLS from the University of Arizona and a bachelor's degree in English from Northern Arizona University. She has a diverse work history outside of the library world, having experience in the hospitality industry as a bartender and waitress—a background that has, surprisingly, contributed greatly to her work as a library manager. She has also worked as contributing editor on several fiction and nonfiction titles.

CAROL SINWELL, MLIS, EdD, is dean emeritus at Northern Virginia Community College (NVCC). She received a master's degree in education and a doctorate in education leadership from the University of Virginia's Curry School of Education and a master's in library and information systems at Catholic University. She teaches in the Masters of Social Foundations in Education program at the University of Virginia. After teaching in K–12 schools for more than 11 years, Sinwell entered Fairfax County Public Library System where she developed a broad array of management skills serving as a children's librarian, reference librarian, and branch manager. In 2003, she received the American Library Association's Movers and Shakers award that recognizes the 50 Most Innovative Librarians in the United States and Canada for the year, and was an "Outstanding NVCC Woman" for Women's History Month.